'Croft's *Radical Construction Grammar* is a welcome contribution bearing on an issue of basic importance to linguistic theory: the nature and status of grammatical categories. His innovative examination of this question from a functionalist and typological perspective refocuses the debate in a fundamental way. It deserves to be seriously considered by all linguists regardless of their theoretical orientation.'

Ronald W. Langacker, University of California, San Diego

'There is no doubt that this book is a landmark in linguistic theory. It is an outstanding work by a brilliant intellect in which Croft demonstrates the depth of his linguistic knowledge and above all vision. It will constitute a source of inspiration for much future linguistic theorizing.'

Anna Siewierska, University of Lancaster

'*Radical Construction Grammar* is an important work that is bound to elicit strong reactions, for it questions basic tenets of linguistic research. Croft argues persuasively that much research on universals suffers from methodological flaws: there are language universals, but linguists have been trying to characterize them at the wrong level of description. Common to all humans is our perceptual/conceptual apparatus and communicative needs: that is where we need to anchor our theory of universals. The fundamental unit of sound–meaning relations in language is the construction. So instead of trying to build up constructions out of some universal inventory of smaller units, we should characterize the constructions in their own terms and seek generalizations (both within and across languages) in terms of the abstract properties of the constructions. Because the arguments are presented in great detail and illustrated with fascinating examples, the book's controversial claims cannot be dismissed lightly. I look forward to the discussion it will provoke.'

Tom Wasow, Stanford University

Radical Construction Grammar

Syntactic Theory in Typological Perspective

WILLIAM CROFT

OXFORD
UNIVERSITY PRESS

Great Clarendon Street, Oxford OX2 6DP

Oxford University Press is a department of the University of Oxford.
It furthers the University's objective of excellence in research, scholarship,
and education by publishing worldwide in

Oxford New York

Auckland Cape Town Dar es Salaam Hong Kong Karachi
Kuala Lumpur Madrid Melbourne Mexico City Nairobi
New Delhi Shanghai Taipei Toronto

With offices in

Argentina Austria Brazil Chile Czech Republic France Greece
Guatemala Hungary Italy Japan South Korea Poland Portugal
Singapore Switzerland Thailand Turkey Ukraine Vietnam

Oxford is a registered trade mark of Oxford University Press
in the UK and in certain other countries

Published in the United States
by Oxford University Press Inc., New York

© William Croft 2001

The moral rights of the author have been asserted

Database right Oxford University Press (maker)

First published 2001

All rights reserved. No part of this publication may be reproduced,
stored in a retrieval system, or transmitted, in any form or by any means,
without the prior permission in writing of Oxford University Press,
or as expressly permitted by law, or under terms agreed with the appropriate
reprographics rights organization. Enquiries concerning reproduction
outside the scope of the above should be sent to the Rights Department,
Oxford University Press, at the address above.

You must not circulate this book in any other binding or cover
and you must impose this same condition on any acquirer.

British Library Cataloguing in Publication Data

Data available

Library of Congress Cataloging in Publication Data
Croft, William.
Radical construction grammar : syntactic theory in typological perspective / William Croft.
p. cm.
Includes bibliographical references.
1. Grammar, Comparative and general—Syntax. 2. Universals (Linguistics)
3. Typology (Linguistics) 4. Semantics. I. Title.
P291.C76 2001
415—dc21   2001036596

ISBN 0–19–829955–9
ISBN 0–19–829954–0 (pbk)

5 7 9 10 8 6 4

Typeset by Best-set Typesetter Ltd., Hong Kong
Printed in Great Britain
on acid-free paper by
Biddles Ltd., King's Lynn, Norfolk

to a lost home

My time comin' any day—don't worry 'bout me, no.
Been so long I felt this way—but I'm in no hurry, no.
Rainbow's end down that highway,
Where ocean breezes blow.
My time comin', voices say.
And they tell me where I'll go.

Don't worry 'bout me;
No, no, don't worry 'bout me, no.
I ain't in no hurry, no, no,
'cause I know where to go.

California!
Preaching on the burning shore
California!
I'll be knocking on the golden door

Like an angel,
Standing in a shaft of light
Rising up to paradise,
And I know I'm gonna shine

The Grateful Dead, 'Estimated Prophet'

Lyrics to 'Estimated Prophet' by John Barlow, © Ice Nine Publishing Company. Used with permission.

Contents

Preface xiii
Acknowledgments xvi
List of Figures xix
List of Tables xxii
List of Abbreviations xxiv
List of Symbols xxviii

PART ONE FROM SYNTACTIC CATEGORIES TO SEMANTIC MAPS

1. Syntactic Argumentation and Radical Construction Grammar 3
   1.1. Introduction 3
   1.2. Methodology and Theory in Syntax 9
       1.2.1. The basic question of syntactic analysis 9
       1.2.2. Distributional analysis: the basic method of syntactic argumentation 11
   1.3. Constructions and Construction Grammar 14
       1.3.1. Arguments for construction grammar 14
       1.3.2. Syntactic and semantic structure: the anatomy of a construction 18
       1.3.3. The organization of constructions in a construction grammar 25
   1.4. Distributional Analysis and Cross-linguistic Universals 29
       1.4.1. Problems in using distributional analysis across languages 29
       1.4.2. Cross-linguistic methodological opportunism and its problems 30
       1.4.3. An alternative view: there is no universal inventory of atomic primitives 32
   1.5. Distributional Analysis and the Representation of Particular Language Grammars 34
       1.5.1. Problems in using distributional analysis in particular languages 34
       1.5.2. Language-internal methodological opportunism and its problems 41
       1.5.3. An alternative view: there are no atomic grammatical primitives 45

	1.6. Radical Construction Grammar: Frequently Asked Questions	47
	1.6.1. How can you have a syntactic theory without atomic primitive units?	47
	1.6.2. Can't these facts be captured by a feature-based approach to categories, or by a categorial grammar approach?	48
	1.6.3. Doesn't RCG create a hopeless proliferation of categories? How do you label them all?	49
	1.6.4. If categories are defined relative to constructions, how do you identify constructions?	51
	1.6.5. How do you capture generalizations for categories across constructions in RCG?	53
	1.6.6. How can a child acquire a grammar without atomic primitive categories?	57
	1.6.7. How does RCG relate to other versions of construction grammar?	58
	1.6.8. How can I use RCG for grammatical description if all categories are construction-specific and constructions are language-specific?	59
	1.6.9. If categories are construction-specific and constructions are language-specific, does this mean that there is no Universal Grammar, and no language universals?	60
	1.7. Conclusion and Prospects	61
2.	Parts of Speech	63
	2.1. Introduction	63
	2.2. The Alleged Absence of Parts of Speech in Particular Languages	65
	2.2.1. A "lumping" typological theory of parts of speech	65
	2.2.2. A critique of "lumping" theories of parts of speech	67
	2.2.3. Semantic shift and zero coding	70
	2.3. From Lumping to Splitting	75
	2.3.1. Distributional analysis and the analysis of parts of speech	75
	2.3.2. Splitting: where does one stop?	78
	2.3.3. Further problems with distributional analysis and parts of speech	81
	2.4. Conceptual Space, Semantic Maps and a Universal Theory of Parts of Speech	84
	2.4.1. Separating the universal from the language-particular	84
	2.4.2. The universal-typological theory of parts of speech	86

		2.4.3. Conceptual space and semantic maps	92
		2.4.4. Typological markedness and the topography of conceptual space	98
		2.4.5. Functional prototypes and the Grammatical Category Structure Hypothesis	102
		2.4.6. The universal-typological and Cognitive Grammar theories of parts of speech	104
	2.5.	Integrating the Language-Particular and the Universal in the Representation of Grammatical Knowledge	105
3.	Syntactic Categories and Semantic Relativity		108
	3.1.	The Relationship between Form and Meaning	108
	3.2.	Hidden Assumptions in Arguments for Semantic Relativity	110
		3.2.1. Contrast	111
		3.2.2. One-to-one form–meaning mapping	112
		3.2.3. Redundancy in expression	119
		3.2.4. The Semantic Uncertainty Principle	124
	3.3.	The Dynamic, Fluctuating Character of Linguistic "Relativity"	126
	3.4.	Semantic Universals, Relativity, and Radical Construction Grammar	129
4.	Clausal Syntactic Roles ("Grammatical Relations")		132
	4.1.	Introduction	132
	4.2.	Language Universals without Universal Syntactic Roles	134
		4.2.1. "Accusative" vs. "ergative" languages	134
		4.2.2. Hierarchies of A/S/P role categories	138
		4.2.3. Hierarchies of coding object roles	142
		4.2.4. Conclusion	146
	4.3.	Language Universals without Global Syntactic Roles	147
		4.3.1. Arguments for and against global (and universal) syntactic roles	148
		4.3.2. The Subject Construction Hierarchy	152
		4.3.3. Diachronic reality of the Subject Construction Hierarchy	155
		4.3.4. A conceptual space representation for the Subject Construction Hierarchy	159
	4.4.	Some Further Complications	161
		4.4.1. Split intransitivity and the subject prototype	162
		4.4.2. Ergativity and quantification	165
		4.4.3. Split ergativity	167
	4.5.	Conclusion	170

x   Contents

Part Two   From Syntactic Relations to Symbolic Relations

5. Dependency, Constituency, and Linear Order — 175
    5.1. Introduction — 175
        5.1.1. The internal structure of constructions — 175
        5.1.2. Coded dependencies and collocational dependencies — 176
    5.2. Collocational Dependencies as Semantic Relations — 179
    5.3. Constituency and Linear Order — 185
        5.3.1. Arguments for constituency — 185
        5.3.2. From constituency to formal grouping — 190
        5.3.3. Linear order and formal grouping — 196
    5.4. Overtly Coded Dependencies — 197
        5.4.1. Typological classification of overtly coded dependencies — 197
        5.4.2. Mismatches among overtly coded dependencies, contiguity, and linear order — 199
    5.5. Conclusion — 201

6. A Radical Approach to Syntactic Relations — 203
    6.1. The Logical Argument against Syntactic Relations — 203
    6.2. Syntactic Relations vs. Symbolic Relations — 206
        6.2.1. Unlikely semantic dependencies — 209
        6.2.2. Proposition vs. Subject-Predicate construal — 213
        6.2.3. Clause collapsing — 216
    6.3. Syntactic Relations vs. Syntactic Roles — 220
        6.3.1. Relative order of three or more elements — 221
        6.3.2. Second position — 223
        6.3.3. Nested relational coded dependencies — 224
        6.3.4. Absence of one of the units in a syntactic relation — 226
        6.3.5. Optionality or absence of an overtly coded dependency — 232
    6.4. Comprehending Constructions without Syntactic Relations — 233
        6.4.1. The identification of semantic roles via morphosyntactic devices — 233
        6.4.2. The identification of constructions — 236
        6.4.3. The scaffolding metaphor and the semi-iconicity of syntax — 237

7. Heads, Arguments, and Adjuncts — 241
    7.1. Introduction — 241
    7.2. Criteria for Headhood — 242

7.2.1. Functor criteria	243
7.2.2. Base criteria	244
7.2.3. Head criteria	245
7.3. Deconstructing Heads	246
7.3.1. Agreement	246
7.3.2. Subcategorization, government, and construction grammar	247
7.3.3. Obligatoriness and distributional equivalence	250
7.3.4. The syntactic category determinant and the morphosyntactic locus	252
7.4. A Semantic Definition of "Head"	254
7.4.1. Heads and profile equivalents	254
7.4.3. Heads and PIBUs	257
7.5. Grammaticalization and the PIBU Profile Equivalent	260
7.5.1. Auxiliaries and articles	260
7.5.2. Numerals, quantifiers, and classifiers	261
7.5.3. Adpositions	263
7.5.4. Complementizers	265
7.5.5. Copulas	266
7.5.6. PIBUs in other syntactic processes	267
7.6. "Heads" and Roots in Morphology	268
7.7. The Argument–Adjunct Distinction	272
7.7.1. Criteria for the argument–adjunct distinction	272
7.7.2. Valence and the autonomy–dependence continuum	273
7.7.3. Symbolic instantiation in constructions	275

PART THREE   FROM UNIVERSAL CONSTRUCTIONS TO SYNTACTIC SPACE

8. The Voice Continuum	283
8.1. Introduction	283
8.1.1. Do language universals need universal constructions?	283
8.1.2. Active, passive, inverse: delimiting the grammatical domain	284
8.2. Prelude: Animacy Constraints in Actives and Passives	288
8.3. The Structural Variety of Actives and Passives	290
8.3.1. Some so-called passives	290
8.3.2. Some so-called inverses	295
8.4. Blurring the Active–Nonactive Distinction	302
8.4.1. Some so-called "passives" and ergatives	303
8.4.2. Philippine voice systems	306
8.4.3. Person-based split ergative systems	309
8.5. A Typological-Universal Analysis of Voice Constructions	310

8.5.1. Syntactic space and the nonuniversality of constructions	310
8.5.2. Universals of syntactic space	314
9. The Coordination–Subordination Continuum	**320**
9.1. Introduction	320
9.1.1. The traditional classification of complex sentences	320
9.1.2. The continuum of complex sentence types	322
9.2. A Gestalt Analysis of Coordination and Adverbial Subordination	328
9.2.1. The semantic parallelism of "coordination" and "adverbial subordination"	328
9.2.2. Adverbial clauses and figure–ground constructions	329
9.2.3. Coordination and complex figure constructions	336
9.2.4. Conventionalized construals: conditionals and comparatives	338
9.2.5. The evolution of complex sentences to deranked clause chains	341
9.3. E-site Elaboration and the Typology of Complements and Relative Clauses	346
9.3.1. E-site elaboration	346
9.3.2. From figure–ground to relative clause	349
9.3.3. From purpose clause to infinitival complement	351
9.3.4. From serial verb to complement	352
9.4. The Syntactic Space of Complex Sentences: the Deranking Hierarchy	354
9.5. Conclusion	361
10. Syntactic Theory and the Theory of Language	**362**
References	369
Index of Authors	393
Index of Languages	397
Index of Constructions, Categories, and Features	401
Index of Subjects	407

Preface

Much to my students' chagrin, it has taken me a long time to figure out what I think syntax is, or at least for a coherent view to evolve of what I think syntax is. But this is due in part to my frustration at the way syntax is generally done.

As a student myself, and afterwards as a researcher and teacher of syntactic phenomena, I have been frustrated with a seemingly endless series of syntactic "theories" whose chief goal appeared to be the construction of a representation language for syntactic description. The result has been a continuing kaleidoscope of notations which have made even five-year-old journal articles—and many reference grammars—difficult to decipher.

I found this notational imperative to be true not merely of "formalist" theories (generative theories and their nontransformational offshoots), but also of some "functionalist" theories, as well as earlier "structuralist" theories (such as tagmemics, well represented in reference grammars of languages around the world). This is not at all to say that I found no important insights about syntax in the work produced in these theories. But the model of representation used by the researcher got in the way of the insights, rather than illuminating them; and I would often find myself giving up before uncovering any insights that were there.

I have also been frustrated at the often distant relationship between these syntactic models, and some of the analyses proposed in those models, and empirical reality. A large class of research articles—again, both "formalist" and "functionalist"—is devoted to claiming that phenomenon X in language Y really is a passive, or really is not a passive. Such research discounted or ignored the opposing evidence, which made me uncomfortable. It also missed the point, which was that phenomenon X was interesting and challenging precisely because it sort of was a passive but sort of wasn't at the same time; both its passivelike and its unpassivelike syntactic properties were equally important. Just as traditional grammarians tried—unsuccessfully—to fit modern European languages into the mold of Classical Latin and Greek, modern linguists are trying to fit languages of the world into the mold of "Standard Average European".

Likewise, a second large class of research articles would demonstrate a remarkable convergence of syntactic factors, or (in functionalist research) functional factors, that led to phenomenon X in language Y being exactly the way it is, based on a complex but calibrated interaction of universal formal or functional principles. But how did the researcher know from looking only at language Y that these principles really were valid for all languages, or that the way they interacted in language Y was governed by universal principles? In fact, they almost never are, when one starts looking at additional languages.

This of course has led to a third class of research articles, namely finding an exotic language Z, or exotic dialect of language Y, and demonstrating that the universal principles in the second class of articles weren't quite right. But the usual conclusion of this class of articles was that a minor adjustment of definitions, or the introduction of a binary-valued parameter, would set things right. This incremental, one-language-at-a-time approach just could not do justice to the facts of languages (plural!) taken as a whole, I felt.

Furthermore, I was frustrated by the lack of explicit discussion of methodology and argumentation for establishing syntactic theories. When I was a student, a supposed virtue of syntax courses (and a selling point to administrations dubious about the "relevance" of linguistics or the "transferable skills" it was supposed to provide to students) was the teaching of proper methods of argumentation. After I became a teacher and researcher myself, colleagues would confide in me quite a different viewpoint. One prominent nontransformational formalist told me that post-1980 generative grammar (Government and Binding theory and its successors) had abandoned standards of syntactic argumentation. A prominent Chomskyan linguist (i.e. a practitioner of post-1980 generative grammar) told me that cognitive grammar had abandoned all standards of syntactic argumentation. Needless to say, it wasn't clear to me just what the standards of syntactic argumentation were supposed to be.

A typical example is to be found in arguments for/against the status of the syntactic category 'adjective' in some languages. The same facts would be used by one linguist to argue that language Y has adjectives, and by another to argue that it doesn't. Another, slightly different sort of example is the argument that one analysis or model is preferred over another because it is "simpler" or "more elegant", or "less redundant". But simplification of one part of a model almost always involves complication of a complementary part; how does one decide if the overall model is simpler? And above all, what reason do we have to believe that simplicity, elegance or nonredundancy are psychologically valid desiderata for grammatical knowledge, rather than being just a reflection of the analyst's ingenuity?

The response of some linguists to these frustrations has been disheartening. We are told that every new notation is progress towards Universal Grammar. If we bring in cross-linguistic data, we are told that Universal Grammar can best be found by examining only one language (see for example Newmeyer 1998: 335). If we try to address methodological issues, we are told that we should not be looking for discovery procedures, but that once we find Universal Grammar, Universal Grammar will give us the methodological clarity we need. I do not find these to be satisfying answers.

Unfortunately, I was also dismayed by the response of other linguists, including a number of typologists and functionalist linguists, to what I presume were similar frustrations with "syntax": namely avoiding the issue, explicitly or implicitly. Many typologists, who were in the best position to deal with the empirical problems mentioned above, explicitly took the position that their work was "model-neutral" or "theory-neutral". That usually meant only that they did not couch their studies in the representational notation of the most popular theory of the day. Such studies in fact often made strong claims as to what was universal in language, and offered some sort of explanation for those universals. But they did not describe the consequences of their universal hypotheses for the representation of speaker's knowledge of their language, let alone call it a syntactic theory.

Functionalist linguists (with some notable exceptions) have increasingly turned to studies of the conceptual semantics and/or discourse function of various syntactic constructions. These studies are invaluable, and I would be the first to say that meaning and use have been much too long neglected in linguistic research. But unfortunately it also means that syntax has been left behind.

The reader has no doubt gathered by this point that this book is intended to present a view of syntax that escapes the quandary created by the frustrations enumerated above. As I said at the beginning, I found it quite difficult myself to escape this quandary, and to discard what I now believe are certain prejudices (both "formalist" and "functionalist"), and come to a theoretically coherent and empirically plausible perspective on syntax. I hope that those who have shared these frustrations will find the following pages useful.

Acknowledgments

I would like first to thank—or perhaps apologize to—the students of "Grammatical Analysis", which I taught at the University of Michigan from 1987 to 1989, and the students of the undergraduate "Introduction to Syntax" which I taught at the Linguistic Society of America Summer Institute at Albuquerque in 1995; they all listened (mostly) patiently and struggled with the issues I was also struggling with. I would also like to thank the students at Summerschool of the German Linguistics Society, Mainz, Germany in September 1998 and the LOT Winterschool in Leiden in January 2000, who listened to and responded to earlier versions of the material in this book.

Fritz Newmeyer played an important role with his 1992 *Language* paper and subsequent correspondence, forcing me to really address the issues I have just criticized others for not addressing in my preface. This exchange led to my 1995 *Language* paper (Croft 1995a) and eventually this book (as well as Croft 2000a). Matthew Dryer made some of these points clearly and articulately in 1995, on the Funknet email list and in a talk at the Albuquerque Functional Approaches to Grammar conference (later published as Dryer 1997b); his arguments convinced me that some gnawing suspicions I had expressed only passingly before were really on the right track.

Radical Construction Grammar also follows naturally from the modules developed for the hypertext Framework for Descriptive Grammars, funded by the US National Science Foundation (grant BNS-9013095 from 1990 to 1993) to the University of Michigan and the University of Southern California. In the effort to develop a hypertext network of pages to organize the grammatical description in terms of the formal structures of any language, we were led to a construction-based representation. In this representation, we defined functional prototypes for category labels, but we also recognized that a grammatical description could eschew all of these labels, or merely use them mnemonically. It was a short step from that recognition to Radical Construction Grammar. I wish to thank the National Science Foundation; my co-principal investigator, Bernard Comrie; our German collaborators Christian Lehmann and Dietmar Zaefferer; our research assistants Tim Clausner, Bruce Harold, and Robin Belvin; and Lehmann's research assistants Jürgen Bohnemeyer and Eva Schultze-Berndt. I also thank Mouton de Gruyter for permission to publish a substantially revised and expanded version of Croft 2000b as Chapter 2 of this book.

This book would not have been written without the generous invitation to spend the 1999–2000 academic year at the Linguistics Department of the Max Planck Institute for Evolutionary Anthropology at Leipzig. My deepest gratitude goes to its director, Bernard Comrie, and to Martin Haspelmath, Mike Tomasello, Elena Lieven, Susanne Michaelis, Claudia Büchel, and Julia Cissewski for intellectual and practical support. A special thanks goes also to the Chester Language Development group, whose interest and enthusiasm provided a spark to this work, and who also commented on several chapters of the first draft.

Jóhanna Barðdal, Matthew Dryer, Jack Hawkins, and Toshio Ohori gave me valuable comments on significant parts of the book. Matt Shibatani and his advanced syntax seminar read and discussed the first six chapters, and gave me detailed comments. Sonia Cristofaro, Östen Dahl, Martin Haspelmath, Mike Tomasello, and an anonymous referee read the entire version of the first draft and contributed many valuable comments and criticisms. I am especially indebted to Martin Haspelmath, who spent hours discussing his comments with me, and above all to Sonia Cristofaro, who not only discussed the first draft with me in detail, but also read and commented on later drafts of several chapters, and discussed the issues at length before, during, and after many dinners in Leipzig. These people have made this a vastly better book, and they are absolved of blame for any errors and inaccuracies that may remain.

I would also like to thank the audiences who contributed many valuable questions, comments, and observations that have improved the content of this book in many ways, at presentations given at the 65th Annual Winter Meeting of the Linguistic Society of America, the Institute for Linguistics of the University of Cologne, the Indiana University Lecture Series in Formal Syntax, the Nineteenth Annual Meeting of the Berkeley Linguistics Society, the Department of Linguistics of the University of Amsterdam, the Workshop on Conditionals at the University of Duisburg, the Typology Mini-Symposium at the University of Stockholm, the Seventh Annual Research Seminar of the Department of English at the University of Tampere, the Department of Linguistics at the University of Essex, The Philological Society, the Linguistic Circle of Copenhagen, the Faculty of Humanities Lecture Series of the University of Copenhagen, the XVI Scandinavian Linguistics Conference, the Department of Linguistics at the University of Manchester, the Fifth International Cognitive Linguistics Conference, the Department of Linguistics at the University of California at Berkeley, the Oxford Linguistics Circle, the Spring 1998 Meeting of the Linguistics Association of Great Britain, the Department of Linguistics at the University of Chicago, the Linguistic Circle of Edinburgh, the Second Meeting of the Association for Linguistic Typology, the "Whither Whorf?" Workshop of the Cognitive Science Program at Northwestern University, the University of Manchester Institute of Science and Technology, the Department of Linguistics at the Catholic University of Leuven, the Workshop on Language Development at the University of Wales, the Workshop on Language and Thought at the Department of Psychology of the University of Chicago, the Sixth International Cognitive Linguistics Conference, the Department of Language and Information Sciences of the University of Tokyo, the Faculty of Integrated Human Studies of Kyoto University, the Faculty of

Letters of Kobe University, the Second Winter Typological School in Moscow, the 22nd Annual Meeting of the German Linguistics Society, and the 28th LAUD Symposium on Cognitive Linguistics.

Above all, I give my thanks to the field linguists who have devoted their lives to describing the languages of the world. Without their work, linguistics would not exist. Yet they struggle to get their work published and to be employed; nobody wants to publish reference grammars (let alone texts) because linguists aren't interested in reading them, and it is well-known that you can't get tenure with "just" a marvelously detailed reference grammar of your field language. Not infrequently I get frustrated at a patchy, incomplete description, or at what I believe is a poor analysis of the facts, in a reference grammar or descriptive article; but are not theoretical linguists as much to blame for this state of affairs? I don't expect that field linguists will like everything I say here, but I hope that this book goes some way towards bringing syntactic theory back to data.

Between May 1997, when I first presented these ideas under the name 'radical construction grammar', and the present writing, a number of my teachers, colleagues, and friends have died. All were too young, and most were much too young. I would like to remember them here. Charles Ferguson at Stanford offered a gentle yet healthy iconoclasm; Jim McCawley was an inspiration from my undergraduate days at Chicago onward. Megumi Kameyama and Keith Denning were both fellow graduate students at Stanford; Keith was also my closest friend in linguistics. Dave Poole, one of the leading folkdancers in Menlo Park and an independent spirit, coaxed me in my first advanced folkdance class and always wanted to talk about linguistics; we'll always dance Pušteno Oro/Devojče, Devojče for you. Barbara Thornton was one of the finest interpreters of medieval music alive; her death has robbed the world, but her voice and vision have been captured in many beautiful recordings. Finally, Sky Evergreen (Bob Bauer), the first of these to die, was my best friend from junior high school onwards; he taught me to love music, one of the most precious gifts I have ever received . . . Death don't have no mercy.

I would also like to thank Bernard, Don, Elena, Julia, Henry, Katja, Martin, Masha, Melissa, Mike, Mira, Penny, Sonia, Susanne, and especially Carol for their emotional support and for showing me light in the darkness.

Lastly, I thank my old friend Don Falk for bringing the Dead back to life for me; and the late Dick Latvala and the folks at Club Front in San Rafael, my home town, for releasing their shows on disc, thereby letting Jerry and the Boys once again speak to me, sing for me, and cry for me.

And we bid you goodnight.

W.A.C.
Leipzig, August 2000

Figures

1.1	The componential model of the organization of a grammar	15
1.2	The symbolic structure of a construction	18
1.3	The relation between form and function in a componential syntactic theory	19
1.4	The relation between form and function in construction grammar	19
1.5	Simplified generative and construction grammar representations of *Heather sings*	20
1.6	Elements, components, and units of a construction	21
1.7	Representation of subject and object in generative grammatical theories	23
1.8	Dependency representation of syntactic relation between *Heather* and *sings*	23
1.9	Roles in the Intransitive construction	23
1.10	The difference between syntactic roles and syntactic relations	24
1.11	A taxonomic hierarchy of clause types	26
1.12	Multiple parents in a construction taxonomy	26
1.13	A reductionist construction grammar representation of the category Verb across constructions	54
1.14	Radical Construction Grammar representation of verbal categories	56
1.15	Radical Construction Grammar representation of construction taxonomy	56
2.1	Conceptual space for parts of speech	92
2.2	The semantic map for the Japanese Nominal, Nominal Adjective, and Adjective constructions	95
2.3	Semantic map of English parts of speech constructions	99
2.4	Distribution of Lango predication/modification constructions	101
2.5	Dynamicization of structural coding/behavioral potential map hypothesis	101
3.1	The relation between syntax, semantics, and conceptualization (Langacker 1976)	109
3.2	Universal polysemy analysis of Ground role	117
3.3	The relation between syntax, semantics, and conceptualization	128
4.1	Distributional properties (occurrence in syntactic position/with case affixes) for syntactic roles of English and Yuwaalaraay	135
4.2	Conceptual space for participant roles in transitive and intransitive situations	137
4.3	Semantic maps of syntactic roles defined by case coding	138

xx Figures

4.4	Conceptual space for intransitive, transitive, and ditransitive participant roles	147
4.5	A conceptual space representation of the Subject Construction Hierarchy, with a semantic map for Asiatic Eskimo	161
4.6	Conceptual space for intransitive event participant roles	163
4.7	Simplified conceptual space for selected "core" participant roles	164
4.8	Argument linking and aspectual constructions in English	168
4.9	Tense/argument linking constructions in Chol	169
4.10	Conceptual space for aspect and participant roles, with a semantic map for Chol	169
5.1	The internal structure of a construction (exploded diagram)	176
5.2	Construction grammar representation of an idiomatically combining expression	183
6.1	The internal structure of a construction without syntactic relations	204
6.2	Syntactic and semantic structures without symbolic relations	207
6.3	Symbolic links for Tzotzil Possessor Ascension construction in example (2)	212
6.4	Symbolic links for English Predicated Passive construction in example (17b)	216
6.5	Symbolic links in the Japanese Evidential Complement Subject Passive construction	219
6.6	Syntactic roles and syntactic relations	220
6.7	Syntactic roles and relations in a construction with three elements	221
6.8	Symbolic relations in example (29)	222
6.9	Symbolic relations in the constructions illustrated in example (37)	224
6.10	Symbolic links for the construction illustrated in example (40)	226
6.11	Symbolic links for the construction illustrated in example (55)	232
7.1	Simplified semantic valence structure for *Hannah sings*	274
7.2	Semantic valence structure for *chase + in the park*	275
8.1	The conceptual space for active–passive–inverse voice	284
8.2	Semantic map for Cree Direct and Inverse constructions	287
8.3	Semantic map for Lummi Active and Passive constructions	289
8.4	Semantic map for K'iche' Active and Passive voice	290
8.5	Semantic map of Upriver Halkomelem voice constructions	294
8.6	Semantic map for Arizona Tewa Active and Passive/Inverse constructions	296
8.7	Semantic map for Tangut Verb Agreement	296
8.8	Semantic map for Yurok Bipersonal, Unipersonal, and Passive constructions	297
8.9	Semantic map for Chukchi Transitive Verb constructions	300
8.10	Semantic map for Seko Padang proclitic constructions	301
8.11	Semantic map for Yimas Agreement constructions	302
8.12	Semantic map of Dyirbal case constructions	310

8.13	Approximate visual presentation of the syntactic space for voice constructions	313
8.14	Paths of grammatical change in voice in syntactic space	314
8.15	Two analyses of topicality and voice constructions	316
8.16	The conceptual space for voice and transitivity	317
9.1	The continuum of complex sentence types	322
9.2	The conceptual space of complex sentence types	327
9.3	Perception of different-sized forms	332
9.4	Perception of bounded and open-ended forms	333
9.5	Figure–ground relations and discourse structure	335
9.6	The principle of good continuation in perception	337
9.7	Syntactic-conceptual space mapping for complex sentence constructions	360

Tables

1.1	Distribution of Verbs and Adjectives in predicate constructions	12
1.2	Traditional constructional tests for subjecthood in English	14
1.3	The syntax–lexicon continuum	17
1.4	Distribution of arguments across tests for Direct Object status	35
1.5	Distributional patterns for Active Object and Passive Subject in English	36
1.6	Subclasses of one word class?	37
1.7	Separate word classes?	37
1.8	Multiple word class membership?	38
1.9	A third word class?	39
1.10	The representation of constructions in reductionist and nonreductionist syntactic theories	54
2.1	Distribution patterns of Noun-Nominal Adjective-Adjective classes in Japanese	83
2.2	Semantic properties of prototypical parts of speech	87
2.3	Overtly marked structural coding constructions for parts of speech	88
2.4	Distribution of Lango property and action words	100
4.1	Distribution of case marking in Yuwaalaraay	135
4.2	Distribution of NP positions in English	135
4.3	Distribution of zero vs. overt case coding in accusative languages	139
4.4	Distribution of zero vs. overt case coding in ergative languages	140
4.5	Distribution of object roles in the English Indirect Object construction	143
4.6	Distribution of object roles in the English Ditransitive construction	143
4.7	Distribution of zero vs. overt case coding in direct object languages	144
4.8	Distribution of zero vs. overt case coding of primary/secondary objects	145
4.9	Arguing for the global category Subject (S+A) in English	148
4.10	Data supporting the Subject Construction Hierarchy	156
4.11	Animacy-based split in Cashinawa	167
4.12	Localist metaphor linking event structure and aspect	169
7.1	Zwicky's criteria for headhood (Zwicky 1985, 1993)	242
7.2	Properties of clustering	267
8.1	Distribution of Guaraní agreement forms	298
8.2	Analysis of Guaraní agreement forms	298
8.3	Paradigm of Dyirbal Split Ergative forms	309

8.4	Summary of structural properties of voice constructions	311
8.5	Localist metaphor linking event structure, participant animacy, and aspect	319
9.1	Gestalt principles accounting for the foreground–background distinction	333

Abbreviations

The abbreviations for grammatical morphemes and categories have been standardized in the examples, in accordance with the abbreviations adopted by the Framework for Descriptive Grammars project (Bernard Comrie, William Croft, Christian Lehmann, Dietmar Zaefferer) in 1991, and subsequently adopted (with some modifications) by the European Typology project. Abbreviations in this list have a maximum length of five, and were designed to eliminate ambiguity, maintain uniqueness of abbreviation, and to render some less-used abbreviations more "natural". Some additional abbreviations found in the examples are also listed below. (Following the conventions adopted in this book—see §1.6.3—the full names of language-specific category labels are capitalized and the full names of semantic category labels are in lower case.)

1	First Person
2	Second Person
3	Third Person
A	transitive agent
ABL	Ablative ('from')
ABS	Absolutive Case
ACC	Accusative
ACCID	Accidental
ACT	Active
ACTR	Actor
ADVR	Adverbializer
AF	Actor Focus (Philippine languages)
AI	Animate Intransitive conjugation (Algonkian languages)
AN	Animate
ANTI	Antipassive
ANTIC	Anticipatory desinence (Papuan languages)
APPL	Applicative
ART	Article
ASP	Aspect
ASSOC	Associative
AT	Attributor
AUX	Auxiliary
CAUS	Causative
CJPRT	Conjunctive Participle
CLF	Classifier
CLn	Noun Class n
CMPL	Completive

COMP	Complementizer
CONN	Connective
COP	Copula
DAT	Dative
DEF	Definite
DEM	Demonstrative
DET	Determiner
DIR	Direct Voice
DISC	Discourse Marker
DIST	Distal (= third person deictic)
DO	Direct Object
DS	Different Subject
DSTR	Distributive
DU	Dual
DUR	Durative
EMPH	Emphatic
ERG	Ergative
EVID	Evidential
EX	Exclusive
F	Feminine
FNI	free null instantiation
FNL	Final position marker
FOC	Focus
FRM	Formal (politeness)
FUT	Future
FZ	father's sister
G	ditransitive "goal"
GEN	Genitive
GENL	General Classifier
GER	Gerund (Verbal Adverb)
GF	Goal Focus (Philippine languages)
HAB	Habitual
HUM	Human
I	INFL (generative grammar)
IMM	Immediate (Past, Future)
IMP	Imperative
IMPF	Imperfect(ive)
IMPR	Impersonal
IN	Inclusive
INAN	Inanimate
INCH	Inchoative
IND	Indicative
INDF	Indefinite

INESS	Inessive ('in')
INF	Infinitive
INFL	Inflection
INST	Instrumental
INTR	Intransitive
INTS	Intensifier/Intensive
INV	Inverse Voice
IO	Indirect Object
IP	INFL Phrase (generative grammar)
IRR	Irrealis
ITER	Iterative
JUSS	Jussive
K	Case (generative grammar)
KP	Case Phrase (generative grammar)
LNK	Linker
LOC	Locative
M	Masculine
MDL	Modal
MED	Medial Verb form (Papuan languages)
MOM	Momentaneous Aspect
N	Neuter
NARR	Narrative (Tense)
NEG	Negative
NFUT	Nonfuture
NNI	nonnull instantiation
NOM	Nominative
NP	Noun Phrase (generative grammar)
NPST	Nonpast
NR	Nominalizer
NSBJ	Nonsubject
NSG	Nonsingular
NUM	Numeral
OBJ	Object role
OBL	Oblique
OBLG	Obligative
OBV	Obviative (Algonkian languages)
P	transitive patient
PART	Participle
PASS	Passive
PIBU	primary information bearing unit
PL	Plural
PNCT	Punctual
PO	Primary Object
POSS	Possessive

PP	Prepositional Phrase
PRED	Predicate
PREF	Prefix
PREP	Preposition
PRF	Perfective
PRN	Pronoun
PRO	"big PRO" (generative grammar)
PROG	Progressive
PROH	Prohibitive
PROX	Proximal
PRS	Present
PRT	Preterite
PRTT	Partitive
PRXT	Proximate (Algonkian languages)
PST	Past
PTCL	Particle
QNT	Quantifier
RDP	Reduplication
REC	Recent Past Tense
REF	Referential
REFL	Reflexive
REL	Relative Clause marker (other than Relative Pronoun)
REM	Remote (past, future)
RL	Realis
S	intransitive subject
SBJ	Subject
SG	Singular
SO	Secondary Object
Spec	Specifier (generative grammar)
STAT	Stative
SUBR	Subordinator
T	ditransitive "theme"
TA	Transitive Animate conjugation (Algonkian languages)
TEMP	Temporal
TI	Transitive Inanimate conjugation (Algonkian languages)
TNS	Tense
TOP	Topic
TR	Transitive
UNDR	Undergoer
V	Verb
VAL	Validator (Quechuan languages)
VP	Verb Phrase
YBr	younger brother

Symbols

The following symbols are used in example sentences in the original language and their interlinear morpheme translations, and in symbolic representations of syntactic structures. These symbols follow the conventions found in Lehmann (1982c), and revised by the Framework for Descriptive Grammar project (Bernard Comrie, William Croft, Bruce Harold, Christian Lehmann, and Dietmar Zaefferer) in 1991.

In both original language and interlinear morpheme translation:
x y	word boundary between x and y
x – y	morpheme boundary between x and y
x + y	x and y form a compound or a derivative stem
x = y	x and y are joined by clisis
$x_i \ldots y_i$	x and y are coreferential elements
t	trace (generative grammar)

In original language only:
Ø	null expression of meaning (optionally represented)
a<x>b	x is an infix, a . . . b is the discontinous root/stem
a>y<b	a . . . b is a circumfix, y is the root/stem

In interlinear morpheme translation only:
(x)	x is not overtly marked in the original (i.e. null expression of meaning)
y<x>	x is the infix, a . . . b = y is the root/stem
<x>y	a . . . b = x is the circumfix, y is the root/stem
x\y	y is an internal modification of lexeme x in the original
x:y	morpheme boundary between x and y not shown in the original
x.y	x and y are grammatical (sub-)categories of one original language morpheme
x/y	x and y are alternative meanings of an ambiguous element
[x]	x is a syntactic constituent in L1
$[x]_Y$	x is a syntactic constituent of category Y in L1
[X Y Z]	a construction consisting of elements X, Y, and Z, whose linear order is not necessarily fixed

PART I

From Syntactic Categories to Semantic Maps

1

Syntactic Argumentation and Radical Construction Grammar

1.1. Introduction

Radical Construction Grammar is a theory of syntax, that is, a theory characterizing the grammatical structures that are assumed to be represented in the mind of a speaker. As such, it is broadly comparable to the successive versions of generative grammar, such as Government and Binding Theory (Chomsky 1981) and Minimalism (Chomsky 1995), and to Head-driven Phrase Structure Grammar (Pollard and Sag 1993), Lexical Functional Grammar (Bresnan 1982), Role and Reference Grammar (Foley and Van Valin 1984; Van Valin 1993; Van Valin and LaPolla 1997), Functional Grammar (Dik 1997), Word Grammar (Hudson 1984, 1990), and Kay and Fillmore's Construction Grammar (Fillmore and Kay 1993; Kay and Fillmore 1999; see §1.3).

One might reasonably ask, does the field of linguistics need yet another model of syntactic representation? There are more than enough available, in the eyes of many linguists. Moreover, it is not obvious what the significant advantages are of any one syntactic theory over the others. All of the aforementioned theories have developed, in their maturity, a complex array of symbolic representations of various grammatical structures. The complexity is justified by their advocates as being necessary to capture the facts of a wide range of languages, or at least a wide range of facts in a single language. As a result, learning a syntactic theory is like learning a human language, and in fact it is. A syntactic theory offers its followers a technical language for describing the structure of utterances in human languages in presumably insightful ways. If this is true, then it is important to get the syntactic theory right. But which theory is the right one?

Radical Construction Grammar differs radically from all of the aforementioned syntactic theories, as its name implies. Radical Construction Grammar was developed in order to account for the diversity of the syntactic facts of a single language as well as the syntactic diversity of the world's languages. Radical Construction Grammar emerged from a reassessment of the methods of syntactic argumentation used by linguists since at least the structuralist period. Again, the reader may reasonably be skeptical. After all, s/he has probably heard such claims before for other syntactic theories. It is the purpose of this book to persuade the reader that Radical Construction Grammar really is different.

Radical Construction Grammar is radical in that it represents a dramatic break from prior syntactic theories. In this book, I argue that virtually all aspects of the formal representation of grammatical structure are language-particular. In other words, Radical Construction Grammar does away with virtually all of the syntactic apparatus that populate other syntactic theories. Thus, the reader will not find a formal vocabulary for representing syntactic structure in this book, because such a vocabulary would be language-specific. In this sense, Radical Construction Grammar is the syntactic theory to end all syntactic theories. There is no longer any need to learn an entire complex technical language in order to describe a complex human language.

Radical Construction Grammar is also radical in that it goes back to the foundations of syntax in order to make this new beginning. The reason why we must discard all of the formal apparatus is a fundamental flaw in the use of the basic method of empirical syntactic argumentation used in linguistics. This method, the DISTRIBUTIONAL METHOD, defines syntactic categories in terms of their possibility of filling certain roles in certain GRAMMATICAL CONSTRUCTIONS. The distributional method will be described in more detail in §1.2, and the generalized notion of a grammatical construction will be described in §1.3. The distributional method and the linguistic facts it describes turn out to be incompatible with the assumption that syntactic structures or constructions are made up of atomic primitive syntactic elements, that is, the elements that make up the building blocks of other syntactic theories.

Instead, constructions are the basic units of syntactic representation, and categories are derived from the construction(s) in which they appear—as the distributional method implies. In the rest of this chapter, I explain just how this could be true. The remaining chapters in Part I apply the argument of this chapter to two of the most fundamental sets of categories posited by syntactic theories: parts of speech such as noun and verb, and syntactic roles ("grammatical relations") such as subject and object.

The primitive status of constructions does not preclude the possibility of forming generalizations across constructions and their constituent ELEMENTS, or of identifying constructions in the first place. In fact, Radical Construction Grammar presents both of these types of generalizations as instances of the general cognitive process of CATEGORIZATION (§§1.6.4–1.6.6). There is a great deal of research into categorization in psychology and in linguistics, which has revealed how rich and complex this cognitive ability is. I will briefly touch on these questions in §1.3.3 and §§1.6.4–1.6.6.

The formation of categories is an important aspect of grammatical theory. However, the reader will not find representations of categorization processes leading to maximally general analyses of grammatical phenomena in English or any other specific language in this book. There are several reasons for not examining categorization in detail in this volume, besides the practical issue of length. First, a full treatment of this issue must await further psychological research and its application to language (see the references in §1.3.3). Nevertheless, the search for maximally general categories and rules for a particular language will not yield what its practitioners believe. Maximally general categories and rules are highly likely not to be psychologically real (see §1.3.3); hence the search for maximally general analyses is probably a search for an empirically nonexistent—that is, a fictional—entity. Moreover, constructing a maximally general analysis inevitably leads to the ignoring of empirical fact—namely, the manifold differences in distributional patterns of different constructions and categories. In other words, maximally general analyses are fictional in a second sense, in that they do not represent empirical reality.

Analyses of maximal generality are often described as "deep" or "detailed" analyses of grammatical phenomena in a language. A common criticism of cross-linguistic studies is that they utilize only a "superficial" analysis of each language. But a genuinely "deep" and "detailed" analysis of a single language would represent all of the distributional differences among the constructions of the language. Universals of language will not be found by constructing maximally general analyses; even if such analyses are not fictional, they are highly language-specific. Instead, universals of language are found in the patterned variation of constructions and the categories they define. The careful analysis of variation in distribution patterns will reveal generalizations about grammatical structure and behavior in specific languages that are ultimately identical to the cross-linguistic patterns revealed by typological research, as will be seen repeatedly in this book.

The primitive status of constructions and the nonexistence of primitive syntactic categories is the central thesis of Radical Construction Grammar. This thesis makes Radical Construction Grammar a NONREDUCTIONIST theory of syntax, in contrast to the previously mentioned theories (see §1.6.1). But this is not all that is radical about Radical Construction Grammar.

All of the aforementioned syntactic theories posit the existence of SYNTACTIC RELATIONS between the syntactic elements in a construction, such as between a subject noun phrase and a verb, or between an attributive adjective and a noun, although the theories vary significantly in exactly how syntactic relations are represented (e.g. constituency or dependency; see §1.3.2 and Chapter 5). Radical Construction Grammar does not posit any syntactic relations in constructions. The only internal syntactic structure to constructions is their MERONOMIC or part–whole structure: the syntactic structure of constructions consists only of their elements (which may also be complex constructions) and the ROLES that they fulfill in the construction.

Again, this thesis emerges from a critical examination of methods of syntactic argumentation. Two classes of evidence are used to argue for the existence of a syntactic relation between two elements. The first are COLLOCATIONAL DEPENDENCIES, such as the idiomatic relationship between *strings* and *pull* in **Strings** were **pulled** *to get him the job.* The second are CODED DEPENDENCIES, such as the agreement of the Verb *sells* with the Subject *Sheila* in **Sheila** *sells seashells.*

In Part II, I argue that neither collocational dependencies nor coded dependencies are evidence for the existence of syntactic relations. Collocational dependencies actually reveal SEMANTIC RELATIONS between components of the semantic structure associated with the construction in question (§5.2, following Nunberg et al. 1994). Coded dependencies actually reveal SYMBOLIC RELATIONS between a formal element of a construction and the semantic component that it stands for (Chapter 6). If the alleged evidence for syntactic relations actually is evidence for semantic and symbolic relations, then there is no evidence for syntactic relations. And indeed there are some good reasons not to posit syntactic relations, as will be seen in Chapter 6. So Radical Construction Grammar does without them. Chapter 7 applies the theory expounded in Chapters 5–6 to the analysis of heads, arguments, and adjuncts.

Finally, I argue that constructions themselves are language-specific. In this case, the method of argumentation that is challenged is the use of a set of necessary formal syntactic properties for identifying putatively universal constructions across languages. In Part III, I argue that the facts of languages demonstrate that any such set of syntactic properties will isolate only a subset of the relevant constructions in the world's languages. Instead, one must describe a SYNTACTIC SPACE in which there is a continuum of construction types in morphosyntactic terms. I illustrate this approach for voice in Chapter 8 and complex sentences in Chapter 9.

Of course, Radical Construction Grammar does not come out of nowhere, and a number of its central points have been anticipated in other approaches. Cognitive Grammar (Langacker 1987, 1991a, 1991b) is broadly compatible with Radical Construction Grammar. Cognitive Grammar also eschews a complex syntactic metalanguage, and relies heavily on the meronomic relations of elements within syntactic structures (constructions) and on taxonomic relations between constructions (see §1.3.2). Radical Construction Grammar in turn also conforms to Cognitive Grammar's CONTENT REQUIREMENT:

the only structures permitted in the grammar of a language (or among the substantive specifications of universal grammar) are (1) phonological, semantic or symbolic structures that actually occur in linguistic expressions; (2) schemas for such structures; and (3) categorizing relationships involving the elements in (1) and (2) (Langacker 1987: 53–4).

Radical Construction Grammar engages in a detailed critique of syntactic methodology and its consequences, and explores cross-linguistic patterns in greater detail than has been done so far in Cognitive Grammar writings. Statements about the differences between Radical Construction Grammar and 'other syntactic theories' in this book should be understood as excluding Cognitive Grammar from the latter category. Nevertheless, it is important to emphasize that the arguments on which Radical Construction Grammar rests do *not* depend on specific semantic theories or analyses in Cognitive Grammar or elsewhere in the cognitive linguistic tradition.

Last but not least, Radical Construction Grammar is a theory of syntactic representation that is consistent with the findings of field linguists and typological theory (Comrie 1989, Croft 1990a). The critique of syntactic argumentation to be found in this book rests in part on the empirical variation of grammatical phenomena, across languages and within them. This empirical variation is well-known to typologists and in fact to most linguists. Again, it is important to emphasize that the critique presented here does *not* depend on the validity of specific cross-linguistic generalizations proposed in typology. But the question remains, once the critique has been made, and "Universal Grammar" has been deconstructed as I have described above, what is left? Where are the universals of language, if there are any?

The universals of language, if any, are of the type proposed in typological research. Radical Construction Grammar allows one to bring what might be called "thinking like a typologist" (Croft 1999) into the analysis of the grammar of a single language. There are certain ways of thinking about language that come naturally to a typologist but which do not always seem to come naturally to other theoretical linguists. The following paragraphs briefly describe typological thinking.

Above all, DIVERSITY (VARIATION) in language is basic. Variation is the normal state of language which we have to deal with. It is dealing mainly with cross-linguistic variation that is the domain of typology. But typologists have also come to integrate diachronic variation into their purview as in grammaticalization theory (Hopper and Traugott 1993). Radical Construction Grammar offers a way to integrate synchronic language-internal variation into typological thinking.

Everything else about doing typology represents typology's way of dealing with the fact of variation. A typologist uses an INDUCTIVE method of analysis, by constructing a sample of the world's languages and seeking language universals via cross-linguistic generalizations. Since diversity is basic, the only safe way that one can discover the range of linguistic diversity is by cross-linguistic research. And it is only through exploring linguistic diversity that one is able to discover the limits to variation, that is, the universals of human language.

The typologist's search for language universals is balanced by the recognition that ARBITRARINESS in language exists and should be accepted as such. Not everything in language can be, or should be, explainable, whether in terms of formal or functional general principles, abstract generalizations, etc. If it were, all languages would be alike, all languages would be internally invariant, and no languages would change.

A typologist endeavors to make his/her language universals explainable, and hence anything arbitrary about language is, we hope, language-particular. But that means that the grammars of particular languages involve some arbitrariness mixed in with the motivated universal principles (Croft 1995a: 504–9). This is because the principled motivations compete with each other, and the resolution of the competition for each language is always partly arbitrary. This way of thinking is quite foreign to many nontypological linguists, both formalist and functionalist, who seek an explanation for everything in a grammar. Having an eye on the slightly different language across the ocean, or down the road, generally reminds the typologist of the futility of this approach (see the Preface).

A typologist also accepts that all things in grammar must pass. Language is fundamentally DYNAMIC, at both the micro-level—language use—and the macro-level—the broad sweep of grammatical changes that take generations to work themselves out (Croft 2000a). Synchronic language states are just snapshots of a dynamic process emerging originally from language use in conversational interaction. This thinking follows from the recognition of arbitrariness. What is arbitrary can change (since it isn't dictated by general principles)—and does. What is basic are the principles that govern the dynamic or diachronic universals.

In fact, anyone who does typology soon learns that there is no synchronic typological universal without exceptions. But a typologist sees not only the counterexamples—which, after all, must be possible language types, since they actually exist—but also the highly skewed distribution. In a diachronic perspective, where every language type comes into existence and passes on to another type with different degrees of frequency and stability, and the gradualness of change means all sorts of "anomalous" intermediate types are found, possibility is much less important than probability. As a result, there has been a shift in typological thinking from constraining possible language types to calculating probable language types.[1]

This, then, is thinking about language like a typologist: variation, arbitrariness, change, and the fundamentally cross-linguistic character of universals. Radical Construction Grammar clears the way to bring typological thinking to syntactic theory.

Radical Construction Grammar does not merely aim to deconstruct syntax as we know it. Another major goal of Radical Construction Grammar is to represent universals of human language in a way that is plausible as a model of the knowledge of an individual speaker of a particular language. Recently, typologists have begun to embrace a model of the representation of language-particular grammatical knowledge in the context of universal patterns of variation. This model is the SEMANTIC MAP model, in which distributional patterns of language-particular categories are mapped onto a CONCEPTUAL SPACE, much of whose structure is hypothesized to be universal. The semantic map/conceptual space model will be introduced in §2.4, and used throughout Parts I and III of this book (Part II is devoted to the internal syntactic structure of constructions).

---

[1] Dryer 1997a offers powerful arguments for why probabilistic ('statistical') language universals are superior to categorical ('absolute') language universals, given that the known distribution of the vast majority of grammatical properties is skewed, often strongly skewed.

1.2. Methodology and Theory in Syntax

1.2.1. *The basic question of syntactic analysis*

Linguistics is an empirical science. That is to say, any syntactic theory must be developed in a conversation with the facts of human languages. Hence, there are two intertwined basic questions of syntactic analysis, one theoretical and one methodological.

The theoretical question posed by contemporary syntactic theories is: 'WHAT IS THE NATURE OF THE GRAMMATICAL KNOWLEDGE THAT THE SPEAKER HAS IN HIS/HER HEAD, AND HOW SHOULD IT BE REPRESENTED?' That is, what is the right theory of syntax, more precisely, of syntactic representation—in particular one that conforms to the empirical discoveries of cross-linguistic research?

The theoretical question is commonly cast as the search for UNIVERSAL GRAMMAR. The term 'Universal Grammar' and its abbreviation, UG, are associated with generative grammar's claim that certain aspects of syntactic structure are not only universal but innately specified. However, one can characterize Universal Grammar more broadly, without necessarily assuming that it is innate: although innate properties are necessarily universal, universals of human language are not necessarily an innate genetic endowment. In the broad sense, Universal Grammar consists of those aspects or properties of grammatical structure which form the makeup of the grammars of all human languages.

The syntactic theories named in §1.1 offer a precise answer to this theoretical question, in terms of the formal language for syntactic representation that each theory provides. Universal Grammar is the formal language for syntactic representation. These syntactic theories are generally called FORMALIST theories of syntax. Formalist theories of syntax are generally contrasted with FUNCTIONALIST theories of syntax. Functionalist theories of syntax are associated with the hypothesis that the principles that govern syntactic structure are not self-contained, that is, they involve semantic and/or discourse principles. In contrast, formalist theories argue that there is a set of self-contained principles governing syntactic structure that make no reference to semantic or discourse principles.

It is not my purpose to discuss the self-containedness of grammar here (see Croft 1995a). Instead, I wish to focus on a fact about grammar accepted by both formalists and functionalists (see Croft 1995a: 509, 516): that the form–function (syntax–semantics) mapping is ARBITRARY to at least some degree, and thus form must be represented independently of function to at least some degree. Formalist theories of syntax incorporate the arbitrariness of language in their models fairly straightforwardly. Functionalists, on the other hand, have rarely addressed the question of how the formal structure of utterances is to be represented (two important exceptions are Langacker 1987 and Givón 1995). This is the question that this book addresses.

All of the syntactic theories mentioned in §1.1 share a fundamental assumption about the nature of Universal Grammar. It is assumed that Universal Grammar consists of a set of atomic grammatical primitives (categories and relations), over which syntactic structures and constraints on those structures are defined, that are the building blocks of the particular grammars of all human languages. This assumption is shared with traditional grammar, which gave us much of the terminology used to describe these atomic grammatical primitives, such as 'noun', 'verb', 'subject', and 'object'. This assumption is presented as fact in introductory linguistics textbooks, such as O'Grady et al. (1997), and in introductory syntax textbooks, such as Haegeman (1994):

A fundamental fact about words in all human languages is that they can be grouped together into a relatively small number of classes, called syntactic categories (O'Grady et al. 1997: 164).

Words belong to different syntactic categories, such as nouns, verbs, etc., and the syntactic category to which a word belongs determines its distribution, that is, in what contexts it can occur (Haegeman 1994: 36).

Syntactic theories have qualified the universality of Universal Grammar in some cases. A strict interpretation of Universal Grammar would assert that all languages possess essentially the same set of categories and relations. A PARAMETERIZED interpretation of Universal Grammar asserts that the presence of some properties are contingent on the presence of other properties. It is usually assumed that a biconditional universal relation holds between the parameterized properties, such that if a language has +α then it has +β, +γ, etc. and if a language has −α then it has −β, −γ, etc. Finally, a "SMORGASBORD" interpretation of Universal Grammar asserts that the set of categories and relations are available to all speakers, but speakers of some languages do not avail themselves of all of the categories and relations available to them (e.g. Zwicky 1993: 315, fn 9). For example, one approach to the category Aux(iliary) proposed that Aux was a part of Universal Grammar, but not every language had a category Aux. These qualifications are intended to accommodate some of the diversity of human languages, but they do not significantly alter the basic reductionist model.

The theoretical question is the one emphasized in most textbooks and presentations of syntactic theories. But in empirical science, there is always a methodological question that is presupposed by the theoretical question. For syntactic theory, the methodological question is: 'IS THERE A GENERAL, LANGUAGE-UNIVERSAL METHOD FOR JUSTIFYING THE EXISTENCE IN A PARTICULAR LANGUAGE OF THE SYNTACTIC ELEMENTS—CATEGORIES AND RELATIONS—THAT ARE THE BASIC UNITS OF SYNTACTIC THEORY?'

If we propose that adjective or subject are categories in Universal Grammar, we must have a method for deciding whether a particular language has adjectives or subjects. Likewise, if we construct a hypothesis about, for instance, an essential grammatical property of subjects across languages, then we must be able to identify subjects in every language in order to observe if the subjects have the grammatical property in question.

It has been suggested to me that the methodological question is of relatively minor importance. In particular, reference is made to Chomsky's argument that it is unreasonable to ask linguistic theory for a discovery procedure for identifying the right grammar for a particular language (Chomsky 1957: 50–3). However, the problem which I am referring to is more basic than that. It is what Chomsky calls the condition of generality (ibid., 50), necessary for any adequate theory of grammar: 'we must characterize the form of grammars in a general and explicit way so that we can actually propose grammars of this form for particular languages' (ibid., 53–4). That is, for a particular language we can argue for and thus justify the analysis of that language's structures as an instance of the structures found in Universal Grammar.

It is the condition of generality that I believe current syntactic theories fail. That is, the methods that linguists use to argue for their syntactic theories carry hidden fallacies which are largely unremarked upon. When these fallacious assumptions are uncovered, their abandonment leads us to a very different approach to syntactic theory than that advocated by formalist theories and even the functionalist syntactic theories referred to above.

1.2.2. *Distributional analysis: the basic method of syntactic argumentation*

There is essentially one single, simple, method that is widely used for syntactic analysis. This method is called DISTRIBUTIONAL ANALYSIS. Distributional analysis stretches far back in the history of linguistics; but it was first codified and given its name by American structuralist linguists in the middle of the last century:

Descriptive linguistics, as the term has come to be used [i.e. structural linguistics, cf. Harris 1951: 1], is a particular field of inquiry which deals . . . with the regularities of certain features of speech. These regularities are in the distributional relations among the features of speech in question, i.e. the occurrence of these features relatively to each other within utterances (Harris 1951: 5).

In distributional analysis, syntactic categories are defined by the occurrence or nonoccurrence of their members in different types of utterances. Utterance types, such as the Information Question (*What did you see?*) or the Passive (*The bride was greeted by the guests*) are defined in structural terms. We will call utterance types CONSTRUCTIONS; constructions will be discussed in greater detail in §1.3. Also, members of a syntactic category do not occur just anywhere in a construction; their occurrence in a construction is relative to the ROLE they fill in the construction; for example, *The bride* fills the Subject role in the Passive construction.

Distributional analysis can be illustrated with a couple of simple examples. Consider the occurrence/nonoccurrence of the English words *cold, happy, dance,* and *sing* in examples 1–4:[2]

---

[2] In these examples and most other examples in this book, the salient morphosyntactic features discussed in the text are highlighted by boldface. This will, I hope, allow the reader to follow the arguments in the book, especially when examples from little-known languages are used as evidence supporting the argument. In some examples (e.g. 19–22 below), the original language form conflates different grammatical categories; in these case, only the relevant part of the gloss is put in boldface.

(1) a. Jack **is** cold.
　　b. *Jack colds.
(2) a. Jack **is** happy.
　　b. *Jack happies.
(3) a. *Jack **is** dance.
　　b. Jack dances.
(4) a. *Jack **is** sing.
　　b. Jack sings.

In the (a) sentences, the four words occur in the Predicate role after the inflected copula *be*. Sentences (1a) and (2a) are acceptable, but (3a) and (4a) are not. In the (b) sentences, the four words occur in the Predicate role without a Copula but with the Tense Agreement inflection (in this case, 3rd Person Singular Present Tense *-s*). Here, sentences 1b and 2b are not acceptable, but sentences 3b and 4b are. Thus, *cold* and *happy* have the same distribution, and contrast with *dance* and *sing*, which share a different distribution pattern. The overall distribution pattern is given in Table 1.1.

Table 1.1. Distribution of Verbs and Adjectives in predicate constructions

	[SBJ *be* __]	[SBJ __-TNS.PERS]
Adjective: *cold, happy*, etc.	√	*
Verb: *sing, dance*, etc.	*	√

In Table 1.1, the columns represent the constructions illustrated in the (a) and (b) sentences of 1–4 respectively. The construction is represented by specifying the role of each element in the construction. If the role represents a category, the category label is given in small capitals; if the role can be filled by only a specific word or morpheme such as *be*, that word or morpheme is given in italics. The role that is being examined is represented by __. The internal syntactic structure of the construction, in particular the order of elements, is not further specified here (see §1.3.3 and Part II for further discussion).

The rows represent the words in 1–4 that occur or do not occur in the specified roles in the constructions. Occurrence is indicated by √ and nonoccurrence by *. In Table 1.1, the words with the same pattern of occurrence/nonoccurrence are put in a single row. The result is two classes of words, which we have labeled with their traditional names, Adjective and Verb. In this book, we will use the convention of capitalized names for language-specific categories, following Comrie 1976a and Bybee 1985 (see §1.6.3). The difference in distribution of the words in 1–4 in the two constructions is taken to be evidence of the existence of the syntactic categories Adjective and Verb in English.

The pattern of occurrence/nonoccurrence of the words in each row across the constructions in the columns in Table 1.1 is called the DISTRIBUTION or the BEHAVIOR of the word(s) in question. Each construction that is used to define a syntactic category in this way is typically called an ARGUMENT, TEST, or CRITERION for the category in question. Thus, SYNTACTIC ARGUMENTATION is the use of one or more constructions to justify the existence of a particular category in the grammar of a language.

What is the explanation of the distribution of the syntactic categories in Table 1.1? The quotation from Haegeman (1994) in §1.2.1 suggests that it is the category membership of the words in question. A purely semantic explanation will not work for parts of speech (see Chapter 2), and so a syntactic explanation is given instead, in terms of the category membership of the words in question. This explanation is considered to be stronger if one can show that the category in question occurs across many constructions. For example, it has been argued that the categories Subject and Object as syntactic roles are found in several different constructions (examples adapted from Croft 1990a: 8, following standard arguments in the syntactic literature; see also §4.3.1):

(5) *Nominative form of the Pronoun*:
   a. **She** congratulated him.
   b. ***Her** congratulated he.
(6) *Agreement of the Verb*:
   a. She$_i$ likes$_i$ horses.
   b. *She like-Ø$_j$ horses$_j$.
(7) *"Null" Noun Phrase in Infinitive Complement "controlled" by Main Clause Argument*:
   a. Jack told Fred$_i$ Ø$_i$ to buy a car.
   b. *Jack told Fred$_i$ to give Ø$_i$ $50.
(8) *"Null" Noun Phrase in Imperatives*:
   a. Ø Learn Hungarian!
   b. *Mary teach Ø Hungarian!
(9) *"Null" Noun Phrase in Conjunction Reduction Coordination* (see e.g. McCawley 1998: 272):
   a. She$_i$ fell and Ø$_i$ broke her hip.
   b. *She$_i$ died and they buried Ø$_i$.

The arguments for Subject vs. Object in English are summarized in Table 1.2 (p. 14).

In standard syntactic argumentation, the more constructions that appear to include a particular category as a role, the stronger the evidence for that category in the language is. That is, the more arguments for a syntactic category that can be offered, the better.

The distributional method is the basic method of empirical grammatical analysis. It is used to identify the basic grammatical units out of which complex syntactic structures or constructions are built. However, the application of the distributional method reveals problems that can only be resolved by taking con-

Table 1.2. Traditional constructional tests for subjecthood in English

	I	II	III	IV	V
Subject	√	√	√	√	√
Object	*	*	*	*	*

I: Nominative Case marking (Pronouns)
II: Agreement of the Verb
III: Controlled null NP of Infinitive Complement
IV: Null NP of Imperative
V: Null NP in "Conjunction Reduction" Coordination

structions—complex syntactic structures and their meanings—rather than categories as the basic units of grammatical representation. Before discussing the problems with the distributional method, I will describe what constructions are and how they are represented in construction-based syntactic theories.

1.3. Constructions and Construction Grammar

In this section, I will give a brief introduction to constructions and construction grammar; this introduction is based on a more detailed explication in Cruse and Croft (to appear, chapters 10–12). In §1.3.1, I will give an outline of some of the arguments in favor of a construction grammar approach to syntactic theory. Needless to say, this section can give only a summary of the more important arguments, and the curious reader should examine the more detailed arguments in Fillmore, Kay and O'Connor 1988, Goldberg 1995, Kay and Fillmore 1999 and Cruse and Croft (to appear). In §1.3.2, I describe the internal structure of a construction. In §1.3.3, I briefly discuss the organization of constructions in a grammar.

Construction grammar exists in a number of variants, such as those found in Lakoff (1987), Fillmore and Kay (1993; see also Kay and Fillmore 1999), Goldberg (1995) and Langacker (1987, 1991). Radical Construction Grammar, as its name implies, is another variety of construction grammar. The introduction here emphasizes the commonalities among the different models of construction grammar, and the particular points where Radical Construction Grammar will be seen to differ from the other construction grammars.

1.3.1. Arguments for construction grammar

Construction grammar represents a reaction to the COMPONENTIAL MODEL of the organization of a grammar that is found in other syntactic theories. In the componential model, different types of properties of an utterance—its sound structure, its syntax and its meaning—are represented in separate components, each of which consists of rules operating over primitive elements of the relevant types (phonemes, syntactic units, semantic units). The only constructs which contain information cutting across the components are words, which represent conventional associations of phonological form, syntactic category, and meaning. More recently, attention has been directed to LINKING RULES that link complex syntactic structures to their semantic interpretation, and link syntactic structures to their phonological realization. The componential model is illustrated in Figure 1.1.

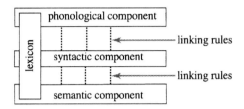

Figure 1.1. The componential model of the organization of a grammar

Many current theories in fact divide grammatical properties into a larger number of components, e.g. a morphological component, an information structure component, or a variety of syntactic components. However these modifications still adhere to the basic concept behind the componential model: grammatical properties of different types are placed in separate components, except for the lexicon.

Construction grammar arose out of a concern to analyze a problematic phenomenon for the componential model, namely idioms (Fillmore et al. 1988). Idioms are linguistic expressions that are syntactically and/or semantically idiosyncratic in various ways, but are larger than words, and hence cannot simply be assigned to the lexicon without some special mechanism. Some idioms are lexically idiosyncratic, using lexical items found nowhere else, such as *kith and kin* 'family and friends'. Such idioms are by definition syntactically and semantically irregular, since the unfamiliar word has no independent syntactic or semantic status. Other idioms use familiar words but their syntax is idiosyncratic, as in *all of a sudden* or *in point of fact*; these are called EXTRAGRAMMATICAL idioms. Still other idioms use familiar words and familiar syntax but are semantically idiosyncratic, such as *tickle the ivories* 'play the piano'.

A theory of grammar should of course capture the differences among these types of idioms and their relationship to the regular lexicon and regular syntactic rules of a language. The need for a theory that can accommodate idioms is even more critical for the idioms that Fillmore et al. (1988) focus their attention on, idioms which are SCHEMATIC to a greater or lesser degree. That is, some idioms are not completely lexically specific or SUBSTANTIVE, like the idioms in the preceding paragraph, but instead include whole syntactic categories admitting a wide range of possible words and phrases to instantiate those categories.

Partially schematic idioms also range over all three types described by Fillmore et al. A schematic idiom which is lexically idiosyncratic is the comparative conditional construction *The X-er, the Y-er* as in *The longer you practice, the better you will become* (the form *the* is not directly related to the definite article, but is derived from the Old English instrumental demonstrative form *þy*). An example of an extragrammatical schematic idiom is the "cousin" construction *Nth cousin (M times removed)*, as in *second cousin three times removed*, which describes different kinds of distant kin relations and has its own unique syntax. Finally, an example of a schematic idiom that is only semantically idiosyncratic is *pull NP's leg* 'joke with NP' as in *Don't pull my leg*; the NP category can be filled by any Noun Phrase denoting a human being.

Schematic idioms pose a serious challenge to the componential model because schematic idioms either have regularities of their own which ought to be captured as regularities (the extragrammatical schematic idioms), or follow regular syntactic rules and ought to be somehow represented as doing so (the grammatical schematic idioms). Moreover, all idioms are semantically idiosyncratic, which means that they do not follow general rules of semantic interpretation. Instead, they have their own rules of semantic interpretation.

Fillmore et al. (1988) argue that we should accept the existence of idioms as CONSTRUCTIONS. Constructions are objects of syntactic representation that also contain semantic and even phonological information (such as the individual substantive lexical items in the partially schematic idioms, or special prosodic patterns or special rules of phonological reduction as in *I wanna go too*). In other words, constructions are like lexical items in the componential model: they link together idiosyncratic or arbitrary phonological, syntactic, and semantic information. The difference between lexical items and constructions is that lexical items are substantive and ATOMIC (that is, minimal syntactic units), while constructions can be at least partially schematic and COMPLEX (consisting of more than one syntactic element).

Beginning with Fillmore et al. (1988) and Lakoff (1987), there have been a number of detailed studies of constructions whose grammatical properties cannot be accounted for by the general syntactic, semantic, and pragmatic rules of English; other major studies following Fillmore et al. and Lakoff's model include Goldberg (1995) and Michaelis and Lambrecht (1996). Also, the studies of syntactic structures with special pragmatic functions by Prince (1978) and Birner and Ward (1998), and the studies of syntactic structures with special semantic interpretations by Wierzbicka (1980, 1987, 1988), strengthen the case for treating those syntactic structures as constructions. Even formal syntacticians who adhere to the componential model have recognized the existence of constructions to some extent; see for example Akmajian (1984) (and compare Lambrecht's 1990 reanalysis of the same phenomenon) and Jackendoff (1990a, 1997).

Constructions can be thought of as the same theoretical type of representation object as lexical items, albeit syntactically complex and at least partially schematic.

Thus, there is a CONTINUUM between the lexicon and syntactic constructions. Fillmore et al. (1988) also make the logical next step: regular syntactic rules and regular rules of semantic interpretation are themselves constructions. The only difference between regular syntactic rules and their rules of semantic interpretation and other constructions is that the former are wholly schematic while the latter retain some substantive elements.

The constructional tail has come to wag the syntactic dog: everything from words to the most general syntactic and semantic rules can be represented as constructions. The final step is to recognize that the internal structure of words are also constructions. After all, a construction like [*The X-er, the Y-er*] or [*pull*-TNS *NP-'s leg*] includes bound morphemes and/or clitic elements in its syntactic representation. One can have fully morphological constructions such as [NOUN-*s*] (partially schematic) or [VERB-TNS] (wholly schematic), while an individual word form like *child-ren* is a wholly substantive morphological construction. The only difference between morphological constructions and syntactic ones is that the former are entirely made up of bound morphemes while the latter are largely made up of free morphemes.

In other words, construction grammar has generalized the notion of a construction to apply to any grammatical structure, including both its form and its meaning. The logical consequence of accommodating idioms in syntactic theory has been to provide a uniform representation of all types of grammatical structures from words to syntactic and semantic rules. The uniform representation is referred to as the SYNTAX–LEXICON CONTINUUM (compare Langacker 1987: 25–7, 35–6), illustrated in Table 1.3.

Table 1.3. The syntax–lexicon continuum

Construction type	Traditional name	Examples
Complex and (mostly) schematic	syntax	[SBJ *be*-TNS VERB-*en by* OBL]
Complex and (mostly) specific	idiom	[*pull*-TNS NP-'s *leg*]
Complex but bound	morphology	[NOUN-*s*], [VERB-TNS]
Atomic and schematic	syntactic category	[DEM], [ADJ]
Atomic and specific	word/lexicon	[*this*], [*green*]

Construction grammar's great attraction as a theory of grammar—not just syntax—is that it provides a uniform model of grammatical representation and at the same time captures a broader range of empirical phenomena than componential models of grammar. For the same reason, construction grammar also provides the most general and neutral way to describe the distributional method (§1.2.2). The notion of a construction in construction grammar is broad enough to represent any morphological or syntactic arguments/criteria/tests for identifying any syntactic category. For example, a description of a distributional argument or test characterized as applying a syntactic or morphological rule to the item in question (such as the Passive rule) can always be recast as a description in terms of occurrence of that item in the construction that is described by the output or result of applying the rule (the Passive construction).

The generality and empirical coverage of construction grammar is a major attraction of construction grammar. However, the arguments in favor of Radical Construction Grammar do not presuppose construction grammar. The arguments to be presented in this chapter and in Chapters 5–6 are methodological arguments and thus apply to other theories of grammar as well as to construction grammar. Nevertheless, the central thesis of this chapter, that constructions are the primitive units of syntactic representation, virtually requires that syntactic theory be a variety of construction grammar. One consequence of the Radical Construction Grammar position, however, is that the penultimate construct in Table 1.3, atomic schematic constructions (syntactic categories), does not exist in the Radical Construction Grammar model (see §1.6.5).

1.3.2. Syntactic and semantic structure: the anatomy of a construction

In this section, I will introduce fundamental concepts and descriptive terms for the analysis of the structure of a grammatical construction. The concepts in this section form the basis of any syntactic theory, including Radical Construction Grammar, although they are combined in different ways in different syntactic theories. I will adhere to conventional terminology in construction grammar as much as possible.

Grammatical constructions in construction grammar, like the lexicon in other syntactic theories, consist of pairings of form and meaning that are at least partially arbitrary. Even the most general syntactic constructions have corresponding general rules of semantic interpretation. Thus, constructions are fundamentally SYMBOLIC units, as represented in Figure 1.2 (compare Langacker 1987: 60).

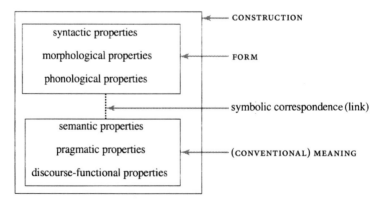

Figure 1.2. The symbolic structure of a construction

The term 'meaning' is intended to represent all of the CONVENTIONALIZED aspects of a construction's function, which may include not only properties of the situation described by the utterance but also properties of the discourse in which the utterance is found (such as use of the Definite Article to indicate that the object referred to is known to both speaker and hearer) and of the pragmatic situation of the interlocutors (e.g. the use of a construction such as *What a beautiful cat!* to convey the speaker's surprise). In this book, I will use the terms 'meaning' and 'semantic' to refer to any conventionalized feature of a construction's function.

The central essential difference between componential syntactic theories and construction grammar is that the symbolic link between form and conventional meaning is internal to a construction in the latter, but is external to the syntactic and semantic components in the former (as linking rules). Figures 1.3 and 1.4 compare construction grammar and a componential syntactic theory on this parameter, highlighting in boldface the essential difference in the two models.

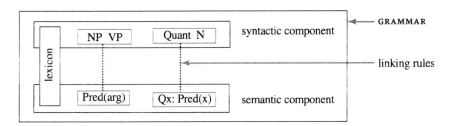

Figure 1.3. The relation between form and function in a componential syntactic theory

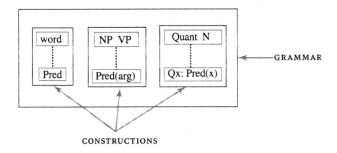

Figure 1.4. The relation between form and function in construction grammar

In the componential model, the various syntactic structures are organized independently of the corresponding semantic structures, as represented by the bold boxes in Figure 1.3. In construction grammar, the basic linguistic units are symbolic, and are organized as symbolic units (see §1.3.3), as represented by the bold boxes in Figure 1.4.[3] As a consequence, the internal structure of the basic (symbolic) units in construction grammar is more complex than that of basic units in the componential model.

The internal structure of a construction is the morphosyntactic structure of sentences that instantiate constructions. For example, a simple intransitive sentence like *Heather sings* is an INSTANCE of the Intransitive construction. If we compare a simplified representation of *Heather sings* in generative grammar to a simplified representation of the same in construction grammar, we can see that they are actually rather similar except that the construction grammar representation is symbolic (Figure 1.5).

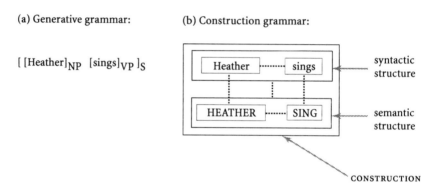

Figure 1.5. Simplified generative and construction grammar representations of *Heather sings*

The box notation used in Figure 1.5b is simply a notational variant of the bracket notation used in Figure 1.5a (Langacker 1987; Kay and Fillmore 1999). Thus, we can see that both the generative grammatical representation and the construction grammar representation share the fundamental part-whole or MERONOMIC structure of grammatical units: the sentence *Heather sings* is made up of two parts, the Subject *Heather* and the Predicate *sings*.

The brackets in Figure 1.5a are labeled with syntactic category labels, while the corresponding boxes in the syntactic structure of Figure 1.5b are not labeled. This does not mean that the boxed structures in Figure 1.5b are all of the same syntactic type. Construction grammarians, of course, assume that syntactic units

---

[3] Other theories that share construction grammar's basis in symbolic units are Head-driven Phrase Structure Grammar (HPSG; Pollard and Sag 1987, 1993), and Semiotic Grammar (McGregor 1997). However, these theories are not explicitly construction-based, although HPSG and Fillmore and Kay's version of construction grammar have converged in many respects.

belong to a variety of different syntactic categories. The boxes have been left unlabeled because the nature of those categories is precisely the issue to be addressed in this chapter. All that it is necessary for us to assume at the moment is the meronomic structure of the syntactic structure of a construction.

Beyond the meronomic structure of grammatical units, generative theories and construction grammar diverge. First, as we have already noted, construction grammar treats grammatical units as fundamentally symbolic, that is, pairings of grammatical form and the corresponding meaning or SEMANTIC STRUCTURE. As a consequence, the representation of a construction includes correspondence relations between the form and the meaning of the construction. We will call these correspondence relations SYMBOLIC RELATIONS.

Since we will be talking about the formal or syntactic structure of a construction and also the semantic structure of a construction, it will be convenient to use different names for the parts of a syntactic structure and the parts of a semantic structure. We will call the parts of the syntactic structure ELEMENTS and parts of the semantic structure COMPONENTS. Thus, a symbolic link joins an element of the syntactic structure of a construction to a component of the semantic structure of that construction. There is also a symbolic link joining the whole syntactic structure to the whole semantic structure (the middle symbolic link in Figure 1.5b). This symbolic link is the construction grammar representation of the fact that the syntactic structure of the Intransitive construction symbolizes a unary–valency predicate–argument semantic structure. Each element plus corresponding component is a part of the whole construction (form + meaning) as well. I will use the term UNIT to describe a symbolic part (element + component) of a construction. That is, the construction as a symbolic whole is made up of symbolic units as parts. The symbolic units of *Heather sings* are not indicated in Figure 1.5b for clarity's sake; but all three types of parts of constructions are illustrated in Figure 1.6 (compare Langacker 1987: 84, Fig. 2.8a; Figure 1.6 suppresses links between parts of the construction for clarity).

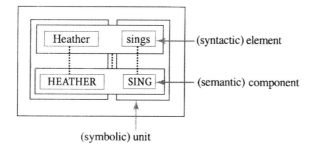

Figure 1.6. Elements, components, and units of a construction

Figure 1.5b has two other relations apart from the symbolic relation: one joining the two syntactic elements and one joining the two semantic components. The link joining the two semantic components describes a SEMANTIC RELATION that holds between the two components, in this case some sort of event–participant relation. Thus, the semantic structure of a construction is assumed to be (potentially) complex, made up of semantic components among which certain semantic relations hold. This is *all* that we need to assume about the nature of semantic structure in order to construct the arguments in this book, in particular, the arguments in Part II. I believe that these assumptions are uncontroversial for most if not all syntactic theorists.

The link joining the two syntactic elements in Figure 1.5b is a SYNTACTIC RELATION. The syntactic relation does not obviously correspond directly to anything in the generative grammar representation in Figure 1.5. This is because the representation of syntactic relations in most syntactic theories is more complex than a simple syntactic link. In fact, we can identify three layers in the usual analysis of syntactic relations:

1 the abstract syntactic relation;
2 the means of representing the abstract syntactic relation;
3 the overt manifestation of the abstract syntactic relation.

The first layer is the ABSTRACT SYNTACTIC RELATION itself, such as the Subject–Verb relation holding between *Heather* and *sings* in the construction grammar representation in Figure 1.5. This is intended to be a neutral way of characterizing the syntactic structure of the construction.

The second layer is the MEANS OF REPRESENTING the abstract syntactic relation. Different syntactic theories use different means for representing abstract syntactic relations. For example, generative grammar uses CONSTITUENCY to represent abstract syntactic relations. The labeled bracketing in Figure 1.5a is a shorthand for representing the constituency structure in (10):

(10)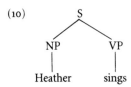

In other words, the generative grammatical representation in Figure 1.5a displays the means of representation of the syntactic relation Subject–Verb, not the abstract syntactic relation itself.

Generative grammar uses constituency relations to represent many different sorts of syntactic relations. For example, constituency is used to distinguish so-called "grammatical relations" such as subject and object, as in Figure 1.7. Other theories, such as Word Grammar, represent a "grammatical relation" more directly as a DEPENDENCY between the Verb and the Subject, as in Figure 1.8. Still further theories, such as Lexical-Functional Grammar, use a combination of constituency and dependency to represent different types of syntactic relations holding between elements of a syntactic structure.

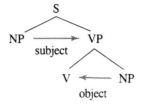

Figure 1.7. Representation of subject and object in generative grammatical theories

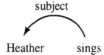

Figure 1.8. Dependency representation of syntactic relation between *Heather* and *sings*

The third layer is the OVERT MANIFESTATION of the abstract syntactic relation, that is, the linguistic evidence supporting the existence of a syntactic relation. Examples of the overt manifestation of the syntactic relation between *Heather* and *sings* are the contiguity of *Heather* and *sings*, the word order (*Heather* precedes *sings*), and the overt expression of the suffix *-s* on the Verb that agrees with *Heather* in Person and Number (3rd Person Singular).

I will continue to represent only abstract syntactic relations in the construction diagrams in the remainder of this book. This is because in Part II, I will argue that Radical Construction Grammar should dispense with abstract syntactic relations entirely. Thus, the means of representation of syntactic relations discussed above are rendered vacuous. Instead, the putative overt manifestation of syntactic relations exemplified above will be argued to be the manifestation of symbolic relations.

One final theoretical/terminological point remains to be made. The analysis of syntactic structure is unfortunately confounded by an ambiguity in much traditional syntax terminology. We can illustrate this with the example of the term 'Subject' in the Intransitive Clause construction in Figure 1.9, illustrated once again by the sentence *Heather sings*.

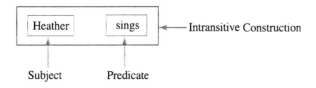

Figure 1.9. Roles in the Intransitive construction

The term 'Subject' can mean one of two things. It can describe the ROLE of a particular element of the construction, that is, a PART-WHOLE or MERONOMIC relation between the element labeled 'Subject' in the Intransitive construction and the Intransitive Construction as a whole. This is the sense in which one says that *Heather* is the Subject OF THE INTRANSITIVE CLAUSE *Heather sings*. This part-whole relation is represented implicitly in Figure 1.9 by the nesting of the box for *Heather* inside the box for the whole construction *Heather sings*.

The Subject role defines a grammatical category, namely those words (more precisely, phrases) that can fill the Subject role. The Subject category is the category of possible fillers of the Subject role in a Clause construction; some examples are given in (11):

(11) a. **Jennifer** ran across the field.
    b. **Larry** found $20.
    c. **The car** hit a tree.

The term 'Subject' can also describe a syntactic RELATION between one element of the construction—the Subject—and another element of the construction—the Verb. This is the sense in which one says that *Heather* is the Subject OF THE VERB *sings*. As noted above, the Subject syntactic relation is assumed to be manifested by a variety of properties, such as the case form of the noun phrase (in English, with Pronouns), agreement of the Verb (in English with 3rd Person Subjects in Present Tense), and word order (in English, preverbal position):

(12) a. **She** sings madrigals.
    b. *Her sings madrigals.
    c. *She sing madrigals.
    d. *Madrigals sings she.

In other words, the term 'Subject' confounds two different types of relations in a construction: the ROLE of the part in the whole, and the RELATION of one part to another part (this terminological distinction is taken from Kay 1997). The difference between the two is illustrated in Figure 1.10.

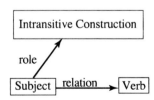

Figure 1.10. The difference between syntactic roles and syntactic relations

In Part II of this book, I will argue against the existence of syntactic relations. On the other hand, I assume the existence of syntactic roles in constructions in

Radical Construction Grammar. In fact, the part-whole structure of constructions is the only sort of syntactic structure that Radical Construction Grammar calls for. While this may appear to be an impoverished view of syntactic structure in comparison to other syntactic theories, it must not be forgotten that Radical Construction Grammar, like construction grammar in general, also posits symbolic relations and semantic relations in a construction. It is in these latter structures that significant cross-linguistic generalizations can be found.

1.3.3. *The organization of constructions in a construction grammar*

In Figure 1.4 (§1.3.2), I presented construction grammar as an inventory of constructions, in the broad sense of the latter term (including words, morphemes, morphological structures, syntactic constructions, etc.). However, constructions are not merely an unstructured list in construction grammar. Constructions form a STRUCTURED INVENTORY of a speaker's knowledge of the conventions of their language (Langacker 1987: 63–76). This structured inventory is usually represented by construction grammarians in terms of a TAXONOMIC NETWORK of constructions. Each construction constitutes a NODE in the taxonomic network of constructions.

Any construction with unique, idiosyncratic morphological, syntactic, lexical, semantic, pragmatic, OR discourse-functional properties must be represented as an independent node in the constructional network in order to capture a speaker's knowledge of their language. That is, any quirk of a construction is sufficient to represent that construction as an independent node. For example, the substantive idiom [SBJ *kick the bucket*] must be represented as an independent node because it is semantically idiosyncratic. The more schematic but verb-specific construction [SBJ *kick* OBJ] must also be represented as an independent node in order to specify its argument linking pattern (or in older generative grammar terms, its subcategorization frame). Finally, the wholly schematic construction [SBJ VERB OBJ] is represented as an independent node because this is how construction grammar represents the Transitive Clause that is described by phrase structure rules in generative grammar, such as S → NP VP and VP → V NP.

Of course, *kick the bucket* has the same argument structure pattern as ordinary transitive uses of *kick*, and ordinary transitive uses of *kick* follow the same argument structure pattern as any transitive verb phrase. Each construction is simply an INSTANCE of the more SCHEMATIC construction(s) in the chain [*kick the bucket*]—[*kick* OBJ]—[VERB OBJ]. Thus, these constructions can be represented in a TAXONOMIC HIERARCHY, as in Figure 1.11.

However, grammatical constructions do not form a strict taxonomic hierarchy. One of the simplifications in the hierarchy of constructions in Figure 1.11 is the exclusion of Tense-Aspect-Mood-Negation marking, expressed by Auxiliaries and Verbal suffixes. If those parts of an utterance are included, then any construction in the hierarchy in Figure 1.11 has multiple parents. For example, the sentence [*I didn't sleep*] is an instantiation of both the Intransitive Clause construction and the Negative construction, as illustrated in Figure 1.12.

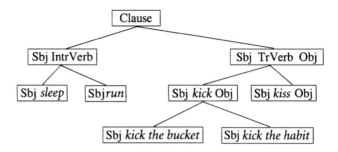

Figure 1.11. A taxonomic hierarchy of clause types

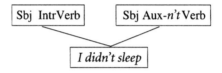

Figure 1.12. Multiple parents in a construction taxonomy

The sentence [*I didn't sleep*] thus has MULTIPLE PARENTS in the taxonomy of constructions to which it belongs. This is a consequence of each construction being a PARTIAL specification of the grammatical structure of its daughter construction(s). For example, the Negative construction only specifies the structure associated with the Subject, Verb and Auxiliary; it does not specify anything about a Verb's Object (if it has one), and so there is no representation of the Object in the Negation construction in Figure 1.12.

A construction typically provides only a partial specification of the structure of an utterance. For example, the Ditransitive construction [SBJ DITRVERB OBJ1 OBJ2], as in *He gave her a book*, only specifies the predicate and the linkings to its arguments. It does not specify the order of elements, which can be different in, for example, the Cleft construction, as in *It was a book that he gave her*. Nor does the Ditransitive construction specify the presence or position of other elements in an utterance, such as Modal Auxiliaries or Negation, whether in a Declarative Sentence (where they are preverbal; see (13a)) or an Interrogative Sentence (where the Auxiliary precedes the subject; see (13b)):

(13) a. He **won't** give her the book.
     b. **Wouldn't** he give her the book?

Hence, any specific utterance's structure is specified by a number of distinct schematic constructions. Conversely, a schematic construction abstracts away from the unspecified structural aspects of the class of utterances it describes. The model of construction grammar conforms to Langacker's content requirement for a grammar: the only grammatical entities that are posited in the theory are grammatical units and schematizations of those units (§1.1).

The taxonomic organization of syntactic knowledge in construction grammar is simply the organization of syntactic structures into categories based on their grammatical properties. As such, it might be expected that syntactic knowledge follows the same principles of organization of other categories, in particular lexical categories, since constructions are part of a representational continuum with lexical items. This in fact appears to be true.

Some constructions are polysemous, with multiple senses or uses. An example of a construction with multiple sense would be the different senses of the English Present Perfect:

(14) a. President Clinton **has visited** Kosovo. [existential reading]
 b. President Clinton **has announced** that America will invade Kosovo!
 ["hot news" reading]

Some constructions have meanings that are metaphorical extensions from their basic meaning, just as many words do. An example of a metaphorical extension of a construction is the Perceptual Deictic *There*-construction, illustrated in (15), which is a metaphorical extension from the Central Deictic *There*-construction illustrated in (16) (Lakoff 1987: 511, 509):

(15) a. **Here comes** the beep.
 b. **There's** the beep.
(16) **There's** Harry.

The Perceptual Deictic describes the impending (15a) or just-realized (15b) activation of a nonvisual perceptual stimulus, for example an alarm clock that is about to go off. To express this meaning, the Perceptual Deictic uses the metaphor of deictic motion of a physical entity in physical space, expressed in the Presentational Deictic (Lakoff 1987: 511; see Goldberg 1995: 81–9 for another example of a metaphorical extension of a construction).

Constructions thus display many of the same properties of lexical items, such as polysemy and metaphorical extensions. More generally, constructions (like lexical items) represent CATEGORIES, and construction grammar draws on cognitive theories of categorization in its modeling of construction taxonomies.

For example, an issue that has attracted attention in the construction grammar literature is the question: where is grammatical information represented in the construction taxonomy? One school of thought argues that information should not be redundantly represented in taxonomy. For example, the representation of [*kick the bucket*] would only specify the idiosyncratic semantic interpretation of that phrase; specification of the position and form of *kick*'s Direct Object would then be INHERITED from the more schematic superordinate constructions in the taxonomy. This school of thought searches for the MAXIMALLY GENERAL construction schema (see §1.1). Kay and Fillmore's (1999) Construction Grammar is a representative of this school of thought.

Another school of thought argues that grammatical information can be, and in many cases should be, redundantly represented in the taxonomic hierarchy. Evidence for redundant representation of grammatical information in the taxonomic hierarchy comes from psycholinguistic evidence that patterns of frequency of use determine the level of representation of grammatical knowledge in a speaker's mind. This school of thought, in other words, advocates a USAGE-BASED MODEL of grammatical representation (see e.g. Bybee 1985; Langacker 1987).

For example, a high token frequency of a particular word form or syntactic construction will lead to the storage or ENTRENCHMENT of that word form or construction even if its grammatical properties are predictable from taxonomically superordinate constructions. Also, it is argued that PRODUCTIVITY, represented by the entrenchment of a more abstract schema, is a function of its type frequency, that is, the frequency of different instances of the schema. For example, the productivity of the Past Tense schema [VERB-*ed*] is taken to mean that this schema is highly entrenched in an English speaker's mind, and that in turn is due to high type frequency, that is, the large number of different Verbs that form their Past Tense according to this schema. Conversely, low token frequency, that is, infrequent activation of the constructional schema in language use, can lead to decay and loss of entrenchment of the construction schema over time. In other words, the degree of generality of construction schemas, and the location of grammatical information in the taxonomic network, is an empirical question to be answered by empirical studies of frequency patterns and psycholinguistic research on entrenchment and productivity of schematic constructions.

A theory of grammar attempts to answer the question posed in §1.2.1: what is the grammatical knowledge of a speaker? The usage-based model attempts to answer that question. The development of usage-based models of grammatical representation, and the psycholinguistic and linguistic evidence for them, is still at an early stage. A considerable amount of research has been done on the usage-based model in morphology, but the usage-based model has only very recently been applied to syntactic constructions (see Cruse and Croft in press, chapter 12 for a survey of the literature). The usage-based model holds out the promise of a psychologically principled way to determine which constructions of a language should be independently represented as nodes in the taxonomic network, that is which constructions are actually entrenched in a speaker's mind.

There is another important principle of the organization of grammatical knowledge, however, which is supported by evidence from typological universals of language. A speaker's knowledge of constructions is also organized by the relations between the meanings of the constructions. The semantic relationships between constructional meanings can be represented in terms of a structured CONCEPTUAL SPACE. Conceptual space and the principles governing it will be introduced in §2.4, and the conceptual space model of grammatical organization will play a significant part in the analyses proposed by Radical Construction Grammar in the rest of this book.

1.4. Distributional Analysis and Cross-linguistic Universals

Up to this point, we have described distributional analysis as it applies to a single language. However, distributional analysis is also a method that has been used for uncovering Universal Grammar, that is, syntactic categories and roles that are found across languages, not just within a single language. However, two serious problems arise when distributional analysis is applied across languages. This section describes these problems and two opposing approaches to resolving the problems.

1.4.1. *Problems in using distributional analysis across languages*

1.4.1.1. Nonuniversality of constructions

The first problem is that the constructions used to define the categories in question in one language (say, English) are missing in the language to be analyzed. For example, inflectional criteria are commonly used to distinguish parts of speech (noun, verb, and adjective) in languages, such that inflection for number, gender, and case identify nouns and inflection for agreement, tense, aspect, and mood identify verbs. However, Vietnamese lacks all morphological inflection (Emenean 1951: 44). Hence inflection cannot be used to define parts of speech in Vietnamese. Likewise, many of the criteria for Subject vs. Object given for English in (5)–(9) above are absent in Wardaman, an Australian aboriginal language. Wardaman lacks infinitival complements and "Conjunction Reduction" coordination (Merlan 1994), the constructions used in (7) and (9) to define Subject in English.

This problem is well-known. It was observed by the American structuralists who codified distributional analysis. Before listing some typical inflectional criteria for defining parts of speech across languages, Nida writes in a footnote, 'There are so many languages in which the following generalizations do not hold that one is tempted to avoid such statements altogether' (Nida 1949: 149, fn 30). This problem is well-known because it is common. Languages differ in the constructions that they possess. English is also lacking in constructions that are taken to be relevant for defining parts of speech and syntactic roles in other languages. For example, the Russian Noun category is defined by its inflection for Case as well as Number, but English lacks case inflection.

Yet the distributional method by itself cannot solve this problem. The distributional method does not tell us whether or not Vietnamese has parts of speech, let alone the same parts of speech that English does. Likewise, the distributional method does not tell us if the syntactic roles of Wardaman are the same as those in English, since Wardaman lacks some of the constructions defining syntactic roles in English.

1.4.1.2. Wildly different distributions across languages

A second serious problem is that even when the relevant constructions exist in the language in question, they give wildly different distributions and hence wildly different categories from those found in English and other familiar European languages. For example, Makah, a native American language of the Pacific Northwest, has inflections for Agreement, Aspect, and Mood, which are used as criteria for the category Verb in English and other European languages. But virtually all semantic classes of words can be inflected for Person-Aspect-Mood in Makah, including what are English Verbs (17), Nouns (18), Adjectives (19), and Adverbs (20; Jacobson 1979: 110–11 see §2.3.1).

(17) k'upšil   ba?as   ?u·yuq
     point:MOM:IND:3   house   OBJ
     'He's pointing at the house.'
(18) babałdis
     white.man:IND:1SG
     'I'm a white man.'
(19) ?i·?i·x̣ʷ?i
     big:IND:3
     'He's big.'
(20) hu·?ax̣is   ha?ukʷ'ap
     still:IND:1SG   eat:CAUS
     'I'm still feeding him.'

Again, the distributional method does not tell us whether or not the category defined by Person-Aspect-Mood inflection in Makah is the same as the category defined by Person-Tense-Mood inflection in English. Like the problem of missing constructions, the problem of wildly different distribution is a cross-linguistically common one. Languages differ considerably in the range of words that occur in either nominal or verbal inflections. Likewise, languages differ considerably in the range of noun phrases that can be "null" (i.e. not be present) in a clause, one of the chief criteria for the category Subject in English and other languages. In Wardaman, for example, any Noun Phrase can be "null", and so the criteria for Subject role illustrated in (7)–(9) cannot be applied to Wardaman, or rather, it would make all Noun Phrases into "Subjects".

1.4.2. Cross-linguistic methodological opportunism and its problems

The commonest solution to these problems is what I will call CROSS-LINGUISTIC METHODOLOGICAL OPPORTUNISM. Cross-linguistic methodological opportunism uses language-specific criteria when the general criteria do not exist in the language, or when the general criteria give the "wrong" results according to one's theory. For example, one can examine other constructions in Vietnamese and Makah that differentiate word classes in a way that corresponds to the parts of speech in European languages; or one can ignore the fact that some constructions defining Subject in English are absent in Wardaman, and use the constructions that do exist in Wardaman to define Subjects in that language.

But cross-linguistic methodological opportunism is just that: opportunistic. It suffers from two interrelated and fatal problems. The first is that there is no a priori way to decide which criteria (if any) are relevant to deciding that a particular category is an instantiation of a universal category like Noun or Subject across languages. One might propose that inflection for agreement and tense-mood-aspect will be the criterion for the category Verb across languages. But why? No reason has been given to do so. And if one does so, then one will have to conclude that all words are Verbs in Makah and no words are Verbs in Vietnamese, which is hardly a savory conclusion for a theory that posits Verbs as a part of Universal Grammar.

The second problem is that the choice of criteria looks suspiciously like serving a priori theoretical assumptions. For example, there has been an ongoing debate about whether native American languages of the Pacific Northwest, including Makah, have the Noun–Verb distinction. Those who argue against the Noun–Verb distinction take the distributional pattern in (17)–(20), that is, inflection in predication, as criterial. Those who argue in favor of the Noun–Verb distinction, such as Jacobsen, use distributional patterns in other constructions to differentiate the word classes. Without prior agreement or some principled means for specifying which constructions define a category across languages, analysts can use whatever constructions they wish in order to come to whatever conclusions they wish.

Cross-linguistic methodological opportunism in identifying categories across languages is unprincipled and ad hoc. In other words, cross-linguistic methodological opportunism is not a rigorous scientific method for discovering the properties of Universal Grammar. Yet it is a very widely used form of cross-linguistic argumentation.

For example, Jelinek and Demers argue that Straits Salish does not distinguish nouns, verbs, and adjectives, because all can appear in the Predication construction ((21a–c), with the enclitics =lə=sxʷ '=PST=2SG.NR'), and in the Determination construction ((22a–c), with the Article cə; Jelinek and Demers 1994: 698–9):

(21) a. t'iləm=lə=sxʷ 'you sang'
 b. si'em=lə=sxʷ 'you were a chief'
 c. sey'si'=lə=sxʷ 'you were afraid'
(22) a. cə t'iləm=lə 'the (one who) sang'
 b. cə si'em=lə 'the (one who) was a chief'
 c. cə sey'si'=lə 'the (one who) was afraid'

But van Eijk and Hess (1986) observe the same distributional facts for the closely related languages Lillooet and Lushootseed, and yet conclude that Lillooet and Lushootseed do distinguish Noun and Verb. Their argument is based on the distribution pattern of Possessive affixes and Aspect inflection, which divide Lillooet and Lushootseed roots into Noun and Verb categories in their analysis (van Eijk and Hess 1986: 321–2).

Jelinek and Demers note that in Straits Salish also, only a subset of roots may take Possessive affixes (Jelinek and Demers 1994: 699). But they point out that "Nouns" may occur in the Predication construction (ibid.; see (21b)), and then argue that the fact that "Nouns" with Possessive affixes may occur in the Predication and Determination constructions is the deciding case: 'they have the same syntax as any other predicate' (ibid.: 700).

Here we see a common pattern in syntactic debate. The distributional facts show that there are some similarities and some differences between two grammatical phenomena. One set of analysts (e.g. Jelinek and Demers) takes a "lumping" approach, arguing that certain distributional differences are superficial compared to the underlying grammatical unity. The other analysts (e.g. van Eijk and Hess) take a "splitting" approach, arguing that the distributional differences really are significant and require a distinct analysis for the two phenomena. Yet there is no a priori way to resolve the question: the "lumper" overlooks the mismatches in distribution, and the "splitter" overlooks the generalizations. Another way must be sought out of this dilemma.

1.4.3. *An alternative view: there is no universal inventory of atomic primitives*

Dryer (1997b) proposes a different solution to the problems posed in §1.4.1, at least for functionalist approaches to syntax (I will discuss formal approaches to syntax below). Dryer bases his argument on the problems posed by identifying grammatical relations such as Subject and Object across languages, but he invokes parallels with phonemes and parts of speech, and I will briefly present Dryer's argument in generalized form.

Dryer suggests that the following four things might be proposed to exist in the domain of grammar (adapted from Dryer 1997b: 116–17):

(23) a. categories and relations in particular languages
   b. similarities among these language-particular categories and relations
   c. functional, cognitive and semantic explanations for these similarities
   d. categories and relations in a cross-linguistic sense

Syntactic theorists, including many functionalist theorists, assume the existence of (23d), that is, UNIVERSAL categories and relations. These universal categories and relations are then instantiated in the grammars of particular languages. In other words, (23a) is just an instantiation of (23d). In this view, (23b)—the fact that categories across languages are similar, not identical—is due to language-particular peculiarities that do not affect the overall architecture of Universal Grammar.

But in fact there is a wide range of cross-linguistic variation in syntactic categories and roles and other basic syntactic phenomena, as we have already seen, and will see in later chapters. Dryer argues that a functionalist syntactician should accept the uniqueness of language-particular grammatical relations, namely accept (23a) and reject (23d). Dryer argues that such an approach is palatable to a functionalist approach to language because there ARE similarities among language-particular grammatical relations, and the functionalist offers functional, cognitive, and semantic explanations for these similarities, (23c). That is, a functionalist can offer an explanatory theory of language without positing universal grammatical relations. Dryer writes:

the search for an understanding of the similarities and differences among grammatical relations in different languages will be impeded if we make the mistake of thinking of grammatical relations as crosslinguistic categories, and will be more successful if we bear in mind that grammatical relations are unique to every language (Dryer 1997b: 140).

the similarities among languages [with respect to grammatical relations] can be explained directly in terms of functional and cognitive principles that underlie language and which cause languages to be the way they are (Dryer 1997b: 139).

Dryer suggests that formal theories of syntax can posit universal grammatical relations without a problem: 'The view that grammatical relations are cross-linguistic notions makes sense if one adopts the view of formal linguistics that explanation of language is largely internal to language' (Dryer 1997b: 115). However, Dryer does not elaborate this point, and it is not clear why it should be true. Formalist linguists face the same methodological problems with distributional analysis, and the same facts of cross-linguistic variation, as functionalist linguists do. If the formalist explanation is largely internal to a language, which is essentially correct, then there are no criteria for identifying categories as the same across languages.

In fact, the argument against universal categories and relations is not functional at all. The problems with applying the distributional method across languages involve constructions and the distributional patterns they define, not any particular functionalist analysis of the constructions and their distributional patterns. The argument against universal categories and relations is a fundamentally EMPIRICAL one. Moreover, the empirical argument against universal categories is not based on an esoteric fact of a single little-known language; it is based on the well-known and pervasive grammatical diversity of languages.

The alternative view, rejecting universal categories and relations, has a number of advantages over the standard view. The alternative view avoids the inconsistencies of cross-linguistic methodological opportunism, which leads to undecidable disputes over questions such as whether Makah has the Noun–Verb distinction or whether Vietnamese can be said to have parts of speech at all. There is no need to ignore distributional patterns that do not fit the assumed universal categories. The alternative view allows each language to be itself: it respects the grammatical diversity of languages, and the uniqueness of each language's grammar.

In this respect, the alternative view is little different from the view espoused by American structuralists: 'no logical scheme of the parts of speech—their number, nature and necessary confines—is of the slightest interest to the linguist. Each language has its own scheme' (Sapir 1921: 119). Instead, the alternative view allows the analyst to focus on the similarities and differences across languages. Positing universal categories would imply identical behavior across languages, which is empirically false. The more interesting and significant task (pace Sapir) is to explain similarities and differences of categories and relations across languages.

Of course, abandoning universal categories and relations leads to a very different view of Universal Grammar. Under the alternative view, Universal Grammar does not consist of an inventory of universal categories and relations available to all speakers. For a functionalist, this is not a serious problem, since a functionalist seeks universals of language in cognition and discourse. This does not mean, of course, that a functionalist can ignore the question of what the structure of a grammar looks like under the alternative view. It just means that the formal structures in grammars are language-particular, and universals of language must be sought elsewhere.

For a formalist, accepting the alternative view poses a more serious challenge. Universal Grammar in a formal sense could not consist of anything more than very general constraints on types of categories and their configuration in syntactic structures or constructions. In principle, that appears to be the direction that Chomskyan generative grammar has headed: general constraints on syntactic structure but a proliferation of syntactic categories. In practice, however, the syntactic categories are assumed to be cross-linguistically universal, and the same categories (or a subset thereof) are posited for every language. This practice also holds for other formal syntactic theories.

Given the actual practice of formal syntacticians, then, the alternative view argued for here is very serious, and one might wish to find ways to accommodate cross-linguistic variation without giving up on universal categories and relations. I do not see how one can do so without falling back into cross-linguistic methodological opportunism. However, the theoretical quandary is in fact more serious, because the same problems arise in the analysis of a single language.

1.5. Distributional Analysis and the Representation of Particular Language Grammars

1.5.1. *Problems in using distributional analysis in particular languages*

1.5.1.1. Mismatch in distribution between constructions

The fundamental problem with distributional analysis across languages is the difference or MISMATCH in distribution patterns for the same criterion or construction across languages. But within a single language, the different criteria (constructions) used to define a particular category often have different distributional patterns as well. That is, there are mismatches in the distribution patterns defined by different constructions in a single language.

A simple example of mismatch in distribution is found with the arguments for distinguishing English Direct Objects from Obliques. English Direct Objects can occur as the Noun Phrase that immediately follows the Verb in the Active Voice and lacks a Preposition, as in (24a):

(24) a. Jack kissed **Janet**.
 b. **Janet** was kissed by Jack.

Another test or criterion for Direct Object status in English is occurrence as the Subject of the Verb in the counterpart Passive Voice, as illustrated in (24b). Obliques contrast with Direct Objects on both counts. Obliques cannot occur without a Preposition (compare (25a) to (25b)), and cannot occur as Passive Subjects (25c):

(25) a. *The old man walked **a cane**.
 b. The old man walked **with a cane**.
 c. ***A cane** was walked with by the old man.

The distribution pattern for Direct Objects vs. Obliques is given in Table 1.4.

Table 1.4. Distribution of arguments across tests for Direct Object status

	[SBJ VERB __]	[__ *be* VERB:PASS *by* OBL]
Direct Object: 24	√	√
Oblique: 25	*	*

Table 1.4 makes it appear that the two tests for Direct Object status coincide. However, that is not the case. There are postverbal prepositionless Noun Phrases that cannot occur as Passive Subjects:

(26) a. Jack weighs **160 pounds**.
 b. ***160 pounds** is weighed by Jack.
(27) a. 1997 witnessed **the demise of 18 years of Tory rule in Britain**.
 b. ***The demise of 18 years of Tory rule in Britain** was witnessed by 1997.

And there are Oblique Objects of Prepositions that can occur as Passive Subjects:

(28) a. Claude Debussy lived **in this house**.
 b. *Claude Debussy lived **this house**.
 c. **This house** was lived in by Claude Debussy.

In other words, all possible distributional patterns for these two constructions are attested, as shown in Table 1.5.

Table 1.5. Distributional patterns for Active Object and Passive Subject in English

Example	[SBJ VERB __]	[__ be VERB:PASS by OBL]
24	√	√
25	*	*
26, 27	√	*
28	*	√

Mismatches in distributional patterns are the norm in languages. The American structuralists were aware of this fact. Moreover, the more constructions that one uses to define categories, the larger the number of distinct categories that would be observed, and the smaller each of those categories would be. In fact, if one takes all distributional criteria seriously, one would end up with a very large number of syntactic categories and relations, each of which would have very few members. Again, the American structuralists were aware of this problem:

Form-classes are not mutually exclusive, but cross each other and overlap and are included one within the other, and so on (Bloomfield 1933: 269).

in many cases the complete adherence to morpheme-distribution classes would lead to a relatively large number of different classes (Harris 1946: 177).

If we seek to form classes of morphemes such that all the morphemes in a particular class will have identical distributions, we will frequently achieve little success. It will often be found that few morphemes occur in precisely all the environments in which some other morphemes occur, and in no other environments (Harris 1951: 244, discussing analysis of a corpus).

This is not simply a matter of speculative extrapolation: this conclusion has also been empirically verified in at least one large-scale formal grammatical model. In a very large grammar of French developed by Maurice Gross and colleagues, containing 600 rules covering 12,000 lexical items, no two lexical items had exactly the same distribution, and no two rules had exactly the same domain of application (Gross 1979: 859–60).

Again, distributional analysis does not provide an answer to the problem as to which construction, or both, or neither should be used to define the category of English Direct Objects, or any other category for that matter.

1.5.1.2. Subclasses and multiple class membership

Some cases of distributional mismatches have been analyzed as instances of syntactic subclasses rather than as distinct syntactic classes. For example, the English

Noun category, which can be defined by occurrence as the Head of a Noun Phrase (see (29a–b)), is traditionally divided into two subclasses, Count and Mass, in part by the occurrence of the former but not the latter with the Plural (see (30a–b)):

(29) a. the **student**/the **book**/*etc.*
 b. the **mud**/the **air**/*etc.*
(30) a. **student**-s/**book**-s/*etc.*
 b. *****mud**-s/*****air**-s/*etc.*

The distributional pattern is given in Table 1.6; one construction defines the class, and the other construction differentiates the subclasses.

Table 1.6. Subclasses of one word class?

	[__-s]	[the __]$_{NP}$
Count Noun: *student, book*, etc.	√	√
Mass Noun: *mud, air*, etc.	*	√

On the other hand, English Nouns and Adjectives do occur in some of the same constructions: they both take the Copula *be* when predicated (31a–b), and they can both occur as prenominal Modifiers (32a–b):

(31) a. She is a **student**/This is a **book**/*etc.*
 b. She is **tall**/She is **sad**/*etc.*
(32) a. **student** discount/**book** warehouse/*etc.*
 b. **tall** girl/**sad** woman/*etc.*

English Nouns and Adjectives can also be differentiated: for example, Nouns can be the Heads of Noun Phrases while Adjectives cannot:

(33) a. the **student**/the **book**/*etc.*
 b. *the **tall**/*the **sad**/*etc.*

The distribution pattern of (32) vs. (33) is given in Table 1.7.

Table 1.7. Separate word classes?

	[the __]$_{NP}$	[the __ NOUN]$_{NP}$
Noun: *student, book*, etc.	√	√
Adjective: *tall, sad*, etc.	*	√

But the distributional patterns in Tables 1.6 and 1.7 are the same. In other words, there is no a priori basis for deciding which constructions provide sufficient conditions for separate word classes and which constructions merely define subclasses of one word class. The distributional method alone cannot decide this question. As Schachter puts it:

> It must be acknowledged, however, that there is not always a clear basis for deciding whether two distinguishable open classes of words that occur in a language should be identified as different parts of speech or as subclasses of a single part of speech.... What this means is that there may in some cases be considerable arbitrariness in the identification of two open word classes as distinct parts of speech rather than subclasses of a single part of speech (Schachter 1985: 5–6).

The same is true of another strategy for dealing with mismatches in distribution, namely allowing for multiple class membership. For instance, another construction distinguishing Adjectives from Nouns is occurrence with the Anaphoric Head *one*:

(34) a. *the **box** one/*the **woman** one/etc.
    b. the **tall** one/the **sad** one/etc.
    c. the **rich** one/the **poor** one/etc.

However, the words in (34c) can also occur as the Head of a Noun Phrase themselves:

(35) a. the **box**/the **woman**/etc.
    b. *the **tall**/*the **sad**/etc.
    c. the **rich**/the **poor**/etc.

Words like *rich/poor* are usually analyzed as being both Nouns and Adjectives, that is, as having multiple class membership. The distribution pattern defined by the constructions in (34)–(35) is given in Table 1.8; the first construction defines Nouns and the second defines Adjectives.

Table 1.8. Multiple word class membership?

	[the __]$_{NP}$	[the __ one]$_{NP}$
Noun: *box, woman*, etc.	√	*
Adjective: *tall, sad*, etc.	*	√
Noun and Adjective: *rich, poor*, etc.	√	√

On the other hand, the Genitive Noun Phrase with the Possessive enclitic *-'s* is usually treated as belonging to a different category from the Attributive Possessive Pronouns and the Pronominal Possessive Pronouns. Distributionally, the Genitive Noun Phrase can function attributively, that is, occur as a prenominal Modifier, like the Attributive Possessive Pronouns:

(36) a. **my** book/**your** book/*etc.*
    b. *****mine** book/*****yours** book/*etc.*
    c. **John's** book/**Sally's** book/*etc.*

And the Genitive Noun Phrase can function pronominally, that is, occur as a Noun Phrase on its own:

(37) a. *bigger than **my**/*bigger than **your**/*etc.*
    b. bigger than **mine**/bigger than **yours**/*etc.*
    c. bigger than **John's**/bigger than **Sally's**/*etc.*

The distribution pattern for (36)–(37) is given in Table 1.9.

Table 1.9. A third word class?

	[__ NOUN]	[*bigger than* __]
Attributive Possessive: *my, your*, etc.	√	*
Pronominal Possessive: *mine, yours*, etc.	*	√
Genitive Noun Phrase: *John's, Sally's*, etc.	√	√

As with Tables 1.6–1.7, the distribution patterns in Tables 1.8–1.9 are the same. In other words, there is no a priori basis for deciding which constructions are only necessary conditions for word class membership (hence permit a third word class analysis) and which constructions are sufficient to define separate word classes (hence multiple class membership for words occurring in both constructions). Again, the distributional method cannot decide this question.

1.5.1.3. Lack of exclusive partitioning of lexical items

A third problem with the distributional method is that there is often a lack of exclusive partitioning of lexical items. For example, some English Nouns are clearly Mass Nouns, as defined by their occurrence in the Bare Singular construction without an Article (see (38)):

(38) a. There's **mud** on your boots.
    b. *I found **two muds** on the carpet.

Other nouns are both Mass Nouns and Count Nouns, as defined by occurrence with Numerals (compare the (a) and (b) sentences in (39)–(40)):

(39) a. There's **chocolate** on your hands.
    b. I ate only **five chocolates**.
(40) a. There's **hair** on the sofa.
    b. There's **a hair** on the sofa.

The lack of exclusive partitioning of the lexical items in (38)–(40) could be accounted for by multiple class membership or by a third class. However, it appears that almost any Count Noun can potentially occur in the Bare Singular construction, as attested examples such as (41b) demonstrate (see also §3.2.3):

(41) a. The Walkers own **three cars**.
b. "There was a huge Buick there; just acres of **car**."
[overheard by Mary Ellen Ryder, Manchester, 30 April 1997]

Another example of the lack of exclusive partitioning of lexical items are the words variously described as Adverbs, Prepositions and/or Particles (e.g. Biber et al. 1999, §§2.4.6, 5.3.2–3). I illustrate the problems with one word, *down*:

(42) a. She walked **down** (from the mountain).
b. She sat **down**.
c. She looked **down** (at the people below).
(43) a. She walked **down** the road.
b. *She sat **down** the table. ['down at the table']
c. She is sitting **down** the table from me.
d. *She looked **down** the people below.
e. She looked **down** the stairwell.
(44) a. The proposal went **down** badly.
b. After she left, he broke **down**.
c. He broke **down** the problem into five parts.
d. *He broke **down** it into five parts.

The examples in (42) are Adverb-like, indicating direction. However, *down* may sometimes act like a spatial Preposition, as in (43a,c,e)—but not (43b,d). The examples in (44) are usually called Particle uses of *down*. However, the examples in (44a–b) are more Adverb-like, while the example in (44c) is more Object-like—except when a pronominal object is involved (44d). *Down* is of course only one of very many words that behave slightly differently, yielding either many sub-classes or many cases of criss-crossing multiple class membership, without any clear picture of how many classes to posit, and with some indeterminacy in some contexts. For example, regarding the attested examples (45a–b), Biber et al. note that *in* in (45a) is more like a Particle because it can be omitted; but omission of *in* in (45b) is 'less freely admissible and therefore behaves more like a preposition' (Biber et al. 1999: 79):

(45) a. I knew that there was a man **in** there. (NEWS)
b. **In** there I feel skinnier than ever. (FICT)

This problem is of a somewhat different type from the other problems described with the distributional method. Indeterminacy of classification implies that distributional patterns may be more flexible and fluid than is usually assumed, and hence word classes are not as sharply defined as is commonly thought.

1.5.2. *Language-internal methodological opportunism and its problems*

The common solution to the problems posed by the distributional method in a single language is analogous to the common solution to the cross-linguistic problem. I will call it LANGUAGE-INTERNAL METHODOLOGICAL OPPORTUNISM. Language-internal methodological opportunism simply selects a subset of language-specific criteria to define a category when the criteria do not all match. That subset of criteria, or possibly just one criterion, defines the category in question. Mismatching distributions are ignored, or are used to define subclasses or multiple class membership.

Language-internal methodological opportunism was proposed by Bloomfield and Harris as a solution to the problems posed in §1.5.1, as can be seen by the continuation of the quotations from §1.5.1.1:

For this reason a system of parts of speech in a language like English cannot be set up in any fully satisfactory way: our list of parts of speech will depend upon which functions we take to be the most important (Bloomfield 1933: 269).

This means that we change over from correlating each morpheme with all its environments, to correlating selected environments (frames) with all the morphemes that enter them (Harris 1946: 177).

For example, the usual solution to the mismatch in the two criteria commonly used to define Direct Objects in English is to select the criterion of Passive Subject, or passivizability in the transformational metaphor, as the defining criterion of Direct Object. Thus, *160 pounds* in (23a) and *the demise of 18 years of Tory rule in Britain* in (25a) are not Direct Objects in this approach.

Language-internal methodological opportunism is just as unsatisfactory as its cross-linguistic cousin. There is no a priori way to decide which of several constructions with mismatching distributions, or which subset of constructions, should be chosen as criteria for identifying the category in question. Why should passivizability be the criterion for defining the Direct Object category? Why shouldn't the criterion be occurrence as the postverbal prepositionless Noun Phrase in the Active construction? The choice of criteria again looks suspiciously like serving a priori theoretical assumptions of the analyst, for example a priori assumptions about what should or should not be a Direct Object. Moreover, if one does choose one construction (or subset of constructions) to define a category, then one still has not accounted for the anomalous distribution pattern of the constructions that have been left out (in this case, occurrence as the postverbal prepositionless Noun Phrase in the Active construction).

Language-internal methodological opportunism, like cross-linguistic methodological opportunism, is unprincipled and ad hoc, and hence is not a rigorous scientific method for discovering the properties of the grammar of a language.

42 *From Syntactic Categories to Semantic Maps*

Yet language-internal methodological opportunism is a widely used form of argumentation in the analysis of particular language grammars.

I will give one illustrative example, from the debate between Larson and Jackendoff on the analysis of the Ditransitive (Double Object) construction in English (Larson 1988; Jackendoff 1990b; Larson 1990). Of course, a proper explication of the arguments and counterarguments in these lengthy articles would take up more space than can be afforded here. Much of the debate between Larson and Jackendoff does not involve a disagreement with the distributional facts that they present, but instead turns on what theoretical construct in generative grammar is preferable to analyze the distributional facts, and on semantic arguments. Here we will restrict ourselves to two essential syntactic arguments presented in these articles.

Larson analyzes the Indirect Object construction in (46a) as a result of Verb movement in the structure in (46b) (Larson 1988: 342–3):

(46) a. send a letter to Mary
     b.

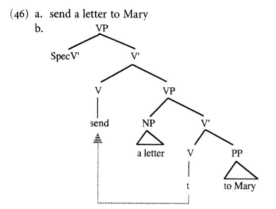

Larson analyzes the Double Object construction in (47a) as a result of the NP movement in the structure in (47b) (Jackendoff 1990b: 438):

(47) a. send Mary a letter
     b.

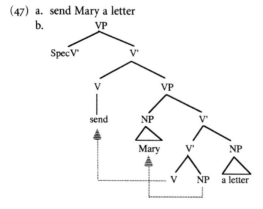

In (47b), the NP *Mary* is moved upwards and the NP *a letter* is "demoted" in comparison to its position in (46b).

Larson further argues that the syntactic operation in (47) is essentially identical to the Passive operation, illustrated in (48) (from Haegeman 1994: 296):

(48) a. This story is believed by the villagers.
  b.

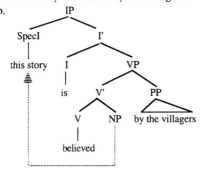

That is, both Passive and Dative Shift involve moving one NP upwards in the tree—recipient in Dative Shift, patient in Passive—and "demoting" one NP—theme in Dative Shift, agent in Passive—in comparison to the "demoted" NP's position in each construction's counterpart—Indirect Object for Dative Shift, Active for Passive.

Larson's justification for the analysis in (47b) is a variety of parallel distributional facts, such as the *each . . . the other* construction (Larson 1988: 338, 354; see Barss and Lasnik 1986):

(49) a. *Dative Shift:* *I showed the other's friend each man. *cf.*:
  b. I showed each man the other's socks.
(50) a. *Passive:* *The other boy was recommended by each mother. *cf.*:
  b. Each mother recommended the other boy.

Larson notes differences between Dative Shift and Passive: for example, the latter occurs in the [V-*en*] morphological construction (in our terms) but the former does not:

(51) *given Mary a letter

However, he argues that other generative principles can account for the 'apparent differences' (Larson 1988: 357).

Jackendoff argues for the traditional analysis of the Double Object construction as having two Object complements, as in (52b) (Jackendoff 1990b: 428), and argues that the distributional facts presented by Larson are in fact due to linear order, not the nested constituent structure given in (47b).

(52) a. show John himself
    b.
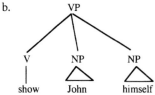

For Jackendoff the difference in distribution between Dative Shift and Passive illustrated in example (51) is not a mere 'apparent difference', but an argument against Larson's analysis.

Jackendoff further notes another distributional difference between Passive and Dative Shift (Larson 1988: 336 and Jackendoff 1990b: 438):

(53) a. *Dative Shift*: I showed Mary herself.
    b. *Passive*: *Bill was hit by himself.

Reflexivization of the "demoted" NP when it is coreferential with the "moved" NP is grammatical in Dative Shift, but not in Passive. In his response to Jackendoff, Larson does not mention this distributional fact, which suggests that this distributional difference is not deemed sufficiently serious for him to abandon his analysis.

Jackendoff also presents distributional evidence that the facts in (49)–(50) are also shared by certain other constructions, including the Locative Alternation constructions in (54) (see Jackendoff 1990b: 433–4):

(54) a. I loaded each set of books into the other's box.
    b. *I loaded the other's box with each set of books.

Jackendoff argues that the presence of the Prepositions and the choice of Preposition in (54) poses a problem for Larson's analysis (Jackendoff 1990b: 442–4). That is, Jackendoff considers the distributional differences—presence of Prepositions in the Locative Alternation construction in (56) vs. absence of Prepositions in Dative Shift—significant enough to reject Larson's analysis. In his response, Larson accepts these distributional facts. However, Larson argues that 'this does not represent a "sharp" difference between dative and *spray-load* pairs' (Larson 1990: 605). Larson then points out still other distributional differences that undermine Jackendoff's analysis which I will not pursue here.

This brief sketch of two central arguments in these articles illustrates the same common pattern in syntactic debate that was noted in §1.4.2. The distributional facts show that there are some similarities and some differences between two grammatical phenomena. One analyst (Larson) takes a "lumping" approach and the other analyst (Jackendoff) takes a "splitting" approach. Yet there is no a priori way to resolve the question: the "lumper" overlooks the mismatches in distribution, and the "splitter" overlooks the generalizations. Again, another way must be sought out of this dilemma.

1.5.3. An alternative view: there are no atomic grammatical primitives

In this section, I argue that the same solution offered by Dryer for cross-linguistic categories should be applied to categories within a language. The following four things might be proposed to exist in a particular language grammar:

(55) a. categories and relations defined by particular constructions
 b. similarities among these construction-specific categories and relations
 c. functional, cognitive, and semantic explanations for these similarities
 d. categories and relations in a cross-constructional sense

All of the syntactic theories referred to in §1.1 assume the existence of (55d), which I will call GLOBAL categories and relations. These global categories and relations are then instantiated in particular constructions in a particular language. In other words, (55a) is just an instantiation of (55d). In this view, the fact that categories across constructions are similar, not identical, is due to construction-specific peculiarities that do not affect the overall architecture of the language's grammar.

But in fact distributional criteria in general do not match, within or across languages. Yet there is no justification for deciding which distributional criteria are the "right" ones for establishing syntactic primitives—categories and relations—demanded by contemporary syntactic theories. These two basic facts call into question the assumption of the existence of (55d)—global categories and relations—by contemporary syntactic theories.

The real problem is in a logical inconsistency in the way the distributional method is used, given the fact of distributional mismatches among constructions. The distributional method is combined with the theoretical assumption that the categories/relations defined by constructions are the syntactic primitives used to represent grammatical knowledge. CONSTRUCTIONS ARE USED TO DEFINE CATEGORIES—this is the distributional method. BUT THEN THE CATEGORIES ARE TAKEN AS PRIMITIVE ELEMENTS OF SYNTACTIC REPRESENTATION AND ARE USED TO DEFINE CONSTRUCTIONS—this is the syntactic model of representation. THIS APPROACH IS CIRCULAR. It would not be circular if there were no distributional mismatches, because the facts of language would then conform to the theoretical assumption. But the facts of language are otherwise.

Given the facts of language and the circularity of the standard approach to those facts, one must discard either the distributional method or the assumption that categories/relations are the theoretical primitives of syntactic theory. But how can one discard the distributional method? What is the alternative? Yet cross-linguistic and language-internal methodological opportunism essentially do abandon the distributional method, at the price of empirical coverage and theoretical consistency. Methodological opportunism selects distributional tests at the whim of the analyst, and ignores the evidence from other distributional tests that do not match the analyst's expectations, or else treats them as superficial or peripheral.

Instead, I propose that we discard the assumption that syntactic structures are made up of atomic primitives (language-universal or language-particular). CONSTRUCTIONS, NOT CATEGORIES AND RELATIONS, ARE THE BASIC, PRIMITIVE UNITS OF SYNTACTIC REPRESENTATION. The categories and relations found in constructions are derivative—just as the distributional method implies. This is Radical Construction Grammar.

So-called theories of syntactic categories, grammatical relations (and also of dependency, constituency, heads, argument vs. adjunct, main clause vs. subordinate clause, etc.) are at best theories of the constructions used by the analyst to argue for the existence of the categories, relations, etc. For example, if one takes passivizability as the criterion for Direct Object in English, then one's conclusions will tell us something about the Passive, not about some allegedly global category Direct Object. At worst, theories of categories, etc. are theories of nothing at all, if the analyst does not apply his/her constructional tests consistently.

Such theories fail because of mismatches across languages and especially within a language between the distributions defined by the constructions that are used by the analyst. The mismatches are a theoretical problem because the assumption of atomic syntactic primitives means that all the distributions should match up. That is, not just similarity but identity of distribution is expected. Again, this argument against existing formal theories of syntax is not functional at all, and hence is not dependent on a belief in (55c), that is, functional, cognitive, or semantic explanations for similarities of categories across constructions. The argument is simply empirical, based on the well-known and pervasive diversity of distributions defined by grammatical constructions.

In Radical Construction Grammar, the grammatical knowledge of a speaker is knowledge of constructions (as form–meaning pairings), words (also as form–meaning pairings), and the mapping between words and the constructions they fit in. The mapping between words and the constructions is many-to-many: a word fits into many different constructions, and constructional roles can be filled by many different words. This knowledge is represented by the distribution tables given in this chapter, though we will see in later chapters that there is more structure to grammatical knowledge than the distributional tables give. This model can of course be extended to constructions that have other constructions, not just words, as component elements.

In Radical Construction Grammar, syntactic categories are derivative of—in fact epiphenomenal to—the representation of grammatical knowledge. Syntactic categories can be defined in two different ways. Categories can be defined construction-specifically, as the class of fillers of a particular role in a single construction. This definition corresponds to the columns in the distribution tables given in this chapter. Categories can also be defined cross-constructionally, as the class of fillers that has an identical distribution across the relevant roles for all constructions of the language, or at least some specified set of constructions in the language. This definition corresponds to the rows in the tables.

Either definition for syntactic categories can be analytically useful in some circumstances. But what is basic are the constructions, and the constructions define the categories, either individually or jointly. Among other things, this approach solves the problem of the lack of exclusive partitioning of lexical items into atomic primitive categories: this fact reflects the more-than-occasional variability and instability of the word–construction relationship, and the priority of constructions in defining categories.

1.6. Radical Construction Grammar: Frequently Asked Questions

The fundamental thesis of Radical Construction Grammar, that constructions and not categories are the primitive units of syntactic representation, is an idea that is difficult to grasp because the opposite view is so deeply entrenched in linguistic theory (indeed, it took me almost ten years to accept this point of view). As a result, certain questions have been repeatedly asked in my presentations of Radical Construction Grammar. This section will offer answers to these frequently asked questions.

1.6.1. *How can you have a syntactic theory without atomic primitive units?*

The main conceptual hurdle to considering Radical Construction Grammar as a logically possible theory of grammar is the assumption that the primitives of syntactic theory must be atomic. But 'atomic' and 'primitive' are logically independent concepts. ATOMIC units are those that cannot be broken down into smaller parts in the theory. PRIMITIVE units are those whose structure and behavior cannot be defined in terms of other units in the theory. Primitive elements need not be atomic. The notions 'atomic' and 'primitive' can be dissociated.

The logical independence of 'atomic' and 'primitive' allows us to give a precise definition of reductionist and nonreductionist scientific theories. Theories in which the primitive theoretical constructs are atomic are REDUCTIONIST theories. A reductionist theory begins with the smallest units and defines the larger or more complex units in terms of combinations of atomic primitive units. All of the theories of syntactic representation referred to in §1.1 are reductionist. Complex syntactic structures, that is, constructions, are defined by—built up from—their ultimately atomic primitive parts: syntactic categories and syntactic relations (such as constituency and dependency). Contemporary syntactic theories differ chiefly in the inventory of syntactic primitives and the rules governing their combination.

Theories in which the primitive theoretical constructs are complex are NONREDUCTIONIST theories. A nonreductionist theory begins with the largest units and defines the smaller ones in terms of their relation to the larger units. The paradigm example of a nonreductionist theory is the theory of perception proposed by Gestalt psychology (Koffka 1935; Köhler 1947; Wertheimer 1950). In Gestalt psychology, evidence is presented to the effect that the perception of features of objects is influenced by the perceptual whole in which the feature is found.

Radical Construction Grammar is a nonreductionist theory of syntactic representation. Constructions, not categories and relations, are the basic, primitive units of syntactic representation. The categories and relations internal to constructions are derived from them, as described in §1.5.3.

A nonreductionist theory does not deny that constructions (syntactic structures) are made up of parts. A nonreductionist theory of grammar, like reductionist theories, assumes that constructions, or more precisely, actual instances of constructions, can be segmented into their constituent words and morphemes. A nonreductionist theory differs from a reductionist theory in that it hypothesizes that the whole is greater than the sum of its parts. The parts take their significance—that is, are categorized—by virtue of the role that they play in the construction as a whole.

The parts qua instances of a syntactic category do not have an independent existence outside of the whole construction (or constructions) in which they play a role. That is, syntactic categories are defined in terms of the construction(s) in which they occur. A nonreductionist construction grammar therefore does not have any atomic schematic constructions (see Table 1.4 in §1.3.1).

1.6.2. Can't these facts be captured by a feature-based approach to categories, or by a categorial grammar approach?

In some contemporary syntactic theories, certain syntactic categories are not atomic but are instead decomposed into features. For example, there is a widely cited decomposition of the major parts of speech into the features [±N, ±V] (Chomsky 1970; Jackendoff 1977). In other syntactic theories, such as Head-driven Phrase Structure Grammar and Fillmore and Kay's Construction Grammar, the categories themselves are features, e.g. <cat v> for Verb; but the category feature is just one feature among many others that play a role in accounting for distributional patterns.

The use of features instead of categories may or may not be in the spirit of Radical Construction Grammar. The use of features illustrated by [±N, ±V] represents an even greater degree of reductionism than that found in theories that treat parts of speech as atomic primitive units. In that respect, decomposition of categories into features is the opposite of what Radical Construction Grammar proposes.

On the other hand, features for defining syntactic categories are—or should be—invoked in order to account for distributional facts about the words or phrases to which the features are attached. Even a feature like [+N], which appears to be a further reduction of syntactic structure, is—or should be—invoked when there is some construction which defines a distribution pattern that permits the parts of speech that are [+N] but disallows the parts of speech that are [−N]. To the extent that features specify occurrence/nonoccurrence of the element with the feature in a construction, the employment of features is in the spirit of Radical Construction Grammar.

I contend that if one takes all distributional patterns seriously, then one would end up with a set of features each of which is in essence indexed whether or not the word (or phrase) in question occurs in each role in each construction. For each mismatch of distributions across constructions, the mismatching words would somehow have to be indexed with a feature that in effect blocks its occurrence in one construction or permits its occurrence in the other construction. For instance, one might attach a feature to the representation of the Object of the English Verb *weigh* that permits it to occur without a Preposition (on the assumption that it is an anomalous Oblique), or prevents it from being passivized (on the assumption that it is an anomalous Direct Object).

The end result of this process would be a notational variant of Radical Construction Grammar, in which the mapping between words and constructions is represented by the values of the features indicating the distribution across constructions of each word or other grammatical unit. For example, the Object of *weigh* would, among other things, have the features which essentially reduce to <weigh <obj = +ActiveDirectObject, −PassiveSubject>>. Although this feature representation is one way of modeling Radical Construction Grammar, it has the drawback that the feature does not separately represent the construction and its relevant role; the feature label simultaneously encodes both.

A similar argument can be applied to a categorial grammar representation of the facts. In categorial grammar, syntactic categories are defined in terms of their combinability with other units to produce a larger unit. For instance, a transitive verb is defined as something that can combine with a noun phrase to produce a verb phrase. The category Transitive Verb is notated VP/NP. The categorial grammar notation also captures distributional relations between words and constructions. The categorial grammar representation X/Y means that a word of category X/Y can combine with element Y in construction X.

Again, I contend that if one takes all distributional patterns seriously, the end result would be a set of categories that indicates the occurrence of each word in each construction. To take the *weigh* example again, one would end up specifying *weigh* as a word which can combine with a prepositionless Noun Phrase to its right to yield an Active Verb Phrase (i.e. *weigh* is of type ActiveVP/NP), but cannot combine with the Passive suffix (or with the Passive Auxiliary) to produce a Passive Verb Phrase (i.e. it is not of type PassiveVP/PassivePrt). Although categorial grammar is another way of modeling Radical Construction Grammar, it has the drawback that all combinations must be represented as binary, whereas many constructions have more than two elements. (Categorial grammar can represent a construction with more than two elements, but only as a series of binary combinations.)

1.6.3. Doesn't RCG create a hopeless proliferation of categories? How do you label them all?

Radical Construction Grammar does appear to create a proliferation of categories, but since categories are not atomic primitive elements, this is not a theoretical problem. The linguist is, in fact, largely free to label the categories as s/he wishes. Naming the categories is, however, a practical problem for a linguist describing a language.

The same question arises with respect to Dryer's argument against universal categories and relations. In Dryer's view, all categories are language-specific. Dryer argues that what to label a category in a language is purely terminological; I will use the word LABEL to describe a name for a category (or construction) that has no theoretical significance in itself.

Dryer does suggest that using labels such as Noun or Verb instead of X and Y for, say, Kutenai word classes is convenient: 'Such a choice of label makes it easier to remember the labels and to follow discussions of the language, and it does draw attention to the similarities between these word classes and word classes in other languages' (Dryer 1997b: 118).

One can suggest a general mnemonic for labeling language-particular categories: Language + Category, such as Kutenai Verb and English Verb. These labels can be treated on analogy to proper names for people, as in Surname + Given Name. The category labels are like given names such as Bill. The fact that the name Verb occurs in Kutenai Verb and English Verb does not mean that they are instances of a universal grammatical category Verb with theoretical content, just as the fact that the name Bill occurs in Bill Croft and Bill Clinton does not mean that these individuals belong to a unified category with conceptual content.

The labeling problem arises even more acutely in Radical Construction Grammar. But the naming of elements in particular constructions is just a terminological problem, and a similar mnemonic can be applied here as well. The simplest mnemonic is for categories defined by the distribution in a role in a single construction. In this case, the category can be named Language + Construction + Category, such as English Passive Subject. Again, English Passive Subject should be treated as a proper name for a category; it should not be assumed that the category labeled by English Passive Subject is identical to the category labeled English Active Object, or for that matter to the category labeled English Active Subject—let alone the category labeled Japanese Passive Subject. Labeling of categories defined cross-constructionally is not so easy, and I have no simple solution to offer here. However, many typological universals only require construction-specific category labels.

Constructions are also language-specific. In Part III, I will argue that there are no universal constructions. The labeling problem thus arises here as well, but the mnemonic solution is straightforward: Language + Construction, as in English Passive. Again, English Passive is a proper name, and should not be assumed to be the name of a universal construction identical to, for example, the construction labeled Japanese Passive.

One advantage of the purely mnemonic labeling of categories and constructions in languages is that a Radical Construction Grammar description or analysis of a particular language can use the terminology already conventionally established for that language without any theoretical consequences. For example, a linguist using Radical Construction Grammar for describing or analyzing Philippine languages can use the traditional descriptions of the verb forms (Actor Focus, Goal Focus, etc.), even though the terms Goal, Focus, etc. are used to describe quite different categories in other languages. All that must be remembered is that the labels do not carry any theoretical significance.

One terminological convention that must be adhered to is the orthographic distinction between the (capitalized) names for grammatical constructions and categories in a particular language on the one hand and the (lower case) names for cross-linguistically valid semantic, pragmatic and discourse-functional categories on the other. For example, it is essential to differentiate the Philippine language construction name Focus (capitalized) from the pragmatic category of focus (lower case), since not only are they different types of categories, the grammatical category may not be an expression of the pragmatic category of the same name.

Although categories (and constructions) are language-specific as morphosyntactic structures, categories and constructions may be compared across languages according to their function (meaning, in the broad sense defined in §1.3.1). The formulation of cross-linguistic universals is in fact dependent on identifying categories and constructions across languages in terms of shared function (see Greenberg 1966b: 74; Keenan and Comrie 1977/1987: 63; Croft 1990b: 11–18). For this reason, when comparing categories and constructions across languages, I will use lower-case names such as 'relative clause'. This name should be read as 'the category/construction in a language that encodes the function named by this term'. These lower-case names do have theoretical significance (hence they are names, not labels).

In discussing language-specific instantiations of these categories and constructions, I will label the construction with the capitalized form of the name, for example 'English Relative Clause'. The assertions that are made about the language-particular categories and constructions labeled in this way should be interpreted as applying only to the use of the category/construction encoding the function with which the name is associated. For example, in a discussion of relative clauses across languages and the English Relative Clause, the lower-case name denotes 'the construction encoding the function of a proposition modifying a referent' (Keenan and Comrie 1977: 63), and any generalization made in the discussion about the grammatical properties of the English Relative Clause construction apply only to the English Relative Clause construction used for the relative clause function.

1.6.4. *If categories are defined relative to constructions, how do you identify constructions?*

This is the most frequently asked question about Radical Construction Grammar. Constructions can be identified even if they are primitive units, that is, not defined in terms of some other theoretical construct. Even though constructions are primitive units, they are complex (§1.6.1) and they have many properties that identify them. The complex wholes that linguists study (and children learn; see §1.6.6) are instances of constructions, that is, utterances. The parts are the words and morphemes making up each utterance.

The identification of constructions is essentially a CATEGORIZATION problem, that is, categorizing the utterances one hears or records into discrete types. In fact, this is the same problem faced by a field linguist with a corpus of the language being described, or for that matter the language user and language learner (see §1.6.5). What occurs in natural discourse are constructions, that is, complex syntactic units; we do not hear individual words with category labels attached to them. Utterances are instances of constructions. A corpus is a set of utterances which can be sorted into different types according to their grammatical properties. In other words, from the points of view of the language analyst, language user, and language learner, the larger units come first.

Categorization of constructions is as easy—or as difficult—as categorization of any other entities. Constructions often do fall into discrete types. There are discontinuities in the corpus of sentences: constructions have distinctive properties and their elements define distinctive distribution classes. For example, there are significant discontinuities between the structure of an English Transitive Active Clause and a Passive Clause, so that the two can be reliably separated. One such discontinuity is that the Passive Clause lacks a Direct Object which the counterpart Transitive Active Clause has. There are also other important cues for the categorization of constructions (see §6.5.2). Many constructions involve some unique combination of substantive morphemes, such as the English Passive construction's combination of *be*, Past Participle Verb form (usually an affix), and *by* (when the agent phrase occurs).

Finally, and perhaps most important of all, constructions are symbolic units. The semantics of a construction plays a significant role in differentiating constructions for the purpose of categorization and identification. The semantics of the participant roles encoded by the Active Subject and the Passive Subject are very different, despite the grammatical similarities of the Subject role in the two constructions and the identity of the counterpart verb stem. Since constructions are symbolic units (§1.3.2), categorization of utterances into construction types utilizes properties of both form and meaning in constructions.

Of course, categorization is not always as simple as I have made it out to be here. The English Transitive Active–Passive example represents a level of schematicity in constructions that has a relatively high CUE-VALIDITY (Rosch 1978): a relatively high number of properties shared by the members with the category plus a relatively low number of properties shared by members across the categories. Constructions form a taxonomy (§1.3.3), and more general and more specific construction types will have a lower cue-validity than the Transitive Active/Passive distinction. Also, construction types in other domains of grammar may not have as high a cue-validity as the example I have used here. Moreover, research in categorization has demonstrated that different members of a category have different status in the category: some are more PROTOTYPICAL members and others are more PERIPHERAL members (Rosch 1978; see §§2.4.3–2.4.4; and see Taylor 1995 for a recent survey).

It is true that the variation in the internal structure of categories, and their discreteness from other categories, is problematic for a linguist analyzing a particular language, and I have not given any detailed principles for categorization of constructions in this section. But I must emphasize again that these facts are problematic to the same extent for the language speaker and language learner. The best way to understand how to identify constructions is to use the results of psychological research into categorization and the formation of taxonomies, a domain that regrettably will not be discussed in detail in this book (see §1.1 and §1.3.3).

1.6.5. *How do you capture generalizations for categories across constructions in RCG?*

In order to answer this question, we must first look at how categories are represented in reductionist theories. To simplify comparison, we will compare reductionist construction grammar to Radical Construction Grammar.

The syntactic structure of any complex construction is made up of elements (§1.3.2). These elements may be constructions themselves. For example, the Intransitive Clause construction illustrated in 56 has as a part the Noun Phrase construction:

(56) [[The girls]$_{\text{Noun Phrase}}$ [sang]$_{\text{Verb}}$]$_{\text{Intransitive Clause}}$

Ultimately, a complex construction will be broken down into its atomic elements—words and morphemes—which form categories. It is the representation of these categories that differentiates a nonreductionist grammatical theory such as Radical Construction Grammar from reductionist theories.

Both reductionist and nonreductionist syntactic theories assume the existence of a meronomic (part–whole) structure to complex constructions. The part–whole relation is indicated implicitly by the nesting of bracketed/boxed elements in the representation of the morphosyntactic structure of a complex construction. For example, in (56) the part–whole relation between *The girls* and *The girls sang* is represented implicitly in the nesting of the Noun Phrase brackets inside the Intransitive Clause brackets. I will refer to this part–whole relation as an INTERNAL meronomic relation.

Reductionist theories of syntax allow for an element—i.e. a category—to be part of more than one construction. For example, the part of the Intransitive Construction [SBJ VERB] labeled 'Verb' is also assumed to be a part of the Transitive Construction as well. If so, the representation of the Verb construction as an independent node in the construction network is required. This independent node is then represented as playing a role in several other constructions. This analysis is represented in Figure 1.13.

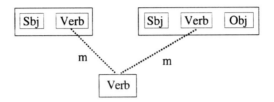

Figure 1.13. A reductionist construction grammar representation of the category Verb across constructions

In the representation in Figure 1.13, we will say that there is an EXTERNAL meronomic link (labeled 'm') between each construction that has a Verb element as a part on the one hand, and the independent construction representing the Verb element on the other. Thus, there are at least two different types of links in the construction network in reductionist construction grammar: taxonomic links between constructions, discussed in §1.3.3, and external meronomic links from parts of constructions to parts of other constructions, illustrated in Figure 1.13.

In a Radical Construction Grammar representation of a construction, the categories of the construction are defined by the construction itself. Hence the categories are unique to each construction. The representations of the Intransitive construction and the Transitive construction in a reductionist syntactic theory (such as a reductionist construction grammar model) and in Radical Construction Grammar are given in Table 1.10.

Table 1.10. The representation of constructions in reductionist and nonreductionist syntactic theories

	Reductionist construction grammar	Radical Construction Grammar
Intransitive construction	[SBJ VERB]	[INTRSBJ INTRVERB]
Transitive Active construction	[SBJ VERB OBJ]	[TRSBJ TRVERB TROBJ]

The Radical Construction Grammar representation captures the fact that the distributional categories defined by the roles in the Transitive construction are not identical to those defined by the roles in the Intransitive construction. For example, the class of "Verbs" that can occur in the Transitive construction is not the same as the class of "Verbs" that can occur in the Intransitive construction. Hence the two categories are labeled "Intransitive Verb" and "Transitive Verb". (In fact, they could be named "Rosencrantz" and "Guildenstern" as far as syntactic theory is concerned; but I will follow the labeling mnemonic proposed in §1.6.3.) However, the Radical Construction Grammar representation does not capture the fact that Transitive Verbs are inflected with the same inflectional affixes as Intransitive Verbs, or that Transitive Subjects occur in the same position and in the same pronominal form as Intransitive Subjects.

In a reductionist theory, this fact is captured by describing the categories in the two constructions as the same category, for example Verb. That is, the Intransitive construction and the Transitive construction share one of their parts, namely, the Verb, as in Figure 1.13. However, the reductionist representation does not capture the fact that not all Verbs that occur in the Intransitive construction can occur in the Transitive construction, or vice versa. Needless to say, an adequate syntactic theory must be able to capture both the fact that Transitive Verbs and Intransitive Verbs are distinct classes, and the fact that they share the same inflections.

The solution to this problem in Radical Construction Grammar can be motivated by considering again the process of identifying constructions described in §1.6.4. Categorizing utterances as instances of constructions is one way of abstracting away from the input. The result of this process is a network of taxonomic relations among constructions. Another process that occurs in categorizing utterances is the analysis of utterances breaking them into their constituent parts. But the analysis of utterances into their component parts is another way of abstracting from the input. The learner (or analyst) abstracts from two or more constructions which have parts that share something in common, say, a set of inflections.

Radical Construction Grammar represents analysis as abstraction from parts of constructions directly. That is, Radical Construction Grammar allows for taxonomic relations among parts of different constructions. Thus, the Transitive Verb category in the Transitive construction and the Intransitive Verb category in the Intransitive construction can be subsumed under a more general category, which I will call Morphological Verb.

It is *absolutely essential* to recognize that the commonalities across the subcategories found in various constructions must themselves be justified linguistically. For example, the justification for a category subsuming Intransitive Verb and Transitive Verb comes in from the occurrence of the Morphological Verb category in another construction, namely the morphological construction of Tense-Agreement (TA) inflection. This is why I have labeled the category Morphological Verb—in order to make clear that I am not positing a global category Verb for English (or any other language). There is no global category Verb; just overlapping XVerb categories defined by various constructions. The representation of this subnetwork of verbal categories in Radical Construction Grammar is given in Figure 1.14 (p. 56; t is used to indicate that the relations between elements is taxonomic).

In other words, no schematic syntactic category is ever an independent unit of grammatical representation in Radical Construction Grammar. Every schematic

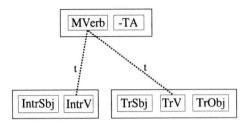

Figure 1.14. Radical Construction Grammar representation of verbal categories

category is a part of a construction, which defines that category. Only words, being completely substantive, may be independent units of grammatical representation in Radical Construction Grammar. Yet even words are often not analyzable as wholly independent grammatical units. Words often exist only embedded in constructions, such as morphological inflections (see Bybee 1985, chapter 5) or syntactic constructions. Words also vary in meaning depending on the constructions in which they appear (see Chapter 3 and Croft 1998a).

The Radical Construction Grammar representation of categories allows us to eliminate external meronomic links. In Radical Construction Grammar, the only type of links between constructions and elements of constructions are taxonomic links. In this respect, Radical Construction Grammar is a simpler model of grammatical knowledge than reductionist construction grammar. In other words, all types of grammatical generalizations are represented as taxonomic generalization, that is, categorization (see §1.6.5).

Figure 1.15 gives a Radical Construction Grammar representation of part of the taxonomic hierarchy in Figure 1.11.

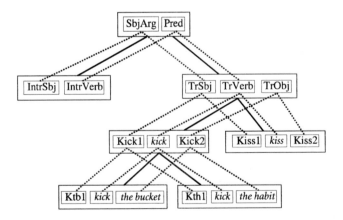

Figure 1.15. Radical Construction Grammar representation of construction taxonomy

The taxonomic hierarchy in Figure 1.15 describes only the taxonomy of argument structure constructions, that is, constructions representing the encoding of arguments of predicates (see Fillmore and Kay 1993; Goldberg 1995; Croft in press). In Figure 1.15, each construction part is given its own category label. The construction parts are linked in taxonomies by broken lines, and the constructions as a whole are linked in taxonomies by heavy black lines.

Each construction and category in the taxonomic hierarchy is motivated by a grammatical fact of English. Different transitive phrases with *kick* share grammatical properties, specifically, the encoding of the two arguments. The *kick* construction thus permits us to establish the grammatical categories Kick1 and Kick2, standing for the two arguments of *kick* in its transitive uses. Likewise, the transitive verb constructions with *kick* and *kiss* share grammatical properties, namely the encoding of the two arguments, and allow us to establish the superordinate categories TrSbj and TrObj. Finally, the Transitive and Intransitive constructions of English share grammatical properties, namely the encoding of the one argument of Intransitive Verbs and one of the arguments of Transitive Verbs (see Chapter 4). The existence of the Clause construction allows us to establish the superordinate categories SbjArg ("subject as an argument") and Pred. Note that the Clause construction does not specify anything about the TrObj element in the Transitive construction. This is because the Clause construction represents only the generalization about the Subject arguments of Transitive and Intransitive clauses.

The actual existence of any of these construction schemas is an empirical question (see §1.6.4). Although the idiosyncrasy of idioms such as *kick the bucket* and *kick the habit*, and the argument structures of verbs such as *kick* and *kiss*, are a sufficient condition for positing the existence of these specific constructions, the positing of more general constructions is not a necessary consequence. Likewise, the elimination of more specific constructions whose properties can be predicted by more general constructions (such as a semantically regular *kick* sentence like *She kicked me*) is not a necessary consequence. Individual speakers may vary as to what grammatical generalizations they do or do not form. The positing of more schematic constructions, and the elimination of more specific constructions with predictable grammatical properties, is an empirical question, which can only be answered by the principles discovered by the usage-based model (see §1.3.3).

1.6.6. *How can a child acquire a grammar without atomic primitive categories?*

The essential structure of a radical construction grammar is the many-to-many mapping between words and constructions (more precisely, between words and the roles in constructions). This structure is not impossible to store or to learn (pace Radford 1988: 63). Of course, the more constraints we can impose on the many-to-many mapping, the easier the grammar is to store or learn. But constraining the many-to-many mapping such that words in a single class have identical distributions, as implied by the standard syntactic theories, is empirically untenable.

Radical Construction Grammar argues that categories and relations are construction-specific. In addition, Radical Construction Grammar argues that constructions are language-specific (see Part III). If so, then virtually all of the formal syntactic properties of grammar are language-specific and therefore must be learned INDUCTIVELY. The inductive learning process is essentially the same process described in the preceding section. A child is exposed to utterances in context—thus, a significant part of the meaning of the utterance is available to the child from the context of use. The child acquires constructions by categorizing utterances into their types, in terms of the grammatical properties of the utterances that the child is able to perceive. (It is possible that the child does not perceive all relevant properties of the input: s/he may not be able to keep track of inflections, for instance, and so the inflections in the input would not be part of the construction type s/he induces.)

In the process of categorizing utterances into constructions, the child has effectively induced the categories of the elements of those utterances, since those categories are defined by the constructions (compare Figure 1.15 above). It makes no sense to ask if children have the same categories as adults do in Radical Construction Grammar, because such a question assumes the existence of global syntactic categories. Categories are defined by constructions, and children do not have the same constructions as adults do. Eventually, as the child becomes able to process all aspects of the input, and is exposed to more and more varied instances of constructions, s/he gradually builds up a taxonomic network of constructions and their categories that comes to equal that possessed by adult speakers of the language.

In fact, this model of syntactic acquisition has much empirical evidence in support of it. A number of recent studies that carefully document in detail children's earliest multiword utterances demonstrate that children start with very narrowly defined constructions and only very gradually expand their production with different combinations of words and inflectional forms (Braine 1976; Tomasello 1992, 2000; Lieven et al. 1997; Tomasello et al. 1997; Pine and Lieven 1997; Pine et al. 1998; Rubino and Pine 1998; Gathercole et al. 1999; see Croft and Cruse in preparation, chapter 12 for a brief summary of their results). This evidence implies a very gradual inductive process, beginning with very specific constructions and very gradually inducing more schematic constructions and producing novel utterances with those schemas.

1.6.7. How does RCG relate to other versions of construction grammar?

Radical Construction Grammar, like other versions of construction grammar, uses a uniform generalized concept of a grammatical construction as a symbolic unit, atomic or complex, from completely substantive to completely schematic (§1.3.1). Thus, Radical Construction Grammar embraces the syntax–lexicon continuum. Radical Construction Grammar also uses the same principles of the taxonomic organization of constructions as most other construction grammar theories

(§1.3.3). In particular, Radical Construction Grammar allows for the polysemy (radial category structure) of some construction types, metaphorical extensions of constructions, and accepts the usage-based model of the representation of grammatical information in the taxonomic network of constructions.

Radical Construction Grammar differs from other versions of construction grammar in the meronomic structure of constructions, that is, the internal structure of constructions (§1.3.2). Radical Construction Grammar retains the symbolic relations of the parts of constructions as in other construction grammar models, in particular Cognitive Grammar (Langacker 1987: 76–86). In Radical Construction Grammar, categories are defined by the roles they play in constructions. Hence the categories are unique to each construction. Radical Construction Grammar rejects meronomic links between parts of different constructions and instead uses taxonomic links between elements of different constructions to capture generalizations across categories in different constructions (§1.6.5).

Also, Radical Construction Grammar does not posit syntactic relations between elements in constructions (see Part II); it posits only semantic relations and symbolic relations (between elements of constructions and the corresponding components of the semantic structure of the construction). Finally, as will be argued in Part III, Radical Construction Grammar argues that constructions are language specific (Part III), a position not held by all construction grammarians (cf. Kay and Fillmore 1999: 1).

1.6.8. How can I use RCG for grammatical description if all categories are construction-specific and constructions are language-specific?

Typical reference grammars have chapters describing lexical categories of the language, such as the parts of speech, and also chapters describing syntactic roles in the clause such as subject and object (or ergative and accusative, or actor and undergoer), and syntactic roles in the phrase such as different types of modifiers and complements of the head noun.

From a Radical Construction Grammar perspective this is a misleading way to describe a human language. In a Radical Construction Grammar description of a language, every chapter would describe a class of constructions of the language. Instead of parts of speech, chapters would describe the propositional act constructions of the language (Chapter 2; Croft 1990b). Instead of syntactic roles, chapters would describe the argument linking constructions of the language (Chapter 4; see Levin 1993, Part One; Goldberg 1995). Since the generalized concept of construction includes morphological structures, the description of a language's morphology in Radical Construction Grammar would also be in constructional terms.

A Radical Construction Grammar description of a language would also describe in some detail the possible fillers of each role in each construction, since category labels in themselves do not provide any significant information about possible fillers. Many descriptions of constructions in traditional grammars do not give a sufficiently detailed description of the behavior of different lexical semantic classes across the constructions of the language. Yet substantial differences in grammatical behavior are found within lexical subclasses. More fine-grained distinctions than simply 'verbs' or 'count nouns' are necessary. Previous studies of lexical classes relevant to various types of constructions include Croft (1991: 95–8) for propositional act constructions; Wierzbicka (1988, Chapter 10) for countability constructions; Craig (1986) and Croft (1994b) for gender/animacy/classifying constructions; Herskovits (1985) for spatial relation constructions; Levin (1993, Part Two) for argument linking constructions; Croft (1990c) for voice constructions; Croft (in preparation) for aspectual semantic classes; and Cristofaro (1998, ch. 5) for clausal complement constructions.

Finally, a Radical Construction Grammar description of a language will also describe in some detail the semantics, pragmatics, and discourse function of each construction, since constructions are symbolic units and the function of a construction is as much a part of linguistic convention as the construction's form. This aspect of grammar is as important as the proper description of morphosyntactic constructions and distributions. In particular, the semantic interpretation of the words or phrases filling roles in constructions often varies depending on the construction (see §2.2.2, §2.5), and conversely the semantics of the construction varies depending on the class of words or phrases filling the constructional roles (see §3.2.2, §3.2.4). These differences in semantic interpretation are a central part of grammatical description.

Constructions are language-specific in their morphosyntactic properties, but their function in structuring and communicating information is not. A Radical Construction Grammar description of a grammar would organize constructions in terms of the functions that they perform. The organization of constructions by functions will in fact not be that different from common practice in reference grammars, because the traditional organization of grammatical descriptions is actually based on function as much as on form.

Radical Construction Grammar essentially allows the descriptive linguist to describe the structure of a language in the language's own terms, since constructions are language-specific. The functional organization of a grammatical description will allow the description to be easily followed by readers unfamiliar with the language. Finally, the typological generalizations presented in this book and in the monographs and reference works cited herein will allow the field linguist to place the constructions of her or his language in a wider grammatical context.

1.6.9. *If categories are construction-specific and constructions are language-specific, does this mean that there is no Universal Grammar, and no language universals?*

If Radical Construction Grammar argues that virtually all of syntactic structure is language-particular, and reduces that structure to the absolute minimum on top of that, then are there any universals of language left? Is there no Universal Grammar?

In one sense, there is no Universal Grammar. That is, there is no universal syntactic template to which the grammars of all particular languages conform. Nor is there an inventory of universal syntactic categories, relations or even constructions which the grammars of all particular languages draw from. This is in fact a good thing, because the endless cycle of syntactic theories witnessed in the last century is a consequence of the futile search for the mirage of the "right" universal template or set of universal categories, relations, and syntactic structures.

There are universals of language, but not in syntactic structure taken by itself. The universals of language are found in semantic structure and in symbolic structure, that is, the mapping between linguistic function and linguistic form. In Chapter 2, I will introduce the notion of a conceptual space, now gaining wider use among typologists, and the principles of typological markedness that govern the form–function mapping. In the following chapters, these theoretical constructs will be used to form positive hypotheses of language universals. Many of these hypotheses are not new, having been proposed in typological research over the past four decades. However, Radical Construction Grammar allows these results to take their rightful place in the context of a cross-linguistically valid theory of syntax.

1.7. Conclusion and Prospects

Radical Construction Grammar has a number of advantages over reductionist syntactic theories. It avoids the inconsistencies and self-fulfilling analyses of methodological opportunism in using the distributional method. There is no need to ignore, dismiss, or treat as exceptional distributional facts that do not fit the global categories posited by reductionist theories. It allows for the proper focus of attention on the richness and diversity of a speaker's knowledge of the constructions of his/her language. It also allows one to capture both the differences and similarities among categories defined by different constructions in the same language, as well as across languages.

The mismatches in distribution within and across languages do fall into systematic patterns. These patterns have been analyzed by typologists and include such phenomena as implicational hierarchies, typological prototypes, grammaticalization paths, etc. Not only do reductionist syntactic theories founder on the mismatches; their models of syntactic representation often do not capture the patterns that the mismatches conform to.

It should be noted that the same arguments against reductionist theories of syntactic representation also apply to reductionist theories of phonological and semantic representation. In phonology, there are problems in defining 'vowel' vs. 'consonant', deciding whether certain syllables exist or not as such for certain prosodic processes ('extrametricality'), and even in defining 'segment' and 'syllable' from a phonetic point of view. In a nonreductionist phonological theory, phonetically specified word forms and schematic phonotactic (and prosodic) templates generalized from them would be the representational primitives, and syllable and segment categories would be derivative.

In semantics, distributional analysis is used to identify semantic categories (see e.g. Cruse 1986). Not surprisingly, problems arise in defining various sorts of semantic categories, and even such basic concepts as identity and distinctness of word senses. In a nonreductionist semantic theory, complex semantic structures such as frames and the complex semantic structures found in constructions would be the representational primitives, and the semantic categories of components of semantic frames and other complex semantic structures would be derivative.

The development of a Radical Templatic Phonology and a Radical Frame Semantics should be a priority for nonreductionist linguistic theory. This book will not present either theory. However, an important aspect of syntactic representation is the counterpart semantic interpretation. In construction grammar, a construction is symbolic: it is a pairing of a morphosyntactic structure with a semantic structure. Hence we cannot entirely avoid the question of semantic representation, although this book focuses on syntactic representation. In particular, one cannot discuss cross-linguistically valid criteria for syntactic representation without addressing the cross-linguistic validity of semantic representation; this is done in Chapter 3.

I assume that the semantic structures in particular constructions function as units; these units would be the primitives of Radical Frame Semantics. These units can be related to one another in a conceptual space, as noted in §1.3.3; conceptual spaces are described in §2.4 and will be used throughout Parts I and III of this book. In Part II, on the internal structure of constructions and their meanings, I make minimal assumptions about the semantic structure of the conventional meaning of a construction. I assume only that a semantic structure is made up of components and relations among those components (see also §1.3.2), and that morphosyntactic elements can denote (symbolize) either semantic components or semantic relations. Hence, the semantic representations in Part II merely indicate semantic components and their relations. Proposing and defending more precise semantic representations would require another volume.

In fact, one of the reasons why this book is half the length of its nearest counterparts—Givón 1984, 1991; Langacker 1987, 1991a; Van Valin and LaPolla 1997—is that the latter volumes (especially Langacker's) discuss semantic issues at greater length than I do here. Nevertheless, it is possible to discuss—and resolve—fundamental issues in syntactic theory without presenting a full-fledged semantic theory, in fact by making only the minimal assumptions presented in the two preceding paragraphs. That is what this book seeks to achieve.

2

Parts of Speech

2.1. Introduction

There appears to be a widely accepted view, among typologists and also many other syntacticians, that the two assertions in (1a–b) about parts of speech—the major syntactic categories noun, verb, and adjective—should be part of syntactic theory:

(1) a. Noun, verb, and adjective are universal (cross-linguistic) categories found in particular languages
   b. But noun, verb, and adjective are not language universals—that is, not all languages possess the parts of speech noun, verb or adjective

In this chapter, as in previous work (Croft 1984, 1986, 1991, 2000b), I argue that the diametrically opposed assertions in (2a–b) should be part of syntactic theory:

(2) a. Noun, verb, and adjective are not categories of particular languages
   b. But noun, verb, and adjective are language universals—that is, there are typological prototypes (Croft 1990a, chapter 6) which should be called noun, verb, and adjective

To set the stage for the problem, I will begin with the analysis of parts of speech in traditional grammar, note its obvious inadequacies, and then turn to the shortcomings of more recent attempts to deal with the question, before presenting the Radical Construction Grammar analysis outlined in (2a–b).

The traditional, so-called notional or SEMANTIC CLASS analysis of parts of speech is given in (3a–c):

(3) a. Nouns denote OBJECTS (persons, things, places)
   b. Adjectives denote PROPERTIES
   c. Verbs denote ACTIONS

It has long been noted that the semantic class definition is inadequate because it is based on the semantic class of lexical items rather than their morphosyntactic behavior (see for example Radford 1988: 57). In fact, words of any of the semantic classes in (3a–c) can be found as Nouns (4a), Adjectives (4b), or Predicates (4c) (they can be outright Verbs in other languages, see §2.3.1):

(4) a. movement, eruption, kiss, strength, whiteness, size
   b. waste (incinerator), electrical (appliance), sleeping (child), broken (mirror)
   c. (be) happy, (be a) doctor

For this reason, the notional analysis has been rejected. But in many cases, nothing has really been put in its place. It is merely assumed that morphosyntactic behavior of some sort will establish parts of speech in a particular language, and that we may label those parts of speech with the terms Noun, Verb, and Adjective in many if not all languages. As Langacker notes: 'Every linguist relies on these concepts but few if any are prepared to define them in an adequate, explicit, and revealing way' (Langacker 1987: 2).

For example, most generative and related syntactic theories posit two binary features, [±N,±V], to define Noun, Verb, Adjective, and Preposition. The features are intended to capture similarities and differences in syntactic behavior among these four parts of speech; but they do not tell us what behavior should be used to determine those four parts of speech in the first place. In fact, most of the effort in X-bar theory in generative syntax has been employed to demonstrate the IDENTITY of syntactic patterning of the major parts of speech, and more recently minor parts of speech and even inflectional affixes. No guidelines are given as to how to DIFFERENTIATE parts of speech in a particular language. It is merely assumed that the inventory of parts of speech are universal because the features [±N,±V] are innately given.

The lack of interest in determining parts of speech in generative theory is illustrated by the lack of coverage in standard textbooks. Haegeman simply assumes that words belong to syntactic categories such as Noun and Verb, and gives no criteria for establishing parts of speech (Haegeman 1994: 36–7). Radford assumes that morphosyntactic behavior can be used to identify categories, and discusses a number of examples (Radford 1988: 57–63), but nothing more specific is said about what sort of morphosyntactic behavior can serve the purpose. It appears that there is no theoretically motivated set of criteria for establishing parts of speech in generative theory.

The situation worsens when we turn to cross-linguistic studies. How do we know that a syntactic category established in an exotic language X corresponds to the category Noun, Verb, both, or neither in our better-known European languages (§1.4.1)? In his survey of parts of speech systems, Schachter argues that grammatical criteria must be employed (Schachter 1985: 3); but in labeling such categories, he proposes a semantic heuristic based on the notional definition in (3a–c) above (Schachter 1985: 4). But heuristic definitions are no substitute for a sound methodology and theory.

Stassen expresses his frustration at the absence of any criteria for parts of speech by noting how in Sundanese, two different linguists arrive at the opposite conclusion as to whether the language has Adjectives (Stassen 1997: 32). Stassen concludes, 'different grammarians may propose different practical solutions, but all of these solutions will inevitably suffer from a certain degree of arbitrariness' (Stassen 1997: 32).

In the next two sections, we will observe the same problem at a much more general level. In the absence of theoretically motivated criteria for parts of speech, we witness two opposing trends in analyzing parts of speech. Some linguists—the "lumpers"—argue for the absence of major parts of speech in certain languages, or more precisely their conflation into one or two broader categories. Other linguists—the "splitters"—argue for the presence of the major parts of speech in every language, and many minor ones as well. In §2.2, I discuss perhaps the most sophisticated "lumping" approach, that of Hengeveld (1992), and argue that lumping is possible only by ignoring important facts about the languages analyzed. In §2.3, I discuss "splitting", and show that once one accepts splitting (as one must do, empirically), there is in principle no end to the splitting that one could do.

In fact, the real problem is that parts of speech are not grammatical categories of particular languages (see (2a) above). Once one accepts that, the analytic problems go away, and one can turn to the proper domain for a theory of parts of speech, typological patterns in conceptual space, explicated in §2.4. In §2.5 I briefly compare the typological and cognitive theories of parts of speech.

2.2. The Alleged Absence of Parts of Speech in Particular Languages

2.2.1. A "lumping" typological theory of parts of speech

Many linguists claim that there are languages that lack Adjectives or even lack the Noun–Verb distinction. The alleged absence of Adjectives is particularly widespread: words denoting qualities are described as (Stative) Verbs or as Nouns, depending on their morphosyntactic properties. Some languages, notably Nootkan, Salishan, Iroquoian, Philippine, and Polynesian languages, are said to lack even the Noun–Verb distinction. These assertions are commonly found in reference grammars of languages, most of which are written with no particular theoretical syntactic approach in mind. However, some recent typological research has begun to analyze parts of speech according to a "lumping" approach.

The most detailed and systematic exploration of a "lumping" approach to the typology of parts of speech systems is found in Hengeveld (1992). Hengeveld uses a Functional Grammar approach to define four parts of speech—Verb (V), Noun (N), Adjective (A), and Adverb (Adv; Hengeveld 1992: 58). The definitions of parts of speech are given in (5):

(5) a. A *verbal* predicate is a predicate which, without further measures being taken, has a predicative use *only*.
   b. A *nominal* predicate is a predicate which, without further measures being taken, can be used as the head of a term [referring expression].
   c. An *adjectival* predicate is a predicate which, without further measures being taken, can be used as a modifier of a nominal head.
   d. An *adverbial* predicate is a predicate which, without further measures being taken, can be used as a modifier of a non-nominal head.

The predicate, modifier, and term (referring expression) roles in Hengeveld's definitions of the parts of speech are in fact PROPOSITIONAL ACT functions. Predication, reference, and modification are pragmatic (communicative) functions, or as Searle described them, PROPOSITIONAL ACTS (see Searle 1969: 23–4; Croft 1990b; Croft 1991: 109–11). The act of REFERENCE identifies a referent and establishes a cognitive file for that referent, thereby allowing for future referring expressions coreferential with the first referring expression. The act of PREDICATION ascribes something to the referent. Predication does not establish a cognitive file for the state of affairs that is predicated, but instead prototypically reports relatively transitory states of affairs, often in a narrative sequence. The act of MODIFICATION (of referents) functions to enrich a referent's identity by an additional feature of the referent, denoted by the modifier.

What Hengeveld means by "without further measures being taken" is the obligatory presence of additional morphemes in order to use the lexical item in a particular function (predicative, term head, modifier). Hengeveld compares the term modifier *intelligent* in *the intelligent detective* to those in *the singing detective*, *the detective **who** is singing* and *the detective **from** London*. The modifiers *sing* and *London* require further measures (indicated in boldface in the examples), while *intelligent* does not. Hence, *intelligent* is an Adjective, while *sing* and *London* are not (Hengeveld 1992: 58–9). These further measures are what I have called 'function indicating morphosyntax' (Croft 1991: 58), and will call here the STRUCTURAL CODING of the propositional act functions. Structural coding does not include inflection; inflection is what I will call the BEHAVIORAL POTENTIAL of a stem in a particular syntactic role (see §2.4.2).

Hengeveld uses the criteria in (5) to determine what parts of speech a language has. In many instances, according to him, languages lack part of speech distinctions, that is, further measures need not be taken to use lexical items in certain functions. Hengeveld argues that such languages fall into two types.

In the first type, which Hengeveld calls FLEXIBLE, there simply is no overt structural coding for two or more part-of-speech functions. Hengeveld gives Quechua as an example of a flexible language with respect to the Noun–Adjective domain (Hengeveld 1992: 63, from Schachter 1985: 17; neither source indicates the variety of Quechua cited):

(6) rikaška: **alkalde**   -ta
    see.PST.1SG **mayor**   -ACC
    'I saw the mayor.'

(7) rikaška: **hatun**   -ta
    see.PST.1SG **big**   -ACC
    'I saw the big one.'

(8) chay   **alkalde** runa
    that   **mayor**   man
    'that man who is mayor'

(9) chay **hatun** runa
    that **big** man
    'that big man'

Hengeveld labels the lumped category N/A, since for him there is no priority of one label over another in a flexible language.

In the second type, which Hengeveld calls RIGID, there is overt structural coding of the part-of-speech function, but the same morphosyntax is used for two or more basic semantic classes (objects, properties, actions, to use the traditional grammar labels). Hengeveld gives Mandarin Chinese as an example of a rigid type with respect to Adjectives (more precisely, property words) and Verbs (action words). Action words and property words both lack overt structural coding in predication but require an overt Relativizer when modifying a term (Hengeveld 1992: 63, from Schachter 1985: 18; tones are not indicated in either source):

(10) neige nühaizi **liaojie**
     that girl **understand**
     'That girl understands.'
(11) neige nühaizi **piaoliang**
     that girl **beautiful**
     'That girl is beautiful.'
(12) **liaojie** de nühaizi
     understand REL girl
     'a girl who understands'
(13) **piaoliang** de nühaizi
     beautiful REL girl
     'a beautiful girl'

Hengeveld describes the lumped category as V, since there is no term modifier type without overt structural coding that could be called A.

2.2.2. A critique of "lumping" theories of parts of speech

Hengeveld's analysis has a clear theoretical basis, but it is not applied consistently across languages, and there is reason to question its utility. The most fundamental problem arises because Hengeveld—and all other "lumping" approaches to parts of speech—do not take into consideration what happens to a lexeme's MEANING when it is used in more than one function.

For example, in the Quechua examples above, the lexical item *hatun* denotes a property (bigness) in its modifying function in (9), but denotes an object possessing that property (a big one) in its term or referring function in (7). This is a substantial semantic difference. However, Hengeveld writes, 'Quechua combines the functions of adjectival and nominal predicates in one part of speech' (Hengeveld 1992: 64). In other words, the semantic difference between 'big' [property] and 'big one' [object] is considered to be irrelevant by Hengeveld.

The semantic differences allowed by Hengeveld are even greater with languages claimed to be extremely flexible or rigid. Hengeveld describes Tongan as 'an extremely flexible language' based on the following data (Hengeveld 1992: 66; examples from Tchekhoff 1981: 4):

(14) na'e **si'i** 'ae **akó**
 PST **small** ABS **school**:DEF
 'The school was small.'

(15) 'i 'ene **si'í**
 in POSS.3SG **childhood**:DEF
 'in his/her childhood'

(16) na'e **ako** 'ae tamasi'i **si'i** iate au
 PST **study** ABS child **little** LOC 1SG
 'The little child studied at my house.'

The absence of overt structural coding for the various uses of *si'i* and *ako* in (14)–(16) is taken by Hengeveld to indicate that Tongan has one category, N/V/A. The meaning shifts in examples (14)–(16) include 'small' and 'childhood' for *si'i* and 'school [n.]' and 'study [v.]' for *ako*.

Hengeveld describes Tuscarora as 'an extremely rigid language', based on the following data (Hengeveld 1992: 66, 67; examples from Williams 1976: 32, 234, 256, as glossed and translated in Hengeveld 1992):

(17) ra- **kwá:tihs**
 M.SBJ- **young**
 "He is young."
 'boy'

(18) ka- **téskr** -ahs
 N.SBJ- **stink** -IMPF
 "It stinks."
 'goat'

(19) ra- **kwá:tihs** wa- hr- ø- atkáhto -? ka- **téskr** -ahs
 M.SBJ- **young** PST- M.SBJ- OBJ- look.at -PNCT N.SBJ- **stink** -IMPF
 "He is young, he looked at it, it stinks"
 'The boy looked at the goat.'

The fact that *kwá:tihs* and *téskr-* take the same, apparently predicative inflection in all of their uses is taken by Hengeveld to indicate that Tuscarora has a single part of speech V (for a critique of the alleged identity of the morphological affixes in all functions in Iroquoian languages, see Mithun 2000). The meaning shifts in examples (17)–(19) include 'be young' and 'boy' for *kwá:tihs* and 'stink [v.]' and 'goat' for *téskrahs*.

It is of course a priori possible to construct a typological classification of parts-of-speech systems using only structural coding and allowing any degree of semantic shift. However, it does not appear that Hengeveld applies this criterion consistently, and there is good reason to believe that these criteria are unworkable and miss important generalizations.

If the sorts of semantic shifts illustrated in the Quechua, Tongan, and Tuscarora examples are allowed, then European languages should be assessed by the same criteria. For example, Spanish also allows Adjectives to function as referring expressions, as in (20) (Hengeveld 1992: 61):

(20) prefiero   es   -a   **modern** -a
      prefer:1SG.PRS that -F.SG **modern** -F.SG
      'I prefer that modern (one).' [e.g. house]

Yet Hengeveld writes, 'it would be incorrect to consider *moderna* 'modern' a noun, since the absolute use of adjectives, as illustrated in [14], is limited to those contexts in which a head noun is understood from the context' (Hengeveld 1992: 61–2). But the contexts in which the Quechua word *hatun* occurs also imply that the object to which it refers is understood from the context.

It is possible that Hengeveld does not analyze Spanish in the same way as Quechua because, on the whole, Spanish Nouns (object words) cannot be used as modifiers without overt structural coding. However, one cannot deny that Spanish Adjectives (property words) can be used as terms. Spanish exhibits a ONE-WAY flexibility: Adjectives can be terms, but Nouns cannot be modifiers. English happens to exhibit the opposite one-way flexibility: any Noun can be a modifier (so-called Complex Nominal expressions such as *piano trio*), but Adjectives cannot be terms without *one* (*the big one*). There is no obvious way to deal with one-way flexibility in Hengeveld's approach.

Likewise, if one allows semantic shift in the analysis of parts of speech, then English is a strong candidate for N/V/A flexibility. A great number of English lexemes, especially in the most frequent and basic vocabulary, can be used as predications and as terms. Compare the English examples in (21)–(23) with the Tongan examples in (14)–(16):

(21) a. The **school** was small.   [Noun]
     b. We **schooled** him in proper manners. [Verb]
(22) a. The little child **studied** at my house. [Verb]
     b. I retired to my **study**.   [Noun]
(23) a. The school was **small**.   [Adjective]
     b. the **small** child   [Adjective]
     c. There are a lot of **smalls** at this fair. [Noun]

Yet Hengeveld analyzes English as possessing the full set of parts of speech word classes (Hengeveld 1992: 69).

It is possible that Hengeveld does not analyze English as an extremely flexible language because N/V flexibility is not possible with all English lexemes that function as terms. Hengeveld does allow for the possibility that a language may have a minor part-of-speech class without it affecting its overall typological classification as a flexible or rigid lumping type. He notes that 'Tuscarora has a reduced number of true nouns' (Hengeveld 1992: 67), and writes:

Note that languages at best show a strong tendency towards one of the types. It is on the basis of these tendencies that I have assigned them a particular position in this classification. For instance, the rigid language Wambon is listed as a language without manner adverbs, but it has at least one. Mandarin, another rigid language, is listed as a language without adjectives but has in fact an extremely limited set of adjectival predicates. The situation is even more complicated in flexible languages (Hengeveld 1992: 69).

On the other hand, Hengeveld allows for the possibility of intermediate language types in his classification, for languages with somewhat larger parts-of-speech classes (Hengeveld 1992: 69–70).

If one allows for the ignoring of small parts-of-speech classes, however, one must quantify this criterion and apply it consistently. Does English have too few N/V lexemes to qualify as a flexible N/V language? If not, then how many is enough? Are basic vocabulary or the most frequent stems weighted more heavily than less common, less basic vocabulary? How do we know that when we read a grammar of an obscure "flexible" language X that the author of the grammar has systematically surveyed the vocabulary in order to identify what proportion is flexible? If English were spoken by a small tribe in the Kordofan hills, and all we had was a 150 page grammar written fifty years ago, might it look like a highly flexible language? And even if one could answer these questions, one cannot ignore "minor" part-of-speech classes. This would be methodological opportunism, both across and within languages.

2.2.3. *Semantic shift and zero coding*

These practical problems are the result of a theoretical decision that is highly questionable. This is the ignoring of semantic shifts in the lexemes that are found in different part-of-speech constructions (referring expressions, predication constructions, attributive constructions). Hengeveld argues that in an extremely flexible language such as Tongan, 'the only limitations on the use of predicates in different [part-of-speech] functions have to do with semantic compatibility' (Hengeveld 1992: 67). The first problem with this criterion is that in practice it is vacuous: if 'stink [v.]' and 'goat' are allowable semantic shifts, or 'school [n.]' and 'study [v.]', then there are likely to be no limitations on semantic compatibility of a lexeme with a part-of-speech function.

A second problem with the semantic shift/compatibility criterion is that semantic shift is actually not required for semantic compatibility in a different part-of-speech function. Semantic compatibility is what allows a property word like *hatun* to be used referentially, with the meaning 'the big one', and might disallow an object word like 'house' to be used attributively (Kees Hengeveld, personal communication). However, the semantic shifts across parts-of-speech uses found in Quechua and Tongan are not necessary to achieve semantic compatibility with different parts of speech constructions. The property concept 'big' can be referred to, as is done with the English Nouns *size* or *largeness*. Likewise, the action concept 'study' can be referred to, as is done with the English Noun *studying*. The translation equivalents of *largeness* and *studying* are the genuine equivalent referring expressions for Quechua *hatun* and Tongan *ako*. Yet these are not described by Hengeveld, and in most cases, these typically require overt structural coding, as in English *largeness* and *studying* (Croft 1991: 68–74).

The third, perhaps most serious, problem with the semantic shift/compatibility criterion, is that the semantic shifts are language-specific conventions. As noted above, English *school* can be used as a Verb just as its Tongan translation equivalent *ako* can; but it does not mean the same thing as *ako* [v.] 'study'. Conversely, the English translation equivalent of *ako* [v.], *study* can be used as a Noun; but then it does not mean the same thing as *ako* [n.] 'school'. The English Verb *stink* can be used as a Noun, but it does not mean the same thing as its Tuscarora counterpart *téskrahs* 'goat'. The English translation equivalent of Tongan *si'i* [adj.] 'small' can also be used as a Noun, but it does not mean the same thing as *si'i* [n.] 'childhood': *small* [n.] is used to refer to non-furniture antiques in the antiques trade, or to refer to underwear in laundry in British English (Carolyn Cook, personal communication). All of these language-specific semantic differences imply that just as in English, Tongan and Tuscarora lexical items have multiple conventional meanings, each of which happens to fall into different parts of speech.

It could be argued that the more general patterns of semantic shift, such as the general shift of a property word to denoting an object possessing the property in Quechua and other languages, is a better example of a flexible parts of speech language type (Hengeveld, personal communication). Yet such general semantic shifts are still language-specific: languages such as English cannot use the phrase **the big* to refer to something that is big; instead *the big one* is required. Hence, such general semantic shifts are due to the conventions of a language just as much as the more idiosyncratic semantic shifts illustrated in (15)–(23).

An analysis that allows a single lexeme to shift meaning freely would have to claim that the lexical stem is vague between the two uses, and the semantic shift is governed by general pragmatic principles. But there are problems with both parts of this analysis, the general meaning and the pragmatic principles.

A vagueness analysis assumes that there is a general meaning for a word that defines all and only the uses of that word. This meaning is supposed to be neutral with respect to the semantic features that vary in particular uses of the word. The problem arises in the specification of the general meaning. A lexical stem cannot be vague between exactly the occurring uses of the lexical stems of the type discussed by "lumping" theorists, for example between 'big' and 'the big one', or between 'school' and 'study'. There is no general semantic definition that covers all and only the meanings 'big' and 'the big one', and all and only the meanings 'school' and 'study'. A vague definition such as 'some concept associated with large size/studying' is too general. If the word were vague, then any concept associated with large size would be equally acceptable for *hatun* and any concept associated with studying would be an equally acceptable use of *ako*.

In other words, such a general definition provides necessary but not sufficient conditions for the proper use of words like Quechua *hatun* or Tongan *ako*. The inability to identify sufficient conditions is the Achilles heel of all vagueness or monosemy definitions (see Cruse 1992 and §3.2.2). The alternative is to specify that the particular use represents a conventional meaning of the expression, that is, that there are two senses of the word in question, each of which may belong to a different part of speech.

Moreover, the pragmatic principles invoked by a general meaning analysis are not general: they would have to be conventions of particular languages and their speech communities. This is contrary to the definition of pragmatics as those aspects of language use that are derivable from general principles governing the interaction of the interlocutors, including their (shared and unshared) general knowledge. Convention means that a speaker is using a form such as *hatun* in a particular context in conformity with previous uses of that form in that context in the speech community (Lewis 1969; Clark 1996: 62–71; Croft 2000a: 95–8), and not on the basis of general pragmatic principles (that is, nonconventional coordination devices that enable the hearer to recognize the intended meaning of the speaker; see Lewis 1969: 33–6, 83–8, 119–20; Clark 1996: 80–1; Croft 2000b: 99–104). A description of a use as the result of a 'pragmatic convention' is equivalent to a polysemy analysis (see also Croft 1998a). That is, the conventional meanings of a word such as *hatun* include reference to a property and reference to an object possessing that property. Calling the latter a 'pragmatic' convention does not make the latter meaning any less conventional—that is, semantic (Ariel 1998)—than the former meaning.

Although one cannot say with absolute certainty that a particular use of a form is conventional, a high frequency of use strongly implies that the use is conventional. Also, conventions are arbitrary to some degree, that is, there are alternatives to the convention adopted by the speech community (Lewis 1969: 68–76). Hence a degree of arbitrariness also implies the presence of a convention. And arbitrariness is indicated by the cross-linguistic variation in semantic shifts described above, and also in the impossibility to come up with a general meaning for the allegedly vague word.

Another argument against the semantic-shift analysis is that it ignores important empirical facts. I have already noted above that Hengeveld's analysis involves methodological opportunism in ignoring small part-of-speech classes. But ignoring semantic differences also involves a sort of methodological opportunism. This conclusion can be demonstrated with an example that does not involve a shift in part of speech. In §1.5.1.1, it was observed that the English Verb *weigh* cannot occur in the Passive construction, as in the following example:

(24) *106 pounds is weighed by Jack.

In fact, however, *weigh* can occur in the Passive construction in its metaphorical meaning of 'consider':

(25) This argument has to be weighed seriously.

In other words, distributional analysis must take into consideration distributional facts RELATIVE TO THE MEANING of the words and constructions being analyzed, or else important linguistic generalizations will be missed (I am grateful to Toshio Ohori for this observation). One would thus naturally expect there to be distributional differences in the case of semantic shift, and these differences require an analysis that recognizes the differences in meaning. The fact that in some cases, the distributional differences occur across constructions used to define parts of speech, makes examples like *hatun* and *ako* no different from other words with multiple meanings.

An objection to the multiple-meaning analysis is that it would require the existence of extensive zero derivation (Kees Hengeveld, personal communication). However, many syntactic theories, including construction grammar theories, do not appeal to derivational processes in representing the relationship between the two meanings. Instead, the semantic shifts are represented as a systematic POLYSEMY between, for example, a property meaning and an object-possessing-property meaning (see §3.2.2 for further discussion of polysemy). The representation of systematic polysemy is straightforward, and moreover, systematic polysemy is pervasive in language (Nunberg 1979). For example, Nunberg points out that all words have a systematic polysemy between reference to the type (e.g. *lion* referring to the species) and an instance of the type (referring to an individual lion), and between use (*lion* referring to the animal) and mention (*lion* referring to the word, as in *Lion is a four letter word*).

But perhaps the most serious objection to the allowance of any semantic shift is that by ignoring semantic shifts, one overlooks an important language universal. It is common cross-linguistically to find a lexical item used in more than one propositional act function without overt morphological derivation but with a significant and often systematic semantic shift. The semantic shifts are constrained by the language universal in (26):

(26) If there is a semantic shift in zero coding of an occurrence of a word (i.e. flexibility) in a part-of-speech construction, even if it is sporadic and irregular, it is always towards the semantic class PROTOTYPICALLY associated with the propostional act function, that is, the semantic classes for parts of speech in (3) (see §2.1) (Croft 1991: 74–7).

In other words, the traditional semantic class definition of parts of speech in (3) is partially correct: it defines the prototypical members of the part of speech category, although as noted above, nonprototypical semantic classes may also belong to the part of speech category. A PROTOTYPE is a privileged subset of members of a category that represent the "best" exemplars of the category; a number of psychological phenomena are manifestations of prototypicality (see Rosch 1978 for a survey). The theoretical concept of a prototype is also relevant to language universals such as the one in (26); other language universals sensitive to prototypicality will be given in §2.4.4.

The following patterns are particularly common cross-linguistically. Property words used as referring expressions shift meaning to an object (person or thing) which possesses the property, as with Quechua *hatun-ta* in example (7). Action words used in referring expressions shift meaning to a person, place, or thing which is a typical salient participant in the action in its semantic frame (in the sense of Fillmore 1982), as with Tongan *ako* in example (15), or K'iche' (Quiché) *tixoh* 'eat' in (27) (Mondloch 1978: 198):

(27) lē   k-   ā-   ∅-   tixoh
     the   PRS-   2SG.ERG-   3SG.ABS-   eat
     'what you eat' [lit. 'the you-eat-it']

Conversely, an object word used in a predication construction shifts meaning to an action typically or saliently associated with the object in its semantic frame, as frequently occurs in English (see Clark and Clark 1979):

(28) **pocket** the change, **tree** a cat, **staple** an envelope, etc.

A simpler semantic shift of object words in predication is to the process 'become an [object]', as in the Makah example in (29) (Jacobsen 1979: 114).

(29) **ɬa·x̣ukš?al**
     man:MOM:NOW:IND:3
     'He's gotten to be a man.' (cf. *ɬa·x̣uk* 'man')

Similarly, it is quite common for property words used in predication constructions to shift meaning to the inchoative process 'become [property]' (Stassen 1997: 163–4). In Biblical Hebrew, the Verbal inflection in (30) (by internal vowel changes) yields an inchoative interpretation, in contrast with the stative Non-verbal predication in (31) (Stassen 1997: 158, from Lambdin 1971: 193, 14):

(30) zāqēn
     old.3SG.M.PRF
     'He became old.'
(31) tôḇ   -îm   hā-   ǎnāšîm
     good   -M.PL   ART-   man.PL
     'The men are good.'

Even where there is no major semantic shift, there is usually a subtle semantic shift towards the semantic class prototypical for the propositional act function. For instance, predicate nominals do not denote an object in itself, but rather a relation. The typical relation is taken to be the relation of membership in the object class, as in *She is a musician* (as it was in Croft 1991 and Stassen 1997). But there is also the relationship of identity, as in *She is the mayor*, and a variety of other relations (see Croft 1991: 69–71; Hengeveld 1992: 75–91; Stassen 1997: 100–6).

Object words as modifiers must also be construed as relational, and become less object-like the more modifier-like their syntax (Croft 1991: 103–4; see Uehara 1998:

105–29 for a more complex pattern in Japanese). For example, the Turkish Izafet construction with the Genitive suffix (overt structural coding for object word modification) has a more specific, object meaning, whereas the Izafet construction without the Genitive treats the modifier more as a property (Lewis 1967: 42–3):

(32) üniversite -nin profesörler -i
     university -GEN professors -3SG.POSS
     'the professors of the university'
(33) üniversite profesörler -i
     university professors -3SG.POSS
     'university professors'

The same is true of the English glosses of the Turkish sentences: the zero coded prenominal Noun in the Complex Nominal construction in (33) is more property-like than the postposed Genitive NP in (32).

Likewise, the more predicate-like the syntax of object words and property words in predication, the more transitory and less inherent is the property asserted (Wierzbicka 1986; Bolinger 1967, 1980a,b; Croft 1991: 105–6). Bolinger provides a nice example of a scalar increase in inherentness from Verb to Adjective to Noun in English (Bolinger 1980b: 79).

(34) a. Jill fusses.
     b. Jill is fussy.
     c. Jill is a fussbudget.

Finally, Langacker argues that even action nominalizations represent an alternative conceptualization or construal of the action as a static whole (Langacker 1987: 207–8).

2.3. From Lumping to Splitting

2.3.1. *Distributional analysis and the analysis of parts of speech*

A more far-ranging criticism of Hengeveld's and other lumpers' analysis of parts of speech in various languages is that other relevant morphosyntactic evidence is ignored. Structural coding constructions represent only one or two constructions providing evidence for parts of speech such as Noun, Verb, and Adjective. Distributional analysis often reveals COVERT categories, that is, categories not obligatorily flagged by overt structural coding. For example, one can distinguish two different classes of predicates indicating transfer of possession, which both have the same form (as English Verbs), according to whether they occur in the Ditransitive or Double-Object construction:

(35) a. Ellen gave/sent the books to Laura.
     b. Ellen donated/contributed $500 to the Save-the-Redwoods League.
(36) Ellen gave/sent Laura the books.
(37) *Ellen donated/contributed the Save-the-Redwoods League $500.

The fundamental fact that is overlooked is that while difference of form entails difference in categorization, identity of form does *not* entail identity of categorization (see also §3.2.2).

A clear illustration of this fact can be found in Jacobsen's excellent critique of claims that Makah and other Nootkan languages lack any major parts of speech distinctions (Jacobsen 1979). Such claims are based on one distributional context, predication, as illustrated in the examples in §1.4.1.2, repeated here as (38)–(41) (Jacobsen 1979: 110–11):

(38) **k'upšil** baʔas ʔu·yuq
point:MOM:IND:3 house OBJ
'He's pointing at the house.'

(39) **babaɬdis**
white.man:IND:1SG
'I'm a white man.'

(40) **ʔi·ʔi·x̌ʷʔi**
big:IND:3
'He's big.'

(41) **hu·ʔax̣is** haʔukʷ'ap
still:IND:1SG eat:CAUS
'I'm still feeding him.'

In all of these examples, the predicated word occurs in the same, initial, syntactic position and takes the "verbal" inflections. Nevertheless, when one looks at other distributional contexts in Makah, not only can Noun, Verb, and Adjective be identified, but so can Adverb and Auxiliary. It is worth reviewing the arguments of this difficult-to-find paper in some detail.

Nouns (generally object words) have some distinctive behavior even as predicates. Predicated Nouns can occur without change of meaning in the (zero coded) Durative Aspect only (Jacobsen 1979: 114; see example (30) above). Although Jacobsen does not note this fact, the use of Nouns in Momentaneous Aspect involves a semantic shift to inchoative process (as in example (29) in §2.2.3) or an associated action (as in (42)) in all the examples given in his paper (ibid.: 114):

(42) **p'atqčil**
baggage:MOM:IND:3
'He's packing' (cf. *p'atuq* 'baggage')

In other words, the Makah examples conform to the universal in (26).

When used as referring expressions, Nouns occur in what appears to be the—zero coded—"Durative Aspect". However, Jacobsen points out that 'in the absence of a contrast it is misleading to speak of nouns as being in the durative aspect' (Jacobsen 1979: 114). That is, there is no reason to assume that the zero coded form of Nouns as referring expressions is the Durative Aspect found in predicates.

As modifiers, Nouns require Possessive suffixes or the suffix *i·c* 'belonging to' (Jacobsen 1979: 139; example from ibid.: 136):

(43) qu?aci·c   t'aši
    human:BELONGING.TO trail
    'human trails'

Verbs (generally action words) occur as predicates in both Durative and Momentaneous Aspect. Verbs can function as Subject referring expressions only when suffixed with -°*iq*, unlike Nouns (which may occur without it). Even then, the -°*iq* form refers to a person/place/thing associated with the action, not the action itself:

(44) da·s?its   t'iqʷasiq
    see:PASS:IND:1SG   sit:on.ground:ART
    'The one sitting on the ground sees me.'

Moreover, the -°*iq* forms take a restricted range of Demonstratives (ibid.: 122). When Verbs are used as modifiers, they require the -°*iq* form, or a prefix (ibid.: 123):

(45) t'iaqʷasiq   ƛ'icuxʷadi
    sit:on.ground:ART   person
    'the person who is sitting on the ground'

Adjectives (generally property words) occur as modifiers without additional morphology (ibid.: 136):

(46) ?usubas   ?i·?i·x̣ʷ   ba?as
    REF:need:IND:1SG   big   house
    'I need a big house.'

Adjectives require -°*iq* when functioning as referring expressions, and moreover refer to a thing possessing the property, not the property itself, just as in Quechua and Spanish (ibid.: 138):

(47) waha·?al   ?i·?i·x̣ʷ?iq
    go:now:IND:3   big:ART
    'A large one goes.'

Certain minor parts of speech can also be identified on distributional grounds. For example, Auxiliaries only occur in a construction with a following Verb in the Absolutive form (ibid.: 133):

(48) wiki·s   ha?uk
    not:IND:1SG   eat(ABS)
    'I'm not eating.'

Auxiliaries do not occur as modifiers of other predicates (ibid.: 134). Adverbs, another minor class, can occur following predicates as modifiers (ibid.: 131), and never take the Object affixes when predicated (ibid.: 132).

In discussing his arguments for parts of speech in Makah, Jacobsen makes the following observation: 'In saying that there are these parts of speech, however,

I am not excluding cases of multiple class membership, of sporadic occurrence in atypical roles, and especially, of lexicalization (internally verbal formations used as nouns), all of which seem to occur' (Jacobsen 1979: 107). In fact, English is not that much different. In English, there are many cases of multiple class membership of polysemous items, of sporadic occurrences of words in atypical roles, and even of verbal lexicalization—compare for example *forget-me-not* and *They'll ask me **heaven knows what** question next*.

Distributional analysis provides a more complete picture of the grammatical patterning of a language. "Lumping" analyses of parts of speech succeed only by ignoring distributional patterns. Even language families claimed to lack a Noun–Verb distinction, such as Nootkan, Salishan (Kuijpers 1968; Kinkade 1983) and Iroquoian (Sasse 1988, 1991), can be argued to have the usual parts of speech under careful distributional analysis (in addition to Jacobsen 1979 for Nootkan, see van Eijk and Hess 1986 and Croft 1991: 42–5 for Salishan, and Mithun 2000 for Iroquoian).

2.3.2. *Splitting: where does one stop?*

The empirical facts appear to favor the "splitters". But the "splitters" have their own problem. There is no way to stop splitting. For example, the Makah data do not allow us to distinguish between the major parts of speech (Noun, Verb, and Adjective) and the minor ones (Auxiliary, Adverb, and Preposition). Worse, careful distributional analysis demonstrates that even the traditional parts of speech should be split.

A simple, cross-linguistically common example is the existence of more than one class of Adjectives (property words) in a language such as Lango (Noonan 1992). Again, I will go into this example in some detail, since it will be used to illustrate the universal typological theory of parts of speech in §2.4.2. Distributionally, Lango has two classes of property words and one class of action words. The first class of property words have distinct Singular and Plural stem forms, all of which are listed in (49) (Noonan 1992: 105):

(49) SG PL
  dìt   dìtò   'big, old, important'
  dwôŋ   dòŋɔ̀ 'large, old'
  ràc   ràcù   'bad'
  bèr   bècò   'good'
  cèk   cègù   'short'
  tídí   tínò   'small'
  bòr   bòcò   'long, high, far away'

In modification, this class normally uses only the Attributive particle, and uses either the Singular or Plural stem forms in Agreement with the Head Noun, whether the latter inflects for Number or not (Noonan 1992: 155). These forms are interpreted by Noonan as being Relative Clauses in the 3rd Singular Habitual—

but "3rd Singular" is a zero prefix and "Habitual" is a zero suffix; recall Jacobsen's warning above about interpreting noncontrastive zeroes:

(50) gwòkk   à   bèr
     dog.SG AT (3SG)**good**.SG(HAB)
     'the good dog'
(51) gwóggî   à   bècò
     dog.PL AT (3SG)**good**.PL(HAB)
     'the good dogs'

When predicated, the first property class inflects with Subject Agreement prefixes. However, they inflect only in Habitual Aspect (ibid.: 104). The Copula can be used with words of this class to indicate past time reference with Perfective form and uninflected (Singular) Adjective (ibid.: 146):

(52) án   àrâc
     I   1SG:bad:HAB
     'I am bad.'
(53) án   **abédò**   rác
     I   1SG:**stay**:PRF bad
     'I was bad.'

The first property class has independent tone in Habitual inflections other than the Gerund. This class also requires the Copula to form Infinitives and Subjunctives, but does not trigger the Plural stem in these contexts (ibid.: 105):

(54) ómìttò   **dɔkɔ**   bèr
     1PL:want:PROG **become**:INF good.SG
     'We want to be good.'

The second property word class lacks distinct Singular and Plural stem forms, unlike the first class. Otherwise its behavior is identical to that of the first property word class. When predicated, the second property word class inflects with Subject Agreement prefixes. The second class inflects only in Habitual Aspect, using the Copula for nonpresent Tenses and for Infinitives and Subjunctives. The second class has independent tone in Nongerund Habitual inflections. In modification, the second class normally uses the Attributive particle only (ibid.: 103):

(55) kùll   à   ɲwé
     warthog AT (3SG)smelly(HAB)
     'a smelly warthog (= 'a warthog that's smelly')'

The third class of words are mostly action words. Like both the property word classes, in predication the action word class inflects with Subject Agreement prefixes. Like the second property word class, the action word class lacks distinct Singular and Plural stem forms. Unlike either property word class, the action word class inflects in Perfective, Progressive, and Habitual aspects: *àgíkò/àgíkô/ágìkkò*

[1SG:stop:PRF/HAB/PROG] 'I stopped/stop/am stopping something' (ibid.: 92). The action word class never requires a Copula. The action word class has Habitual tone in Nongerund Habitual inflection (H HL for disyllables, HL for monosyllables; ibid.: 91, 97):

(56) nɛ́nɛ́
  3SG:see:HAB
  'he sees it'

The action word class forms Infinitives and Subjunctives directly (Noonan 1992: 213), and uses Plural Subjunctive inflectional forms (unlike the first property word class; ibid.: 92–3):

(57) àdâg kwànnò bukkì
  1SG:refuse:HAB read:INF book:this
  'I refuse to read this book.'

In modification, the action word class occurs in Relative Clauses, inflectable in any tense/aspect, with either the Attributive particle + Relative Pronoun, the Attributive particle, or even zero (ibid.: 217–18):

(58) gwókk **àmê/à/Ø** òtɔ́ɔ̀
  dog AT:REL/AT/Ø 3SG:die:PRF
  'the dog that died'

These three options are possible with the two property word classes as well, but the Attributive particle + Relative Pronoun with attributive property concept words is less normal for the property classes, but preferred for the action word class (Noonan, personal communication).

All linguists would call the action word class Verb; but what about the two property word classes? If the second, larger property word class is called Adjective, what is the first class to be called? One could say there are two subclasses of the class Adjective. But the only justification for doing so is the semantic heuristic—property word classes should be called Adjectives—not a theoretically motivated principle. (One might argue that the main difference between the two property word classes in Lango is morphological; but morphological properties are often used to define parts of speech, and other languages, such as Japanese described below, anyway distinguish property word classes by syntactic means.)

Even standard European languages have the same problems. Property words—Adjectives—in English can be defined in part by their occurrence in the Simple, Comparative, and Superlative Degree. But degree is expressed in three different ways in English, defining three different classes of property words:[1]

---

[1] The distinction between Class II and III is not phonological—cf. *ill/*iller/*illest, whole/*wholler/*whollest*. Class II has been shrinking over the history of English; many more property words fell into Class II in Shakespeare's time.

(59) Class I: Suppletive degree forms—*good/better/best, bad/worse/worst*
Class II: Inflectional degree forms—*tall/taller/tallest, small/smaller/smallest*
Class III: Periphrastic degree forms—*loquacious/more loquacious/most loquacious*

Again, distributional analysis does not tell us whether to treat these as three parts of speech or as three subclasses of one part of speech. Only the semantic heuristic suggests they are subclasses of Adjective, and this heuristic has long been discredited as a grammatical criterion for parts of speech.

2.3.3. Further problems with distributional analysis and parts of speech

The splitting into multiple classes of what seems to be a single major part of speech is a serious theoretical problem. But the problems with establishing parts of speech in the grammar of a single language do not end there.

Traditional Japanese grammarians long ago decided that Japanese has not three but four major parts of speech: Nouns, Verbs, Adjectives, and Nominal Adjectives. This is another manifestation of the problem described in the preceding section. However, the application of the usual distributional criteria for establishing the categories of Noun, Adjective, and Nominal Adjective in Japanese demonstrates that there are more categories than just those three.

Nouns are characterized by a Copula construction in predication and a construction with the Genitive particle *no* in modification (Uehara 1998: 64, 56):

(60) Hon   da.
     book   COP
     'It is a book.'
(61) Ainu-go   no   kenkyuu
     Ainu-language   GEN   research
     '(the) study of the Ainu language'

Nominal Adjectives also use the Copular construction in predication but use a linking particle *na* in modification (ibid.: 88):

(62) Kirei   da.
     pretty   COP
     'It is pretty.'
(63) kirei   na   hon
     pretty   LNK   book
     'a pretty book'

Adjectives use an Adjectival inflection in predication and in modification (ibid.):

(64) Yasu   -i.
     cheap   -INFL
     'It is cheap.'
(65) yasu   -i   hon
     cheap   -INFL   book
     'a cheap book'

But there are other classes defined by different distributional patterns. A class that I will call Type I Nominal Adjective/Adjective occurs with either the Adjectival inflection or the Copula construction in predication, and either the Adjectival inflection or *na* in modification (ibid.: 89):

(66) Atataka -i.   / Atataka da.
     warm   -INFL / warm   COP
     'It is warm.'
(67) atataka -i   hi / atataka na   hi
     warm   -INFL day / warm   LNK day
     'a warm day'

A fifth class, which I will call Type II Nominal Adjective/Adjective occurs only with the Adjectival inflection in predication but with either the Adjectival inflection or *na* in modification (ibid.):

(68) Tiisa -i.   / *Tiisa da.
     small -INFL / small   COP
     'It is small.'
(69) tiisa -i   hon   / tiisa na   hon
     small -INFL book / small LNK book
     'a small book'

Finally, there is a class which alternates between Nominal Adjective and Noun (ibid.: 106):

(70) heiwa   na   kuni
     peace(ful) LNK country
     'a peaceful country'
(71) heiwa   no   sisya
     peace   GEN messenger
     'a messenger of peace'
(72) kenkoo   na   hito
     health(y) LNK person
     'a healthy person'
(73) kenkoo no   zyootai
     health GEN condition
     'health condition'

The corresponding English translations of (70)–(73) use the same lexical root but in different syntactic category forms—in both of the examples here, a base Noun and a derived Adjective form. However, the Japanese lexical forms are identical except for their syntactic occurrence, which is ambivalent between Noun and Nominal Adjective behavior, corresponding to the English Nominal-Adjectival formal difference.

The distribution patterns of Japanese words across the constructions used to define Noun, Nominal Adjective, and Adjective are summarized in Table 2.1 in the format introduced in §1.1.2.

Table 2.1. Distribution patterns of Noun-Nominal Adjective-Adjective classes in Japanese

	no Mod	*na* Mod	*i* Mod	*da* Pred	*i* Pred
hon, etc.	√	*	*	√	*
kirei, etc.	*	√	*	√	*
yasu, etc.	*	*	√	*	√
atataka, etc.	*	√	√	√	√
tiisa, etc.	*	√	√	*	√
heiwa, kenkoo, etc.	√	√	*	√	*

One could argue that there are in fact only the three traditionally named word classes, Noun, Nominal Adjective, and Adjective, and the three additional classes described above represent multiple class membership. But distributional analysis cannot tell us whether to describe the latter three classes as examples of multiple class membership or simply three additional classes with different distribution patterns (§1.5.1.2).

On top of this, speakers vary as to which words have which distributions, and words fit into different constructions with varying degrees of (un)grammaticality (Uehara 1998: 98–9, 103–15). Hence category membership is not clearcut even for individual lexical items (§1.5.1.3). Distributional analysis not only reveals a large number of syntactic classes, but also reveals sometimes fuzzy category behavior at the boundaries of those classes.

We may summarize the fundamental problem of the standard approach to parts of speech, in fact to grammatical categories in general as follows. Distributional analysis is the basic method for determining what categories exist in a language. It is assumed that distributional analysis will reveal parts of speech, in fact it is assumed that it will reveal grammatical categories which we can take as the primitive atomic elements that syntactic theories use to describe grammars. But distributional analysis does nothing of the sort.

First, distributional analysis reveals a myriad of classes, and gives us no method for deciding between parts of speech and minor syntactic categories (§1.5.1.2). Second, the systematic application of distributional analysis does not yield a small number of parts of speech with sharp boundaries (leaving aside fixes such as subclasses and multiple class membership, which must be motivated by other means). This latter fact suggests that the categories which distributional analysis defines are not only not the traditional parts of speech, but that they are not the sort of atomic primitives that we would like to use as the building blocks of our models of syntactic representation for particular languages.

2.4. Conceptual Space, Semantic Maps and a Universal Theory of Parts of Speech

A proper theory of parts of speech that applies to all languages must satisfy the following three conditions in order to be successful. First, there must be a criterion for distinguishing parts of speech from other morphosyntactically defined subclasses. Second, there must be a cross-linguistically valid and uniform set of formal grammatical criteria for evaluating the universality of the parts of speech distinctions. Third, there must be a clear distinction between language universals and particular language facts.

It should be clear from the discussion at the end of §2.2.3 that the first condition is lacking in the theories of parts of speech that have been discussed here. The second condition is closely tied to the first. It has not really been addressed in any of the aforementioned theories except Hengeveld's, which I will argue is too limited. It may not be obvious to many readers that the third condition is important or relevant to a theory of parts of speech. But I believe that the failure to satisfy the first two conditions follows directly from not recognizing the importance of distinguishing language universals from language-particular facts. So I will first address the third condition.

2.4.1. *Separating the universal from the language-particular*

There are two common responses to the paradoxes presented in §2.3. The first is to say that there are no parts of speech in syntactic theory, and that 'languages could differ from each other without limit and in unpredictable ways', in Joos' famous passage (Joos 1957: 96). This is in effect a denial of the existence of language universals in the description of parts of speech (or of any other grammatical phenomenon) in particular languages.

The other response is essentially methodological opportunism. Haegeman (1994) assumes that category membership determines distribution, not the other way around (see §1.2.1). In practice, Haegeman and most others use only the distributional facts they find useful for their theoretical hypotheses. They ignore some distributional patterns, focusing on a small subset of constructions (or even just one, like predication), and using those to construct a syntactic theory with parts of speech and other atomic syntactic primitives. This strategy tends to lead to a "lumping" approach. For example, looking only at the presence/absence of structural coding constructions in predication leads to the idea that there is only one part of speech in Makah. Hengeveld's (1992) theory also examines referring expressions and adnominal and adverbial modifiers, but still examines only structural coding constructions. Together with the allowance of semantic shift, it still leads to a broadly "lumping" approach. The "lumping" approach is expressed in hypothesis (1b) at the beginning of this chapter: parts of speech are not necessarily found in all languages.

There is a third way, which combines the positive features of both of the earlier responses. To reach this third way, however, we must abandon the negative features of both of the earlier responses. The aim of the selective abandonment of distributional analysis is to preserve hypothesis (1a) in §2.1: that parts of speech which we label Noun, Verb, Adjective, etc. are universal categories instantiated in particular languages. But we do not need to preserve it. In fact, distributional analysis tells us that we must abandon it. That is the positive feature of the Joos intepretation of American structuralism (*pace* Anward et al. 1997: 168). As was argued in Chapter 1, categories in a particular language are defined by the constructions of the language. The constructions are the primitive elements of syntactic representation; categories are derived from constructions.

Radical Construction Grammar offers a solution to the problem of representing syntactic categories, relations, and constructions for particular languages without compromising empirical accuracy and completeness. Radical Construction Grammar takes the Joos view seriously. But in Radical Construction Grammar, parts of speech cannot be categories of particular languages. We could choose to label certain English syntactic categories defined by certain English constructions as Noun, Verb, and Adjective. But we would then have no theoretical motivation to label the categories defined by constructions in any other language with the same labels. We have only the discredited semantic heuristic, or terminological convenience (Dryer 1997a). And anyway, the constructions of English taken as a whole would still define many more classes than the three major parts of speech, or even the dozen or so usually found in traditional grammars.

We may now return to the analyses of parts of speech that I have criticized and reexamine them from a Radical Construction Grammar perspective. Following Jacobsen, I criticized those linguists who used only the predication construction to define parts of speech, and so for example argued that Makah had no parts of speech (or just one, Verb). But what is wrong with those linguists' analyses is not what they discovered about Makah and other languages. What is wrong with their analyses is that they believed that their discoveries were about parts of speech. They were not. What they discovered was a typological pattern about the predication construction, or more precisely, the family of inflectional constructions they used to define predication (subject and/or object agreement, tense-aspect-mood inflection, etc.). More specifically, they discovered typological patterns about the relationship between the predication construction and the semantic classes of lexical items that fit into the predication construction.

All of that is legitimate, interesting and important empirical and theoretical linguistic research. Just how interesting it can be is found in Stassen's massive and brilliant study of the predication of various semantic classes (actions, properties, objects, and locations)—appropriately titled *Intransitive Predication* (Stassen 1997; see also Wetzer 1996). (Unfortunately, Stassen and Wetzer still refer to the semantic classes by syntactic category labels and use potentially misleading terms like "nouny" and "verby".) But no reference to parts of speech is necessary to do such research, or to appreciate it.

Hengeveld's (1992) study is broader in scope, in that he examines not just predication but also reference (terms in his terminology) and modification. My objection to Hengeveld's work (besides the empirical, methodological, and semantic problems I raised in §2.2.2) is his claim that it is about parts of speech. It is in fact about structural coding constructions—copular and noncopular constructions, relativizing or other attributive constructions, and nominalization constructions. Nevertheless, Hengeveld's model (properly carried out) does survey the interaction between a family of constructions and a family of semantic classes of lexical items (predicates in his terminology).

However, the universal-typological theory I presented in earlier work (Croft 1984, 1986, 1991), and which finds an antecedent in Dixon's seminal study of adjectives (Dixon 1977), is still more general. In fact, it is a theory which I believe is general enough to be thought of as a theory of parts of speech as language universals. It is broader than Stassen's or Hengeveld's models, although it is sketched out in less detail and tested on a much smaller sample. (Nevertheless, the results of Stassen's and Hengeveld's larger-scale studies do not contradict the theory in Croft (1991).) It is broader in that the typological interactions among a much wider family of constructions are analyzed. It is more general in that it is couched in terms of independently motivated typological principles, which allows us to compare the results to other typological patterns. In §2.4.2, I will outline the theory, and in §2.4.3, introduce the conceptual space model as a means to represent an individual speaker's knowledge of their specific language constructions and their knowledge of language universals.

2.4.2. The universal-typological theory of parts of speech

In order to construct a genuinely universal theory of parts of speech, we must discard the main negative feature of the Joos approach (and much of the generative grammar that followed American structuralism). This is the narrow view that universals of language are only categories and structures which are found in all languages, or almost all languages. That is, we must discard the view that universals of language are only what typologists call UNRESTRICTED UNIVERSALS, properties true of all languages. In this narrow view, Universal Grammar is just a template of pre-given syntactic categories and structures which particular languages are fitted into, or which particular language grammars choose from (see §1.6.9). This view of Universal Grammar is not only too narrow; Radical Construction Grammar shows that it is simply untenable. Grammatical categories of particular languages are irreducibly language particular; in fact, they are also construction-specific. Instead, Universal Grammar is manifested in IMPLICATIONAL UNIVERSALS of the sort discovered by typology. In this section, I describe the universal-typological theory of parts of speech and its foundations in the interaction of semantic class and discourse function.

The range of constructions in the universal-typological theory of parts of speech includes constructions for predication, reference, and modification, as with Hengeveld's (1992) model. The three propositional act functions (§2.2.1) are in fact the foundation for the three-way distinction of the traditional major parts of speech. This is the first step towards satisfying the first condition, a means of identifying the major parts of speech as opposed to other, "lesser", categories (either language universal or language particular). Predicating, referring, and modifying constructions encode the propositional acts. That is, I will use the lower-case terms 'predicative', 'referring', and 'attributive' to describe constructions in any language that encode the three propositional acts (see §1.6.2).

The lexical items that fill the relevant roles in the propositional act constructions can be divided into semantic classes. The hypothesis of Croft (1991) is that the semantic classes of OBJECTS, PROPERTIES, and ACTIONS are the TYPOLOGICAL PROTOTYPES of referring, attributive, and predicating constructions respectively. I will first define the three semantic classes and then turn to the typological analysis.

The semantic classes of objects, properties and actions are only a small subset of the semantic classes of words found in human languages. They are defined in terms of four semantic properties. The first is RELATIONALITY, that is, whether a definition of a concept inherently requires reference to another concept (Langacker 1987: 214–16). For example, one cannot conceive of an action such as running without the involvement of a runner, or of a property such as height without something that is tall. On the other hand, one can conceive of a chair or a dog without the involvement of another concept. The second property is STATIVITY—whether the concept represents a state or a process. The third property is TRANSITORINESS—whether the concept represents a transitory state or process or an inherent or permanent state of the entity in question (only states can be permanent). The fourth and final property is GRADABILITY—whether the entity is gradable along a scalar dimension, such as height. The three semantic classes in Figure 2.1 below are defined by the four semantic properties in Table 2.2 (adapted from Croft 1991: 65, Table 2.4).

Table 2.2. Semantic properties of prototypical parts of speech

	Relationality	Stativity	Transitoriness	Gradability
Objects	nonrelational	state	permanent	nongradable
Properties	relational	state	permanent	gradable
Actions	relational	process	transitory	nongradable

In comparing lexical items within and across languages, semantics is held fixed to the greatest extent possible. This allows us to make a consistent and systematic comparison across languages, in terms of the semantics of the lexical item, in contrast to Hengeveld's theory (see §2.2.2).

A typological prototype category is a functionally defined category that is typologically unmarked with respect to the relevant constructions. In the case of parts of speech, the relevant constructions include those constructions used for reference, modification, and predication, as noted above. Table 2.3 (see Croft 1991: 67, Table 2.6) gives the traditional labels normally used for the three propositional act constructions combined with the three semantic classes defined in Table 2.2.

Table 2.3. Overtly marked structural coding constructions for parts of speech

	Reference	Modification	Predication
Objects	UNMARKED NOUNS	genitive, adjectivalizations, PPs on nouns	predicate nominals, copulas
Properties	deadjectival nouns	UNMARKED ADJECTIVES	predicate adjectives, copulas
Actions	action nominals, complements, infinitives, gerunds	participles, relative clauses	UNMARKED VERBS

The constructions that were examined by Hengeveld are structural coding constructions: the constructions that actually encode the propositional act function. These constructions can be divided into two types by the number of morphemes that are used to encode the function in question. If one or more morphemes are used to encode the function, then we may speak of OVERT structural coding in the language. For example, English employs overt Nominalization of property words and action words when they are used as referring expressions (74a–b); the Genitive enclitic -'s and Prepositions used with object words as modifiers (75a–b); the Complementizer *that* used for action words as arguments (Finite Complements (76a)) and modifiers (Finite Relative Clauses (76b)); the *-ing* form for action words as arguments (Gerund (77a)) and modifiers (Participle (77b)); the Relative Pronoun for action words as modifiers (78); and the Copula *be* for object and property words as predicates (79a–b), and also the Article *a* for object word predication (79a).

(74) a. good**ness**, happi**ness**
 b. destruc**tion**, produc**tion**
(75) a. Bill**'s** book
 b. the book **on** the dresser
(76) a. She realized **that** he was not going to leave her.
 b. the man **that** left the party early

(77) a. Runn**ing** is bad for your knees.
    b. the woman runn**ing** down the road
(78) the tree **which** fell on my house
(79) a. That **is a** cypress.
    b. That cypress **is** big!

Other referring, modifying, and predicating constructions do not employ any morpheme whose function is to express the propositional act function. We will call these ZERO structural coding constructions. Examples of zero structural coding constructions in English include reference to an object (80), modification by a property (81), and predication of an action ((82); recall from §2.2.1 that inflection is not part of structural coding):

(80) I found the **ring**.
(81) The **big** cookie is hers.
(82) I **ate** it.

The structural coding constructions display a pattern in English that is repeated across languages: if there is zero coding of propositional acts, it is found for object reference, property modification and/or action predication. These three pairings of semantic class and propositional act are the TYPOLOGICALLY UNMARKED combinations, that is, they form typological prototypes. I believe that the terms NOUN, ADJECTIVE, and VERB (all lower case) may be used to describe these typological prototypes (Croft 1991):

(83) a. noun = reference to an object
    b. adjective = modification by a property
    c. verb = predication of an action

The typological prototypes for noun and verb have a high degree of cue validity as contrasting categories (Rosch 1978): objects and actions differ for the first three semantic properties in Table 2.2, and are associated with the most opposed propositional act functions.

The typological evidence for the prototypes for parts of speech is given by the theory of TYPOLOGICAL MARKEDNESS (Greenberg 1966a; Croft 1990a, 1996a). The theory of typological markedness is a general theory of the relationship between form and meaning across languages. It is often misunderstood because of important differences between it and the Prague School theory of markedness (see Croft 1996a for historical discussion). The theory of typological markedness (along with the distributional method) satisfies the second condition given above: it provides valid cross-linguistic grammatical criteria for testing the universality of the three parts of speech across individual languages.

Typological markedness has two important features that differentiate it from Prague School markedness. First, typological markedness is a universal property of a CONCEPTUAL category, not a language-particular property of a language-particular grammatical category as it is in Prague School markedness. When it is argued that object reference is typologically unmarked, a hypothesis is being put forward about the conceptual category of object reference (or noun) as it is encoded in the world's languages, not the grammatical category labeled Noun in English or any other particular language.

Any other combination of propositional act and semantic class is typologically marked. These unmarked and marked combinations are conceptual categories. The assertion that the combinations in (83) are unmarked and all other combinations are marked refers to a hypothesis about a pattern of variation with respect to how those conceptual categories are encoded across languages.

The formal criteria of typological markedness apply to structural coding constructions and constructions exhibiting the behavioral potential of the categories in question. The proper definition of the structural coding criterion of typological markedness reveals the second significant difference between typological markedness and Prague School markedness. In Prague School markedness, an unmarked category is expressed by zero, and a marked category is expressed by an overt morpheme. If this were a typological universal claim, it would amount to an absolute universal. The Prague School formulation is untenable cross-linguistically: counterexamples are abundant.

Instead, the structural coding criterion specifies only that the marked member is encoded by *at least as many* morphemes as the unmarked member (Croft 1990a: 73). This generalization is an implicational universal:

(84) *Structural coding*: If a language codes a typologically unmarked member of a grammatical category by n morphemes ($n \geq 0$), then it codes a typologically marked member of that category by at least n morphemes.

The formulation in (84) allows for overt structural coding of both unmarked and marked concepts in a language—for example, overt coding of various modifier classes including properties in Japanese and Lango—and for zero coding of both—for example, in languages such as Makah that allow predication of properties and object classes without overt derivation and without a copula. The only excluded type is a language where the unmarked member is expressed by *more* morphemes than the marked member—if, for example, a language required a copula or auxiliary for the predication of actions but had zero coding of the predication of properties and/or object classes.

In §2.4.1, I stated that there are additional constructions that are relevant to a universal-typological theory of parts of speech beyond the structural coding constructions. These are constructions that encode some other conceptual dimension but secondarily make reference to the conceptual categories in the conceptual space in question. These constructions indicate the BEHAVIORAL POTENTIAL of the categories defined on the conceptual space.

For example, the inflectional constructions of tense, aspect, and mood encode the temporal, aspectual, and modal properties of situations. But the inflectional constructions are also defined over semantic classes and propositional acts. For example, of the three semantic classes named above, only action words allow for inflection for tense in English. Thus, these inflectional constructions are relevant for a universal theory of parts of speech. These constructions are the usual inflectional categories associated with parts of speech: case, number, gender, size, possessor agreement, etc. for referring expressions; degree and gender/case/number agreement for modifiers; and tense, aspect, mood, and argument agreement for predications.

Typological markedness also constrains the distribution of constructions exhibiting the behavioral potential of the categories in question. English conforms to the implicational universal governing behavioral potential.

(85) *Behavioral Potential*: If a construction encoding the behavioral potential of members of a grammatical category is found in that category, then it is found with at least the unmarked member of that category for that construction.

The behavioral potential criterion specifies that the unmarked member displays *at least as wide a range* of grammatical behavior as the marked member. The behavioral potential criterion is again formulated as an implicational universal. It allows for the possibility of marked members to have the same inflectional possibilities as unmarked members in some language—for example, Subject Agreement in all predicated classes in Lango. The behavioral potential criterion only excludes the case of marked members having *more* inflectional possibilities than unmarked members.

Typological markedness also allows for differences in degree. As noted at the end of §2.3.2, English splits its property words into three classes depending on the type of degree expression, suppletive, morphological, or periphrastic. These different means of expression define a hierarchy of markedness such that suppletion is the least marked and periphrasis the most marked (Croft 1990a: 79–80). Thus we may arrange the English adjectives on a scale of behavioral potential, with *good/bad* the least marked, and the property words requiring periphrastic *more/most* the most marked.

In the universal-typological theory of parts of speech, any asymmetry in structural coding or behavioral potential constitutes evidence for the typological unmarkedness of the semantic class in the relevant propositional act construction. Thus, small closed classes as well as larger classes of any size are relevant to the theory. No empirical cross-linguistic data are ignored. It is hypothesized, however, that the cross-linguistic distribution of word meanings will conform to the prototype patterns displayed in Table 2.3.

Typological markedness represents a cross-linguistic universal about the encoding of function by linguistic form. It is formulated in a fashion to allow for cross-linguistic comparison of morphosyntactic properties of constructions. Structural coding compares the number of morphemes used to encode the function in question by a construction. Behavioral potential compares the presence of grammatical distinctions (by means of inflectional morphology or periphrastic constructions) expressing associated functions. Thus, typological markedness does not presuppose the existence of universal grammatical categories that was argued against in Chapter 1.

Typological markedness also allows us to construct generalizations about categories *across* constructions. The typological prototypes for noun, verb, and adjective are cross-constructional categories, across the various structural coding and behavioral potential constructions of languages. As we will see in §2.4.4, the prototype patterns defined by the relevant constructions are found within languages as well as across languages.

2.4.3. *Conceptual space and semantic maps*

In Chapter 1, I argued that a speaker's knowledge of a language includes the many-to-many mapping between constructions and categories—the fillers of the relevant roles in the constructions. I illustrated the category–construction mapping with tables giving distribution patterns in Chapter 1, also illustrated for Japanese in Table 2.1 in §2.3.3. In §2.4.1 I presented a universal-typological theory of parts of speech, proposing a set of universals that define and constrain a range of variation in the structure and distribution of constructions encoding the propositional acts of reference, predication, and modification. In this section, I will integrate the language-particular distribution patterns and the universals of parts-of-speech constructions into a general model of the speaker's knowledge of their language. The means for doing so is the semantic map theory in typology.

The theory of parts of speech advocated in §2.4.1 (and references cited therein) is not simply a list of functional properties. The functional properties define a CONCEPTUAL SPACE, also known as a mental map, cognitive map, semantic map, or semantic space. The conceptual space for parts of speech (in simplified form) is essentially the same as the structure of Table 2.3. It is illustrated in Figure 2.1, retaining the row and column headings of Table 2.3 (two additional functions, to

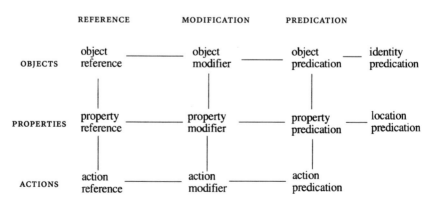

Figure 2.1. Conceptual space for parts of speech

be discussed below, have been added at the right hand side of the conceptual space).

The conceptual space approach to cross-linguistic research has increased in importance in recent cross-linguistic research (see for example L. Anderson 1974, 1982, 1986, 1987; Croft et al. 1987; Croft 1991; Kemmer 1993; Haspelmath 1997a, b, to appear; Stassen 1997; Kortmann 1997; van der Auwera and Plungian 1998). In fact, conceptual space is central to typological theory in general and Radical Construction Grammar in particular. Much of what is universal in language, as discovered through cross-linguistic research in typology, can be represented in the structure of conceptual space.

Conceptual space is a structured representation of functional structures and their relationships to each other. I have chosen the term 'conceptual' instead of the term 'semantic' for two reasons. First, I wish to emphasize the fact that the structures are not merely semantic in the traditional, narrow truth-functional sense of that term. Conceptual space also represents conventional pragmatic or discourse-functional or information-structural or even stylistic or social dimensions of the use of a grammatical form or construction (see §1.3.2). Second, there are some good reasons to differentiate between a language-universal conceptual structure and a language-specific semantic structure; this terminology follows that used by Langacker (1976; see §§3.1, 3.3 for further discussion). I have also chosen the term 'space' instead of 'map' in order to distinguish the universal conceptual space from the map of a particular language's categories onto the space (see below).

A conceptual space representation such as that in Figure 2.1 is only one small part or region of conceptual space. For convenience, I will call a region of conceptual space a conceptual space as well, and henceforth speak of CONCEPTUAL SPACES for different functions that are expressed by language. Conceptual space is also multidimensional, that is, there are many different semantic, pragmatic, and discourse-functional dimensions that define any region of conceptual space. Of course, the written medium is only two-dimensional, and we will by necessity reduce the conceptual space representation to two dimensions.

Moreover, for any particular domain of language, we need only to refer to the relevant dimensions of conceptual space. The relevant dimensions of conceptual space are the functions or conventional meanings of the constructions whose analysis we are interested in, and the meanings of the elements that fill the relevant roles in the construction.

For the sorts of coarse-grained conceptual spaces described in this book, I will use the convention of representing the constructions that encode the functions being analyzed along the horizontal dimension of the two-dimensional conceptual space diagram. In Figure 2.1, these are the constructions used for the propositional acts of reference, modification, and predication; the values along the vertical dimension are given in capital letters. The vertical dimension of the diagram will be used to represent the members of the categories defined by the relevant roles in the constructions ranged along the horizontal dimension of the space. In Figure 2.1, these are the semantic classes of the words that fill the relevant roles in the propositional act constructions; the values along the vertical dimension are also given in capital letters. The relevant roles are the roles normally described as the HEADS of the propositional act constructions. Of course, this requires a semantic definition of headhood. Such a definition will be provided in Chapter 7; for now, the reader may assume the traditional analysis of the content word as the head of each construction.

The vertical dimension of the conceptual space for parts of speech should of course include all semantic classes, not the three narrowly defined classes from Table 2.1. In fact, the vertical dimension could be as finely divided as single word concepts if necessary. A fine-grained division would be necessary to capture the variation in expression of the Japanese concepts represented by the distribution in Table 2.1 (see Figure 2.2). Also the vertical dimension actually involves multiple dimensions representing at least the four semantic dimensions in Table 2.2, and probably other semantic dimensions as well.

The horizontal dimension of the conceptual space for parts of speech could also be elaborated. Figure 2.1 only represents modification of a referent; modification of a predicate (adverbial modification) would also have to be represented. One might also argue that other propositional acts should be posited. For example, Croft (1990b) proposes a set of minor propositional acts including classification, selection (including quantification) and situating (including the determination function of articles and demonstratives). Thus, Figure 2.1 should not be taken as the final word on the structure of this region of conceptual space.

The distribution pattern of parts-of-speech constructions in any language can be MAPPED onto the conceptual space in Figure 2.1. For example, we can map the Japanese categories in Table 2.1 onto the upper right subregion of the conceptual space of Figure 2.1, namely the subregion for objects and properties in modification and predication. This is done in Figure 2.2.

Figure 2.2 represents a SEMANTIC MAP of a particular language's categories onto the relevant conceptual space. That is, the conceptual space is the underlying conceptual structure, and a semantic map is a map of language-specific categories on the conceptual space (see above). Two elements of the conceptual space of Figure 2.1 have been suppressed in Figure 2.2 for visual clarity. The names of the points in the conceptual space have been suppressed. Only the dimensions of the conceptual space are named, the horizontal dimension of modification and predication and the vertical dimension of the different semantic classes (in fact, specific word concepts from Uehara's examples). It should be assumed of course that the conceptual space consists of points that could be labeled 'book as modifier', 'book as predication', 'peaceful as modifier', etc. Also, the connections between the points in conceptual space in Figure 2.1 have been suppressed in Figure 2.2, since the points have been suppressed. The part played by these connections in the representation of conceptual space will be described below.

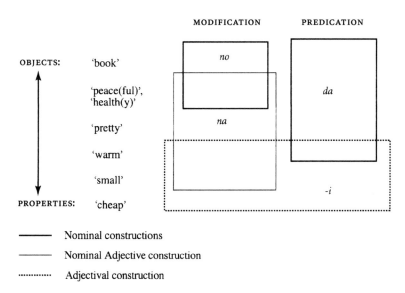

Figure 2.2. The semantic map for the Japanese Nominal, Nominal Adjective, and Adjective constructions

The diagram in Figure 2.2 captures all of the information in Table 2.1. Members of the Noun category such as *hon* 'book' combine with *no* in modification and with *da* in predication (see examples (60)–(61)). This can be inferred from the fact that the semantic map for *no* includes the 'book as modifier' region in the upper left of the conceptual space in Figure 2.1, and the semantic map for *da* includes the 'book as predicate' region in the upper right. Members of the Adjective category such as *yasu* 'cheap' combine with the suffix *-i* in both modification and predication (see (64)–(65)). This can be inferred from the fact that the semantic map for *-i* includes both the 'cheap as modifier' and 'cheap as predicate' regions at the bottom of the conceptual space. The various other categories of Japanese are represented in the middle of Figure 2.2. The overlapping semantic maps indicate that alternative modification constructions are possible for certain lexical items; for example, *atataka* 'warm' may occur with either *-i* or *na* in a modification construction, or with either *-i* or *da* in a predication construction.

Figure 2.2 is superior to the distribution table in Table 2.1 as a means of representing a Japanese speaker's knowledge of this portion of his/her grammar. Figure 2.2 imposes more structure on the speaker's knowledge of his/her language, by virtue of the structure of the conceptual space representing the meanings of the constructions and lexical items that occur in the constructions. The structure of the conceptual space in Figure 2.2 is intended to conform to a number of general principles, and is intended to yield a conceptual space that makes sense as part of a speaker's knowledge about language and the world it communicates.

The central principle governing representations of conceptual space is given in (86):

(86) *Semantic Map Connectivity Hypothesis*: any relevant language-specific and construction-specific category should map onto a CONNECTED REGION in conceptual space.

In theory, if there is a coherent mapping of form onto function in the grammatical domain, one should be able to arrange the concepts in the conceptual space so that any relevant grammatical category in any language will form a connected region in the space. Not only should construction of the space be empirically possible, but the structure of the conceptual space should also make sense in semantic, pragmatic, and/or discourse-functional terms (see below). The hypothesis of typological theory, including Radical Construction Grammar, is that most grammatical domains will yield universals of the form–function mapping that can be represented as a coherent conceptual space. In fact, given the methodological arguments in Chapter 1, this is the only hope for universals of language.

The connections in Figure 2.1 are necessary for specifying what counts as a connected region in conceptual space. One cannot assume from a two-dimensional visual representation of the conceptual space that contiguous points are in fact connected; points may be neighbors simply for visual convenience. However, in the conceptual space in Figure 2.1 contiguous points on the vertical or horizontal dimensions can be assumed to be connected (except for identity predication and location predication).

Figure 2.2 indicates that the Semantic Map Connectivity Hypothesis holds for the conceptual space for parts of speech in Figure 2.1 with respect to the relevant subset of Japanese word classes and constructions. In the following section, we will see that the hypothesis also holds for English and Lango word classes and constructions related to parts of speech.

The conceptual space for parts of speech also makes conceptual sense. For example, the conceptual space for parts of speech implies that properties are intermediate between objects and actions. There is some typological evidence supporting both of those hypotheses. It appears that overt expression of predication—copulas or an auxiliary (as it is called when it accompanies action word predications)—conforms to the hierarchy *object < property < action* (Croft 1991: 130, Stassen 1997: 127). Stassen also proposes a more detailed hierarchy of properties spread between objects and actions: *object < material, gender < value, age, form < dimension, color < physical properties < human propensity < action* (Stassen 1997: 168–9).[2] Stassen's research demonstrates that detailed cross-

---

[2] Wetzer argues that color belongs to the left of age, value, and dimension on the hierarchy of properties (Wetzer 1992: 242).

linguistic research—his sample consists of 410 languages—reveals further fine-grained detail of the topography of conceptual space that could not be discovered otherwise.

The conceptual space for parts of speech also implies that modification is intermediate between reference and predication. It also appears that overt expression of propositional act function with actions—nominalization—conforms to the hierarchy *reference < modification < predication*. That is, if nominalized forms are found in modification of actions, then they are also found in reference to actions; further research is necessary to confirm this hypothesis. Also, participial (modifying) derivation appears to be dependent on the existence of nominalization (Croft 1991: 131), further suggesting the intermediate status of modification.

Finally, there is a plausible functional explanation for the intermediate status of properties and of modification. Properties are relational (like actions) but stative and permanent (like objects; see Table 2.2 and Croft 1991: 131–2). Modification both helps to enrich reference (cf. Wierzbicka 1986) and to give a secondary assertion about the referent (Croft 1991: 131).

The two-dimensional conceptual space in Figure 2.1 is of course a gross oversimplification of the actual relationships among semantic classes and propositional act functions. There are many other semantic classes, and they will not necessarily line up in a single dimension with respect to the propositional act functions. Stassen's (1997) account of intransitive predication, which incidentally supports the universal-typological theory of parts of speech presented here, includes the category of predication of location, and it represents a "branch" linked to the predication of properties but not directly linked to the predication of actions or objects. Stassen also suggests that identity predication is linked to object predication, but not directly to the predication of other semantic classes. Stassen's discoveries have been included in Figure 2.1.

In an earlier work, I argued that properties and modification are not only intermediate in their dimensions, but that adjectives are also less prominent as a typological prototype than nouns and verbs (Croft 1991: 130–3). The exact grammatical status of other sorts of modification—quantification, enumeration, deixis, determination, etc.—with respect to property modification remains an interesting and open question. Hence the universal-typological theory of parts of speech outlined here is only the first step in a more comprehensive mapping of this region of conceptual space and the dynamic patterns of the syntactic constructions that occupy that space.

The conceptual space model allows us to relate functional categories identifiable across languages—propositional act function and semantic class—to their syntactic expression within particular languages—the constructions used to express the propositional act functions of various semantic classes, and the constructions used to express cross-cutting conceptual distinctions for those classes. The conceptual space represents a typologically valid language universal:

a universal conceptual structure and universal constraint that syntactic categories (construction-specific and language-specific) are mapped onto conceptual categories that form connected regions in conceptual space.

Each point in conceptual space represents a semantic structure for a particular construction, and the connections represent semantic relations among constructional meanings. The connections between points in conceptual space lend themselves to a network representation of conceptual structure, as is found in activation network models of knowledge representation (Elman and McClelland 1984; Elman et al. 1996).

In the next section, I will describe another set of typologically valid universals, the universals of form–function mapping found in typological markedness theory.

2.4.4. *Typological markedness and the topography of conceptual space*

The typological-universal theory of parts of speech also has implications for the universal topography of the conceptual space for parts of speech in Figure 2.1. Typological markedness theory makes the following predictions for the grammatical encoding of functions in conceptual space:

(87) *Structural Coding Map Hypothesis*: Constructions encoding a function should code that function in at least as many morphemes in typologically marked points in conceptual space as in typologically unmarked points in conceptual space.
(88) *Behavioral Potential Map Hypothesis*: Constructions expressing the behavioral potential of a category should be found in at least the typologically unmarked points in conceptual space.

Figure 2.3 is the semantic map for the primary parts of speech constructions in English, including both constructions of structural coding and behavioral potential.

The solid boxes in Figure 2.3 indicate the distributions of constructions that overtly encode reference, modification, and predication in English, as described in §2.4.2. Overt Nominalization (indicated by -NR in Figure 2.3; see examples (74a–b) in §2.4.2) is found with property words and action words in reference. Nouns as modifiers use the Genitive enclitic -'s or Prepositions (indicated by Prep; see examples (75a–b)). The Complementizer *that* is used for action words as arguments (Finite Complements) and modifiers (Finite Relative Clauses) and the -*ing* form is used for action words as arguments (Gerund) and modifiers (Participle); this distribution is indicated by 'COMP that, -ing' in Figure 2.3 (see also examples (76)–(77)). The Relative Pronoun (WH-Rel) is used for action words as modifiers (see example (78)). Finally, the Copula *be* is used for object and property words as predicates, with addition of the Article *a* for object predication; the former is indicated by 'COP be' and the latter by 'COP+ART be a' in Figure 2.3 (see example (79)). All of these patterns conform to the Structural Coding Map Hypothesis.

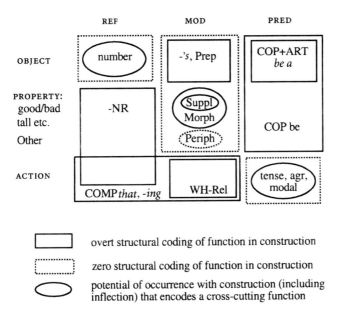

Figure 2.3. Semantic map of English parts of speech constructions

The dotted boxes indicate the distributions of constructions that use zero coding of reference, modification, and predication in English. For reference and predication, the zero coding constructions are found only with object words and action words respectively, as predicted. For modification, there also exists the zero coding construction for English object word modifiers, the Complex Nominal construction, illustrated by *piano stool, music stand, chamber music recital,* and so on. This pattern does not violate the Structural Coding Map Hypothesis, which only specifies that the semantic map for the zero coding construction include the prototype.

The constructions expressing behavioral potential for parts of speech in English are given as ovals in Figure 2.3. The behavioral potential constructions in English are restricted to the relevant prototype regions in conceptual space, which conforms to the Behavioral Potential Map Hypothesis. Further, the differences in the formal expression of degree in English allows us to identify more and less prototypical property words as adjectives. The degree of prototypicality conforms with Dixon's (1977) generalizations: the most prototypical adjectives—the English property words with morphological or suppletive degree forms—include the concepts of value (*good/better/best, bad/worse/worst*), age (*older/oldest, younger/youngest, riper/ripest,* etc.), and dimension (*taller/tallest, wider/widest,* etc.).

We will now turn to a more complex example of the principles of typological markedness governing the encoding of function by grammatical form, the semantic map for Lango property words and action words, based on the data in §2.3.2. Lango has two classes of property words, which we will call core properties (the small closed class) and peripheral properties. Lango also has a class of action words, which shares some distributional patterns with the property words. The distribution of the Lango property and action word classes is given in Table 2.4.

Table 2.4. Distribution of Lango property and action words

	I	II	III	IV	V	VI	VII
Core properties	√	√	√	√	*	*	*
Peripheral properties	*	√	√	√	*	*	*
Actions	*	*	√	(√)	√	√	√

I: distinct singular/plural stems
II: nonhabitual copula
III: subject agreement
IV: attributive particle ((√) = attributive particle + relative pronoun preferred)
V: habitual tone in nongerund habitual forms
VI: inflections for nonhabitual forms
VII: possess distinct infinitive and subjunctive forms

The distributional pattern gives the facts about Lango grammar but it does not differentiate the language-universal from the language-particular. As such, it is an inadequate description of what Lango speakers know about their language. Universals of parts of speech are brought into the picture by mapping the distributional pattern of Lango lexical classes and constructions in Table 2.4 onto the conceptual space for parts of speech, as in Figure 2.4 (adapted from Croft 2000b: 92, Figure 2).

The distribution of semantic classes across constructions in Lango, like that of English, conforms to the universal principles governing conceptual space and language-particular semantic maps. The distributional patterns for each construction occupy a connected region of the conceptual space, thus conforming to the Semantic Map Connectivity Hypothesis. The overt structural coding constructions include the nonprototypical regions of the conceptual space, in conformity to the Structural Coding Map Hypothesis. In addition, the overt structural coding construction for modification, the Attributive particle, also covers the prototypical region, property modification. However, a construction combining the Attributive particle and the Relative Pronoun—hence with more morphemes coding the function than the Attributive particle alone—is preferred in the less prototypical region of action modification. Finally, the zero structural coding construction for predication includes the prototypical region in conceptual space (action predication).

The behavioral potential constructions in Lango include the prototypical regions of the conceptual space. The employment of distinct Singular and Plural

Parts of Speech 101

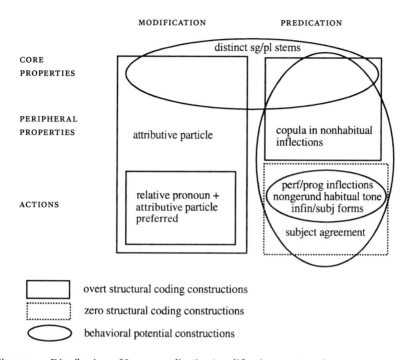

Figure 2.4. Distribution of Lango predication/modification constructions

stems is also found in the nonprototypical region of core property predication, and the employment of subject agreement is also found in the nonprototypical region of property predication. These facts are still in conformity to the Behavioral Potential Map Hypothesis.

The combination of the conceptual space approach to typological universals with Radical Construction Grammar also allows us to DYNAMICIZE the universal-typological theory of parts of speech advocated here, following the general principles of the dynamicization of typological markedness patterns (Croft 1990a: 214). For both (overt) structural coding constructions and behavioral potential constructions, two directions of change are possible; see Figure 2.5.

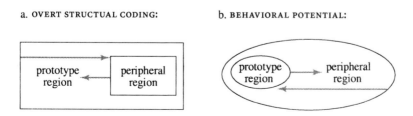

Figure 2.5. Dynamicization of structural coding/behavioral potential map hypotheses

An overt structural coding construction (such as modification or predication) may arise in a marked/nonprototypical region of conceptual space first and spread to an unmarked/prototypical region later (the left-pointing arrow in Figure 2.5a). Conversely an overt structural coding construction may be lost from a unmarked/prototypical region of conceptual space first and from a marked/nonprototypical region last (the right-pointing arrow in Figure 2.5a). One of these scenarios is what is hypothesized to have happened with the Attributive particle in Lango. It appears that the Relative Pronoun is now spreading to property words: it is a possible but less preferred construction for that semantic class. Likewise, the Copula appears to have arisen with predicated property words, though it has yet to spread to all Tenses of Lango; or perhaps it may be that the Copula construction is retreating.

Likewise, a behavioral potential construction may arise in the unmarked/prototypical region of conceptual space first, and then spread to marked contexts later (the right-pointing arrow in Figure 2.5b). Conversely, a behavioral potential construction may be lost from a marked/nonprototypical region of conceptual space first and from the unmarked/prototypical region last (the left-pointing arrow in Figure 2.5b). One of these scenarios is presumably what has happened with Subject agreement and suppletive Number Agreement in Lango. Suppletive Number Agreement is used in only a limited fashion in predication—it is not found in the Subjunctive, for instance—which suggests either that it is just now spreading to the marked predication function, or is retreating from it. Either way, we would expect to find suppletive Number Agreement among core property words as modifiers in Lango if it is found in any predicated property word constructions.

2.4.5. *Functional prototypes and the Grammatical Category Structure Hypothesis*

In §2.4.2, I argued that the parts of speech should be identified with functional prototypes, not language-specific grammatical categories. This view is not without precedent; Sapir expressed the same view over three quarters of a century ago:

There must be something to talk about and something must be said about this subject of discourse once it is selected. This distinction is of such fundamental importance that the vast majority of languages have emphasized it by creating some sort of formal barrier between the two terms of the proposition. The subject of discourse is a noun. As the most common subject of discourse is either a person or a thing, the noun clusters about concrete concepts of that order. As the thing predicated of a subject is generally an activity in the widest sense of the word, a passage from one moment of existence to another, the form which has been set aside for the business of predicating, in other words, the verb, cluster about concepts of activity. No language wholly fails to distinguish noun and verb, though in particular cases the nature of the distinction may be an elusive one (Sapir 1921: 119).

In Radical Construction Grammar, the terms noun, verb, and adjective do not describe language-particular grammatical categories; they describe functional prototypes, if they describe anything at all. A prototype describes the core of a category; it does not say anything about the boundary of a category (cf. Cruse 1992, Croft and Cruse to appear). In fact, the universal typological theory of parts of speech defines only prototypes for the parts of speech; it does not define boundaries. Boundaries are features of language-particular categories.

The boundaries of prototype categories may be either sharp or fuzzy. The category defined by the presence vs. absence of Gerund Habitual tone in Lango predications has a sharp boundary, at least according to the available description. On the other hand, the boundary between the language-particular Japanese categories of Adjective and Nominal Adjective appears to be fuzzy, as noted in §2.3.3 (see Uehara 1998 and references cited therein). The status of boundaries of language-particular grammatical categories is a matter of empirical linguistic and psycholinguistic investigation of the speakers of that language. It is not a matter to be decided by a universal theory of parts of speech.

The behavioral potential criterion also allows for the limited or "defective" behavior of a peripheral member of a category—for example no tense/aspect marking of predicated property words, restricted range of demonstratives with action words in reference, etc.—without having to commit to the peripheral member being "in" or "not in" the category in a universal-typological sense. Consider again Lango predicated properties, which lack certain verbal inflections (such as the Gerund Habitual tone), but possess other verbal inflections (such as Subject Agreement), and yet require a Copula in certain tense/mood forms. Are they verbs or adjectives? This question simply makes no sense in language-particular terms. The different inflections represent different constructions: the Lango property words simply have a different distribution from the Lango action words, and hence belong to a different language-particular grammatical category (in fact two different categories) from action words.

The universal theory of parts of speech defines universal prototypes for the three major parts of speech, but does not define boundaries for these categories. Boundaries are aspects of language-particular grammatical categories, determined by distributional analysis. Boundaries may be sharp or fuzzy depending on the distributional patterns found with words in the language. I propose the following hypothesis for the relationship between the universal and the language-specific, following a more general proposal in Cruse and Croft (in press):

(89) *Grammatical Category Structure Hypothesis*: the internal category structure of a grammatical category (e.g. a prototype point in conceptual space and links to its extensions) is provided by the universal theory of grammar, while its boundaries are provided by the particular language grammar.

Finally, we may ask the question of why particular regions in the conceptual space for parts of speech are prototypical. The answer to that question is again found in the theory of typological markedness. In the theory of typological markedness, structural coding and behavioral potential are a consequence of the token frequency of the conceptual category in discourse: typologically unmarked categories have at least as high a token frequency in discourse as typologically marked categories. In Croft (1991: 87–93), text counts are given of the nine combinations of semantic class and propositional act function in oral narratives from four diverse languages (English, K'iche', Soddo, and Nguna). The text counts demonstrate the overwhelmingly greater frequency of object reference and action predication, and the significantly greater frequency of properties as modifiers compared to other propositional act functions of properties (properties were found to be highly frequent as modifiers, but not always the most frequent modifier; ibid.: 93).

2.4.6. The universal-typological and Cognitive Grammar theories of parts of speech

Langacker (1987) has proposed a conceptual analysis of parts of speech which is broadly compatible with the universal-typological theory of parts of speech presented in this section. For Langacker, a noun is conceptually a thing, that is, a concept construed as nonrelational and summarily scanned (that is, conceived statically and holistically). A verb is a process, that is a concept construed as relational but sequentially scanned (that is, mentally scanned through time). Modifiers, including adjectives, are concepts construed as relational but summarily scanned.

The semantic shifts we have described in §2.2 conform with Langacker's conceptual analysis. However, it must be pointed out that the construals of particular concepts is conventionally established for a particular language, and often for particular lexical items. For example, the construal of the Makah word for 'baggage' as the process of packing is language particular; English does not use *baggage* but instead *pack* to describe this process. And as noted in §2.2.2, some languages (such as English) do not allow the general construal of a property word to indicate an object possessing that property.

Nevertheless, there is no inherent conflict between these two theories of parts of speech. The solution is to recognize that the language-particular categories which linguists prefer to call Noun, Verb, and Adjective are what Lakoff (1987) calls RADIAL CATEGORIES. Radial categories are categories with internal structure, typically a prototype with extensions that are conceptually motivated but linguistically conventional. These extensions themselves involve a degree of conceptualization, which sometimes manifests itself as a fairly dramatic semantic shift.

The difference between the cognitive and typological theories of parts of speech is chiefly a matter of emphasis. The cognitive theory emphasizes the uniformity of the semantic construals found over and over again across languages with respect to constructions expressing the propositional act functions. The typological theory focuses on the variation found in the distributional patterns of constructions and lexical classes within and across languages, and the varied topography of the conceptual space that underlies the typological universals.

2.5. Integrating the Language-Particular and the Universal in the Representation of Grammatical Knowledge

In this chapter, I have applied the principles of Radical Construction Grammar to the analysis of lexical syntactic categories (the parts of speech). Other approaches to syntactic categories have foundered on the fact that distributional analysis gives no a priori criteria for either lumping or splitting word classes, given the conflicting distributional patterns found within and across languages. Radical Construction Grammar accepts the verdict of distributional analysis and rejects the notion that parts of speech are global categories of particular language grammars, let alone categories of Universal Grammar. Instead, language-particular categories are construction-specific. Existing typological research on parts of speech systems, where conducted carefully and systematically, can be reinterpreted as typological generalizations about the constructions encoding the propositional act functions of reference, predication, and modification.

Radical Construction Grammar also adopts the semantic map model of typological theory for the representation of language universals and of language-particular distribution patterns. The universals of language are found in conceptual structure and in the mapping of conceptual function onto grammatical form. A number of universals are proposed in typological theory, and are adopted by Radical Construction Grammar:

- conceptual space represents a universal structure of conceptual knowledge for communication in human beings;
- language-specific and construction-specific grammatical categories should map onto connected regions of conceptual space (Semantic Map Connectivity Hypothesis);
- diachronic changes in the distribution of a construction should follow connected paths in conceptual space (dynamicized version of the Semantic Map Connectivity Hypothesis);
- constructions encoding a function should code that function in at least as many morphemes in typologically unmarked points in conceptual space as in typologically marked points in conceptual space (Structural Coding Map Hypothesis);
- constructions expressing the behavioral potential of a category should be found in at least the typologically unmarked points in conceptual space (Behavioral Potential Map Hypothesis);
- the constructions encoding the typologically unmarked points in conceptual space should have at least as high a token frequency in discourse as those encoding the typologically marked points in conceptual space (frequency criterion);
- the conceptual space provides the internal structure of grammatical categories; the boundaries of grammatical categories are defined language-specifically, and may be fuzzy (the Grammatical Category Structure Hypothesis).

We can now see how the universal and the language-particular are integrated in the representation of a language speaker's grammatical knowledge. All speakers possess (or acquire—see §1.2.1) the universal structure of conceptual space, including its topography (prototypical vs. nonprototypical regions, for example). The acquisition (and use) of language involves identifying the distribution pattern of each construction acquired. This process is the discovery of the semantic map for that construction. This process is constrained by the hypotheses presented in §2.4. The result is a semantic map representing the distribution patterns of the constructions of the language.

It is worth returning to the hypotheses on what there is in grammatical knowledge outlined in §1.5.3, repreated below:

(88) a. categories and relations defined by particular constructions
    b. similarities among these construction-specific categories and relations
    c. functional, cognitive, and semantic explanations for these similarities
    d. categories and relations in a cross-constructional sense

In Radical Construction Grammar, (a)—categories (and relations; see Chapter 4) defined by particular constructions—are represented by individual semantic maps on conceptual space. Item (b)—similarities among these construction-specific categories—are represented by the amount and nature of the overlap of the semantic maps. Item (c)—functional, cognitive, and semantic explanations for these similarities—are represented by the universal topography of the conceptual space itself, and the sorts of explanations that we may offer in order to account for its topography. All of this is achieved without any reference to (d)—global categories or relations.

The same is also true for cross-linguistic comparison. In §1.4.3, I presented Dryer's original points on what there is in Universal Grammar; they are repeated below:

(89) a. categories and relations in particular languages
    b. similarities among these language-particular categories and relations
    c. functional, cognitive, and semantic explanations for these similarities
    d. categories and relations in a cross-linguistic sense

In Radical Construction Grammar, (a)—categories (and relations) in particular languages—are represented by the semantic maps of the categories defined by functionally equivalent constructions across languages. Item (b)—similarities among these language-particular categories and relations—are represented by the amount and nature of the overlap of semantic maps on regions of conceptual space. Item (c)—functional, cognitive, and semantic explanations for these similarities—are represented by the universal topography of the conceptual space itself, and the sorts of explanations that we may offer in order to account for its topography. All of this is achieved without any reference to (d)—universal categories or relations.

The reader has no doubt noticed the parallels between the Radical Construction Grammar analysis at the language-particular level and the cross-linguistic level. The highly repetitive nature of the last two pairs of paragraphs actually contains a major insight: GRAMMATICAL VARIATION WITHIN A LANGUAGE AND GRAMMATICAL VARIATION ACROSS LANGUAGES ARE GOVERNED BY THE SAME UNIVERSAL STRUCTURES AND PRINCIPLES. (This is not to ignore the equally important, but different, social variation within language; see Croft 2000a, especially chapter 7.)

Moreover, Radical Construction Grammar demonstrates that one might even propose typological universals on the basis of grammatical variation within a single language. The fact that English coding constructions for predication require two morphemes for object words (*be a*), one for property words (*be*), and none for action words (see Figure 2.3) is evidence for the implicational hierarchy *object* < *property* < *action* across languages as well as within languages. In other words, Radical Constructon Grammar integrates typological theory and the analysis of a single language.

Radical Construction Grammar and typological theory will be applied to syntactic roles ("grammatical relations") in Chapter 4. But before we turn to syntactic roles, we must examine more closely the nature of conceptual space as a universal of human communication.

3

Syntactic Categories and Semantic Relativity

3.1. The Relationship between Form and Meaning

In the preceding chapters, I have argued that syntactic categories are construction-specific. One consequence of this argument is that universals of language are not to be found in syntactic structure per se. Instead they are found in the structure of conceptual space, and in general principles of form–function mapping such as typological markedness. The hypothesis underlying the use of conceptual space is that at some level semantic structure is universal. Indeed, the universality of semantics is a fundamental principle underlying cross-linguistic comparison. This principle is invoked explicitly in typology and implicitly in other syntactic theories. How does one identify nouns across languages, if one's theory assumes that Noun is a universal syntactic category? One looks at the encoding of objects in referring expressions, and assumes that the relevant construction(s) defines the category Noun in the language in question. This is the heuristic method described by Schachter (1985) (see §2.1).

Radical Construction Grammar argues that the distributions of all constructions should be accounted for in syntactic representation; but it then argues that the distributions can be organized by means of conceptual space, such that the distributions are semantic maps on the space. The crucial aspect of the universal semantics hypothesis to Radical Construction Grammar is the independence of semantics from syntactic structure. Since syntactic structure is language-specific in Radical Construction Grammar, then if syntactic structure determined semantic structure, languages would be incommensurable in meaning as well as in form.

In fact, typologists have hypothesized that if anything, the causal relation between form and meaning is the other way around: 'the structure of the language reflects in some way the structure of experience, that is to say, the structure of the world, including (in most functionalists' view) the perspective imposed on the world by the speaker' (Croft 1990a: 164). This hypothesis goes under the name of the ICONICITY of form with respect to meaning (Haiman 1980a, 1983c, 1985). The principle of iconicity implies that there is a parallelism between syntactic structure and semantic structure. It also implies that semantic structure determines or, better, motivates grammatical structure.

Syntactic Categories and Semantic Relativity 109

However, the universality of semantics is not universally accepted. There is a tradition that extends back at least as far as Humboldt which argues that not all aspects of semantics are universal. More precisely, the semantics of a linguistic expression is at least in part determined by syntactic structure. This hypothesis goes under various names (the semantic relativity hypothesis, the Sapir/Whorf hypothesis) and various guises (for surveys, see Lucy 1992a; Lee 1996).

A recent approach to grammatical semantics which seems to support semantic relativity comes from cognitive linguistics. Traditional grammarians and generative grammarians have analyzed many grammatical categories, such as Noun or Subject, as being "meaningless". If this were true, the existence of these elements would be problematic for iconicity, since they have no counterparts in semantic structure. One of the more significant hypotheses of cognitive linguistics is that most if not all grammatical categories in fact do have meaning. But the meaning contributed by these categories is conceptual; that is, it represents a way of conceptualizing experience in the process of encoding it and expressing it in language:

Meaning reduces to conceptualization ... Semantic structures incorporate conventional "imagery", i.e. they construe a situation in a particular fashion ... The lexical and grammatical resources of a language are therefore not semantically neutral—inherent to their nature is the structuring of conceptual content for symbolic purposes (Langacker 1988: 49, 50, 63).

If one language says *I am cold*, a second *I have cold*, and a third *It is cold to me*, these expressions differ semantically even though they refer to the same experience, for they employ different images to structure the same basic conceptual content (Langacker 1987: 47).

Langacker's view (articulated fully in an earlier paper, Langacker 1976) combines both a universal and a language-particular representation of meaning. For Langacker, SEMANTIC STRUCTURE is language-specific, that is, shaped by the syntactic structure of expressions. But semantic structure represents a conventionalized construal ("image") of CONCEPTUAL STRUCTURE, which is universal and represents the richness of human experience. Langacker's model is described in Figure 3.1.

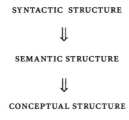

Figure 3.1. The relation between syntax, semantics, and conceptualization (Langacker 1976)

Syntactic structure directly represents the corresponding semantic structure; thus, semantic structures in Cognitive Grammar are homomorphic with the syntactic structures that symbolize them. Semantic structure represents a construal of conceptual structure, that is, one of several different ways to construe the experience being communicated.

Nevertheless, Langacker does not consider the conventional construal or imagery of semantic structure to have a significant impact on thought (I am grateful to Ewa Dąbrowska for pointing out this passage to me):

> When we use a particular construction or grammatical morpheme, we thereby select a particular image to structure the conceived situation for communicative purposes. Because languages differ in their grammatical structure, they differ in the imagery that speakers employ when conforming to linguistic convention. The relativistic view does not per se imply that lexicogrammatical structure imposes any significant constraints on our thought process—in fact I suspect it to be rather superficial (cf. Langacker 1976). The symbolic resources of a language generally provide an array of alternative images for describing a given scene, and we shift from one to another with great facility, often within the confines of a single sentence. The conventional imagery invoked for linguistic expression is a fleeting thing that neither defines nor constrains the contents of our thoughts (Langacker 1991b: 12).

There is a more radical interpretation of conceptualization, however: grammatical structure determines semantic structure, but there is no foundation on which the semantic structures of different languages rest. That is, this approach does away with the universal conceptual structure at the bottom of Figure 3.1. This radical relativist approach is explicitly advocated by Sasse (1991):

> if there are differences in expressions, there are also differences in meaning. This fundamental unity of expression and meaning defines meaning as language-specific and rules out universal semantics as a legitimate field of study (Sasse 1991: 93).

If a strong version of the semantic relativity hypothesis were true, Radical Construction Grammar—and other syntactic theories as well—would not be able to compare languages, and there would be no basis for language universals at all.

However, a closer examination of arguments for semantic relativity demonstrates that there are some important hidden assumptions in the arguments which ultimately undermine the most radical version of semantic relativity (the one advocated by Sasse). In this chapter, I will argue that the universalist position is broadly valid for conventionalized constructions, as Langacker argues, though the universalist position must be qualified to allow for some degree of semantic relativity in the use of novel, nonconventionalized expressions. I will call this the CONVENTIONAL UNIVERSALIST position.

3.2. Hidden Assumptions in Arguments for Semantic Relativity

The radical relativist conclusion, that syntactic structure determines the conceptualization of experience manifested in semantic structure, involves a series of hidden assumptions. The first three hidden assumptions are all controversial; in fact, I will argue that all of them are implausible and hence the burden of proof rests on the radical relativist. Even if these three hidden assumptions can be supported, the fourth hidden assumption results in a paradox, the Semantic Uncertainty Principle, that cannot be avoided by a radical relativist, although it is not a paradox for a less radical position.

3.2.1. Contrast

Let us begin with the example used by Langacker regarding the three ways to express the sensation of coldness, illustrated more concretely with three languages that actually differ in the way Langacker describes:

(1) a. *English*: I **am** cold.
 b. *French*: J'**ai** froid. [lit. 'I have cold']
 c. *Hebrew*: Kar **l**-i. [lit. 'It is cold to me']

The conclusion that these constructions differ semantically is based on the Principle of Contrast, which is widely accepted not only among cognitive linguists but linguists in other approaches as well (see e.g. Bolinger 1977; Haiman 1980c; Clark 1993).

(2) *Principle of Contrast*: if two grammatical structures occur in the same language to describe the "same" experience, they will differ in their conceptualization of that experience in accordance with the difference in the two structures.

The Principle of Contrast is closely associated with the principle of synonymy avoidance, in which two synonymous words or constructions develop distinct meanings or social/stylistic differences in most cases (Croft 2000a: 175–8).

There is, of course, a major difference between the Principle of Contrast as it is formulated and its use in arguments for semantic relativity. The Principle of Contrast is a within-language principle. It is motivated by the hypothesis that individual speakers will attempt to identify some difference in meaning or social context, given contrasting words or constructions. But arguments for semantic relativity are across languages, not within a language, and so there is a hidden assumption in the argument for semantic relativity:

(3) *Hidden Assumption #1*: if there is no contrast within a language, there is still a difference in conceptualization in comparison with different structures in other languages.

Yet if two grammatical structures do not occur in the same language, and so no contrast exists in the mind of any particular speaker, does the same difference in conceptualization hold? Instead, whatever way the language has chosen—'I am hungry', 'I have hunger', etc.—is the only conventional way to express this experience (which I will call a BODILY STATE). So the speakers do not have available to them alternative ways to conceptualize bodily states, and so it may not be the case that the conventional expression encodes any particular conceptualization of bodily states for the speakers of the language.

In fact, Langacker himself makes this point with respect to another grammatical phenomenon. In some languages the causee participant role of a causative construction (i.e. *John* in *Mary made John bake a cake*) can be encoded with either an accusative case or an oblique case (usually dative or instrumental case), while in other languages there is no choice of case marking for the causee. In considering the semantic differences in using the accusative case vs. using an oblique case (dative or instrumental), Langacker writes:

> That is, it does so [the oblique confers a greater degree of volition on the causee] when the language allows an option [between accusative and oblique case for causees]. If the same case is used in all circumstances, its meaning is neutral in regard to agentivity and directness of causation (Langacker 1991: 412, fn. 14).

Hidden Assumption #1 is very likely to be invalid. That is, it is much more likely that speakers of different languages represent similar experiences in similar ways, despite differences in the conventional linguistic expression of those experiences. This is the conventional universalist position. However, there is a plausible relativist response to the argument against Hidden Assumption #1; yet the response itself contains a further hidden assumption.

3.2.2. One-to-one form–meaning mapping

The response to the argument against Hidden Assumption #1 identifies a source of genuine contrast. The different ways to express cold, hunger, etc. across languages do exist in the same language. For simplicity, I will look at only the first two possibilities, 'I am cold' and 'I have cold'. Even if a language uses only 'I am cold', there will exist 'I have X' or the appropriate possessive construction in that language, which contrasts with 'I am cold'. Conversely, a language using exclusively 'I have cold' will have 'I am X' or the appropriate predicate adjectival construction which contrasts with 'I have cold'. The conceptualization is encoded by the constructions [SBJ PRED ADJ] vs. [SBJ POSS OBJ]—or whatever the predicate adjective and possession constructions are; these too vary considerably across languages.

ENGLISH

(4) [SBJ PRED PROPERTY]
  a. I am **American**.
  b. I am **cold**.
(5) [SBJ POSS OBJECT]
  I have **a car**.

FRENCH

(6) [SBJ PRED PROPERTY]
    Je suis **Américain**.
(7) [SBJ POSS OBJECT]
    a. J'ai **une voiture**.
    b. J'ai **froid**.

In the argument for semantic relativity, the conceptualization of cold, hunger, etc. depends on whether it is categorized as the ascription of a property (the predicate adjectival construction) or as the possession of an object (the possession construction). In other words, the grammar of the construction confers the conceptualization of the experience.

The argument given above has another hidden assumption. In order for such an argument to follow logically, it must be assumed that the grammatical element is the same and has the same meaning in all its uses. This approach to semantics is called MONOSEMY:

(8) *Hidden Assumption #2*: all analyses of linguistic forms must posit monosemy; that is, there should be a 1:1 correspondence between linguistic form and linguistic meaning.

This assumption is asserted explicitly by Sasse in a footnote:

One of the fundamental heuristic strategies in linguistic analysis should be the attempt to find a uniform function or meaning for each formal linguistic phenomenon, i.e., not to assume *a priori* that there are irregular mapping relations between form and function (homonymy, etc.), but to proceed from the assumption that there is, *in principle*, a 1:1 relation, each form having one and only one basic function, the subfunction being determined by and explainable in terms of the environment. Assuming [sic] of homonymy is acceptable only as the result of the inability to discover a uniform meaning, i.e., as a last resort, so to speak, but never as an acceptable working principle (Sasse 1991: 94, fn. 8; emphasis original).

Hidden Assumption #2 can be challenged at two levels. One can challenge the necessity or even plausibility of a unitary, monosemy analysis of the meaning in question. This challenge has been discussed extensively (see below). But one can also challenge the unitary analysis of the linguistic FORM in question. This question has rarely been raised in discussions of semantic relativity, but it is in fact quite lethal to relativistic analysis.

There are often subtle differences in the proper formal syntactic representation of the two apparently identical constructions. In some cases, there are phonetic or phonological differences in the realization of what appears to be the same morpheme in different contexts of use. For example, the English *going to* Future in (9a) appears identical to the *go* + Destination construction in (9b); but the former allows reduction to *gonna* (10a) while the latter does not ((10b); Heine 1993: 51):

(9) a. John is **going to** get sick soon.
    b. John is **going to** town soon.

(10) a. John is **gonna** get sick soon.
　　b. *John is **gonna** town soon.

In other cases there are differences in distribution of the forms in a syntactic category. For example, Mandarin Chinese is sometimes argued not to have a separate category of Prepositions; the "Prepositions" are described as simply Verbs. It is true for many members of the "Preposition" category, such as *cháo* 'face', that they occur as "Prepositions" and as Verbs (Li and Thompson 1981: 363):

(11)　[S*BJ* ["P*REP*" O*BJ*] V*ERB*]
　　　tā　　**cháo**　nán　　bài
　　　3SG　**face**　south　worship
　　　'She worships facing [towards the] south.'
(12)　[S*BJ* **V*ERB*** O*BJ*]
　　　tā　　de　　wūzi　　**cháo**　hăi
　　　3SG　GEN　room　　**face**　sea
　　　'Her room faces the sea.'

However, other members of the "Preposition" category do not occur as Verbs:

(13)　[S*BJ* ["P*REP*" O*BJ*] V*ERB*]
　　　bié　　**hé**　　wǒ　　kāiwánxiào
　　　don't　**with**　1SG　joke
　　　'Don't joke with me.'
(14)　[S*BJ* **V*ERB*** O*BJ*]
　　　*bié　**hé**　wǒ

In other words, the category represented by the blank (underlined) role in the [S*BJ* [___ O*BJ*] V*ERB*] construction is not identical to the Verb category in the [S*BJ* **V*ERB*** O*BJ*] construction. Hence the blank role category in the [S*BJ* [___ O*BJ*] V*ERB*] construction cannot be labeled Verb. It is a distinct syntactic category, which could be labeled Preposition (of course, category labels in Radical Construction Grammar are merely mnemonic; the point here is simply that the two categories are not the same).

In still other cases, there are differences in behavioral potential of the category in question which differentiate the category from the source. For example, directional adverbs in many languages are identical in form to verbs describing the path of motion of the directional. For example, the K'iche' Verb *ca:n* 'remain' is also the Directional 'behind' (Mondloch 1978: 168):

(15)　x-　　　e:-　　　　**ca:n**　　-aj　　**ca:n**　　le:　　ajchaqui:b
　　　PST-　3PL.ABS-　**remain**　-TR　**behind**　the　workers
　　　'the workers remained behind.'

However, the K'iche' Directionals cannot be inflected with the prefixes and suffixes which are found on the same forms when they are used as Verbs.

In our original example of different constructions for 'cold' in English and French, the constructions appear to be identical for English properties and bodily states and for French possession and bodily states. But they are not identical in syntactic behavior. The French Bodily State construction allows Degree Adverbs such as *très* 'very' while the possession construction does not.

(16) [SBJ *avoir (très)* STATE]
  a. J'ai froid.
  b. J'ai **très** froid.
(17) [SBJ *avoir* OBJECT]
  a. J'ai une voiture.
  b. *J'ai **très** une voiture.

Likewise, the English Bodily State construction allows a Quantifying Adverb such as *always* while the property construction does not:

(18) [SBJ *be (always)* STATE]
  a. I am cold.
  b. I am **always** cold.
(19) [SBJ *be* PROPERTY]
  a. I am American.
  b. *I am **always** American.

Thus, the French [SBJ *avoir (très)* STATE] construction and the [SBJ *avoir* OBJECT] construction are not the same; nor are the English [SBJ *be (always)* STATE] construction and the [SBJ *be* PROPERTY] construction.

In fact, the differences in grammatical behavior of the English and French bodily state constructions are due to the semantics of bodily states: bodily states are gradable transitory states, unlike properties (which are inherent) or possession (which is not gradable). This is precisely what one would expect under the conventional universalist hypothesis: the semantics of bodily states, distinct from the semantics of properties or of possession, determines at least some aspects of the grammatical structure of the construction encoding bodily states.

In other words, not only do subtle differences in the linguistic form argue against the relativist position, but the differences themselves can be accounted for by adopting the universalist position. This is one of the strongest arguments against a radical relativist position. If we take the analysis of form seriously, as we must, we will be able to identify formal differences that support the universalist position in almost any putative example of linguistic relativity.

Nevertheless, even if it were possible to demonstrate formal identity, there still remains the question of a unitary analysis of linguistic meaning, that is, a monosemy analysis. Sasse assumes that there are only two possible types of semantic analyses, monosemy or homonymy. However, monosemy and homonymy are not the only possible analyses of word, morpheme, or constructional meaning.

An alternative analysis of the meaning of a linguistic element distinct from homonymy is POLYSEMY (see e.g. Lakoff 1987; Croft 1998a; see also §2.2.2). A polysemy analysis for a word or construction proposes that two uses of a form are semantically related to each other by a semantic process (such as metaphor) without those two uses being semantically identical (= having a single overarching meaning). The semantic process extending the original meaning to its extension occurred historically and may still govern the speaker's knowledge of the two uses (Gibbs 1990).

Polysemy analyses play a central role in cognitive linguistics; Lakoff (1987) for example discusses them in detail, calling them radial categories. Cross-linguistic comparison offers an important perspective on polysemy analyses of grammatical elements. This perspective can be illustrated by an analysis of Russian and Finnish cases by Dahl (1979/1987).

Russian and Finnish use different cases to distinguish location and motion. For location, Russian uses the Locative Case (20b) and Finnish uses a set of Cases, including the Inessive (20c). For motion, Russian uses the Accusative Case (21b) and Finnish a second set of Cases, including the Illative (21c; Dahl 1987: 151–2):

(20) a. John lives in London.
    b. *Džon živët v Londone.* [Locative]
    c. *John asuu Lontoossa.* [Inessive]
(21) a. John went to London.
    b. *Džon poexal v London-Ø.* [Accusative]
    c. *John meni Lontooseen.* [Illative]

However, for a class of predicates including 'remain', 'stay', and 'leave [something somewhere]', Russian uses the Locative Case (22b) while Finnish uses the Illative Case ((22c); ibid.):

(22) a. He remained in London.
    b. *On ostalsja v Londone.* [Locative]
    c. *Hän jäi Lontooseen.* [Illative]

Dahl first entertains a monosemy analysis of the two cases in each language, exploiting the spatial and temporal properties of the predicates involved. Location involves one point in time and one place (i.e. one point in space). Motion involves at least two points in time and at least two different places: one moves from one place to another over an interval of time. The anomalous predicates involve just one place, but over an extended time period, that is at least two points in time.

Given this semantic analysis of the predicates, one could formulate the following monosemy analysis of the cases in Russian and Finnish:

(23) Russian: Accusative = involves at least two different places ('go')
                  Locative = involves only one place ('live', 'remain')

(24) Finnish: Inessive = involves only one point in time ('live')
                Illative = involves at least two points in time ('go', 'remain')

One effect of the monosemy analysis of the Russian and Finnish cases is that the cases appear to be defined on completely different semantic parameters, the Russian ones on space and the Finnish ones on time. From a typological perspective, this appears odd; one would expect more similarity in case systems than this analysis provides. On the other hand, this difference may be considered to be support for a relativistic analysis.

There is a major shortcoming of monofunctional/monosemy analyses: it is almost impossible to find necessary *and sufficient* conditions for category membership. Without sufficient conditions, speakers' knowledge of their language is not captured by the analysis (see also Cruse 1992). For example, the aforementioned Russian and Finnish cases have many other uses than those illustrated in examples (20)–(22), and those uses cannot be subsumed under the monosemous definitions given above. The cases must be polysemous in a broader perspective, which raises the possibility that they are polysemous in (20)–(22) as well.

Dahl offers an alternative polysemy analysis for both the Russian and Finnish cases, which is illustrated graphically in Figure 3.2.

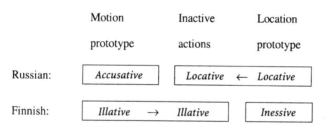

Figure 3.2. Universal polysemy analysis of Ground role

The polysemy analysis posits two PROTOTYPES, for motion and location, and a nonprototypical intermediate type, called INACTIVE ACTIONS in Figure 3.2 (Croft 1991: 97). The motion prototype is defined as involving at least two points in both time and space. The Russian Accusative and Finnish Illative both encode the motion prototype. The location prototype involves only one point in both time and space. The Russian Locative and Finnish Inessive both encode the location prototype. The intermediate nonprototypical category of inactive actions involves one point in space but at least two in time. In Russian, the case for the location prototype is EXTENDED to inactive actions, based on its similarity with respect to spatial properties. In Finnish, the case for the motion prototype is extended to inactive actions, based on its similarity with respect to temporal properties.

The prototype analysis has a number of desirable features. It captures our intuition that motion and location are salient spatiotemporal situation types. We are more likely to encounter (and communicate about) motion and location situations. Also, motion and location are opposed on both dimensions, spatial and temporal. Categories that are opposite on a number of identifying features have a high degree of cue validity and so are more natural as basic-level categories (Rosch 1978). The inactive action situation type is less common and less clearly differentiated from motion and location, and hence is an unlikely candidate for a category prototype.

The prototype analysis also suggests that grammars of many if not all languages are, so to speak, designed by their speakers to encode the more salient and common situations that they encounter in their experience. This is the respect in which a semantic universal (the prototype) is expressed in language—in DuBois' aphorism, 'grammars code best what speakers do most' (DuBois 1985: 363). The less prototypical situation type, on the other hand, varies in its expression across languages (probably arbitrarily—not a problem for a typologist; see §1.1).

The prototype analysis also makes an empirical prediction. The three situation types define a simple one-dimensional conceptual space. Figure 3.2 gives the semantic maps of Russian and Finnish cases on the conceptual space. As was argued in §2.4.2, languages are predicted to have categories mapping connected regions in conceptual space (the Semantic Map Connectivity Hypothesis). Thus, it is predicted that a language type that codes the location argument of 'go' and 'live' in the same way, but codes the location argument of 'remain' differently, will not occur. (This is a nonvacuous competing motivations analysis; see Croft 1990a: 193.)

The prototype analysis captures both universal and language-specific aspects of grammatical categories. The universal aspect of categories is the underlying structure of the conceptual space. The language-specific aspect of categories is the boundary of a language-specific category delimiting a connected region of conceptual space. The prototype analysis is thus an instantiation of the Grammatical Category Structure Hypothesis (§2.4.5).

The prototype analysis suggests that it is the properties of the situation type, as encoded by the lexical item, that influences the choice of grammatical case, not that the grammatical case imposes a "spatial" or "temporal" construal of the situation type. The prototype analysis, by respecting the semantic distinctness of the peripheral category member, also predicts that there will be formal divergence between prototype and peripheral category. This divergence in formal structure of the construction is exactly what is the usual case, as I argued above in challenging the hidden assumption of unity of form.

It is possible that Russian and Finnish speakers have both analyses simultaneously, that is, they distinguish the prototype and its extension but also form a monosemous semantic category for the cases. This may be the case; but it would only apply to the subset of uses described here, as noted above. And the existence of a language-particular general meaning does not have to deny the existence of the prototype-extension pattern internal to the category. In fact, the Grammatical Category Structure Hypothesis (§2.4.5) proposes that the internal structure of grammatical categories is universal, and it is only the boundaries that are language-specific. I will return to this point in §3.4.

3.2.3. *Redundancy in expression*

Another type of relativity argument is offered for the difference between languages such as English and languages that have (sortal) numeral classifiers, used whenever a noun is modified by a numeral. In all languages, a partitive or measure classifier is used when counting entities encoded by what are usually called mass nouns:

(23) *Partitive classifiers*: two pieces of bread, three slices of cheese, four blades of grass
    Measure classifiers: two cups of sugar, three pounds of chocolate, six yards of muslin

All languages also have group or arrangement classifiers that can be used when counting sets of entities encoded by what are usually called count nouns:

(24) *Group classifiers*: two flocks of sheep, a box of chocolates
    Arrangement classifiers: three rows of trees, four stacks of paper

Numeral classifier languages are distinguished from non-numeral classifier languages by the requirement that even what are usually called count nouns require a classifier, called a SORTAL classifier, when modified by a numeral. In the following Yucatec Mayan examples, the classifier suffixed to the number is grammatically required (Lucy 1992b: 52):

(25) 'un-   **túul**   máak
     one-   CLF.ANIM   man
     'one man'
(26) 'um-   **p'éeh**   nàah
     one-   CLF.GENL   house
     'one house'

The grammatical difference between English and Mayan with respect to classification has led many researchers to analyze languages with sortal numeral classifiers as lacking any distinction between mass nouns and count nouns. Under this analysis, languages with sortal numeral classifiers construe all nouns as unbounded (uncountable), and the classifier—partitive, measure, group, arrangement, or sortal—UNITIZES the kind denoted by the noun so that it can be counted. A characteristic description of such a language is given by Lucy (see also e.g. Rijkhoff 1992: 77, 79–80):

If we look to English for parallels, we find a similar phenomenon in those lexical nouns such as *zinc* and *cotton* which are not usually modified by a numeral, for example, *two zincs, *two cottons. These lexical nouns have traditionally been called "mass" nouns... Such mass nouns are generally conceptualized as lacking any intrinsic specification of unit as part of their referential meaning... This interpretation of English mass nouns can illuminate the pattern of numeral modification for Yucatec lexical nouns. It suggests, by analogy, that all the lexical nouns of Yucatec are unspecified as to unit since they all require supplementary marking (i.e. numeral classifiers in the context of numeral modification). Under this analysis, the numeral classifiers serve to specify the unit or boundedness of the referent of the lexical noun, that is, they are unitizers which supplement the meaning of the lexical noun head so that it will accept numeral modification (Lucy 1992b: 73).

The relativistic argument for the difference between languages like English and languages like Yucatec Mayan can be challenged on the basis of nonunity of linguistic form (§3.2.2). That is, it is not at all clear that the "mass noun" construction with partitive/measure classifiers is syntactically identical to the "count noun" construction with sortal classifiers. For example, sortal classifiers are associated with particular count nouns, while there is no single classifier associated with particular mass nouns, since various partitive and measure classifiers are used with each classifier (Greenberg 1977). This syntactic difference is a consequence of a semantic difference between sortal and measure classifiers: measure classifiers describe a temporary state of the material, while sortals describe the inherent state of the object (Berlin 1968: 175). Measure classifiers are an open class, but sortals are a closed class (De León 1987: 84, cited in Aikhenvald 2000: 116).

In some languages, sortals are optional, that is, they are not found in all contexts, for example not with larger numerals (Aikhenvald 2000: 117). Aikhenvald writes that, for example, 'In Minangkabau classifiers are often omitted in everyday language, and this does not change the semantics of a numeral phrase' (ibid.). Measure nouns, on the other hand, are syntactically as well as semantically necessary in numeral expressions (ibid.: 116). All of these differences suggest that the measure classifier construction and the sortal classifier construction are syntactically distinct, and that some of the syntactic differences are due to the semantic differences between uncountable substances and countable objects—just as the universalist position predicts (§3.2.2).

If we overlook these differences in form between sortal classifiers and other classifiers, we still find a hidden assumption in this argument for semantic relativity:

(27) *Hidden Assumption #3*: Linguistic analysis should minimize syntagmatic redundancy.

Hidden Assumption #3, like Hidden Assumption #2, is not a necessary assumption about the nature of language and the representation of the grammatical knowledge of speakers. The alternative analysis is one in which there is semantic redundancy. In the case of classifiers, the redundancy analysis is that the count noun as well as the classifier includes unitization in its semantics. The redundancy in semantics does not imply that the count noun can combine SYNTACTICALLY with the numeral by itself. The requirement of a classifier in a numeral classifier construction is a syntactic fact about the numeral classifier construction, not a semantic fact about the meaning of the count noun.

Hidden Assumption #3 represents the principle of nonredundancy in the representation of a grammatical structure. Nonredundancy in representation assumes a maximum of SYNTAGMATIC PARSIMONY in the expression of information in an utterance and the construction type it instantiates. But there is no a priori reason to assume that linguistic representations maximize syntagmatic parsimony. A consequence of syntagmatic parsimony is to add complexity to the computation of an utterance. In this case, the hearer would have to compute that the head noun of the sortal classifier construction is to be unitized when it is parsed in combination with the sortal classifier.

The universalist analysis, in which count nouns are unitized in classifier languages as in English, allows for redundancy in the storage of the semantic information in the construction—unitization is found in the noun's semantics as well as in the sortal classifier's semantics. But the redundant storage allows for more parsimonious computation, in that the noun is already specified as a count noun.

Hence on grounds of parsimony, neither analysis is to be preferred a priori. If anything, psycholinguistic evidence tends to favor redundancy and computing parsimony (Barsalou 1992: 180). Nevertheless, if one assumes nonredundancy, it leads to serious analytical problems.

If one assumes nonredundancy in analysis then, in fact, English has just as much evidence favoring the absence of a difference between count and mass nouns as Yucatec does, if not more. English has two constructions which are taken to differentiate count nouns and mass nouns. The Counting Construction consists of the Indefinite Article or a Numeral in combination with a Count Noun:

(28) [a(n)/NUM NOUN{-Ø, -s}]
    A dog/Two dogs came out of the alley.

The Bare Singular construction consists of a simple Noun stem without an Article in combination with a Mass Noun:

(29) [Ø NOUN-Ø]
    I spilled **soup** on my shirt.

In fact, however, either construction can be used in principle with virtually any Noun, as these (mostly) attested examples illustrate:

(30) a. "When you're 6 or 7 years old, that's quite a lot of **dog** bearing down on you." [Maggie W., 16.2.94]
    b. "They figured they needed that much **car** to ferry everybody around." [Carol T., 14.3.00]
    c. We'd like three **soups**, two white **wines** and an **orange juice**, please.
    d. "That's one of the best . . . **lightnings** I've ever seen." [Debra, 12.4.96]

These English facts can be analyzed in the same way that Lucy analyzes Yucatec: the Nouns have no inherent countability, and countability (or the lack thereof) is represented only in the construction with which the Noun is combined. The only difference between English and Yucatec is that there is a separate morpheme in

Yucatec which can be associated with unitization, while in English unitization is associated with the construction as a whole. But in a construction grammar model, this difference is trivial. In even a reductionist grammar model, rules of semantic interpretation are associated with the English Counting construction, and unitization could be associated with the numeral, for example. Hence, there is no difference between Yucatec and English. Either language can be analyzed as having a count-mass distinction or lacking it, depending on whether one assumes nonredundancy or not.

But assuming nonredundancy, as is done in the analysis of numeral classifier constructions (but not the English Counting construction), causes serious difficulties in other grammatical domains. The nonredundant analyses of numeral classifier constructions assumes that unitization must be attributed to the grammatical element, the sortal classifier, otherwise it would have no meaning; and hence unitization is not part of the meaning of the content word (the noun).

If we applied this argumentation more widely in grammar, we would end up with bizarre results. Consider nonredundant analyses of the following English grammatical constructions:

(31) a. **Three** books
 b. **She** lives here
 c. **Yesterday** I biked to work
 d. I **insert**ed the floppy **into** the drive.
 e. I **gave** her a book.

The Number suffix in (31a) encodes plurality and nothing else. A nonredundant analysis would then have to conclude that plurality is not part of the meaning of the Numeral *three*. The Verbal suffix -*s* in (31b) encodes third person singular. A nonredundant analysis would have to conclude that third person and singular is not part of the meaning of the Personal Pronoun *she*. (The suffix also indicates present tense, but since it contrasts with non-3rd-singular present -Ø, it must have some other meaning, namely 3rd person singular.) The Verbal suffix -*ed* in (31c) encodes past time reference and nothing else. A nonredundant analysis would have to conclude that past time reference is not part of the meaning of the Temporal Adverb *yesterday*. The Preposition *into* in (31d) encodes penetration to the interior of an object. A nonredundant analysis would have to conclude that penetration to the interior of an object is not part of the meaning of the Verb *insert*. The Ditransitive construction in (31e) encodes transfer of possession (Goldberg 1995: 32). A nonredundant analysis of the construction vs. Verb meaning would have to conclude that transfer of possession is not part of the meaning of *give*.

All of these nonredundant analyses make no sense, and put into serious question the assumption of semantic nonredundancy itself. If we do not assume semantic nonredundancy in (31a–e), there is no reason to assume semantic nonredundancy in the sortal classifier construction in (25)–(26).

The nonredundancy assumption plays a role in another argument in the analysis of parts of speech. It is often argued that nouns do not refer by themselves; only noun phrases refer. This argument is based on a syntactic distributional fact of English, that Nouns require Articles, and the semantic fact that the Articles function to specify reference:

(32) a. **The cat** is scratching the furniture.
 b. *****Cat** is scratching the furniture.

From these two English facts and the nonredundancy assumption, it is concluded that nouns—not just English Nouns, but nouns in general—do not refer. Not all theorists take this position; for example, Langacker analyzes both nouns and articles as being of the same semantic type, 'things' in his terminology. However, most formal semantic analyses take this position, and the more recent analysis of determiners as heads of their phrases follows from this analysis (see Chapter 7).

This analysis has also been used to question the universal-typological theory of parts of speech given in §2.4.2 (Ewald Lang, personal communication 1992; Nikolaus Himmelmann, lecture, Marburg, Germany, 2000). The universal-typological parts of speech theory hypothesizes that the prototypical noun is an object word used in reference. In the nonredundant analysis of noun phrases/determiner phrases, the noun does not refer; only the determiner refers. In fact, this criticism does not represent the theory accurately, because the structure of the conceptual space is defined by the whole construction, which does perform the function of reference, not just the head noun (see also Chapter 7). Nevertheless the nonredundant analysis of noun semantics has similar shortcomings to the nonredundant analysis of count noun semantics.

First, there are languages in which nouns stand alone in referring expressions, namely languages without articles, such as Russian (Pulkina and Zaxava-Nekrasova n.d.: 93):

(33) Nesmotrja na **morozy jabloni** ne pogibli.
 in.spite.of on **frost:PL apple.tree:PL** NEG perish:PST.PL
 'In spite of **the frosts, the apple trees** did not perish.'

A relativistic analysis that consistently applied the nonredundancy assumption would conclude that Russian nouns semantically refer, in contrast to English nouns. In fact, the relativistic analysis is not usually advocated for Russian. Yet there is no a priori reason to apply the relativistic analysis in the case of Yucatec classifiers but not in the case of Russian nouns.

Instead, an analysis based on English is usually applied to Russian. In this analysis Russian Nouns do not refer any more than English Nouns do. Instead Russian Nouns are found in Noun Phrases: these Noun Phrases are analyzed as having zero Determiners, or an NP node above the N node without any Determiner branch, or as undergoing head-to-head movement of the noun from N to D position. If this approach were consistently applied, then one would have to posit a classifier phrase for all languages including English, and thus posit a null Numeral Classifier for English. Again, no a priori reason is given to justify extending the nonredundant analysis of English Nouns to Russian nouns but not extending the nonredundant analysis of Yucatec Nouns to English Nouns.

A further problem is the actual distribution of article usage in languages such as English. In English, there are some contexts in which Articles are not used, with mass nouns and bare plural count nouns:

(34) a. **Arsenic** is poisonous.
    b. **Cats** have tails.

A nonredundant analysis would have to posit a null Article, or assume that Nouns are referring expressions in some contexts but not others.

Finally, there are languages which use articles with proper names, as in Modern Greek (Holton et al. 1997: 278):

(35) o **Días** íne planítis
    the Jupiter is planet
    'Jupiter is a planet.'

Here a nonredundancy analysis would imply that the Greek Proper Name does not refer. This analysis is nonsensical, as was the case for the examples in (31a–e). All of these facts suggest that a universalist analysis in which nouns in English and other languages are referential is to be preferred over a relativist analysis.

3.2.4. *The Semantic Uncertainty Principle*

The hidden assumptions we have described so far call into question many of the most common arguments for semantic relativity based on grammatical differences in languages. Even if these assumptions could be justified for particular cases, however, there remains a logical flaw in the argument for semantic relativity. We can illustrate this with Sasse's argument against a universal semantics (Sasse 1991).

Sasse argues that certain languages lack a noun–verb distinction, that is, all semantic classes of words take the same inflections and can occur as referring expressions or as predications. However, not all such languages behave alike. According to Sasse, Tongan is a language in which all Clauses are nominal phrases, as illustrated by his "literal translation" of example (36) (Sasse 1991: 79):

(36) na'e **ui** 'a Sione
    PRT **call(ing)** ABS/GEN S.
    'It was calling of Sione.'   [Sasse's "literal translation"]
    'Sione called/was called.'

Cayuga, on the other hand, is a language in which all words are verbal sentences in Sasse's view, again illustrated by his "literal translation" of example (37) (Sasse 1991: 84):

(37) a- hó- **htǫ:'** ho- **tkwę't** -a' nękyę́ h- **ǫkweh'**
    PST- 3SGN/3SGM- **lose** 3SGN- **wallet** -NR this 3SGM- **man**
    'It was lost to him, it is his wallet, this one, he is a man' ["literal translation"]
    'The man lost his wallet.'

In fact, there are distributional differences which indicate that "nominal" and "verbal" uses are not identical. The Tongan "nominal" Verb takes a tense-mood Auxiliary while the other nominals do not. Likewise, the Cayuga "verbal" Noun for '[it is his] wallet' takes a Nominal suffix that the Verb does not take, and the Verb takes a tense prefix which is not found on the "verbal" Nouns in Cayuga (for a more detailed critique of Sasse's analysis of Cayuga, see Mithun 2000). These distributional differences imply that in fact the Noun Phrase and Verbal Clause constructions are grammatically distinct in these two languages, and undermine any claim that they are identical in their semantics. However, even if we ignore these distributional differences—thus strengthening Sasse's argument—there is still a logical flaw in the argument.

Let us assume Sasse's analysis, that all Tongan utterances are nominal phrases and all Cayuga words are verbal sentences, and that this reflects fundamentally different underlying conceptualizations of experience. How does Sasse arrive at this conclusion? By looking at the grammatical elements: the inflections and associated grammatical particles. But one can arrive at this conclusion only by assuming that the grammatical elements have the same meaning in Tongan and Cayuga that they do in familiar European languages. It is assumed that we can identify the Genitive marker of Tongan with that of English and other languages, thereby demonstrating the "nominality" of Tongan Clauses; and likewise identify the Pronominal affixes of Cayuga with those of other languages, thereby demonstrating the "predicational" character of Cayuga Noun Phrases. That is, we must assume that the semantics of the grammatical elements is universal, in order to demonstrate that the semantics (conceptualization) of the concepts denoted by the lexical items is radically relative.

This argument also applies to the case of 'cold'. The alleged difference in conceptualization of states/sensations can only be asserted by assuming the universal semantics of the predicate adjective and possession constructions. One could equally reasonably argue that the predicate adjective and possession constructions of French differ conceptually from the predicate adjective and possession constructions in English. After all, the French constructions range over a different set of situation types from the English constructions. Likewise, the relativistic interpretation of nouns in classifier languages can only be asserted by assuming the universal semantics of partitive, measure, and group expressions (as well as the identity of those expressions with sortal classifiers).

But there is no a priori reason to assume that the grammatical elements always are universal. It could be that the semantics of the lexical items is universal and the semantics of the grammatical elements is determined at least in part by that of the lexical items. That is, the "nominal" grammatical element '*a* in Tongan is polysemous between a (nominal) Genitive meaning and a (verbal) Absolutive argument meaning; and the Cayuga Pronominal prefixes are polysemous between a (verbal) agreement function and a (nominal) gender function. Likewise, one could just as easily assume that the semantics of bodily states is universal and the semantics of the constructions used to predicate a bodily state of a person is determined at least in part by the lexical semantics of the bodily state words. And one could just as easily assume that the semantics of individuatable objects is universal and the semantics of the constructions used to enumerate objects is determined at least in part by the lexical semantics of the object words (i.e. count nouns).

This is the core hidden assumption in radical linguistic relativity arguments, which I call the Semantic Uncertainty Principle (Croft 1993a: 374–5):

(38) *Hidden Assumption #4: Semantic Uncertainty Principle*: determining the relativity of the conceptualization given by one constructional element can only be done by assuming the universality of the conceptualization given by another element in the construction.

One important consequence of the Semantic Uncertainty Principle is that there is some model of universal semantics assumed by all linguists; semantics is not radically relative. The question is, what is the relationship between universal semantics and language-specific conceptualizations? In the following section, I offer an interpretation of linguistic relativity and conceptualization that conforms to what we know about the dynamic nature of language.

3.3. The Dynamic, Fluctuating Character of Linguistic "Relativity"

A solution to the iconicity-conceptualization puzzle emerges when we consider how patterns like those found in Tongan and Cayuga arise. The process of grammaticalization, well studied by typologists, gives an account (see for example Lehmann 1982b/1995; Heine et al. 1991; Traugott and Heine 1991; Hopper and Traugott 1993). In grammaticalization, constructions acquire new semantic uses over time, and can diverge syntactically as well (through replacement, renewal, or split). For example, a nominalized verb form plus its genitive dependent may grammaticalize into a main verb predication plus its core argument. Something like this may have happened in Polynesian, and has led to the Genitive case preposition also encoding the core argument of the main predication, which itself is identical to an action nominal. Also, pronouns often grammaticalize into argument indexing affixes ("agreement" affixes) on verbs, and into determiners and thence into gender markers on nouns. Both of these processes have happened in Iroquoian, with approximately the same original Pronouns (in fact, the grammaticalization into verbal indexes and nominal gender markers occurred at separate stages in the history of Iroquoian; Mithun 2000).

The grammaticalization process can be seen to involve three steps at the microlevel. The first step in the process is that a construction is extended to a new function, previously encoded by some other construction. This initial step is a crucial one, because the old and new constructions contrast in the function in question. Many linguists argue that when there are two different constructions for a single function in the same language, the two contrasting constructions offer alternative conceptualizations of the same experience, each highlighting different aspects of the function they are competing to express, to the extent that they can contrast in use (§3.2.1). That is, the new construction at least partially imposes the conceptualization of its original structure and function. This is likely to be true (if at all) at the initial stage of the process, when the new construction is not yet conventionalized.

In the next step, the old construction in the new function is eliminated, or marginalized to the point that it no longer significantly contrasts with the old one. At this point, the "new" construction has become conventionalized in the new function, which has now become one of its normal functions. At this point too, the highlighting of particular aspects of the function expressed by the new construction fades, because of the absence of grammatical contrast. The conceptualization of the experience encoded by the lexical items (content words) occurring in the construction reasserts itself, so to speak, in the new function.

At this point, the construction has become conventional in its new function. The construction is polysemous with respect to its original meaning. The independence of the construction in its new function is demonstrated by the last step in the grammaticalization process: the new construction undergoes shifts in grammatical structure and behavior in keeping with its new function. These shifts will manifest themselves as syntactic, morphological, and phonological changes that occur only to the construction in its new function, thereby making it distinct from the old construction in its original meaning. In fact, these grammatical differences manifest themselves rapidly: all of the examples discussed in this chapter have grammatical differences (see also Mithun 2000, Croft 1998a).

There is a complex interplay of conceptualizations offered by lexical items and grammatical constructions in any actual utterance. Every utterance, whether novel or conventional, involves the combination of a large number of grammatical units. The grammatical system is therefore always in a state of tension. Variation and change in linguistic structures in a single language suggest that the conceptualizations underlying different structures are not only not incommensurable, but also simultaneously available to speakers of a language at any given time.

The simultaneous availability of alternative conceptualizations is sometimes manifested directly by schizophrenic grammatical behavior. The following example illustrates the competing conceptualization of nouns denoting a collective entity in British English:

(39) Section 278 of the Highways Act 1980, therefore, provides that if **a** highway authority
are satisfied that it would be of benefit to the public for the authority to enter into

an agreement with any person ... for the carrying out of highway works, the authority may do so on terms that that person pay the whole or part of the cost (Victor Moore, *A Practical Approach to Planning Law*, 6th edn London 1997, p. 262).

A collective entity is conceptually both singular and plural: it is singular because it functions as a single unit, but it is also plural in that it is made up of a multiplicity of individuals (in this case, the people employed by the highway authority). The singular conceptualization motivated the use of the Indefinite Article *a*, and the plural conceptualization motivated the use of the Plural Verb form *are*, at least at the inception of the collective noun constructions in British English. At this point, the use of the Singular Article and the Plural Verb form are conventions of the language.

This example demonstrates that a universalist analysis cannot simply posit a single way to conceptualize experience, valid to all speakers of all languages. In the conventional universalist analysis advocated here, all speakers have essentially the same understanding of collective entities (or bodily states, or individuatable objects, etc.) available to them: but that understanding lends itself to alternative conceptualizations, any one of which may become established as the new conventional way to communicate that experience. The alternative conceptualizations drive grammatical change through the reconstrual of the experience.

We may summarize the relation between syntax, semantics, and conceptualization as in Figure 3.3 (cf. Figure 3.1).

SYNTACTIC STRUCTURE

⇓ ⇑

SEMANTIC STRUCTURE

⇓ ⇑

CONCEPTUAL STRUCTURE

Figure 3.3. The relation between syntax, semantics, and conceptualization

All speakers possess roughly the same conceptual structure (including conceptual space). But conceptual structure, which Langacker treats as the raw material which is shaped by linguistic semantics, is itself not a single resolvable structure. Instead, conceptual structure is an experience in which alternative, conflicting conceptualizations are simultaneously immanent. The alternative conceptualizations are rendered available by the different grammatical elements, from lexical items to grammatical constructions, that make up a speaker's utterance in context.

The multidimensional character of experience can allow for a novel construal of the semantic structure for a conceptual experience. The novel reconstrual of semantic structure is expressed by the use of a nonconventional syntactic structure for that experience (such as the earliest uses of *avoir* 'have' for bodily states), which encodes the reconstrual in the process that I have described in this section. This part of the process is represented by the downward arrows in Figure 3.3.

Once the new syntactic structure has become conventionalized, however, other, universal, properties of the experience reassert themselves. These other properties of the experience (such as the gradient character of bodily states) alter the semantic structure of the construction in its newly conventionalized function, which leads in turn to the alteration of the formal syntactic structure. This part of the process is represented by the upward arrows in Figure 3.3. This analysis of the interplay between universality and relativity is the conventional universalist analysis.

3.4. Semantic Universals, Relativity, and Radical Construction Grammar

In this chapter, I have subjected arguments for semantic relativity to a critique that reveals a set of hidden assumptions, all of which question the plausibility of a relativist analysis. The first assumption is that syntactic differences across languages imply semantic differences (Hidden Assumption #1). But if there is no contrast within the language, and the construction is the normal conventional way to express the meaning, it is at least equally plausible to assume that it does not encode any specific conceptualization.

This criticism can be countered by comparing constructions within a language, but such comparison assumes a one-to-one relation between form and meaning (Hidden Assumption #2). In fact, there is almost always a difference in form between the grammatical construction used in its prototypical function and its use in another function where it is claimed to impose its conceptualization. Moreover, the differences in form reflect the universal aspects of the semantics of the function to which the construction has been extended.

Another assumption found in arguments for semantic relativity is that the syntagmatic semantic analysis of a construction should minimize semantic redundancy between the meanings of the elements (Hidden Assumption #3). However, a nonredundant analysis may end up leading to the conclusion that languages are similar, not different (as with the Yucatec Numeral Classifier construction vs. the English Counting construction). And in many domains, a nonredundancy analysis is simply nonsensical.

Finally, even if all of the preceding hidden assumptions could be justified, relativistic analyses of the meanings of content words in various languages assume the universality of the meaning of the grammatical inflections, particles, or constructions that are claimed to impose their conceptualization on the meaning of the content words (the Semantic Uncertainty Principle). If, however, we take a diachronic perspective, we find that the pattern of change implies that if anything, it is the universal features of the meanings of content words that influence the evolution of the grammatical inflections and constructions they occur in.

What are the consequences of the conclusions of this chapter for Radical Construction Grammar? There exists a conceptual structure that represents universal aspects of human experience, even if that conceptual structure is multifaceted. Hence we may posit a (multidimensional) conceptual space that is largely the same for human beings. The conceptual space must allow for alternative conceptualizations of experience, as manifested by the extension of constructions to describe situations that they were not used to describe in earlier stages of the language. This is captured by the structure of the conceptual space. Extension of constructions to new uses is a change in the distribution of that construction, and such changes are theorized to follow connected paths in conceptual space. For example, the predication of bodily states would be situated between the predication of inherent properties and the predication of possession, thereby representing its conceptually intermediate—and conceptually ambivalent—status. The structure of conceptual space should capture the similarities and differences of neighboring points in the space, which invite alternative conceptualizations.

The relativistic conceptualization that is found at least in the early, nonconventionalized stages of the extension of a construction implies that the structure of the semantic map of a particular language can affect the speaker's behavior. That is, the formal similarities in the grammar used for certain situations can focus attention on the similarities among those situations. Conversely, formal differences can focus attention on the differences between situation types expressed by the different constructions.

There is psycholinguistic evidence that the semantic maps of a language do affect a speaker's behavior (Kay and Kempton 1984; Choi and Bowerman 1991; Bowerman 1996). For example, Choi and Bowerman compare the semantics of English and Korean putting constructions and their acquisition by children. In both languages, a morpheme encodes the path of the motion, in terms of the relationship between the thing put (the figure, in the terms of Talmy 1974) and the ground object onto/into which the figure is put. In English, the path is expressed by prepositions such as *in* and *on*, while in Korean the path is expressed by the verb, such as *kkita* and *nehta*. The English constructions use prepositions such as *in* and *on* which focus attention on the containment vs. contact or attachment:

(40) a. put a wallet in a handbag, a ball into a box, a cassette into a cassette case
b. put a top on a pen, ring on a finger

The Korean verbs, on the other hand, are identified with tightness of fit (*kkita*) vs. looseness of fit (*nehta*); other verbs identify other spatial configurations of figure and ground objects (Choi and Bowerman 1991: 163):

(41) a. *kkita*: cause one 3-dimensional object to 'fit'/'unfit' from another (cassette–cassette case, top–pen, ring–finger)
  b. *nehta*: put something into a loose container (wallet–handbag, ball–box)

Choi and Bowerman observed the earliest uses of spatial terms by English and Korean children, well before the age of two in both cases. Children used the spatial terms of their language semantically appropriately from the earliest age (English-speaking children typically use prepositions alone in their earliest utterances about motion; Choi and Bowerman 1991: 96). English children consistently differentiate containment from surface contact/attachment from their earliest uses of *in* and *on* (Bowerman 1996: 166). Korean children, on the other hand, consistently differentiate tight fit from loose fit from their earliest uses of *kkita* and *nehta* (Bowerman 1996: 166).

In addition, Choi and Bowerman observed that Korean children differentiate spontaneous from caused motion in their earliest utterances, just as Korean does, while English children used *in* and other path expressions for both spontaneous and caused motion from their earliest utterances, just as English does. Similarly, English children use *up* and *down* for vertical motion in a wide variety of contexts, just as English does, while Korean children differentiate vertical motion depending on the manner or path of motion, in accordance with the earliest verbs they learn; Korean children do not learn general verbs meaning 'go up' (*olla kata* or causative *ollita*) and 'go down' (*naylye kata* or causative *naylita*) until quite late compared to English children's learning of *up* and *down* (Choi and Bowerman 1991: 107).

In other words, there is a wide range of evidence that English and Korean children do not categorize spatial situations in accordance with a universal set of semantic primitive concepts—which usually look suspiciously similar to English prepositional semantics—onto which they map their language-specific categories. Instead, English and Korean categorize spatial situations differently and in accordance with the specifc categories of their language. This is what would be expected from a Radical Construction Grammar perspective, in which there are no universal primitive categories.

In sum, speaker behavior is affected both by the universal conceptual space and the language-specific semantic maps on conceptual space. The semantic map model nicely captures both the universal and relativistic aspects of human linguistic behavior. Having established the semantic map methodology more securely, we now turn our attention to another type of allegedly primitive syntactic category, that of syntactic roles.

4

Clausal Syntactic Roles ("Grammatical Relations")

4.1. Introduction

The syntactic roles ("grammatical relations") traditionally named 'subject' and 'object' are among the most intensively studied categories in language. They are of course central to the structure of the clause and to the semantic structure of the state of affairs denoted by the clause. For the same reason, the status of 'subject' and 'object' has been central to theories of syntax.

The terms 'subject' and 'object' are ambiguous: they are used to describe clausal syntactic roles in argument structure constructions, and also to describe a syntactic relation between an argument and the verb (§1.3.2). This chapter discusses subject and object as clausal syntactic roles; subject and object as syntactic relations will be discussed in Part II. In fact, I will examine only the syntactic roles of CORE clausal arguments, that is, those arguments that fill what are typically described as subject and object roles. The arguments presented here are based on the general principles presented in Chapter 1. Thus, the analysis of core clausal syntactic roles presented here applies to all syntactic roles.

One of the central bones of contention between formalist and functionalist theories of syntax is the status of syntactic categories of various kinds, such as parts of speech or syntactic roles. The usual way that the differing positions are presented is that formalist theories argue that categories such as syntactic roles are purely syntactic, while functionalist theories argue that such categories are purely semantic. However, this is not the proper way to formulate the question, and the usual formulation has led to controversies that actually miss the point.

We may begin with one of the first assertions of the formalist position by Chomsky:

Such sentences as "John received a letter" or "the fighting stopped" show clearly the untenability of the assertion that the grammatical relation subject–verb has the 'structural meaning' actor–action, if meaning is taken seriously as a concept independent of grammar. Similarly, the assignment of any structural meaning as action–goal to the verb–object relation as such is precluded by such sentences as "I will disregard his incompetence" or "I missed the train" (Chomsky 1957: 100).

In fact, one way of interpreting Chomsky's claim is that it is simply wrong. For each of the examples that Chomsky gives in this passage, the semantics of the Subject and Object syntactic roles is straightforward:

(1) John received a letter.
(2) The fighting stopped.
(3) I will disregard his incompetence.
(4) I missed the train.

Using the terms most commonly used to name the participant roles encoded by syntactic roles, the Subject in 1 is the recipient and the Object is the possessed item. In 2, the Subject is an undergoer. In 3, the Subject is an experiencer and the Object is the stimulus (see §4.3.3). In 4, the Subject is again an experiencer and the Object is the stimulus. In other words, for each sentence, the participant role encoded by the syntactic role is straightforward.

This interpretation of Chomsky's claim will strike formalists as beside the point, but I have deliberately chosen it here to highlight a hidden assumption about the semantics of syntactic roles made by Chomsky and others (e.g. Rosen 1984). The hidden assumption is Hidden Assumption #2 from Chapter 3, namely, that any semantic account of syntactic roles will be monosemous, that is, a single general meaning would have to be posited for each syntactic role by the semantic account. But a semantic account need not be monosemous, and in fact a polysemy account is necessary to account for the variation within and across languages for describing the semantics of syntactic roles.[1]

Thus, the debate between formalist and functionalist accounts of syntactic roles should be posed rather differently. The question should not be, is there a semantics of syntactic roles? There is. The formalist claim is rather that a semantic account of syntactic roles will require a nonuniform (polysemy) account, yet from a syntactic point of view all subjects (or objects) have a unified, uniform syntactic behavior. Hence a semantic analysis of syntactic roles will not capture the unified, uniform syntactic behavior of syntactic roles.

The real question that should be posed to the standard formalist analysis of syntactic roles is this: is a uniform characterization of the subject role better found in syntax than in semantics? In this chapter I will argue that the answer to this question is no. The syntactic roles subject and object are not unified, uniform syntactic categories. Instead, syntactic roles are construction-specific, and thus syntactic and semantic accounts of syntactic roles are at a par. This is not to deny the

[1] There are cognitive linguistic analyses of syntactic roles as uniform construals of participant roles (Croft 1991, 1998b; Langacker 1991a). For example, in my own work, I argue that the subject role represents a construal of the participant as the initiator of the causal chain denoted by the verb. But these cognitive linguistic analyses of syntactic roles require language-specific conventional construals of particular participant roles. As with the cognitive linguistic analysis of parts of speech described in §2.5, and more generally with construal analyses discussed in Chapter 3, positing conventionalized construals is equivalent to a polysemy account.

existence of language universals governing syntactic roles. But as with parts of speech, the universal properties of syntactic roles are in fact the properties of particular constructions encoding those roles, and the conceptual space onto which the constructions are mapped.

4.2. Language Universals without Universal Syntactic Roles

4.2.1. "Accusative" vs. "ergative" languages

Most syntactic theories posit universal syntactic roles, which are traditionally named subject and object. In some theories, particularly generative syntactic theories, the syntactic roles are themselves defined in terms of more primitive syntactic constructs. In generative theories, a subject is the argument phrase that is sister to the verb phrase in the sentence, while the object is the argument phrase that is sister to the verb within the verb phrase (see §1.3.2, Figure 1.7). In either case, syntactic roles are treated as universals that can be identified across languages.

However, there are many languages in the world in which it appears that the syntactic roles define quite different categories than do the syntactic roles in most European languages. Compare examples (5)–(6) from Yuwaalaraay (Williams 1980: 36) to their translations to English in (7)–(8):

(5) ḍuyu   -gu   ṇama **dayn** -∅   yi: -y
    snake -ERG that **man** -ABS bite NFUT
    'The snake [A] bit **the man** [P].'
(6) wa:l ṇama **yinar** -∅   banaga -ṇi
    NEG   that **woman** -ABS   run   -NFUT
    '**The woman** [S] didn't run.'
(7) **The snake** [A] bit the man [P].
(8) **The woman** [S] didn't run.

In Yuwaalaraay, the "transitive object" *ḍayn* 'man' in (5) is encoded with the same case marking as the "intransitive subject" *yinar* 'woman' in (6), while the "transitive subject" *ḍuyu* 'snake' is encoded with a special case marking -*gu* 'ergative'. In English, the Intransitive Subject *the woman* in (8) is encoded in the same way as the Transitive Subject *the snake* in (7): both occur before the Verb, and would trigger Subject Agreement in the Present Tense. The Transitive Object *the man* in (7) is coded differently: it occurs after the Verb, does not trigger Agreement, and would take the Object form if it were a Pronoun.

We can describe the difference between Yuwaalaraay and English in terms of distributional patterns. First, we must have a common denominator of comparison. Following Comrie (1978) and Dixon (1979), we use the following abbreviations for the fillers of transitive and intransitive syntactic roles (Dixon uses O instead of P):

(9) A = "subject" of transitive verbs (from a Eurocentric perspective)
    P = "object" of transitive verbs
    S = "subject" of intransitive verbs

I used these abbreviations in examples (5)–(8) in order to facilitate comparison of the two different distribution patterns. In Yuwaalaraay, the Case marking constructions have the distribution in Table 4.1.

Table 4.1. Distribution of case marking in Yuwaalaraay

	__-Ø	__-gu
A	*	√
S	√	*
P	√	*

In English, the constructions encoding syntactic roles—including Case marking for Pronouns, but chiefly position—have the distribution in Table 4.2.

Table 4.2. Distribution of NP positions in English

	[__ V NP]	[NP V __]
A	√	*
S	√	*
P	*	√

The distributions of English and Yuwaalaraay are compared in Figure 4.1.

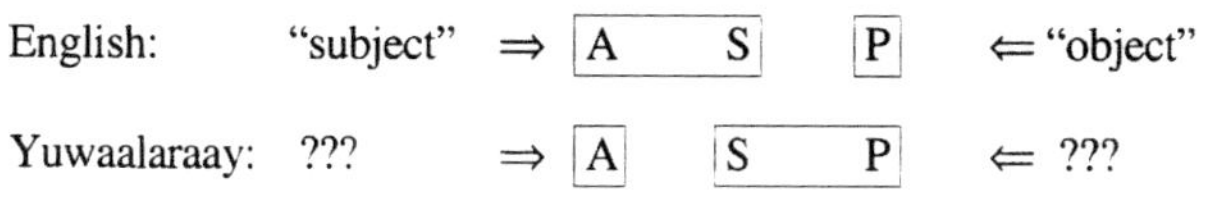

English: "subject" ⇒ [A   S]   [P]   ⇐ "object"

Yuwaalaraay: ???   ⇒ [A]   [S   P]   ⇐ ???

Figure 4.1. Distributional properties (occurrence in syntactic position/with case affixes) for syntactic roles of English and Yuwaalaraay

The question is, does Yuwaalaraay have the syntactic roles Subject and Object, and if so, which is which? The problem we are faced with here is the same problem described in §1.4.1.2: wildly different distributions for the same or similar constructions across languages. The case marking construction contrasts A+S against P in English, but S+P against A in Yuwaalaraay.

Several options are available to us (§1.4.1.2). We may deny that Yuwaalaraay has the syntactic roles Subject or Object. We may say that Yuwaalaraay has the category Subject, but then we must decide whether to identify it with the A category or the S+P category. Or we may look for other constructions in Yuwaalaraay that define the A+S category, and call that category Subject, in analogy to English Subject.

But there is no a priori motivation for any of these choices. Defining Subject in Yuwaalaraay as either A or S+P violates most linguists' intuitions about the category subject, and certainly weakens any theoretical content in this notion. Defining Subject by some other construction in Yuwaalaraay that groups A+S— a common strategy, as we will see in §4.3.1—simply assumes that the English category are universal Subjects. Likewise, denying that Yuwaalaraay has the category subject, while asserting that English and other languages like English have the universal (cross-linguistic) category subject—the smorgasbord approach to universal grammar (§1.2.1)—elevates the English category to a universal theoretical status while denying the Yuwaalaraay categories equal status.

The Radical Construction Grammar alternative, also advocated by Dryer (1997b), is that each language has its own categories for syntactic roles. English Subjects have no different theoretical status than the Yuwaalaraay category S+P: both are language-specific categories. In fact, syntactic roles are also construction-specific (see §4.3). Instead, Radical Construction Grammar examines the similarities and differences between language-specific categories in order to find universals such as those found with parts of speech.

In order to compare syntactic roles across languages, we must have a semantic basis of comparison. That is, the terms A, S, and P must be interpreted SEMANTICALLY. A, S, and P each stand for a polysemous category made up of a cluster of semantic PARTICIPANT ROLES found in one-participant situations (S) and two-participant situations (A, P). For many two-participant situation types, the participant roles are divided in the same way across languages, that is, we can identify one participant role as the A role and the other role as the P role. A and P are in fact mnemonic for agent and patient respectively. However, other participant roles are not so easily identified across languages. That is, the terms A, S, and P hide a substantial degree of language variation in the assignment of semantic participant roles to syntactic roles. The category S in particular covers a wide range of semantic participant roles. We will not discuss most of that variation here (but see §§4.3.3–4.3.4 and §4.4.1). The amount of variation found in the distribution patterns of prototypical A, S, and P participant roles across and within languages is sufficient to make the case for a Radical Construction Grammar approach to syntactic roles.

We also need more neutral terms to describe the common groupings of participant roles of languages like English and Yuwaalaraay. We will adopt the widely used terms in (10) for higher-order groupings of participant roles:

(10) A+S NOMINATIVE   P ACCUSATIVE
     S+P ABSOLUTIVE   A ERGATIVE

Clausal Syntactic Roles 137

These are also semantic categories, despite the use of traditional case terminology. For example, nominative is a polysemous semantic category made up of the clusters of participant roles included in the A and S categories. As semantic categories, their role names are given in lower case; language-specific categories with the same names will be capitalized (see §1.6.3).

We will also follow common usage to describe languages with constructions possessing one or the other distribution patterns of participant roles. Languages possessing constructions defining nominative and accusative roles, such as English, will be called ACCUSATIVE languages. Languages possessing constructions defining ergative and absolutive roles, such as Yuwaalaraay, will be called ERGATIVE languages. These terms are actually misnomers (see §4.3), but they will suffice for now for the purposes of this section.

Having identified A, S, and P as semantic roles, we can see that Figure 4.1 is in fact a simple conceptual space for semantic roles, including the semantic maps for both English and Yuwaalaraay. Thus, Figure 4.1 is a first step towards developing universals of syntactic roles in Radical Construction Grammar. A more precise representation of the conceptual space for A, S, and P is given in Figure 4.2.

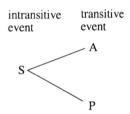

Figure 4.2. Conceptual space for participant roles in transitive and intransitive situations

In Figure 4.2, as in the conceptual spaces introduced in Chapter 2, the horizontal dimension represents constructions, that is, the clausal constructions encoding intransitive and transitive events, and the vertical dimension represents semantic participant role clusters, which are specific to each event type.

The connections between A, S, and P indicate possible case marking systems. Under the assumption that syntactic categories are mapped onto connected regions of conceptual space, the case marking systems in Figure 4.3 are the ones that are expected to be found.

The first two semantic maps in Figure 4.3 have already been illustrated in this chapter. The third semantic map in Figure 4.3 is represented by nonpronominal noun phrases in many languages, as in English. However, it is much rarer as a pattern for all noun phrases, because pronouns commonly distinguish A and P.

The fourth semantic map in Figure 4.3, with all three distinct, is quite rare, except with limited subclasses of S, A, and P (see for example the Cashinawa 3rd

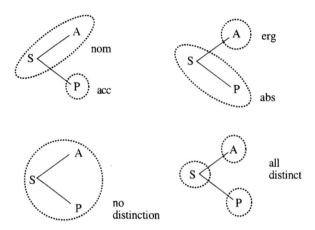

Figure 4.3. Semantic maps of syntactic roles defined by case coding

Person Pronouns in §4.4.3, Table 4.11). Dixon reports several languages in which tripartite marking is found on a subset of nouns, or in a subset of contexts; the only languages in which all noun phrases are reported to be consistently marked with distinct forms for S, A, and P are some Australian languages in southeast Queensland, including Wangkumara and Galali (Dixon 1994: 41).

The one type that is not predicted to occur is the type in which one marking is used for A and P, and another for S. The only instance of this pattern that I know of is found in the Past Tense only of Rushan, an Iranian language (Payne 1980: 155; see Dixon 1994: 39, fn 1). Moreover, the anomalous pattern is being replaced by the nominative-accusative Present Tense pattern by younger speakers.

The following sections will offer more evidence for universals of syntactic roles without having to posit the existence of universal syntactic roles. That is, I will present cross-linguistic universals of how clausal syntactic roles are mapped onto conceptual space, without having to assume the existence of universal syntactic primitives 'subject' and 'object'.

4.2.2. Hierarchies of A/S/P role categories

The existence of ergative languages like Yuwaalaraay poses difficulties for syntactic theories that posit universal syntactic roles (§4.2.1). One can preserve the notion of universal syntactic roles, but there is no a priori basis for choosing among the alternative analyses of Yuwaalaraay. Radical Construction Grammar does away with the problem by denying the existence of universal syntactic roles. Abandoning universal syntactic roles not only does away with this problem; it also allows one to discover and represent language universals that could not be captured with universal syntactic roles (see Siewierska 1997 for a detailed survey of the universals illustrated below).

Case marking constructions that encode participant roles across languages can be divided into two formal types in terms of structural coding: zero coding vs. overt coding of the role (§2.4.3). The distribution of zero vs. overt coding of semantic roles falls into the pattern illustrated in Table 4.3, with few exceptions (Croft 1990a: 104).[2]

Table 4.3. Distribution of zero vs. overt case coding in accusative languages

	nominative A+S	accusative P	
Latvian	ruden-s	ruden-i	'autumn'
Hungarian	ember-Ø	ember-t	'man'

Latvian: Lazdiṇa 1966: 302; Hungarian: Whitney 1944: 18–19, 22

The pattern in Table 4.3 can be described by the following implicational universal:

(11) If a language has overt coding of the nominative set of participant roles, then it has overt coding of the accusative set of participant roles.

The implicational universal in (11) can summarized by the hierarchy in (12):

(12) nominative < accusative...

A hierarchy is a relative ranking of conceptual categories according to a cross-linguistic pattern of grammatical variation. The pattern of variation can be described by a chained set of implicational universals about the distribution patterns of construction types across the conceptual categories in question. In this case, the hierarchy is defined with respect to the cross-linguistic variation in the distribution patterns of zero and overt case marking constructions in accusative languages. This is of course the structural coding criterion for typological markedness. The hierarchy in (12) will be called the ACCUSATIVE CASE MARKING HIERARCHY.

The same hierarchy is found in the distribution of verb agreement[3] in accusative

---

[2] There is one logical possibility that is attested in languages but is not included in Table 4.3: zero marking of A, S, and P. However, one cannot decide whether zero marking of A, S, and P is "really" zero marking of A+S and P or zero marking of A and S+P. In fact, in §4.3, I will argue that one cannot decide this question, because syntactic roles are construction-specific and thus zero case marking is simply neutral among A, S, and P. Thus, languages with neutral case marking, and with no agreement, are left out of the discussion in this section and the following section on object roles.

[3] The term 'agreement' is used here to describe affixes, usually expressing the category of person, usually found on the verb, indexing a participant in the verbal event, and usually allowing expression

languages, with very few exceptions. The common patterns of verb agreement are given in the following examples (Croft 1990a: 106):

AGREEMENT WITH NOMINATIVE (A+S) ARGUMENT ONLY: SPANISH

(13) Los   soldado   -s   quebr -aron   las   ventana   -s
     the.M.PL   soldier.M -PL   break -3PL.SBJ.PST the.FPL window.F -PL
     'The soldiers broke the windows.'

AGREEMENT WITH NOMINATIVE (A+S) AND ACCUSATIVE (P) ARGUMENTS: KANURI (Hutchison 1981: 135)[4]

(14) nzú-   rú   -kɔ́   -nà
     2SG.OBJ- see   -1SG.SBJ -PRF
     'I saw you.'

It is the role that is higher (leftwards) on the hierarchy that triggers agreement: if a verb agrees with accusative roles, then it agrees with nominative roles. Agreement by the verb is part of the behavioral potential of a participant role, and behavioral potential is associated with the typologically less marked categories.

If we turn to ergative languages, we also find cross-linguistic universals concerning the distribution of zero vs. overt case marking of participant roles. Again with very few exceptions, we find the distribution patterns in Table 4.4 (Croft 1990a: 105).

Table 4.4. Distribution of zero vs. overt case coding in ergative languages

	absolutive S+P	ergative A	gloss
Tongan	'a he talavou	'e ha talavou	'a young man'
Yup'ik	nuna-Ø	nuna-m	'land'

Tongan: Churchward 1953: 66, 68; Yup'ik: Reed et al. 1977: 41

The distribution patterns found here conform to the implicational universal in (15), which can be described by the hierarchy in (16):

of the participant as a noun phrase argument of the verb. There are many analyses of agreement which under certain circumstances analyzes the affix as pronouns (referring expressions) that happen to be bound morphemes. In §6.3.1, I will argue that all cases of agreement should be analyzed this way (see Barlow 1988). I continue to use the term 'agreement' following convention, but it should be interpreted in the sense of what Barlow calls anaphoric agreement; see §6.3.1.

[4] There are a number of Oceanic languages in which the A+S agreement marker is not morphologically bound to the verb stem, while the P agreement marker is, such as Woleaian (Sohn 1975: 93); I analyze this as agreement (see §5.4.1, example (68)).

(15) If a language has overt coding of absolutive roles, then it has overt coding of ergative roles.
(16) absolutive < ergative ...

As in accusative languages, the behavioral potential of triggering verb agreement follows the same hierarchy as the structural coding of participant roles by case marking. Again with very few exceptions, the following agreement distribution patterns are found (Croft 1990a: 106):

AGREEMENT WITH ABSOLUTIVE ONLY: CHECHEN-INGUSH (Nichols 1984: 186)

(17) bier   -Ø   d-   ielxa   [CM agrees with 'child']
     child   -ABS CM-   cries
     'The child is crying.'
(18) a:z   yz   kiniška -Ø   d-   ieš [CM agrees with 'book']
     1SG.ERG this book   -ABS CM-   read
     'I'm reading this book.'

AGREEMENT WITH ABSOLUTIVE AND ERGATIVE: K'ICHE'
(Mondloch 1978: 46)

(19) c-   at-   in-   tzucu: -j
     PRES-   2SG.ABS- 1SG.ERG- look.for -TR
     'I look for you.'

Another distributional pattern associated with the markedness hierarchy of roles is the formation of relative clauses. Relative clauses are defined as the coding of actions functioning as modifiers of one of their participants (§2.4.3), and include nonfinite constructions performing that function, such as participles. Many languages have different relative clause constructions depending on the participant role being modified, or have restrictions on which roles can be modified in direct form.

For example, in English Nonfinite Participles are used for nominative and accusative roles, while a Finite Relative Clause is required for other participant roles:

(20) a. the sleep**ing** boy [S]
     b. the boy read**ing** a book [A]
(21) the book read by the boy [P]
(22) the boy **that** I gave the book to Ø.

In English, overt coding of all Relative Clauses is the norm (though English Finite Clauses may lack an overt Complementizer). The coding of relative clauses conforms to the hierarchy in (12), but does not offer positive evidence for the asymmetrical typological markedness relation. However, many languages have an ergative pattern for relative clause formation which does offer positive evidence for typological markedness.

For example, Aguacatec forms Relative Clauses modifying S or P arguments with a zero coded Active Voice Verb form, but Relative Clauses modifying A arguments require an overtly coded Focus Antipassive Voice Verb form (Larsen 1981: 131):

(23) ja   Ø-   w-   il   xna?n   (ye)   m-   Ø-   u?l
     PRPST 3SG.ABS-   1SG.ERG- see woman   (the) PRPST   3SG.ABS arrive.here
     'I saw the woman who arrived.' [S]

(24) ja   Ø-   w-   il   b'u?y (ye)   n-   Ø-   x-   tx'aj xna?n
     PRPST 3SG.ABS-   1SG.ERG- see rag   (the) PRPST 3SG.ABS- 3SG.ERG- wash woman
     'I saw the rag that the woman washed.' [P]

(25) ja   Ø-   w-   il   xna?n   n-   Ø-   tx'aj   -oon b'u?y
     PRPST 3SG.ABS-   1SG.ERG- see woman   PRPST 2SG.ABS-   wash   -FOC rag
     'I saw the woman who washed the rag.' [A]

The cross-linguistic facts described in this section demonstrate that there are language universals defined by the distribution patterns of certain constructions—case marking, verb agreement and relativization—which need not presuppose universal syntactic roles. Indeed, forcing ergative languages into universal syntactic roles of subject and object would obscure the language universals described in this section. Ergative languages would provide counterexamples to the accusative role hierarchy, for example the overt case marking of A vs. zero case marking of P in Yup'ik. Moreover, the ergative role hierarchy displayed by ergative languages taken as such would be overlooked.

The accusative and ergative hierarchies are found with essentially the same types of constructions across accusative and ergative languages. In fact, the two hierarchies can be subsumed under a single general explanation. The causal factor for structural coding and behavioral potential in typological markedness is token frequency in use: the ranking of categories in a hierarchy is predicted to correspond to the ranking of categories in token frequency. This is true for both the accusative and ergative hierarchies. The nominative (A+S) category has a higher token frequency than the accusative (P) category because the nominative category is found in both transitive and intransitive clauses while the accusative category is found in transitive clauses only. Likewise, the absolutive category (S+P) has a higher token frequency than the ergative (A) category because the absolutive category is found in both transitive and intransitive clauses while the ergative category is found in transitive clauses only.

In the next section, we will observe the same patterns with different categories of object syntactic roles.

4.2.3. *Hierarchies of coding object roles*

In §4.2.2, we did not include ditransitive verbs. In English, ditransitive verbs encode their arguments in two different constructions, illustrated in (27)–(28):

(26) I saw Mira [P].
(27) I gave the book [T] to Mira [G].
(28) I gave Mira [G] the book [T].

In (27), the Indirect Object construction, *the book* is coded like the accusative P role in (26), while *Mira* is coded as an Oblique with an overt Preposition. This coding pattern corresponds to the traditional categories of Direct Object (Accusative) and Indirect Object (Dative). In (28), the Ditransitive construction, however, *Mira* is coded like the Accusative P role in (26), being the first argument immediately following the Verb, while *the book* is coded as the second argument following the Verb.

I will use the following names for the groupings of participant roles found in ditransitive verbs (Croft 1990a: 102):

(29) P = "object" of monotransitive verb
T = "theme" object of ditransitive verb
G = "goal" object of ditransitive verb

P, T, and G are polysemous semantic categories representing clusters of semantic participant roles. Following Dryer (1986), we will use the following names for the higher-order groupings of participant roles:

(30) P+T DIRECT OBJECT   G INDIRECT OBJECT
P+G PRIMARY OBJECT   T SECONDARY OBJECT

Again, these are polysemous semantic categories, which can be compared across languages.

In this case, English displays both patterns, which shows that syntactic roles are construction-specific as well as language-specific. We can compare the two English patterns with the following distribution tables, Tables 4.5 and 4.6.

Table 4.5. Distribution of object roles in the English Indirect Object construction

	[VERB __]	[VERB NP *to* __]
Direct Object: P+T	√	*
Indirect Object: G	*	√

Table 4.6. Distribution of object roles in the English Ditransitive construction

	[Verb __ NP]	[Verb NP __]
Primary Object: P + G	√	*
Secondary Object: T	*	√

We will set aside the fact that object roles are construction-specific for the moment, and in the rest of this section we will turn to languages which use just one pattern or the other.

The data in Table 4.7 provide evidence for the hierarchy of direct and indirect objects in (31).

Table 4.7. Distribution of zero vs. overt case coding in direct object languages

	direct object P+T	indirect object G	
Hungarian	ember-**t**	ember-**nek**	'man'
Big Nambas	Ø dui	**a** dui	'person'

Hungarian: Whitney 1944: 18–19, 22; Big Nambas: Fox 1979: 41, 125–6

(31) direct object < indirect object

If the direct object is overtly case marked, so is the indirect object, and if the verb does not agree with the direct object, then it does not agree with the indirect object:

AGREEMENT WITH DIRECT OBJECT ONLY: K'ICHE' (Mondloch 1978: 200; compare example (19) in §4.2.2)

(32) k-   Ø-   (ii-)   yaa   xun   nu-   kej
     IMPF- 3SG.ABS 2PL.ERG   give one   1SG.POSS- deer
     'Give me a deer.'

AGREEMENT WITH DIRECT OBJECT AND INDIRECT OBJECT: Amele (Roberts 1987: 279, 280)

(33) uqa   qet   **-ud**   -i   -na
     3SG   cut   **-3SG.DO**   -PRED   3SG.SBJ.PRS
     'He is cutting him.'

(34) uqa   jo   ceh   **-ad**   **-ut**   -en
     3SG   house   build   **-3PL.DO**   **-3SG.IO**   -3SG.SBJ.REMPST
     'He built houses for her.'

There are very few languages in which the distribution pattern defined by case marking distinguishes primary objects from secondary objects. Yoruba codes the secondary object with the Locative Preposition *ní* (Rowlands 1969: 21):

(35) a   fẹ́   ówó
     we   want money
     'We want money.'
(36) nwọ́n kọ́   wa   ní   yorùbá
     3PL.SBJ teach 1PL.PO SO   Yoruba
     'They taught us Yoruba.'

Yokuts codes the primary object with the Objective form, and codes the secondary object with the suffix -ni (Newman 1944: 198, 201):

(37) ka:ẏu'   te:w   -a   'amin   xatta
     Coyote   rabbit -PO   3SG.POSS ate
     'Coyote ate his cottontail rabbit.'
(38) 'ama' ṭan   kaẏiw wana: -'an   hexa: -ni   'amin
     and   DEM.PO Coyote give   -DUR.PRS fat   -SO   3SG.POSS
     'And Coyote gives him his fat.'

These two languages do provide evidence for the structural coding criteria for typological markedness, as can be seen in Table 4.8 (Croft 1990a: 105).

Table 4.8. Distribution of zero vs. overt case coding of primary/secondary objects

	Primary Object (P+G)	Secondary Object (T)	Gloss
Yokuts	hexa:-**in**	hexa:-**ni**	'fat'
Yoruba	**Ø** yorùbá	**ní** yorùbá	'Yoruba'

Yokuts: Newman 1944: 201; Yoruba: Rowlands 1969: 21

The case marking data provide evidence for the hierarchy of object roles in (39):[5]

(39) primary object < secondary object

Verb agreement in a primary/secondary object distribution pattern is much more frequent across languages. The one widely attested type is given in (40)–(41):[6]

---

[5] Marathi and some other Indic languages appear to be a counterexample to this generalization:

(i) mi hyA   mANsa -lA   mazi mulgi   geto
    I   this man   -ACC/DAT my   daughter give
    'I give this man my daughter.'

However, the reason for this pattern is that the Dative case marker -lA that is used to code G referents has been extended to P+T referents that are high in animacy/definiteness (in the case of Marathi, pronouns, humans, and definite animates). In other words, the Dative is becoming a generalized P+T+G marker, starting with high animacy/definiteness P+T referents. In Ditransitive clauses, however, a human nominal T is not given the Dative case marking when a human nominal G is present (I am grateful to Masayoshi Shibatani for bringing these examples to my attention).

[6] I do not know of any languages that agree with both T and G in a primary object–secondary object pattern. Kinyarwanda allows agreement of the verb with both T and G, but the agreement forms

AGREEMENT WITH PRIMARY OBJECT ONLY: HUICHOL (Comrie 1982: 99, 108)

(40) uukaraawiciizɨ   tɨɨri   me-   **wa-**   zeiya
     women   children   3PL.SBJ-   **3PL.PO-**   see
     'The women see the children.'

(41) nee   uuki   uukari   ne-   **wa-**   puuzeiyastia
     I   man   girls   1SG.SBJ-   **3PL.PO-**   show
     'I showed the man to the girls.'

The agreement pattern supports the hierarchy in (39) as well.

Again, we find universals of the distribution patterns of constructions, in fact the same constructions as were discussed in §4.2.2, despite the cross-linguistic variation in syntactic role categories. And again, there is a single explanation for the patterns despite the variation in categories across languages. The direct object (P+T) role category has a higher token frequency than the indirect object (G) role category, because the direct object roles are found in transitive and ditransitive clauses, while the indirect object roles are found in ditransitive clauses only. The primary object (P+G) role category has a higher token frequency than the secondary object (G) role category, because the primary object roles are found in transitive and ditransitive clauses, while the secondary object roles are found in ditransitive clauses only.

More generally, we can make the following generalization. Languages vary in the distribution patterns that are defined by paradigmatic sets of categories that they possess. But typological markedness predicts that the following implicational universals will hold across languages, no matter what the distribution pattern of the category is (compare §2.4.2):

(42) *Structural coding*: the category with lower token frequency will be encoded by at least as many morphemes as the category with higher token frequency.
(43) *Behavioral potential*: the category with higher token frequency will display at least as much grammatical behavior as the category with lower token frequency.

These are universals of symbolic relations in constructions, that is, the encoding of function (conceptual categories) by form, which we have already seen operating in the encoding of propositional act functions in Chapter 2.

We have at this point the conceptual space in Figure 4.4 (p. 147) for participant roles.

4.2.4. Conclusion

In this section, we have focused on some of the more common variations in the encoding of participant roles in languages. With respect to the constructions examined in this section, we have found that none of the categories defined by combinations of A, S, P, T, and G are universal, in the sense of categories found

are identical. The order of pronouns is fixed in the verb complex, but even so, the simplest generalization is that P+T is the last element in the Verb (agreement for beneficiary can precede agreement with G; Kimenyi 1980: 182).

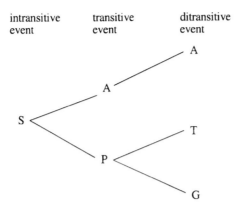

Figure 4.4. Conceptual space for intransitive, transitive, and ditransitive participant roles

in all languages. There is no theoretically privileged combination of these clusters of semantic roles. In particular, subject (A+S), direct object (P+T) and indirect object (G) should not be accorded a more privileged position in syntactic theory than ergative (A), absolutive (S+P), primary object (P+G), and secondary object (T). All of the combinations conform to the general principles governing structural coding and behavioral potential given in (42)–(43).

These general principles demonstrate that the diversity in how languages encode participant roles in syntactic roles does not preclude the existence of universals of grammar. Universals of grammar exist, but only in relation to the concepts encoded by grammar. The distribution patterns (semantic maps) of syntactic roles in languages reflect the structure of the conceptual space of events and their participant roles. The encoding of participant roles largely respects the aforementioned general principles of the form–function mapping.

The analyses and arguments presented in this section assume that syntactic roles are global in human languages, that is, all constructions make reference to the same syntactic roles in a language. This is in fact not true, as I argued in Chapter 1 (see also examples (33)–(34) in §4.2.3). We now address this issue.

4.3. Language Universals without Global Syntactic Roles

Different constructions in a single language have different distribution patterns. This is true of the constructions that make reference to syntactic roles just as much as it is true of any other syntactic category. This fact has led to methodological opportunism in arguments for syntactic roles within and across languages. In this section, I argue that most analyses dealing with this fact are guilty of methodological opportunism, and overlook important universals of coding of participant roles.

4.3.1. Arguments for and against global (and universal) syntactic roles

There are many constructions in English and other languages that define distribution patterns with respect to participant roles. All of these constructions are potentially relevant to defining syntactic roles in a language. Table 4.9 gives some of the commonly invoked constructions that have been used to support the global (cross-constructional) category Subject in English (adapted from Croft 1990a: 8; see also §1.2.2).

Table 4.9. Arguing for the global category Subject (S+A) in English

Intransitive sentences (S)	Transitive sentences (A)
Coding:	
Nominative/Accusative case marking:	
She/*Her slept.	**She** congratulated him.
Subject Agreement:	
Teresa sing-**s**/*sing-Ø	Teresa like-**s**/*like-Ø horses.
Preverbal position:	
Teresa sang/*Sang Teresa.	**Teresa** ate the muffins.
Behavior:	
"Control" of reflexive:	
N/A	Teresa$_i$ cut herself$_i$ /*Herself$_i$ cut Teresa$_i$.
"Null NP" in Nonfinite forms:	
Jack told Fred$_i$ Ø$_i$ to leave.	Jack told Fred$_i$ Ø$_i$ to buy a house.
	*Jack$_j$ told Fred$_i$ to give Ø$_{i,j}$ $50.
"Null NP" in imperatives:	
Ø Sing!	Ø Learn Hungarian!
	*Mary teach Ø Hungarian!
"Null NP" and its controller in Coordination:	
She$_i$ died and Ø$_i$ went to heaven.	She$_i$ fell and Ø$_i$ broke her hip.
	*She$_i$ died and they buried Ø$_i$.
	*She found them$_i$ and Ø$_i$ were starving.

The syntactic analyses of the constructions used as criteria for the English Subject syntactic role in formalist theories have changed considerably over the years, and diverge considerably at present. However, these changes have not affected the methodological principle of distributional analysis—and its opportunistic use—found in the syntactic arguments for the subject category.

Table 4.9 divides distributional criteria for subject status into CODING and BEHAVIORAL criteria, from an important early paper on subjecthood (Keenan 1976). Coding criteria are those constructions (in the broad construction grammar sense) whose main function is to encode events and their participants. These constructions are case marking, agreement, and linear order (§§5.3–5.4). Keenan's terminology thus differs from the same terms used in typological markedness, where only case marking is genuinely a coding construction.

Behavioral criteria are constructions whose main function is not the encoding of events and their participants, but which make reference to participant roles. For example, the reflexive construction performs the function of expressing the identity of the referent of two distinct participant roles. However, the reflexive construction in most languages constrains the possible coreferential participant roles in a way that defines syntactic roles in the reflexive construction. Likewise, the coordination construction performs the function (among others) of tracking the identity of referents across the events expressed by the conjoined clauses. But in English and other languages, the reference-tracking possibilities are constrained in terms of participant roles in a way that defines syntactic roles in the coordination construction. Again, Keenan's terminology differs from that used in typological markedness.

In Table 4.9, all of the English constructions appear to converge on the same syntactic role, the Subject role. In fact, that is an oversimplification of the English facts, as will be seen below. The oversimplification has served the purpose of perpetuating the idea that the grammar of English (and other languages) supports a syntactic theory with atomic primitive categories and relations out of which all syntactic structures or constructions can be built. Nevertheless, the differences in distribution patterns of these constructions are relatively small compared to the very different division of participant roles into syntactic roles in ergative languages.

The divergent nature of the categorization of core participant roles in ergative languages has led many linguists to try to explain ergativity away in the name of preserving subject (A+S) and object (P) as universal syntactic roles. This goal appeared to be achievable since there exist other constructions in most ergative languages that differentiate A+S from P. But it is only by methodological opportunism that such a goal might be achievable: by ignoring the ergatively patterning constructions that do exist in many languages. Doing this renders such analyses empirically inadequate. Moreover, these analyses miss language universals that do govern the behavior of the constructions "defining" subjecthood—precisely because those universals can only be captured if one gives up global syntactic roles and accepts that syntactic roles are construction-specific. I begin here by describing the arguments for a universal subject role and offering a critique. In §§4.3.2–4.3.3 I describe the universal missed by this search, the Subject Construction Hierarchy, in its synchronic and diachronic manifestations. In §4.3.4 I present a Radical Construction Grammar account of the Subject Construction Hierarchy in terms of a constraint on the structure of conceptual space.

In an influential paper, S. Anderson (1976) argued that virtually all ergative languages had the category subject, in fact, the category subject defined as S+A as in English and other European languages. Anderson's argument rests on the fact that in virtually all ergative languages, there are constructions whose distribution follows the A+S vs. P pattern. For example, in Tongan, the case marking of arguments, a coding criterion, follows an ergative/absolutive distribution pattern, the Preposition 'a codes S+P while the Preposition 'e codes A (S. Anderson 1976: 3–4):

(44) na'e   lea   'a   etalavou
     PST   speak ABS young.man
     'The young man spoke.'

(45) na'e   ma'u   'e   siale   'a   e   me'a'ofa
     PST   receive ERG Charlie ABS DEF gift
     'Charlie received the gift.'

However, the control of the Infinitival complement of Verbs such as *lava* 'be possible' follows the same pattern as the English Infinitive in Table 4.9 (ibid.: 13):

(46) 'oku   lava   'a   **mele**   'o   hū   ki   hono fale
     PRS   possible ABS **Mary**   TNS enter to   his   house
     'Mary$_i$ can Ø$_i$ [S] enter his house.'

(47) 'okul ava   'e   **siale**   'o   taa'i 'a   e   fefine
     PRS   possible ERG **Charlie** TNS hit   ABS DEF woman
     'Charlie$_i$ can Ø$_i$ [A] hit the woman.'

(48) *'oku   lava   'a   e   **fefine** 'o   taa'i 'e   siale
     PRS   possible ABS DEF **woman** TNS hit   ERG Charlie
     *'The woman$_i$ can Charlie hit Ø$_i$ [P]'

The "missing" argument of the Complement is the S role of the Complement Verb *hū* 'enter' in (46), or the A role of the Complement Verb *taa'i* 'hit' in (47); but it cannot be the P role of *taa'i* (cf. (48)).

A similar pattern is found in Abaza, a Northwest Caucasian language. In Abaza, Verb agreement follows an ergative/absolutive distribution pattern, with the 3rd person agreement prefix *d-* coding S+P and the 3rd person prefix *l-* coding A (Anderson 1976: 4):

(49) a-   phʰəs   **d-**   qa-   cʷa   -d
     the-   woman **3.ABS-** hither- sit   -PST
     'The woman sat up.'

(50) a-   phʰəs   a-   qac'a **d-**   **l-**   šə   -d
     the-   woman the- man   **3.ABS-** **3SG.ERG-** kill -PST
     'The woman killed the man.'

But it is the accusative (P) argument's agreement prefix that is replaced by the Reflexive prefix *c-* in (51), just as it is the accusative (P) argument phrase that is replaced by the Reflexive Pronoun *herself* in the English translation (ibid.):

(51) **c-**   l-   ba   -x   -d
     REFL 3SG.ERG.F see -back -PST
     'She$_i$ saw **herself$_i$**.'

In these and other languages that Anderson discusses, the ergative distribution pattern is restricted to the coding constructions, while the accusative distribution pattern is found in the behavioral constructions. Anderson concludes from these facts that the languages in question do have the universal syntactic roles subject and object. Languages such as Tongan and Abaza that have ergative patterning in their coding constructions are described as "morphologically ergative" but "syntactically accusative" or as being "superficially ergative" but "deep accusative": 'most ... morphologically ergative languages are ergative only superficially: in syntactic terms, they are accusative' (Anderson 1976: 18).

Anderson's analysis reflects the syntactic theory of the time, when case marking and agreement patterns were not represented as part of the syntax, and the structure of sentences was derived from a deep structure configuration that could differ radically from the surface structure. Many contemporary syntactic theories do not make the same sharp distinction between morphology and syntax, and many such theories do not have a distinct level of deep structure. Thus, the letter of Anderson's analysis has been superseded by changes in syntactic representation.

However, the spirit of Anderson's analysis is still widely followed, in downplaying the diversity of the ways that languages encode participant roles. This is because the spirit of Anderson's analysis is the widely practiced opportunistic use of the distributional method which I described in §§1.4–1.5. Anderson finds constructions which have a nominative/accusative distribution pattern in the so-called ergative languages. This pattern is then used to justify the existence of global syntactic roles of subject and object in the ergative languages. The alleged existence of subject and object as global syntactic roles in these languages is then used to justify the existence of universal subject and object syntactic roles in linguistic theory.

Anderson's methodological opportunism suffers from the theoretical and empirical flaws described in §§1.4–1.5. Anderson's analysis downplays the constructions in Tongan and Abaza that define an ergative distribution pattern. One reason that these constructions are downplayed is the a priori theoretical commitment to a reductionist syntactic theory that posits global categories in the grammars of particular languages. That is, Tongan and Abaza must have a single coherent set of syntactic roles, and conflicting evidence is downplayed.

The other reason that the coding constructions, rather than the infinitive and reflexive constructions, are downplayed is because of an a priori theoretical commitment to a universalist syntactic theory in which a universal grammar posits the categories and relations that are available to the grammars of particular languages. The categories defined by coding constructions are less uniform across languages than those defined by behavioral constructions.

Empirically, the coding constructions that define ergative distribution patterns in languages like Tongan and Abaza are of equal theoretical status to the behavioral constructions defining accusative distribution patterns in those languages. More importantly, the coding constructions conform to universals of language of the sort described in §4.2, which must be accounted for in any syntactic theory. Finally, even if one restricted one's attention to behavioral constructions in defining syntactic roles, there are languages in which even these pattern ergatively.

In Dyirbal, an Australian aboriginal language, behavioral constructions, including the Coordination constructions, define an S+P category. In a Coordinate Sentence, if the P argument of the second Clause is coreferential with an S argument in the first Clause, the basic Verb form is used, as in (52). If the A argument of the second clause is coreferential with an S argument in the first Clause, then an overtly coded Antipassive Verb form is used (and the P argument is then coded as a Dative), as in (53) (Dixon 1994: 162, 164):

(52) ŋuma   banaga -ɲu   yabu   -ŋgu   **bura** -n
     father return -NFUT   mother   -ERG   **see**   -NFUT
     'father$_i$ [S] returned and mother saw him$_i$ [P]'
(53) ŋuma   banaga -ɲu   **bural** -ŋa   -ɲu   yabu   -gu
     father return -NFUT   **saw**   -ANTI   -NFUT   mother   -DAT
     'father$_i$ [S] returned and Ø$_i$ [A] saw mother'

Anderson was aware of this case (Anderson 1976: 17). One is then faced with the choice of either saying that all languages have subjects but not all subjects are A+S (this appears to have been Anderson's position), or saying that subject is A+S and not all languages have subjects. This is of course the quandary of any syntactic theory committed to global and universal categories when faced with the typological facts of human languages.

4.3.2. The Subject Construction Hierarchy

In the late 1970s, when the issue of ergativity attracted a great deal of attention, (at least) two proposals were made that moved in the direction of Radical Construction Grammar (the second will be discussed in §4.4.2). Dixon starts to decompose syntactic roles along the lines of the constructions which referred to them (Dixon 1979). He proposes that S, A, and P [= his O] are universal 'semantic–syntactic' categories (Dixon 1979: 59; he does not define 'syntactic–semantic'). He introduces the notion of a pivot, that is, a category specific to certain types of constructions such as the reference-tracking coordinate constructions. He treats ergative patterns as a 'surface' phenomenon—a description that retains the negative connotations but at least recognizes that coding constructions need not define the same categories as the pivot constructions. (Dixon also proposed that 'subject' be defined as A+S, and is always available to grammars, along the lines of the smorgasbord approach to universal grammar referred to in §1.2.1.)

Dixon also recognizes that some of the tests listed in Table 4.9 indicated categories other than syntactic roles. For example, the English Imperative construction is sensitive to the ability and volition of the participant role, so that some S roles and even some A roles are unacceptable Imperatives:

(54) a. *Ø Be tall!
  b. *Ø Understand catastrophe theory!

There are other mismatches among the constructions (criteria) used for defining the Subject role in English. For example, the category defined by the Reflexive Pronoun role in the English Reflexive construction does not coincide with the P argument, and nor does the category defined by the NP controlling the reflexive coincide with the A argument:

(55) a. **Paul**$_i$ shaved **himself**$_i$.
  b. **Paul**$_i$ sent a letter **to himself**$_i$.
  c. I talked to **John**$_i$ **about himself**$_i$. [McCawley 1998: 367]

Example (55a) is a typical P argument expressing the reflexive. In (55b), however, the role coded by the Reflexive Pronoun is not the P role, and in (55c), the controller of the argument coded by the Reflexive Pronoun is not the A argument.

Dixon's proposal is a step away from the concept of global syntactic roles. But the empirical facts are even more complex, and ultimately call for a shift to construction-specific syntactic roles. One reason for this shift is the diversity of distribution patterns across constructions within languages. But another reason for this shift is the existence of a language universal that can only be described using construction-specific syntactic roles.

First, the coding criteria for syntactic roles do not always line up. In a number of languages including Wardaman, case marking follows an ergative pattern while Agreement follows an accusative pattern (Merlan 1994: 110):

(56) ... wurre -wuya -Ø **ngawun-** da -wa ngayug -ji
    child -DU -ABS 1SG.NOM/3NONSG.ACC- see -FUT 1SG -ERG
    '... I have to see the two children myself.'

The A argument *ngayug* 'I' takes the Ergative suffix *-ji* in contrast with the Absolutive zero suffix on the P argument *wurrewuya* 'child-DUAL'. The Agreement prefix is difficult to analyze, but to the extent that it is analyzable, it follows a nominative–accusative pattern. One could call this pattern "split morphological ergativity". The significant fact is that across languages, it is always ergative case marking combined with accusative verb agreement, and not the other way around.

Not surprisingly, the behavioral criteria that are invoked to identify global "deep subjects" do not always line up either (Croft 1991, chapter 1; Kazenin 1994). For instance, many Mayan languages have extraction constructions that pattern ergatively. Extraction constructions are constructions which pragmatically focus or foreground one participant, and syntactically divide the construction between the constituent denoting the focused/foregrounded participant and the rest. Examples of extraction constructions are relative clauses, clefts, information (WH) questions, and constituent negation. These are illustrated for English in (57a–d), with a vertical stroke giving the syntactic division:

(57) a. the woman | that I gave the documents to
 b. It was Sally | that I gave the documents to.
 c. Who | did I give the documents to?
 d. It wasn't Sally | that I gave the documents to.

In Aguacatec, as in English, Cleft constructions are formed with a Relative Clause. If the S or P argument is clefted (focused), the Verb remains in the zero coded Active Voice (Larsen 1981: 137):

(58) yaaj | m- ∅- **u?l**
 man PROX.PAST- 3SG.ABS- **arrive.here**
 'It was the man [S] that arrived'
(59) b'u?y | n- ∅- x- **tx'aj** xna?n
 rag PROX.PAST- 3SG.ABS- 3SG.ERG- **wash** woman
 'It was the rag [P] that the woman washed.'

If the A argument is clefted, the Verb must be put into the overtly coded Focus Antipassive Voice (ibid.; cf. example (31) above):

(60) xna?n | n- ∅- **tx'aj** -oon b'u?y
 woman PROX.PAST- 3SG.ABS- **wash** -ANTI rag
 'It was the woman who washed the rag.'

On the other hand, Coordination with the particle -tz in Aguacatec follows an accusative pattern. The particle -tz is used to indicate coreference of the A or S participant with an A or S participant in an earlier Clause. This pattern is illustrated with the following passage from a narrative (Larsen 1981: 141; note that -tz need not be suffixed to the coreferential Noun Phrase):

(61) b'een tilool **Lu?** ye teele?n tzaaj chichoojo?n kob'ox ajpayaaj
 he.saw.it **Pedro** the its.leaving hither their.pay some merchant
 '**Pedro** [A] saw some merchants receiving their pay, ...
 niin tzun b'een ii? -**tz** tan k'otle?n juun jul tzi b'ee?
 and then he.went he to its.being.dug one hole at.edge road
 '**he** [S] went to dig a hole at the side of the road,'
 niin kyaaj kyeen tq'ol q'aaq' -**tz** tk'u?l jul
 and he.left.it fire in.it hole
 'and **he** [A] left a fire inside the hole; ...'

Again, the "split syntactic ergativity" found in Aguacatec and other languages follows a typological pattern. Ergative extraction constructions are combined with accusative coordination constructions, but not the other way around. Kazenin examined coordination, purpose constructions, and relative clauses; I examined coordination, relative clauses, agreement and case marking. In the languages examined, the choice of ergative vs. accusative distribution patterns conformed to the following implicational hierarchy:

(62) *The Subject Construction Hierarchy*:
coordination < purposive < relativization < verb agreement[7] < case marking

The constructions in the Subject Construction Hierarchy are defined cross-linguistically as discussed in §1.6.3. That is, the constructions to be compared across languages are those that include the function in question (for the functional characterization of agreement and case marking, see §5.4; for coordination and purposive, see §9.3 and §9.4 respectively). The Subject Construction Hierarchy defines an implicational scale such that for any construction on the scale, if the construction patterns ergatively, then all the constructions to the right of it on the scale also pattern ergatively; and if the construction patterns accusatively, then all the constructions to the left of it on the scale also pattern accusatively.

Table 4.10 (p. 156) summarizes the data in languages examined by Kazenin and myself with respect to the Subject Construction Hierarchy.

The Subject Construction Hierarchy leads us to two conclusions. First, syntactic roles must be defined construction-specifically, because any two constructions can potentially differ in their distribution patterns with respect to syntactic roles in a single language. Second, once we have accepted that syntactic roles are defined construction-specifically, we can then seek—and find—universals of language that govern the distribution of construction-specific syntactic roles. I believe that it is appropriate to use the term 'subject' in describing the Subject Construction Hierarchy, because the Subject Construction Hierarchy is a hypothesis about syntactic roles that extend across constructions. The Subject Construction Hierarchy is, at any rate, the closest thing in Radical Construction Grammar to subjects as they are traditionally understood.

4.3.3. *Diachronic reality of the Subject Construction Hierarchy*

There is evidence that at least a simplified version of the Subject Construction Hierarchy also constrains diachronic shifts in syntactic role distributions in languages. The evidence comes not from diachronic patterns in the acquisition or loss of ergative patterns, but in the evolution of a more specific participant role, namely experiencers in mental or psych verbs.

MENTAL VERBS denote psychological states or processes, typically emotion, cognition, and perception. The person whose mental state is being described is called

---

[7] Some languages such as Chavante and Xokleng have ergative verbal number agreement but accusative nominal case marking; but verbal number agreement behaves differently from person agreement (see §4.4.1). There are also some languages with accusative pronominal case marking but ergative person agreement, such as Hittite and Sumerian. I am grateful to Anna Siewierska for bringing these examples to my attention.

Table 4.10. Data supporting the Subject Construction Hierarchy

	Coord.	Purp.	Rel.	Agr.	Case
Dyirbal	E	E	E	E	(E)
Yidiny	E/A	E	E	—	(E)
Kalkatungu	n	E	E	—	E
Mam	n	E	E/n	(E)	—
Aguacatec	A	E	E	(E)	—
Jacaltec	A	E	E	(E)	—
Asiatic Eskimo	A	A	E	n?	E
Coast Tsimshian	n	n	E	?	?
Avar	A	?	?	E	E
Chukchi	n	n	n/E	n	(E)
Basque	n?	A	A	E	E
Tongan	?	?	A	n	E
Warrungu	n	(E/n)	?	A	A/E?
Warlpiri	A	A	A	A	E
English	A	A	A	A	A

E = ergative/absolutive   n = neither
A = nominative/accusative   — = construction doesn't exist
E/A = strategies alternate   ? = no information
(E) = morphological split ergativity (animacy, aspect; see §4.2.6)
Data from Kazenin 1994: 92, except Warlpiri from Bresnan and Simpson 1982, and Dyirbal, Avar, Basque, and Tongan from Anderson 1976

the EXPERIENCER, and the entity that brings about the mental state or is the object of attention of the mental state is called the STIMULUS. Examples of mental state verbs are given in (63)–(64):

(63) a. **I** like classical music.
     b. **I** remembered the answer.
     c. **She** saw me.
(64) a. Classical music pleases **me**.
     b. The dog frightened **her**.
     c. The music is barely audible **to me**.

Examples (63a–c) have experiencers coded as Subjects. Examples (64a–c) have experiencers coded as Objects or as Obliques governed by the Preposition *to*, while the stimulus is coded as Subject. Both of these patterns for coding experiencers are found in the world's languages (for some discussion of the semantics and typology of argument linking in mental verbs, see Croft 1991: 213–25; Croft 1993b).

What interests us here is that there is evidence for a diachronic change in grammatical relations such that experiencers move across the Subject Construction

Hierarchy, or at least the simplified version of the hierarchy given in (65) (using Keenan's terminology):

(65) behavioral constructions < coding constructions

Cole et al. (1980) describe the process as the 'acquisition of subjecthood', and illustrate it in Germanic and Georgian. In the first stage of the process, experiencers are coded as Obliques and have the behavior of Obliques. For example, in Gothic, the experiencer *uns* 'us' is in Dative Case and does not trigger Verb Agreement (Cole et al. 1980: 721):

(66) galeikaida **uns** ei biliþanai weseima
pleased.3SG 1PL.DAT that left might.be.1PL
'It pleased us that we might be left.'

Likewise, it is the stimulus, not the experiencer, that controls the missing argument in the second clause in Coordination (ibid.):

(67) hwaiwa **skuluþ**$_i$ gaggan jah Ø$_i$ galeikan guda
how should.2PL go.INF and Ø$_i$ please.INF god.DAT
'how you$_i$ should live and Ø$_i$ please God' (I Thess. 4:1)

The same state of affairs still holds for German. As in Gothic, the experiencer *mir* 'me' is in the Dative Case and does not trigger Verb Agreement (ibid.: 727–8):

(68) **Mir** gefallen diese Damen
1SG.DAT please:3PL these ladies
'I like these ladies.'

The experiencer cannot be deleted with a Nominative Case antecedent in the Coordination construction (ibid.; Martin Haspelmath, personal communication):

(69) **Er**$_i$ kam und Ø$_i$ besuchte die Kinder
3SG.M.NOM came and visited:3SG the children
'He$_i$ came and Ø$_i$ visited the children.'
(70) *****Er**$_i$ sah die Damen und Ø$_i$ gefielen sie
3SG.M.NOM saw the ladies and please:3PL they
'*He$_i$ saw the ladies and they pleased Ø$_i$.'

In the second stage of the process, experiencers are coded as obliques, but have subject behavioral properties. That is, the experiencer is now included in the distribution pattern for the constructions on the left side of the Subject Construction Hierarchy, and equally importantly, the stimulus is excluded from the distribution pattern. For example, in Early Middle English, the experiencer is still coded in the Object (Accusative) Case (ibid.: 729–30):

(71) a foreward þat þe mai full well like
an agreement that you.ACC may full well please
'an agreement that may full well please you' (AD 1275)

However, the experiencer can be the null argument of the second clause in Coordination (ibid.):

(72) **Us**$_i$ sholde neither lakken gold ne gere But Ø$_i$ ben honoured
1PL.ACC$_i$ should neither lack:3PL gold nor gear but Ø$_i$ be honored
whil we dwelten there
while we dwelt there
'We should not lack gold nor gear, but be honored while we dwelt there.'
(Chaucer, *Troilus and Criseyde*, IV: 1523)

(73) **Arthur**$_i$ loked on the sword and Ø$_i$ liked it passynge well (Malory, *Morte D'Arthur*, AD 1470)

In the third stage, experiencers are coded as subjects and have the behavior of subjects. That is, experiencers are included in the distribution pattern of constructions all the way across the Subject Construction Hierarchy. The third stage is illustrated by Modern English. Experiencers use the Subject Pronoun form and control Verb Agreement:

(74) **I** liked the sword.
(75) **We** do not lack anything.

Experiencers, not stimuli, are allowed as the null argument in Coordination:

(76) **She**$_i$ saw the house and Ø$_i$ liked it.

Evidence from Georgian confirms the relative positions of agreement and case marking in the Subject Construction Hierarchy. In Old Georgian, experiencers were already included as Subjects in the distribution patterns of the behavioral constructions (Cole et al. 1980: 736). In Old Georgian, experiencers were assigned Dative Case, but 3rd Person Subject Number Agreement on the Verb was triggered by the stimulus (Cole et al. 1980: 739–40)

(77) me miqvaran isini
1SG.DAT me.love.**they** they.NOM
'I love them'

In Modern Standard Georgian, the experiencer is still encoded with the Dative case. However, if both the experiencer and the stimulus are 3rd person, then the experiencer triggers the 3rd Person Subject Number Agreement, as in (78). If the stimulus is 1st or 2nd Person, then the experiencer does not trigger 3rd Person Subject Number agreement, as in (79) (Cole et al. 1980: 739–40):

(78) mat uqvart is
3PL.DAT them.love.he.**PL** 3SG.NOM
'They love him.'
(79) mat vuqvarvar me
3PL.DAT him.loves.I.(SG) 1SG.NOM
'They love me.'

In Modern Colloquial Georgian, the experiencer is still assigned Dative Case marking, but a 3rd Person experiencer now triggers 3rd Person Subject Number Agreement regardless of the Person of the stimulus (ibid.):

(80) mšoblebs   vuqvarvart   me
     parents.DAT them.love.I.PL 1SG.NR
     'My parents love me.'

The reader may have the impression that the unidirectional changes from oblique experiencer to subject experiencer in languages such as English implies that the "natural" category to which experiencers belong is the nominative or subject category. If this were true, then eventually all languages would have subject experiencers. In fact, however, new oblique experiencer constructions have arisen in English even as the old oblique experiencer constructions have become wholly subject experiencers. The new constructions involve experiencers governed by *to*:

(81) a. The performers were barely visible **to the ticketholders** in the second gallery.
     b. It seems **to me** that you should move it a couple of feet to the left.
     c. The news of their engagement was already known **to everyone**.

The unidirectional change of oblique experiencers to "subjects" is simply a constant cycle of grammaticalization and renewal of oblique experiencers.

4.3.4. *A conceptual space representation for the Subject Construction Hierarchy*

In Radical Construction Grammar, an explanation for the Subject Construction Hierarchy is sought in the relationship between the function of the constructions in the hierarchy and the semantics of the syntactic role category. Givón hinted at an explanation in his functional-typological survey of grammar: 'The great bulk of so-called subject properties used to define the behavior of "deep" ergative languages turn out to be pragmatic topic properties, associated with deletion under identity in various grammatical environments' (Givón 1984: 166).

The three behavioral constructions in the Subject Construction Hierarchy all involve a null expression of an argument in one clause that is coreferential with an argument in the other clause (this was formerly represented as deletion under identity in transformational grammar):

(82) a. *Relative clause*: the man$_i$ that Ø$_i$ came to dinner
     b. *Purpose*: She$_i$ went downtown Ø$_i$ to find some shoes.
     c. *Coordination*: She$_i$ went downtown and Ø$_i$ bought some shoes.

It is generally accepted that A arguments are on the whole more topical than P arguments: A arguments are generally human or animate and P arguments are generally inanimate or at least nonhuman, and topicality is associated with empathy on the hierarchy of animacy. S arguments are on the whole intermediate in topicality, since they range widely over all semantic referent types.

Hence the nominative A+S category will be more topical than the absolutive S+P category. Likewise, experiencers (Ex) are always human while stimuli (St) may be human or nonhuman, and so experiencers are on the whole more topical than stimuli. Hence the A+Ex category will be more topical than the A+St category.

Kazenin argues that the behavioral constructions that he examines differ in their degree of foregrounding (Kazenin 1994: 93). Coordinated clauses are the most foregrounded, since they express both events approximately equally (see §9.2.3). Relative clauses are the most backgrounded, since the event they encode is used simply to identify a referent in the main clause event and thus has a grounding function (see §9.3). Purpose clauses are intermediate: the event described by the purpose clause is not backgrounded like the event in a relative clause, but it exists only as an intention of the agent of the first clause (see §9.4.2). The more foregrounded a clause is, the more likely it is that the participant will be topical, because topical participants are generally tracked on the foregrounded events; in fact, it is relatively continuous participation in the foregrounded events that signals the topicality of a referent (compare Givón 1983).

Agreement and case marking do not involve reference tracking across clauses, and so there is no interaction of topicality with degree of foregrounding. There is considerable evidence that agreement is correlated with a higher degree of topicality, including conventionalized restriction to human and/or definite referents (Givón 1976, Croft 1988). On the other hand, case marking is not particularly correlated with a higher degree of topicality, instead being sensitive to the relationship between the referent's type (speech act participant, human, inanimate) and the participant role played by the referent in the event (Silverstein 1976; Dixon 1979, 1994; see also Chapter 8).

In Radical Construction Grammar, a pattern such as the Subject Construction Hierarchy must be represented in the structure of the relevant region of conceptual space. According to Kazenin's hypothesis, the situation types can be arranged on a conceptual dimension corresponding to degree of foregrounding of the event relative to another event (at least for the behavioral properties). Also, the participant roles can be arranged on a conceptual dimension that corresponds to the topicality of the referent in the participant role. If we combine these two patterns, we will have a conceptual space like that in Figure 4.5.

Following the principles for setting up a conceptual space in Chapter 2, the horizontal dimension represents the function of the construction and the vertical dimension represents the semantics of the elements filling the relevant role of the construction. Each of the constructions in the Subject Construction Hierarchy encodes a situation type.

The Subject Construction Hierarchy is represented as a constraint on possible semantic maps in the structure of the conceptual space in Figure 4.5. The natural semantic correlation of foregrounding with topicality is represented by disallowing semantic maps in which the boundary between the semantic

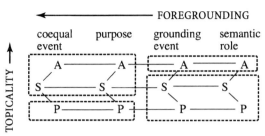

Figure 4.5. A conceptual space representation of the Subject Construction Hierarchy, with a semantic map for Asiatic Eskimo

maps for participant roles in the constructions on the left side of the conceptual space diagram in Figure 4.5 is higher than the boundary between the semantic maps for participant roles in the constructions on the right side of the conceptual space diagram. Figure 4.5 illustrates the Subject Construction Hierarchy with a semantic map for Asiatic Eskimo (since Agreement in Asiatic Eskimo does not have either an ergative or an accusative pattern, it is left out of the figure).

4.4. Some Further Complications

The data presented so far in this chapter has focused on well-known cross-linguistic and cross-constructional variation in the mapping of participant roles into syntactic roles. The Radical Construction Grammar analysis recognizes this variation by analyzing syntactic roles as construction-specific (and language-specific). On the other hand, there are also universals of the encoding of participant roles that can only be discovered by accepting that syntactic roles are language-specific and construction-specific, such as the participant role hierarchies and the Subject Construction Hierarchy. These universals are captured by structuring conceptual space such that the hierarchies reflect sequentially connected regions in conceptual space.

Of course, the data presented so far is a simplification of the actual state of affairs. A, S, and P are crude groupings of participant roles, and we have already seen that experiencers and stimuli cannot be simply grouped under A and P. A more fine-grained analysis of participant roles will reveal a more complex conceptual space. Section §4.4.1 will describe one specific example which has important implications for the structure of the conceptual space, namely the possibility of a subject prototype.

Likewise, if we look at other constructions than those in the Subject Construction Hierarchy, the picture again becomes more complicated. It is clear that a number of other constructions commonly have ergative distribution patterns in languages. Some of these additional constructions are discussed in §4.4.2 and §4.4.3.

4.4.1. *Split intransitivity and the subject prototype*

If one examines the typological markedness data for participant roles in §4.2, it appears to be possible to propose a subject prototype. The cluster of participant roles that is subsumed under S, the single role of a one-participant event, is at the top end of both of the accusative and ergative hierarchies, because S is shared by the nominative category (A+S) and the absolutive category (S+P). Across the two hierarchies, S is the first category, if any, to have zero case marking and to trigger verb agreement. Thus, S is a candidate for a subject prototype, like the parts of speech prototypes proposed in Chapter 2.

However, the constructions involved in the typological markedness of participant roles, case marking and verb agreement, split the S participant roles in many languages. For example, Transitive Verbs in Lakhota agree with both A and P, which are glossed as ACTOR and UNDERGOER respectively (Croft 1991: 9):

(83) ó-   ma-   ya-   kiye
     LOC-   1.UNDR-   2.ACTR-   help
     'You help/helped me.'

However, Intransitive Verbs are split between those that use the Actor Agreement prefixes (as in 84) and those that use the Undergoer Agreement prefixes (85; ibid.):

(84) **wa-**   ʔu
     1.ACTR-   come
     'I am coming.'
(85) **ma-**   khuže
     1.UNDR-   sick
     'I am sick.'

This phenomenon goes under the name of SPLIT INTRANSITIVITY.

The semantics underlying split intransitivity appear to vary significantly across languages. However, some of this variation is due to the theoretical assumption that the two subgroups of S, which we will abbreviate Sa (actor intransitive) and Su (undergoer intransitive) are global and universal categories. For example, the splits in agreement and case marking are often lumped together with a split in choice of a 'be' or 'have' auxiliary in the perfect construction in various European languages (see e.g. Van Valin 1990).

But the perfect construction is a different construction from the case marking and agreement constructions, and performs a different function, namely an aspectual function. It appears that the split in auxiliary choice in the perfect construction is defined, or at least motivated, by aspectual properties of the verbal event. The split in case marking and agreement, on the other hand, is motivated by the causal structure of the event, as with argument linking in general (Croft 1991, 1994a, 1998b; see especially Croft 1998b: 50–5). In other words, Sa and Su, like other syntactic categories, are construction-specific.

Sa and Su are also language-specific, that is, Sa and Su do not have identical distributions across languages even when comparing similar constructions, such as case marking and agreement. In Croft (1998b), I survey the data presented by Holisky 1987, Mithun 1991, and Gregores and Suárez 1967, and propose the following partially-ordered hierarchy of intransitive participant roles, defined in terms of event semantic class (Croft 1998b: 53):

(86) *Hierarchy of A-like to P-like marking of the intransitive participant role*
controlled < inactive < bodily actions, < temporary states
activities   actions   uncontrolled activities,
                         dispositions/properties,
                         inchoatives

The conceptual space for intransitive participant roles implied by the split intransitivity hierarchy would not be completely linear, because the intransitive event semantic classes are only partially ordered (Figure 4.6).

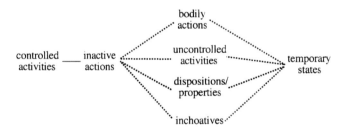

Figure 4.6. Conceptual space for intransitive event participant roles

The conceptual space in Figure 4.6 requires a constraint that prevents an intransitive participant construction with its syntactic role category from extending diachronically across two consecutive dotted links before extending to all parallel gray links (this constraint captures the partial ordering in (86); I am grateful to Masayoshi Shibatani for pointing out this to me).

For now, we will simplify this region in conceptual space as a pair of clusters of intransitive participant roles, without being specific as to which participant roles are included in which cluster for any specific language with split intransitive case marking or verb agreement.

If we incorporate split intransitivity and also the experiencer and stimulus participant roles from mental verbs, we end up with the conceptual space in Figure 4.7.

The horizontal dimension in Figure 4.7 represents a rough division of event

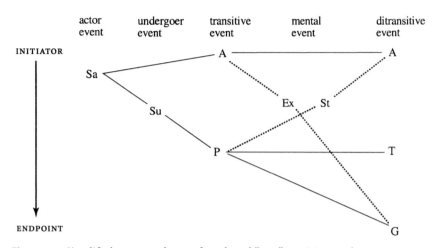

Figure 4.7. Simplified conceptual space for selected "core" participant roles

semantic classes. The event semantic classes are divided roughly by the number of participants; but it should be clear that the transitivity of the event classes correlates with the number of participants. For example, the ditransitive events are events of various types of transfer, while transitive events are prototypically cause-change-state events, and intransitive events are of the types given in Figure 4.6.

The vertical dimension in Figure 4.7 corresponds to the positions of the participant roles in the event's causal chain (Talmy 1976, Croft 1991) or force-dynamic structure (Talmy 1988, Croft 1998b), such that the participants at the top are more like initiators in transmitting force, and the participants towards the bottom are more like endpoints of the transmission of force in each event type.

The exception to this pattern are mental events, indicated by the gray links in Figure 4.7. In Croft 1993b, I argue that mental events involve two opposing force-dynamic patterns. In the first pattern, the experiencer attends to the stimulus, not unlike the transitive A–P (agent–patient) type. In the second pattern, the stimulus causes a change in the mental state of the experiencer, which can be assimilated to the transitive A–P type or to an A–G (agent–goal) pattern, with the goal representing the dative experiencer.

The empirical manifestation of this two-way causation is that languages encode either experiencer or stimulus as the causally antecedent participant (and some languages even encode experiencer and stimulus with the same case marking). Thus, there are connections from experiencer and stimulus to both the agent–patient event type and the agent–goal (dative experiencer) type in Figure 4.7, in order to capture the cross-linguistic variation in argument linking.

We may now ask the question, is either Sa or Su the typological prototype for subject? Here, the case marking and agreement evidence clashes, unlike the situation with A and P. Svan, Laz, and Lhasa Tibetan have overt coding of Sa (plus A) and zero coding of Su (plus P; Siewierska 1997: 192), though Eastern Pomo has traces of overt Su+P case marking in its 1st/2nd pronouns (McClendon 1978: 2). However, Kewa, Tsou, Arawakan, Tariana, and Bare have agreement with A+Sa only (Anna Siewierska, personal communication). The answer appears to be that neither is unequivocally the typological prototype for subject, or more accurately that case marking and agreement are sensitive to different functional properties (Croft 1988; see §6.4.1).

In sum, the typological markedness patterns for the individual clusters of case roles yields the partially-ordered markedness hierarchy in (87):

(87) *Hierarchy of typological markedness of participant role clusters*:
Sa, Su < A, P < T, G

This hierarchy is more or less identifiable with the horizontal dimension of the conceptual space for participant roles in Figure 4.7: zero case marking and agreement begins at the upper left side of the space, and spreads rightward and downward.

4.4.2. Ergativity and quantification

In §4.3.2, I referred to two papers from the 1970s which proposed the decomposition of syntactic roles by construction type. The first paper, Dixon (1979), was discussed in that section. The other paper, Moravcsik (1978), argues that ergativity is a property of constructions, not languages as a whole, and thus is an antecedent to this position on syntactic categories taken by Radical Construction Grammar.

One of the examples of construction-specific ergativity that Moravcsik uses are certain constructions in Russian. All of the constructions involve quantification associated with the verbal event. The participant roles that can be used in the quantification constructions are the absolutive roles (S+P; Moravcsik 1978: 249–50; Anastasia Bonch-Osmolovskaya, personal communication):

(88) cvet   -**ov**   narvali
flowers -GEN   pick:PST.PL
'We picked a lot of flowers.'

(89) vod   -**y**   nateklo
water   -GEN   flowed
'Lots of water flowed.'

(90) Vanja   i   Saša   kupili   **po**   pjat'   biletov
Vanja   and   Sasha   bought   DSTR   five   tickets
'Vanja and Sasha bought five tickets each.'

(91) U   nix   bylo   **po**   zolotomu   kol'cu
at   them   was   DSTR   golden   ring
'They each had a golden ring.'

(92) On   **ne**   čitaet   stix   **-ov**
     he   not   read:PRS.3SG   poetry   -GEN
     'He doesn't read poetry.'
(93) Otvet   **-a**   **ne**   prišlo
     answer   -GEN   not   arrive:PST
     'No answer came.'

Examples (88)–(89) illustrate the Partitive construction, in which the event is carried out on a part of the P argument (88) or the S argument (89); in Russian, S or P are expressed in the Genitive. Examples (90)–(91) illustrate the Distributive construction, which in Russian is expressed by the Distributive Preposition *po* combined with the P argument (90) or the S argument (91). Examples (92)–(93) illustrate the Negative construction; in Russian the P argument (92) or S argument (93) of the Negated Verb is expressed in the Genitive.

Another ergative quantification pattern that has been observed in many languages is the expression of verbal number. For example, in Coast Tsimshian (Sm'algyax; Mulder 1994: 74–5), a Plural Verb form is triggered by a Plural S argument (as in (94)) or a Plural P argument (as in (95)):

(94) ła   **mik-**   **miig**   -a   magooxs   di   -ł   maayi
     about   PL-   ripe   -CONN.PRED   salmonberry   and   -CONN   huckleberry
     'The salmonberries and huckleberries are almost ripe.'
(95) ada   wil   -t   ksa-   **has-**   **hayts**   -tga   smʻooygyit   -ga
     and   then   -3A   out-   PL-   send   -CONN.PRED   chief   -CONN.PRED
     hananax -t   -ga
     women   -3.POSS   -DEM
     'Then the chief sent out his women.'

This pattern is not the only one found across languages; in other languages it is the A and S arguments that trigger plural verb forms. Durie argues persuasively that in those languages in which the absolutive (S+P) argument triggers verbal number agreement, the verbal number is expressing the plurality of the event, not the argument (Durie 1986). When arguments of an event are quantified, then the event may be quantified as well. For example, action on plural objects and intransitive events with plural objects are actually plural events, even in the case of a single agent acting on plural objects.

The ergative patterns associated with event quantification do not conform to the Subject Construction Hierarchy. For example, Russian does not have an ergative distribution pattern for any of the constructions on the Subject Construction Hierarchy, and Coast Tsimshian has only some ergative patterning in Agreement (Mulder 1994: 111). In the Radical Construction Grammar analysis presented here, this fact cannot only be accommodated, it can be predicted.

In Radical Construction Grammar, all syntactic roles are construction-specific, and so the ergative distribution patterns of the constructions illustrated in this section can be easily represented as categories specific to these constructions. The reason that these ergative patterns do not conform to the Subject Construction Hierarchy is that the function of these constructions has nothing to do with foregrounding or topicality, and hence they do not fall in that dimension of conceptual space. Instead, the function of these constructions has to do with quantification, in particular event quantification. Very little has been done on the typology of event quantification, so we cannot propose a model for this region in conceptual space. In principle, however, this can be done.

4.4.3. Split ergativity

Another type of construction-based variation in the distribution patterns of syntactic roles goes under the name of SPLIT ERGATIVITY. The term 'split ergativity' is actually used for two quite different sorts of variation in syntactic roles. One type of split ergativity is called an animacy-based or person-based split, in which ergative and accusative case marking patterns depend on person or animacy of the referent. An example of an animacy-based split ergative case marking system in Cashinawa is given in Table 4.11 (Dixon 1979: 87; ... ṽ represents final stem vowel nasalization).

Table 4.11. Animacy-based split in Cashinawa

	A	S	P
1st/2nd person pronouns	-Ø	-Ø	-a
3rd person pronoun	habũ	habu	haa
proper names, common nouns	...ṽ	-Ø	-Ø

The Cashinawa case marking system is split between ergative and accusative patterns in the paradigm. If one compares 1st/2nd Pronoun forms, there is a contrast between Nominative (A+S) zero and Accusative (P) -a. If one compares Common Noun forms, there is a contrast between Ergative (A) nasalization and Absolutive (S+P) zero.

But ergative and absolutive patterns are only found in an abstract paradigm. In actual sentences of Cashinawa, one can find any combination of A and P. Thus for example a 1st/2nd Person Pronominal A and a Common Noun P will both be zero coded, and a Common Noun A and 1st/2nd Person Pronominal P will both be overtly coded (albeit with different case morphemes). Even the Cashinawa case paradigm is not a properly split ergative. There is an overlap of the Ergative nasalization and the Accusative -a suffix (with loss of stem-final b) in the 3rd Person Pronoun, so that the 3rd Person Pronoun has distinct forms for A, S, and P. The Cashinawa pattern represents a distinct (though related) phenomenon, which will be discussed in §8.4.3.

Another class of split ergative patterns, the aspect- (or sometimes tense-) based splits, do represent different constructions with different distribution patterns. For example, in Chol, the Present Tense construction uses prefixed Agreement for A and S vs. suffixed Agreement for P (examples (96)–(97)), while the Past Tense construction uses prefixed Agreement for A only, vs. suffixed Agreement for S and P (examples (98)–(99); Comrie 1978: 352–3).

(96) mi   h-   k'el   -et
     PRS   1SG.NOM-   see   -2SG.ACC
     'I see you.'

(97) mi   a-   čəmel
     PRS   2SG.NOM-   die
     'You are dying.'

(98) ca   h-   k'eley   -et
     PST   1SG.ERG-   see   -2SG.ABS
     'I saw you.'

(99) ca   čəmiy   -et
     PST   die   -2SG.ABS
     'You died.'

The construction-specific character of aspect- and tense-based split ergativity can easily be captured in Radical Construction Grammar. The reason that aspect- and tense-based split ergativity appears to be anomalous is that in English and other European languages, argument linking in single clauses is independent of other clause-level constructions. For example, in English the constructions encoding arguments of any predicate are independent of the constructions positioning Auxiliaries and Nonfinite Verb forms that are used to express tense-aspect-mood categories, such as the Perfect or the Progressive, as illustrated in Figure 4.8 using the box notation but suppressing the boxes for the smallest units (compare Figure 1.12 in §1.3.3).

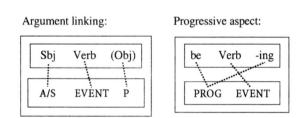

Figure 4.8. Argument linking and aspectual constructions in English

In Chol, on the other hand, the constructions encoding aspect or tense also have distinct ways to encode the arguments of the verb. Thus, unlike English, one cannot abstract away from tense–aspect distinctions in the argument linking constructions of Chol. Instead, there are two tense/argument linking constructions in Chol (Figure 4.9).

Present (Accusative): 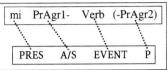 Past (Ergative):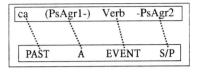

Figure 4.9. Tense/argument linking constructions in Chol

As with the Subject Construction Hierarchy, there is a functional explanation for the cross-linguistic patterns of variation in syntactic role distributions in tense–aspect constructions. Cross-linguistically, aspect splits almost always have accusative distribution in present tense or imperfective aspect, and ergative distribution in past tense or perfective aspect. Tense constructions such as those of Chol presumably arise via the grammaticalization of aspect constructions, into tense such that past tense results from perfect and possibly perfective aspect and present tense from imperfective aspect (Bybee and Dahl 1989; Bybee et al. 1994, chapters 3 and 5). DeLancey (1981, 1982) argues that this pattern is due to a localist metaphor which links causal structure and aspectual structure (and also person deixis; see §8.5.2). DeLancey's analysis is presented in Table 4.12 (adapted from DeLancey 1982: 172).

Table 4.12. Localist metaphor linking event structure and aspect

event structure	Agent (Initiator)	→	Patient (Endpoint)
aspect	Onset (Imperfective)	→	Termination (Perfective)

The relationship between the semantics of aspectual constructions and the semantics of participant role categories can be represented in conceptual space in the same way as the Subject Construction Hierarchy (Figure 4.10).

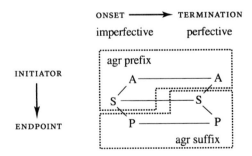

Figure 4.10. Conceptual space for aspect and participant roles, with a semantic map for Chol

We must also impose the same constraint on this conceptual space as we did for the Subject Construction Hierarchy. The boundary between the two semantic maps for participant roles in the constructions on the left of the conceptual space cannot be higher in the space than the boundary between the semantic maps for participant roles in the constructions on the right side of the conceptual space. Chol, whose semantic maps are given in Figure 4.10, uses the same pair of Agreement affixes in the Present and Past Tenses, and so the semantic maps for both sets of participant roles extend across the breadth of the conceptual space diagram. For Chol, the constraint expressed just above specifies that the boundary between the categories must be no higher on the left than on the right.

4.5. Conclusion

We may now return to the question posed at the beginning of this chapter: are syntactic roles as purely formal grammatical categories more unified in their structure and behavior across languages than the cluster of participant roles that are grouped under each syntactic role?

The answer to that question is no. Syntactic roles must be defined construction-specifically, and the patterns of distribution that they define are varied both within and across languages. Terms such as 'subject' and 'object' do not define some fixed category or syntactic structure. Within a language, there are no categories defined by syntactic role—independent of the constructions they occur in. Instead, constructions are the primitive units of syntactic representation, and the categories they define distributionally are found in relations to each other defined in terms of their meaning or function.

Thus, syntactic and semantic characterizations of syntactic roles/grammatical relations are on an equal footing. Both syntactic and semantic characterizations are heterogeneous, varying within and across languages. The focus of syntactic theory should be on the interplay between form and function, not on some supposed supremacy of one over the other.

In Radical Construction Grammar, and in typological theory more generally, the complex patterns of syntactic and semantic variation are captured by representing the interplay of form and function as semantic maps on a structured conceptual space. Syntactic roles define regions in conceptual space that represent semantically related groupings of participant roles of events. The dimension(s) of conceptual space that represent participant roles interact with the dimensions of conceptual space that represent the functions of various constructions that make reference to participant roles. These conceptual dimensions include event structure itself (case marking and agreement), referent salience (agreement), foregrounding/reference-tracking (relative clauses, purpose clauses, and coordinate clauses), event quantification (partitive, distributive, negative, and verbal number), and tense/aspect (perfective/past and imperfective/present). The structure of the conceptual space reflects the hierarchies of implicational relations governing the participant role distribution patterns of these constructions across and within languages.

PART II
From Syntactic Relations to Symbolic Relations

5

Dependency, Constituency, and Linear Order

5.1. Introduction

5.1.1. *The internal structure of constructions*

In Part I of this book, very little has been assumed about syntactic structure and organization in Radical Construction Grammar. The syntactic structure of constructions has been assumed to consist only of (i) the construction itself as a whole, independently represented entity, and (ii) its parts or ELEMENTS, which define syntactic categories or ROLES (see §1.3.3). That is, the only syntactic structure for constructions that we have assumed so far is the part–whole relation between roles and constructions respectively. In Part I, I argued that constructions must be taken as basic and the categories or roles found in constructions are derivative, defined by the constructions in which they are found. Hence there do not exist global syntactic categories in the grammar of a single language, nor universal categories in a Universal Grammar.

Part II of this book explores in more detail the internal structure of constructions in Radical Construction Grammar. The internal structure of a construction in ordinary construction grammar (see §1.3.2, Figure 1.6) is illustrated in an exploded format in Figure 5.1 on page 176 (compare Langacker 1987: 84, Fig. 2.8b).

Both the formal (syntactic) and functional (semantic) structures may be made up of parts, which define roles in the construction. Syntactic relations, indicated by a dotted arrow for reasons to be explained below, hold between elements of the syntactic structure, and semantic relations hold between components of the semantic structure. Finally, there are symbolic relations between syntactic elements and the corresponding semantic components, and between the syntactic structure of the construction as a whole and its semantic structure.

Radical Construction Grammar differs from other construction grammars and from componential syntactic theories, however, in that it dispenses with syntactic relations, that is, relations between the syntactic elements of a construction. That is, the structure of a grammatical unit in Radical Construction Grammar is the structure in Figure 5.1 minus the dotted arrow for syntactic relations.

Of course, there are certain morphosyntactic properties of constructions that are taken to be the overt manifestation of syntactic relations (§1.3.2). Thus, any

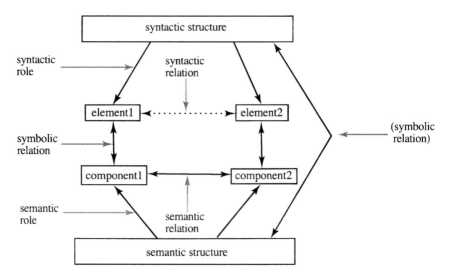

Figure 5.1. The internal structure of a construction (exploded diagram)

argument against the existence of syntactic relations will have to account for the morphosyntactic properties of constructions that are taken to be evidence for the existence of syntactic relations, and also make a critique of constituency and dependency analyses.

In this chapter, I argue that evidence for syntactic relations falls into two types, coded dependencies and collocational dependencies. In §5.2, I present the argument by Nunberg et al. (1994) that collocational dependencies are in fact the overt manifestation of semantic relations, not syntactic relations, and show that Nunberg et al.'s analysis has a natural interpretation in Radical Construction Grammar. In the remainder of this chapter, I present a brief critique of constituency and coded dependency relations, showing that in both cases, there is no single constituency or dependency analysis for a construction.

In Chapter 6, I argue that coded dependencies, including constituency, are evidence for symbolic relations, not syntactic relations. Finally, in Chapter 7, I offer a Radical Construction Grammar analysis of head–dependent relations and the argument–adjunct distinction.

5.1.2. Coded dependencies and collocational dependencies

Arguments for syntactic relations are based on grammatical evidence that falls into two distinct classes. One class comprises what I will call CODED DEPENDENCIES. These are syntactic relations that are manifested by some overt aspect of the grammatical structure of an utterance, such as (1a):

(1) a. She understands him.

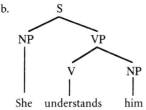

In (1a), there is assumed to be grammatical evidence from coded dependencies of a syntactic relation between *she* and *understands* (the Subject relation) and between *understands* and *him* (the Object relation). The Pronoun Case forms encode the two syntactic relations. The presence of Verb Agreement with *she* also codes the Subject relation. The linear order or position of the two Pronouns also encodes the Subject (preverbal) and Object (immediate postverbal) relations. Finally, the analysis of the constituent structure (phrase structure) of (1a), given in (1b), defines the Subject relation (the NP that is sister to the VP) and Object relation (the NP that is sister to the verb inside the VP). All of these properties are taken as evidence of these two syntactic relations.

Another class of evidence for syntactic relations that is appealed to in syntactic arguments comprises what I will call COLLOCATIONAL DEPENDENCIES. A collocational dependency is a constraint on the choice of a word in a sentence by another word or words in the sentence, as illustrated in (2):

(2) The cherry trees **burst into bloom**.

The choice of noun in the prepositional phrase *into bloom* is constrained by the verb *burst*: *bloom* or *flower* are the only possibilities. This collocational relation is evidence of some sort of dependency between the Verb and the Prepositional Phrase (a governed oblique phrase). Also, the choice of Noun Phrase for the Subject of *burst* is constrained by *burst* in this context: it must be a flowering plant (including flowering trees). This collocational relation is evidence for a dependency relation of some sort between the initial Noun Phrase and the Verb. (There is, in fact, another collocational dependency with *burst*, pointed out to me by Kim Allen and illustrated by *The cherry trees burst into flames*. In this construction, the Noun Phrase may denote any combustible object. Nevertheless, the constraint on the initial Noun Phrase still indicates a dependency between it and the Verb.)

Some collocational dependencies appear to be best described as constraints on single lexical items (or phrases) or syntactic categories of lexical items/phrases, like *burst into bloom/flower*. Others appear to be better described as constraints on semantic classes of lexical items/phrases, like *The cherry trees/apple trees/etc. burst*... The fact that some collocational dependencies seem to be syntactic and others semantic poses a problem for their analysis; this problem is addressed in §5.2.

Despite this problem in defining the nature of collocational dependencies, collocational dependencies of the more syntactic sort have played a significant role in syntactic argumentation, because collocational dependencies and coded dependencies often do not line up:

(3) a. Tom **spilled** the **beans**.
    b. The **beans** were **spilled** by Tom.

In (3a), there is a collocational dependency between *spill* and *beans*: in the idiomatic meaning intended here, *spill* allows only the word *beans*. This collocational dependency is called an IDIOM CHUNK, and it is evidence for a relation between *spill* and *beans*. This relation is also supported by coded dependencies in (3a)—immediate postverbal position, and a constituency relation between Verb and NP. Both collocational and coded dependencies appear to support an Object relation between *spill* and *beans* in (3a). In (3b), however, the Object-like collocational dependency clashes with the Subject coded dependency (preverbal position, auxiliary agreement, etc.).

In transformational grammar, the mismatch between collocational and coded dependencies was resolved by establishing two sets of syntactic relations. One set of syntactic relations was called SURFACE STRUCTURE (later, S-structure) and is supported by coded dependencies. The other set of syntactic relations was called DEEP STRUCTURE (later, D-structure) and is supported by collocational dependencies. Transformational (movement) rules operate on deep structures to derive surface structures. For example, the D-structure of a Passive has the collocational Object (*beans*) in the Object syntactic relation to the Verb *spill*. A movement rule then moves the collocational Object to the Subject syntactic relation in S-structure, producing a passive sentence.

Since the 1970s, generative grammar also posits a (syntactic) anaphoric relation between the moved element and the position from which the element was moved. The anaphoric relation is illustrated in this example from a 1992 textbook (Cowper 1992: 84):

(4) a. The **book** was **taken**.
    b. [[ ] was [taken [the book]]] ⇒ [[The book]$_i$ was [taken t_i]]

The anaphoric relation holds between *the book* and the postverbal position which represents its collocational dependency with *take*.

In other cases, collocational dependencies call for anaphoric relations between an overtly expressed syntactic element and a zero element, even when no movement is assumed to have taken place in transformational theory. For example, the Infinitival Complement in (5a) is analyzed as having a (collocationally appropriate) Subject which is anaphorically related to the Main Verb's Object (example from Cowper 1992: 162):[1]

---

[1] In earlier versions of the theory, the deep structure for (5a) had an overt Subject for the Infinitival phrase which was deleted under identity with the Main Clause Object.

(5) a. George begged **Judith** to **feed** the baby.
   b. [George$_j$ [begged [Judith$_i$] [PRO$_i$ [to feed [the baby]]]]]

The existence of collocational dependencies has been widely used as an argument for syntactic relations between elements in generative grammar and related syntactic theories. Where the collocational dependencies do not match with coded dependencies, it has been necessary to find a means to represent the different syntactic relations. This perceived need has resulted in much of the complexity of generative syntactic representations.

In §5.2, I will present the argument by Nunberg et al. (1994) that collocational dependencies are in fact evidence for semantic relations, not syntactic relations. This argument lends support to NONTRANSFORMATIONAL syntactic theories, which make do with only one level or stratum of syntactic representation. Nontransformational theories include Head-driven Phrase Structure Grammar and all construction grammars, including Radical Construction Grammar.

Hence, evidence for syntactic relations in nontransformational theories must be based on coded dependencies: both constituency and other coded dependencies. In §§5.3–5.4, I will present a critique of coded dependencies. The evidence for coded dependencies, like the evidence for global primitive categories, is based on various tests or criteria. As with the criteria for global primitive categories, the various tests are often missing in other languages, and often do not match. Thus, the arguments against global primitive categories also work against global constituency and dependency relations. There are as many types of dependency and constituency relations as there are tests for dependency or constituency. Our goal, as before, is to try to identify cross-linguistically valid tests—more precisely, cross-linguistically valid formal coding properties of "syntactic relations"—and examine which factors determine the language-internal and cross-linguistic variations in the domain of application of the tests.

5.2. Collocational Dependencies as Semantic Relations

Some collocational dependencies appear to be better described in syntactic terms, and others appear to be better described in semantic terms (§5.1.2). In fact, there is a continuum between "syntactic" collocational dependencies and "semantic" ones. The continuum requires a uniform treatment of all collocational dependencies as varying on a single continuous parameter. The question is, what is this parameter?

The most "semantic" of collocational dependencies go by the name of SELECTIONAL RESTRICTIONS. Selectional restrictions are restrictions on possible combinations of words which are determined only by the semantics of the concepts denoted by the word. For example, the restrictions on the use of *mud* and *car* in (6)–(7) follow from the fact that mud is a viscous substance and a car is a machine:

(6) a. **Mud oozed** onto the driveway.
    b. ?*The **car oozed** onto the driveway.
(7) a. The **car started**.
    b. ?***Mud started**.

The restrictions on *mud* and *car* are not dependent on the conventional form in which the concepts are expressed. If one used the word *goo* instead of *mud* or *lawnmower* instead of *car*, the judgments in (6)–(7) would remain the same. The combinations in (6a) and (7a) are SEMANTICALLY COMPOSITIONAL. That is, the meaning of the whole construction is a function of the meaning of the elements of the construction. More precisely, the semantics of the whole construction follows the general rules of semantic composition of expressions in the language. In a componential model of grammar, there are general rules of semantic composition in the semantic component. In a construction grammar model, the general rules of semantic composition correspond to the symbolic relations linking form and meaning in the most schematic or general constructions in the language.

An intermediate point on the continuum of collocational dependencies involves what are called COLLOCATIONS proper. Collocations are combinations of words that are preferred over other combinations which otherwise appear to be semantically equivalent. For example, Matthews argues that *toasted* and *roasted* describe essentially the same process, but are restricted in their acceptable combinations (Matthews 1981: 5):

(8) a. roasted meat
    b. toasted bread
(9) a. ?*toasted meat
    b. ?*roasted bread

Most linguists would analyze (8a–b) as semantically compositional as well. In both cases, the meaning of the whole can be predicted from the meaning of the parts. It is just that speakers of English conventionally use *toasted* with *bread* and *roasted* with *meat*, but not the other way around. This convention does not affect the semantic compositionality of the expressions in (8a–b).

However, the collocational facts in (8a–b) must be represented in a grammar of English. In a construction grammar model, they would be represented as two constructions, something like [*roasted* MEATNoun] and [*toasted* BREADNoun]. Both constructions are instances of the superordinate construction [TRVERB-PASSPART NOUN].

Typically, collocations are expressions that can be interpreted more or less correctly out of context, but cannot be produced correctly if the conventional expression is not already known to the speech community (Nunberg et al. 1994: 495). For example, the expressions in (10a) and (10b) are the American and British terms for the same type of object; each is compositional to the speakers of that dialect, but a speaker of the other dialect would not be able to know what conventional expression is used to refer to that type of object:

(10) a. thumb tack [American English]
   b. drawing pin [British English]

Nunberg et al. argue that exactly the same analysis given above for collocations applies to the great majority of idiom chunks, those that they call IDIOMATICALLY COMBINING EXPRESSIONS. In an idiomatically combining expression, the syntactic parts of the idiom (e.g. *spill* and *beans*) can be identified with parts of the idiom's semantic interpretation ('divulge' and 'information').

Nunberg et al. argue that idiomatically combining expressions are not only semantically analyzable, but also semantically compositional, contrary to the received view. Idiomatically combining expressions are largely fixed in their choice of words. Any substitution leads to ungrammaticality, as in (11b–c) and (12b):

(11) a. Tom **pulled strings** to get the job.
   b. *Tom pulled ropes to get the job.
   c. *Tom grasped strings to get the job.
(12) a. She **spilled** the **beans** about Tom.
   b. *She spilled the succotash about Tom.

However, given the meanings of the words in the idiomatically combining expression, the meaning of the whole expression is compositional:

By convention . . . *strings* can be used metaphorically to refer to personal connection when it is the object of *pull*, and *pull* can be used metaphorically to refer to exploitation or exertion when its object is *strings* (Nunberg et al. 1994: 496).

When we hear *spill the beans* used to mean 'divulge the information', for example, we can assume that *spill* denotes the relation of divulging and *beans* the information that is divulged, even if we cannot say why *beans* should have been used in this expression rather than *succotash*. This is not to say, of course, that *spill* can have the meaning 'divulge' when it does not co-occur with *the beans*, or that *beans* can have the meaning 'information' without *spill*. The availability of these meanings for each constituent can be dependent on the presence of another item without requiring that the meaning 'divulge the information' attach directly to the entire VP. Rather it arises through a convention that assigns particular meaning to its parts when they occur together (ibid.: 497).

At first, Nunberg et al.'s analysis may look odd. To say that *pull* and *strings* each have a meaning found only in *pull strings*, and that those meanings are compositional in the idiomatically combining expression, seems ad hoc. The more natural description appears to be the traditional one, that the meaning of the idiomatically combining expression is noncompositional. In fact, it is sometimes said that one of the strongest pieces of evidence for constructions as independent syntactic objects is that there is some degree of noncompositionality in the meaning of the construction. But there is evidence that Nunberg et al.'s analysis is the right one.

Some English words exist only in idiomatically combining expressions, such as *heed* in *pay heed*. It makes sense to say that *heed* has a meaning that is of course found only in *pay heed*. It appears that the distribution of *heed* is idiosyncratic, because *heed* seems to be essentially synonymous with *attention* in *pay attention*, and yet does not behave the same way (Nunberg et al. 1994: 505, citing an argument from Radford 1988):

(13) a. You can't expect to have my **attention/*heed** all the time.
  b. He's a child who needs a lot of **attention/*heed**.

Nunberg et al. argue that in fact *heed* does not mean the same thing as *attention* does, when *attention* is the object of *pay* (Nunberg et al. 1994: 505):

(14) a. You can't expect to have my **attention/*heed** all the time.
  b. He's a child who needs a lot of **attention/*heed**.
(15) a. The children paid rapt **attention/?*heed** to the circus.
  b. I pay close **attention/?*heed** to my clothes.

The semantic differences are related to the difference between the verbs *attend* and *heed*: 'we clearly attend to much that we do not heed ... one can take heed but not attention, and ... attention but not heed can wander' (ibid.: 506). In other words, *heed* in *pay heed* does have its own meaning even though it occurs (as a noun) in only that combination. Nunberg et al. write:

[The] highly restricted distributions [of *heed* and *dint*] indicate that their meanings are so highly specialized as to be compatible with only one or two predicates. Such dependencies are simply the limiting case of selectional restrictions, which are generally recognized to be semantic in nature (ibid.: 506).

Hence, it is reasonable to assume that other words have specialized meanings in idiomatically combining expressions, and that those meanings are semantically compositional.

Another piece of evidence for the compositionality of idiomatically combining expressions is psycholinguistic. Speakers of English recognize the meanings of words in idiomatically combining expressions, and recognize them as figurative meanings, even though the figurative meanings are found only in the idiomatically combining expressions (Gibbs 1990). The clearest manifestation of this fact is the syntactic modification of parts of idiomatically combining expressions, as in *My life rug had been pulled out from under me* (a woman on Jerry Garcia's death; Associated Press, 9 Aug. 2000). These two pieces of evidence point to Nunberg et al.'s conclusion that 'The dependency among the parts of idiomatically combining expressions is thus fundamentally semantic in nature' (Nunberg et al. 1994: 505).

Nunberg et al.'s analysis of idiomatically combining expressions is more natural in construction grammar than in a componential grammar. An idiomatically combining expression such as *spill the beans* is a construction. As a construction, it has unique syntax: the verb must be *spill* and its object must be *the beans*. It also has a semantic interpretation, namely 'divulge information'. All Nunberg et al. are saying is that this construction has its own semantic interpretation rules, mapping *spill* onto 'divulge' and *the beans* onto 'information.' The constructional analysis is presented in the diagram in Figure 5.2 (p. 183).

The whole construction *spill the beans* has the meaning DIVULGE THE INFORMATION; this fact is represented by the symbolic relation joining *spill the*

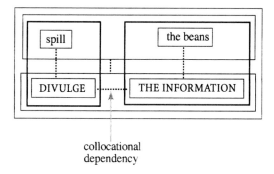

Figure 5.2. Construction grammar representation of an idiomatically combining expression

beans and [DIVULGE THE INFORMATION], and the box indicating the entire construction. The syntactic structure is divided into two elements, and the semantic structure is divided into two components. Nunberg et al.'s semantic analysis of *spill* and *the beans* in the context of the idiomatically combining expression is represented by the two symbolic units in boldface boxes. The collocational dependency between *spill* and *the beans* is semantic, as indicated in Figure 5.2.

Nunberg et al.'s analysis is even more natural in Radical Construction Grammar than in a reductionist construction grammar. In Radical Construction Grammar, the whole construction is the primitive unit of representation and the parts are derivative. Thus, the meaning of the whole construction, [DIVULGE INFORMATION], is basic and the analysis into parts, in this case [*spill*/DIVULGE] and [*the beans*/INFORMATION] is derived from the meaning of the whole and the breakdown of the whole into parts.

What Nunberg et al. have done is dissociate conventionality from noncompositionality. Idiomatically combining expressions are not noncompositional. There are truly noncompositional expressions: these are IDIOMATIC PHRASES such as *saw logs* and *kick the bucket*. However, idiomatic phrases appear to be far less common than idiomatically combining expressions; compare the list of idiomatic phrases in Nunberg et al. (1994: 532, example 70), with the appendix of idiomatically combining expressions in their paper.

Other analysts have assumed that an idiomatically combining expression is noncompositional because the meaning of the whole is not predictable from the meaning of the parts when those parts appear in expressions other than the idiom. But what is unusual about idiomatically combining expressions is not that they are noncompositional but their meanings do not conform to the semantic interpretation rules of the more schematic syntactic structures such as [VERB OBJECT]$_{VP}$ in the case of *spill the beans*. *Spill the beans* is compositional: the parts of the syntactic expression can be mapped onto components of the meaning of the idiom, as in Figure 5.2. The way that *spill the beans* differs from regular syntactic expressions is that there are rules of semantic interpretation associated with just that construction, which are not derivable from the superordinate [VERB OBJECT]$_{VP}$ construction of which *spill the beans* is an instance. In other words, idiomatically combining expressions differ from more regular expressions in their LACK OF GENERALITY, NOT in their compositionality. Degree of generality is the parameter on which collocational dependencies vary.

Thus, the common perception that a particular construction must be represented as an independent syntactic unit because it is noncompositional is incorrect. Idioms (other than idiomatic phrases) are compositional. The reason that they must be represented as independent constructions is that semantic interpretation rules associated with the construction are very specific, in fact unique to that construction, and not derived from another more general syntactic pattern, as construction grammarians carefully note (see, e.g., Goldberg 1995: 13 and Michaelis and Lambrecht 1996: 219).

Conversely, one can think of the most schematic constructions of a language as highly general idiomatically combining expressions. Consider for example the English Predicate Adjective construction, illustrated in (16), and its semantic interpretation:

(16) Hannah **is smart**.

The English Predicate Adjective construction has the form [PREDADJSBJ *be* PREDADJ] in Radical Construction Grammar. The members of the PredAdj category have a meaning which requires them to be combined with the Copula *be* in order to be interpreted as ascribing a property to a referent (unlike Verbs). The Copula *be* has a meaning that requires combination with a member of the PredAdj category in order to be interpreted as doing the job of ascribing (a property) to the Subject phrase.

This analysis is no different from the description of the semantics of idiomatically combining expressions given above. In fact, this is essentially the same semantic analysis that Langacker argues for (Langacker 1987: 214–22, 1991a: 204–5). Using Langacker's terminology, PredAdj denotes an atemporal relation, and the Copula *be* denotes a process with which PredAdj meanings must be combined in order to be predicated. It would also be identical to a categorial grammar analysis in which PredAdj must be of a semantic type which, when combined with *be*, can then be combined with constituents of type Sbj to yield a proposition.

The consequences of Nunberg et al.'s analysis of collocational dependencies for syntactic theory are substantial. Coded dependencies are represented in syntactic structure, while collocational dependencies are represented in semantic structure (see Figure 5.2). The clashes between collocational dependencies and coded dependencies disappear, because the former are semantic and the latter are not. (One of the great ironies of syntactic theory is that generative grammarians claim that syntactic representation is autonomous from semantic representation; yet much of the syntactic machinery of generative grammar is justified on the basis of evidence that is in fact semantic, not syntactic.) Nunberg et al.'s argument immensely strengthens the case for nontransformational theories of syntactic representation. Nunberg et al. draw this conclusion, not surprisingly, since they are associated with a nontransformational syntactic theory. Their argument also strengthens the case for construction grammar, which also uses only a single level of representation of syntactic structure.

Treating collocational dependencies as semantic makes more sense than treating them as syntactic. One can find examples of collocations or idiomatically combining expressions, such as *mad inventor* in (17), where syntactic representation of the collocational dependency would call for an extremely abstract deep structure:

(17) Mr Wichterle, a Czech, was a bit **mad** in an **inventor**ish sort of way (*The Economist*, 5 September 1998, p. 107).

The consequences of Nunberg et al.'s argument for methods of syntactic argumentation are also great. One is of course left with many fewer arguments for particular syntactic relations, namely only those arguments from constituency, linear order and overtly coded dependencies. Moreover, we must search for cross-linguistically valid methods for identifying these, which will turn out to be fewer than those usually appealed to in the syntactic literature. Nevertheless, as we will see in the rest of this chapter, even the remaining criteria for syntactic relations do not match up within languages.

5.3. Constituency and Linear Order

5.3.1. *Arguments for constituency*

CONSTITUENT STRUCTURE, also called phrase structure, is a grouping of elements in a syntactic structure. These groupings are commonly represented in syntactic theory by the bracketing of constituents, as in (18a), or by a tree diagram, as in (18b):

(18) a. [I [put [the book]$_{NP}$ [on [the shelf]$_{NP}$]$_{PP}$]$_{VP}$]$_S$
     b.

The constituent structures illustrated in (18) represent the simpler structures used in earlier versions of generative grammar. More elaborate structures are employed in more recent versions of the theory for a number of reasons, including the representation of null elements in order to capture collocational dependency relations, and the syntactic representation of inflectional categories such as agreement and case. I have argued that collocational dependencies are in fact semantic dependencies (§5.2); for agreement and case marking, see §5.4 below. Hence, the central question for us to examine is the status of constituents of the type illustrated in (18).

Constituent structure is assumed to represent a global (§1.5.3), abstract structure of syntactic constituent relations for a given sentence. Thus, arguments must be provided for the constituent structure of a sentence. Textbooks which discuss arguments for constituency (e.g. McCawley 1998) use a variety of criteria to establish constituency relations. But these arguments are also instances of language-internal methodological opportunism (§1.5.2). In the rest of this section, I will discuss a number of arguments for constituency, and show how they do not satisfy the requirement for a cross-linguistically valid criterion for putative constituency relations.

Before proceeding, however, an important methodological point must be made. Semantic relations, including of course collocational dependencies, are NOT evidence for or against syntactic constituency (or any other type of syntactic relation). Thus, the semantic structure of (19a), something like (19b), is not evidence that [*the girl*] and [*a new violin*] are separate constituents, even though *the girl* and *a new violin* denote two separate referents, each of which is a participant in the main verb event:

(19) a. Mary gave **the girl a new violin**.
  b. *Give(Mary,girl,violin)*

Yet our intuitions about basic constituency relations in sentences are almost entirely based on semantics. The semantic basis of constituency is the principle of iconicity (see §3.1, §6.4), namely that in most cases, syntactic contiguity reflects semantic relations. While this principle holds in most cases (see §6.5.1), it is possible that syntactic relations will not reflect semantic relations.

In fact, the conflict between semantically based intuitions and syntactic contiguity as criteria for constituency can be illustrated by so-called "discontinuous constituents". An example of a "discontinuous constituent" is the pair of bracketed elements in the Warlpiri example in (20) (Hale 1973: 214):

(20) [**tjaṇṭu-ŋku**] ∅-tju   yalku-ṇu   [**wiṛi-ŋki**]
  dog-ERG   (AUX)-me bite-PST   **big-ERG**
  'The big dog bit me.'

The Adjective *wiṛi-ŋki* 'big-ERG' appears to be a modifier of the Noun *tjaṇṭu-ŋku* 'dog-ERG', since it describes a property of the dog, and agrees with it in Case. In other words, Adjective plus Noun appear to be a constituent. However, the two words are not contiguous.

But "discontinuous constituent" is a syntactic oxymoron. It simply means that there is a mismatch between the criterion of contiguity and the semantic relations holding among the corresponding components in the semantic structure of the construction. The only reason that the two elements in (20) are treated as constituents is because of the semantic relation holding between the dog and its property of large size.

In some languages, including Warlpiri, each noncontiguous element must be inflected for the relevant Case enclitic. In contrast, when the two elements are contiguous, only one Case enclitic is found (Hale 1973: 214):

(21) [tjaṇṭu   wiṛi-ŋki]   ∅-tju   yaḷku-ṇu
     dog   big-ERG   (AUX)-me   bite-PST
     '[The big dog] bit me.'

This structural difference indicates that there are two separate consituents in (20), each marked by the Case enclitic.

In (20), the two constituents occur at the beginning and the end of the sentence. This pattern appears to be common among languages with "discontinuous constituents": the two constituents are performing different discourse functions. In Polish, the initial and final elements have the function of contrastive focus and contrastive topic, as in the following double-contrastive sentence (as a response to a remark like 'Apparently they have a beautiful house'; Siewierska 1984: 60):

(22) Nie!   [Piękny]   mają   [ogród].   [Dom]   mają   [kiepski]
     no   beautiful   have   garden   house   have   crummy
     'No! They have a beautiful garden. Their house is crummy.'

In Wardaman, the two constituents are almost always found at the beginning and end of intonation units (Merlan 1994: 241):

(23) [lege   walanja]   nga   -ga   -ndi   go   [yidinen   -bi]
     one(ABS)   goanna(ABS)   1SG-   take   -PST   3SG.DAT   whole   -ART
     'I took one goanna for him whole (i.e. one whole goanna)'

Merlan suggests that the initial element is thematic, while the final element is the information focus (e.g. it is contrastive; Merlan 1994: 242).

In other words, the structure of the grammatical unit conforms to information structure, which conflicts with the object–property relationship. The object–property relationship is instead encoded by overt expressions of coded dependencies, that is the identical case forms of the two constituents in both Polish and Wardaman. The "discontinuous noun phrase" is a distinct construction, for Wardaman [TOPICNP-CASE$_i$ ... FOCUSNP-CASE$_i$]. Other examples of so-called "discontinuous constituents" may turn out to be distinct constructions with a distinct discourse function and their own constraints on contiguity and position of elements (Siewierska 1984: 70).

I now turn to properly syntactic criteria for constituency, drawn partially from McCawley (1998, ch. 3). One commonly used criterion for constituency is PRONOMINALIZATION, that is, the possibility of substituting a single word unit for a complex unit (McCawley 1998: 67). For example, the two putative constituents bracketed in (24) can be replaced by simple Pronouns, as in (25):

(24) [**The little girl**] sat [**on the couch**].
(25) [**She**] sat [**here**].

However, pronominalization is not a fully universal test for constituency. It presupposes the universal existence of pro-forms for the putative constituent. Pro-forms such as pronouns are probably universal for phrasal arguments and adjuncts, but probably not always for finite and nonfinite clausal arguments and adjuncts. For other proposed constituents, for example those bracketed in (26), overt pro-forms are not widely found across languages:

(26) a. the [**blue flowers**]$_{N'}$
     b. I [**bought some bread**]$_{VP}$.

Even if pro-forms exist, however, the construction for pro-forms may be different from that for full phrases. In Spanish for example, the Object Noun Phrase constituent follows the Verb (*compré* 'I bought' in (27)), but the Object Pronoun occurs in a proclitic construction before the Verb (28):

(27) Compré [**el libro**]$_{NP}$ ayer.
     'I bought the book yesterday.'
(28) [**Lo**]$_{Prn}$ compré ayer.
     'I bought it yesterday.'

Another often-used test for constituency is ELLIPSIS, which can be thought of as null pronominalization (McCawley 1998: 67). The classic example in English is what is called Verb Phrase Deletion (or V'-Deletion):

(29) Lydia won't [**go to San Francisco**]$_{VP}$, but I will [Ø].

In the majority of the world's languages, argument phrases can be null (see the Spanish examples in (30)), thereby appearing to offer evidence that argument phrases are constituents:

(30) a. [**Los gatos**]$_{NP}$ estaban durmiendo.
        'The cats were sleeping.'
     b. [Ø] Estaban durmiendo.
        '(They) were sleeping'

Ellipsis as a criterion for constituency suffers from the same problems as pro-forms. Elliptical constructions are found for only a subset of putative constituents.

The elliptical construction is a distinct construction from its nonelliptical counterpart, and so it may not be valid to infer a constituent structure for the nonelliptical construction on the basis of what is elided in the elliptical construction.

Finally, one would have to identify cross-linguistically valid criteria for distinguishing constructions in which the elided material is claimed to be a constituent, as with VP-Deletion, and those in which the elided material is not a constituent, as with the Stripping construction in (31) (McCawley 1998: 55):

(31) John plays poker on Fridays, but not bridge.

In (31), the elided material is the discontinuous string *John plays . . . on Fridays*.

Yet another commonly invoked criterion for constituency is the ability to CONJOIN the constituents in a coordinate construction: it is assumed that only constituents can be conjoined (McCawley 1998: 58). Examples of various putative constituents in English coordinate constructions are given in (32):

(32) a. [**The boys**]$_{NP}$ and [**the girls**]$_{NP}$ should come to the front.
 b. I [**went outside**]$_{VP}$ and [**looked for my cat**]$_{VP}$.
 c. I'm not going because [**I'm tired**]$_S$ and [**my feet hurt**]$_S$.

However, not all languages have coordinate constructions for many constituent types (Mithun 1988: 336). Also, some English coordinate constructions support "constituents" that are not supported by other criteria (the transformational names for these constructions are given in the examples):

(33) *Gapping*: Jenny gave [**the books to Randy**]$_?$ and [**the magazines to Bill**]$_?$.
(34) *Right Node Raising*: [**Jenny makes**]$_?$ and [**Randy sells**]$_?$ the prints.

Coordination of grammatical units, including even the types of units conjoined in Gapping and Right Node Raising, is argued by Wierzbicka (1980, ch. 7) to represent a certain kind of conceptual grouping, what she calls a 'general formula' (see §9.2.3). This kind of conceptual grouping is a linguistic phenomenon in its own right. But it is a property of coordinate constructions, not an indicator of a global constituent structure.

The criteria for constituency described in this section fail as cross-linguistically valid criteria for a global constituent structure. The tests do not necessarily exist in all languages. Different test constructions give different results: compare VP Deletion to Stripping for null anaphora, and Conjunction Reduction to Gapping and Right Node Raising for coordination. A decision to choose one construction over another as a "test" for constituency is opportunistic. In many cases, the choice of construction as a criterion for constituency is based on intuitions about semantic relations, not syntactic ones. Yet the use of semantic criteria leads to mismatches with syntactic criteria such as contiguity ("discontinuous constituents").

In sum, we must abandon the goal of finding a global constituent structure. Instead, we must look at genuinely cross-linguistically valid criteria for something like constituency, and not assume that the criteria will yield a single global constituent structure. In fact, because of the connotations of 'constituency', it is probably best not to use the term and instead speak of (FORMAL) GROUPING, as Langacker suggests in a 1997 article:

> constituents are neither essential nor fundamental to linguistic structure, but emerge in special circumstances. They reflect the basic psychological capacity for *grouping*, which is guided by the gestalt principles of *contiguity* and *similarity* (Langacker 1997: 9, emphasis in original).

The next section describes three cross-linguistically valid criteria for the formal grouping of elements.

5.3.2. *From constituency to formal grouping*

The single cross-linguistically valid syntactic criterion for formal grouping is the CONTIGUITY of elements in the utterance. The converse of contiguity is SEPARABILITY, that is, the ability to insert other elements between the two elements in question. However, contiguity/separability is not as simple a criterion as it appears at first sight.

Separability depends on what is interrupting the putative constituent:

(35) a. I found [the Ø tieclasp]
 b. I found [the **gold** tieclasp]
 c. I found [the ***yesterday** tieclasp]
 d. I found [the **whatsitcalled** tieclasp]

The words *the* and *tieclasp* in (70a) are contiguous, but they are separated by the modifier *gold* in (70b). The usual analysis of (70b) is that *gold* is part of the same constituent as *the* and *tieclasp*, in contrast with *yesterday* in (70c). This leaves the problem of parentheticals such as *whatsitcalled* in (70d), although in most cases, the parenthetical is modifying the contiguous element (in this case, *tieclasp*) in one way or another.

English is generally assumed to be a relatively rigid language when it comes to linear order and consituency, and thus contiguity relations are relatively easy to identify. In (35), I give some attested examples that suggest that even in English, contiguity relations in constructions are not as tightly fixed as constituent structure analyses imply (for further examples, see McCawley 1991: 75, under 'Misplacements'):

(36) a. "I never [got **really** the full story]"—Carol T., 24.5.84
 b. "and [the father **in the meantime** of this family] . . ." [speaker went on to describe the father]—Melissa B., 31.5.98
 c. "These things aren't yet in [wide **enough** spread] use"—Terry W., 23.4.84

The examples in (35)–(36) suggest that contiguity is a matter of degree, and should be defined along a continuum, where the highest degree of contiguity is morphological attachment. It may be argued that examples (36a–c) are due to performance errors. However, without an independently motivated theory of performance, such examples cannot be dismissed in this fashion. On the other hand, there have not been any detailed studies of patterns of syntactic contiguity in actual discourse to my knowledge.

Contiguity is a property of the syntactic structure of constructions. As such, it is important to decide whether two sentences with different patterns of contiguous elements are instances of the same construction. Sometimes is it not obvious whether two different sentences are instances of a single construction or of two different constructions. For example, (37a–b) might be analyzed as instances of the same construction which happens to allow permutation of its constituents:

(37) a. **A guy [who I hadn't seen since high school]** came in.
b. **A guy** came in **[who I hadn't seen since high school]**.

If (37a–b) are instances of the same construction, then the separation of the Noun Phrase *a guy* and the Relative Clause *who I hadn't seen since high school* in (37b) would be evidence against analyzing [*a guy who I hadn't seen since high school*] as a syntactic group in the construction in (37a).

However, a more careful constructional analysis demonstrates that (37a) and (37b) are instances of two different constructions. In order to demonstrate that (37a–b) are instances of a single construction with variable positions of the relative clause, one must come up with a schematic characterization of the superordinate construction's structure (§1.6.4). This is not possible for (37a–b). First, the schematic description of a construction subsuming both (37a) and (37b) would have to say that the position of the Relative Clause is free, but in fact it can occur only either next to the Noun Phrase it modifies or at the end of the Sentence. Second, there are instances of the construction illustrated by (37b) that have no counterparts in the construction type illustrated by (37a) (McCawley 1998: 771):

(38) **A man** entered and **a woman** left [who had met in Vienna].

The only equivalent to (38) that looks like (37a) is actually quite different; in fact it involves yet another construction type:

(39) **A man and a woman [who had met in Vienna]** entered and left **respectively**.

Hence (37b) represents a distinct construction from (37a), the Extraposed Relative Clause construction. Therefore the constituent structure of (37b) does not tell us anything about the constituent structure of (37a).

Another type of formal grouping in syntax is defined not (just) by syntactic contiguity but also by prosodic unity: the occurrence of a grammatical unit in a single INTONATION UNIT. Patterns of occurrence of grammatical units in intonation units have been investigated in detail for English (Quirk et al. 1964; Crystal 1975; Chafe 1980, 1994; Altenberg 1987; Croft 1995c) and Wardaman, (Merlan

1994; Croft 1997). The same general principles governing the distribution of grammatical units (GUs) over intonation units appear to hold in both languages, although they are typologically quite different; this is an indication that we have captured a level of grammatical description that is cross-linguistically valid.

First, both languages largely conform to the following condition:

(40) *The Full Grammatical Unit (GU) Condition*: virtually all intonation units are grammatical units, as the latter are usually analyzed on syntactic and semantic criteria (Croft 1995c: 845).

The Full GU Condition applies to 97 percent of the English IUs studied and 96.5 percent of the Wardaman IUs. The Full GU Condition is a manifestation of the close relationship between prosodic structure and grammatical structure.

Three general constraints on the occurrence of grammatical units in intonation units were found to hold in both languages. First, PARALLEL units, such as conjuncts in coordination or apposition, are broken into separate intonation units (Croft 1995c: 851 and Merlan 1994: 494; the numbers index the number of the text and the lines excerpted from the text):

(41) 10,186   [1.0] I mean it's just .. it wasn't .. I didn't get a specific feeling like **this is** [1.8 [.95] u—m [.5]] **this is Mexico,**
       10,187   **or this is** [2.3 [1.2] u—m [.6]] **the southern part of the United States,**
       10,188   or anything like that.

(42) XVI,10   wujujurlma   -ya   Ø-   gaygba   -rri   -ya   **lege**   -yi
              pocket.RDP   -LOC   3SG-   call   -PST   -NARR   **one**   -ADVR
      XVI,11   **ngarnaj**   -bi
              self   -ART
              'in the pocket he called alone, by himself'

The parallelism constraint implies that with respect to prosody, parallel units are separate constituents, in contrast to the most common constituent structure analyses of parallel units where they form a single larger constituent. Only parallel grammatical units that are conceived of as a single conceptual unit (see §9.2.3) are found under a single intonation contour (Mithun 1988: 331–6). For example, in Gurung, a cape and dress constitute a Gurung girl's costume, replacing the ragged dress baby girls wear; hence, the phrase 'cape and skirt' is found in a single intonation unit (Mithun 1988: 332, from Glover 1974: 210.22):

(43) jxa·lé   ŋxywí   coló   pi̧   -m
      then   **cape**   **skirt**   give   -NPST
      'The (we) give (the girls) a cape and skirt.'

The second constraint is that the more COMPLEX a grammatical unit is, in terms of the number of elements in the grammatical unit and their type (lexical, phrasal, clausal), the more likely it is to be broken across separate units. Examples (44)–(45) illustrate this principle with a Relative Clause Verb with two heavy NPs and two Adverbs (English; Croft 1995c: 859) or a Noun Phrase with a Phrasal modifier (Wardaman; Merlan 1994: 410, glosses modified).

(44) 14,100 [1.55 [.95] a—nd [.15]] then you switch back to the ma—n,
 14,101 that's [.4] **climbing down out of the tree,**
 14,102 **again with another .. pouchful of .. of pears.**
(45) III,338 yibarnang
  FZ(ABS)
  'aunties'
 III,339 nganinggin -gu yibiyi wu
  mine -DAT father -DAT
  'my father's'
 III,340 wok wurr- yana -rri -ya
  work 3NSG- do -PST -NARR
  'worked'
  'My father's aunties worked [for whites].'

The third general constraint is DISTANCE: the greater the semantic distance between two elements of a grammatical unit, the more likely they are to be broken into separate intonation units. For example, the semantically more distant circumstantial dependents boldface in (46) and (48) are in separation intonation units, in contrast to the verbal dependents in boldface in (47) and (49) (Croft 1995c: 863 and Merlan 1994: 465, 446).

(46) 13,86 [.2] and **in exchange,**
 13,87 .. the boy gives him three pears.
(47) 7,85 and they each have a pear **in their hands,**
(48) XI,32 **alibala -wan wirrig** na
  early -DISC tomorrow now
 XI,33 Ø- galma -rri na
  3SG- mount -PST now
  'and early the next day he got on a horse'
(49) IX,37 **yi- wol** Ø- na -rri nangarrij -marla
  YI.CL- shadow(ABS) 3SG- see -PST shift -ITER
  'he saw the shadow moving'

I hypothesized that the GUs that occur in a single IU are stored in the mind as whole constructions, thereby putting an upper limit on the syntactic complexity of stored linguistic units (the IU Storage Hypothesis; Croft 1995c: 872). Constructions that are broken across multiple IUs are computed, and it is the greater processing load, at least for complex structures, that leads to production in separate intonation units.

For parallel constituents and more distant constituents, there is probably a different sort of process involved, namely EXTENSION (Ford et al. 1997). Extension is the addition of a grammatical unit after a point of closure for interactional reasons. A point of closure is defined by completion of the grammatical unit; hence extensions are more distantly related to the GU than the units that precede closure. Extensions are typically semantic adjuncts, but the additions and elaborations expressed by conjoined phrases and appositive phrases respectively also satisfy the functional definition of extensions.

Another criterion for formal grouping that comes from the structure of naturally occurring discourse is the UNIT OF FIRST-POSITION SELF-REPAIR (Fox and Jasperson 1995). The proximate cause for repair in conversation is that the speaker wishes to re-execute an utterance, usually but not always with changes to the grammatical structure of the utterance (hence, "correcting errors" is not completely appropriate as a description). Ultimate causes for repair include real time response to hearer feedback, holding the floor, problems in realizing simultaneous but independent interactional goals, and memory failure (Fox and Jasperson 1995: 125).

Fox and Jasperson investigate first-position self-repair, that is, repair by the speaker of the same turn constructional unit (TCU), that is before the point of projected closure of utterance. Fox and Jasperson note that the Full GU Condition also applies to repair: 'The repairing segment of an utterance is integrated using normal syntax. . . . The segment that follows the site of repair initiation is always syntactically coherent in our data, that is, it forms a syntactic constituent' (Fox and Jasperson 1995: 108). The choice of a repairing segment is motivated by the need of the hearer to fit the repairing segment in with the previous material, usually with some repetition. However, only certain syntactic choices are actually found in first-position self-repair.

Fox and Jasperson observe that it appears that repair can always occur at word-level, as in example (50) (Fox and Jasperson 1995: 103, 99; their Types A and B; the repaired segment is in brackets and the repairing segment in italics):

(50) a. ^C: He's a [good-*] *good* student
    b. ^G: .hh VI (1.0) [is:*] (1.2) *h-has* (0.2) modes associated with it.

Also, repair can always occur at the level of the whole TCU (Fox and Jasperson 1995: 101, their Type G; their notation in (51) is modified to show the extent of the repair):

(51) ^M: [You have to figure out the uh-*] (1.0) *I don't know what it was.*

The remaining types of repair represent RECYCLING (backing up to the beginning of) certain grammatical units. Repair within phrases can recycle to the beginning of the Noun Phrase, or the beginning of the Prepositional Phrase (i.e. NP or PP recycling is found; Fox and Jasperson 1995: 101, 102, 103):

(52) B: .hh Hey do you see [V-*] (0.3) *fat old Vivian* anymore?
(53) ^K: Now I'm going to look (0.5) [at my*] (1.1) *at this,*
(54) H: .hh And tshe- this girl's fixed up on [a da-*] *a blind date.*

In repair within clauses, repairs from the Verb onwards recycle the whole Clause, not the Verb Phrase (Verb plus arguments; Fox and Jasperson 1995: 98, 97):

(55) ^D: you know you got this 300 electron volts, [and you go-*] *and you always go*, oh my god what (0.4) is an electron volt
(56) ^M: Taking physics 302. [I didn't have-*] (0.4) *I had* 301, but I had it a long time ago at Arizona State.

In other words, first-position self-repair defines a type of formal grouping for the English Noun Phrase, the Prepositional Phrase, and the Clause, but not Verb Phrases.[2]

Fox and Jasperson's data also indicate that some "parenthetical" expressions are part of the grammatical units, that is, they are constituents with respect to this criterion of constituency:

(57) ^D: for instance- [you might have*], in this case you don't, but *let's say you might have* the mass, of one of these things on both sides
(58) ^G: Now this terminal (1.2) is smart enough to show you (0.4) that you're in (1.6) [ins-*] *what they call insert* mode or append mode.

That is, first-position self-repair formally groups parenthetical elements with the unit it modifies.

First-position self-repair can also be used to identify more complex constructions. Hopper illustrates Pseudocleft sentences including the following example from the Collins Cobuild corpus of spoken English (Hopper 2000):

(59) And in defence I mean [what snakes or what animals try-*] *like what most animals try to do is* if they tha have got a poisonous property is another animal attacks them they give them er a dose of venom which will not kill them it will just deter them next time

In (59), a first-position self-repair recycles to the beginning of the clefted Clause (*what* . . .) in the Pseudocleft construction.

This section has examined three cross-linguistically valid criteria for formal grouping of elements in a construction: syntactic contiguity/separation, occurrence in a single intonation unit, and unit of first-position self-repair. All three of these properties can be identified in any language given a corpus of utterances and the relevant prosodic properties. As such, the various formal grouping properties described in this section are available to the hearer without positing any abstract constituent structure. The three criteria do not match, and yield different formal groupings. Also, at least the first two are gradient. But this is not a problem in a theory such as Radical Construction Grammar without a unique abstract constituent structure. Instead, the formal structure of the construction also indicates separability of elements and prosodic groupings.

---

[2] There is a possible confounding factor in the examples in Fox and Jasperson's paper: all of the examples of clause recycling involve a Pronominal Subject. It may be that the English Pronominal Subject is really a proclitic and that is why recycling does not stop before the Subject.

5.3.3. *Linear order and formal grouping*

Linear order, like formal grouping, is a cross-linguistically observable property of the syntactic structure of utterances. Also like formal grouping, the linear order of elements in a construction can encode semantic roles in a construction's meaning. For example, in Cantonese, linear order is used to encode semantic roles without any overt coded dependency (Matthews and Yip 1994: 68):

(60) **ngóh** ngoi **kéuih**
     1SG   love 3SG
     'I love her.'

(61) **kéuih** ngoi **ngóh**
     3SG   love 1SG
     'She loves me.'

In (60)–(61), there is no change in form of either the Pronouns or the Verb to indicate which NP has the A semantic role and which has the P role; only linear order indicates the semantic role.

Linear order is a much more straightforward property of utterances than the various properties that indicate formal grouping. However, linear order is usually combined with constituent structure in syntactic representations. That is, a phrase structure syntactic representation such as [NP [V NP]] not only specifies that [V NP] is a subconstituent of [NP [V NP]], it also specifies that the order of elements is the order given in the representation, namely NP < V < NP. However, there is evidence that linear order can vary independently of formal grouping. That is, a conventional grammatical constraint of contiguity may not specify the relative order of the contiguous elements.

For example, in many languages, such as Ute, the relative order of elements in the finite clause construction is not fixed. In example (62), the Subject follows the Verb, while in (63), the Subject precedes and the Object follows the Verb, and in (64), both the Subject and the Object precede the verb (Givón 1980a: 318–19):

(62) 'u-náàga̲   kwaví- -pọrọ -pu̲gá   tuá-ci-u   'úmu̲
     there.in   lie.PL- -go   -REM   child.PL   they.SBJ
                         V   S
     'they were swimming in there, the children were'

(63) 'ú   paví   -ci̲   páay   -pu̲gá -amu̲   'umú̲   tuá-ci-u-av
     that.SBJ   Beaver -SBJ call   -REM   -them them.OBJ child.PL.own
     S   V   O
     'so Beaver called them, those children of his'

(64) xwa̲-'urá ta'wá -ci̲   'u   piwá   -av   'uwáy   máy -pu̲gáy -u
     then   man   -SBJ that.SBJ spouse -own   her.OBJ say -REM   -her
               S   O   V
     'so then one day the man told his wife ...'

A highly schematic construction covering all Ute Clauses would be of the form [SBJ, OBJ, VERB], the comma notation explicitly indicating that the order of elements is not fixed.

It has been observed by many analysts that word order in so-called "free word order" languages such as Ute is in fact not "free", but instead encodes discourse function (information structure). For example, in O'odham (Papago), a language closely related to Ute, Payne's analysis of a corpus of texts indicated that virtually every order of Subject and Object were found, but that Focused and Indefinite NPs are consistently preverbal and Definite NPs are consistently postverbal (Payne 1987: 788, 794–5). This generalization can be captured by abstracting a construction schema such as [INDEF/FOCUSNP < VERB < DEFNP], which indicates information structure only, not argument structure. Thus, the argument structure constructions linking participants to syntactic roles will lack specification of the linear order of their elements.

Even in a relatively rigid word order language such as English, linear order is not specified in many of the more schematic constructions. For example, a schematic argument structure construction such as the ditransitive construction [SBJ, VERB, OBJ1, OBJ2] does not specify linear order of its elements. Instead, linear order is specified by other English constructions:

(65) a. *Active Declarative*: I gave Becky a bottle of champagne.
 b. *"Topicalization"*: Becky I gave a bottle of champagne.
 c. *Information Question*: What did you give Becky?
 d. *Relative Clause*: the bottle of champagne that I gave Becky

Thus, linear order should be dissociated from the theoretical concept of formal grouping.

5.4. Overtly Coded Dependencies

5.4.1. *Typological classification of overtly coded dependencies*

Syntactic relations are often explicitly or overtly coded by morphemes whose chief function appears to be expressing that dependency relation. Nichols (1986) proposes a typological classification based on the syntactic status of the element to which the morpheme is affixed. However, this classification is problematic. Instead, a classification based on the semantics of the morpheme expressing the dependency provides a means to identify types of coded dependencies across languages (Croft 1988).

Nichols proposes a typological classification distinguishing head-marking and dependent-marking languages. Nichols classifies whole languages as head-marking or dependent-marking, but this raises problems when some constructions are head-marking and others are dependent-marking in a single language (Croft 1990a: 33–4). For this reason, I will apply Nichols's classification to specific constructions.

A head-marking construction encodes the dependency relation between head and dependent on the head element, while a dependent-marking construction encodes the dependency relation on the dependent element. The Russian Finite Clause construction illustrates both head-marking and dependent-marking:

(66) pis'm   -o   lež   -it   na   stol   -e
     letter.N -NOM.SG   lie   -3SG.PRS on   table.M -LOC.SG
     'The letter is lying on the table.'

The head is the Verb 'lie' and one of the dependents is the Subject 'letter'. The Verb is marked for 3rd Person Singular Agreement with the Subject (the suffix -*it*); this is a typical example of head marking. The Subject is marked with a Nominative Case suffix -*o* indicating the syntactic relation that holds between 'letter' and 'lie'. This is a prototypical example of dependent marking.

However, there are a number of problems in this typological classification of coded dependencies. It requires that one can identify heads and dependents across languages; in fact, it presuppose a syntactic theory of heads and dependents. But the notion of 'head' is beset with the same problems as the other syntactic notions discussed so far (see Chapter 7). Hence the basis for the classification is thrown into doubt.

Another problem with Nichol's classification is the status of morphologically independent elements that encode dependencies. In many languages, case marking is not found on nouns, but instead adpositions encode dependencies, as in Rumanian (Nandris 1945: 145) and of course English:

(67) pune   cartea   **pe** masă!
     put:IMP   book:DEF   on   table
     'Put the book **on** the table!'

In some languages, the person agreement form is not affixed to the verb, but is a morphologically independent element, as in Woleaian (Sohn 1975: 93):

(68) Sar   kelaal   **re** sa   tangiteng
     child   those   3SG   ASP   cry.RDP
     'Those children over there cried and cried.'

Finally, it is not clear that head marking vs. dependent marking is a useful natural class. In typological research, "head marking" is de facto identified with person agreement of verbs with their core arguments, nouns with their possessors, and adpositions with their complements. "Dependent marking" is de facto identified with case marking of noun phrase dependents in the same constructions. But there are languages in which a case-like function is expressed by a morpheme affixed to the head, as in Mokilese (Harrison 1976: 164):

(69) Ngoah insingeh   **-ki**   kijinlikkoau   -o   nah   pehnn   -o
     I   write.TR   **-with** letter   -DET   his   pen   -DET
     'I wrote that letter with his pen.'

And there are languages in which an agreement-like function is expressed by a morpheme affixed not to the head but to the first constituent in the clause, as in Ute (example (70), from Givón 1980a: 311); or to any constituent, including the agreed-with constituent, as in Bartangi (example (71), from Payne 1980: 163, 165; see also Santali, cited in Sadock 1991: 46):

(70) kavzá -yi -amụ -'ura maĝá -x̂a -páa-ni
    horse -OBJ -3PL -be feed -PL -FUT
    'They are going to feed the horse.'
(71) äz -um tā -r kitob vuj
    I -1SG you -to book bring.PRF
    'I have brought you a book.'

In other words, both elements with case functions and elements with agreement functions are found affixed to dependents, as independent particles, and affixed to heads.

For this reason, overtly coded dependencies are better classified semantically. A semantic classification can be used consistently across languages because it is based on a semantic distinction. The most obvious semantic classification of overtly coded dependencies divides them according to whether they are RELATIONAL or INDEXICAL (see Croft 1988, where the latter are called 'deictic').

Relational coded dependencies are also called CASE MARKING constructions. Relational morphemes encode the semantic relation between the denotations of the elements that they relate. Relational morphemes include case markers (including adpositions), and possibly some possessive classifiers (Lichtenberk 1983).

Indexical coded dependencies are also called AGREEMENT constructions. Indexical morphemes index the referent of one of the members of a dependency. Indexical morphemes include agreement markers, both person agreement typically found on verbs, possessed nouns and adpositions, nonperson agreement typically found on modifiers of nouns, and also numeral classifiers and possessive classifiers.

5.4.2. *Mismatches among overtly coded dependencies, contiguity, and linear order*

Some languages use a variety of overtly coded dependencies. In a construction grammar, the different types of coded dependencies in a single language are treated as different constructions. And since there are multiple criteria for establishing a putative syntactic relation in a language with multiple overtly coded dependencies, one might expect there to be mismatches in languages as well as across languages. This is in fact what we find.

First, in some languages different overtly coded dependency constructions imply that an element has a syntactic relation with two different elements. For example, the Russian Relative Pronoun *kotoraja* in (72) exhibits two different coded dependency relations (Pulkina and Zakhava-Nekrasova n.d.: 569):

(72) my pošli po doroge **kotor** **-aja** vela
    we went:PST:PL along road:F:DAT.SG **which** **-FSG.NOM** lead:PST.FSG
    k reke
    towards river:FSG.DAT
    'We went along the road that leads to the river.'

On the one hand the Relative Pronoun *kotoraja* agrees in Gender and Number (Feminine Singular) with the Head Noun of the Relative Clause, *doroge* 'road'. On the other hand, *kotoraja* inflects for Case with respect to the Relative Clause Verb *vela* 'leads' (*kotoraja* is Nominative because it is the Subject of that Verb), and also triggers Subject Agreement (Feminine Singular) on the Relative Clause Verb.

Second, two different overtly coded dependencies may link the same two elements, but the two codings will categorize the elements differently. For example, in languages with ergative case marking and accusative agreement (§4.3.2), both case marking and agreement indicate a dependency of the arguments on the verb, but categorize that dependency differently. In the Wardaman example in (73) (from §4.3.2), the P argument is categorized with S arguments by case marking (i.e. absolutive), but the A argument is categorized with S arguments by verb agreement (i.e. nominative):

(73) ... wurre -wuya -Ø **ngawun-** da -wa ngayug -ji
 child -DU -ABS 1SG.NOM/3NONSG.ACC- see -FUT 1SG -ERG
 '... I have to see the two children myself.'

In other cases, the dependency categorization clashes with the putative syntactic relations defined by linear order. A well-known example of this mismatch is the English *There*-construction. In the English *There*-constructions, Verb Agreement in most dialects indicates a Subject syntactic relation between the Verb and the postverbal NP (indicated in boldface in (74)), while linear order indicates a Subject syntactic relation between the Verb and preverbal *There* (indicated by italics):

(74) *There* **are** [PL] **fifteen geese** [PL] in your geraniums.

In Early Middle English, the experiencers that are coded with Objective Case marking in Early Middle English are put in the preverbal position otherwise associated with arguments coded with Nominative Case marking (from §4.3.3):

(75) a foreward þat **þe** mai full well like
 an agreement that **you.OBJ** may full well please
 'an agreement that may full well please you' (AD 1275)

That is, the category of preverbal arguments does not match the category of Nominative Case arguments in Early Middle English.

The example of so-called "discontinuous constituents" in (76) (from §5.3.1), which I described therein as representing a mismatch between syntactic contiguity and semantic relations, also represents a mismatch between overtly coded dependency and contiguity:

(76) [tjaṉṭu-**ŋku**] Ø-tju yaḻku-ṉu [wiṟi-**ŋki**]
 dog-ERG (AUX)-me bite-PST big-ERG
 'The big dog bit me.'

There is an overtly coded dependency in (76) between *tjaṇtu-ŋku* 'dog' and *wiṛi-ŋki* 'big', as seen in the shared Ergative Case enclitic, but no contiguity between the two elements.

Another common source of mismatches between formal grouping and overtly coded dependencies is in the encoding of semantic predicate-argument structure by one and information (discourse) structure by the other. For example, in many languages, information questions constitute two formal groups defined by contiguity/separability. This structure corresponds to the information structure of information questions. The use of contiguity/separability for information structure can be illustrated with the following Tzutujil example and its English translation (Dayley 1985: 333):

(77) [**naq**]_{Focus} [n- Ø- ee- choy -b'ee -j ja q'aayiis]_{Presupp}.
     what INCMPL- 3SG.ABS- 2PL.ERG- cut -INST.FOC -TR the weed
     '[What] [do you all cut the weeds with]?'

The initial element corresponds to the focused part of the information question—the information being requested—and the rest of the Clause forms a syntactic group corresponding to the backgrounded part of the information question—the presupposed information. Event–participant relations are not encoded by formal contiguity, but instead by the overtly coded dependencies of Person Agreement and by the Instrumental Focus suffix *-b'ee* which encodes the semantic relation between the focused element participant and the verbal event. Thus, overtly coded dependencies do not match with syntactic contiguity/separability in Tzutujil and English information questions.

In other languages, syntactic contiguity/separability will reflect semantic predicate-argument structure, and information structure is expressed in other ways. For example, in many languages, information questions have the same formal grouping relations and linear order as declaratives, as in Usan (Reesink 1987: 295):

(78) [[munon wonou bur sig âib **mâi-mâi**]_{Object} guma -ib -â]_{Clause}
     man his pig very big **how.many** spear -FUT.SG -3SG
     'How many of the man's very big pigs will he spear?'

In (78), the information question is expressed by the Indefinite form *mâi-mâi*, which appears contiguous with the Noun denoting the unit quantified, rather than separated from the rest of the Clause.

5.5. Conclusion

Arguments for syntactic relations fall into two types, those built on evidence from collocational dependencies and those built on evidence from coded dependencies. Collocational dependencies are in fact evidence for semantic relations, not syntactic relations (Nunberg et al. 1994). In fact, Nunberg et al.'s analysis looks more natural in Radical Construction Grammar than in a componential grammar theory or even a reductionist construction grammar theory.

Coded dependencies, including constituency and linear order, are therefore the only proper types of evidence for syntactic relations that remain. Constituency is not an abstract global structure for the syntax of constructions. Arguments for constituency in the syntactic literature are guilty of methodological opportunism. Different tests for constituency yield conflicting results. All tests are construction-specific. Some of the constructions do not exist in some languages, and hence cannot be used as cross-linguistically valid tests. Instead of a global constituent structure, there are different types of formal groupings that are defined by a variety of properties of utterances, including contiguity/separability, occurrence in a single intonation unit, and the unit of a first-position self-repair.

Overtly coded dependencies are best analyzed in terms of the meaning that they encode (indexical and relational); this classification gives us a cross-linguistically valid basis for comparing overtly coded dependencies across languages. However, there are common mismatches of "evidence" for dependency: between different overtly coded dependencies in a single language, between overtly coded dependency and linear order, and between overtly coded dependency and formal grouping. Each type of structure that defines a coded dependency defines its own set of coded dependencies.

In the next chapter, I will argue that coded dependencies encode symbolic relations, not syntactic relations.

6

A Radical Approach to Syntactic Relations

6.1. The Logical Argument against Syntactic Relations

In this chapter, I will argue that a theory of syntactic representation should posit virtually no syntactic relations. That is to say, the representation of the syntactic structure of a construction should not include any syntactic relations between the elements that make it up. In other words, the only syntactic structure in constructions is the part–whole relation between the construction and its elements. This is another respect in which Radical Construction Grammar is radically different from other contemporary syntactic theories.

Lest the reader find this hypothesis too difficult to entertain at first, let me make some important qualifications at the outset. There still remains the part–whole structure of constructions. Moreover, the part–whole structure of constructions can be nested. For example, the elements of a clause include phrases that denote the participants in the event denoted by the clause. Those phrases are themselves complex constructions. Thus, there is some nested hierarchical structure to constructions (see §6.4.1).

Also, I am not denying the existence of the formal properties of utterances that were described in §5.4, such as contiguity, linear order, prosodic structure, and so on. These structures exist, of course. But they are not the manifestation of abstract syntactic relations; they are formal properties of construction types, as instantiated in particular utterances.

Finally, it must not be forgotten that constructions are symbolic units. They consist of syntactic structures paired with semantic structures. Thus, even in a theory that eschews syntactic relations, the elements of a construction are not cast adrift. Besides being structured in the ways described in the preceding two paragraphs, the elements of a construction are also linked to semantic structures by symbolic relations. And symbolic relations are where what is interesting about grammar takes place.

I first present a logical argument demonstrating that one does not need syntactic relations in order to model the use of a construction grammar in language use, that is, the comprehension and production of language. The argument against the necessity of syntactic relations follows directly from the model of a speaker's knowledge of a construction in construction grammar. In other words, the logical argument holds for ordinary construction grammar as well as Radical Construction Grammar.

A construction is a pairing of a complex syntactic structure and a complex semantic structure. Consider a construction in which the complex syntactic structure consists of only the elements of the construction, without any syntactic relations holding between the elements of the construction. This construction is depicted in Figure 6.1 (which is the same as Figure 5.1, minus syntactic relations).

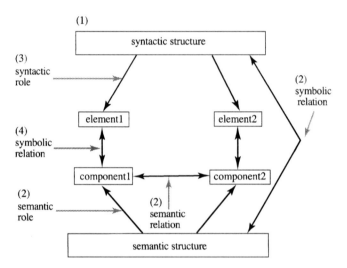

Figure 6.1. The internal structure of a construction without syntactic relations

The complex semantic structure of the construction in Figure 6.1, on the other hand, consists of both the components of the semantic structure and the semantic relations that hold between the components of the semantic structure.

The representation of a construction must also specify the symbolic relations in the construction, that is, the correspondences between elements of the syntactic structure of a construction with the appropriate components of its semantic structure. The existence of these symbolic relations is one of the chief features of construction grammar that differentiate it from the componential model of grammar (see §1.3.2, Figures 1.3–1.4).

Given this representation of a construction, it is straightforward to demonstrate that it is not necessary to assume the existence of syntactic relations for the purpose of communication. Consider the situation of a hearer with his grammatical knowledge organized as in Figure 6.1. The hearer hears an utterance; for communication to succeed, the hearer must arrive at an understanding of the meaning conveyed in the utterance. The process of understanding can be described in four steps, indicated as 1–4 in Figure 6.1 (these steps are not necessarily sequential, of course).

In Step 1, the hearer recognizes the utterance as an instance of a particular construction. That is, the hearer is able to identify the box labeled 'syntactic structure' in Figure 6.1 as the syntactic structure of a particular construction. In Step 2, the hearer accesses the semantic structure of that construction in his or her memory via the symbolic relation between the syntactic structure as a whole and the semantic structure as a whole. By this step, the hearer also accesses the semantic components and semantic relations between components. In Step 3, the hearer identifies the elements of the syntactic construction via the syntactic roles of the construction. Finally, in Step 4, the hearer utilizes the symbolic relations to identify the appropriate semantic component corresponding to each syntactic element.

That is, the hearer has now understood what the speaker has said—the overall semantic structure plus the components of that structure—without any recourse to syntactic relations. And understanding the meaning of an utterance is the goal of communication. Syntactic relations are not necessary to achieve this goal.

Of course, the logical argument only demonstrates that a speaker *can* get away without syntactic relations (assuming that the speaker's grammatical knowledge is represented as in construction grammar). It does not follow that a construction grammarian *should* abandon syntactic relations. The argument in the preceding paragraph is an application of Ockham's razor to render an analysis simpler and more "elegant": if a theoretical entity is not necessary in the analysis, eliminate it. In this case, the "unnecessary" theoretical entities are syntactic relations between elements in a construction.

However, with constructions we are talking about a psychological entity, namely the speaker's knowledge of a construction (§1.2.1). The simplicity or elegance of an analysis is not a sufficient argument for the nonexistence of some psychological entity. There is a considerable body of psychological research that strongly suggests that psychological representations possess redundant information (see Barsalou 1992: 180 and references cited therein). All that the preceding paragraph indicates is that if we have empirical linguistic reasons for abandoning syntactic relations, then doing so will not render our model of grammatical knowledge inadequate for the purposes to which language is put.

There have to be some good positive reasons to abandon syntactic relations, given that one can do without them. That is, we must demonstrate that the model represented in Figure 6.1 is empirically superior to alternative models in which syntactic relations are posited.

One plausible alternative model is the componential model of grammar (see §§1.3.1–1.3.2), which utilizes syntactic relations but not symbolic relations, since form and meaning are in separate components; instead, general linking rules join form and meaning. The logical argument presented above demonstrates that one can dispense with syntactic relations if one utilizes symbolic relations to map the elements onto the corresponding semantic components. One might ask whether the converse is true, that is, whether one can dispense with symbolic relations if one utilizes syntactic relations. In other words the question is whether symbolic relations are merely a notational variant of syntactic relations (I am grateful to John A. Hawkins for raising this question).

In §6.2, I will argue that symbolic relations in a construction grammar are not notational variants of syntactic relations in a componential model. A plausible componential model will not be able to maintain general linking rules in the face of the complexity of the form–meaning mapping in human languages. At best, the general linking rules will have to be construction-specific. That is, the "general linking rules" will turn out to be the symbolic relations of a specific construction—just as in Figure 6.1. In other words, the model in Figure 6.1 is superior to a componential model in accounting for the cross-linguistic facts.

Another plausible alternative model is one that uses syntactic relations instead of syntactic roles. The logical argument given above demonstrates that one can dispense with syntactic relations if one utilizes syntactic roles to identify the elements of the construction. One might ask whether the converse is true, that is, whether one can dispense with syntactic roles and use only syntactic relations. In other words, the question is whether syntactic roles are merely a notational variant of syntactic relations (I am grateful to Matthew Dryer for raising this question).

In §6.3, I will argue that syntactic roles are not notational variants of syntactic relations. In fact, syntactic relations impose additional syntactic structure on a construction. But that additional syntactic structure assumed by the positing of syntactic relations run into very serious—indeed, fatal—problems when faced with widespread and common cross-linguistic phenomena. However, a model with only syntactic roles can easily handle these phenomena. In other words, the model in Figure 6.1 is superior to a syntactic relation model in accounting for the cross-linguistic facts.

6.2. Syntactic Relations vs. Symbolic Relations

In §6.1, it was demonstrated that a model of grammatical representation with symbolic relations and no syntactic relations can perform the functions of communication, and hence syntactic relations are not logically necessary for a model which has symbolic relations. The question then arises, can it be done the other way around? That is, can one dispense with symbolic relations if one uses syntactic relations? If so, then symbolic relations are merely a notational variant of syntactic relations.

A model with syntactic relations and without symbolic relations would posit only the relations given in Figure 6.2 (cf. Figure 6.1).

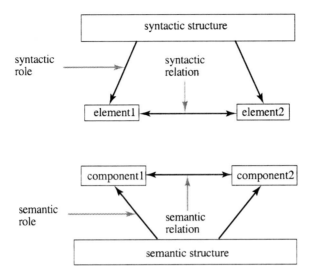

Figure 6.2. Syntactic and semantic structures without symbolic relations

Strictly speaking, it is impossible to have syntactic relations without symbolic relations. The speaker and hearer have no way to link utterances they hear with the meaning that is intended to be conveyed. However, the componential model makes up for this deficiency by positing linking rules that link syntactic structures to semantic structures. Thus, an account without symbolic relations would be an example of the componential model of grammar, not of construction grammar.

In §1.3.1, I presented a summary of the arguments against the componential model. In essence, if one analyzes the full range of utterances carefully enough, one would eventually have to posit linking rules for each construction. Such a model would in fact be a notational variant of construction grammar: the construction-specific linking rules would simply be the symbolic relations of a construction grammar representation. In other words, a model of grammatical representation cannot do without symbolic relations, even though it can do without syntactic relations.

There is one possible counterargument that could be made to the critique in §1.3.1. The additional syntactic structure provided by syntactic relations (over and above the structure provided by syntactic roles) *might* allow us to have construction-independent linking rules that would successfully identify the semantic components and the semantic relations that hold between them. For the sake of argument, I will set aside the critique in §1.3.1 here and pursue this possible counterargument.

The most obvious way in which the additional structure provided by syntactic relations could aid in identifying the semantic interpretation of an utterance is by mapping onto semantic relations. If the syntactic relations map onto semantic relations, then a syntactic element can be identified with the corresponding semantic component. For example, if there is a syntactic relation linking elements A–B in an utterance, and we know that this syntactic relation maps onto semantic relation X–Y by virtue of some linking rule, and both relations are asymmetric, then the hearer can identify A with X and B with Y and thereby understand the utterance.

In other words, a componential model with syntactic relations and linking rules between the syntactic and semantic components would have to assume ICONICITY (more precisely, DIAGRAMMATIC ICONICITY) in the linking of syntax and semantics in order to perform the function of communication. The principle of iconicity was explicated in §3.1: that syntactic structure reflects semantic structure. In particular, syntactic elements and syntactic relations should map onto semantic components and semantic relations.

Although the concept of iconicity is associated with functionalist syntactic theories, it is also a part of formalist syntactic theories that advocate the componential model (Newmeyer 1992). The most general mapping rules in formalist theories are essentially iconic. An example of a formalist iconic mapping rule is the Theta Criterion of Government and Binding Theory: 'Each argument is assigned one and only one theta role. Each theta role is assigned to one and only one argument' (Haegeman 1994: 73). Other important formalist principles indirectly link semantics to syntax by linking lexical information, which includes semantics, to syntactic structure. These principles include the Projection Principle of Government and Binding Theory (Chomsky 1981: 29; Haegeman 1994: 55) and the Uniqueness, Completeness, and Coherence conditions of Lexical-Functional Grammar (Kaplan and Bresnan 1982: 181, 204).

In this section I will present many examples of constructions in which it is implausible to maintain that there is a semantic relation corresponding to a putative syntactic relation. Some of these examples are typologically rare, others are quite common. These data question the possibility of saving syntactic relations through general linking rules to semantic relations. At best, a componential model with syntactic relations would require a linking rule specifically for the constructions possessing the anomalous syntactic relations. This may not appear to be a problem for componential models—after all, they do not assume universal iconicity. However, taken to its logical conclusion—linking rules for each construction—this model reduces to a construction grammar, and the alleged value added by positing syntactic relations is lost.

If we abandon syntactic relations, however, then the problems of noniconic mappings between syntactic relations and semantic relations disappears. We can still maintain the principle that every piece of syntactic structure corresponds to a matching part of the semantic structure. This is possible because if there are no syntactic relations, then there cannot be a noniconic mapping onto semantic relations.

6.2.1. Unlikely semantic dependencies

The first example is the phenomenon usually described as possessor ascension. In some languages, the semantic possessor of a referent appears to have a syntactic relation to the verb, not the noun phrase expressing the referent. One such language is Tzotzil (Aissen 1980: 95):

(1) 1-   i-   k'as   -b   -at   j-   k'ob
    PRF-   1SG.ABS-   break   -IO.APPL -PASS   1SG.POSS-   hand
    'My hand was broken.'

In (1), the 1st Person semantic possessor is encoded as the (Passive) Subject of the verb, with the Agreement prefix *i-*. It is also encoded as a morphosyntactic Possessor of the NP denoting the possessum (*j-*).

Possessor ascension with verbs of this type is a common type of possessor ascension across languages. It can plausibly be argued that there really is a semantic relation between the 1st Person referent and the action: the breaking of my hand affects me.

Such an iconic analysis is plausible for many such examples in many languages. But in some languages, including Tzotzil, one can find an indirect object/semantic possessor of a verb for which a verb-possessor semantic relationship is much less plausible (Aissen 1987: 130; 3rd Person Singular Absolutive marking is zero, but the Indirect Object suffix *-be* indicates that this is an example of Possessor Ascension):

(2) ta   j-   nujan   -be   s-   p'in   -al
    IMPF   1SG.ERG-   turn.face.down   -IO.APPL   3SG.POSS- pot   -POSS
    'I'll turn its [the soup's] pot face down.' [i.e. the pot that the soup was cooked in]

Since the soup is already cooked and out of the pot, it is implausible to assume that the soup is affected by someone turning face down the pot it was cooked in.

A similar observation can be made for the phenomenon usually described as quantifier float. In quantifier float, a quantifier is in an apparent syntactic relation with a verb rather than the noun phrase whose referent it quantifies. A language exhibiting quantifier float is Pima (Munro 1984: 273):

(3) hegai   'uuvi   'o   **vees**   ha-   ñeid   **hegam**   **ceceoj**
    that   woman   3.AUX   **all**   them-   see   **those**   **men**
    'The woman saw all the men.'

In (3), the Quantifier *vees* 'all' occurs immediately preceding the Verb, functioning as a verbal Modifier rather than a Modifier of the Noun Phrase *hegam cecoj* 'those men'.

As with the possessor ascension example in (1), it is plausible to argue that there is a semantic relation between quantifier and event in example (3): the seeing event is either collective and so 'all' describes its collectiveness, or the verb+quantifier sums up all of the individual seeing events of the woman seeing a man.

Again, the iconic analysis applies to most cases of quantifier float in the literature. But some languages, including Pima, extend the Quantifier Float construction to cases where it is implausible to assume a corresponding semantic relation (Munro 1984: 275):

(4) **vees** ñei 'ant heg **heñ- navpuj** ha- maakaika
 all see 1SG.AUX ART **my- friends** their- doctor
 'I saw the doctor of all of my friends.'

It seems implausible that seeing a single doctor can be construed as a collective or summation event that could be described as 'all'.

Another noniconic pattern is ANOMALOUS AGREEMENT. In anomalous agreement, one element in a syntactic structure agrees with another element, and there is no plausible semantic relation corresponding to the putative syntactic relation defined by the agreement pattern. Again, there are cases in which a semantic relation may plausibly be posited, but there are other cases in which it is implausible that there is a semantic relation corresponding to the putative syntactic relation defined by the agreement pattern.

For example, in several languages of the Caucasus, and some Indo-Aryan languages, the Adverb agrees with the Absolutive NP, as in the following example from Avar (Elena Kalinina, personal communication):

(5) roq'o =b **video** b= ugo
 at.home =N **video.N** N= be.PRS
 'There is a video at home.'

In (5), the Adverb *roq'o* 'at home' agrees with the Absolutive NP *video*. In this example, it is plausible to posit a direct semantic relation between the Adverb and the Absolutive NP. There is a locative relationship between the video and the home, with the video functioning as the figure of the locative relationship (see §9.2.2) and the home as the ground.

However, Adverb Agreement is also extended to other situations where a semantic relationship between the Adverb and the Absolutive NP is less plausible. Example (6) gives a similar example from Marathi, an Indo-Aryan language (Hook and Chauhan 1988: 179):

(6) ti haa **bhaag tsaangLaa** vaatsel
 she this **part.MSG good.MSG** will.read
 'She will read this part well.'

In (6), the Adverb *tsaangLaa* 'well' agrees with *bhaag* 'part', but there is at best only an indirect semantic relationship between the part and the quality of the reading.

In the following example from Tsakhur, the semantic relationship between Adverb and Absolutive NP is even less plausible (Elena Kalinina, personal communication):

(7) ma -na zaʕfa   sa<r>k'yl   t'ufli -bi -shi   lqa aʕlh -a: -nGaʕ
    this -AT woman.CL2 <CL2>-turn.PF   shoe -PL -OBL.PL   -LOC go   -IMPF -TEMP
    ibrehim-pashe   javash **=ba** **sumk'a**   alja<p'>t'   -u
    Ibrahim-Pasha.CL1   quiet =ADV.CL3 handbag.CL3   <CL3>-take   -PF
    qyʁych' -u wo =r
    go.out -PF FOC =CL1
    'When this woman turned back and went to fetch the shoes [lit. went for/after the shoes], Ibrahim-Pasha quietly took the handbag and went out.'

In (7), the Adverb *javash* 'quiet' agrees with the Absolutive NP *sumk'a* 'handbag', but it seems implausible to posit a direct semantic relation between the quiet manner of the action and the handbag.

Other types of anomalous agreement exist. In some Turkic languages, the Head Noun of a Relative Clause agrees in Person and Number with the Relative Clause Subject, as in the following Uzbek example (Sjoberg 1963: 141):

(8) **men** -iŋ   oqi   -gan   kitɔb **-im**
    1SG   -GEN   read   -PART   book   -1SG.POSS
    'that book that I read/have read'

In (8), the Possessive Agreement suffix on the Head Noun *kitɔb* 'book' agrees with the Subject *men* 'I', which is itself encoded as a Genitive dependent on the Participle *oqi-gan* 'reading'. In fact, the Subject Noun Phrase may be eliminated, leaving the 1st Person semantic argument of the predicate as an apparent syntactic dependent on 'book' (ibid.):

(9) oqi   -gan   kitɔb **-im**
    read   -PART   book   -1SG.POSS
    'that book that I read/have read'

In Tsez, another Caucasian language, there is Agreement in Noun Class by the Main Clause Verb with the Absolutive NP of the Verb's Sentential Complement (Polinsky and Comrie 1999: 117; cf. Haspelmath 1999):

(10) eni   -r   [už -ā   **magalu**   b- āc' -ru   -λi] **b-** iy   -xo
     mother -DAT boy -ERG **bread.CL3:ABS** CL3- eat -PSTPRT -NR CL3- know -PRS
     'The mother knows that the boy ate bread.'

In (10), the Verb *iy* 'know' agrees with the Absolutive NP *magalu* 'bread', but there is no plausible direct semantic relationship between the knowing and the bread.

In the above cases, it would be difficult to identify a semantic relation corresponding to the putative syntactic relation. But if we abandon the assumption that there is a syntactic relation, the remaining syntactic structure—the part–whole relation—is iconic with the semantic structure. And there is no insuperable difficulty for the hearer to figure out the semantic relations. The hearer can find the possessor or quantifier easily enough in the possessor ascension and quantifier constructions, and also identify the NP argument to whose denotation the possessor referent or quantifier applies. Likewise, the hearer can find the controller of the anomalous agreement pattern. Figure 6.3 illustrates an analysis of the Tzotzil Possessor Ascension construction in (2).

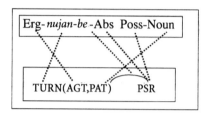

Figure 6.3. Symbolic links for Tzotzil Possessor Ascension construction in example (2)

In Figure 6.3, the relational coded dependency, -*be*-, denotes a semantic relation;[1] but in the Possessor Ascension construction, it is not a (nonexistent) semantic relation between the verbal event and the Absolutive indexed referent, but the possessor relation between the Absolutive indexed referent and the stimulus denoted by the possessed noun.

Of course, it is not impossible to account for this pattern in a componential grammar. Special linking rules linking the Indirect Object referent to the semantic possessor of the Direct Object referent could be devised. But such linking rules would be specific to the Possessor Ascension construction, and would be notational variants of the construction grammar analysis presented in Figure 6.3. That is to say, positing syntactic relations does not offer any advantage (such as a more general set of linking rules) over a Radical Construction Grammar representation with symbolic relations and without syntactic relations. This same conclusion applies to the examples in this section and §§6.2.2–6.2.3 as well.

Finally, there is a plausible explanation as to how these noniconic constructions arose. The constructions originated in the cases where there is a motivated semantic relationship underlying the apparent syntactic relation. For example, in most cases, there is a plausible semantic relation of affectedness underlying the possessor ascension construction, and of event quantification underlying the quantifier float construction. This is why these cases are widely found. Then in some languages, the construction was extended to other verb classes where the possessor/quantifier is not in a direct semantic relation with the situation denoted

---

[1] For this reason, the semantic relation between possessor and patient is overtly represented in the semantic structure of the Possessor Ascension construction in Figure 6.3. Where no syntactic element encodes a semantic relation, then the relation will be left implicit in the simplified predicate calculus semantic representations used in the figures. (Recall that only the division of a semantic representation into components and their semantic roles and relations need be assumed in the arguments for Radical Construction Grammar; see §1.7.)

by the verb; these examples are found only in languages where the plausibly iconic cases are also found. A similar scenario may hold for the anomalous agreement constructions, although this remains to be confirmed.

I return to English for the last example in this section. In English, there is a construction which is called Neg-raising after its transformational analysis, illustrated in (11):

(11) I don't think [she's coming back]. [= 'I think she isn't coming back']

One proposed analysis of (11) is that (11) has its literal meaning—it is not the case that I think that she is coming back. The meaning associated with Neg-raising, given in brackets in (11), is an implicature: I would not be informing you of my not believing she is coming back unless I actually believed that she is not coming back, hence you may conclude the more informative assertion that I believe that she is not coming back.

However, the implicature analysis is not acceptable for (12), an attested example from a television commentary on the kidnapping of the American newspaper heiress Patty Hearst (Horn 1979: 168):

(12) "I don't think that [ever before have the media played such a major role in a kidnapping]."

The implicature analysis fails in (12) because the occurrence of the Adverb *ever* and the inversion of *have* and *the media* in the Subordinate Clause normally occur only in the presence of negation in that clause. Thus, the Negator *-n't* in (12) is semantically related to the Subordinate Clause assertion, but is syntactically (indeed, morphologically) related to the Main Clause Verb—another noniconic structure.

Again, there is a plausible diachronic scenario for the occurrence of sentences like (12). The Main Clause *I don't think* is probably grammaticalizing to a negative epistemic marker, on the basis of the implicature reading of sentences like (11). As a negative epistemic marker, *I don't think* triggers the Negative Adverb *ever* and the Subject–Auxiliary inversion characteristic of English Negative Sentence constructions.

6.2.2. Proposition vs. Subject-Predicate construal

This section describes syntactic constructions which divide the elements of a clause into two distinct parts, a Subject and a Predicate, and the implication of that syntactic division for the mapping of syntactic structure onto semantic structure in those constructions.

The sentence in (13b) illustrates a construction that I will again call by its transformational name, Raising to Object:

(13) a. I believe [**that he ate the bagel**].
b. I believe [**him**] [**to have eaten the bagel**].

In (13a), the object of *believe* is a Clause, which encodes the proposition that I believe. In (13b), we find instead two units, one of which is encoded as a Direct Object Noun Phrase, and the other as an Infinitival Predicate. An iconic analysis of the semantic structure for a Raising to Object construction would be that a belief can be construed here as ascribing a property (in the Infinitival Complement) to the Object referent of *believe*. In fact, Langacker gives just such an analysis (Langacker 1995).

A similar analysis can be given to the so-called Tough-Movement construction in (14b):

(14) a. It is hard **to find Tina**.
     b. **Tina** is **hard to find**.

In (14a), the Complement of the Predicate *be hard* is an Infinitival Complement that encodes a generic state of affairs and ascribes the property denoted by *be hard* to that state of affairs. In (14b), the generic state of affairs is divided into a Noun Phrase that is coded as the Subject of *be hard* and an Infinitival Complement missing its Object. It is plausible to analyze the semantic interpretation of (14b) as attribution of the complex predicate denoted by *be hard to find* to the Subject referent.

Such an analysis appears to be less plausible, though not impossible, for the Moose Cree example in (15) (James 1984: 210; see also examples (23)–(24) below):

(15) ālimēliht -ākosi -w **meri** [kihči- tot   -aw -iyan [kihči- tāpwē -ht -amān
     be.hard -AI   -3 **Mary** SUB- make -TA -2→1 SUB-   believe -TI -1
     [ē- āhkosi -t]]]
     SUB- sick:AI -3
     [literally:] 'Mary is hard to you make me believe (she) is sick.'

In both the English Tough-Movement construction in (14) and the Moose Cree Tough-Movement construction in (15), the syntatic role of Mary as an apparent NP Dependent of the Main Clause Verb *ālimēliht* 'be hard' is more a result of the information structure of the constructions. In the Tough-Movement construction, Mary is the topic, in that the assertion is about Mary, not about the state of affairs which is being described as hard.

Another construction that divides a clause into a Subject and a Predicate is the Copula construction, as in (16):

(16) Susan **is** tall/intelligent/etc.

In (16), the putative Subject syntactic relation holds between *Susan* and *be*, not *Susan* and *tall/intelligent*, even though it is tall height and intelligence that is being ascribed to Susan. Nevertheless, the Copula encodes predication, that is, ascription of the predicated property to the Subject (see §5.2). Hence it seems plausible to consider there to be a semantic relation between the Subject and the Copula.

The verb *be* is also found as the Passive Auxiliary in the Passive construction in English:

(17) a. The neighbor's kid broke the window.
b. The window **was** broken by the neighbor's kid.
c. the window broken by the neighbor's kid

In the Predicated Passive in (17b), the Passive Subject is the P argument, unlike the Active Subject in (17a). This shift in perspective is due to topicality, as argued in many studies of the Passive construction (e.g. Kuno 1987). The Auxiliary *be* in (17b) encodes predication of the process to the P argument, just as it does in (16): the Copula is absent when the Passive functions as a modifier of the P argument, as in (17c).

However, it is rather tenuous to consider the Subject as the semantic argument of the copula *be* in (17b), and perhaps even in the simple Nonverbal Predication construction in (16). In other languages, the functions of predication and passive are not encoded with an agreeing auxiliary. For example, there is no Copula in Nonverbal predication in Classical Nahuatl. Instead, the word stem is inflected directly (Andrews 1975: 148):

(18) ah-   **ni-**   **tīcitl**
NEG- 1SG- doctor
'I am not a doctor.'

In Hebrew, the Passive *gudal* 'be brought up' is a morphological derivation of the Verb, without a Copula (Keenan 1985: 252):

(19) ha-   yeled **gudal**   al   yedei ha-   saba
the- child bring.up.PASS on   hands the- grandfather
'The child was brought up by the grandfather.'

In Tok Pisin, Auxiliaries such as *inap* 'can' (from English *enough*) do not inflect (Verhaar 1995: 138):

(20) bai   yupela **inap** kisim   graun bilong ol
FUT   2:PL   **can**   get:TR   land   POSS   them
'You [pl.] will be able to get their land.'

Hence there is no overt coding of a syntactic relation between the Subject and the Auxiliary Verb in Tok Pisin, and so *inap* could be analyzed as a Verbal Operator, and *yupela* as the Subject of *kisim*.

Finally, in the Luganda sentence in (21), both the Auxiliary and the Verb agree with the Subject Noun Phrase *olu-kiiko* 'council' (Ashton et al. 1954: 292):

(21) ku   ssaawa ennya   **olu-**   kiiko   **lu-**   naa-   ba **lu-**   tudde
LOC ten.o'clock   LU.CL- council LU.CL- NEAR.FUT- be LU.CL- sit.PART
'At 10 o'clock the council will be in session [literally: will be sitting].'

It could be argued that English construes the Subject NP as a semantic argument of the Passive Auxiliary/Copula *be*, as demonstrated by the putative syntactic relation between the NP and *be*; but Classical Nahuatl, Hebrew, Tok Pisin, and Luganda do not make a similar construal. But to support such an analysis, the hidden assumptions discussed in Chapter 3 would have to be addressed and defended: absence of contrast, identity of syntactic form or behavior, constructional monosemy, nonredundancy, and the Semantic Uncertainty Principle.

The Radical Construction Grammar analysis is that there is no subject syntactic relation as such. This analysis would represent an example such as (17b) as in Figure 6.4.

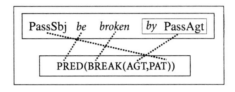

Figure 6.4. Symbolic links for English Predicated Passive construction in example (17b)

In Figure 6.4, the coding morphosyntax simply links the phrase in the Copula Subject role to the relevant participant of the event denoted by the Predicate (the Passive Verb in (17b)) in the semantic structure of the construction. This noniconic structure is only partially noniconic, of course, because it reflects the information structure of the utterance (not explicitly represented in Figure 6.3) instead of its event-participant structure.

Again, there is a diachronic explanation for the noniconic apparent syntactic relation. An auxiliary or copula verb begins life as a full verb denoting a state of affairs with participants (for typical verbal sources of copulas and passive auxiliaries, see Clark 1978; Keenan 1985; Siewierska 1984). But the verb form has been grammaticalized to the point of encoding merely the predication function and the voice function, which are semantic operations on the state of affairs denoted by its complement's predicate. However, in the grammaticalization process, the auxiliary/copula has retained its source construction's morphosyntax, including syntactic agreement indexing a participant of the state of affairs denoted by its complement's predicate.

6.2.3. *Clause collapsing*

The last set of examples pose similar problems to those in §6.2.2, for similar reasons. A class of English constructions that indicate tense, aspect, mood, and evidentiality also split a Clause denoting a state of affairs:

(22) a. [Sara] wants [**to sit down**].
     b. [Janet] seems [**to be ill**].

c. [**The cats**] will [**scratch the furniture**].
   d. [**Sara**] began [**to sing**].

In (22a–d) the state of affairs is split into a Subject NP, which is apparently syntactically dependent on the Main Verb (or Auxiliary in (22c)), and a Nonfinite Complement of the Main Verb or Auxiliary, denoting a state of affairs in which the Subject has a participant role (Sara sits down, Janet is ill, the cats scratch the furniture, Sara sings).

An iconic analysis of the constructions in (22a–d) would require that the state of affairs minus the Subject referent be construed as in the semantic scope of the Main Clause predicate, while the Subject referent is a semantic argument of the state of affairs denoted by the Main Verb or Auxiliary. Such a semantic analysis is decreasingly plausible from (22a) to (22d).

In (22a), the Subject referent is the person who has the desire described in the Complement. The semantic structure does reflect the putative syntactic relations in (22a): in mental space terms (Fauconnier 1985), the Subject referent anchors the mental space built by the Main Verb *want*.

Evidentials such as *seem* in (22b) also build a mental space, but the mental space is anchored by the speaker, not the Subject referent: it is the speaker of (22b) to whom the state of affairs (Janet is ill) only appears to be true. Hence there is no special status of the Subject referent with respect to the evidentially qualified state of affairs. In fact, in Moose Cree, either the Subject or the Object NP can occur as an apparent syntactic dependent of the Main Clause Verb (James 1984: 209, her glosses):

(23) **ni-** itēliht -ākosi -n [ē- **kiskēli** -m -iyan]
     1-   seem   -AI   -1   SUBR- **know**   -TA -2→1
     'I seem to be known by you.' [literally: 'I seem you know me']

For tense marking (22c), the temporal location of the event as well as the event itself is being ascribed to the Subject referent. This makes sense: in the last sentence of (22c), I am stating of the cats that the event of their scratching the furniture will occur in the future. However, this is equally true for any argument of the predicate, not just the Subject referent. Hence there is no semantic motivation to divide the state of affairs into the parts corresponding to Subject and Complement. The same applies to aspect in (22d): the aspectual phase is ascribable to any participant, not just the subject.

In sum, it is implausible to treat the Subject and Complement as semantic arguments of the main verb/auxiliary in most instances. On the other hand, identifying the Subject referent as the remaining participant in the state of affairs denoted by the Complement is straightforward in the constructions exemplified in (22a–d).

Again, there is a diachronic explanation for the noniconic mapping of arguments in (22a–d). These constructions are in the middle of a grammaticalization process sometimes called CLAUSE COLLAPSING: a complex sentence structure with a main verb and a complement verb is being reanalyzed as a single clause with a tense, aspect, and/or mood indicating form (the former main verb) and a main verb (the former complement verb). This diachronic change is a gradual process, and the examples in (22)–(23) show that for some languages, one of the last steps in this process is the reassignment of syntactic arguments to the former complement verb. In other languages, argument phrases denoting other participants of the Complement are instead reassigned into the main clause.

In Italian, in what is called the Clitic Climbing construction, a clitic Pronoun denoting a participant of the Complement state of affairs appears as if it were in a syntactic relation with the auxiliary verb. Two examples are given below, both of the Direct Object clitic *lo* (Napoli 1981: 861, 863; examples attested):

(24) l'-   ho   appena   finito   di   **fare**
     it-   I.have   just   finished   of   **do**:INF
     'I just finished doing it.'

(25) me   **lo**   sa   **dire**?
     to.me it   you.can   **tell**:INF
     'Can you tell it to me?'

There is no semantic relation holding directly between the Perfect Auxiliary *ho* '(I) have' in (24) or the Auxiliary *sa* '(you) can' in (25) and the participant denoted by the Object clitic.

In Ancash Quechua, full Noun Phrase arguments of the Infinitival Complement, such as *Huaraz-chaw* 'in Huaraz' in (26), can appear as apparent dependents of the Main Clause Verb *muna* 'want' (Cole 1984: 111):

(26) noqa   **Huaraz** **-chaw**   muna   -a   [wayi   -ta   **rura**   -y   -ta]
     I   **Huaraz** **-in**   want   -1   house   -ACC   **make**   -INF   -ACC
     'I want to make a house in Huaraz.'

In (26), it is the house-building, not the wanting, that is located in Huaraz.

It seems implausible to argue that the various nonsubject arguments in (24)–(26) are semantic arguments of 'have', 'can', and 'want'. Yet in a construction grammar without syntactic relations, it is again straightforward to map the argument phrases of the construction's syntactic structure into the appropriate participant roles of the construction's semantic representation, on the model of Figure 6.4.

I close with two particularly complex examples. In Moose Cree, a participant of the state of affairs denoted by a doubly-embedded Verb—the Verb 'be sick'—may be coded as an apparent dependent of the Main Clause Verb (James 1984: 210):

(27) itēliht -ākosi -w   **mēri**   [ē-   kī-   alamotam -ātan   [ē-   **ākhkosi** -t]]
     seem   -AI   -3   **Mary**   SUBR- PST-   tell   -TA:1→2   SUBR-   **sick**:AI -3
     [literally:] 'Mary seems that I told you that (she) is sick.'

And in Japanese, the Subject referent of the Sentential Complement of an evidential Verb can be coded as an apparent Subject argument of the Passive of the evidential Verb (Tsukiashi 1997: 49; attested example):

(28) **watasi** wa [**hait** -te-iru -koto] o satorarenu -yoni
　　　I　　TOP　**be.in**　-PROG　-COMP　OBJ　notice:PASS:NEG　-so.that
　　　[literally:] 'so that I will not be noticed to be in'

What seems to be going on here is a combination of encoding a more topical participant as an element of the main clause, and the first steps in the collapsing of a complex sentence with evidential meaning.

In all of these examples, it is pushing common sense plausibility, to a greater or lesser degree, to posit a semantic relation corresponding to the putative syntactic relation. Although a plausible iconic analysis can sometimes be provided for particular cases, and in some cases motivates the creation of the construction, I believe that one cannot always provide a plausible iconic motivation. But in all of these examples, if we assume knowledge of a construction that specifies only symbolic relations between syntactic elements and semantic components, it is not at all difficult for the hearer to identify who did what to whom where, in the common sense intuition of the meaning of these sentences. A representation of the Japanese Evidential Complement Subject Passive is given in Figure 6.5.

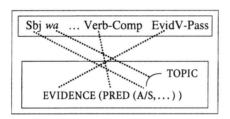

Figure 6.5. Symbolic links in the Japanese Evidential Complement Subject Passive construction

If we abandon syntactic relations, the remaining syntactic structure is iconic. Most important of all, hearers can still succeed in understanding what the speaker said, with the knowledge of construction structure that remains in Radical Construction Grammar.

The existence of noniconic relationships between syntactic and semantic structure raises a question in semantic analysis. Since form–meaning mappings can be noniconic, how do we decide when the mapping is noniconic and when the mapping is iconic, reflecting an alternative construal of the state of affairs? This question is not a priori decidable for the reasons given in Chapter 3: constructions change in their semantic structure because of competing alternative conceptualizations. Decisions must be made on a case by case basis, along the lines discussed in Chapter 3.

The structure of the English Passive can serve as an example. The P argument triggers Agreement on the Auxiliary *be*, and exhibits no direct syntactic relationship to the Past Participle form of the Verb. Nevertheless, we may conclude that the P argument is not a semantic argument of the Auxiliary because there is no contrast with a predicated passive lacking *be* (§3.2.1). On the other hand, the Passive Subject role of the P argument contrasts with the Active Object role in the Active construction, and that contrast should be expressed in semantic structure. This contrast is usually described in information-structural terms, but it also can be analyzed as representing an alternative construal of the event (Croft 1998b).

More generally, it can be said that many of the apparently noniconic patterns are due to the fact that syntactic structure reflects information structure as well as the event–participant structure of the state of affairs denoted by the construction. Since the two do not always match, the structure of the utterance iconically reflects sometimes one, sometimes the other (see §5.4.5).

6.3. Syntactic Relations vs. Syntactic Roles

The data presented in §6.2 support the argument for a construction-based approach to syntactic representation, and specifically demonstrate that positing syntactic relations does not have any advantage over positing symbolic relations. In fact, positing syntactic relations causes problems for any attempt to replace construction-specific symbolic relations with more general linking rules, because there often is no simple isomorphic/iconic mapping of syntactic relations to semantic relations.

If we accept the existence of symbolic relations, based on the arguments in §1.3.1 and §6.2, we may then turn to examine the other necessary premise to the logical argument in §6.1, syntactic roles. The relevant structures are illustrated in Figure 6.6.

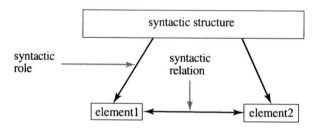

Figure 6.6. Syntactic roles and syntactic relations

Syntactic roles relate a syntactic element to the whole construction, while syntactic relations relate a syntactic element to another syntactic element. In §6.1, I argued that if one posits syntactic roles (as well as symbolic relations), then one can dispense with syntactic relations. Again, we may reverse the question, and ask

A Radical Approach to Syntactic Relations   221

if one posits syntactic relations, can one do without syntactic roles? That is, are syntactic roles and syntactic relations notational variants?

Strictly speaking, a model of syntactic structure cannot do without syntactic roles. That is, one must posit at least a generic part–whole relation. The real question is, can syntactic relations replace specific syntactic roles such as Subject and Predicate that uniquely specify elements of the construction? In the following sections, I argue that they cannot. Syntactic relations impose more structure on constructions than syntactic roles. But there is very strong evidence that the additional structure is problematic, or—fatally—is simply not there.

6.3.1. Relative order of three or more elements

Syntactic roles and syntactic relations are only notational variants in a binary branching meronomic (part–whole) structure, such as the one given in Figure 6.6. Consider a construction C with only two elements, X and Y. One can describe the roles of X and Y in C as X/C and Y/C, and a relation between X and Y as X–Y. If one knows that X and Y are parts of C, and the relation X–Y, then one can define the roles of the two elements as the first and second members respectively of the syntactic relation X–Y. If one knows only the roles of the two elements in a binary branching meronomic structure, that is, X/C and Y/C, then one can define the syntactic relation as the one holding between X/C and Y/C.

If the structure in question is made up of more than two parts, however, the syntactic role representation is not a notational variant of the syntactic relation representation. The syntactic relations cannot be inferred from the syntactic roles alone. Consider a ternary branching meronomic structure as in Figure 6.7.

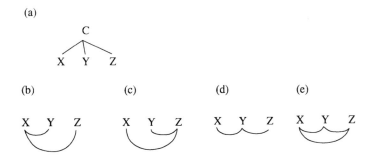

Figure 6.7. Syntactic roles and relations in a construction with three elements

Figure 6.7a gives the syntactic roles holding between elements X, Y, and Z and construction C. Figure 6.7b–e gives all possible models of syntactic relations from which the roles in Figure 6.7a could be inferred. That is, knowing the syntactic relations in any of the structures in Figure 6.7b–e, one can derive the roles X/C, Y/C, and Z/C in Figure 6.7a. However, one cannot decide which part of Figure 6.7b–e is the correct representation given only the information in Figure 6.7a. That is, syntactic relations represent a richer syntactic structure than syntactic roles.

However, there is good reason to assume that the additional syntactic structure is not there. Consider a concrete example, from Kilivila (Senft 1986: 110):

(29) eseki   luleta   yena   guyau
     he.give his.sister   fish   chief
     VERB **NP1**   **NP2** **NP3**
     'The chief gives his sister the fish.'

According to Senft, the order of arguments is fixed, such that the first Noun Phrase after the Verb is the recipient (the chief's sister), the second the gift (the fish) and the third the donor (the chief). In this case, there are four elements. Putative syntactic relations would be coded by linear order. But there is no way to justify which syntactic relations should actually be represented. One plausible analysis is that each Noun Phrase is in a syntactic relation with the Verb, and the syntactic relation is coded by the relative position of each Noun Phrase. But this analysis is essentially justified on semantic grounds, not syntactic ones. Another plausible analysis is to posit a binary branching constituency analysis. But there is no way to justify which of the binary branching analyses in (30) is the right one, because linear order is fixed. Any choice between the binary structures in (30a–e) is arbitrary.

(30) a. [V [NP1 [NP2 NP3]]]
     b. [[[V NP1] NP2] NP3]
     c. [[V NP1] [NP2 NP3]]
     d. [V [[NP1 NP2] NP3]]
     e. [[V [NP1 NP2]] NP3]

A binary branching analysis simply imposes greater syntactic structure than is actually present in (29).

In a syntactic role analysis, the syntactic description of the construction is straightforward: relative position directly codes the syntactic roles of the NPs and the symbolic links to their respective participant roles. The relative order of elements is specified by the construction, and each element is mapped onto the appropriate participant role, as in Figure 6.8.

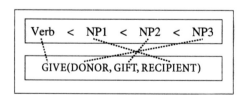

Figure 6.8. Symbolic relations in example (29)

6.3.2. Second position

In §5.3.3, as in most of the syntactic literature on the subject, it was assumed that the specification of linear order is relative, that is, the position of an element is specified relative to the position of other elements, as in the Kilivila example in Figure 6.8. The position of certain elements in some constructions are informally described as occurring in absolute position, such as first or last position. For example, the English Complementizer is informally described as occurring in initial position in the Complement Clause:

(31) She thought [**that** perhaps Bill would come in the afternoon].

Likewise, the Relativizer in Mandarin Chinese is informally described as occurring in final position (example from Li and Thompson 1981: 580):

(32) [zhòng shuǐguǒ **de**] nóngrén
grow fruit REL farmer
'(the) farmer(s) who grow fruit'

Initial and final position can be described in relative terms: the initial element occurs before all other elements in the construction, and all other elements precede the final element in the construction. However, there are elements which occur only in second position in a construction. For example, in O'odham, the Auxiliary occurs in second position in the Clause (see example (33)), while all of the other elements of the construction can occur in any order (example (34); Zepeda 1983: 31):

(33) huhu'id 'o g ban g cu:wĭ
chase AUX DEF coyote DEF jackrabbit
'The coyote is chasing the jackrabbit.'
(34) a. ban 'o g cu:wĭ huhu'id.
b. cu:wĭ 'o huhu'id g ban.
c. huhu'id 'o g cu:wĭ g ban.
d. cu:wĭ 'o g ban huhu'id.

The existence of second position elements means that one must allow for the representation of absolute position in the syntactic structure of constructions. Second position elements, however, pose potential problems in defining syntactic relations, because they break up apparent syntactic constituents. For example, the free word order of O'odham prevents us from defining a Verb Phrase constituent, hence the Verb plus NP arguments would be a whole constituent. If the Auxiliary is a separate constituent from the Clause, as a sort of operator, then the Clausal "constituent" is interrupted by the Auxiliary.

The same is true of the second position Definite Article in the Bulgarian Noun Phrase (Scatton 1983: 314):

(35) nóva -ta mi kníga
new:FSG -the:FSG my book:FSG
'my new book'

The usual analysis of an Article as a separate constituent from the rest of the Noun Phrase would imply that the rest of the Noun Phrase is interrupted by the Article.

Worse for the constituent structure analysis, second position is sometimes defined as the second word in a construction, not the second constituent, as in examples (36) and (37):

SECOND POSITION AUXILIARY/PRONOUN COMPLEX: SERBIAN-CROATIAN
(Comrie 1989: 22):

(36) [[taj **mi** pesnik] čita   knjigu danas]
     that **to.me** poet   reads book   today
     'That poet reads the book to me today'

SECOND POSITION ENCLITIC ARTICLE: MACEDONIAN (Sadock 1991: 118, from Koneski 1967: 327):

(37) [[četiri **-te** stotini] lug'e]
     four   -the   hundred   people
     'the four hundred people'

In (36)–(37), the second position element breaks up subconstituents as well as the main construction constituent.

The specification of elements by absolute position is most naturally accomplished by relating the second position element to the whole construction—in other words, by treating second position as a syntactic role [... Def$_{2nd}$ ...]. The syntactic role representation of second position easily allows a hearer to identify the relevant semantic component for the second position element. Conventions of relative position, such as [Num < Base] and [NumP < Noun] in Macedonian, are also easily represented with syntactic roles, and allow for the identification of the other components of the semantic structure. These structures are illustrated in Figure 6.9, in which the second position Definite construction is combined with the Numeral construction.

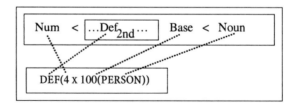

Figure 6.9. Symbolic relations in the constructions illustrated in example (37)

6.3.3. *Nested relational coded dependencies*

Another problem with syntactic relations vs. syntactic roles involves relational coded dependencies. In §5.4.1, I argued that certain overtly coded dependencies, relational coded dependencies, can be analyzed as encoding the semantic relation between the relevant components of the construction. For example, the Russian Genitive case marker encodes the possession relation in (38):

(38) kniga Ivan -a
    book Ivan -GEN
    'Ivan's book'

As noted in §5.4.1, a relational overtly coded dependency may also be an independent element, that is, an adposition, as in the Margi example in (39) (Hoffman 1963: 240):

(39) bzə́r n͜ índà ár wù
    boy sits LOC tree
    'The boy sits in the tree.'

In (39), however, the question arises as to the status of the locative preposition *ár*. Is *ár* merely an indicator of a syntactic relation between the Verb *n͜ índà* and the Noun *wù*, or is it a syntactic element in its own right, with a syntactic relation to *n͜ índà* on the one hand and to *wù* on the other? The latter solution is usually taken, but that analysis means that there is no direct syntactic relation between 'sit' and 'tree', although there is a direct semantic relation between the two.

This may not be a serious problem, but then there is no reason to stop at adpositions: why not treat the case suffix in (38) as an independent syntactic element in its own right, with a syntactic relation to *kniga* on the one hand and *Ivan*- on the other? This is in fact the direction which contemporary generative grammar has gone, by positing syntactic constituents headed by inflectional affixes. As a result, a phrase such as the Russian example in (40) will have a syntactic structure something like that in (41):

(40) nadejat'sja na pobed -u
    hope   for victory -ACC
    'to hope for victory'

(41)

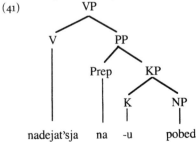

In (40), the Verb *nadejat'sja* determines the choice of the Preposition *na*, and the Preposition determines the choice of the Accusative Case suffix *-u*. But the Verb–Preposition and Preposition–Case relations are collocational dependency relations. Collocational dependencies are constraints in the choice of one word imposed by the choice of another word in the same construction (see §5.1.2). And collocational dependencies are semantic (§5.2). Hence, there is no evidence of syntactic relations on the basis of the adposition and case affix.

This conclusion is not a problem for Radical Construction Grammar. In Radical Construction Grammar, the adposition and the case affix are present to encode a symbolic relation, namely the participant role of the referent of the noun phrase governed by the adposition and case affix. These symbolic links are illustrated in Figure 6.10.

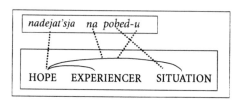

Figure 6.10. Symbolic links for the construction illustrated in example (40)

The collocational relations are evidence of the semantic relation that holds between the emotion expressed and the content of that emotion. That is, the adposition and case affix help the hearer to identify which participant role is filled by which Noun Phrase referent in the construction.

6.3.4. *Absence of one of the units in a syntactic relation*

The problems described in §§6.3.1–6.3.3 present major difficulties for a model utilizing syntactic relations instead of specific syntactic roles. In all of the examples, it is impossible to decide which syntactic relations hold. However, far and away the most serious, perhaps fatal, problem for a model of syntactic representation with syntactic relations is that some part of the syntactic relation simply is not there. Yet this is very common in human languages. In many cases, one of the elements in a putative syntactic relation is absent; these are discussed in this section. In many other cases, the morpheme that encodes the putative syntactic relation is absent; these are discussed in the next section. The problem posed by the absence of some part of a syntactic relation is critical, and is essentially impossible for a model with syntactic relations to avoid.

In §5.4.1, I described indexical coded dependencies, also known as agreement. In agreement, the syntactic relation between two elements is overtly coded by a morpheme on one element (the TARGET) that agrees with or indexes the other element (the CONTROLLER). For example, in the Warlpiri example (42), the 1st Person Singular Agreement suffix -*rna* agrees with or indexes the Subject Noun Phrase *ngajulu-rlu* 'I' (Jelinek 1984: 49, corrected by Kenneth Hale, personal communication):

(42) **ngajulu** -rlu kapi -**rna** -∅ wawirri -∅ panti -rni yalumpu -∅
    I   -ERG FUT -1SG.SBJ -3SG.OBJ kangaroo -ABS spear -NPST that   -ABS
    'I myself will spear that kangaroo.'

A very common phenomenon in the world's languages, however, is that the putative controller is absent from the sentence, as in the Warlpiri example (43) (Jelinek 1984: 43, from Hale 1983: 6):

(43) wawirri   -∅   kapi   -**rna**   -∅   panti   -rni   yalumpu   -∅
    kangaroo -ABS FUT   -1SG.SBJ   -SG.OBJ spear   -NPST that   -ABS
    'I will spear that kangaroo.'

The same phenomenon is found in nonperson agreement of modifiers with nouns. In Spanish, Demonstratives and Adjectives agree with the Head Noun in Gender and Number (Hengeveld 1992: 61):

(44) es   -**a**   **casa**   modern   -a
    that -FSG   house:F(SG)   modern   -FSG
    'that modern house'

However, in the appropriate discourse contexts, the Noun may be absent, but the Demonstrative and Adjective still "agree with" the absent Noun (ibid.; see §2.2):

(45) prefier -o   es   -a   modern   -a
    prefer   -1SG.PRS   that -FSG   modern   -FSG
    'I prefer that modern one.'

The absence of the controller in a construction poses a serious problem for the analysis of agreement markers as indicators of syntactic relations. How can there be a syntactic relation between two elements if the other element is not there? This problem has spawned a number of proposed solutions, all of which are unpalatable in one way or another.

One solution is to argue that sentences like (43) actually have a null Subject Pronoun that acts as the controller. This solution is unpalatable to many linguists because the positing of null elements is an unconstrained theoretical device. Another solution is to argue that the putative target in sentences like (43) is really a bound pronoun, and so the syntactic relation is encoded by the position and form of the bound pronoun. In this approach, examples like (42) are now a problem. One would have to analyze the affix in (42) as an Agreement affix, in which case the same affix would be an Agreement affix in one context and a Bound Pronoun in another (see the analysis of Chichewa in Bresnan and Mchombo 1987). Or one would have to analyze the Independent Subject Pronoun as an "adjunct" rather than an argument of the verb (Jelinek 1984; Jelinek and Demers 1994; Foley 1991: 227–8). Yet it is not clear in what sense the Independent NP is an "adjunct".

Support for the view that person affixes are bound pronouns in at least some languages is the fact that in some languages, the person affix is not used if there is an independent noun phrase. For example, in Breton, the Verb does not occur with the 1st Person Singular suffix if there is a 1st Person Singular Independent Pronoun (Stump 1984: 290, 291):

(46) levrioù   a   lennan
     books   PTCL   read:1SG
     'I read books.'

(47) **me**   a   lenn   [*lennan]   levrioù
     I   PTCL   read   [*read:1SG]   books
     'I read books.'

However, in Emphatic sentences the 1st Person Singular suffix is used even with the 1st Person Emphatic enclitic (ibid.: 302):

(48) levrioù   a   lennan   -**me**   [*lenn   -me]
     books   PTCL   read:1SG   -1SG.EMPH   [*read   -1SG.EMPH]
     'I read books.'

In languages such as Kanuri, illustrated in (49)–(50), the Person prefix is optional (Hutchison 1981: 139):

(49) **nyí**   -à   rú   -kə́   -nà
     2SG   -ASSOC   see   -1SG -PRF
     'I saw/have seen you.'

(50) **nyì**   -à   **nzú-**   rú   -kə́   -nà
     2SG   -ASSOC   2SG-   see   -1SG -PRF
     'I saw/have seen you.'

Similar problems arise with the absence of the head noun in noun phrases. Lehmann argues that nonperson agreement in noun phrases agrees not with the head noun, but with the noun phrase of which the modifier is a part (Lehmann 1982a: 221–3). In some languages, the property with which the modifier "agrees" is not overtly expressed on the controller (ibid.: 204). For example, in Rushi, Case is expressed on the Demonstrative but not the Head Noun; and in Lithuanian, Definiteness is expressed on the Adjective but not on the Head Noun (ibid.: 204–5). In this analysis, the noun phrase is always present even if the head noun is absent. Lehmann describes this as NP-internal agreement. However, Lehmann notes that this solution leads to an unpalatable conclusion: if the only element of the noun phrase that expresses the category is the head noun, then one would have to say that the head noun agrees with the noun phrase (ibid.: 223–4).

These problems arise because of a widely accepted assumption, namely that there is exactly one syntactic argument per semantic referent in a clause. This assumption is expressed in the Theta Criterion in Government and Binding Theory (Haegeman 1994: 73; see §6.4) and the Uniqueness Condition in Lexical-Functional Grammar (Kaplan and Bresnan 1982: 181), inter alia. Thus, in examples like (42) either the 1st Person suffix must be analyzed as "merely" an agreement marker, or the 1st Person Independent Pronoun must be analyzed as "merely" an adjunct. Yet there is no a priori reason to accept one of these analyses over the other. Conversely, in example (43), the absence of an independent argument phrase requires analysis of the 1st Person suffix as a bound pronominal argument. Yet there are many languages in which there is no overt expression of an argument at all, either as an independent noun phrase or as a person agreement affix. The Japanese sentence in (51) is an example of this phenomenon (Gundel et al. 1993: 298):

(51) toori   e   dete   shibaraku   hashitteku
     street   to   go.out   for.some.time   run
     '[He] goes out onto the street and runs for some time.'

The alternative is to abandon this assumption, and treat an agreement affix as expressing a symbolic relation, not a syntactic relation. That is, agreement indexes the referent rather than the phrase denoting the referent. "Agreement" is then simply double indexation, by the independent argument phrase and by the agreement affix. Language-specific constructions specify when double indexation is prohibited (as in the Breton example (47)), optional (as in the Kanuri examples (49)–(50)), or obligatory (as in the Warlpiri example (42) and the Breton example (48)).

In other words, all indexes refer. There is an asymmetry between an independent noun phrase and a pronominal affix, and between a modifier gender/number/case affix and a head noun; but the asymmetry is not one of referring expression ("argument") vs. a nonreferring expression ("mere agreement").

This analysis has been proposed by Barlow (1988). In a survey of patterns of agreement, Barlow compares patterns of agreement in various features in a local context (i.e. where agreement is taken to express syntactic relations) and in anaphoric contexts (where the agreement marker is analyzed as a pronoun, its features dictated by semantic coreference relations; Barlow 1988: 139–52). Barlow concludes that 'there are many similarities and no major distinction between local and anaphoric agreement' (ibid.: 154).

Barlow argues that the reference relation holds between a syntactic element—noun phrase, pronoun, agreement affix—and a DISCOURSE REFERENT. A discourse referent is a conceptual entity that is set up by interlocutors whenever a referring expression is used, including indexical expressions. A discourse referent is semantically (not grammatically) linked to prior discourse referents with the same identity (Barlow 1988, ch. 5). Barlow argues that a discourse referent represents a 'perspective' on a semantic referent (Barlow 1988: 188–9; see below), and hence a single real-world referent may be manifested in multiple discourse referents.

The chief objection that might be offered to Barlow's analysis is that agreement is often grammatical rather than semantic. For example, the Gender of Spanish *casa* 'house' is not semantically based: there is no obvious ways in which houses are female. Hence, the agreement of the Demonstrative and Adjective with the Gender of 'house' should not be described in semantic structure but in syntactic structure, that is as an indicator of syntactic relations. But one cannot draw a sharp line between the syntactic domains in which agreement is grammatical and agreement is semantic; and it is not clear that 'grammatical' vs. 'semantic' is the best description of the two types of agreement.

Corbett presents data for the hierarchy of agreement given in (52) (Corbett 1979):

(52) *Agreement Hierarchy:*
attributive < predicate < relative pronoun < personal (anaphoric) pronoun

If a construction uses grammatical agreement in any construction on the hierarchy, then it will also use grammatical agreement for any construction to the left on the hierarchy. If a construction uses semantic agreement in any construction on the hierarchy, then it will use semantic agreement in any construction to the right on the hierarchy.

The following examples illustrate the hierarchy for Number Agreement in a gradient fashion in Serbian and Croatian. The Numerals 2–4 require a special grammatical agreement form ('Dual Survival'), which is required on the Noun and the Attributive Adjective (Corbett 1979: 206):

(53) ova dva **dobra** [DUAL] čoveka.
'these two good men'

Either the Dual Survival form or the Plural form is possible for the Predicate and the Relative Pronoun, but in text counts the Dual Survival form is found 82 percent of the time for the Predicate and only 38 percent for the Relative Pronoun (Corbett 1979: 206). The Anaphoric Pronoun must always be the Plural *oni* (ibid.). These facts conform to the Agreement Hierarchy.

In other words, one cannot divide the domain of linguistic phenomena into "grammar" and "semantics/pragmatics", and assume that "grammatical" agreement will be found in the former and "semantic" agreement will be found in the latter. Any or all of the construction types that involve specification of the features of referents may use either grammatical or semantic agreement.

But there is some question as to whether the difference between the two types of agreement is best described as "grammatical" vs. "semantic" (Barlow 1988: 220–5). Instead, the two types of agreement represent two different semantic properties. For example, in §3.3, we observed that both Singular and Plural agreement are found with Group Nouns in British English: . . . *if* **a** *highway authority* **are** *satisfied that* . . . But both Singular and Plural features are semantically motivated, since a group is both a single unit and a group of individuals.

Barlow gives a number of similar examples. In the Chichewa example in (54), the Plural Agreement of the Possessive Pronoun indicates respect for the referent (the speaker's father; Barlow 1988: 95, from Corbett and Mtenje 1987: 10):

(54) bambo   **anga**
     father.SG my.POSS.PL
     'my father'

In the Modern Standard Arabic example in (55), the Feminine Singular Agreement on the Verb indicates that the Plural Subject is nonhuman (Barlow 1988: 124):

(55) ʔal-   jimaalu   naam -**at**
     DEF-   camel.M.PL   sleep -**FSG**
     'The camels slept.'

In all of these cases, the form of the "controller" contributes one semantic feature to the referent's description, and the form of the "target" contributes another type of semantic (or pragmatic) feature to that referent's description. In these cases, it is better to analyze the two types of indexes as offering different perspectives (Barlow 1988: 189) on the referent.

Even in the case of less semantically motivated agreement patterns, such as the grammatical genders of a language like Spanish, a semantic analysis can be offered. First, the description of grammatical gender in Spanish as grammatical, that is not semantic, only argues against a monosemous semantic analysis of gender (see §3.2.2 and §4.1). But a monosemous analysis of gender is not the only possible semantic analysis. One can have instead a polysemy, or at least homonymy, account of "grammatical" gender as encoding a symbolic relation. That is, a gender denotes a class of referents, albeit a heterogeneous class, and thus a symbolic relation can be established between a gender and a referent. This is the analysis proposed by Barlow, who posits properties of discourse referents such as <IN-FEMININE-CLASS(x)>, etc. (Barlow 1988: 182, ex. 211e).

The properties need not be mutually exclusive, because they are properties of discourse referents, not of the underlying real-world entities. For example, in *an authority are*..., the discourse referent of *an authority* has the property <INDIVIDUAL(x)> and the discourse referent of the agreement form *are* has the property <COMPOSED-OF-INDIVIDUALS(x)>. The properties are kept separate because each discourse referent imposes a different perspective on the group entity. Likewise, the discourse referent for French *le vélo* 'the [Masculine] bicycle' has the property <IN-MASCULINE-CLASS(x)> and the discourse referent *la bicyclette* 'the [Feminine] bicycle' has the property <IN-FEMININE-CLASS(x)>. The properties are kept separate; the two perspectives are the two names that the object has in French.[2]

An analysis of indexical coded dependencies as distinct syntactic roles which indicate symbolic relations instead of syntactic relations avoids the problem of

---

[2] In Barlow's analysis the Agreement Hierarchy must be reformulated. Barlow reformulates the Agreement Hierarchy as follows: moving along the Agreement Hierarchy, there is a likelihood that the discourse referents will display new properties from those associated with the noun name for the entity referred to, and/or further salient properties of the entity (Barlow 1988: 217–24).

missing elements of the relation. All indexical elements refer, and agreement is analyzed as coreference relations in the semantic structure of the construction. The symbolic analysis for the Modern Standard Arabic example (55) is illustrated in Figure 6.11; the coreferential linking of the discourse referents of *jimaalu* and *-at* is indicated by the dotted line in the semantic representation.

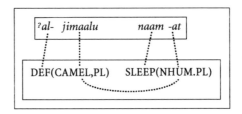

Figure 6.11. Symbolic links for the construction illustrated in example (55)

6.3.5. *Optionality or absence of an overtly coded dependency*

Another cross-linguistically widespread phenomenon is the optionality or absence of the morpheme indicating the existence of an overtly coded dependency. For example, agreement is optional in some languages, such as the Kanuri examples (49)–(50) in §6.3.3. Numeral classifiers are often found only on lower numerals, or not on bases (Aikhenvald 2000: 117; see §3.2.3).

Another quite common example of this phenomenon is the variation in the presence/absence of an adposition or case marking. For example, P arguments in Rumanian sometimes are marked by the Preposition *pe* (a Locative Preposition), sometimes not (Nandris 1945: 183–5). The rules are complex, and only a few examples will be given here. *Pe* is obligatory for Pronouns, Common Nouns, and Proper Names when they refer to human and definite Ps, and in certain constructions for definiteness; it is optional for Ps that are human and specific (referential) indefinite or nonhuman and Pronominal; and it is prohibited for Ps that are non-specific (nonreferential) indefinites, or are partitive or generic:

(56) a   întrebat   **pe**   al   diolea   copil
     PRF   ask.PART   ACC   POSS.ART   second   child:DEF
     'He asked the second child.'

(57) îşi   alese   mire   **(pe)** un   fiu   de   împărat
     REFL   choose.PST   groom   (ACC)   a   son   of   emperor
     'She chose as her bridegroom an Emperor's son.'

(58) n'a   avut   **(*pe)**   copii   niciodată
     NEG'PRF   have.PART   (ACC)   children   never
     'She has never had children.'

The variable presence/absence of overt coded dependencies poses a problem for syntactic relations. It would appear to imply that syntactic relations come and go as the morphosyntax indicating them comes and goes, either optionally or subject to inherent properties of the related elements (animacy, verbal transitivity, cardinality of numeral, etc.). It would be odd to say that particular syntactic relations come and go in such a fashion.

One might respond that the overt coding morpheme is only a superficial manifestation of an underlying syntactic relation. But the arguments for syntactic relations not based on coded dependencies are based on collocational dependencies, which are semantic, not syntactic (§5.2). One might instead argue that other formal properties of the construction, such as word order, encode the syntactic relation. But the criteria for different types of coded dependencies do not match up (§5.4.2), so each coded dependency must be taken on its own. We have only coded dependencies to rely on for putative syntactic relations; and yet they come and go.

In Radical Construction Grammar, the variable presence/absence of overt coded dependency morphemes is not a problem. When present, the overt coded dependency symbolizes a semantic relation, which itself facilitates the identification of the symbolic relation between the syntactic element in question and the corresponding component of the semantic structure. The absence of the overt coded dependency in some contexts does not entail the disappearance of the semantic relation; the semantic relation is simply not overtly coded (it is instead recoverable from other information in the construction or the discourse context). Of course, it is important to understand the conditions under which overt coded dependencies are present or absent; I will address this issue in §6.4.1.

6.4. Comprehending Constructions without Syntactic Relations

In §§6.2–6.3, I have argued that a speaker does not need syntactic relations in comprehending utterances in a construction grammar, and in fact positing syntactic relations poses a number of problems, some serious enough to be fatal. But if we abandon syntactic relations, these problems become pseudoproblems, and simply go away. In this section, I elaborate on the implications of the Radical Construction Grammar model of syntactic structure without syntactic relations.

6.4.1. *The identification of semantic roles via morphosyntactic devices*

Syntactic structure in Radical Construction Grammar is not completely flat, as noted in §6.1. Constructions can be nested inside other constructions; the universal example of this is phrasal constructions nested in clausal constructions. Hence there is some hierarchical structure to constructions in Radical Construction Grammar. Also, I am specifically arguing against syntactic relations *between* elements in a construction. A syntactic element still has a formal relation to the construction as a whole, namely the syntactic ROLE. After all, a hearer must be able to identify which part of the construction is which.

The logical argument against syntactic relations given in §6.1 goes through only if a hearer hears an utterance and is able to identify the construction (Step 1, §6.1), its meaning (Step 2), the elements of the construction (Step 3), and the correspondence between the elements and the components of its semantic structure (Step 4). In the rest of this section, I will argue that the formal properties of constructions that are interpreted as evidence for syntactic relations in standard syntactic theories can be analyzed, and are better analyzed, as aiding the hearer in Steps 1, 3, and 4.

What I called coded dependencies in §5.4—morphemes such as case marking, adpositions, agreement markers, classifiers, etc., and groupings based on contiguity, prosody, etc.—are of course present in the world's languages. I argued in §§6.2–6.3 that overtly coded dependencies do not code relations between syntactic elements. However, overtly coded dependencies do perform other important functions. First, they help to identify which element of the construction is which—Step 3. But equally important, overtly coded dependencies code the correspondence relation between a syntactic element and its counterpart semantic component in the construction—Step 4. In other words, overtly coded dependencies code symbolic relations, not syntactic relations.

The radical approach explains why "syntactic relations" are so massively polysemous—they are not much more than the minimum needed to identify the semantic roles of the components symbolized by the syntactic elements of the construction. It also explains why sentences are interpretable even when the cues provided by coded dependencies go awry (e.g. wrong linear order) or are missing. The coded dependencies are only cues to the symbolic relations in a construction; they are not the glue holding a construction together. The symbolic relations and the semantic relations are the glue holding a construction together.

Why do the various types of coded dependencies appear when and where they do in constructions? Cross-linguistically, coded dependencies tend to show up when the hearer needs them, and to be absent when the hearer does not need them.

Overt relational coding—case marking and adpositions—is typically found in clauses when the referent is unexpected for the participant role it is playing in the event (Croft 1988; there I used the term 'less prototypical' rather than 'unexpected'). For example, the Rumanian Object Preposition *pe* is present when the Object referent is most likely to be mistaken for the Subject referent, that is when it is human and/or definite.

Overt case marking is there when the hearer might have difficulty identifying the referent's participant role in the state of affairs. In general, overt relational coding is found when the participant role is low on the hierarchy of participant roles given in §4.4.1. This is because the lower participant roles are less salient in the event and thus less expected to be overtly expressed by the speaker. Overt relational coding is also found when the A argument is low in animacy and/or definiteness, and (much more commonly) when the P argument is high in animacy and/or definiteness (see §8.4.3); these are the less typical fillers of these participant roles.

Similarly, overt relational coding is less likely to occur for a locative role when the locative role is filled by a phrase denoting a place, but more likely to occur when the locative role is filled by a phrase denoting a person. For example, Modern Eastern Armenian has four locative relational coding devices: -Ø, -*um* '-LOC', -*i mej* '-GEN in', and -*i vəra* '-GEN on' (Comrie 1986: 86–9, from Minassian 1980; see also Aristar 1997). Zero is used when the filler is a place and the state of affairs has a salient locative role, such as 'live' (Comrie 1986: 86):

(59) Aprum   em   Yerevan -Ø
living   I.am Erevan   -(LOC)
'I live in Erevan.'

Either zero or the monomorphemic, affixed Locative morpheme -*um* is used when the filler is a place and the state of affairs does not have a salient locative role, as in (60), or when the filler is not a place but the state of affairs has a salient locative role, as in (61) (ibid.: 87, 88):

(60) Utum   em   Yerevan -um/?-Ø
eating   I.am Erevan   -LOC
'I am eating in Erevan.'
(61) gəndaseɣ -ə   tup^h -um e
pin   -DEF box   -LOC is
'The pin is in/*on the box.'

Finally, the bimorphemic Postposition plus Genitive Case suffix is used when the filler is a person (here, the person acts as only a metaphorical place; ibid.: 88):

(62) ays   avazak -i   mej mi k^{h}ani lav hatkut^{h}yunner kan
this brigand -GEN in   some good   qualities   there.are
'There are some good qualities in this brigand.'

There is no need for overt relational coding with prototypical role-fillers, because their role can be reconstructed from the semantics of the state of affairs denoted by the verb and the semantic type of the participants denoted by the argument phrases.

Indexical coded dependencies—agreement—are used for highly salient referents (Givón 1976, Croft 1988): those high on the participant role hierarchy, or those that are high in animacy or definiteness. These referents are the referents whose identity the hearer is most required to keep track of in discourse. Often, salient referents are likely to be left unexpressed as NPs because they are highly accessible (Ariel 1990). This is most likely with fillers of participant roles high on the participant role hierarchy in §4.4.1 (Croft 1988). Fillers of participant roles lower on the hierarchy are less likely to be highly accessible, and so are typically overtly expressed as argument phrases. In these cases, agreement is much rarer cross-linguistically (or in the case of obliques, virtually absent). Agreement markers are thus more likely to be found when the referent is otherwise left unexpressed.

Also, despite the fact that I showed in §6.2 that there are many cases of non-iconic syntactic structures, one cannot overlook the fact that the great majority of constructions in the world's languages do have a substantially iconic relationship between syntactic structure and semantic structure. Many of the "noniconic" patterns reflect competition between grammatical structures reflecting the structure of the state of affairs and grammatical structure reflecting the information-structural status of the components of the semantic structure (see §5.4.2).

Why is syntactic structure mostly iconic? Because an iconic mapping between function and form is one of the easiest ways to allow a hearer to identify the semantic components corresponding to the syntactic elements of a construction. But as the examples in §§6.2.1–6.2.3 show, an iconic mapping is not the only way. Any reasonable way for the hearer to get the symbolic relations from the speaker's utterance will do.

6.4.2. *The identification of constructions*

So far I have discussed how a hearer can identify the elements of the syntactic structure of a construction, and the symbolic relations between syntactic elements of a construction and the semantic components of that construction, thereby identifying the relevant semantic roles of the syntactic elements. This task presupposes that the hearer can identify the construction in the first place—Step 1—and as a consequence access the semantic structure of the construction—Step 2. But there are clues in the structure of constructions that aid the hearer in this task as well.

For example, the English Passive construction has two unique parts—the Auxiliary verb *be* and the Past Participle Verb form—which jointly specify that this construction is a Passive (and not a Progressive or a Perfect); the Agent Phrase provides a third unique part, the Preposition *by*. These cues taken as a whole provide a structural Gestalt which aids the hearer in identifying the Passive construction as a whole—Step 1 in comprehension.

Functionalist analyses of grammatical structure have been criticized because language possesses substantial redundancy, and this redundancy is assumed to be dysfunctional. For instance, Durie describes redundancy as a case of functional 'overkill':

> with respect to *The farmer killed a duckling* it is clear that ducklings don't kill farmers, and if English did have 'free' word order, there would be no need for a speaker to further disambiguate the sentence. Such further disambiguation would be redundant. As a disambiguating device, English SVO word order displays functional over-generalization, or *overkill*: it is there even when you don't need it (Durie 1995: 278, emphasis in original).

But word order and other role-identifying devices have another function besides identifying roles: they identify constructions as a whole—in Durie's example, the English Nontopicalized Declarative Transitive Active construction. Without being able to identify constructions, semantic roles would be much harder to identify.

Much functional "overkill" in language is not redundant because it (also) serves the function of identifying constructions; it is there because the hearer still needs it. (Conversely, functional "underkill"—ambiguity, including polysemy—is tolerated because the hearer can figure out the semantic role of the referent in the semantic structure of the construction most of the time.)

Even the structure of the discourse may play a significant role to help the hearer to identify the construction, via the significant presence of repetition. For example, Weiner and Labov conducted a study of English Agentless Passives, and discovered that occurrence of an Agentless Passive construction in the immediately preceding clause is a significant factor in the use of the Agentless Passive, independent of other pragmatic/discourse factors (Weiner and Labov 1983: 52–4). Since the Agentless Passive is much rarer in discourse than the Active, one might expect it to require more effort to recognize, and hence repetition facilitates recognition.

Repetition is also found in self-repairs. Fox and Jasperson note that 'the repairing segment carefully reproduces the exact format of the TCU so far, with the exception of replacing the repairable' (Fox and Jasperson 1995: 106), as in the following example:

(63) ^G: That's something [you] can* (.) *each individual user can* change.

Tannen writes, 'repetition and variations [i.e. repeating the construction with different word(s)] facilitate comprehension by providing semantically less dense discourse' (Tannen 1989: 49). Repetition also provides syntactically less dense discourse; 'this facilitation is due to the priming effect: recently activated material is easier to access again' (Bybee 1988: 431).

Finally, the discourse context and the shared knowledge between speaker and hearer, including knowledge of their immediate surroundings, offers clues as to what the semantic structure of the speaker's utterance is. In other words, even the construction's semantic structure, in some schematic form, may be identifiable to the hearer in context. What a speaker will say at a certain point in the conversation is not entirely unpredictable. In fact, many aspects of what a speaker will say are probably quite predictable in many cases. To the extent that what a speaker will say is predictable, certain constructions will be primed in the hearer's mind, and that will facilitate recognizing the syntax of the speaker's utterance when it does come.

6.4.3. *The scaffolding metaphor and the semi-iconicity of syntax*

The abandonment of syntactic relations allows us to escape a number of serious empirical problems in syntactic analysis, some of which were illustrated in §§6.2–6.4. It also dramatically simplifies the syntactic structure of our grammatical knowledge. Instead, analysis is focused on the symbolic relations of a construction: the relation between the construction as a whole and the complex semantic structure it symbolizes, and the relation between the elements of the syntactic structure and the corresponding components of the semantic structure. This is in fact where the real work by speaker's grammars is done in actual language use, and where the real work should be done in syntactic theory.

A closer examination of the mapping from syntactic structure to semantic structure demonstrates that it is in fact more complex than most theories suggest. Langacker compares two approaches to the meaning of complex linguistic expressions:

> the *building block metaphor* . . . sees the meaning of a composite expression as being constructed out of the meanings of its parts simply by stacking them together in some appropriate fashion. . . . In lieu of the building block metaphor, we might adopt the *scaffolding* metaphor: component structures are seen as scaffolding erected for the construction of a complex expression; once the complex structure is in place (established as a unit [construction]), the scaffolding is no longer essential and is eventually discarded (Langacker 1987: 452, 461, emphasis in original).

Langacker illustrates the scaffolding metaphor with the example of Causative Verb constructions in Eastern Mono, a Uto-Aztecan language. Eastern Mono Causatives are formed from an Instrumental prefix attached to an Intransitive verb (Langacker 1987: 292):

(64) ma-   **ma'-**   -k^{w}aca?i   -'ti
 it-   hand-   -descend   -TNS
 'He dropped it.'

But the causative meaning in (64) is more than the sum of the parts, as can be seen by the translation: dropping is not merely the descent of one's hand.

In this chapter, I have argued that what appears to be the coding of syntactic relations is in fact scaffolding to help the hearer to identify which element of the construction symbolizes which component in the semantic structure of the construction. Examples such as (64) suggest that even the coding of the main elements of a construction are only scaffolding for a richer semantic structure.

Examples like (64) can be multiplied. As observed by a number of analysts, the two nouns in the English Complex Nominal construction, illustrated in (65), are only scaffolding for a much more specific semantic relationship between the two Nouns (Clark and Clark 1979: 767):

(65) "Ruling in death of **Ferrari woman**"

Example (65) is a newspaper headline; *Ferrari woman* refers to a woman whose will stipulated that she be buried in her Ferrari.

Syntactically more complex constructions also turn out to be merely scaffolding for an elaborate semantic interpretation:

(66) The shop managed to run out of yogurt.

The interpretation of (66) is that because of prior poor planning on the part of the shop manager (in the opinion of the speaker), customers bought the entire supply of yogurt from the aforementioned shop.

Another interesting example of the scaffolding character of a construction's syntactic form is found in Noun Incorporation in Gunwinggu, an Australian aboriginal language (Oates 1964). Gunwinggu Noun Incorporation expresses a wide range of semantic relations between the Incorporated Noun and other elements of the construction in which it occurs. In (67), the Incorporated Noun indicates a classifying or agreeing function (Oates 1964: 110; gloss on 113):

(67) galug   bene-   wam   bene-   ṟed-   naŋ   ṟed   -gereŋe   -ni
     then   3DU-   go:PST   3DU-   camp-   see:PST   camp   -new   -this
     'Then they came close to the camp which they saw was newly made ...'

In (68), the Incorporated Noun can be interpreted as having a classifying function (a cashew tree as opposed to a cashew nut), but unlike (67), (68) can also be interpreted as a sort of part–whole relation (Oates 1964: 104, gloss on 112):

(68) bene-   dulg-   naŋ   mangaralaljmayn
     3DU-   tree-   saw   cashew.nut
     '... They saw a cashew tree.'

In (69), the part–whole relation is the reverse of (68): the Incorporated Noun denotes a part of the referent of the External Noun (ibid.: 99, with gloss on 103):

(69) dja   baṇdadgen   ŋale-   baye   -ŋ   galug baṇdadgen   ŋale-   wogdayn
     and   stone.axe   handle-   (3SG)bite -PST then   stone.axe   handle-   (3SG)speak:PST
     '[the chicken hawk] bit the handle of his stone axe and rattled its handle [arousing himself to kill the wirwiriyag].'

In (70), two very different sorts of relations are found. The first Incorporated Noun, *gele-* 'fear' indicates the manner of the action. The second Incorporated Noun, *gug-* 'body' indicates that it is the possum as a physical object (a body), not a sentient or volitional being, that is being referred to (ibid.: 92 with gloss on 95):

(70) galug   namaṇde   gele-   waʔwume   -ŋ   dja   djorggun gug-   babalnʔmey   ...
     then   devil   fear-   (3SG)call.out -PST and   possum   body-   (3SG)drop:PST   ...
     'Then the devil called out in fear and dropped the [dead] possum ...'

S arguments may be incorporated, and may retain the Pronominal index, which is then coreferential with the Incorporated Noun (Oates 1964: 105; gloss on 112):

(71) **bene-**   **gug-**   mangaŋ
     3DU-   body-   fall:PST
     'Their bodies fell together.'

Gunwinggu Noun Incorporation illustrates scaffolding at the more conventionalized end of the grammatical spectrum. However, scaffolding is found throughout the grammatical spectrum, even to very broad conventions of discourse. For example, in answering a question about what someone was doing, speakers of Kalam must report the movement to and from the locus of the activity, as well as the activity itself (Pawley 1993: 111):

(72) a. nad   etp   g   -ab   -an   o   -p   -an?
         you   what   do   -REC.PST   -2SG   come   -PF   -2SG
         'What have you been doing?'
    b. **am**   wog-day   olok   kpl   g   -ab   -yn   **o**   -p   -yn
        go   garden   here.and.there weeding   do   -REC.PST   -1SG   **come** -PRF   1SG
        'I went to the garden, weeded here and there, and came here.'

English speakers report only the activity: a typical response to the question in (72) would be *I weeded*.

In contrast, Ojibwe speakers report only the first subactivity (Rhodes 1977: 508):

(73) a. a:ni: -š   ga:-   ž-   bi-   dogšnan   ma:npi:?
         how   -then   PST-   like-   come-   arrive   here
         'How did you get here?'
    b. n-   gi:-   bi-   **bo:z**
        1-   PST-   come-   **embark**
        'I set out.'

English speakers would report the means of traveling, for example *I got a ride*, and would not normally express the initial subactivity at all.

Both the Kalam and Ojibwe response patterns represent highly general but nevertheless language-specific conventions for describing activities. The cross-linguistic variation thus reveals that the English responses also represent language-specific conventions. Each language chooses different parts of an activity as scaffolding in communicating the activity to other speakers.

Elements of constructions functioning as scaffolding for the meaning to be conveyed is the norm, not the exception, for the symbolic relation between elements of a construction and components of its semantic interpretation. Syntax is iconic chiefly in the one-to-one mapping of elements onto components of the semantic structure. The semantic relations between those components, and to other unexpressed components of the meaning of the utterance, are complex and often highly context-sensitive. Abandoning syntactic relations avoids the problem of linking putative syntactic relations to these complex and variable semantic structures.

7

Heads, Arguments, and Adjuncts

7.1. Introduction

In this chapter, I will offer a Radical Construction Grammar critique of the syntactic relational concepts of heads, arguments, and adjuncts. In §§7.2–7.6, I will offer a critique of the syntactic notion of head, and offer an alternative theoretical analysis in which 'head' is a symbolic relation between a syntactic role and a semantic component, following the proposals in Chapter 6. In §7.7, I offer a critique of the argument–adjunct distinction, and suggest that although the semantic counterparts to argument and adjunct form a continuum, there is a cross-linguistically valid distinction between argument and adjunct in terms of two type of symbolic relations.

The contemporary syntactic notion of head is a generalization over the concepts of agreement, government, and modification in traditional grammar. In its most general form, headhood represents the hypothesis that there is a general characterization of the DOMINANT member of any asymmetric syntactic relation in a construction (syntactic structure). In other words, head is assumed to be a global syntactic category (§1.4.3) which is defined relative to the other member of the syntactic relation, which in turn is called the DEPENDENT. Dependents are further divided into two types, ARGUMENTS and ADJUNCTS.

As with other proposed global categories, criteria or tests have been proposed for the analysis of heads. The most thorough discussion of criteria for headhood is offered by Zwicky (Zwicky 1985, 1993; see also Hudson 1987). Zwicky offers six criteria for headhood in his 1985 paper, and adds four more in his 1993 paper (see Table 7.1 below). In the 1985 paper, Zwicky argues that most of the criteria for headhood that he discusses are in fact irrelevant—a position not unlike the Radical Construction Grammar critique that I offer in §7.3. In his 1993 paper, however, Zwicky argues that there are three distinct global syntactic categories which he calls functor, head, and base.

I present Zwicky's criteria in §7.2 and a critique of them in §7.3. Some criteria turn out to be not clearly defined; the remaining criteria do not match up—not a surprising conclusion by this point. Since Radical Construction Grammar rejects syntactic relations, any concept of head in Radical Construction Grammar must be formulated as a symbolic relation between a syntactic role and a semantic component. In §§7.4–7.5, I argue that the intersection of two semantic properties, profile equivalence and primary information-bearing unit (PIBU), represent the concept of head. In §7.6, I argue that at the word level, the relevant role is root (vs. affix), and root is defined only in terms of PIBU status.

7.2. Criteria for Headhood

Zwicky (1985) examines a series of grammatical criteria as candidates for determining headhood; he adds several other criteria in his 1993 paper. Zwicky applies the criteria to the following English constituent combinations (Zwicky 1985: 4):

(1) a. Det + N
    b. V + NP
    c. Aux + VP
    d. P + NP
    e. NP + VP
    f. Comp + S

To illustrate his criteria, I will use here only (1b), V + NP. This combination probably has the most widely accepted dependency analysis of the six constructions Zwicky discusses: namely, the Verb is the head and the Object NP is the dependent. In fact, all of Zwicky's criteria generally point to that conclusion (problematic cases will be reserved for the next section). Zwicky's syntactic criteria are presented in Table 7.1 according to the three-way taxonomy of functor, base, and head from his 1993 paper (Zwicky's semantic criteria are discussed in §7.4.1).

Table 7.1. Zwicky's criteria for headhood (Zwicky 1985, 1993)

Functor
Agreement target (Zwicky 1993: 295); 'determination of concord' [Zwicky 1985: 8–9])
Subcategorizand (Zwicky 1985: 5; replaced by 'lexical subcategorization' [Zwicky 1993: 295])
Governor (Zwicky 1985: 7–8; 1993: 295–6)

Base
Obligatoriness (Zwicky 1985: 13; 1993: 297, 310)
Distributional equivalent (Zwicky 1985: 11; renamed 'external representation' [Zwicky 1993: 297])

Head
Morphosyntactic locus (Zwicky 1985: 6–7; 1993: 298)
Syntactic category determinant (Zwicky 1993: 297)

Zwicky describes three other criteria, all of which are weaker than the criteria in Table 7.1. Zwicky also argues that heads in his narrow sense are of WORD RANK (Zwicky 1993: 297). However, word rank is not a sufficient condition for head status. For example, an Adverb modifier such as *very* in *very happy* is of word rank, yet is not the head of the Adjective Phrase in Zwicky's sense. Zwicky himself notes that heads are merely 'typically specified as of Word rank' (ibid.).

UNIQUENESS is the property that only one element can fill the relevant role. For example, there may be only one Subject phrase; in contrast, there may be many Adjectival modifiers. In Zwicky's analysis, only one syntactic type is not unique: modifiers. But even Adjectives can be semantically divided into unique subgroups. The Noun Phrase *little red book* may have two Adjectival modifiers, but they are of different types: one cannot say *big large book or *red pink book. On the other hand, as we saw in §6.3.1, there are reasons not to assume that uniqueness is a universal property for elements of certain types of constructions.

OPTIONALITY applies only to nonrequired units (Zwicky 1993: 310). Zwicky observes that in English, some are optional, others are obligatory, but draws no language-universal (or even language-specific) generalizations from this observation. An analysis of optionality in Radical Construction Grammar is presented in §7.7.3.

7.2.1. *Functor criteria*

Zwicky (1993) identifies one set of criteria with the semantic FUNCTOR, that is, the element that is analyzed as a functor in formal semantic theories as opposed to an argument. This semantic concept will be discussed in §7.4.1; here I will describe the morphosyntactic criteria that Zwicky believes are associated with the functor.

The first functor criterion is the presence of AGREEMENT on the functor ('determination of concord', Zwicky 1985: 8–9; 'target of agreement', Zwicky 1993: 295): the functor's argument(s) trigger agreement by the functor (see §§5.3.3, 6.3.1). This criterion does not hold in English for V + NP, but can be found in languages with Object Agreement, such as Yimas, where the NP generally determines the concordial properties of the V (Foley 1991: 203):

(2) **wanwa**   wa-   ka-   tar-   wapi
    knife.CL.IX.SG CL.IX.SG.O-   1SG.A-   CAUS-   sharp
    'I sharpened the knife.'

The Class IX Noun *wanwa* 'knife' determines the choice of the Class IX Object prefix *wa-*.

The second criterion for functors is the SUBCATEGORIZAND (Zwicky 1985: 5–6).[1] According to this criterion, the element in a construction that requires a subcategorization frame is the functor. This item must be lexical in Zwicky's model of

---

[1] Zwicky (1993) replaces this concept with LEXICAL SUBCATEGORIZATION. He describes lexical subcategorization as restriction to 'a class of lexemes eligible to serve in that function in the construction' (Zwicky 1993: 295; see also Pollard and Sag 1987: 136).

syntax (Zwicky 1985: 5), since the subcategorization frame is listed in the lexicon. In the V + NP case, we have the archetypal use of subcategorization frames in syntax—representing the argument structure associated with the Verb—and the V is the subcategorizand:

(3) [*hit* NP]:
   a. Tina **hit** the ball.
   b. *Tina **hit**.
(4) [*sleep* __]:
   a. Tina **slept**.
   b. *Tina **slept** the ball.

Zwicky argues that the functor is the constituent that GOVERNS the grammatical form of its sister constituent(s) (Zwicky 1985: 7–8; 1993: 295–6). Zwicky defines subcategorization as present when an element (necessarily lexical) specifies what sister constituents it can have; government, on the other hand, indicates what FORM those constituents are found in, for example accusative vs. instrumental case of objects (see §7.2.1). Zwicky also argues that there are also semantic interpretation rules associated with subcategorizations.

Zwicky also distinguishes two types of government. In the first type, the morphological form is determined by virtue of the construction itself. In the second type, the lexical class of the head determines the form of the dependent. English V + NP illustrates the first type: the Pronominal Objective form is required by virtue of the fact that the Pronoun is the Object of the Verb. The second type is illustrated in a language with a richer Case system than English, Russian:

(5) a. *čitat' gazetu* (ACC) 'to read a/the magazine'
    b. *pravit' mašinoj* (INST) 'drive a car'
    c. *mešat' rabote* (DAT) 'to interfere with the work'

Example (5a) (Accusative) is usually analyzed as the default pattern and represents Zwicky's first type of government. The selection of Instrumental and Dative Case forms of the Object NP in (5b–c), however, is determined by the Verb, and hence are examples of the second type of government.

7.2.2. *Base criteria*

The category of BASE is proposed in Zwicky (1993) as possessing distinct properties from that of the head as he defines the latter concept (see §7.2.3). The base is identified with a semantic property, which Zwicky describes as 'classifying' (Zwicky 1993: 310) or 'characterizing' (Zwicky 1993: 296). I will return to this semantic property in §7.4, and describe the morphosyntactic criteria here.

One of Zwicky's original criteria for headhood is the OBLIGATORY CONSTITUENT in a construction (Zwicky 1985: 13); he later redefines obligatoriness and argues that this criterion applies to the base (Zwicky 1993: 297, 310). Zwicky (1985) characterizes obligatoriness as an operational criterion which has nevertheless been treated as definitional in the literature. The head should be the obligatory constituent in the unit; the following example suggests that V is the head because it is obligatory whereas the NP is not.

(6) a. Janet ate lunch.
    b. Janet ate.
    c. *Janet lunch.

Zwicky (1993: 297) redefines this criterion as the REQUIRED constituent: a constituent that is either present or, if absent, is to be understood elliptically. For example, the VP *turkey* in (7) is missing its Verb, but (6b) is acceptable only if the Verb is elliptically understood as *ate* (ibid.):

(7) I ate chicken, and Kim [Ø turkey]$_{VP}$.

Zwicky's redefinition of this criterion is the same as the definition of syntactic arguments to be proposed in §7.7.3.

The last base criterion is what Zwicky first calls the DISTRIBUTIONAL EQUIVALENT (Zwicky 1985: 11) and later calls its external representation (Zwicky 1993: 297). Zwicky derives this criterion from Bloomfield's notion of 'same form class' (Bloomfield 1933: 194; see Zwicky 1993: 297). Zwicky (1985) describes this criterion as 'the one consituent that belongs to a category with roughly the same distribution as the construct as a whole' (Zwicky 1985: 11). Of course, much depends on how strictly one interprets the word 'roughly' in Zwicky's definition. We can use (6a–c) again to illustrate that V has a similar distribution to VP, while NP does not.

7.2.3. Head criteria

Zwicky uses the name 'head' to describe the element associated with the last set of criteria. Zwicky does not identify this concept with any semantic property, but instead most closely identifies it with the criterion of the MORPHOSYNTACTIC LOCUS (Zwicky 1985: 6–7; Zwicky 1993: 298). The element in the constituent which bears the morphosyntactic marks linking that constituent with higher-level constituents is the head. Zwicky intends this as not merely overt inflectional coding on the head of the constituent, but abstract syntactic properties that must be attributed to the putative head constituent in syntactic analysis. This can be illustrated in our example in that morphosyntactic properties dictated by constituents into which V + NP is embedded, such as tense and finiteness, are located on the V, not the NP, of the V + NP:

(8) a. I barbecu**ed** the steak.
    b. *I barbecue the steak**ed**.

Zwicky (1993) adds another head criterion, the SYNTACTIC CATEGORY DETERMINANT, to the set of head criteria (Zwicky 1993: 297). He argues that the syntactic category determinant is the element which shares its category with that of the head, albeit not its rank. In our example, Verb and Verb Phrase are of the same category—Verb—but of different ranks: Verb is a word, and Verb Phrase is a phrase.

We now turn to a critical review of these different criteria.

7.3. Deconstructing Heads

Based on the empirical facts presented in earlier chapters, we should not be surprised to discover mismatches in the various head criteria proposed by Zwicky. Zwicky (1985) discards all the syntactic criteria for headhood but one, while Zwicky (1993) distributes the criterion across three theoretical entities (functor, base, and head).

In Radical Construction Grammar, each criterion potentially has its own distribution pattern. In the following sections, I will examine each criterion critically. Some criteria will turn out to be invalid; other criteria are construction-specific, and the criteria which remain do not match up.

Another problem with most of Zwicky's criteria, that I briefly raise here, is variation within a category with respect to the criteria for headhood. For example, English Determiners behave differently with respect to distributional equivalence. The Demonstratives *this/that* are distributional equivalents of NP, since they can occur as pronouns in *This is beautiful*; but the Articles *the* and *a* are not distributional equivalents of NP, since they cannot: **The/a is beautiful*. Should one say that Determiners pass the distributional equivalents test, because some of them do, or that they fail the test, because some of them do not? This is relevant because the theoretical claim that is being made with the concept of head is that this concept is general to all asymmetric dependency relations in grammar. This means that the criteria used to define heads should be relatively easily applicable to all such relations—another way in which the criteria must be theoretically relevant to the grammatical construct being studied.

7.3.1. Agreement

Agreement gives conflicting evidence for headhood across languages; this can be observed in genitive constructions. In some languages, the Genitive Modifier agrees with the Head Noun, as in Bulgarian (Scatton 1983: 317):

(9) sestr   -ina   -ta   **kŭšta**
    sister -GEN.FSG -ART.FSG   **house.FSG**
    '[the] sister's house'

In other languages, the Head Noun agrees with the Genitive Modifier, as in the Mam example in (10) (England 1983: 142):

(10) t-   kamb'   **meeb'a**
     3SG.POSS- prize   **orphan**
     '[the] orphan's prize'

The explanation for this conflict is that agreement is sensitive to a semantic property that is independent of headhood. Agreement morphemes agree with (are triggered by) semantic arguments (Lehmann 1982a). The reason for this, I argued in §6.3.1 (following Barlow 1988), is that agreement morphemes index discourse referents, which are expressed as syntactic arguments (when they are expressed at all).

The reason there is a cross-linguistic mismatch in agreement in genitive constructions is that a genitive modifier is an argument, and it is a modifier within a larger noun phrase which is also an argument (see also Zwicky 1993: 309). So either argument can trigger agreement, and cross-linguistically either one does.

7.3.2. Subcategorization, government, and construction grammar

Zwicky argues that subcategorization and government should be related to the notion of semantic functor, not head as he wishes to define it (Zwicky 1985: 3, 9–10). However, there are syntactic difficulties with treating subcategorization and government as reflections of semantic functor. Specifically, a construction grammar analysis of government and subcategorization eliminates the directionality that supports the head-dependent or even functor–argument asymmetry.

The extent to which there is an asymmetric syntactic relationship analogous to a semantic functor–argument relationship depends on the extent to which the syntactic relationship between a lexical item and its subcategorization or pattern of government is a function in the mathematical sense. That is, it depends on the degree to which there is a unique subcategorization/government pattern for each lexical item. If so, then it is reasonable to assume that the functor determines the subcategorization. If not, then it is difficult to maintain this claim. I will argue that the relationship is not a (mathematical) function.

The usual characterization of subcategorization in generative syntax assumes there is a particular directionality, so that the subcategorizand determines the subcategorization that it requires. This is questionable to the extent that the subcategorization is not a function in the mathematical sense, that is that there is a unique subcategorization for each lexical head. This is not generally the case, particularly in English. Many Verbs can be used with or without an Object—that is, they may occur in either the Intransitive or Transitive subcategorization frames:

(11) *eat, drink, smoke,* etc.: either [_] or [_ NP]

Many Ditransitive Verbs take one of two subcategorization frames: [_ NP NP] or [_ NP *to* NP], as Zwicky himself notes:

(12) *give, send, tell,* etc.: [_ NP NP] or [_ NP *to* NP]

Levin (1993) describes a large number of argument structure alternations in English ('argument structures' are generally defined as subcategorization frames linked to particular thematic roles). It appears from her inventory that most Verbs in English allow multiple argument structures.

In order to maintain the mathematical function relationship between a Verb and its subcategorization frame, one could postulate two distinct Verbs, each one taking a single subcategorization frame, thereby preserving the function-like character of the word–subcategorization relationship. However, there are also subtle semantic differences depending on which subcategorization frame is used with a particular Verb, which can be argued to be contributed by the subcategorization frame itself. This position has been argued for Transitives by Rice (1987), and for Ditransitives and several other constructions by Goldberg (1995). Another example of more than one subcategorization per Verb with a difference in meaning between the subcategorizations is the well-known Locative Alternation (Anderson 1971; Dowty 1991):

[_ NP LocPrep NP]:

(13) a. Mary **sprayed** paint on the wall.
b. They **loaded** hay on the truck.

[_ NP *with* NP]:

(14) a. Mary **sprayed** the wall with paint.
b. They **loaded** the truck with hay.

The Direct Object is interpreted as more completely affected by the action than the Oblique, and this appears to be an effect of Direct Object status in these argument structures, not the verb meaning.

These facts have a natural analysis in construction grammar. The subcategorization frame is an argument structure construction (§1.3.2), and there is a many-to-many mapping between verbs and the constructions they occur in. No directionality is involved, and so there is no direct connection between subcategorization and functor status.

A similar argument applies to government. Zwicky argues that with government, there is directionality because it is the form of the governed complement that is chosen, while there is no such mark found on the governing constituent itself (e.g. the Verb governing the Case of an Object in German or Russian, or an Auxiliary governing a Nonfinite Verb form in English). Again, this argument is weakened to the extent that the shape of the governed element is not uniquely determined by the lexical class of the head, and instead varies, possibly systematically, in relation to the head.

For example, the relationship between the English Auxiliaries *have* and *be* and the Nonfinite Verb forms they govern (*to* Infinitive, Bare Infinitive, Present Participle, Past Participle) is a many-to-many relation:

(15) *have* + *to* Infinitive: obligation
have + Past Participle: perfect

have + NP + Bare Infinitive: indirect causation
be + *to* Infinitive: obligation
be + Present Participle: progressive
be + Past Participle: passive

There is no systematic semantic predictability in either direction, although there are relationships that suggest that the semantics of both the Auxiliary and the Verb form are involved. Similarly, the choice of the Case of Objects in Russian or other languages is often dependent on semantic interpretation.

Worse, from the point of view of the traditional government analysis, the governed alternations are productive in some languages. For example, the Warlpiri Absolutive-Dative Alternation for P arguments follows a pattern of degree of affectedness and is quite general (Hale 1982: 250):

(16) kurdu -ngku ka -ju **ngaju** paka -rni
 child -ERG PRS -1 **me(ABS)** strike -NPST
 'The child is striking me.'
(17) kurdu -ngku ka -ju -rla -jinta **ngaju** -ku paka -rni
 child -ERG PRS -1 AUX -3SG.DAT **me** -DAT strike -NPST
 'The child is striking "at" me.'
(18) ngarrka -ngku ka -rla **karli** -ku warri -rni
 man -ERG PRS AUX **boomerang** -DAT seek -NPST
 'The man is looking for a boomerang.'

We may analyze Warlpiri as having the the ERG-ABS construction [NP-ERG, AUX, NP-ABS, VERB] and the ERG-DAT construction [NP-ERG, AUX, NP-DAT, VERB]. Some verbs can take either ERG-ABS or ERG-DAT with a systematic semantic shift, while others take only ERG-DAT because of their semantic compatibility with ERG-DAT constructional semantics; hence the verb–case government mapping is not a function either.

Also, the argument based on the definition of government can be turned on its head in some cases. In a number of languages, the Transitivity of the Verb is overtly coded on the Verb by an affix such as the Tok Pisin Transitive suffix *-im* (Verhaar 1995: 304):

(19) Yu mas karamap **-im** gut olgeta poteto...
 2SG OBLG cover **-TR** carefully all potatoes
 'cover all the potatoes carefully...'

One could argue that the presence of an Object triggers a formal property of the Verb, namely its Transitivity marking. Zwicky (1993: 296) argues instead that *-im* is an indicator of the lexical subcategory of the Verb, reversing the directionality of the relationship. But these two analyses are equivalent, and there is no real directionality in the relationship.

The complexity and range of possibilites of the relationship between a verb and its pattern of government is analogous to that between a verb and its subcategorization frame. Government too can be analyzed by having constructions as independently stored grammatical entities along with lexical items. Government merely specifies more precise structural information about the constructions, e.g. [Verb NP$_{\text{Instrumental}}$]. As a matter of fact, Prepositions in English subcategorization frames correspond to "government" of Case in languages with extensive NP Case morphology such as Russian; the two phenomena are essentially identical.

7.3.3. Obligatoriness and distributional equivalence

Obligatoriness again gives conflicting evidence for headhood across languages. We may illustrate this with the Adj + N construction. In English, the Noun is the obligatory constituent: one cannot say *the big. The nearest construction to this involves the use of the Pro-form *one*, which functions as the head: *the big ones*. In other languages, such as Quechua, however, the Noun is no more syntactically obligatory than the Adjective, as we observed in §2.2 (Schachter 1985: 17):

(20) **hatun** -kuna -ta
     big   -PL   -ACC
     'the big ones [Object]'
(21) **alkalde** -kuna -ta
     mayor   -PL   -ACC
     'the mayors [Object]'

The Adjective is also thereby the distributional equivalent of the Noun Phrase in Quechua, if we ignore the semantic shift it undergoes (see §2.2).

Another example in which cross-linguistic variation plays havoc with distributional equivalence for reasons not having to do with headhood is the Det + N example discussed in §7.3. There it was pointed out that in English, some Determiners (e.g. *that*) are distributional equivalents, while others (e.g. *the*) are not: *these books/these* vs. *the book* vs. **the*. The reason for this, however, is that the Pronominal equivalent of *the* is *he/she/it*, and it just happens that in English there is a suppletive relationship between the Article and the 3rd Person Pronoun. In other languages, however, this is not the case and 'the' is in fact a distributional equivalent for NP; the example here is from Luganda (Ashton et al. 1954: 41):

(22) eki-   kwaso **eky-** o
     CL.SG- pin   CL.SG-   **the**
     'the pin'
(23) **eky-** o
     CL.SG-   **the**
     'it, "the one"'

But, in still other languages, attributive demonstratives are not the distributional equivalent of NP; attributive and pronominal demonstratives are consistently different in form. Japanese represents this language type (see Kuno 1973: 27):

(24) *Attributive:* **kono** hito 'this man' vs. ***kono**   'this'
     Pronominal: **kore**   'this'   vs. ***kore** hito 'this man'

A slightly different explanation accounts for the differences in behavior for the combinations NP + VP, V + NP. The optionality of the object illustrated for English *eat* in (6b) is not general for all Transitive Verbs in English, and involves some distinct semantic properties which suggest that there are in fact two different verbs, *eat* [tr.] and *eat* [intr.] (see §7.7.3). If we are interested in distributional equivalence for NP + VP and V + NP in general, we must look at other languages. When we do so, we find distributional equivalence for the VP and V respectively depends on whether the language has null subject/object anaphora (pro-drop) or not.

In English, in general, there is little Null Subject/Object Anaphora (but see §7.7.3). In other languages such as Japanese, Mandarin Chinese, and Rennellese, from which the following example is taken (Elbert and Momberg 1965), Null Anaphora is quite general and also quite common:

(25) aano   tutuku   i   mu'a   Hangemangama
     and.then   spill   in   front   H.
     'And then [he] spilled [it (earth)] in front of Hangemangama.'

The evidence from Null Anaphora in Rennellese suggests that the V is the head of V + NP by the distributional equivalence and obligatoriness criteria. But an NP can also be the distributional equivalent of the VP, if the language uses NPs in predicate nominal constructions without the addition of copulas or verbal inflections, as in Russian:

(26) ona   čitala   knigu
     she   read:PRS   book
     'She was reading a book.'
(27) ona   spala
     she   sleep:PST
     'She was sleeping.'
(28) ona   student
     she   student
     'She was a student.'

With the combination Aux + V, the obligatoriness/distributional equivalence of the Auxiliary depends on whether the language has the VP-Deletion construction, as in English (Zwicky 1985: 13), or lacks it, as in French (Zwicky 1985: 14):

(29) You haven't been to Rumania, but I have ∅.
(30) a. *Tu n'es pas allé en Roumanie, mais moi je suis ∅.
     b. Tu n'es pas allé en Roumanie, mais moi j'**y** suis **allé**/mais moi **si**.

In other words, obligatoriness depends on the constructions available in the language—Null Anaphora, VP-Deletion, copula-less Predicate Nominals, etc.—not on some universal concept of headhood.

As noted in §7.2.2, Zwicky redefines the obligatoriness criterion as required rather than obligatory. A required element may be absent, but then is interpreted as elliptical. This analysis causes the examples in (20), (23), and (25) to conform to Zwicky's criterion, because they are all elliptical. However, this strategy leads to the opposite problem: more than one element in a construction is required. For instance, in the Rennellese sentence in (25), both the Verb and its required arguments are required in Zwicky's sense, since the absent arguments are elliptical.

There are other cases in which more than one element is not only required but obligatory. In Palauan, every NP (and in fact also every VP) must be accompanied by a particle that might be described as a Determiner (Josephs 1975: 113):

(31) a   ngalęk   a   męnga   ęr   a   ngikęl
     DET   child   DET   eat   OBJ   DET   fish
     'The child is eating the fish.'

Both the Determiner particle and the Noun or Verb are obligatory elements of their respective constructions. Another example is O'odham: every Finite Clause contains an Auxiliary as well as a Verb (Zepeda 1983: 8):

(32) 'i:da   'o'odham   'o   ñeok
     this   person   AUX   speak
     'This person is/was speaking.'

In fact, "distributional equivalence" of a construction and its base element (in Zwicky's terms) does not make sense. Zwicky notes that to apply this criterion, morphology must be ignored (Zwicky 1993: 297–8). But syntax must also be ignored; an English Transitive Verb Phrase, [TrVerb Object], does not have the same syntactic distribution as the Transitive Verb; in particular [TrVerb Object] cannot fill the TrVerb role in [TrVerb Object]. In other words, the "distributional equivalence" criterion cannot be coherently applied because one must ignore distribution patterns in order to define "distributional equivalence".

With respect to the obligatory and required element criteria, I have argued that they are due to a variety of grammatical facts: whether there are distinct attributive and pronominal forms for any or all determiners or other modifiers; whether there is general null anaphora for subjects and/or objects; whether a copula is required for predicate nominals; whether a Verb Phrase Deletion construction exists in the language or not; whether multiple elements are required. None of these grammatical facts has any obvious connection to headhood, either some intuitive semantic notion or any specific formal notion. Instead, as with subcategorization and government, the obligatoriness or requirement of the element of the construction is a property of the construction as a whole, not of any element or of any specific class of elements of a construction (see §7.7.3). In other words, Zwicky's grammatical criteria for base evaporate, although the semantic definition Zwicky offers survives (see §7.4.1).

7.3.4. *The syntactic category determinant and the morphosyntactic locus*

We now turn to the grammatical criteria that Zwicky (1993) associates with head in his narrow sense of the term: syntactic category determinant and morphosyntactic locus. Zwicky introduces the first in his 1993 paper with little explication: '[the syntactic category determinant] determines the syntactic category of the construct as a whole' (Zwicky 1993: 297). It is hard to see how this criterion is much more than true by stipulation. If categories are defined by distribution (see Chapter 1), then the syntactic category determinant is identical to the distributional equivalent; and I have argued in §7.3.3 that the criterion of distributional equivalent does not make sense.

This leaves the one morphosyntactic criterion that Zwicky does consider to be an indicator of headhood, the morphosyntactic locus of grammatical inflection. Zwicky's chief interest in his 1985 paper is in what is called percolation, a principle that morphosyntactic features of the head match the morphosyntactic features of the constituent of which it is the head. These features are generally inflectional features, such as gender, number, tense, etc. But this definition of headhood seems circular. Since the purpose of percolation is (as the name implies) to percolate features from one level to another, it is not surprising that the head is the element at the lower level bearing those features. Zwicky seems to feel some of this circularity, by suggesting that morphosyntactic locus is the primitive concept (Zwicky 1985: 3, 10), and concludes, 'unless there is very good reason for doing otherwise, the morphosyntactic locus should be identified as the head in syntactic percolation' (ibid.: 10).

Again, the criterion of morphosyntactic locus fails cross-linguistically. The inflectional repertory of some languages is very limited, possibly nonexistent in some languages. Hence morphosyntactic locus is not a cross-linguistically valid criterion. In those languages where inflection occurs, there is cross-linguistic conflict as to which element is the head by the morphosyntactic locus criterion.

Languages differ as to whether the Auxiliary or the Verb is the morphosyntactic locus for inflections associated with the clause. The morphosyntactic locus is sometimes Aux, sometimes V, sometimes both. In Basque, only a handful of Verbs inflect (Lafitte 1962: 238, 273–4); the Verbs appear in various Participial forms and require an inflected Auxiliary instead (Saltarelli 1988: 227):

(33) erosketa   -k   gaur   goiz   -ean   egi   **-n**
     purchase   -ABS.PL today   morning -LOC.SG do   -PRF
     d-   it-   u   -t
     3ABS-   ABS.PL- TR.AUX -1SG.ERG
     'I did/have done the shopping this morning.'

In Kiowa, Verbs inflect; separate forms indicating Tense–Aspect–Mood are uninflected particles (Watkins 1984: 146–7, 217–24; example from ibid.: 159):

(34) á·kʰḭ·gyà   hègɔ́   **mîn**   gyá-   kʰḭ·   -mà
     flowers   now   IMM.FUT   PL-   bloom   -IMPF
     'The flowers are about to bloom'

In O'odham, the Auxiliary inflects for some categories (Tense–Aspect–Mood and Subject), while the Verb inflects for Object (Zepeda 1983: 33):

(35) a:ñi **añ**   g   wipsilo **ha-**   cecposid
     I   1SG.AUX DET   calves   3PL.OBJ- brand.RDP
     'I am/was branding the calves.'

Similar conflicting evidence is found cross-linguistically for determiner (demonstratives and/or articles) and noun as the morphosyntactic locus of inflections associated with the noun phrase. In many languages the morphosyntactic locus is the noun; it is inflected for number, gender, case, etc. In Yurok, for example, Demonstratives and Articles do not inflect, while Nouns inflect for Possessor, and a few nouns have irregular Plurals (Robins 1958). But in other languages, the only manifestation of inflectional categories is on the determiner. For example, in Rennellese, the Determiner inflects for Number and Definiteness, while the Noun does not inflect (Elbert 1988: 131, 133):

(36) **te** hage/**naa** hage
    'the house/the houses'

Finally there are languages like English in which both the Noun and (some) Determiners inflect, in this case for Number:

(37) a. this book/**these** books
     b. that book/**those** books
     c. a book/**some** books
     but:
     d. the book/the books

In the end, no single syntactic criterion is able to provide a cross-lingustically valid, uniform means to identify "heads" as a universal and global primitive member of asymmetric syntactic relations. The question now is: is there a coherent, linguistically significant notion of a "dominant" element of a construction? If so, what is its proper definition? In the next two sections, I will argue that there is such a notion.

7.4. A Semantic Definition of "Head"

7.4.1. *Heads and profile equivalents*

The traditional notion of head is relatively recent. The first reference to heads by name that I am aware of is Sweet:

> The most general relation between words in sentences from a logical point of view is that of **adjunct-word** and **head-word** . . . *book (books)* is an adjunct-word in *book-seller, book-selling, sale of books, he sells books, he sold his books,* the corresponding head-words being *seller, selling, sale, sells, sold* (Sweet 1891: 16).

Sweet unfortunately does not define what a head-word is in general; the head-adjunct distinction is taken as self-evident. These terms evoke the syntactic asymmetry rather than any pretheoretical characterization of the "dominant" element.

More specifically, they do not provide any clue as to how to determine independently which element is the head, except through the morphosyntactic criteria which I have argued to be largely irrelevant to the question.

Jespersen appears to subscribe to the same position as Sweet's, though he does not use the word 'head':

In any composite denomination of a thing or person . . . , we always find that there is one word of supreme importance to which the others are joined as subordinates. This chief word is defined (qualified, modified) by another word, which in turn may be defined (qualified, modified) by a third word, etc. We are thus led to establish different 'ranks' of words according to their mutual relations as defined or defining. In the combination *extremely hot weather* the last word *weather*, which is evidently the chief idea, may be called primary; *hot*, which defines *weather*, secondary, and *extremely*, which defines *hot*, tertiary (Jespersen 1924: 96).

As with Sweet, Jesperson focuses on the asymmetric relation, but not the property that determines which is the 'dominant' one in the relationship. However, he gives a hint in his example: '*weather*, which is evidently the chief idea . . .'.

Bloomfield's position is the starting-point of structuralist and generative theories of headhood:

If all of the syntactic constructions which go to make up a phrase are endocentric, then the phrase will contain among its ultimate constituents some word (or several words, members of a co-ordination) whose form-class is the same as that of the phrase. This word is the *center* of the phrase. In the phrase *all this fresh milk*, the word *milk* is the center, and in the phrase *all this fresh bread and sweet butter*, the words *bread* and *butter* are the centers (Bloomfield 1933: 195).

Bloomfield was a strict behaviorist by the time he wrote this passage, and so uses the criterion of distributional equivalence ('same form-class'), which we have argued is not relevant to headhood. But in addition to using the term 'head' (in another passage on the same page), Bloomfield here uses the term 'center', which is reminiscent of Jespersen's concept of the 'chief idea'.

Before presenting his morphosyntactic criteria for headhood, Zwicky suggests a semantic definition, inspired by Jespersen (1924): 'Like Jespersen . . . we could take the head/modifier distinction to be at root semantic: in a combination X + Y, X is the "semantic head" if, speaking very crudely, X + Y describes a kind of the thing described by X' (Zwicky 1985: 4). Zwicky's definition describes the head as a syntactic role, that is, headhood is defined in terms of a relationship between a syntactic element and the construction as a whole. Zwicky's definition is also symbolic, in that it describes a relationship between a syntactic element and the semantic structure it symbolizes.

Zwicky's definition of semantic head is essentially the same as Langacker's notion of head in Cognitive Grammar (Langacker 1987, §8.2.1). Langacker uses the term PROFILE to name the part of a semantic structure that is actually symbolized by a construction. In discussing the question of how the profile of a composite (complex) construction is related to the profiles of its component parts, Langacker writes: 'For the most part, a composite structure simply inherits the profile of one of its components. The component structure whose profile is inherited will be termed the PROFILE DETERMINANT of the construction' (Langacker 1987: 289). For example, in the phrase *broken vase*, *vase* is the profile determinant because the whole phrase profiles the vase. In contrast, in the clause *the vase broke*, *broke* is the profile determinant because the clause profiles the breaking event.

The formulation of Zwicky's criterion and Langacker's—hedged—definition of profile determinant suggests that constructions have a conventionally specified element that determines the profile of the construction as a whole. This definition is not able to account for certain noncanonical construction types. In some constructions, such as the English appositive construction *my brother the geophysicist*, the profile of the whole is identical not to just one but both of the component NP profiles.

In some other constructions, no element determines the profile of the whole construction because no element has a profile that is identical to that of the whole construction. These are EXOCENTRIC or headless constructions. For example, the Quechua example *hatun* 'the big one' profiles an object whereas the word *hatun* profiles a property of the object (in the analysis advocated in Chapter 2). Other examples include headless relative clauses, as in (38), and sentential complements, as in (39):

(38) [**What really bothers me**] are all of those square brackets.
(39) I said [(**that**) **I was going to do it**].

In (38)–(39), no element profiles the same thing as the whole construction in brackets.

Another example of an exocentric construction are coordinate constructions such as the conjoined NP *Matt and Rina*. The entity denoted by the whole is a pair of people; neither proper name denotes that composite entity, nor does the connective. So we are inclined to call this construction headless also. This is a generally accepted analysis (see e.g. Matthews 1981).

The only way that one might argue that either construction has a head would be to analyze *what* in (38) and *that* in (39) as denoting the same thing as the whole construction. Likewise, one could argue that in Coordination, the semantics of *and* is such that it denotes a composite entity and hence is the profile determinant for the Coordinate construction. This is arguably Wierzbicka's analysis of *and* (Wierzbicka 1980; see also §9.2.3). Such an analysis would make *and* the head (profile determinant) of the coordinate construction because its denotation most closely matches the denotation of the whole construction X *and* Y. These semantic analyses must of course be justified.

Langacker, in discussing similar examples (Langacker 1987: 291), suggests that we reserve the term 'profile determinant' to constructions in which there is a single element which possesses the relevant property as against other elements in the same construction. However, we can modify the Zwicky/Langacker definition to make it applicable to any construction:

(40) *Profile equivalent*: In a combination X + Y, X is the PROFILE EQUIVALENT if X profiles/describes a kind of the thing profiled/described by X + Y.

In other words, we have reversed the direction of determination of headhood from 'word to construction' to 'construction to word'. We begin with construction X + Y and see what it profiles. Then we look among its constituents, and discover which constituent, if any, has a profile that best matches the profile of X + Y.

Reversing Zwicky's (and Langacker's) definition makes it clear that profile equivalence is a property of a construction; it is a property of a particular word only by virtue of the construction it occurs in. This definition fits exactly with Radical Construction Grammar, in which constructions are the primitive elements of syntactic representation and elements and the grammatical category of an element is derivative.

Another advantage of reversing Zwicky's definition is that it naturally allows for noncanonical construction types. A construction may have more than one profile equivalent; this is possible if the profile of the whole construction happens to coincide with the profile of more than one of its elements. A construction may also lack a profile equivalent entirely, if no element's profile coincides with the profile of the whole construction. For the definition in (40), which starts from the construction instead of some specific element, both of these possibilities are perfectly natural. Finally, profile equivalence may be a matter of degree, namely, the degree to which some element's profile matches the profile of the whole in semantic type. The match in profiles may not be perfect. This latter possibility is excluded if the denotation of a construction X + Y is something inherited from a (unique) component element X.

However, profile equivalence is not the entire story for the concept of head.

7.4.3. Heads and PIBUs

Decisions about profile equivalents are going to hinge on the semantics of the elements of the construction and how they relate to the semantics of the whole. Once closer attention is paid to those elements, it appears that many constructions lack a unique profile equivalent. In this section, I review some of these examples, and introduce a second semantic property that accounts for diachronic linguistic patterns.

There are two widely held views about what is the head in a prototypical noun phrase. The traditional view is that a noun, such as *turkey*, is the head, and so the phrase is properly described as a noun phrase (NP). A more recent proposal (originating in Abney 1987) is that the article, for example *the*, is the head, and so the phrase is properly described as a determiner phrase (DP). Neither proposal is universally accepted, though the latter is now dominant in generative grammar. What does the profile equivalent analysis imply is the head?

One semantic argument in favor of articles rather than nouns as the heads of the phrases they are found in is that the phrases as a whole refer, but simple nouns do not. In most English NPs, a referring expression is not complete without an Article. It appears to be the Article that appears to fix reference and therefore most closely denotes the same thing as the whole phrase, namely a thing whose identity is established and is situated in the domain of discourse and the speaker's and hearer's shared knowledge. This is the intuitive semantic motivation behind the DP analysis.

In §3.2.3, I argued that the syntactic fact of (mostly) obligatory Articles in some languages such as English is not a sufficient reason for assuming this semantic analysis. It presupposes a nonredundancy analysis of construction meaning which is not tenable in general. A more plausible analysis is that both article and noun refer in noun phrases in general (see for example Langacker 1991a: 95). If this analysis is accepted, then phrases with articles have two profile equivalents, the article and the noun.

A similar argument applies to verb and auxiliary. An English Clause with an inflected Auxiliary does not denote a complete predication without the Auxiliary. Of course, there are clauses with inflected Verbs and no Auxiliary, and a Clause also requires the Verb as well as the Auxiliary. More generally, the same arguments as those offered in §3.2.3 for the joint profile equivalence of articles and nouns in phrases can be applied to auxiliaries and verbs in clauses. Again, if this argument is accepted, then clauses with auxiliaries have two profile equivalents, the auxiliary and the verb.

In the analyses of phrases and clauses just presented, most if not all phrases and clauses have two profile equivalents. It is probably not an accident that the morphosyntactic locus of phrases is typically the article, the noun or both, and that the morphosyntactic locus of clauses is typically the verb, the auxiliary, or both. The morphosyntactic locus is essentially sensitive to a profile equivalent. Hence, we may formulate the implicational universal in (41):

(41) If inflectional categories relevant to a phrase or clause exist in a language, then they are expressed on at least one of the profile equivalents of the phrase/clause.

Does the existence of two profile equivalents for clauses and phrases mean that we must accept a two-headed analysis for them? In other words, does the search for a single "dominant" element in most constructions ultimately fail? The search may fail synchronically, but diachronically there is in fact an asymmetry between the two profile equivalents of clauses and phrases.

The noun and the verb each possess a semantic property that the article and the auxiliary lack: the noun and the verb are the PRIMARY INFORMATION-BEARING UNITS (PIBUs) of the phrase and clause respectively. In common parlance, they are the content words. PIBUs have major informational content that functional elements such as articles and auxiliarties do not have. I therefore propose the semantic definition of headhood in (42):

(42) A (*semantic*) *head* is the profile equivalent that is the primary information-bearing unit, that is, the most contentful item that most closely profiles the same kind of thing that the whole constituent profiles.

There is a simple semantic definition of a PIBU, or rather, what makes the PIBU more contentful than its potential competition. If the criterion of profile equivalence produces two candidates for headhood, the less schematic meaning is the PIBU; that is, the PIBU is the one with the narrower extension, in the formal semantic sense of that term.

Consider again Langacker's analysis of English articles in a phrase such as *the violinist*. In Langacker's analysis, both *the* and *violinist* profile a 'thing' (his technical term for what a noun profiles). However, *the* profiles a thing at a very high degree of generality (schematicity): the only restriction is that it is uniquely available to speaker and hearer in the discourse context. *Violinist*, on the other hand, is a much more specific kind of thing, and so in formal semantic terms its extension is much more limited. Hence, *violinist* is also the PIBU and hence the head.

A similar argument can be constructed for auxiliaries and verbs. I suggested above that auxiliaries and verbs both profile the state of affairs denoted by the clause. The auxiliaries profile the process as very generally grounded in a mental space/possible world or discourse space (such as present vs. past time reference). The verb profiles a much more specific situation type; and hence is the head.

There is a cross-linguistically common grammatical phenomenon that is sensitive to PIBU status as well as profile equivalence, and that is grammaticalization and reanalysis. If there are two candidates for headhood by the definition in (42), the one that is not the PIBU will undergo grammaticalization. In fact, if the functional element-to-be originates as the head of the construction, then in the process of grammaticalization head status gradually shifts. The construction's profile will shift towards that of the PIBU, and the profile equivalent that is not the PIBU may expand its extension—that is, bear even less information than it did before. At this point, the formerly dependent structure becomes the head according to the definition in (42). If the grammaticalization process continues, the functional elements end up losing their status as autonomous syntactic units, becoming affixed to the lexical head.[2]

In other words, the so-called functional heads—determiner and auxilary—grammaticalize, and get reduced in their grammatical behavior. The lexical heads—noun and verb—do not. We may formulate this diachronic implicational universal as follows:

(43) If there is more than one profile equivalent for a phrase/clause, the profile equivalent that is not the PIBU will eventually undergo reduction and attachment to the PIBU profile equivalent (head).

In the next section, I present evidence supporting the universal in (43).

---

[2] These processes are echoed in the Clitic Principle (reduction) and Incorporation Principle (reduction + attraction) of Autolexical Syntax (Sadock 1991: 105).

7.5. Grammaticalization and the PIBU Profile Equivalent

7.5.1. Auxiliaries and articles

In §7.4.2, I argued that shift of profile equivalence and PIBU status occurs concomitant with the grammaticalization of determiners and auxiliaries. This presupposes that in fact the situation was different in an earlier stage of the grammaticalization process, that is, which element is the best candidate for headhood (under the semantic definition in (42)) was different. This is certainly the case with auxiliaries, at least those auxiliaries that originated as main verbs (see Bybee et al. 1994 for extensive documentation of this process).

Auxiliaries often begin as main verbs, that is, as the profile equivalent of the clause, and the main-verb-to-be is a dependent. In the grammaticalization process, the construction's profile shifts to include the dependent verb. The verb is now the PIBU as well as a profile equivalent, and the auxiliary becomes even less of an information-bearing unit than it was before.

An example of this process can be found in Avar (Harris and Campbell 1995: 188–9, from Čikobava and Cercvadze 1962: 328–30):

(44) ebel   ret'el   b-   uq'ule -y   y-   ugo
     mother(ABS) clothing(ABS)   N-   sewing -F   F-   is
     'Mother is a sewer of clothing/one who sews clothes.'

(45) ebel   -ał'a   ret'el   b-   uq'ule -b   b-   ugo
     mother -ERG   clothing(ABS)   N-   sewing -N   N-   is
     'Mother is sewing clothing.'

Example (44) is an Equative construction, hence the profile equivalent is the Verb *ugo* 'is'. Equative constructions have two Absolutive NPs. The Verb *ugo* agrees with its Subject *ebel* 'mother [fem.]' with its Feminine suffix *-y*. The Participle *uq'ule* 'sewing' agrees with its Object *ret'el* 'clothing [neu.]' by the Neuter prefix *b-*, and with the Subject *ebel* by the Feminine suffix *-y*.

Example (45) is an Auxiliary construction with a Transitive Verb. Both Auxiliary *ugo* and Verb *uq'ule* are profile equivalents, but *uq'ule* is the PIBU. The profile equivalent status of *uq'ule* leads to the employment of the Transitive construction for (45): the A argument of *uq'ule* is coded in the Ergative case, and both Auxiliary and Verb agree with the sole Absolutive argument (the P argument), which is Neuter.

The auxiliary in an auxiliary construction may eventually come to be affixed onto the verb, as has happened with *lenda* 'may' in the last three generations of Kituba speakers (Heine and Reh 1984: 21–2):

(46) *two generations ago:*   *present generation:*
     munu   **lenda**   ku-   sala   mu-   le-   sala
     I   **may**   INF-   work   1SG-   **MDL-** work
     'I may work.'   'I may work.'

In the grammaticalization process, the construction as a whole changes meaning. That is, the construction has changed its profile so that the main-verb-to-be is now a profile equivalent, and the auxiliary-to-be profiles only the tense–aspect–mood of the situation profiled by the main-verb-to-be. At that point, both auxiliary and verb are profile equivalents, but the verb is the PIBU; and reduction and absorption of the auxiliary takes place.

The historical scenario with articles is similar (Greenberg 1978a; Heine and Reh 1984; Diessel 1999: 128–9). Articles begin their lives as demonstratives. They are transformed into articles, as in the well-known case of the development of the Romance articles from Latin, such that the Latin Demonstratives *ille, illa* evolve into the French Articles *le, la*. Articles often then come to be affixed to the head noun, as in Standard Ewe, where *atí lá* 'the tree' is being replaced by *atí-á* (Heine and Reh 1984: 23). When this final stage is accomplished, the noun-plus-article-affix becomes a single word carrying out the referring function, and it is the sole profile equivalent. The affixed article may disappear, leading to an articleless NP in which the noun is the only candidate for headhood.

If the demonstrative source of a determiner is originally a pronoun, then it would be in apposition to the noun phrase and would profile the same thing as the noun phrase (Diessel 1999: 60–2, 129). The demonstrative pronoun of course generally has more semantic information than a typical determiner, that is, deictic information and possibly some classifying information, and so is a better candidate for PIBU than an article. As the demonstrative becomes an article and is more tightly integrated into the phrase, then its profile competes with that of the noun, which is clearly the PIBU, and leads to the reanalysis of the article as a modifier and eventual loss of independent syntactic status of the article.

7.5.2. *Numerals, quantifiers, and classifiers*

A well-known example of syntactic change is found with numerals and quantifiers in combination with nouns (e.g. **three** books, **many** CDs). In a number of languages, particularly in the circum-Baltic area (Koptjevskaja-Tamm 2001), quantifiers and numerals frequently start out their lives as the "head" of their phrases, in the traditional syntactic sense: they inflect for case marking in the clause in which they occur, while the nouns that categorize the entities being quantified are in dependent genitive phrases. But frequently, the noun changes from being a case-marked dependent of the numeral or quantifier. The change can be described as [**Qnt** [N-CASE]] > [Qnt **N**], using bold face for the head. This syntactic change appears to be unidirectional. In many cases, the synchronic situation is such that lower numerals have the syntactic behavior of adjectives, and so resemble modifiers, and higher numerals have the syntactic behavior of nouns, and so resemble the heads of noun phrases (Greenberg 1978b: 285, Universal 47).

How is this reanalysis to be accounted for? The quantifier and the noun profile are virtually the same thing: a REPLICATE MASS (Langacker 1991a: 83–4), whose quantity is denoted by the quantifier, and whose type is denoted by the noun. Both quantifier and noun appear to be profile equivalents. Choice of one or the other as head focuses attention on either the quantity or the type of replicate mass. If the quantity is large, then it is more salient, and hence is more likely to be the PIBU, if 'primary' is taken to include salience as well as semantic extension. On the whole, however, the noun is the PIBU, and grammaticalization ensues.

The grammaticalization of quantifiers involves a subtle profile shift. In [Qnt [N-CASE]], the quantifier/numeral profile is nonrelational (see §2.4.2), denoting the replicate mass itself, while the case-marked noun is relational because of the case marker (see §5.4.1): the case marker relates the noun type to the replicate mass. The nonrelational entity is the best profile equivalent of the referring expression, which is itself nonrelational (see §2.4.2). Hence, in [Qnt [N-CASE]], the quantifier profile is the better candidate for profile equivalent. In the [Qnt N] structure, the noun profile is nonrelational, profiling the object itself while the quantifier/numeral is relational, expressing the measurement of the quantity. Hence, in [Qnt N], the noun's profile is the better candidate for profile equivalent.

One can illustrate the profile shift with Measure Classifiers in English. They have the syntactic form of [**NOUN** [*of* NOUN]], which suggests that the first Noun is the Head (as indicated by bold face). But the behavior of the two Nouns in clauses indicates that the Genitive "Dependent" is functioning as the Head:

(47) a. Tim drank a **cup** of coffee.
b. *Tim broke a **cup** of coffee.

The P participant of *drink* must be a potable liquid; the P participant of *break* must be a physical object. The phrase *a cup of coffee* denotes the liquid and not the physical object. Hence *coffee* is the profile equivalent, even though it appears to be a "Dependent Genitive". In contrast, the profile equivalent for the Complex Nominal *coffee cup* is the profile of *cup*:

(48) a. Tim broke a coffee **cup**.
b. *Tim drank a coffee **cup**.

In fact, the Genitive *of* in (47a) is now reduced to *a cuppa coffee*, demonstrating that the Preposition has lost its syntactic identity and no longer can be thought of as indicating that the following Noun is a dependent.

Another example of syntactic change associated with numerals involves numeral classifiers. In numeral classifier constructions, the classifier is almost always contiguous to the numeral cross-linguistically. This [[NUM CLF], NOUN] structure appears to be an appositive one, that is, both [NUM CLF] and [NOUN] are profile equivalents. This is obvious from the commonest etymology of numeral classifiers, namely nouns; at some point in the past, [NUM CLF] was simply a [NUM NOUN] noun phrase.

When a numeral classifier system grammaticalizes, it is most common for the classifier (or what is left of it) to attach to the numeral, not to the noun whose profile it shares, as in the Ponapean examples in (49) (Rehg 1981: 125–6):

(49) a. *waluh* 'eight [inanimate]'
 b. *welimen* 'eight [animate]'
 c. *weluhmw* 'eight [yams or bananas]'

The grammaticalization of Numeral and Classifier in Ponapean has progressed quite far; it is difficult to identify morpheme boundaries in (49a–c), although the first part is clearly the original Numeral. Eventually, the classifier system breaks down; generally one classifier spreads at the expense of others. In other words, the classifer, not the noun, loses much of the information it bore, in contrast to the noun, which retains its PIBU status.

We may explain the grammaticalization of classifiers by the concepts of profile equivalence and PIBU. Numerals have the profile of the cardinality of replicate mass. The classifier as well as the noun is a profile equivalent. However the noun is the PIBU, with respect to both the classifier and the numeral. The non-PIBU profile equivalent—the classifier—is reduced and eventually absorbed by the numeral. In the end, the noun is both the profile equivalent and the PIBU, and is the head of the reanalyzed numeral construction.

Koptjevskaja-Tamm notes that numeral and quantifier phrases in many languages consist of simple juxtaposition of the numeral/quantifier and noun (Koptjevskaja-Tamm 2001: 560). It may be, in this case, that the subtle difference in profile that was invoked to describe the grammaticalization of non-juxtapositional quantifier constructions is in fact absent in juxtapositional quantifier constructions. Instead, both quantifier/numeral and noun profile the (nonrelational) replicate mass.

7.5.3. *Adpositions*

Adpositions represent problematic cases for syntactic definitions of headhood. In generative grammar, adpositions are generally taken to be the heads of adpositional phrases. However, in Functional Grammar (Dik 1997) and Role and Reference Grammar (Van Valin and LaPolla 1997), nouns are the heads of adpositional phrases, and in generative grammar there is some uncertainty as to how to handle them in the recent literature on "functional heads". Haspelmath writes: 'Abney 1987: 63 notes that adpositions seem to "straddle the line" between functional and lexical categories, and Ouhalla 1991: 202 states that "the status of prepositions with respect to the division worked out here is not clear"' (Haspelmath 1994: 5).

Yet the diachronic facts here are again unequivocal: adpositions grammaticalize and eventually may come to be fused with the noun as case markers. This process is illustrated with the Hungarian Noun *béle* 'innards' in (50) (Lehmann 1982b: 85) and the English Noun *side* in (51) (*Oxford English Dictionary*):

(50) *bél-e [innards-DAT]
  > vilag-bele 'into the world' (old literary language)
  > vilag-ba 'into the world' (modern language)
(51) 16c. *in the side of NP* > 17–19c. **inside** *of NP* > 19–20c. **inside** NP

The qualification 'ultimately' is the important word here. We must consider the two extreme ends of the continuum of adpositions. The diachronic source of adpositions are most commonly (serial) verbs with meanings such as 'take' or 'use' for the instrumental relation or (relational) nouns with meanings such as 'face' for the benefactive relation, or body-part terms for various spatial relations (in addition, directional adverbs are a prominent source in Indo-European languages).

In nominal or verbal phrases in which adpositions originate, the serial verb/relational noun is the sole profile equivalent. Their head status is reflected grammatically in that the dependent NP is a genitive dependent of the relational noun or an object dependent of the serial verb. The NP argument is only a part of the phrase's profile by virtue of its being a participant in the verbal event or the entity to which the relational noun is related.

However, as grammaticalization progresses, two things happen. First, the meaning of the adposition is broadened in extension. This makes it a less likely candidate for PIBU. Second, that meaning overlaps more and more with the meaning of the verb. This is clearest with adpositional phrases or oblique case NPs that are governed by the verb. In a sentence such as *Put the book back on the bookshelf*, the profile of the Verb *put* includes the destination of the Object *book*. This component of *put*'s profile overlaps considerably with the limited range of meanings that are permissible in the Locative PP argument of *put* (roughly, they must indicate a location which is the final location of the Direct Object). In this example, the Preposition still provides more semantic content for that aspect of the action than the Verb—compare *Put the picture over the couch*. But the content of the object NP of *put* and the NP governed by the Preposition highly determine that locative relationship anyway.

If we turn to nonspatial relations, the overlap is more complete. In *I agree with you*, the Preposition *with* still possesses a meaning but its contribution to the Verbal profile is minimal; *agree* already contains the symmetrical meaning of *with* and in fact chooses that meaning of *with* in contrast to the many other meanings that *with* possesses. In the case of markers of core participant roles, such markers generally have a very broad semantic extension, and the verb contributes the more specific meaning. The adposition thus loses its PIBU status relative to the verb, leaving the argument NP as the profile equivalent for the argument phrase. As a consequence, the adposition is reduced and eventually attaches to the noun.

In §7.5.2, we saw that in the evolution of quantifier phrases, the profile of the quantifier shifts towards that of the noun. In contrast, in the evolution of adpositional phrases, the profile of the adposition shifts towards that of the verb that governs it (see also Croft 2000a: 121–4), leaving the noun the head of its phrase by default, so to speak. This is the reason why the adposition looks more like a "head" until later stages of grammaticalization, especially for oblique relations. For obliques or less-grammaticalized direct object markers, it is unclear what the profile of the PP is, as the adposition's profile gets absorbed by the verb and the NP's inherent properties come to dictate more of its semantic relation to the situation denoted by the verb.

7.5.4. Complementizers

Subordinate clauses introduced by complementizers, such as *She said [that she didn't love him]*, are now usually analyzed as having the complementizer as the head of CP, governing the complement clause. This analysis is not based on a semantic analysis of the complementizer in formal syntactic theories. However, Langacker offers a semantic analysis of complementizers in cognitive grammar (Langacker 1991a: 417–49), which we may use as a starting point for our analysis.

Langacker analyzes complementizers as profiling a nonprocessual interpretation of the state of affairs denoted by the complement clause, which is required for the complement clause to function as an argument. The complementizer shares its profile with the predicate—a very abstract characterization of a state of affairs—but it contributes an atemporal construal of the predicate profile.

The sources of complementizers are varied, including pronominal elements and nouns (Lehmann 1982b/1995: 62), as in (52a–b) from English, and the verb 'say' as in example (53) from Ewe (Lord 1976: 182; Lehmann 1982b/1995: 62; see also §9.4.5):

(52) a. She said **that**.
      b. She said **that** [she didn't love him].
(53) fia   gbé   **bé**   [wómagàvá   o]
     chief   refuse say   they.PROH.come   NEG
     'The chief forbade that they should come.'

A pronominal element or noun is the profile equivalent as much as the head of the complement clause (its predicate), subject to the construal of the complement's state of affairs so that it can function as an argument of the main clause predicate. The verb 'say' and adpositions originate as the sole profile equivalent. The process of grammaticalization to complementizer status leads to a profile shift of 'say'/adposition such that the profiles of complementizer and complement overlap in the way described in the preceding paragraph. In all of these cases, the complement clause predicate is the PIBU by the time that the complementizer has developed. We would therefore expect the non-PIBU complementizer to grammaticalize, and it does.

The fate of complementizers is twofold. Complementizers come to be attached to the main verb, as with the Dative Subordination suffix in the Yidiny example in (54) (Dixon 1980: 459):

(54) waguja -ŋgu gurŋga   wawa -l   maŋga -nyu-nda
     man   -ERG kookaburra(ABS) see -PRS laugh -DAT.SUBR
     'The man is watching the kookaburra laughing.'

In this case, grammaticalized complementizers are often best analyzed as nominalizers (Lehmann 1982b: 65–6).

The other fate of complementizers is to simply disappear, as in English *He believes (that) she is right*. When this happens, the verb takes on the atemporal construal in its profile in this constructional context. In either case, complementizers behave in the same way as the other elements described in this section; and the verb ends up being the sole profile equivalent of its phrase.

7.5.5. *Copulas*

Another example of grammaticalization is the merging of copulas with predicative nouns and adjectives, leading to inflected nominal and adjectival predications, or a special predicative nominal/adjectival form distinct from the form of nouns and adjectives found in NPs. Stassen (1997) presents many examples of a copula affixed to predicate nominal/adjective, such as Beja, about which he writes: '[Beja] employs predicative suffixes, which strongly resemble deictic pronouns, and which differ formally from the [agreement] suffixes used with verbs' (Stassen 1997: 79; example, ibid., from Tucker and Bryan 1966: 543):

(55) barú:k ha'á -bwa
     2SG.M   sheik -2SG.M
     'You are a sheik.'

A copula occurring with a predicative noun or adjective appears to be the profile equivalent, because the overall clause profiles the assertion classifying the subject as belonging to the category of the predicate nominal, or possessing the property of the predicate nominal. However, the copula verb itself is of minimal semantic content, adding only a predicative function to a maximally schematic categorization of the referent of the S argument. It can be argued that the profile of the whole clause is determined partly by the copula and partly by the predicate noun/adjective—categorization of the S referent as being of the type profiled by the predicate noun, or ascription of the property profiled by the predicate adjective.

A plausible diachronic analysis is that the predicate noun/adjective itself comes to profile the predicating act; the profile of the predicate noun/adjective thus comes to overlap with that of the copula. The predicate noun/adjective is the PIBU and therefore absorbs the copula, becoming an inflected predicate form by itself. Another possible diachronic analysis is that the two forms simply fuse morphologically and jointly provide the profile of the whole clause as a single word. The former analysis is preferable in a situation where the predicate noun/adjective develops its inflections at the same time as regular verbs do: the verb forms are acquiring a predicational profile, so it is reasonable to assume that the nonverbal predications are doing so also.

7.5.6. *PIBUs in other syntactic processes*

Profile equivalence is a necessary condition for headhood in the definition in (42), and the PIBU only enters into the picture when there are two or more profile equivalents. This in turn causes a syntactic change because there is a shift in meaning of the article, auxiliary, quantifier, adposition, classifier, complementizer, or copula such that its profile changes, overlapping with another profile equivalent that is a PIBU (in the case of articles, auxiliaries, and quantifiers) or overlapping semantically another element which then absorbs its meaning, leading to its fusion with another word (in the case of adpositions, classifiers, complementizers and copulas). While the details of the diachronic process differ significantly in each case, there is a commonality to all of them: a shift in semantic profile leads to another element with higher information content becoming a profile equivalent and the non-PIBU element grammaticalizes.

But can the syntactic processes of grammaticalization occur without the shift in profile? It appears so. The phenomenon called VERBAL ATTRACTION involves the attachment of pronominal and even nominal arguments to the verb (Heine and Reh 1984, §1.1.3.1; see also Mithun 1984). Myhill (1988a) argues that the 'most informationally important' element of the sentence, which he calls the nucleus (Myhill 1988a: 261) and is the same as the PIBU, syntactically attracts lesser information-bearing units. This phenomenon he calls CLUSTERING, and gives the examples shown in Table 7.2.

Table 7.2. Properties of clustering

High-PIBU nucleus	Low-PIBU element attracted to nucleus (>bound form)
Verb	pronoun (>agreement marker)
Verb	low-salience NP (>incorporated N)
Verb	auxiliary (>tense–aspect–mood affix)
Foregrounded verb	continuing topic NP
Foregrounded verb	coordinating conjunction (>narrative verb form)
Process verb	result or "framing" (Talmy 1991) particle (>affix)
Presentative NP	existential verb
Predicative NP	copula (>bound predicator)
Focused NP	equational verb in cleft (>focus NP form)
Emphasized element	pronoun

It may be that attraction of a low-PIBU profile equivalent to its high-PIBU partner in the diachronic processes described in (43) is part of a more general process, which can be proposed as a diachronic implicational universal:

(56) If two elements in a phrase or clause differ significantly in information-bearing status, the non-PIBU element may be reduced and attracted to the PIBU element.

If the universal proposed in (56) is valid, then "headhood" is simply the result of the interaction of two separate phenomena: the synchronic language universal about profile equivalents in (41), and the diachronic language universal about PIBUs in (56).

7.6. "Heads" and Roots in Morphology

It is commonly assumed in syntactic approaches to morphology, and also by certain semantic models, including Cognitive Grammar (e.g. Langacker 1991a: 76), that the notion of headhood can be applied within a word as well as outside of it. Some have questioned the validity of this move (e.g. Bauer 1990), and heads do not have an obvious place in word-based approaches to morphology such as Bybee (1985) and Anderson (1992).

It is not entirely clear what aspects of morphological structure should be comparable to what goes on in syntactic change. The most salient aspect of morphological organization, at least in those cases where morphemes are easily segmentable, is the distinction between ROOT and AFFIX. I argue here that the semantic notion of PIBU, but not the notion of profile equivalent, is relevant to morphological organization at the word level with respect to the root–affix distinction. The problems encountered with attempts to apply the notion of head below the word level can be attributed to this fact. For bound morphology, the relevant concept is the ROOT, semantically defined as the PIBU.

The root–affix distinction is generally defined in phonological terms. Their definition is ultimately based on the structuralist notion of an affix as a bound morpheme and the root as a free one. However, in a language with obligatory inflection of root forms, in particular a language with obligatory inflection and no zero-coded inflectional categories, the root in the intuitive sense is just as dependent as the inflection. For example, in K'iche', Verbs must always appear with Aspect, Agreement, and Voice affixes, and do not occur without at least one overt affix. Hence the K'iche' Verb root is as bound as the K'iche' Verbal affixes. Yet there is rarely any doubt as to which morpheme is the root and which is the affix in such languages. The root is the PIBU.

In §7.5.1, I argued that the grammatical fusion of articles (and their meaning and inflectional categories) with the head noun and that of auxiliaries with the main verb led to the unification of both profile equivalents within a single word. Within such a word, advocates of morphological heads have argued that the inflection is the head. But the same arguments with respect to a semantic definition of headhood presented in §7.4 apply here also: both inflection and root are profile equivalents of the whole; but the root is the PIBU.

This conclusion is rather different from that found in Haspelmath (1992), following Williams (1981) and others. Haspelmath argues that the head-dependent relations of syntax are continued into the morphology, and specifically the functional heads of syntax are continued into the inflectional morphology. I have argued for a different analysis of heads in syntax. I agree that what is found in the morphology is a continuation of the syntax to some extent, and that the syntax–morphology distinction is gradient. However, gradience need not imply continuity. That is, a phenomenon relevant to syntax such as headhood may not be continued all the way into the depths of the word, although the boundary between syntax and morphology may be unclear.

Instead, what matters is how the relevant semantic criteria operate in syntax and morphology. Profile equivalence and PIBU behave differently in the morphology, and profile equivalence is not helpful in defining morphological structure, in particular the root–affix structure of words.

As Haspelmath notes, there are mismatches between the syntactic head-dependent pattern and the morphological root–affix pattern. In so-called head-marking languages (see §5.4.1), affixes are etymologically dependents, namely pronominal arguments. For example, the Agreement prefixes in K'iche' are transparently related to the Independent Pronouns (Mondloch 1978: 46):

(57) c-   at-   in-   tzucu: -j
     PRS-   2SG.ABS-   1SG.ERG-   look.for   -TR
'I look for you.' [compare *aat* 'you' and *'iin* 'I']

But in so-called dependent-marking languages, affixes are ultimately etymologically heads, namely former auxiliaries, adpositions, etc. For example, the Tzutujil Preposition *majk* 'because of, on account of', developed from the Noun *majk* 'sin' (Dayley 1985: 153):

(58) xch'ejyi   jar   iixoq   ruu-   **majk**   jar   aachi
     was.hit   the   woman   3SG.POSS-   **because.of**   the   man
'The woman was hit because of the man [etymologically 'the man's sin].'

The head-dependent distinction, to the extent that it is applicable to morphemes, does not account for the root–affix structure; and that is because PIBU status, not profile equivalence, is the most relevant semantic property for this structure.[3]

The properties of profile equivalence and PIBU part with each other in morphology in many derivational forms. For example, in agent nominalizations, the root (verbal or nominal) is the PIBU, but the agent-nominalizing affix is the profile determinant. It is believed that agent nominalizations (and other derivational affixes; Haspelmath 1992: 71) often originate from compounds, not unlike English *mailman, garbageman*, etc. In a compound, both morphemes are roots. In English agent compounds are clearly endocentric and *-man* is the profile equivalent. But by this point in its diachronic development, *-man* is not the PIBU.

In order to demonstrate this, we must extend the definition of PIBU to apply

---

[3] This is not to mention the problems for syntax-based morphology found in nonconcatenative morphology (see Haspelmath 1992: 81–2; Anderson 1992; Spencer 1993).

to cases in which the two candidate elements do not share profiles (see §7.5.6). When they do share profiles, it is relatively straightforward to determine which is more specific in meaning because its extension (in the formal semantic sense) is smaller. When they do not share profiles, one can employ the concept of PARADIGMATIC CONTRAST to determine which is the PIBU:

(59) Whichever form is in paradigmatic contrast with more elements is the primary information-bearing unit.

With the agent nominalization example in the preceding paragraph, the root satisfies the definition of PIBU in (59): there is a large number of contrasting verbal and nominal forms that can take agent nominal affixes, but the agentive affixes are in at most a paradigmatic contrast with a small number of other nominalizing affixes (patient, instrument, location, action nominalizations).

This criterion is used in grammaticalization theory, where it is called PARADIGMATICIZATION (Lehmann 1982b, 1985). Essentially, the semantic change by which a root comes to be used only in contrast to a small number of other forms in paradigmatic contrast is the loss of information content, which we take to be a defining characteristic of affix status.

Even if one accepts the notion that the affix is the profile equivalent in inflection as well as in derivation, the semantic account of headhood given here explains why the syntactic notion of headhood is difficult to apply below the word level. I have argued that a syntactic notion of headhood results from the intersection of profile equivalence and PIBU status. Above the word level, these two semantic properties often coincide; if they do not, grammaticalization often aligns the two. Below the word level, however, the nonalignment of profile equivalence (if inflectional and derivational affixes are analyzed as profile equivalents) and PIBU status is the rule, not the exception. Moreover, diachronic morphological processes do not come into play to align the two (except for complete fusion of stem and derivational affix).

Above the word level, profile equivalence and PIBU status work together to define the (lexical) head. Below the word level, they do not work together; instead, the primary morphological division, between root and affix, is determined by PIBU status and (by definition) boundness of the morpheme.

Earlier in this section, I argued that when both root and affix are bound forms, that is, neither can occur without the other, the semantic property of PIBU status identifies which is the root. There are also instances of the converse phenomenon: two morphemes have similar PIBU status, and cross-linguistically one is sometimes found as a root, sometimes the other.

For example, personal pronouns and case relations both form fairly compact semantic paradigms with a small number of contrasts. In other words, both personal pronouns and case relations have relatively low PIBU. Consider the meaning 'to her/him'. In some languages, such as Djabugay, the root is the Pronoun 's/he' to which is affixed a Case suffix meaning 'to' (Patz 1991: 275):

(60) gulu   -nda
     s/he   -DAT
     'to her/him'

The Djabugay Case suffixes are affixed to Nouns as well as Pronouns. Therefore, the Case suffixes have a smaller number of contrasts than the Pronouns plus Nouns, and hence the latter are roots.

In other languages, such as Mam, the root is the Preposition or Relational Noun meaning 'to', to which is attached a Personal prefix meaning 's/he' (England 1983: 153):

(61) t-   ee
     3SG- to
     'to her'

The Mam Personal prefixes are affixed to Nouns (and Verbs) as well as Prepositions. Therefore, the Personal prefixes have a smaller number of contrasts than the Prepositions plus Nouns and Verbs, and hence the latter are roots.

Another cross-linguistically common example of this phenomenon are personal pronouns and auxiliaries: each generally forms a relatively small paradigm and thus have an equally low PIBU status. In a language such as English, the contracted Auxiliary cliticizes onto the Subject Pronoun as in (62a), as well as to high-PIBU NPs. In other languages such as Spanish, Subject Pronominal endings are affixed to Auxiliaries as in (62b), as well as to high-PIBU verbs:

(62) a. They're sleeping.
     b. Est-án [3PL] durmiendo.

The definitional properties of the morphological root presented here have a different ontological status from the definitional properties of the syntactic head presented in §7.4. Profile equivalence is a necessary condition for headhood but not a sufficient one: a constituent may have more than one profile equivalent. PIBU status is a sufficient condition for headhood only jointly with profile equivalence. If the PIBU is not a profile equivalent, it is not the head.

For a root, however, PIBU status is sufficient. If no morphemes in a word occur alone, the PIBU is the root. If both forms are roughly equal in PIBU status, then distribution with other higher-PIBU forms disqualifies the morpheme as a root. If both morphemes are roughly equal in PIBU status and do not occur with other higher-PIBU forms, then we have two roots, that is, a compound. Profile equivalence is not relevant to root status. Profile equivalence can be applied in principle to compounding and to a lesser extent to derivation, but its applicability to inflection is questionable. If profile equivalence is applicable, then it is almost always divergent from the PIBU morpheme. These differences clarify what word-internal structure and syntactic structure have in common and how they differ, in a typological and diachronic perspective.

7.7. The Argument–Adjunct Distinction

Now that we have established a semantic characterization of heads in Radical Construction Grammar, we may turn to the status of DEPENDENTS in a construction. Syntacticians generally distinguish two types of dependent elements, ARGUMENTS and ADJUNCTS. The term 'modifier' is equivalent to 'adjunct': adjuncts modify their heads.

The examples of argument and adjunct given in (63) are taken to be uncontroversial:

(63) a. Randy chased [the dog]_{Argument} [in the park]_{Adjunct}.
    b. *Randy chased in the park.
    c. Randy chased the dog.

The intuition behind the argument–adjunct distinction is that arguments are syntactically and semantically required, in some sense, while adjuncts are not. In this section, we will look for a cross-linguistically valid characterization of arguments and adjuncts, in conformity with the principles of Radical Construction Grammar. Since the intuitive notion of the argument–adjunct distinction is both syntactic and semantic, we will examine both syntactic and semantic properties of dependents here.

7.7.1. Criteria for the argument–adjunct distinction

As with other grammatical phenomena, the usual strategy is an opportunistic one: enumerate a list of criteria for justifying the argument–adjunct distinction. Again, Radical Construction Grammar expects the various criteria that are proposed to be independent. Here, we will begin with the criteria proposed by Matthews (1981: 124–6). We summarize the criteria here, and then turn to their analysis in the following sections.

Matthews' first criterion is the type of semantic relation that holds between the dependent and its head. For example, in (63a), the dog is a participant in the event, while the park is a CIRCUMSTANTIAL dependent, which describes the location at which the event took place. In some sense, the dog is a more "necessary" part of the event than the location is. This criterion is obviously semantic, and hence can be used to establish only the semantic argument–adjunct distinction.

The second criterion Matthew proposes is the presence of COLLOCATIONAL RELATIONS. The presence of a collocational relation, such as *give protection* but not **give defense*, implies that the syntactic dependent is an argument, and the absence of collocational relations between a verb and adverbials indicating time reference (such as *yesterday*) implies that the syntactic dependent is an adjunct (Matthews 1981: 124–5). As we argued in §5.2, collocational relations are indicators of semantic relations, not syntactic relations, and so they can be used only for the semantic distinction.

Matthews' third criterion is whether or not the expression of the dependent is

OBLIGATORY. For example, *the dog* in (63a) is an obligatory element of the English Transitive Clause construction (cf. (63b)); but *in the park* is an optional element of the same construction (cf. (63c)). This criterion is clearly syntactic, and hence could be the basis of a syntactic argument–adjunct distinction.

The last criterion Matthews discusses is LATENCY. Latency is the requirement for a definite interpretation of a dependent if that dependent is left syntactically unexpressed. One can say *I didn't finish* only when a definite referent for the Direct Object is accessible in the discourse context (the job, the book I was reading, etc; Matthews 1981: 126). The latency criterion captures the same fact as Zwicky's notion of required element (see §§7.2.2, 7.3.3), namely that an absent element may not be simply optional, but is elliptical, thereby calling for a definite interpretation. Latency cannot be separated from the obligatory/optional distinction, and we will treat them together in §7.7.3.

Two further criteria are sometimes offered for the argument–adjunct distinction (e.g., Zwicky 1993: 295–6): arguments are governed or subcategorized for by their heads, and adjuncts agree with their heads. However, the facts discussed in §7.3 require us to give up these further criteria. Government and subcategorization are properties of constructions, not of words taken by themselves (§7.3.2). Likewise, agreement is a distinct phenomenon from the argument–adjunct distinction: agreement may be with either head or dependent (§7.3.1). Thus we may discard these two criteria for the argument–adjunct distinction.

In §7.7.2, I will argue that the semantic criteria are properties of the semantics of the individual words or phrases that enter into the semantic relation. There is a continuum of semantic relations from argument-like to adjunct-like, but it cuts across the semantic head-dependent distinction. In §7.7.3, I will argue that the syntactic criteria, by contrast, support a categorical distinction, but it is a general property associated with constructions as a whole, and again is not restricted to dependents.

7.7.2. Valence and the autonomy–dependence continuum

The standard semantic analysis of the argument–adjunct distinction is that an argument is a SEMANTIC ARGUMENT of the head, whereas an adjunct is a FUNCTOR or PREDICATE whose argument is the head. To return to our example of (63a), *chase* denotes a predicate taking two arguments, one of which is filled by the dog. Hence, the dog is a semantic argument of the chasing event. On the other hand, being or occurring in the park is a predicate taking one argument, which is filled by the chasing event taking place in the park. Hence, the location of the chasing event is a semantic adjunct of the chasing event.

To put the standard semantic analysis in the semantic terms used in Table 2.2 in §2.4.2, the chasing event is RELATIONAL and the dog fills one of the semantic roles in the chasing relation. Conversely, being in the park is relational and the chasing event fills the semantic roles in the being-in-the-park relation. As can be seen from this example, one and the same semantic component can be a relation and at the same time be the filler of a role in a relation. In this example, the chasing event is both a relation (one of whose roles is filled by the dog), and the filler of a role in a relation (the being-in-the-park relation). Hence the relation–role filler distinction is relative to the two semantic components in a semantic structure that are being compared by the analyst.

Langacker (1987) presents an analysis of semantic relations, or semantic VALENCE as he calls it, which not only accounts for the relativity of the relation–role filler distinction, but also demonstrates that the relation–role filler distinction is gradient. We will begin by looking at a straightforward example, and then examine Langacker's extension of valence to other semantic relations.

In a sentence such as *Hannah sings*, singing is relational relative to Hannah. The reason for this is the fact that singing requires a singer. Hence, the semantic structure for *sings* includes a schematic singer as a SUBSTRUCTURE. In *Hannah sings*, Hannah fills the role of the singer for *sings*. Langacker's description of an argument filling the role of a predicate is that the argument ELABORATES the relevant substructure of the predicate. The substructure that can be elaborated by an argument is an ELABORATION SITE or E-SITE (Langacker 1987: 304). These relations are illustrated in Figure 7.1.

Figure 7.1. Simplified semantic valence structure for *Hannah sings*

As we noted above, a unit in a construction may be simultaneously a relation and the filler of a relation. This is captured straightforwardly in the valence analysis. In (63a), for example, the dog elaborates a substructure of the chasing event, namely one of the participant roles; hence the chasing event is a relation. On the other hand, the chasing event itself elaborates a substructure of the being in the park, namely the entity located, called the FIGURE (see §9.2.2); hence, the chasing event is also a role filler.

Not only is valence relative, it is gradient. The description of valence relations for (63a) in the last paragraph is an oversimplification. Chasing is a localizable activity: chasing takes place in a location, as well as involving a chaser and a thing chased. This is not true of all predicates; one cannot say for instance that **Randy was widowed in the park* or **Randy inherited a million dollars in the park*. Hence the location of the chasing event is a substructure of the semantic structure of *chase*, and *in the park* also elaborates that substructure of *chase*. As Langacker puts it: 'The valence relations uniting linguistic expressions depend ... on the sharing of elements. It is only by virtue of having certain substructures in common that two component expressions can be integrated to form a coherent composite expression' (Langacker 1987: 278).

However, the substructure of *chase* elaborated by *in the park* is much less salient in the characterization of the chasing event than the substructures of *chase* elaborated by *Randy* and *the dog*. Conversely, the substructure of *in the park* that is elaborated by *chase* is highly salient in the characterization of the spatial relation. *In the park* is more of an adjunct of *chase* than an argument because *chase* elaborates a salient substructure of *in the park*, while *in the park* elaborates a not very salient substructure of *chase*. The relative strength of the two relations is illustrated in Figure 7.2.

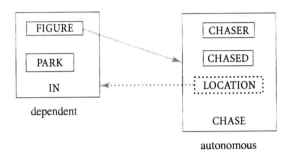

Figure 7.2. Semantic valence structure for *chase + in the park*

Langacker adopts the terms AUTONOMOUS and DEPENDENT to describe the gradient reinterpretation of the predicate–argument distinction. The definition of autonomy and dependence is: 'one structure, *D*, is dependent on the other, *A*, to the extent that *A* constitutes an elaboration of a salient substructure within *D*' (Langacker 1987: 300); and conversely *A* is autonomous relative to *D* to the extent to which it does not elaborate a salient substructure of *D*. In (63a), *In the park* is dependent on *chase* because *chase* elaborates the highly salient figure role of the locative relation *in the park*. Conversely, *chase* is autonomous relative to *in the park* because *in the park* elaborates only the not very salient substructure of the location of the chasing event.

What language universals are associated with autonomy-dependence? The one generalization that one can form is that agreement (indexical coded dependencies) symbolizes autonomous semantic entities relative to a dependent entity in the semantic structure of the construction (§7.3.1). However, as was argued in §7.3.1, agreement does not correspond to the head-dependent distinction: agreement can be with "heads" or "dependents". Hence it is not a reliable criterion for the argument–adjunct distinction.

7.7.3. *Symbolic instantiation in constructions*

The two syntactic criteria for the argument–adjunct distinction that survived scrutiny in §7.7.1 are obligatoriness and latency. These two criteria are crosslinguistically valid, that is, they can be applied to grammatical phenomena in any language. Obligatoriness and latency are related (§7.7.1). In this section, I describe a general framework for describing obligatoriness and latency in a single dimension, INSTANTIATION, based on Fillmore (1986) and Fillmore and Kay (1993, chapter 7). I will then argue that instantiation is always a property of constructions, and applies to heads as well as dependents. In other words, instantiation is a characterization of the symbolic relation between syntactic elements and semantic components.

Fillmore and Kay observe that when an element is absent from a construction, as in (64a) (cf. (64b)), it does not entail that no referent exists for the absent element:

(64) a. She wrote a letter Ø.
b. She wrote a letter **on blue stationery**.

Fillmore and Kay describe this phenomenon as NULL INSTANTIATION, the instantiation of a referent without any overt expression of that referent.

Fillmore and Kay argue that the pragmatic status of the referent varies in different contexts, and can be divided into three types. The type illustrated in (64a) is FREE NULL INSTANTIATION (FNI). There is something on which the letter is written, but the identity of that paper can be freely identified by the hearer. In particular, the referent may be accessible in context:

(65) She took some **blue stationery**$_i$ out of the cupboard and wrote a letter Ø$_i$.

Or the referent may not have been mentioned previously, and is not further specified, as in (64a) (assuming there is no previous mention of the paper on which the letter was written).

Fillmore and Kay contrast free null instantiation with INDEFINITE NULL INSTANTIATION (INI), illustrated in (66):

(66) The dog just ate Ø.

In indefinite null instantiation, the referent is indefinite; in (66), there is some indeterminate food that is instantiated.

The third and last type that Fillmore and Kay discuss is DEFINITE NULL INSTANTIATION (DNI). In definite null instantiation, the referent must be accessible. Definite null instantiation corresponds to Matthews' latency and Zwicky's required (but absent). The so-called pro-drop or null anaphora found in most languages is definite null instantiation, as seen in the Rennellese example (25), repeated below:

(67) aano   tutuku   i   mu'a   Hangemangama
     and.then spill   in   front H.
     'And then [he$_{DNI}$] spilled [it$_{DNI}$—earth] in front of Hangemangama.'

Fillmore and Kay's analysis is a significant step forward in understanding the relationship between syntax and semantics, and captures observations made by others such as Matthews and Zwicky. However, their classification must be modified in order to be used for describing the syntactic argument–adjunct distinction. Also, Fillmore and Kay argue that null instantiation is sometimes associated with lexical items and sometimes with constructions. I argue that null instantiation is always associated with constructions.

First, in order to fill out the taxonomy of referent expressions, we must add overt expression of referents to the taxonomy. We may call overt expression of referents NONNULL INSTANTIATION (NNI). Nonnull instantiation requires the hearer to access a referent in accordance with the information provided by the overt expression. Nonnull instantiation is a feature of the Subject role in the English Declarative construction:

(68) a. **Tina** slept.
 b. *Ø Slept.
 c. **It** seems that she is sleeping.
 d. *Ø Seems that she is sleeping.

A Subject must have nonnull instantiation in the English Declarative construction, even in an example such as (68c), which is sometimes analyzed as having no semantic argument corresponding to *It*, or as having an obligatory Subject referring cataphorically to the state of affairs in the Complement Clause following the Verb.

The English Declarative construction contrasts with the English Imperative construction, which has definite null instantiation of the Subject role (always instantiated as the addressee):

(69) Ø$_{DNI}$ Come here!

We now turn to the question of what type of grammatical entity may have a particular type of instantiation associated with it. I will argue that all types of instantiation are the property of constructions, not of words that fill roles in constructions.

Fillmore and Kay argue that some cases of DNI in English are lexical, not constructional. But what makes some null instantiation look "lexical" (Fillmore and Kay 1993: 7.5, 7.11) is that the construction accepts only a limited set of subclasses of words. For example, Fillmore and Kay argue that a subset of Verbs in English allow for DNI Objects or Obliques, such as *arrive, win, lose*, etc.:

(70) a. The Germans lost **the war**.
 b. The Germans lost Ø$_{DNI}$.
(71) a. The children arrived **at the station** at ten o'clock.
 b. The children arrived Ø$_{DNI}$ at ten o'clock.

Other Verbs, such as *bend, break, destroy, create, move, lift*, do not allow DNI Objects:

(72) a. She lifted **the corner of the bed**.
 b. *She lifted Ø$_{DNI}$.

These facts can be given a constructional analysis. English has a Transitive DNI construction, with the form [SBJ VERB $\emptyset_{DNI}$] ($\emptyset_{DNI}$ is implicit, not a null formal element) and a semantic structure specifying a highly accessible participant corresponding to the overt Object in the ordinary English Transitive construction [SBJ VERB OBJ]. Unlike the Transitive construction, however, the Transitive DNI construction is restricted to a subclass of verbs including *win*, *lose*, etc.

There is further evidence to support the constructional analysis of "lexical" DNI in examples (67)–(68). If DNI Objects were associated with the lexical items and not the construction, then we would expect DNI Objects to occur in other constructions with the same lexical item. However, the Object of *win*, etc. cannot be DNI in the Passive:

(73) a. The Germans lost $\emptyset_{DNI}$.
b. *$\emptyset_{DNI}$ Was lost (by the Germans).

One would not want to say that (73b) is unacceptable because (73a) is intransitive, because (73a) is not Intransitive; it is Transitive with a DNI Object. Yet (73a) cannot be Passivized. This fact can be explained if instantiation is a property of constructions: DNI is part of the Transitive DNI construction, but the Passive construction requires NNI for its Subject role.

Two other examples of putative lexical DNI offered by Fillmore and Kay can also be analyzed constructionally. One construction is restricted to verbs of induced action with personal direct objects, and allows for a DNI Complement that describes the action inducively caused by the causer (Fillmore and Kay 1993: 7.5, esp. fn. 4):

(74) [NP INDUC.V PRN.OBJ $\emptyset_{DNI}$]:
She didn't want to come back, but I persuaded her $\emptyset_{DNI}$.

The other construction is restricted to certain prepositions which in their spatial meaning allow a DNI Prepositional Object describing the ground or reference point of the spatial meaning (Fillmore 1986: 103):

(75) [NP SPAT.V SPAT.PREP $\emptyset_{DNI}$]:
I opened the door to the kitchen and walked in $\emptyset_{DNI}$.

The examples in (69)–(75) demonstrate that there is "null anaphora" or "prodrop" (i.e. DNI) in English, and that it is a gross oversimplification to divide languages into two types, "null anaphora" and "nonnull anaphora". Different constructions with varying degrees of generality that are DNI and NNI can almost certainly be found in all languages.

Free null instantiation is quite different from definite null instantiation. FNI is not really associated with any particular construction. FNI is simply the principle that any component of the semantic structure of a construction that is left unspecified by NNI or DNI is interpreted freely as defined above. It is only NNI and DNI that specify particular interpretations on semantic components of constructions. The FNI principle applies to all unelaborated components of all types of constructions.

The FNI–DNI distinction is also not associated with semantic obligatoriness (autonomy with respect to a dependent component; see §7.7.2). For example, in English, the Active construction requires NNI expression of the A participant (or DNI expression in the Imperative):

(76) a. **The kids** let the dogs out of the backyard.
   b. Ø$_{DNI}$ Let the dogs out of the backyard.

But in the English Passive construction, the A participant is expressed by FNI (Fillmore and Kay 1993: 7.10):

(77) The dogs were let out of the backyard Ø$_{FNI}$.

In other words, free or definite null instantiation is an idiosyncratic conventional property of a construction.

Fillmore and Kay argue that indefinite null instantiation is lexically specified in English, with examples such as *eat* and *drink*. However, one can make the same argument for INI that was made above for DNI. INI is the result of a construction with a restricted distribution pattern. In addition, INI imposes constraints on the semantic type of the otherwise freely instantiated[4] participant, for example food for *eat*, alcoholic drink for *drink* (*drink* also occurs in the Transitive DNI construction, in which case the null instantiated object is not necessarily an alcoholic drink). Thus, INI constructions are really semantically restricted FNI constructions, such as [SBJ *eat* Ø$_{Food.FNI}$] or [SBJ *drink* Ø$_{Alcohol.FNI}$].

These examples of English INI Objects makes INI appear to be the functional equivalent of two constructions found in other languages, antipassive voice and certain types of noun incorporation. The English INI verbs are not unlike the overtly coded antipassive constructions with indefinite object meaning described by Cooreman (1994). An example is the Mam Antipassive Verb *aq'naan* 'work' in (78) (England 1988: 533; see Cooreman 1994: 53):

(78) ma   chin   **aq'naa**   -n   -a
     REC.PST   1SG.ABS   **work**   -ANTI   -1SG
     'I worked.'

In (78), there is no implication of what was worked; it simply describes an agent engaging in a work activity. The fact that something has to be worked (or drunk,

---

[4] Fillmore and Kay argue that the referent in INI is not accessible in the discourse, citing the following exchange as odd: A–*What happened to my sandwich? B–The dog just ate* Ø. However, FNI is equally odd: A–*What happened to my blue stationery? B–Diane wrote a letter* Ø (I am grateful to Martin Haspelmath for pointing this out to me). The relative accessibility of null-instantiated referents will have to be judged by the analysis of naturally occurring discourse.

or eaten), is part of our real-world knowledge of these activities. But the detransitivized verb form shifts perspective onto the agent and her/his activity, and defocuses the object of that activity.

The English INI Objects are also parallel to what Mithun calls Type I Noun Incorporation, illustrated in (79) by Ponapean (Rehg 1981: 214; see Mithun 1984: 850):

(79) i **keng** -**winih** -la
    I eat -medicine -CMPL
    'I completed my medicine-taking.'

In (79), what is completed is the agent's medicine-taking activity, not the medicine; this sentence is acceptable even if some medicine remains after the agent has completed her/his medicine-taking.

Nonnull instantiation is a symbolic property of a construction. Null instantiation is also a symbolic property of a construction, albeit in an odd way: the construction as a whole symbolizes a complex semantic structure requiring a definite (accessible) referent for a specified semantic role. However, instantiation is a property of any semantic component of a construction, not just nonhead components. There are a number of elliptical constructions that require definite null instantiation of their heads (in the semantic sense), such as the English Gapping coordinate construction in (80) and Headless Possession construction in (81):

(80) [[Sheila sells seashells] and [Monica $\emptyset_{DNI}$ moonstones]].
(81) My piece of cake is big, but [Johnny's $\emptyset_{DNI}$] is bigger.

In other words, instantiation is not a specific property of dependents, or of heads for that matter (compare §7.3.3). Instead, instantiation is a fundamental property of the symbolic relations in constructions.

In other words, under scrutiny, arguments and adjuncts as global syntactic roles evaporate. In their place, however, there is a general and powerful gradient concept of semantic valence developed by Langacker, and an equally general and important classification of symbolic relations in constructions in terms of the syntactic instantiation of semantic components in a construction.

Part III
From Universal Constructions to Syntactic Space

8

The Voice Continuum

8.1. Introduction

8.1.1. *Do language universals need universal constructions?*

In the first two parts of this book, I have argued for a model of syntactic representation which takes constructions as the basic units of syntactic representation, and also defined the internal syntactic structure of constructions as a part–whole structure. The model therefore puts a correspondingly greater weight on the form–function mapping for language processing and language universals. Constructions are held together by symbolic and semantic relations, not syntactic relations. Since categories are construction-specific, universals in distribution patterns are defined over conceptual space.

In Part I, I also asserted that constructions are language-specific, but did not elaborate on that point. In Part III, I develop this thesis. As in Parts I and II, the thesis pertains to syntactic structure. Constructions are comparable across languages in terms of their function, such as expressing reference and predication or expressing participant roles in states of affairs. The thesis advanced here is that constructions as cross-linguistically valid configurations of morphosyntactic properties do not exist.

The concept of a universal construction type does not play a central role in contemporary syntactic theories in the way that it did a generation ago (see, e.g., Perlmutter and Postal 1983). In practice, however, particularly in typological studies, much attention is devoted to identifying constructions in a particular language as belonging or not belonging to a particular type, such as passive, active, or inverse voice, to use the phenomenon to be examined in this chapter.

Typologists also worry about the identification of constructions because many typologists formulate language universals in terms of cross-linguistically identifiable construction types. That is, hypotheses are formed about the passive or the inverse construction as a type (see, e.g., Foley and Van Valin 1984: 149–68; Klaiman 1991: 182–4).

In this part of the book, I will argue that typologists will be unsuccessful in identifying universal or cross-linguistic construction types. Constructions are language-specific, and there is an extraordinary range of structural diversity of constructions encoding similar functions across languages. But I will also argue that this fact does not preclude the possibility of discovering and formulating language universals. Using the techniques described and developed in Parts I and II, we may describe universals of language that pertain to the syntactic structure of constructions. In this chapter, I will explore a subset of the phenomena that go under the name of grammatical VOICE from a Radical Construction Grammar perspective.

8.1.2. *Active, passive, inverse: delimiting the grammatical domain*

In order to do a cross-linguistically valid study of grammatical constructions, one must identify the relevant region of conceptual space whose grammatical expression is to be examined. The region of conceptual space that will be discussed here is given in Figure 8.1.

```
              P:
              1,     2  <  3
       A:  1,        —
           2                —
          < 3
```

Figure 8.1. The conceptual space for active–passive–inverse voice

The conceptual space covers only a two-participant event, called V in the rest of this chapter, and the SPEECH ACT PARTICIPANT (SAP) status of the A and P participants in the event (1 = speaker, 2 = addressee, 3 = other). SAP status is given in a partial ordering or ranking on both the vertical (A) dimension and horizontal (P) dimension. SAP status is not totally ordered in conceptual space, as indicated by the notation 1,2 < 3: in some semantic maps, 2 will be ordered before 1, and in other maps neither 1 nor 2 will be ordered with respect to the other. A and P are clusters of participant roles, as defined in §4.2.1. However, I will not be concerned with the problem of identifying which participant role is A and which is P. I add a further restriction, indicated by the dashes in the conceptual space: I will restrict my attention to REFERENTIALLY DISJOINT A and P, and thus exclude reflexive and reciprocal event types.

The constructions encoding this region in conceptual space represent a subset of what has been called voice in the linguistic literature. The term 'voice' has sometimes been extended to constructions for three-participant events, namely causatives and applicatives; others use the term 'diathesis' for these cases. Even in the space of two-participant events, I will narrow the scope of my investigation still further, for reasons of length. I will not look at middle or reflexive voices, since they are associated with the excluded regions in the space in Figure 8.1. Nor will I examine the antipassive voice, which certainly encroaches on this space (but see §8.5.2). Instead, I will examine the voice types usually labeled, with greater or lesser controversy, as active, passive, and inverse voice.

Given this semantic space, one must identify structural properties of the constructions encoding configurations in this space that are cross-linguistically valid in order to compare voice constructions across languages. I will make use of two theoretical notions from typological theory, BASIC TYPE (Croft 1990a: 34–5) and a DERIVED STRUCTURAL definition of a construction (ibid.: 16).

The first step in the analysis is to identify, if possible, the BASIC voice construction of the language in question. This is the canonical voice type in the language. A number of criteria are generally used, of which the simplest one is text (token) frequency: the most frequent type is the basic type. In most cases, the choice of the basic voice construction is straightforward, and I have followed the grammarian's judgment. In other languages, it is not obvious which voice construction is the basic one. These languages will be analyzed in §8.4 after developing an analysis based on less controversial cases.

The basic voice type will be called the ACTIVE voice, following the usual terminology. Example 1 is a sentence in the English Active Voice:

(1) They took the boy to school.

The basic voice type will provide the basis for defining the encoding of Subject, Object, and Oblique roles. The A participant in the Active Voice is by definition the (Active) Subject, and (Active) Subject coding is by definition the case marking and agreement associated with the A in the Active Voice. The P argument is by definition the (Active) Object, and its coding is (Active) Object coding. (I will not use the qualifier 'Active'; reference to Subject and Object should be assumed to apply to the Active or basic voice construction of the language.) Any other argument, such as *to school* in (1), is by definition an Oblique, and its coding is by definition the coding of Obliques. These definitions are construction-specific, in particular the coding constructions for A, P, and V found as part of the Active construction.

Other voice constructions in a language (if any) will be given DERIVED STRUCTURAL definitions. That is, the other voice constructions will be defined not in functional terms, but in structural terms in comparison with the active voice, specifically the coding of A, P, and V in the active voice. This is in fact how universal models of the passive and inverse voices are constructed.

For example, we can take the English Passive Voice as an example of the "canonical" passive:

(2) The boy was ta**ken** to school (**by** his parents).

The English Passive can be described in contrast to the English Active, as in (3):

(3) *Passive:*
    a. A is encoded like an Oblique (if it is expressed at all)
    b. P is encoded like a Subject
    c. V is morphologically distinct from V in the Active

This derived structural definition is an acceptable method for typological comparison as long as it is ultimately grounded in functional categories, namely the functional categories of A, P, and V as encoded in the counterpart, basic Active Voice.

The three properties in (3a–c) represent the English Passive as a structural type: oblique A, subject P, morphologically distinct V. The English Passive, with these three properties, has been taken as the model for a cross-linguistic structural characterization of the passive voice as a universal construction. Nonactive voice forms in other languages are identified as passive (or not) in comparison to the Passive of English and other European languages. The universal passive model also allows for passive constructions in which conditions (3b–c) are satisfied but the agent is not expressed, for example the Lithuanian Passive (Mathiassen 1996: 143). Agent suppression is a common phenomenon among passive constructions that otherwise conform to the English model. Even in English, the vast majority of Passive clauses occur without an overtly expressed A (80 percent in one text count by Svartvik 1966: 141, cited in Shibatani 1988: 93).

However, there is a long tradition in descriptive and typological studies that identifies a construction type distinct from both the active and the passive (in their putative universal form). This construction type is modeled on its occurrence in Algonkian languages, and is called the INVERSE construction. The inverse construction, like the passive construction, is given a derived structural definition. The counterpart basic voice form is usually called the DIRECT form instead of active. A Direct construction from the Algonkian language Cree is given in (4) (Wolfart and Carroll 1981: 69):

(4) ni-   wāpam   -ā   -wak
    1-   see   -DIR   -3PL
    'I see them'

Again, we define the coding of A in the basic (Direct) construction as Subject, the coding of P as Object, and the expression of V, with the Direct suffix, as the basic verb form.

The Inverse in (5) can then be compared to the Direct, as described in (6) (ibid.):

(5) ni-   wāpam   -**ikw**   -ak
    1-   see   -INV   -3PL
    'They see me.'
(6) *Inverse*:
    a. A is coded like an Object
    b. P is coded like a Subject
    c. V is morphologically distinct from V in the Direct

Thus, the Cree Inverse differs from the passive type in (3) with respect to property (6a); cf. (3a).

Another grammatical property distinguishes the Cree Direct and Inverse from the English Active and Passive. Unlike the English voice forms, the Cree Direct and Inverse forms have near complementary distribution when mapped onto the conceptual space in Figure 8.1, as shown in Figure 8.2.

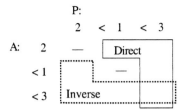

Figure 8.2. Semantic map for Cree Direct and Inverse constructions

The distribution of the Cree Direct and Inverse constructions can be described with the SAP hierarchy 2 < 1 < 3. If A outranks P on the SAP hierarchy, the Direct construction is required; if P outranks A, the Inverse construction is required. For example, if A is 1st Person and P is 3rd Person, then the Direct form is used, as in (4). But if A is 3rd Person and P is 1st Person, as in (5), then the Inverse form is used. The Direct construction occupies the region towards the upper right corner of the conceptual space, and the Inverse occupies the region towards the lower left of the space.

There is only one context in which either the Direct or Inverse may be used (indicated by the overlap of the Direct and Inverse semantic maps in Figure 8.2). This context is when 3rd Person A acts on 3rd Person P (such combinations are henceforth represented as 3→3). In this case, the distribution of the constructions is determined by the grammatical category of OBVIATION, with the values Proximate and Obviative. If A is Proximate, then the Direct construction is used (example (7)), but if P is Proximate, then the Inverse construction is used (example (8); Wolfart and Carroll 1981: 30–1):

(7) wāpam -ēw   nāpēw -∅   sīsīp -a
    see   -DIR:3SG man   -PRXT duck   -OBV
    'The man [PRXT] sees the duck.'
(8) wāpam -ik   nāpēw -a   sīsīp -∅
    see   -INV:3SG man   -OBV   duck   -PRXT
    'The man sees the duck [PRXT].'

The Proximate/Obviative distinction is related to the relative information status or topicality of A and P, not to the A and P semantic roles (as can be seen by (5)–(6)): the Proximate is the more topical of the two referents. We will return to this point in §8.5.2.

The Algonkian Inverse is taken as a model for a cross-linguistic inverse type. Using the same derived structural definition for Inverse that I have used for Passive, A is coded like an Object, P is coded like a Subject, and V is morphologically distinct from the Direct form. In addition, the conformity of the distribution pattern to the SAP hierarchy 1,2 < 3 (as in the conceptual space in Figure 8.1) is generally taken as a defining property of the inverse type.

288   *From Universal Constructions to Syntactic Space*

In this chapter, I will argue that the structural passive type modeled on the English Passive and the structural inverse type modeled on the Cree Inverse are not the only combinations of the relevant structural features found in voice constructions in the world's languages. An extraordinary range of combinations of structural features are found in the non-Active/Direct voice constructions in the world's languages. A broad sample of this variety will be illustrated in §8.3. Some of these voice constructions blur the distinction between Active/Direct and non-Active/Direct; these will be illustrated in §8.4. The reason for illustrating this diversity in such detail is twofold: first, to demonstrate the broad range of structural diversity of voice constructions, and second, to demonstrate that the problematic cases for a theory with universal construction types are in fact quite common, and cannot be evaded with a structural quick fix, or by explaining away the facts of just one or two languages.

Hence, the structural types modeled on the English Passive and Cree Inverse should not have a privileged position in syntactic theory. Instead, the structural diversity of voice constructions must be represented in syntactic theory. The structural diversity of syntactic constructions can be represented in a SYNTACTIC SPACE (see §8.5). The syntactic space then can be mapped onto conceptual space. In the case of active–passive–inverse voice constructions, there is a systematic mapping of syntactic space onto conceptual space, which represents the universals of this subset of voice constructions across the world's languages.

8.2. Prelude: Animacy Constraints in Actives and Passives

In §8.1.1, it was noted that typologists generally consider the SAP hierarchy constraints found in the Cree Inverse construction a defining property of the inverse voice type. However, SAP hierarchy constraints are found in constructions which are otherwise relatively uncontroversial examples of the passive type as defined above.

Lummi has Active and Passive voice constructions, illustrated in (9) and (10) respectively (Jelinek and Demers 1983: 168):

(9) x̌či   -t   -sxʷ   cə   swəy?qə?
    know -TR -2   the   man
    'You know the man.'

(10) x̌či   -t   -ŋ   -sxʷ   ə   cə   swəy?qə?
     know -TR -PASS -2   by   the man
     'You are known by the man.'

The Lummi Passive codes A as a Oblique (with ə 'by') and P as a Subject (triggering verb agreement), like the canonical passive; but it retains the suffix -t otherwise associated with Transitive verbs in the language. However, there is near complementary distribution of the Active and Passive forms, as in Figure 8.3 (prn = pronoun, CN = common noun).

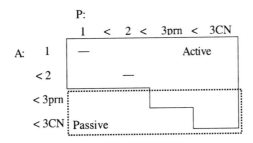

Figure 8.3. Semantic map for Lummi Active and Passive constructions

The Lummi Active is required if A is 1st or 2nd Person, and may be used if P is a Common Noun or if both A and P are 3rd Person Pronouns. The Passive is always possible if A is 3rd Person, and is required if in addition P is 1st or 2nd Person, and if P is a 3rd Person pronoun and A is a Common Noun.

The semantic map of the Lummi Active, like that for the Cree Direct, includes the upper right corner of the conceptual space. The map for the Lummi Passive, like that for the Cree Inverse, includes the lower left corner of the conceptual space.

Other languages allow for greater overlap between Active and Passive constructions in conceptual space, but partially limit the distribution in accordance with the pattern found in Cree and Lummi. For example, K'iche' has a canonical Passive with Oblique A and Passive V form, as in (11) (all examples from Mondloch 1978: 46, 59):

(11) ca-   cun   -ax   la   r-   **uma:l**
     PRS-   cure   -PASS   2SG.FRM   3SG.POSS-   **by**
     'You (formal) are cured by him.'

However, the Active is prohibited for 3→2Formal (compare (11) to (12)); while the Passive is prohibited for 1,2→3 (compare (13)–(15) to (16)):

(12) *c-   u-   cun   la
     PST-   3SG.ERG-   cure   2SG.FRM
     'He cures you (formal).'

(13) c-   Ø-   a:-   tzucu:j
     PRS-   3SG.ABS-   2SG.ERG-   look.for:TR
     'You look for him.'

(14) c-   at-   u:-   tzucu:j
     PRS-   2SG.ABS-   3SG.ERG-   look.for:TR
     'He looks for you.'

(15) x-   Ø-   in-   cunaj   le: achi
     PST-   3SG.ABS-   1SG.ERG-   cure:TR   the   man
     'I cured the sick man.'

290 *From Universal Constructions to Syntactic Space*

(16) *x-   Ø-   cun   -ax   le: yawa:b   w-   uma:l
     PST-   3SG.ABS-   cure   -PASS   the   sick.one   1SG.POSS- by
     'The sick one was cured by me.'

The K'iche' constraints are illustrated in Figure 8.4 (F = formal, f = familiar).

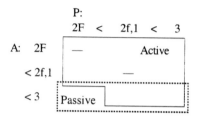

Figure 8.4. Semantic map for K'iche' Active and Passive voice

As with the Cree Direct and the Lummi Active, the K'iche' Active semantic map includes the upper right corner of the space; as with the Cree Inverse and the Lummi Passive, the K'iche' Passive's semantic map includes the lower left corner.

The English Passive also has a marginal SAP constraint on its Passive not unlike K'iche's categorical restriction: the Passive is only marginally acceptable for 1,2 → 3 (DeLancey 1981: 638):

(17) ??Mary Summers was flunked by me.

The pattern found in Cree, Lummi, K'iche' and English is found wherever SAP constraints exist on voice constructions: the basic voice form includes the upper right corner of the conceptual space in Figure 8.1, while the nonbasic voice form includes the lower left corner. This is indeed part of the typological universal underlying voice constructions (see §8.5.2). But before explicating this universal, we must explore the structural diversity of different voice forms.

8.3. The Structural Variety of Actives and Passives

In this and the following section, I will present examples of the basic and nonbasic voice constructions for each language, and then briefly describe the structural properties of the nonbasic voice form and compare it to the passive type in (3) and/or the inverse type in (6).

8.3.1. *Some so-called passives*

Some so-called passives differ from the passive type in (3) in the coding of P, as in the examples of the Welsh Active and Impersonal Passive in (18) and (19) respectively (Comrie 1977: 55):

(18) fe'i   lladdodd   draig
     PTCL'OBJ   killed.ACT   dragon
     'A dragon killed him.'

(19) fe'i   lladdwyd   **gan**   ddraig
     PTCL'OBJ   killed.PASS   **by**   dragon
     'He was killed by a dragon.'

In (19), A is Oblique, V is morphologically distinct, but P is coded like an Object. This is clearest for Pronominal P; nonpronominal Ps do not undergo lenition, in the way Direct Objects normally do.

The Finnish Indefinite ("Passive") is similar to Welsh (Shore 1988: 156, 157, 158):

(20) Miehet   vietiin   poliisiasemalle
     man:PL.NOM   took:INDF   police.station:to
     'The men/Men were taken to the police station.'
(21) **Hänet**   vietiin   poliisiasemalle
     3SG:ACC   took:INDF   police.station:to
     'The men/Men were taken to the police station.'
(22) **Heitä/Miehiä**   vietiin   poliisiasemalle
     3SG:PRTT/men:PRTT   took:INDF   police.station:to
     'Some of them/the men were taken to the police station.'

In the Finnish Indefinite in (20)–(22), A is unexpressed, as with many canonical passives; it is interpreted as an indefinite human (sometimes the context can indicate otherwise; Shore 1988: 160). Although P is coded like a Subject in (20), P is coded like an Object with either Accusative Case (pronouns; (21)), or Partitive Case (Nouns, when appropriate; (22)). As in Welsh, nonpronominal Ps can be found in the Nominative Case (Comrie 1975). V is Impersonal (no Agreement), and is morphologically distinct from the Active V (Shore 1988: 154).

The Russian Impersonal construction in (24) is somewhat similar to the English Passive in that A is expressed as an Oblique (Zolotova et al. 1998: 127):

(23) voln   -y   unes   -li   lodk   -u
     waves.F   -NOM.PL   carry.away   -PST.PL   boat.F   -ACC
     'The waves carried away the boat.'
(24) voln   **-ami**   unes   **-lo**   lodk   **-u**
     boat.F   -INST.PL   carry.away   -PST.IMPR   boat.F   -ACC
     'The boat was carried away by the waves.'

However, P is coded as an Object, and the verb is put into the Impersonal (3rd Singular Neuter) form. Also, the Russian Impersonal construction is restricted to As representing natural forces (ibid.):

(25) *Mal'čik   **-om**   sloma   **-lo**   vetk   **-u**
     boy.M   -INST.SG   break.off   -PST.IMPR   branch.F -ACC.SG
     '*The branch was broken off by the boy.'

Thus, the Russian Impersonal includes the lower left corner of the conceptual space diagram, and excludes the upper right corner (I am grateful to Östen Dahl for this example).

The Maasai Passive illustrates yet another variation on this theme. The Maasai

Active is illustrated in (26)–(27), and the Passive in (28) (Nilo-Saharan; Greenberg 1959/1990: 413):

(26) a-   dɔl
     1SG.SBJ- see
     'I see him/her/them.'
(27) aa-   dɔl
     1SG.OBJ- see
     'He/she/they see me.'
(28) **aa-** dɔl -i
     1SG.OBJ- see -PASS
     'I am seen.'

In the Maasai Passive, A is not expressed (Payne et al. 1994: 301–2), though it could be expressed in earlier times (see Tucker and Mpaayei 1955). P is coded as Object, in both Agreement (compare (28) to (27)) and in Case, for Nominal Ps. V is morphologically distinct; but the -*i* suffix is etymologically a 3rd Person Plural Subject form (Greenberg 1959/1990). Similar constructions can be found in Turkana (Dimmendaal 1983: 72, 131–4) and Kimbundu (Givón 1979: 211–12), among other languages.

Menomini has a Passive construction in addition to the Inverse construction—a demonstration that the two are not mutually exclusive (Bloomfield 1962: 152, 154–5). The Menomini Passive is structurally quite divergent. A typical Active Direct form is given in (29), and a Passive Direct form in (30):

(29) ke- na·n   -a·   -w   -ak
     2-   fetch -IND -3   -PL
     'You [sg] fetch them.'
(30) na·n   -a·   -w   -ak
     fetch -IND -3   -PL
     'They are fetched.'

In the Direct Passive, A is not expressed and P is coded like an Object. The verb conjugation is the same in both (29) and (30) (Transitive Animate[1])—except that it is lacking the 1/2 Subject Agreement prefix *ke*-. Finally, V is not morphologically distinct.

The Menomini Inverse Active and Passive are illustrated in (31) and (32) respectively:

(31) ke- nɛ·qn -ek   -o   -q
     2-   kill   -INV   -IND.3INAN   -1IN
     'It kills us [incl.].' [Transitive Animate Inverse, inanimate actor form]
(32) ke- na·tom -ek   -ɛ·   -q
     2-   call   -INV   -IND.1/2PASS -1IN
     'We [incl.] are called.' [Transitive Animate Inverse, 1st/2nd passive form]

---

[1] This construction is also found with Transitive Inanimate conjugation verbs (Bloomfield 1962: 157–8).

In the Inverse Passive, A is not expressed, P is coded like a Subject (because it is Inverse), and the suffix *-ɛ-* distinguishes the Inverse Passive from the Inverse Active.

Another passive type, found in some Mande languages, is the same as the passive type in (3) except that V is identical to the Active form. An example is Bambara (Chris Culy, personal communication, and from Bailleul 1977):

(33) n'ye   kini   dun
    1SG'CMPL.TR rice eat
    'I ate rice.'

(34) o   fo'ra   dugutigi **fè**
    3SG greet'CMPL.INTR chief   **with**
    'S/he was greeted by the chief.'

In the Bambara "Passive", A is Oblique and P is Subject. The Bambara "Passive" uses the aspect inflections otherwise associated with Intransitive Verbs. Yet V is not morphologically distinct from the V in the Active.

In the Spanish Reflexive Passive, a type found in a number of European languages, P is coded simultaneously as Subject and (Reflexive) Object (Stockwell et al. 1965: 235):

(35) **Se**   abri   **-eron**   las   puertas
    3REFL open -3PL   the windows
    'The windows were opened.'

In the Spanish Reflexive Passive, A may be expressed as an Oblique. Overt expression of A is rejected by some speakers, but example (36) is an attested utterance (overheard 23 May 2000):

(36) **Se**   am   **-a**   **por**   la   gente
    3REFL love -3SG **by**   the people
    'He [King Juan Carlos] is loved by the people.'

P is coded as Subject by V Agreement and Object by virtue of the Reflexive Object Pronoun. V is not morphologically distinct, at least not distinct from Active Reflexive Vs. However, the Reflexive Object marking in Spanish and other European languages is being reanalyzed as a derivational category of the Verb, the Reflexive Middle Voice. The Reflexive Middle Voice occurs with a number of Vs denoting one participant events, such as *bañarse* 'to bathe (onself)', *vestirse* 'to dress oneself', *peinarse* 'to comb one's hair'; *romperse* 'break', *arrodillarse* 'kneel'. As such, one could argue that the Reflexive Passive V is Intransitive, and the Reflexive form is morphologically distinct from the (nonreflexive) Active.

The Upriver Halkomelem Passive is similar and different from the Spanish Reflexive Passive. Examples of the Active and Passive are given in (37) and (38) respectively (Galloway 1993: 425–6):

(37) tás   -l   -əxʷ   -əs   θúƛ'à   tə   swíyəqə
    bump.into -ACCID -3SG.OBJ -3SG.SBJ she   ART man
    'She bumped into the man' [V–A–P order]

(38) tə́s   -l   -əm   θúƛ̓à   tə   swíyəqə
     bump.into -ACCID -3SG.PASS she   ART   man
     'She was bumped into by the man' [V–P–A order]

In the Active in (37), the order of elements is V–A–P, which is the basic voice Verb–Subject–Object order. In the Passive, A is coded like Object with respect to position (second NP after the Verb), but it does not trigger Object Agreement. P is coded like Subject with respect to position, and triggers agreement on V. However, P triggers Agreement suffixes that are distinct from both the Active A and the Active P Agreement suffixes. This particular structural property—special P Agreement forms—is a common phenomenon that does not fit either the passive type in (3) or the inverse type in (6) (see Payne 1999: 249–52). The 3rd Singular Passive Agreement suffix *-əm* has also evolved into a Middle Voice marker: *xʸakʼʷəm* 'to bathe (onself)', *ʔíθʼəm* 'to dress oneself', *ɬícʼəqʷəm* 'to comb one's hair', *yá·kʼʷəm* 'to break (of its own accord)', *θʼqʼəɬxé·m* 'kneel' (Galloway 1993: 301–7).

V takes Control suffixes such as *-l* 'accidentally', otherwise found only with Active Transitive Verbs (Galloway 1993: 244). V is not morphologically distinct from the Active. The Passive also has some SAP hierarchy constraints. The Passive must be used if 3→2, or if P is a 3rd Person Pronoun (as in (38)), and the Active must be used if P is 1st Person Plural (ibid.: 187). The semantic map for the Upriver Halkomelem Voice constructions is given in Figure 8.5.

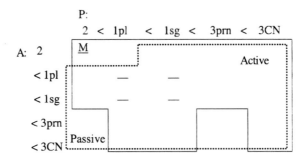

Figure 8.5. Semantic map of Upriver Halkomelem voice constructions

Although some of the restrictions on the Upriver Halkomelem Voice semantic maps are typologically unusual, the Upriver Halkomelem Voice constructions do follow the universal that the Passive map includes at least the lower left hand corner of the conceptual space and the Active map includes at least the upper right hand corner of the conceptual space.

The Passive of Bella Coola, another Salishan language, is structurally slightly different from the Upriver Halkomelem Passive. An example of the Bella Coola Passive is given in (39) (Forrest 1994: 151–2):

(39) kʼx -im   ci-   xnas   -cx   x-   ti-   ʔimlk -tx
     see -3SG.PASS ART- woman -ART   PREP- ART- man   -ART
     'The woman is seen by the man.'

Like the Upriver Halkomelem Passive, the Bella Coola Passive V is not morphologically distinct from the Active V. Also, the P is coded like Subject in position, but takes special P Agreement forms. However, P never takes the Nominative -s (ibid.), and A is coded as an Oblique, unlike the Upriver Halkomelem Passive. The Bella Coola Voice system also has SAP hierarchy constraints: the Passive must be used if 3→1/2, and the Passive is used with more topical Ps for 3→3, not unlike the Cree Inverse.

In sum, the constructions illustrated in this section vary with respect to every structural property of the passive type in (3): whether A is coded as an Oblique or not, whether P is coded like a Subject or not, and whether V is morphologically distinct from the Active V or not. In addition, at least some of the so-called passives exhibit SAP hierarchy constraints. In the next section, we will see that a similar state of affairs holds for so-called inverses.

8.3.2. *Some so-called inverses*

The constructions that have been categorized as inverse are at least as diverse structurally as those that have been categorized as passive. One reason for this is that almost any non-passive-like construction that exhibits SAP hierarchy constraints has been described as an inverse, no matter what its structure is.

I begin with an Arizona Tewa construction that has been described as both a Passive (Kroskrity 1985) and an Inverse (Klaiman 1991). Two examples of the Arizona Tewa Passive/Inverse are given in (40)–(41) (Kroskrity 1985: 311, 313):

(40) hẹ'i sen **-di** né'i kʷiyó 'ó:- tụ́ -'án -'i dó- tay
that man -OBL this woman 3SG/3.PASS- say -CMPL -REL 1SG/3.ACT- know
'I know the woman who was spoken to by the man.'

(41) ụ kʰóto hẹ'i sen **-di wó:-** mégi
you bracelet that man -OBL 2/3.PASS- give
'You were given a bracelet by that man.'

In the Arizona Tewa Passive/Inverse, A is coded partly like an Oblique, with the Case marker -*di* (Kroskrity 1985: 314). P is coded partly like a Subject, with respect to Case marking; it is also the argument that can be relativized and whose reference is tracked (ibid.: 313–14; see §4.3.2). However, A and P are coded with special portmanteau Agreement forms. No morphology distinguishes V from the Active form.

The Arizona Tewa Passive/Inverse is also subject to the SAP hierarchy, as illustrated in Figure 8.6 (p. 296). Although the Arizona Tewa Passive/Inverse construction has a wider distribution than the Active construction, it resembles the distributions of the other constructions discussed above in that the Passive/Inverse distribution includes the lower left corner of the conceptual space, and the Active distribution includes the upper right corner of the conceptual space.

The remaining examples in this section all represent structurally complex paradigms of transitive verb constructions. These systems are usually analyzed simply as the set of Active Transitive V forms of the language. However, some of these systems have recently been reanalyzed as examples of direct vs. inverse

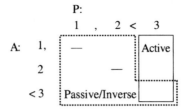

Figure 8.6. Semantic map for Arizona Tewa Active and Passive/Inverse constructions

coding of A and P by a closer examination of the structure of the different forms in the paradigms.

The first example is a simple one, the Tangut Inverse (Kepping 1979; Comrie 1980b; DeLancey 1981). The Tangut Inverse differs from the Cree Inverse in that only one argument is indexed with Agreement affixes on the verb, *-nga* '1st Person' or *-na* '2nd Person'. A number of examples are given below (Kepping 1979: 273; cf. DeLancey 1981: 631):

(42) ni   tın   nga ın   ldıə   thı   **-nga**
     you   if   I   ACC   indeed chase -1
     ku   that tsı viə-thı **-na**
     then her   also chase   -2
     'If indeed you are chasing me, then chase her too.'
(43) ni   pha   ngi-mbın ndı-siei **-na**
     you   other wife   choose   -2
     'You choose another wife.'
(44) mei-swen   manə   na   khe   **-na**
     Meng Sun   formerly you hate -2
     'Meng Sun formerly hated you.'

As can be seen from the examples, V agrees with either A or P. The distribution of V Agreement in Tangut is mapped in Figure 8.7.

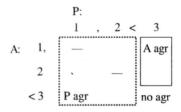

Figure 8.7. Semantic map for Tangut Verb Agreement

If we interpret verb agreement as an indicator of Subject status, in the sense described in §8.1.2 (i.e. coding of A in the 'basic' voice form), then Figure 8.6 is not unlike the Cree example in Figure 8.1, except that a Tangut Verb agrees with only one argument. Subject-like Ps are associated with the lower left part of the space, and Subject-like As are associated with the upper right part of the space.[2]

The next examples represent complex patterns of V agreement with both A and P. We begin with the Yurok Transitive constructions, as analyzed by Robins (1980). Yurok has three different Transitive constructions. The Bipersonal construction possesses a V that agrees with A and P (Robins 1980: 361, 363):

(45) ki   kemeyonem   -es   -ek'
     FUT   take.home   -3SG.OBJ   1SG.SBJ
     'I'll take him home.'

The Unipersonal construction possesses a V which agrees with only A:

(46) (nek)   nekcen   -ek'   neto:ʔmar
     (1SG.SBJ) meet   -1SG   my.friend
     'I meet my friend.'

The Passive construction uses a morphologically distinct form for V:

(47) (yoʔ)   nowkʷoy   (nekah)
     (3SG)   care.PASS (1PL.OBJ)
     'He/she cares for us.'

(48) neto:ʔmar   kelac   nowkʷoy   -eʔm
     my.friend   2SG.OBJ   care.PASS   -2SG.SBJ
     'My friend cares for you.'

In the Passive construction, A is coded like a Subject, with Subject case marking, but without triggering Agreement. P is coded both like an Object, with Object case marking, and like a Subject, triggering Subject Agreement.

The Bipersonal, Unipersonal, and Passive forms are mutually exclusive except for 3PL→1SG, and largely respect the SAP hierarchy 1 < 2 < 3, except for 1SG P forms, as can be seen in Figure 8.8.

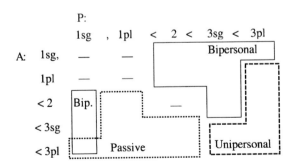

Figure 8.8. Semantic map for Yurok Bipersonal, Unipersonal, and Passive constructions

[2] In addition, it should be noted that A may take an optional Ergative Case form *ndźe-vie*, and P may take an optional Accusative case form *In₁* (Comrie 1980b). Also, Agreement is always optional, and T, G, or a Possessor can trigger Agreement (ibid.).

The Bipersonal construction is the most "direct" and the Passive construction the most "inverse", with the Unipersonal construction in between. The Bipersonal construction is used only when A and P are both human and P is Pronominal (ibid.: 361, 362). The Bipersonal forms for 1SG P are "anomalous" in this system, because they are associated with the lower left corner as well as upper right corner of the conceptual space, and the semantic map does not define a connected region in conceptual space. However, in the 3PL→1SG, the Passive form is taking over from the "anomalous" Bipersonal form (ibid.: 363). In effect, what is happening is that the Passive construction is being integrated into the general Yurok Transitive paradigm.

A similar analysis can be made for other agreement systems, which suggests a similar historical scenario of the integration of former "passive" or "inverse" constructions into the transitive paradigm. For example, the Guaraní Verb Agreement inflections appear to be largely but not entirely monomorphemic (Gregores and Suárez 1968: 131–2) (Table 8.1).

Table 8.1. Distribution of Guaraní agreement forms

A:	P: 1SG	1PE	1PI	2SG	2PL	3
1SG	—	—	—	ro-	po-	**a-**
1PE	—	—	—	ro-	po-	**ro-**
1PI	—	—	—	—	—	**ya-**
2SG	*še-*	ore-	—	—	—	**re-**
2PL	*še-*	ore-	—	—	—	**pe-**
3	*še-*	*ore-*	*yane-*	*ne-*	*pene-*	**o-**

In Table 8.1, the most "direct" forms are indicated in boldface, the most "inverse" forms in italics, with the intermediate forms in roman. The forms in Table 8.1 can be analyzed as in Table 8.2.

Table 8.2. Analysis of Guaraní agreement forms

Direct	Inverse	Portmanteau
a-: 1SG	še-: 1SG	po-: 1→2PL
ro-: 1PE	ore-: 1PE	ro-: 1→2SG
ya-: 1PI	yane-: 1PI	
re-: 2SG	ne-: 2SG	
pe-: 2PL	pene-: 2PL	
o-: 3		

The agreement prefixes are easily analyzed as encoding 1st or 2nd person A (direct) or P (inverse). The P Agreement forms in the second column are like an inverse P Agreement system. The prefixes conform to the SAP hierarchy 1 < 2 < 3, but there are special forms for 1→2. Examples of the Direct and Inverse agreement prefixes are given in (49)–(50) (Gregores and Suárez 1967: 156, 131):

(49) ho-   ʔú   soʔó
     3.DIR- eat   meat
     'He eats meat'
(50) ne-   peté
     2.INV- hit
     'He/she/it/they hit thee.'

D. Payne (1994) suggests that the prefix *ne-* may derive historically from an overt expression of Inverse (but see below).

Payne et al. (1994) analyze part of the Transitive paradigm of Maasai as an inverse system. The Direct and Inverse constructions are illustrated in (51) and (52) respectively (Payne et al. 1994: 291, 294):

(51) á-   tá-   dʊ́   -a   ntáy
     1.DIR- PRF-   see -PRF   2PL.ACC
     'I see you (PL).'
(52) kí-   nyál -à   ntáy   nánú
     1/2PL.INV-   spoil -PF.PL 2PL.NOM   1SG.ACC
     'You (PL) insulted me.'

In the Inverse construction in (51), A is coded like a Subject with respect to tone (tone encodes Case), but unlike a Subject is not triggering V Agreement. P is coded like an Object with respect to Case tone, and triggers Agreement like Subject, but again with special forms (Set II), which can be interpreted as Inverse forms. V is not morphologically distinct. The Inverse Agreement forms conform partly to the SAP hierarchy and partly to a number hierarchy singular < plural: they are used for 2→1SG, 3SG→2SG, and all plural→2SG (Payne et al. 1994: 295).

Another complex example of verb agreement is the Chukotko-Kamchatkan Transitive paradigm, as analyzed by Comrie (1980a, 1980b). In the Present I tense in Chukchi, there is a complex system of Verb Agreement forms. 1st Person forms are invariant and are interpreted by Comrie as Direct forms. Comrie analyzes the prefix *ine-* and the suffix *-tku* as unipersonal Antipassive forms (Comrie 1980a: 64). Comrie hypothesizes that the prefix *ne-* is an Inverse marker; Comrie suggests that it may be in the process of being reanalyzed as a 3rd Person Subject prefix (ibid.: 65; but see below). P is always encoded by personal suffixes, which also encode S in Intransitives; that is, the suffixes are Absolutive. In Chukchi, *ine-* can also be used for a general Antipassive in 3→3 forms (Comrie 1980b: 230–1).[3] Semantic maps for the Chukchi Transitive Verb forms are given in Figure 8.9.

---

[3] This analysis applies only to the Present I tense in Chukchi. In the Present II tense, *n(i)*- occupies the prefix position, and for 1/2→3, the Verb is Antipassive and the suffixes agree with A, which is the higher participant on the SAP hierarchy (Comrie 1980b: 231). Koryak, a closely related language differs from Chukchi in using *ne-* in place of *-tku* (Comrie 1980a: 65).

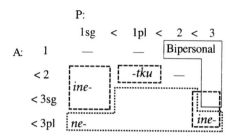

Figure 8.9. Semantic map for Chukchi Transitive Verb constructions

The most inverse construction is the *ne* -construction. In this construction, A is not coded like Subject (it lacks Agreement) or Object (no Object Agreement). If A is low in animacy, the Noun Phrase is coded as an Oblique. P is coded as Subject with Absolutive affixal Agreement, but without any prefixal Agreement, unlike Direct Subjects. V is morphologically distinct (unless *ne*- is a 3rd Person Subject form).

Similar patterns have been reported for Chinook (Silverstein 1976), Ngandi and Nunggubuyu (Heath 1976), and Wardaman (Merlan 1994). This is in fact a fairly common phenomenon in languages in which both A and P are expressed by person agreement on the verb.

The agreement paradigm for Seko Padang, a Western Austronesian language, suggests that some inverse patterns arise from a 3rd person A marker. In Seko Padang, there is a Primary set of Person proclitics on the Verb, in which the A proclitic is closer to the Verb than the P proclitic (Payne and Laskowske 1997: 427–8):

(53) u=   ki=   kini'
      2=   1EX=   pinch
      'We (excl.) pinch you.'

(54) ki=   u=   kini'
      1EX= 2=   pinch
      'You pinch us (excl.).'

However, if A is 3rd Person, the proclitic Pronoun *na*= is used instead of the Primary ∅= proclitic (ibid.):

(55) ki=   **na=**   kini'
      1EX=   3A=   pinch
      'He/she pinches us (excl.).'

Also, a special form (*u*)*du*= is optionally used for the 2nd Person P if A is 1st Person, as in (56); and a special form *mi*= is used for 1st Person P if A is 2nd Person, as in (57) (ibid.; note that the order of affixes also changes in (57)):

(56) (u)du=   ki=   kini'
      2.P=   1EX=   pinch
      'We (excl.) pinch you.'

(57) u=   mi=   kini'
    2=   1.P= pinch
    'You pinch me/us.'

The special form *mi=* may also be used for 3→1 situations (ibid.).

The semantic map for the Seko Padang proclitics is given in Figure 8.10 (Pr. = primary transitive proclitics, indicated by solid line).

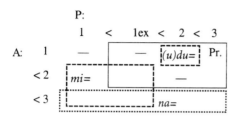

Figure 8.10. Semantic map for Seko Padang proclitic constructions

The most inverse-like construction is the 3A *na=* proclitic, and the most direct are the Primary proclitics. The special *mi=* and *(u)du=* proclitics occupy intermediate regions of the conceptual space. Another way of describing the situation is that 3rd Person As have a special proclitic and 1st/2nd Person Ps have a special proclitic, in which case the 1/2P forms are also inverse-like. However, the 1/2P forms do not appear to have originated in the lower left region, but are being extended to it, which suggests that an intermediate-status analysis of the 1/2P forms is more accurate. The *na=* proclitic could be reanalyzed as an inverse marker. A similar reanalysis might have occurred in the Guaraní and Chukchi cases (cf. D. Payne and Comrie), and in the case of Panare discussed in Payne (1999).

A subtler SAP-constrained pattern is found in Yimas, a Papuan language (Foley 1991). Yimas verbs agree with both A and P, with one exception to be discussed below. The A and P forms for each Person are distinct, except for 1st Person Dual. However, the order and form of agreement prefixes varies in a complex way in accordance with the SAP hierarchy. For all→3, the order of prefixes is [P–A–VERB] as in (58); for all→1 and 3NPL→2, the order of prefixes is [A–P–VERB], as in (59) (Foley 1991: 206):

(58) na-   kay-   tay
     3SG.P-   1PL.A-   see
     'We saw him.'
(59) ma-   kra-   tay
     2SG.A-   1PL.P-   see
     'You saw us.'

In the case of 3PL→1,2, the P form of the 3rd Person Plural marker is used (Foley 1991: 201):

(60) **pu-** ŋa- tay
3PL."P"- 1SG.P- see
'They saw me.'

The forms 1→2 are anomalous: for 1→2SG, a portmanteau prefix is used ((61); Foley 1991: 207), and for 1→2NSG, only the 2nd Person Nonsingular Agreement prefix is allowed, the 1st Person A being inferred from the context ((62); ibid.):

(61) **kampan-** tay
1/2SG- see
'I/we two/we saw you.'

(62) **ŋkul-** cay
2DU- see
'I/we two/we saw you two.'

The semantic map for the Yimas Agreement constructions is given in Figure 8.11.

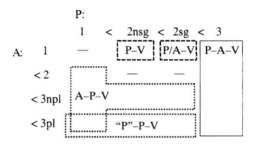

Figure 8.11. Semantic map for Yimas Agreement constructions

The constructions with A prefixes ordered before P prefixes include the lower left corner of the conceptual space; those with P before A include the upper right corner; the two anomalous constructions are in between. The construction with two P forms may be thought of as a more extreme case of the A–P–V construction; it overlaps with the A–P–V construction in the most "inverse" corner of the conceptual space.

The constructions described in this section vary according to all of the properties of the inverse type given in (6): whether A is coded as an Oblique or not, whether P is coded like Subject or not, and whether V is morphologically distinct from the Direct form or not. All of the constructions interact with the SAP hierarchy to at least some extent.

8.4. Blurring the Active–Nonactive Distinction

The last set of examples in §8.3.2 treat as "inverse" the forms that in fact form part of the basic transitive constructional paradigm of the language. In other words, technically, all of the forms are Active. If we examine the range of transitive constructions in a language to observe their structural differences, then it turns out that many other constructional types belong in the same voice continuum.

8.4.1. *Some so-called "passives" and ergatives*

Acehnese has a construction which Durie (1985, 1988) argues is not a passive, despite certain structural properties seemingly shared with the passive type in (3). I will call this the Acehnese Ergative construction. The Ergative construction is illustrated in (63) (Durie 1988: 105):

(63) lôn   ka   **geu-**   côm   **lé-**   gopnyan
     1   INCH   3-   kiss   PREP-   she
    'I was kissed by her.'

In the Acehnese Ergative construction, A is coded partly like a Subject in that it triggers Subject Agreement.[4] But A is also apparently coded like an Oblique, with the preposition *lé-*. P is coded like an Object; if P is enclitic, A may drop *lé-* (Durie 1985: 194). V is not morphologically distinct. However, Durie argues that *lé-* is not an Oblique but simply an Ergative case marker on the A NP (Durie 1988: 111).

Durie's analysis makes Acehnese relatively unremarkable: another ergative case marking language. But there is still a puzzle here. If we take the Active Intransitive construction instead of the Active Transitive construction as the defining construction for Subject, then in ergative languages the A argument in Active Transitives is not coded the same way as S. Instead it has a case marking that is often synchronically (and always diachronically) identical to an oblique case marking.

It is true that A does often share distribution patterns with S in other constructions, including Agreement (see §4.3.2). But in Radical Construction Grammar, we are entitled to examine the distribution patterns of each construction. The advantage of the Radical Construction Grammar approach is that we may now examine languages in which it is not obvious what the Active construction is, and simply compare the different transitive constructions in a language in accordance with the structural properties and the conceptual space described in this chapter, and fit them into the larger typological pattern.

Thus we may look at ergative constructions in their own right, as something intermediate between the passive type in (3) and the basic active construction. Since some ergatives are believed to have arisen from passives, it should not be surprising to find some constructions that appear to be structurally intermediate between the passive type in (3) and the active type.

One such example may be Pukapukan (Chung 1977: 15–16). Pukapukan has

---

[4] More precisely, the verb agrees with A+Sa, that is, the Actor argument (Durie 1985: 41; see also §4.4.1).

three transitive constructions, described by Chung as Active, Passive, and Ergative. The Active construction is illustrated in (64):

(64) tulituli loa   Lua Tulivae ia   i   tana wawine ma   na   tama
     chase   EMPH   Lua Tulivae that ACC his   woman   and the.PL boy
     'Lua Tulivae chased his wife and the children.'

The Passive construction is illustrated in (65):

(65) kai -na   loa   na   tamaliki e   te   wui   aitu   pau
     eat -PASS EMPH   the.PL children AGT the PL   spirit done
     'The children were all eaten by the spirits.'

If we use the Active construction as the standard of comparison, as we have done in the other languages we have examined, then the Passive construction conforms straightforwardly to the passive type in (3): A is coded as an Oblique, P is coded as a Subject, and V is morphologically distinct, with the suffix *na-*.

The functional relationship between the Pukapukan Active and Passive, however, is not the same as the functional relationship between the English Active and Passive. The Pukapukan Active is used only in the formal register, which suggests that it is the archaic construction. The Pukapukan Passive is the normal construction used for two-participant events (Chung 1977: 16). In other words, the Pukapukan Passive is the basic Transitive construction. In general, Passives in Polynesian languages have high text frequency, sometimes higher even than Actives (Chung 1977: 13–14). Moreover, the P in the Pukapukan Passive has already climbed up the Subject Construction Hierarchy (§4.3.2), although the A is still a possible role filler for some of the constructions in the hierarchy.

The Pukapukan Ergative construction is illustrated in (66):

(66) lomilomi ai   e   tana wawine ma   na   tama lua   tulivae ia
     massage   PRN ERG his   woman   and the.PL boy   two   knee   that
     'His two knees were massaged by his wife and the children.'

The Ergative construction is identical to the Passive construction except that it lacks the suffix *-na* that distinguishes the Passive V form from the Active V form. The Ergative construction is also the usual two-participant event construction in casual speech. This suggests that it is the result of the loss of the Passive suffix *-na*—a final step to becoming the zero coded, basic transitive V form.

Similar phenomena are found in other Austronesian languages. The Karo Batak Passive construction is illustrated in (67) (Woollams 1996: 191):

(67) itimai   Raja Aceh denga Putri Hijau
     PASS:wait.for   King Aceh still Putri Hijau
     'The King of Aceh still waited for Putri Hijau.'

In the Karo Batak Passive, P is coded as Subject, but A is not coded like either Subject or Oblique. NPs encoding A are 'incorporated', that is, they precede auxiliaries like *denga* in (67). Pronominal As are coded by special Agreement affixes—

the mirror image of the special P agreement affixes described in §§8.2–8.3. V is morphologically distinct from the Active form.

However, text frequency indicates that the Karo Batak Passive is in fact the basic transitive clause type. In Karo Batak, A is present in 85 percent of Passive clauses (Woollams 1996: 193), compared to 20 percent of English Passives, in one count (Svartvik 1966: 141, cited in Shibatani 1988: 93). Passives occur more than twice as often in texts as Actives (ibid.: 212), though Actives are more common in dependent clauses. This compares to only 12 percent Passives in English texts (Svartvik 1966: 46, cited in Shibatani 1988: 94–5). There are also Subjectless Passives in Karo Batak which typically translate to Intransitive Verbs with Oblique PPs in English (Woollams 1996: 197):

(68) É   maka   turiken   Bunga Ncolé   me   kerna   nipina   é
     and   then   PASS:relate   Bunga Ncole   EMPH   about   dream.her   that
     'And so Bunga Ncole told about the dream that she had.'

The Karo Batak Passive construction is functionally quite different from the English Passive construction. It is the basic Transitive construction in Karo Batak, using the text frequency criterion for basic voice form (see §8.1.2). The higher frequency of the Active in dependent clauses suggests that the Active construction is passing out of use.

The Nilo-Saharan language Shilluk displays a similar pattern in its Active and Passive constructions (Westermann 1912/1970; I am grateful to Matthew Dryer for bringing this example to my attention). In the Shilluk Active construction, A is coded by a preverbal Pronoun or NP and P is coded by a Pronominal suffix or a postverbal NP (Westermann 1912/1970: 61, 76):

(69) á   chwọ̀l   -à
     ASP   call:PRF   -1SG
     'He called me.'
(70) yá   mạ̈tị̈   pi
     1SG   drink:PRF   water
     'I drank water.'

If A is a 3rd Person Pronoun, as in (69), it is replaced by the Aspect particle *a*.

If the A follows V in the Perfect Active construction, then the Pronominal suffix is used for A (Westermann 1912/1970: 74):

(71) à   chwọ́l   -í
     ASP   call:PRF   -2SG
     'You called [. . .]'

In the Shilluk Passive construction, V typically has a falling tone. P is coded like A in the Active, that is, by a prenominal Pronoun or NP, and A is postnominal. If A is Pronominal, it is coded by the same suffixes used for P in the Active or A in the Postverbal Active Perfect. However, only the Singular suffixes are used; the Plural uses the Singular suffixes and devoices the last consonant of the root (Westermann 1912/1970: 78):

(72) á   kwộp   -à
     ASP speak.PASS.PL -1SG
     'It was spoken by us.' (*kwob* 'speak')

If A is Nominal, it is coded by an Oblique NP with the Preposition *yì* 'by' (Westermann 1912/1970: 78):

(73) byél a   châm   yì jál   éní
     dura ASP eat.PASS by this man
     'The dura was eaten by this man.'

The Shilluk Passive codes P like a preverbal A in the Active. But the A form has either a Preposition, not unlike the Acehnese Ergative, or a partially unique Pronominal inflection, not unlike the Karo Batak Passive. However, as in Karo Batak, the Shilluk Passive is in fact the preferred voice form (Westermann 1912/1970: 78).

The Indonesian Passive is similar to the Karo Batak Passive but with the presence of Oblique marking on some As (Myhill 1988b: 113–14). The Indonesian voice system originally has overt coding of all Voice forms, not unlike the Philippine voice systems (see §8.4.2), which dates at least as far back as Classical Malay. In the past three centuries, the Passive (more precisely, patient-oriented) form increasingly occurred with the prefix *di-* (Ariff 2002); this is the form illustrated in (74)–(75) (Myhill 1988b: 113–14):

(74) dalam rapat   itu   **di-**   majukan   pertanyaan **oleh**/*∅ orang-orang Nippon
     at   meeting that PASS-   put.forward   question   PREP   people   Japanese
     'At the meetings, questions would be asked by the Japanese.'
(75) dan letnan   Gedergeder **di-** bunuh Jepang
     and Lieutenant G.   PASS-   kill   Japanese
     'And Lieutenant Gedergeder was killed by the Japanese.'

In the Indonesian Passive, P is coded as Subject, and V is morphologically distinct, with the prefix *di-* (a relatively recent addition to the Passive Verb form). A is coded by the Oblique Preposition *oleh*, except when A immediately precedes V, in which case it is incorporated and not marked with *oleh*. *Oleh* is a recent innovation with the Passive (Myhill 1988b: 132).

The preceding examples demonstrate that the construction that corresponds more closely to the passive type in (3) than its active counterpart may be (or may become) the basic transitive construction in the language, while retaining some of its "passive" morphosyntactic properties. In particular the construction may retain A Oblique marking, which is then reanalyzed as ergative marking.

8.4.2. *Philippine voice systems*

Many Philippine Austronesian languages display a voice system that looks quite different from the familiar active–passive system represented by English. In the context of the sort of cross-linguistic variation that I have surveyed in this chapter, the Philippine voice system does not look quite as odd.

Philippine languages typically have Verb forms that vary depending on which participant of V is "in Focus". The A Focus form is traditionally called the Actor Focus (AF) and the P Focus form, Goal Focus (GF). Focus is a grammatical category whose function varies across the Philippine languages and within a particular language. In some cases, Focus appears to be associated with topicality, although in other contexts, Focus is sensitive to syntactic and semantic factors (see, e.g., T. Payne 1994: 320).

The first language we will examine is Cebuano (T. Payne 1994; Shibatani 1988). Examples of the Actor Focus and Goal Focus constructions are given in (76) and (77) respectively (Shibatani 1988: 88–9):

(76) ni- hatag si Juan sa libro sa bata
AF- give TOP Juan GEN book OBL child
'Juan gave the book to the child.'

(77) **gi-** hatag **ni** Juan ang libro sa bata
GF- give GEN Juan TOP book OBL child
'Juan gave the book to the child.'

In the Cebuano Goal Focus construction, A is coded with a Genitive particle (*ni* in (77)), like the P argument in the Actor Focus construction, and P is coded as Focus. V is morphologically distinct from the Actor Focus form; each uses its own affix. In this respect, the Actor Focus–Goal Focus contrast looks much like the Cree Direct–Inverse contrast: A and P reverse their coding, and both Vs are overtly and distinctly coded. The only difference is the absence of an SAP hierarchy effect.

T. Payne (1994) argues that in all constructions except the Perfective Main Clause construction, choice of AF or GF is determined by syntactic or semantic factors. However, these factors are indicative of the status of AF, GF, and Focus in general. In argument foregrounding constructions such as the Relative Clause and Cleft (see §4.3.4), the relativized or focused element must be the Focus element, as in other Philippine languages (T. Payne 1994: 328–30). In §4.3.4, I argued that this element is more topical. This observation fits with the hypothesis that the prominence associated with Focus is similar to the prominence associated with Subject, although it is grammaticalized differently in Philippine languages. In other Dependent Clauses, the GF form is higher in transitivity than the AF form, in terms of the semantic properties that cluster with transitive clause status according to Hopper and Thompson (1980). This fact suggests that the Karo Batak Passive (analogous to GF) is more like the basic transitive construction than the Active.

In the Perfective Main Clause construction, GF and AF forms are about equally common (Shibatani 1988: 96; T. Payne 1994: 336). The GF–AF distinction does not correspond to foregrounding–backgrounding, as one might expect if the distinction is pragmatic (T. Payne 1994: 337). However, the reason for this appears to be that the Goal Focus construction is in fact two distinct constructions: the Goal

Focus P(A) construction with P immediately following the verb and A optional, and its opposite, the Goal Focus A(P) construction. The Goal Focus P(A) construction has higher topicality P on average, while the Goal Focus A(P) construction has a higher topicality A (T. Payne 1994: 321). Hence the Goal Focus A(P) construction is functionally most like the other constructions discussed here. It is illustrated in (78), where it is translated with an English Passive (T. Payne 1994: 352):

(78) gi-   pilde   gayod   siya   ni   Iyo Baresto
     GF-   defeat   INTS   3SG:FOC   GEN   Iyo Baresto
     'He was really defeated by Iyo Baresto.'

Thus, there is evidence that Focus status is associated with topicality, albeit grammaticalized, and that the Goal Focus form is the basic Transitive construction. This state of affairs is complicated by the fact that the Goal Focus construction appears to be splitting into two constructions based on the relative order of A and P phrases. This latter fact is, however, further evidence that the GF form is the basic clausal form, spawning new constructions with distinct discourse functions.

Another Philippine language, Kapampangan, is structurally somewhat different from Cebuano in that there are Pronominal Agreement clitics which are triggered by A and/or P in different constructions. We may compare this to other Voice forms where A and/or P trigger Agreement. Examples (79) and (80) illustrate the Kapampangan Actor Focus and Goal Focus constructions respectively (Mirikitani 1972: 166–7; see also Shibatani 1988: 128)

(79) mi-   garal   ya   ng   Ingles   i   Nena
     AF-   studied   she$_i$.SBJ   NSBJ   English   SBJ   Nena$_i$
     'Nena studied English.'
(80) pi>garal<an   ne (= na + ya)   ng   Nena   ing   Ingles
     <GF>-studied   she$_i$.AGT.NSBJ + it$_j$.SBJ   NSBJ   Nena$_i$ SBJ   English$_j$
     'Nena studied English.'

If we take the Actor Focus construction as canonical, then the A is Subject, with the Subject particle and Agreement clitic. P is Object, or at least Nonsubject, with the Nonsubject particle. In the Goal Focus construction, P is coded as a Subject, triggering the same Agreement clitic as in the Actor Focus construction. A is coded as Nonsubject, but unlike Nonsubject P, it triggers a special non-Focus A Agreement clitic, not unlike Karo Batak. V is morphologically distinct. Again, there is similarity with the Cree Direct–Inverse pattern in that A and P reverse their "Case" marking; but there are differences, such as different behavior of the Agreement clitics and the absence of SAP hierarchy effects.[5]

---

[5] However, in Tagalog, if the P is definite then the Goal Focus form must be used (Schachter 1977b: 281). Since 1 and 2 are always definite, this constraint means that in Tagalog, the Goal Focus form is required for 1/2 Ps. Thus the definiteness constraint entails an SAP hierarchy constraint in those Philippine languages that have it.

8.4.3. Person-based split ergative systems

The last example that I will discuss are the person-based Split Ergative constructions of Dyirbal and similar languages. Person-based split ergativity is not considered an example of a voice system. However, person-based split ergativity is sensitive to the SAP hierarchy, and displays asymmetries of expression that can be explained by the same principles.

Person-based split ergativity was briefly discussed in §4.4.3. There, it was pointed out that the description as "split ergativity" depends only on the paradigmatic description of the forms of A and P. The paradigm for the Dyirbal Split Ergative Case forms is given in Table 8.3.

Table 8.3. Paradigm of Dyirbal Split Ergative forms

	A	S	P
1,2	-Ø	-Ø	-na
3	-ŋgu	-Ø	-Ø

The 1/2 forms display an accusative paradigm (A+S vs. P), while the 3 forms have an ergative paradigm (A vs. S+P). In fact, of course, it is only when both A and P are 1/2 person or both are 3rd person that the "split ergative" pattern is found in a clause, as in (81) and (82) (Dixon 1972: 60, 1980: 303):

(81) ŋinda   ŋayguna balgan
    2SG.NOM   1SG:ACC   hit
    'You're hitting me.'

(82) bala   yugu   baŋgul   yara   -ŋgu gunba -n   baŋgu   bari -ŋgu
    ART.ABS   tree(ABS) ART:ERG   man   -ERG   cut   -PRS ART.INST axe   -INST
    'The man is cutting the tree with an axe.'

In clauses where 1,2→3, A is Nominative, that is, zero coded (other than the pronoun stem alternant), and P is Absolutive, that is, also zero coded (Dixon 1972: 73):

(83) ŋada   bayi   yaṟa   balgan
    1SG.NOM ART.ABS   man(ABS)   hit
    'I hit the man.'

Conversely, in clauses where 3→1,2, A is Ergative, that is, overtly coded, and P is Accusative, that is, overtly coded (Dixon 1972: 60):

(84) ŋayguna   baŋgul   yara   -ŋgu balgan
    1SG:ACC   ART:ERG man   -ERG   hit
    '[The/a] man is hitting me.'

The case patterns of Dyirbal arguments can be mapped onto the conceptual space in Figure 8.1; this is done in Figure 8.12, with zero coding indicated by Ø and overt coding indicated with the Case label in the order A marking–P marking.

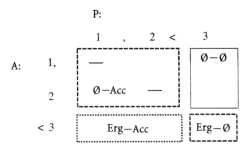

Figure 8.12. Semantic map of Dyirbal case constructions

The most "direct" construction has zero-coding of both A and P. The most "inverse" construction has overt coding of both A and P. The construction with overt coding of just one of A or P is intermediate. In the next section, I will show how the Dyirbal Split Ergative pattern is accounted for by the same principles that account for the other patterns discussed in this chapter.

8.5. A Typological-Universal Analysis of Voice Constructions

8.5.1. *Syntactic space and the nonuniversality of constructions*

The voice constructions illustrated in §§8.3–8.4, covering the conceptual space in Figure 8.1, are structurally extraordinarily diverse. Table 8.4 (p. 311) summarizes the structural properties of the voice constructions described in this chapter, with the models for "universal" active/direct, passive and inverse in boldface.

The structural diversity of voice constructions is not news to typologists. In her typological survey of passive type constructions, Siewierska concludes that 'The analysis of the various constructions referred to in the literature as PASSIVE leads to the conclusion that there is not even one single property which all these constructions have in common' (Siewierska 1985: 1). In a paper surveying inverse constructions, Thompson concludes, 'I know of no structural features which can define inverse constructions and distinguish them from passives' (Thompson 1994: 61). Shibatani argues that 'passives form a continuum with active sentences' (Shibatani 1985: 821).

If this is true, however, then typological universals cannot be formulated using only the "passive", "active", or "inverse" as cross-linguistic structural types of voice constructions. A proper typological explanation must respect the structural diversity of voice constructions in the world's languages, and yet find a cross-linguistically valid means to compare the structure of voice constructions and account for language universals, if there are any.

Table 8.4. Summary of structural properties of voice constructions

	A agr	A case	P agr	P case	V form
ACTIVE/DIRECT	**sbj**	**sbj**	**obj**	**obj**	**(ident)**
Karo Batak P	—	dir/inc	—	sbj	dist
Shilluk P	"spec"	obl	—	sbj	dist
Acehnese E	sbj	"obl"	—	"obj"	ident
Dyirbal SE	—	"obl"	—	"sbj"	ident
Seko Padang "I"	spec	—	(spec)	—	ident
Cebuano GF	—	dir	—	"sbj"	dist
Kapampangan GF	spec	dir	"sbj"	"sbj"	dist
Tangut I	no	sbj/obl	"sbj"	obj (?)	ident
Indonesian *di*-P	—	obl/inc	—	sbj	dist
Arizona Tewa P/I	spec*	obl	spec*	sbj	ident
Chukchi "I"	no	sbj/obl	sbj/no	obj	dist
Yurok "I"	no	dir	sbj	obj	dist
Guaraní "I"	no	dir	spec	dir	ident
Maasai "I"	no	sbj	spec	obj	ident
Menomini P	proh	proh	obj	dir	id (3), dist (1/2)
Cree I pronominal	**obj**	—	**sbj**	—	**dist**
Cree I obviative	obj	obv	sbj	prox	dist
U. Halkomelem P	no	"obj"	spec	"sbj"	ident
Bella Coola P	no	obl	spec	sbj	ident
Maasai P	proh	proh	obj	obj	dist
Spanish RP	no	obl	refl	sbj	ident
Russian IP	no	obl	—	obj	ident
Welsh IP	no	obl	—	obj	dist
Finnish ID	proh	proh	no	obj	dist
Bambara "P"	—	obl	—	sbj	ident
Pukapukan E	—	"obl"	—	sbj	ident
Pukapukan P	—	obl	—	sbj	dist
English P	no	obl	sbj	sbj	dist
Lithuanian P	**proh**	**proh**	**sbj**	**sbj**	**dist**

P = Passive
IP = Impersonal Passive
RP = Reflexive Passive
I = Inverse
E = Ergative
SE = Split Ergative
GF = Philippine Goal Focus
ID = Finnish Indefinite
* = fused forms

sbj = subjectlike
obj = objectlike
obl = obliquelike
dir = direct (non-oblique) argument
inc = "incorporated"
spec = special agreement
no = does not trigger agreement
proh = prohibited
— = case/agr does not exist in language for this category

ident = same as Active form
dist = distinct from Active form

Radical Construction Grammar accepts the structural diversity of constructions. All grammatical constructions are language-specific; the names used for constructions in particular languages are arbitrary from a theoretical point of view (§1.6.3). The generalizations of typological theory presented in Chapters 2, 4, and 5, in combination with the conceptual space model, allow us to compare constructions across languages and formulate language universals.

The syntactic properties in Table 8.4 are grounded in functional categories. Agreement and case marking are indexical and relational coded dependencies respectively (§5.4.1). Coding of A and P can be defined as Subject-like, Object-like, and Oblique-like in comparison with the basic voice construction (§8.1.2). Morphological marking of V relative to the basic voice construction can be categorized as overt or zero across languages. That is, these structural properties of voice constructions can be compared across languages. The properties define a multidimensional SYNTACTIC SPACE. Constructions in a particular language can be plotted on the syntactic space according to the structural properties they possess.

Figure 8.13 (p. 313) gives a simplified representation of the syntactic space for voice constructions, reduced by necessity to two dimensions.

The upper right corner of the syntactic space in Figure 8.13 is the reference point for comparing voice constructions across languages, namely the basic (transitive) voice type of a language. The two major dimensions merge case marking and agreement patterns together to describe the coding of A and P respectively. The two major dimensions are scaled with respect to the similarity of the coding of A and P in the voice construction compared to the canonical Subject (A) and Object (P) coding in the Active/Direct construction. Typefaces are used in the figure to offer some information on the structural properties of V in the voice constructions.

A syntactic space, defined on structural properties of constructions that are cross-linguistically valid, allows one to develop a proper typological classification of languages that respects the continuum of constructions found in the world's languages for any given region of conceptual space. We now turn to universals underlying the syntactic space for voice.

In §8.1.1, I presented the third and final major thesis of Radical Construction Grammar: constructions are language-specific. This chapter has presented evidence for this thesis in one grammatical domain, a subset of voice constructions. Of course, this thesis must be confirmed in all grammatical domains, which is a task far beyond the scope of this book. However, there are two good reasons to believe that this thesis is valid.

First, language change is gradual. There is overwhelming evidence in support of this hypothesis (see, e.g., the references in Croft 2000a, §3.2). The consequence of this for syntactic theory is that syntactic change in constructions will also be gradual. Each intermediate step in the process represents an intermediate con-

The Voice Continuum 313

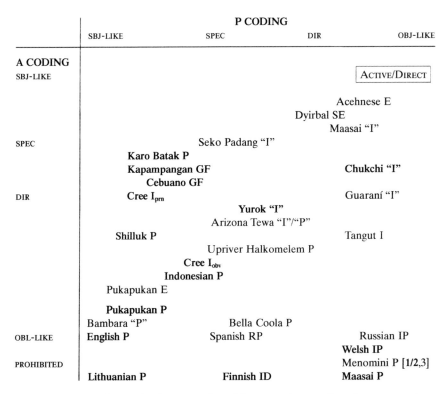

Figure 8.13. Approximate visual presentation of the syntactic space for voice constructions

A = Active
P = Passive
IP = Impersonal Passive
RP = Reflexive Passive
ID = Indefinite
I = Inverse
E = Ergative
SE = Split Ergative
GF = Philippine Goal Focus

boldface: verb form distinct from Active/Direct verb form

Scaling (A top to bottom, P left to right):
A case: sbj < erg < dir < obl < prohibited
A agr: sbj < nonsbj < special < none < prohibited
P case: sbj < dir < obj
P agr: sbj < special < obj/none

struction type in structural terms. Hence a cross-linguistic survey that uncovers the intermediate construction types will yield a synchronic continuum of construction types in structural terms.

Second, there are usually multiple paths of grammatical change. For example, it is known that there are different paths by which passives arise (e.g. Haspelmath 1990). There are also different paths by which ergatives arise, and presumably also inverse systems. Known or hypothesized paths of grammatical change exemplified by the languages discussed in this chapter are given in (85a–j):

(85) a. indefinite subject transitive active > passive: Maasai, Turkana, Finnish (?)
   b. active reflexive > middle voice > passive: Spanish, Upriver Halkomelem
   c. goal focus > passive: Indonesian (?)
   d. passive > ergative (active): Pukapukan, Dyirbal (?)
   e. goal focus/passive > active: Shilluk, Karo Batak (?)
   f. goal focus > ergative (active): Acehnese (?), Kapampangan (?)
   g. passive > inverse: Bella Coola, Lummi, Arizona Tewa
   h. passive > inverse > transitive: Yurok
   i. inverse > transitive: Wardaman, Chinook, Ngandi, Nunggubuyu
   j. third person agent > inverse > transitive: Seko Padang, Chukchi (?), Guaraní (?)

The uncovering of the multiple paths of grammatical change and their intermediate stages further fills out the syntactic space of structural possibilities for a given construction type.

The gradualness of language change and the multiple paths of grammatical change ensure that the careful and systematic cross-linguistic examination of any grammatical phenomenon will reveal a near-continuous multidimensional syntactic space of attested construction types in structural terms. For this reason, we may accept the final thesis of Radical Construction Grammar with reasonable confidence, although of course more cross-linguistic studies will improve our understanding of the structure of syntactic space.

As in earlier chapters, however, we can go beyond the critique of universalist theories of syntactic structures, and seek to uncover the genuine language universals that underlie the diversity of syntactic constructions in a particular grammatical domain such as voice.

8.5.2. Universals of syntactic space

The grammatical changes proposed in (85a–j) are unidirectional. We may then trace out the paths of grammatical change in (85) on the syntactic space in Figure 8.13. The paths of change are illustrated in Figure 8.14 (the letters correspond to the processes in (85a–j)).

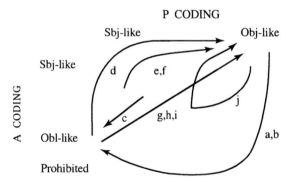

Figure 8.14. Paths of grammatical change in voice in syntactic space

Broadly speaking, there appears to be a cycle of voice changes that proceeds approximately clockwise around the conceptual space (Indonesian is an exception to the general pattern, being a goal focus form acquiring passive-like grammatical properties). A basic voice construction of a particular subtype (indefinite A, reflexive A/P, 3rd person A) becomes a non-basic construction (paths a, b, and the first half of j). Nonbasic voice constructions, whether they originate as a special subtype of basic voice or from another course, may increase in use until they become the new basic voice type (paths d–i and the second half of j).

The most important step in the analysis is to compare the syntactic space in Figure 8.13 to the conceptual space in Figure 8.1. As the figures in the chapter have demonstrated, the syntactic space maps fairly directly onto the conceptual space. The maps conform to the following language universal:

(86) If there is a contrast between a basic and non-basic voice (as defined in §8.1.2), then the semantic map of the basic voice will include the upper right corner of the conceptual space in Figure 8.1, and the semantic map of the nonbasic voice will include the lower left corner of the conceptual space in Figure 8.1.

The uniformity of this mapping of form and function allows us to make the following generalizations. If there are two or more voice constructions for two-participant Vs in a language, then the construction in which A most clearly outranks P in the SAP hierarchy—i.e. 1,2→3—is the basic voice construction. If there is an alternation between two constructions which satisfy the first condition, then the most frequent construction will be—or become—the basic voice construction (see also Dryer's (1995) Frequency Hypothesis).

The universal in (86) has been formulated in terms of the SAP hierarchy. Not all the voice constructions in this chapter are sensitive to the SAP hierarchy. Instead, topicality is another, or the sole, property that appears to correlate with choice of voice form. It is widely accepted, however, that the SAP hierarchy is a conventionalized stand-in for topicality. Speaker and addressee are by definition more topical or salient to the interlocutors, since they *are* the interlocutors. Thus, we may generalize the conceptual space in Figure 8.1 to the one in which the degree of topicality or SALIENCE of the participants define the A and P dimensions (see Figure 8.16 below).

Again, the relationship between voice and topicality is familiar to typological researchers. Two analyses of the relationship between topicality and voice constructions, Thompson (1994) and Cooreman (1987), are summarized in Figure 8.15 (p. 316).

Thompson's and Cooreman's analyses must be modified to allow for the voice continuum. The vertical dimension in Figure 8.15 roughly corresponds to the diagonal from upper right to lower left in Figure 8.13. Of the two models, Thompson's model does not help us determine the "normal" topicality of A and P without already knowing which is the Active/Direct construction. Cooreman's formula-

Thompson (1994: 48):			Cooreman (1987: 76):
A	P	Active/Direct	AGT > PAT
A↑	P↑		
A	P↑	Inverse	AGT < PAT
A↓	P↑		
A↓	P	Passive	AGT << PAT
A↓	P↓		
A	P↓	Antipassive	AGT >> PAT
A↑	P↓		
A↑	P		

Figure 8.15. Two analyses of topicality and voice constructions

tion does not have this problem, since it is based on the relative topicality of A and P.

Thompson and Cooreman also include antipassive voice constructions, which we have not discussed here. The antipassive voice is found in the region beyond the upper right corner of the conceptual space in Figure 8.13. The antipassive represents a transition from two-participant events, where P is rendered nonsalient (see §7.7.3), to one-participant events of the so-called "unergative" type and only "A" remains, as the sole Sa participant role (see §4.4.1 and Figure 4.7). A further extension from the antipassive, where the P argument may still be salient enough to be overtly expressed as an oblique, is noun incorporation, which also comes in degrees (Mithun 1984).

Passives give way to one-participant events in the opposite direction in the conceptual space, the "passive" direction, as well. Shibatani demonstrates the structural and functional resemblances of passives to spontaneous and potential constructions. In Japanese, the Spontaneous (87) and Potential (88) constructions both use the Passive suffix *(r)are* in Japanese (Shibatani 1985: 823):

(87) mukasi   ga   sinob   -**are**   ru
     old.time NOM   think.about   -PASS   -PRS
     'An old time comes to mind.'

(88) boku   wa   nemur   -**are**   -nakat   -ta
     I   TOP   sleep   -PASS   -NEG   -PST
     'I could not sleep.'

Spontaneous constructions are also known as anticausatives (Haspelmath 1993; see also Croft 1990c, Levin and Rappaport Hovav 1994), such as English *break* (tr.)/*break* (intr.), in which A is rendered nonsalient or nonexistent, and only P remains as the sole participant in the event. These are the so-called "unaccusative" type of one-participant situations, where "P" is the lone Su participant role (§4.4.1). Potential constructions also focus on P at the expense of A; compare the English potential Deverbal Adjective in *-able*, such as *unbreakable*, also intransitive in form.[6]

We may now include the transitive and intransitive situation types in a single conceptual space, given in Figure 8.16 (see also Figure 4.7 in §4.4.1).

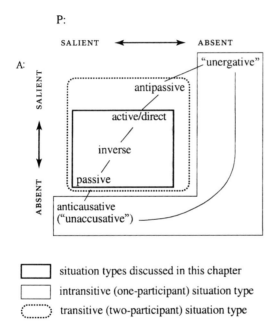

Figure 8.16. The conceptual space for voice and transitivity

The dashed and dotted boxes indicate the regions that represent intransitive and transitive situation types respectively. The boundary between transitive and intransitive situation types is not sharp. For example, the situation denoted by

---

[6] Shibatani argues that there is also a passive prototype (Shibatani 1985). However, he treats non-subject-like A marking as an essential ('primary', 'fundamental', 'basic'; ibid.: 830, 831, 834) property of the passive prototype. His identification of this property as essential is due to his attention to the part of the voice continuum extending into the region of one-participant events. I argue below that the only typologically unmarked voice for two-participant events is the active/direct voice.

a detransitivized verb form such as *drink*, or its antipassivized counterpart in other languages, can be analyzed as either a two-participant situation type with an obligatorily nonsalient second participant, or as a construal as a one participant situation type (see §7.7.3 for discussion of this example).

We have seen that the syntactic space of Figure 8.13 can be mapped onto the conceptual space, such that a topicality/salience dimension is overlaid on the A→P causal structure of 2-participant events; and the salience dimension can be extended to include intransitives in a transitivity continuum, as in Figure 8.16. We may now turn to the question of whether any structural properties of different voice constructions correlate with points or regions of the conceptual space.

In Chapters 2 and 4, I argued that the principles of typological markedness impose constraints on the structural type of constructions coding particular regions of conceptual space for parts of speech and syntactic roles ("grammatical relations"). Voice is closely related to the expression of syntactic roles; in fact, we have focused on case marking and agreement for A and P in describing the structural variety of voice constructions. The principles of typological markedness also constrain the distribution of structural voice types over conceptual space. The upper right corner of the conceptual space is generally occupied by the typologically least marked voice construction. We have already used the text frequency criterion of typological markedness to define the basic voice construction of a language, and that construction generally occupies the upper right corner.

Turning to structural coding, the non-Active/Direct V form is coded by at least as many morphemes as the Active/Direct V form. Where the two V forms are different, the non-Active/Direct V form is overtly coded while the Active/Direct is zero coded, as in English. Exceptions to this generalization are the high frequency overtly coded "Passives" (§8.4.1). However, in one of them, Pukapukan, it appears that the Passive construction loses its overt coding (yielding the Ergative construction) as it becomes the basic construction of the language. Most striking, the overt coding of A and P in Dyirbal increase from the upper right (zero coded A and P) to the lower left (overtly coded A and P) in the conceptual space (see Figure 8.12).

In §4.2.2, I argued that the ability to trigger agreement is part of the behavioral potential of an argument, and thus an indicator of typological unmarkedness. In the Yurok and Chukchi transitive paradigms, agreement with both A and P are associated with the upper right corner of the conceptual space in Figure 8.1, and as one moves to the lower left, agreement is limited to one of A or P (see Figures 8.8 and 8.9; an exception to this generalization is the Yimas 1→2NSG form in (62), which is unipersonal, while the inverse-like [A–P–VERB] construction is bipersonal).

In sum, the typologically least marked SAP alignment is 1/2→3, and hence is the typological prototype for the transitive (active/direct) construction. The typologically most marked SAP alignment is 3→1/2. The intermediate alignments are 1/2→1/2 and 3→3. One frequently finds special forms used for 1/2→1/2, as in Guaraní and Yimas (see Table 8.2 and Figure 8.10). One also finds intermediate forms for 3→3 (as in Yurok and Chukchi), and also overlap in voice forms, such that some pragmatic or conventionalized topicality property determines the choice of voice construction, as in Cree.

It should be noted that the typologically unmarked transitive voice type is *not* the farthest point in the transitive region of the broader conceptual space in Figure 8.16; the antipassive lies "beyond" it. The typologically unmarked transitive voice type must have a sufficiently salient P argument as well as a salient A argument, and hence the antipassive is typologically marked (often expressed with an overt verbal affix or an overt P case marking).

Finally, one can seek an explanation for the interactions between the dimensions of causal A→P relations and SAP/topicality. DeLancey argues that the interactions are motivated by a localist metaphor, given in Table 8.5 (adapted from DeLancey 1982: 172; see also DeLancey 1981 and §4.4.3, Table 4.11).

Table 8.5. Localist metaphor linking event structure, participant animacy, and aspect

participant deixis	1st/2nd person	→	3rd person
causal structure	agent (initiator)	→	patient (endpoint)
temporal aspect	onset (imperfective)	→	termination (perfective)

In the localist metaphor, one mentally starts from the speech participants, the initiator of the event, and the temporal beginning of the event, and moves away from the speech participants, towards the causal endpoint and temporal end of the event. The typologically unmarked alignment is that given in Table 8.5. Any other alignment of participant deixis, causal structure, and temporal aspect may exhibit symptoms of typological markedness.

All of the universals in this section—the universal in (86) and the universals implicit in Figures 8.14 and 8.16—are formulated without reference to any universal structural definition of any voice type. Instead, the concept of a syntactic space was introduced to represent the full cross-linguistic syntactic diversity of voice constructions (in fact, only a subset of that diversity). Using the conceptual space model and the universals of the coding of function into form introduced in §2.4, we are able to discern universals of grammatical voice while at the same time accommodating the full range of syntactic diversity of the world's languages.

9

The Coordination–Subordination Continuum

9.1. Introduction

In Chapter 8, I demonstrated that voice constructions in the world's languages are much more diverse in structure than most syntactic theories would lead one to believe. However, the structural diversity of voice constructions can be represented as relatively continuous dimensions in syntactic space. Moreover, the structure of the syntactic space can be mapped isomorphically onto the structure of the conceptual space coded by voice constructions. The isomorphism represents the universals of the form–function mapping manifested by voice constructions.

Of course, this requires identifying the right dimensions of the syntactic space to map onto the right dimensions of the conceptual space. In the case of voice constructions, this was not difficult, especially as most of the generalizations described in Chapter 8 are already well-known among typologists. The conceptual space is structured by the salience and/or SAP hierarchy for A and P, and the syntactic space by the coding of A and P and patterns of typological markedness.

In this chapter, we will approach the problem of complex sentences from the same perspective. The form and function of complex sentences is much more complicated than that of grammatical voice, and I will be able only to sketch an outline of an analysis here. As with voice, the standard analysis is inadequate for the analysis of both the form and the function of complex sentences across languages.

9.1.1. *The traditional classification of complex sentences*

The traditional analysis of complex sentences makes a primary distinction between COORDINATION, illustrated in (1), and SUBORDINATION, illustrated in (2):

(1) a. [He gave her the book] and [she thanked him].
    b. [She locked the door] and [left].
(2) a. [He read the newspaper] after [he mowed the lawn].
    b. [He read the newspaper] after [mowing the lawn].

In coordination, the two clauses are syntactically equal: in particular, both clauses are FINITE, that is, of the form that can function as a simple main clause. A simple main clause is taken as the basic clause type (see §8.1.2): among other things, it is the most frequent clause type, since it is found in simple sentences as well as complex sentences.

In subordination, the two clauses are not syntactically equal. In (2a–b), the clause following *after* is the SUBORDINATE clause, and the unit consisting of *after* plus the subordinate clause is analyzed as a dependent of the Main Clause. Also, the subordinate clause may be in a form that differs from the form that normally occurs in a main clause (see (2b)), either lacking typical main clause inflections, traditionally called NONFINITE, or with a special set of inflections, often called SUBJUNCTIVE.

One must have a cross-liguistically valid characterization of the syntactic properties of main clause and subordinate clause verb forms. The definition of verb forms found in complex sentences is a derived structural definition, like the definition of non-active voice forms used in §8.1.2. Verb forms found in complex sentences are classified in terms of their relation to verb forms found in simple main clauses (Givón 1980b: 337–8; Stassen 1985: 77; Croft 1991: 83; see §9.6.1). Verb forms in complex sentences are found to differ from those in main clauses in a limited number of ways, listed in (3):

(3) a. Elimination of tense, mood, and aspect markings, or use of special forms distinct from those used on simple main clause verbs
   b. Elimination of agreement markings used on simple main clause verbs, or use of special forms distinct from those used on simple main clause verbs
   c. Overt morpheme attached to verb form

The phenomena in (3a–c) define what has been called DERANKING (Stassen 1985: 77; Koptjevskaja-Tamm 1993; Cristofaro 1998), desententialization (Lehmann 1988: 193–200), and deverbalization (Croft 1991: 83); I will use the term 'deranking' here. Clauses containing verb forms that possess one or more of the properties in (3) are called DERANKED. Clauses containing verb forms that are identical to main clause verb forms, that is, that lack all of the properties in 82, are called BALANCED (Stassen 1985; see §9.4).

The traditional analysis of complex sentences also divides up subordinate clauses into three types, according to their propositional act function (see §2.4.2). The examples in (2a–b) are ADVERBIAL CLAUSES, that is, clauses that function as adverbials in the main clause (i.e. modifiers of the verb in the main clause). Examples (4a–c) are instances of COMPLEMENT CLAUSES, that is, clauses that function as arguments of the verb in the main clause:

(4) a. [She told him that [she had found a job]].
   b. [She wanted [to cook dinner]].
   c. [She said, ["Will you cook dinner tonight?"]]

Complements, like adverbial clauses, may be balanced (as in (4a)) or deranked (4b). In addition, there exist complements which directly express another utterance without alteration, as in (4c); these are called DIRECT SPEECH complements.

The third and last type of subordinate clause are RELATIVE CLAUSES, that is, clauses that function as a modifier of a noun in the main clause:

(5) a. [I found the book [that you lent me]].
    b. [Forms [filled out improperly] will be returned].

Relative clauses, like other subordinate clauses, can be balanced or deranked; traditional analysis describes the verbs of deranked relative clauses as PARTICIPLES.

9.1.2. *The continuum of complex sentence types*

In this section, I will demonstrate that there are syntactic constructions in languages that encode any pair of the four traditional types of complex sentence constructions, as indicated in Figure 9.1.

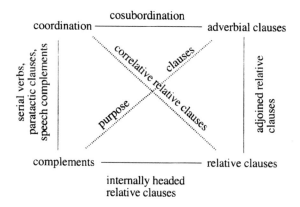

Figure 9.1. The continuum of complex sentence types

This continuum is ultimately a conceptual space, since (as will be argued in the following sections) the traditional classification is best captured by conceptual distinctions. Although Figure 9.1 links all pairs of the four traditional types, two links (indicated by gray lines) are definitely "weaker" than the others. Those two links will be discussed last in this section.

The so-called COSUBORDINATION constructions (Foley and Van Valin 1984) span the region between coordination and adverbial subordination. In cosubordination, one of the clauses is deranked while the other remains balanced. Thus, cosubordination constructions appear to have the syntactic structure of adverbial subordination in European languages, but are translated with coordinate structures, as in the examples from Tamil in (6)–(7) (Annamalai 1970: 137; see Stassen 1985: 77):

(6) [avaru   kavide   eṭudiiṭṭu]   [naaval   moṛipeyarttaaru]
    he.NOM   poetry.ACC write.PRF.GER   novel.ACC translate.PST.IND.3SG
    'He wrote poetry and then translated a novel.'

(7) [naan   paṇam   kuḍuttu]   [avan   sinimaa   -vukku   poonaan]
    I.NOM   money.ACC   give.PRF.GER he.NOM   movie   -to   go.PST.IND.3SG
    'I gave (him) money and he went to the movie.'

These constructions have been called Conjunctive Participles, Gerunds, Absolutives, Converbs, Medial Verb forms, and Deranked Chaining constructions. In some languages, these structures are translated into English as either Coordination or Adverbial Subordination, as in the Burushaski examples below (Tikkanen 1995: 509, from Lorimer 1935, v. 2: 112, l. 18–19):

(8) [má   -a   gúṭaš   -o   d-   ú-   ću   -n]   já   -a   díš   -ulo   bése
    you   -ERG   corpse -PL D-   3HPL.OBJ- bring -CP   I   -GEN place -INESS why
    yáar   -e   ó-   č-   -á   -an
    down -LOC 3HPL.OBJ-   do(DUR) -AUX -HPL.SBJ
    a. 'Why do you bring your corpses and bury them on my land?'
    b. 'Why do your bury your corpses on my land, after bringing them?'

The ambiguity between a coordination and subordination interpretation is found in the difference in what is questioned in (8a–b). Interpretation (8a) questions the combination of the two clauses, indicating that both clauses are ASSERTED (Cristofaro 1998: 38–45), and is thus appropriately translated with a coordinate construction. Interpretation (8b) questions only the main clause state of affairs, indicates that the deranked clause is NONASSERTIVE and thus is appropriately translated into English with an Adverbial Clause construction. In those languages in which there is such an ambiguity, the cosubordinate form spans both coordination and adverbial subordination.

SERIAL VERB constructions and PARATACTIC constructions span the region between coordination and complementation. A serial verb construction is a construction containing two or more verbs which appear to be integrated into a single clause to some degree. Nevertheless, serial verb constructions in many languages, including the Barai examples in (9)–(10), can be translated into English by either coordinate or complement constructions in the appropriate context (Foley and Olson 1985: 43, 44; compare Li and Thompson 1981: 595–8 on Mandarin Chinese):

(9) a   na   ine   tua   kore   -j   -ie
     you   I   stick break.off throw   -TR   -2SG
     'You broke off and threw a stick at me.'

(10) fu   na   ire   ifej   -ie   i
     he   I   food   help   -1SG eat
     'He helped me eat food.'

In (9)–(10), the NPs expressing participants of both events precede both Verbs, as if they were part of a single Clause (Barai is a Verb-final language).

The Lango Paratactic construction has two Verbs both of which are inflected as in Main Clauses. In some instances, such as (11), the Paratactic construction may be translated into English as either a Coordinate sentence or as a Complement (with the implication that I actually closed the door; Noonan 1985: 78):

(11) [án àpóyò   ] [àcégò   dɔ́gólá]
     I   **remembered**.1SG   **closed**.1SG   door
   a. 'I remembered to close the door.'
   b. 'I remembered; I closed the door.'

Noonan also suggests that cross-linguistically, paratactic and serial constructions may be diachronically related (1985: 140).

ADJOINED RELATIVE CLAUSES span the region between adverbial subordination and relative clauses. Adjoined relative clauses in many Australian languages can be translated into English as either Adverbial Clauses or as Relative Clauses to a Head Noun, as in the Warlpiri example in (12) (Hale 1976: 78):

(12) [ŋatjulu -ḷu   na   **yankiri** pantu -ṇu] [kutja- lpa   ŋapa   ŋa   -ṇu]
     I   -ERG AUX **emu**   spear -PST   COMP- AUX   water drink -PST
   a. 'I speared the emu while it was drinking water.'
   b. 'I speared the emu which was was drinking water.'

Similar examples can be found in other languages, including Papuan languages, Old English and Japanese. Foley (1986: 201–2) notes that adverbial clauses and relative clauses are similar or identical in many Papuan languages. For example, adverbial clauses and relative clauses are both indicated by the subordinating suffix -*a* in Iatmul and Alamblak and -*ma* in Hua (ibid.). Wiegand (1987) observes that a class of Old English constructions using the Complementizer *þe* resembles the Australian adjoined relative clauses (see §9.3.2). In Japanese, a construction with the Nominalizer *tokoro* can be translated as an adverbial clause or as a relative clause (Ohori 2001: 280):

(13) [Yoogisya -ga   heya -kara dete.kita] **tokoro** -o   tukamae -ta
     suspect -NOM   room -from came.out   NR   -ACC catch   -PST
   a. 'As the suspect came out of the room, (X) caught (him/her).'
   b. '(X) caught the suspect who came out of the room.'

Morever, there is evidence from a range of languages that the complement of 'say', especially if the complement is a direct speech complement, is not integrated into the clause with the 'say' verb. Hence the speech complement is not subordinate; instead it resembles "coordinate" or at least paratactic structures (Munro 1982). For example, Direct Speech Complements prohibit the Complementizer *that* in English (example (14)), the Object Case marker in Chickasaw (15), and the Object Agreement prefix in Cahuilla ((16); Munro 1982: 302, 303, 306):

(14) He said (***that**) "I'm going."
(15) "Hilha"   (*-**a**)   aachi
     dance   (-OBJ)   say
     'He says, "She's dancing."'
(16) (***pe**-)   ni-   ya   -qa   "Hen-   hichi   -ka"
     (3SG.OBJ-) 1SG-   say   -PRS   1SG-   go   -IMPF
     'I say, "I'm going."'

In Pima, the Auxiliary always occurs in second position. However, if a Direct Speech Complement is initial, then it is not counted as the first constituent. In (17), the particle *b* 'here', cliticized to the auxiliary, is the first constituent preceding the Auxiliary (Munro 1982: 310):

(17) ["S-   heepit   'añ"   ]   [b=   **añ**   kaij]
     STAT-   cold   1SG.AUX   here=   1SG.AUX   say
     '"I'm cold," I said.'

These facts indicate that in these languages, the direct speech complement is a separate clause very much like an independent main clause.

INTERNALLY-HEADED RELATIVE CLAUSES span the region between relative clauses and complements. In an internally headed relative clause, the phrase denoting the participant in the main clause event remains inside the relative clause. The subordinate clause as a whole is found in the syntactic role normally occupied by the participant phrase. Example (18) illustrates an Internally-Headed Relative Clause in Imbabura Quechua (Cole 1982: 55):

(18) [ñuka   chay   **punlla**   -pi   chaya   -shka]   -ka   sumaj   -mi   ka   -rka
     I   that   **day**   -in   arrive   -NR   -TOP   beautiful -VAL   be   -PST(3)
     'The day that I arrived (on) was beautiful.'

In (18), the whole Relative Clause occupies the position of the Topic role, and the Topic clitic -*ka* is suffixed to the Clause as a whole. Moreover, in Imbabura Quechua, the structure of Internally-Headed Relative Clauses is identical to that of Complements, including the Nominalizing suffixes used in both (Cole 1982: 47; example from ibid.: 46):

(19) Juan   -man   ni   -rka   -ni   [Juzi   shamu   -shka]   -ta
     Juan   -to   say   -PST   -1   José   come   -NR   -ACC
     'I told Juan that José had come.'

Although finding a genuinely ambiguous example would not be easy, it is clear that the same construction is used for both relative clause and complement functions in Imbabura Quechua.

Even in languages with externally headed relative clauses, the morphosyntax of complement clauses and relative clauses is often quite similar. For example, English uses *that* plus a balanced clause for both complement and relative clause functions, and the deranked -*ing* Verb form for both Nominals and Participles performing the same two functions respectively:

(20) a. *Complement*: I told her **that** [I was writing a letter].
　　 b. *Relative Clause*: the letter **that** [I was writing]
(21) a. *Nominalization*: I like [play**ing** the piano].
　　 b. *Participle*: the boy [play**ing** the piano]

The above examples indicate the continua in the coding of the four traditional complex sentence types that are marked with solid lines in Figure 9.1. The last two possibilities are not as clearcut, and their peculiar status is implicitly indicated by the arrangement of the four complex sentence types in the figure.

CORRELATIVE clauses may be instances of a coordinate-like structure used for the relative clause function. Examples of Bambara and Hindi Correlative Clauses are given in (22) (Lehmann 1986: 665, from Bird 1968: 43) and (23) (Comrie 1989: 146) respectively:

(22) [n　ye　tyɛ̀　**mì**　ye]　[ò　　　　be　finì　　　fère]
　　 I　CMPL　man　REL　saw　DIST.DEM　IMPF　cloth:DEF　sell
　　 'The man I saw sells the cloth.' [lit. 'I saw which man, he sells the cloth']
(23) [ādmī　ne　**jis**　cākū　se　murgī　ko　mārāthā]
　　 man　ERG　which　knife　with　chicken　ACC　killed
　　 [us　cākū　ko　rām　ne　dekhā]
　　 that　knife　ACC　Ram　ERG　saw
　　 'Ram saw the knife with which the man killed the chicken.'
　　 [lit. 'The man killed the chicken with which knife, that knife Ram saw']

In (22) and (23), both clauses are balanced, and the relative clause is not embedded. However, in both cases, there is a special relative morpheme in the relative clause itself. Comrie argues that 'it is preferable to treat [correlative relative clauses] . . . as instances of adjoined relative clauses' (Comrie 1989: 146).

PURPOSE clauses are often used for infinitival complements, as in English (see Haspelmath 1989 and §9.4.2):

(24) We all lined up [**to** watch the whales].
(25) We want [**to** watch the whales].

This relationship between complementation and adverbial subordination is restricted to purpose clauses, however. Also, purpose clauses are found in the border region (so to speak) between adverbial subordination and coordination (see §9.3.3). For example, Serial Verb constructions in Mandarin may be translated as English Coordination, Purpose, or Adverbial constructions in certain contexts (Li and Thompson 1981: 596; their names for the interpretations are given in square brackets):

(26) [hē　　diǎn　　　jiǔ]　[zhuàng-　　-zhuang　　dǎnzi]
　　 drink　a.little　wine　strengthen-　-strengthen　gall.bladder
　　 a. 'Drink a little wine, and it will give you courage.' [Consecutive]
　　 b. 'Drink a little wine to give yourself courage.' [Purpose]
　　 c. 'Get some courage by drinking a little wine.' [Circumstance]

Confronted with this sort of cross-linguistic variation in the form and meaning of complex sentence constructions, some linguists (e.g. Haiman and Thompson 1984; Lehmann 1988; Foley and Van Valin 1984; Van Valin 1993) have essentially abandoned the coordination–subordination distinction. In its place, these linguists have put a continuum between "more independent" and "more subordinate" structures.

Foley and Van Valin argue for a single continuum, the Interclausal Relations Hierarchy (Foley and Van Valin 1984: 270; Van Valin 1990: 79), while Haiman and Thompson and Lehmann present several more or less independent syntactic parameters for determining complex sentence types. Each parameter, for example degree of reduction of one of the clauses, is treated as a continuum (or at least as not being binary), with one end being more coordinate-like (or main-clause-like) and the opposite end being more subordinate-like (to the point of clause fusion, as Lehmann notes).

However, the semantic map approach used by some typologists and in Radical Construction Grammar allows us to find some pattern to the range of constructions used in various functions. In particular, we may define a conceptual space underlying the traditional analysis as in Figure 9.2.

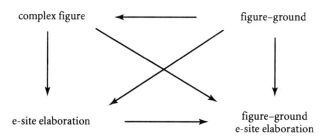

Figure 9.2. The conceptual space of complex sentence types

In §9.2, I argue that the basic conceptual distinction between the traditional categories of coordination and adverbial subordination is a Gestalt distinction, between what I call COMPLEX FIGURE sentences and FIGURE–GROUND sentences. Nevertheless, these two constructions paths appear to spread and converge, leading to ambiguous cosubordination constructions of the type illustrated above. In §9.3, I argue that complements and relative clauses (and also nominalizations, as indicated in Figure 9.2) share the property of e-site elaboration (§7.7.2), which leads to the spread and convergence of those two constructions, apparently in either direction diachronically. The process of adverbial clauses evolving into relative clauses is also a case of the development of e-site elaboration functions of figure–ground adverbial constructions. In §9.4, I address the formal structural properties of complex sentences and, argue that the syntactic variation is structured according to a Deranking Hierarchy, which can be mapped onto the conceptual space in Figure 9.2.

9.2. A Gestalt Analysis of Coordination and Adverbial Subordination

9.2.1. *The semantic parallelism of "coordination" and "adverbial subordination"*

A cross-linguistically valid approach to the coordination–adverbial subordination distinction is to examine the function of these two complex sentence types. One of the most fundamental semantic dimensions would appear to be the semantic relation that holds between the two events: cause, temporal sequence, comparison, etc. However, both "coordinate" and "adverbial" constructions can encode approximately the same range of semantic relations. Examples (27)–(30) illustrate this fact in English for temporal sequence, temporal simultaneity, causal relation, and conditional relation (Haiman 1983a; Culicover and Jackendoff 1997) respectively:

(27) a. Fred ate his lunch and went to the hardware store.
 b. After Fred ate his lunch, he went to the hardware store.
(28) a. I held down the boards and Janet nailed them in.
 b. I held down the boards while Janet nailed them in.
(29) a. He didn't turn in his final paper and he failed the course.
 b. He failed the course because he didn't turn in his final paper.
(30) a. He does that and I'll fire him.
 b. If he does that, I'll fire him.

There is one cross-linguistically valid syntactic property that distinguishes the Coordinate and Adverbial Subordinate constructions in (27)–(30). Where temporal or causal sequence are involved, the clauses in Coordinate constructions must be TENSE-ICONIC (Haiman 1983b: 120). That is, the temporal order of Clauses must match the temporal order of the events denoted by the clauses:

(31) a. Cindy left and Jim was promoted.
 b. Jim was promoted and Cindy left.

Examples (31a) and (31b) do not mean the same thing: the causal order of events differs in accordance with the different order of Clauses.[1]

---

[1] Östen Dahl (pers. comm.) points out that in the following context, the reverse temporal order may hold:
A: What happened during my absence?
B: Cindy left and Jim was promoted.
In this case, however, it is better to say that the temporal sequence of events is deemed to be irrelevant; A has requested a list of 'events during his/her absence', and that time interval is construed as a single time during which many things have happened.

In contrast, the Clauses in Adverbial Subordinate constructions may occur in either order:

(32) a. Cindy quit because Jim was promoted.
b. Because Jim was promoted, Cindy left.

Tense iconicity has been discussed in the discourse literature as a possible criterion for distinguishing coordination from subordination (see, e.g., Labov 1972; Haiman 1983b; Chafe 1988: 18–19, and references cited in Thompson 1987: 435–6). However, embedded constructions generally have conventionalized word orders that may have little to do with tense iconicity.

The freedom of order of the subordinate clauses in (27)–(30) allows us to distinguish them from coordinate sentences by another syntactic property. In the coordination construction, the coordinating conjunction (where present) remains between the two clauses whose order is fixed. In the subordinate construction, the subordinator (as it will be called here) is more closely associated with the adverbial clause, so that when that clause is first, the subordinator is not between the two clauses, and for that reason does not behave as a syntactic linking element.

In the following sections, I argue that the difference between coordination and adverbial subordination can be analyzed in terms of the Gestalt distinction between figure and ground.

9.2.2. Adverbial clauses and figure–ground constructions

The adverbial clause (subordinator + clause) is like the adverbial phrase (adposition + NP), which may also be initial or final:

(33) a. The commission had never met before last year.
b. Before last year, the commission had never met.

In fact, this is more than a syntactic parallel; it is a diachronic and conceptual pattern as well. Diachronically, subordinators in adverbial clauses evolve frequently from adpositions, or directly from relational nouns, a source common to both adpositions and adverbial subordinators. The former has been well documented for the Bodic subgroup of Sino-Tibetan languages (Genetti 1986, 1991). It is also found in the Romance languages, which employ adpositions followed by a complementizer that nominalizes the subordinate clause (Meillet 1915/1921; Lehmann 1982b: 67). In fact, the use of nominalized noun forms or nominalizers such as Spanish *que* is frequently found with adverbial clauses. Hence there is reason to believe that the asymmetrical relation found in adverbial clauses is similar if not identical to that found in adpositional relations.

Talmy (1972, 1974) observes that spatial adpositional relations are conceptually asymmetric. The asymmetry stems from the Gestalt psychology distinction between FIGURE and GROUND (see e.g. Koffka 1935, ch. 5). Thus, the pairs of sentences below are not synonymous in conceptual semantic terms, and in fact the asymmetry makes the second member of each pair bizarre ((34a–b) are from Talmy 1978: 628):

(34) a. The bike is near the house.
  b. ??The house is near the bike.
(35) a. The bike is in front of the house.
  b. ??The house is behind the bike.

Talmy argues that the Subject position of the locative predication is occupied by the figure, while the Object of the Preposition is the ground. The (a) sentences in (34)–(35) have the smaller, more mobile entity as the Subject, and the larger, immobile entity as the Object of the preposition. This is in conformity with Gestalt principles, which demonstrate a certain natural perceptual preference to conceptualize spatial relations according to properties of the objects to be related (Wertheimer 1950). In this case, size and mobility imply that the bike will be taken as the figure, with the house functioning as the ground in the perceptual scene.

If the syntactic roles of the two entities are reversed, the Gestalt roles are reversed as well, and the (b) sentences of (34)–(35) sound odd since they represent an unnatural Gestalt construal of the scene. This is not to say that a situation cannot be constructed in which the house does act as a figure and the bicycle as the ground. It is only to say that the most NATURAL construal of figure and ground, the one that will be most acceptable out of context, is that with the smaller, more mobile entity as figure and the larger, more immobile entity as ground.

In the case of some semantic relations, such as the two illustrated above, either object can be made figure or ground. In (34a–b), the objective semantic relationship is symmetrical, and the same preposition, *near*, is used in both sentences. In (35a–b), the objective semantic relationship is asymmetrical, but there are English Prepositions that encode both relations, that is *behind* and its inverse, *in front of*. This is actually rather unusual; in most cases, there is a "natural" direction to the asymmetry, so that, for example, there is a preposition *in* but no inverse, at least for the use of *in* illustrated in (36a):

(36) a. There's a crocodile in the water.
  b. ??There's water "being-a-suspending-medium-for" the crocodile.

Talmy applies his figure–ground analysis to complex sentences, specifically adverbial relations, and finds essentially the same phenomena (Talmy 1978). We will call these FIGURE–GROUND complex sentences. Simultaneous figure–ground constructions are like *near*: either sentence can be in the main clause, but the sentences are cognitively different:

(37) a. When Jerry was chair of the department, everything was all right.
  b. ??When everything was all right, Jerry was chair of the department.

Temporal sequential figure–ground constructions are like *in front of/ behind*: *before* and *after* are inverses of each other, but again there is a semantic difference in the sentences:

(38) a. After Tom resigned, all hell broke loose.
    b. Tom resigned before all hell broke loose.

Although these example pairs supposedly describe the same truth-conditional situation, the first members of each pair give a very different view of the role of the chair in the wellbeing of the department. In (37a), the healthy state of affairs is presumed to be due to Jerry's chairmanship. (37b) on the other hand is odd, making Jerry look like an opportunist who has the extraordinary ability to take advantage of a healthy state of affairs to assume the chairmanship of the department. In (38a), Tom's resignation is presumed to let loose the forces of chaos; whereas in (38b), Tom succeeded in cutting out when he saw what was happening (or perhaps before the consequences of his actions became apparent to everyone).

In all cases, the event in the ground/subordinate clause is conceptualized as the basis or ground—that is a cause or precondition—for the event in the figure/main clause. The interpretation implicated in (37) and the one implicated in (38) are equally natural. In contrast, the coordinate construction does not have exclusively either implication about the relation:

(39) Jerry resigned and (then) all hell broke loose.

Figure–ground asymmetry may lead to outright anomaly, as in example (40) (Talmy 1978: 636):

(40) a. He dreamed while he slept.
    b. *He slept while he dreamed.

The two events could be coextensive, but since dreaming is contingent on sleeping, sleeping must function as the ground and therefore (40a) is acceptable while (40b) is not.

In these few cases, it is syntactically simple to construct both a semantic relation and its inverse (*before–after*), with standard figure–ground differences. However, for most figure–ground subordinators, there is no natural inverse for the figure–ground relation specified by the subordinator (Talmy 1978: 637):

(41) a. She slept until he arrived.
    b. ??He arrived "immediately-and-causally-before-the-end-of" her sleeping.
(42) a. We stayed home because he had arrived.
    b. ??He arrived "to-the-occasioning-of-(the-decision-of)" our staying home.

Talmy notes that the pattern of the simple figure–ground expression of one semantic relation but not its inverse is not random. In general, the temporally and/or causally prior event is always in the subordinate clause, that is, it is always the ground.[2] These generalizations support the notion that figure–ground sentences involve a figure–ground asymmetry, since the ground functions as the reference point for the figure, and the figure event is temporally or causally contingent on the ground event.

Reinhart (1984) argues persuasively that the foreground–background distinction in narrative discourse is actually the figure–ground distinction (see also Matthiessen and Thompson 1988: 290; Nakhimovsky 1988: 38). The foreground–background distinction has primarily been applied to narrative texts, in which the foreground is defined as those events on the "timeline" of the events reported in the narrative that are presented sequentially in the narrative. Other events, including descriptive material as well as "out of sequence" events, are background. Adverbial subordinate clauses and relative clauses generally encode events that are not on the timeline (Tomlin 1985; Thompson 1987; certain exceptions will be discussed below).

Reinhart identifies the requirement that narrative foreground must be on the timeline with the Gestalt principle of good continuation (see Koffka 1935: 151). A figure is conceptualized as continuous; the timeline provides continuity; hence, events on the timeline can be conceptualized as figures.

Not all events on the timeline are necessarily foregrounded; other Gestalt principles determine which ones are foregrounded. The preference of punctual events as foreground is due to the Gestalt preference to treat a small object as the figure against a large object (Koffka 1935: 183) as in Figure 9.3.

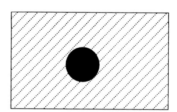

Figure 9.3. Perception of different-sized forms

Likewise, in the temporal dimension the smaller, punctual, event is perceived as figure against the larger, durative, event.

The preference for completed events as foreground (Hopper 1979) is due to the Gestalt principle of closure. We perceive a bounded form as closed and therefore

---

[2] *Until* appears to be anomalous, since the temporally later clause is subordinate; but the subordinate clause denotes the causally prior event, its occurrence causing the end of the event described in the main clause. *Before* is the lone truly anomalous case, since it does not have the causal implications of *until*. However, in just these types pleonastic negative marking is found in some languages (Croft 2000a: 135–7), precisely because the posterior event in the subordinate clause is lacking the ground property of presupposed existence.

a figure. For example, in Figure 9.4, we perceive the closed shape in (a) as the figure; we do not identify (a) as being composed of the line segments in (b) (see Wertheimer 1950: 83; Koffka 1935: 151, 168).

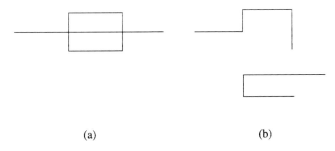

(a)   (b)

Figure 9.4. Perception of bounded and open-ended forms

Likewise, in the temporal domain a bounded event will be treated as a closed temporal unit and therefore the figure.

The properties of foregrounding and the Gestalt principles justifying them are summed up in Table 9.1.

Table 9.1. Gestalt principles accounting for the foreground–background distinction

Foregrounded event	Gestalt principle
on timeline	good continuation
punctual event	size/proximity
completive event	closure

In addition, the phenomenon described in (38a–b), where the grounding adverbial clause represents the motivating or explaining event for the event represented in the main clause, is due to functional dependency (Koffka 1935: 184): 'the ground can determine the interpretation of the figure, but not conversely' (Reinhart 1984: 788).

It is important to point out that the figure–ground distinction is not the same as certain other distinctions that have been proposed to explain the foreground–background distinction. The figure does not correspond to the 'important information' or the 'focus of attention' in the sentence (Reinhart 1984: 787). Although they often coincide, the two are logically distinct; for example, backgrounded material may be more important than foregrounded material. Figure–ground is an asymmetry of contrast based on natural perceptual principles; importance is a matter of focus of attention. The two are distinct and logically independent cognitive phenomena (see Langacker 1987, ch. 3; Cruse and Croft in press, ch. 4). Nor is the ground/background the 'given', 'presupposed', or 'unchallengeable' proposition, as Matthiessen and Thompson (1988: 312–15) empirically demonstrate.

The figure–ground analysis of adverbial subordination allows us to account for two widely occurring counterexamples to the foreground–background analysis. In the following examples, a situation that is part of the narrative sequence is found in an adverbial subordinate clause (Hobbs 1985/1990: 90 and Thompson 1987: 443 respectively):

(43) a. And one Sunday morning about ohhhh five o'clock in the morning I sat down in the Grand—no no, not in the Grand Central, in the Penn Station,
 b. and **while I was sitting there** a young cat came up to me, ...
(44) a. Only after he stopped smiling and shrieking did he go to Stephanie and hug her. That hug was also interrupted by additional shrieks. Quite a lot of noise from a normally silent chimpanzee!
 b. **After spending about fifteen minutes with Stephanie**, Nim went over to WER, Josh, and Jeannie, and hugged each of them in turn.

In (43), the first and second sentences are in narrative sequence. The adverbial subordinate clause in (43b) represents an event in the narrative sequence clause (sitting in Penn Station). This is due to the fact that it recapitulates the event in (43a) in order to serve as the true ground to the main clause figure in (43b). Also, the event description in the first sentence (43a) is punctual and completive, while the description of the same event in the adverbial clause (43b) is durative and incompletive—exactly what one would expect given the figure–ground analysis of foreground and background.

This is essentially the same phenomenon noted by Thompson (1987: 442–3), namely that subordinate clauses that appear to be part of the narrative timeline actually summarize or recapitulate preceding events (and sometimes bring the narrative back to the timeline after a digression). This phenomenon is also common in narratives in Papuan languages, where it is called 'tail-head linkage' (Foley 1986: 200–1).

Another problematic case for the foreground–background analysis are meta-comments and evaluative comments in discourse. Tomlin (1985) examines narratives based on a short animated film from which an objective characterization of foreground and background could be derived. Tomlin was testing the hypothesis that backgrounded events are coded as subordinate clauses, while foregrounded events are coded as main clauses. One significant class of exceptions involve META-COMMENTS: the meta-comment is coded in the main clause, and a foregrounded narrative event may be subordinated to it (Tomlin 1985: 116):

(45) a. Scene goes back to little fish [meta-comment]
 b. **who** is headed toward open mouth of shark with crab at her tail [foreground]

Another class of exceptions involves EVALUATIVE COMMENTS, which are like meta-comments in function and distribution. The evaluative comment is found in a main clause, and may have a narrative event subordinated to it (ibid.):

(46) a. This brings about a complication,   [evaluative comment]
    b. **since** the fish gets caught in one of the portals,   [foreground]

In other words, a figure–ground construction is used, with the meta-comment or evaluative comment functioning as figure and the narrative as ground.

This is anomalous from the point of view of the hypothesis that complex sentence structure reflects the organization of discourse into foreground and background: the narrative line is usually foreground, but in these constructions it is backgrounded. But in a Gestalt analysis of the organization of complex sentences, this is exactly what one would expect. Background information of the usual type functions as a ground for the narrative line. However, the narrative line (or perhaps the whole narrative) functions as the ground for the speaker's evaluation and commentary, since the latter is functionally dependent on the former.

Figure 9.5 represents the possible figure–ground alignments in discourse: the typical narrative–background relation (Figure$_1$–Ground$_1$), the recapitulated event–new event relation (Figure$_1$–Ground$_2$), and the meta-comment/evaluative comment–narrative relation (Figure$_2$–Ground$_2$).

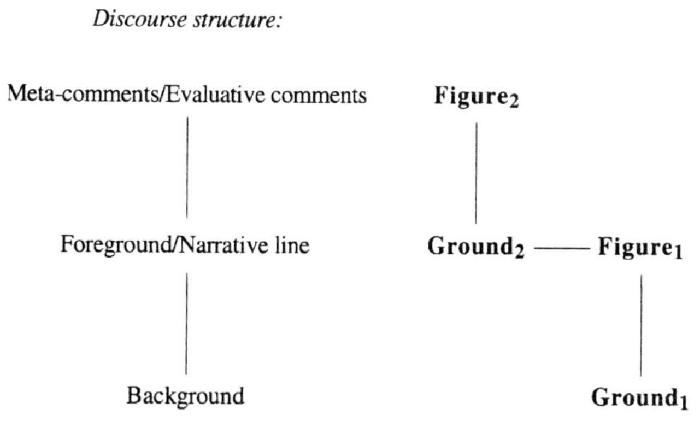

Discourse structure:

Meta-comments/Evaluative comments   **Figure$_2$**
|
Foreground/Narrative line   **Ground$_2$** ——— **Figure$_1$**
|
Background   **Ground$_1$**

Figure 9.5. Figure–ground relations and discourse structure

In other words, the Gestalt organization of information into figure and ground is the basic principle underlying the organization of information in discourse. Whether the narrative line in a discourse is expressed as a main clause or as a (figure–ground) subordinate clause depends on the Gestalt construal of the narrative event in the discourse context.

9.2.3. Coordination and complex figure constructions

The work of Talmy and Reinhart, supported by empirical observations such as those of Matthiessen and Thompson, establish a Gestalt conceptual structure for complex sentences involving adverbial subordinate clauses. What of coordinate sentences, which appear to encode the same sort of truth-conditional semantic relations? I argue here that their semantic analysis also has a Gestalt conceptual structure that differs from that found in figure–ground complex sentences.

As noted in §9.2.3, the most salient syntactic (more accurately symbolic) characteristic of coordinate constructions is their tense iconicity: the temporal (and/or causal) sequence implicated by the order of coordinate clauses is reversed when the order of those clauses is reversed:

(47) a. The vase fell and broke.
b. The vase broke and fell.

Of course, not all conjoined sentences involve sequence, and the sequential relation may be looser than a temporal or causal one. I introduce here terms coined by Stassen (1985, ch. 4) for the description of these semantic relations. Stassen calls two or more clauses in temporal sequence, as in (47a–b), CONSECUTIVE CHAINS, or C-chains. Two or more clauses representing simultaneous events are called SIMULTANEOUS CHAINS or S-chains, as in (48):

(48) The vase is Chinese and the candlestick is German.

Although coordination appears to be quite free in its use, not everything can be naturally conjoined (Wierzbicka 1980: 254, 227):

(49) The sun was shining and the birds were singing.
(50) ??John kissed Mary on the nose and kangaroos are mammals.

Wierzbicka (1980: 230, 246–54) argues that joining two sentences with a conjunction (not just 'and' but also 'but') is possible only when a speaker can conceive of the two events as a single whole. The single whole corresponds to the Gestalt notion of a single, unified figure. For this reason, I will call these types of sentences COMPLEX FIGURE sentences.

Wierzbicka argues that the conceptualization of two events as a single whole requires finding a COMMON DENOMINATOR for the two sentences. That is, the process of explicitly conjoining two sentences (or in (27a–b), two predicates), involves the speaker conceptualizing the paired elements as a whole unit having something in common.

According to Wierzbicka, a common denominator underlies all conjoined elements, even of conjoined sentences that do not share a participant. Thus, the relative felicity of (49) compared to (50) is due to our ability to construct a common denominator for (49) but not for (50). As with the anomalous figure–ground sentences in (37b) and (40b), the oddness of the anomalous sentence in (50) is due to unnaturalness and can be canceled in the appopriate context. It is possible to make (50) acceptable if one can indeed come up with a common denominator to link these sentences (an exercise I will leave to the reader).

Wierzbicka's notion of common denominator is essentially the same as the principle of good continuation in Gestalt psychology. Good continuation is a set of perceptual properties that allows one to construe two entities as actually parts of a single larger entity. For example, it is easier to perceive the two line segments in Figure 9.6a as extending behind the circle than to do so in Figure 9.6b because the former exhibits good continuation and the latter does not (see Koffka 1935: 154–5).

Figure 9.6. The principle of good continuation in perception

The parallel between Wierzbicka's common denominator and the Gestalt concept of good continuation does not end here (although she does not refer to Gestalt principles). Wierzbicka argues (following the medieval scholastic Peter of Spain) that the conjoined entities make up a single larger entity. The common denominator is the means; the end to be achieved is a conceptualization of the conjoined entities as a single unit. The two conjoined entities are naturally perceived to make up a single unit due to the Gestalt principle of good continuation. In describing sentences such as *Mary is big and strong*, Wierzbicka writes:

Each of these sentences does more than ascribe two different and unrelated predicates to the subject. Each sentence suggests that the two predicates which are explicitly mentioned have something in common, and in fact ascribes this third something to the subject, in addition to those two other predicates (Wierzbicka 1980: 249).

This is the Gestalt principle that a whole figure is more than the sum of its parts (see for example Köhler 1947, ch. 5).[3]

Tense iconicity fits into the Gestalt analysis of coordination. Tense iconicity is an example of good continuation for C-chains. Tense iconicity is one of the most

---

[3] Wierzbicka applies her analysis to all conjoined structures, not just conjoined clauses but conjoined smaller constituents, including those found in the constructions known as Conjunction Reduction, Gapping, and Right Node Raising (see §5.3.1). Wierzbicka argues that in constructions such as gapping and right node raising, which appear to conjoin nonconstituents (see §5.4.1), the meaning must also involve a general formula as well as the common denominator to define the whole (Wierzbicka 1980: 252–3). We will not discuss the extension of Wierzbicka's analysis to these constructions here, except to note that these latter constructions also belong in the complex-figure category.

natural means to join two consecutive events into a single Gestalt. Another very natural means is to assume a causal relation between the two events. The Gestalt analysis gives a natural explanation as to why a coordinate sentence *A and B* is often interpreted with more than the truth-conditional meaning 'A is true and B is true': the Gestalt unity requires a common denominator such as temporal or causal continuity linking A and B.

Another common denominator that can unify the events denoted by two sentences in a coordinate construction is shared tense, aspect, and/or mood between the two sentences, or a shared salient participant (typically A, S, or P) in the two events. Shared tense–aspect–mood unifies the two events in the same location in time (tense) and in the same mental space or possible world (mood). A shared participant unifies the two events in that both are brought about by and/or happen to a single referent.

Coordinate sentences contrast with adverbial clauses, in which these variables need not be the same. An adverbial subordinate clause functions as a ground or reference point for the event (figure) in the main clause. The figure event is construed as distinct from the ground event. The figure event is anchored in the discourse by establishing a relation to the distinct ground event, not by uniting figure and ground through some common denominator.

The diachronic sources of coordinators also suggests that the complex figure conceptual analysis is the correct one for the semantics of coordination. There are three common sources for coordinators, illustrated in (51a–c) (Mithun 1988: 344–9):

(51) a. Comitative, especially for phrasal coordination: Sarcee *ihílà* 'with, and', Jacaltec *boj* 'with/and'
  b. Additive adverb: Mohawk *tanū'* 'and' < *tahnū* 'besides'
  c. Sequential adverb: Tiwi *ki* 'then, and'; Mohawk *tahnū* < *ta* 'so' + (?)*nū:wa* 'now'

All of these are additive or linking morphemes, which connect entities of like kind in some fashion or another. The result is a whole, composite entity—that is, a complex figure.

Finally, the figure can be identified with what is asserted in coordination and adverbial subordination (§9.1.2). In coordination, both clauses are asserted, in line with its complex figure construal. In adverbial subordination, only the main clause is asserted, because only the main clause is the figure of the sentence.

9.2.4. *Conventionalized construals: conditionals and comparatives*

In §9.2.1, I pointed out that certain semantic relations between events are encoded as either coordinate or subordinate in English. In most cases, the alternative encoding of these semantic relations represent alternative conceptualizations of the two events as a complex figure or as figure–ground. Causal and temporal relations (simultaneous or consecutive) can function as the common denominator for the complex figure construal. Alternatively, an event may be used as the reference point to which a second event is related temporally or causally in a figure–ground manner.

Although English avails itself of both construals for these semantic relations, it is of course possible for a single construal to be conventionalized in a language (see Chapter 3). This appears to be common across languages for two categories of semantic relations, conditionals, and comparatives.

A typical adverbial conditional construction, as illustrated by the English Conditional sentence *If she leaves, then I will leave too*, consists of a PROTASIS (the *if*-clause), which sets up a hypothetical situation, and an APODOSIS (the *then*-clause), which describes a consequence of the state of affairs described in the protasis.

In English, conditional relations can be expressed by a Coordinate construction as well as an Adverbial construction, illustrated above in (30a–b), repeated as (52a–b) here:

(52) a. He does that and I'll fire him.
   b. If he does that, I'll fire him.
   c. Even if he does that, I'll fire him.

However, the Coordinate sentence in (52a) cannot be interpreted as a concessive (cf. (52c); Haiman 1986: 220–4). This may be explained by the fact that a concessive cannot be construed as a composite whole with its apodosis, since the apodosis will occur DESPITE the occurrence of the protasis.

Other languages can also use a coordinate construction for conditional relations. Coordinate structures can be interpreted conditionally (but not concessively) in Vietnamese, Khmer, Mandarin, Hua, and other Papuan languages, and Early Modern English (*an* 'if' < *and*; Haiman 1987: 218–19, 224; see also Traugott 1985: 296). Although conditional clauses can be reversed without changing the implicational relations, protases are typologically overwhelmingly initial (Greenberg 1966b: 84). Even with the English *if*-conditional, a figure–ground construction, protases are mainly initial (Ford and Thompson 1986 found 77 percent [$n = 490$] in written texts, 82 percent [$n = 406$] in oral texts). The anomalous postposed *if*-clauses are a varied lot, sometimes postposed due to syntactic factors (e.g. *if*-clauses modifying Noun Phrases are postposed; ibid.).

There is a semantic motivation for coding conditionals with complex figure constructions. Iconic sequence involves strongly linked sequential events; the link between the protasis and the apodosis is generally causal in character, although the protasis is hypothetical (Haiman 1986). The situations denoted by protasis and apodosis are in the same hypothetical world. Haiman further notes that paratactic conditionals are restricted to iconic relations between the clauses, and specifically exclude the possibility of a concessive (*Even if...*) interpretation.

On the other hand, there is also typological evidence for coding conditionals with figure–ground constructions. The most common sources of conditional markers are temporal adverbial markers (usually *when*), followed by topic markers

(Traugott 1985: 291–2). The reason for the former is straightforward: *when* adverbials are semantically very much like conditionals with given (factual, rather than hypothetical) protases, and in many languages the two are identical in form (Haiman 1978; Traugott 1985: 291).

Haiman argues that the (initial) protasis functions as the topic for the apodosis; it expresses 'shared knowledge which serves as a framework for the following material' (Ford and Thompson 1986: 361). This resembles the Gestalt principle of functional dependency that is used to distinguish figure and ground (see §9.2.2). Haiman argues that subordinate protases, as opposed to coordinate structures functioning as protases, are backgrounded (Haiman 1987: 224). Finally, it is worth noting that there is no simple way to express the inverse relation to the conditional, so that the protasis is a main clause and the apodosis is an adverbial clause dependent on the protasis.

Thus, there is diachronic and typological evidence for both construals of conditionals, and a semantic explanation for the alternative construals. The fact that protasis and apodosis are strictly sequenced and often causally related invites a complex figure construal (albeit with both clauses hypothetical), while the fact that the protasis is topical implies a backgrounding, figure–ground construction (which appears to be the more common one typologically).

Stassen's (1985) extensive study of comparative constructions reveals that comparatives also vary as to how they are expressed in the world's languages. As with conditionals, one finds both complex–figure and figure–ground constructions for comparatives. A complex–figure-like comparative is biclausal, involving two conjoined clauses that contrast the target and standard of comparison in the relevant property, as in this example from Sika (Stassen 1985: 44, from Arndt 1931):

(53) [dzarang tica gahar] [dzarang rei kesik]
     horse   that big   horse   this small
     'That horse is bigger than this horse.'

Figure–ground comparatives generally use an adverbial phrase rather than a clause, so they are not complex sentences per se; but the use of the adverbial phrase for the standard of comparison is parallel to adverbial locative/temporal phrases. The following example is from Mundari (Stassen 1985: 39, from Hoffmann 1903):

(54) sadom -ete   hati   mananga -i
     horse -from elephant big   -3SG.PRS
     'The elephant is bigger than the horse.'

Again, there is a semantic motivation for the typological variation in the expression of this complex sentence type. On the one hand, the predications for the target and the standard of comparison are parallel. This favors the construal of a comparative as a complex figure construction, specifically a simultaneous chain.

On the other hand, the target–standard relation is a classic figure–ground relation (see Langacker 1987, ch. 3), with the target functioning as the figure and the standard as the ground. This favors the construal of the comparative as a figure–ground construction, with the standard expressed in a subordinate phrase (or possibly clause) using an adposition.

One of Stassen's universals for the distribution of comparative constructions associates complex–figure comparatives with complex–figure chaining constructions: 'If a language has a Conjoined Comparative, it must have a balanced simultaneous chaining construction' (Stassen 1985: 108). This suggests that the conjoined comparative represents an extended use of a prototypical complex–figure construction, the finite coordinate sentence. Stassen's universals for the types of comparatives that resemble figure–ground constructions associate them with deranked chaining constructions (ibid.: 106–7), many of which are probably figure–ground constructions (see §9.2.5).

In the case of both conditionals and comparatives, the semantic relation between the two situations denoted by the two clauses possesses properties that are amenable to both a complex figure and a figure–ground conceptualization, and the structure and etymology of conditional and comparative constructions across languages indicate that both types are found. However, this is not to imply that the choice of one type of construction over another necessarily implies that a complex–figure or figure–ground construal is imposed on the conditional and comparative situation types by the language. Under the conventional universalist hypothesis argued for in Chapter 3, the conventional expression may not share the construal of its source construction.

9.2.5. The evolution of complex sentences to deranked clause chains

The first step in the grammaticalization of complex sentences is the evolution of balanced coordinate and adverbial subordinate clauses into deranked structures. It appears that deranked clause chains may be diachronically derived from either complex–figure or figure–ground constructions. Deranked clause chains may retain formal and functional properties of their source constructions, or they may allow either a complex–figure and figure–ground construal.

Haiman presents evidence that medial verb constructions, including medial-verb switch-reference, in Papuan languages result from the grammaticalization of a coordinating conjunction (Haiman 1983b, 1987). These constructions are tense-iconic: reversing the order of clauses (including reversing the inflections) will indicate a reverse order of events for temporal or causal sequence.

In switch-reference systems, deranked clauses may have either the same subject as the full clause (SS) or a different subject (DS); these are usually morphologically expressed. An example of a DS construction is given in (55), from Hua, with a Switch-Reference suffix -*ga* and an Anticipatory inflection -*da* for the Subject of the Final Clause (Haiman 1980b: 396):

(55) fumo   dmi   -**ga**   -da   u   -e
     pork   he.gave.me -**DS**   -1SG.ANTIC went   -FNL
     'He gave me pork and I went.'

In the languages that Haiman examines, there are two strategies used for expressing switch reference. In the first strategy, the DS forms consist of a person affix while SS forms are bare root forms or have an invariant affix. Haiman argues that these originate in coordinate structures in which gapping has occurred (Haiman 1983b: 106ff), and in several instances the invariant affix (if present) appears to have its source in a morpheme meaning 'and' (something like *kV/*gV; ibid.: 110–12).

In the second type, the type illustrated in (55), the SS forms have personal affixes, and the DS forms have personal affixes plus an additional suffix. Again, this suffix is often derived historically from 'and'. Haiman contrasts these with subordinate constructions that mark switch reference whose medial forms use a distinct suffix -ma (among other forms). This suffix is also found on adverbial and relative clauses (ibid.: 120); both of these are figure–ground constructions (§9.2.2).

This phenomenon is found in languages outside of the Papuan family as well. In some Melanesian languages such as Big Nambas, there are Sequential Verbs which lack Person–Mood Agreement affixes, using instead a Verb form with a prefix glossed as 'and' (Fox 1979: 127, Text 2):

(56) a-   v-   əln   talei   **ka**-   v-   ruh   **ka**-   v-   mi'i
     3PL.RL- PL- leave knife   AND-   PL-   run.away AND-   PL-   go.over
     arna   pitha   ...
     on   mountain ...
     'So they left their knives and ran away and climbed over the hill...'

Lenakel (Lynch 1978) possesses a Conjunctive Verb prefix, glossed 'and' by Lynch, which is used only for Coordinate constructions, and not for Subordinate constructions such as Relative Clauses or Conditionals (Lynch 1978: 46–7; example from Text 1, p. 126):

(57) kani   am   ka   teramsumas   r-   im-   ipk   tehe   **m**-   leliɣ
     and   just that Teramsumas   3SG- PST-   take   sea   AND-   return
     m-   va
     AND-   come
     'And Teramsumas went to the sea and came back.'

This phenomenon is also found in African languages (Haspelmath 1995: 21–2), as in the Swahili ka- Tense forms (Givón 1991: 880, from Mbotela 1934: 37; morpheme glossed AND here):

(58) Wa-   Ingereza   wa-   li-   wa-   chukua   wa-   le   maiti
     PL-   British   3PL-   PST-   3PL-   take   2PL-   DEM   corpses

wa-	ka-	wa-	tia	katika	bao	moja		
3PL-	AND-	3PL-	put	on	board	one		
wa-	ka-	ya-	telemesha	maji	-ni	kwa	utaratibu	w- ote
3PL-	AND-	3PL-	lower	water	-LOC	with	steadiness	3PL- all

'... then the British took the corpses, put them on a flat board, and lowered them steadily into the water.'

Since these languages are SVO, it is the first Verb rather than the last which is fully inflected. It is possible that Big Nambas *ka-* and Swahili *ka-* are grammaticalizations of 'and', although this is quite speculative. Nevertheless one can also compare the English Conjunction Reduction coordinate construction in which a reduced form of *and*, *'n'*, is cliticized to Verbs lacking Pronominal Subjects in narrative sequence:

(59) I got up'n'took a shower'n'ate breakfast.

These examples exhibit semantic and discourse-functional properties of complex–figure sentences. They are tense-iconic; since the medial form is a nonfinite form, this means that they are nonreversible. They are used for the narrative line in narratives, not background information; as Haiman notes, a distinct medial and switch-reference construction is used for backgrounded clauses in Papuan languages.

Certain other deranked coordinate constructions which display the same discourse-functional behavior may also belong in this category, although their diachronic source is not attested. A study of foregrounding and deranked C-chains in Soddo and Japanese by Myhill and Hibiya (1988) supports their analysis as complex–figure in origin. The deranked C-chains in Soddo (the *m*-form) and Japanese (the gerund or *-te* forms) display foregrounding features (same subject and above all temporal sequence, the defining feature of C-chains) in association with the following finite clause, though not the preceding clause. This is to be expected since the deranked C-chain in both languages consists of one or more deranked clauses associated with a following balanced clause (Soddo and Japanese are both SOV).[4]

Another significant property that the Papuan Medial Verb constructions possess is that the Papuan Medial Verbs must have the same tense, mood, and illocutionary force as the main verb they are dependent on (Foley 1986: 194). This constraint means that the two events denoted by the conjuncts are situated in the same location in time, the same temporal contour and the same possible world/mental space. This allows the two events to be construed as a single complex

---

[4] Myhill and Hibiya also investigate two other deranked Verbal forms in Japanese. The Stem form appears to be used for S-chains, and the function of the *-to* form is somewhat unclear. The explanation offered here is different from those offered by Myhill and Hibiya; they argue that the deranked clauses are only partially foregrounded because they do not share foregrounding features with the preceding clause. I suggest that this is due to the looser grammatical link between the deranked clause and the preceding clause compared to the following clause, with which it forms a C-chain.

event, individuated and situated as a unit. This is also a property that figure–ground sentences lack (see §9.2.2).

Complex sentences with adverbial subordinate clauses—the prototypical figure–ground sentences—have a subordinator which is often diachronically derived from an adposition or case marker. Adverbial subordinate clauses are also not tense-iconic. If the subordinator grammaticalizes, then one would expect to find constructions which are not tense-iconic and which share the semantic properties of the figure–ground sentences, not complex–figure sentences.

The older Indo-European participial constructions, including possibly the English participle, may be examples of this phenomenon. The English gerund is not tense-iconic:

(60) a. [Having eaten his fill], the leprechaun went to sleep.
     b. The leprechaun went to sleep, [having eaten his fill].

The same is true of the absolute constructions found in Latin, Greek, and the Slavic languages. The Latin Ablative Absolute, illustrated in (47) (Stassen 1985: 74), is not tense-iconic:

(61) [urbe   destructā]   gaudebimus
     city.ABL.FSG destroy.PARTPRF.PASS.ABL.FSG   be.happy.FUT.IND.1PL
     'When/because/although the city has been destroyed, we will rejoice.'

The Latin Ablative Absolute can be interpreted to indicate temporal sequence, causal, or concessive relations—in contrast, coordinate structures do not indicate concessive relations (see §9.2.4).

The Absolute constructions in Indo-European are governed by particular cases (e.g. the Ablative in Latin). Case relations are a paradigm example of figure–ground asymmetry, as we have discussed with regard to adverbial clauses. These constructions are thus best analyzed as figure–ground constructions.

In many South Asian languages such as Tamil, the Conjunctive Participle (deranked) clause can follow the balanced clause (Peter Hook, Madhav Deshpande, personal communication). However, this is generally possible only as an afterthought, and so this may not be a genuine counterexample to the principle of tense iconicity for complex figure constructions. In other respects, the deranked clauses behave like complex figure constructions: same subject is required, 'compatibility' in tense and aspect are required (Masica 1991: 399), and the linked structures must have 'natural relevance' or represent 'closely related actions' (ibid.), all of which sounds very much like the notion of a common denominator found in complex figure constructions.

Masica (1991: 323) identifies a common New Indo-Aryan Conjunctive Participle form in -*ii*, but he does not propose a lexical or grammatical source for it or other Indo-Aryan forms. These are to be distinguished from Coordinating suffixes such as Sinhalese -*t* and Tamil (Dravidian) -*um* (ibid.: 398), both of which mean 'also' and have the diachronic origins and behavior typical of complex figure constructions (§9.2.3). In Bodic languages of the Tibeto-Burman family of south Asia, the Nonfinal Verb forms evolved from an Ablative adposition (Genetti 1986: 393). However, I have no information on whether or not these forms are tense iconic. Masica (1976: 124) suggests these are a late development.

Masica (1976: 137–8) notes that there are in fact two general areas with deranked chaining constructions in the Eurasian area, Europe and South (and Central) Asia. The latter area participle overwhelmingly uses a "past" participle form, while the European languages use a "present" form (including the English gerund). Since the South Asian constructions appear to be complex figure constructions for the reasons given in the preceding two paragraphs, and the European ones figure–ground constructions, there may be some semantic significance to the choice of participle type. For example, the "present" participles have a large and confusing array of functions, with attributive functions prominent among them (Masica 1976: 113–20)—and the attributive function is associated with relative clauses, which are figure–ground constructions (see §9.3.2). In contrast, the "past" participles of South Asia are not used attributively or nominally (ibid.: 127). It is possible that "present" participles employ oblique case marking (e.g. ablative) when used as deranked chaining constructions, whereas the "past" participles do not; and for that reason "present" participles resemble figure–ground constructions.

Haspelmath (1995: 12–17) describes a class of constructions which he calls CONVERBS—adverbial verb forms not unlike the English gerund. They are most commonly derived from adpositional constructions (ibid.: 17), and so appear to be more grammaticalized versions of adverbial subordinate clauses. Haspelmath distinguishes converbs from medial constructions of the type discussed in §2.1.3 above by the following criteria of "subordination" (ibid.: 12):

(62) a. clause-internal word order (ability to interrupt main clause)
 b. variable position
 c. possibility of backwards pronominal anaphora and control
 d. semantic restrictiveness
 e. possibility of extraction

Haspelmath argues, partly following Roberts (1988), that medial verbs fail the criteria for "subordination" (Haspelmath 1995: 23–7). In fact, two of these criteria pertain not to "subordination" in general, but to figure–ground constructions in particular. Criterion (62b) is (lack of) tense iconicity. Criterion (62d) refers to the function of the "subordinate" clause to restrict the reference of the main clause. This function is the prototypical function of relative clauses, and renders the modified element (the main clause in this case, the head NP for relative clauses) functionally dependent on the modifying clause in the Gestalt sense. This will be discussed further in the next section.[5]

The deranked clause chains surveyed in this section are largely identifiable as either complex–figure or figure–ground constructions. However, once a complex–figure or figure–ground construction is grammaticalized to this degree, it may no longer exhibit the behavior characteristic of its source construction. As seen in §9.1.2, in some languages deranked clause chains exhibit both complex–figure and figure–ground semantics. Thus, either type spreads to either end of the conceptual space in Figure 9.2.

9.3. E-site Elaboration and the Typology of Complements and Relative Clauses

9.3.1. *E-site elaboration*

In §7.7.2, I presented Langacker's analysis of semantic valence and the autonomous–dependent relation, a generalization of the predicate–argument relation found in formal semantic theories. In brief, dependent concepts have a salient substructure that is elaborated (made more specific) by another concept, the autonomous concept in the relation. The salient substructure of the dependent concept is called an elaboration site or e-site. The prototypical e-site corresponds to an argument variable in a predicate representation in formal semantic theories.

In the complex sentence constructions described so far in this chapter, neither sentence denotes a concept that elaborates a salient substructure in the concept denoted by the other sentence. However, complements and relative clauses both essentially involve elaboration of an e-site of the main clause event by the subordinate clause event. In other words, e-site elaboration is a second significant dimension in the conceptual space underlying complex sentences.

Complements are straightforwardly examples of e-site elaboration by the "subordinate" clause. Complements are standardly analyzed as denoting events or states of affairs that fill an argument position of the main clause verb. Relative clauses are not e-site elaborations of a main clause event in the same way that complements are. In fact, in the most common analysis of relative clauses, a relative clause is a modifier of an argument, not the argument itself. Relative clauses by themselves do not appear to fill an argument position of the main clause verb; the head noun of the relative clause does. Instead, the most salient feature

---

[5] The other criteria do not seem to have an obvious Gestalt motivation. For example, some indubitably coordinate structures can violate the Coordinate Structure Constraint (criterion (e)); see Ross (1967), Schachter (1977a), Goldsmith (1985), Lakoff (1986), which suggests that the Coordinate Structure Constraint is sensitive to some other property of complex sentences. Criterion (a) is a criterion for syntactic embeddedness, which is found in both complex–figure and figure–ground constructions.

of relative clauses appears to be that a main clause participant elaborates a salient e-site (participant role) of the relative clause event.

The common analysis of relative clauses is based on the relative clause type found in English and other well-known languages and illustrated in (63): an embedded clause modifying a head noun.

(63) [The tree$_i$ [that Ø$_i$ was struck by lightning] finally fell over.]

However, the analysis of relative clauses as e-site elaborations is appropriate in Langacker's theory; and examination of other relative clause constructions across languages suggests that this analysis is accurate and insightful.

Elaboration in Langacker's theory is not the same theoretical notion as argument-filling. Elaboration simply means that the referent is more narrowly specified than in the unelaborated description. A relative clause elaborates an e-site of the main clause event because it describes the referent more specifically than the head noun does. For example, the Relative Clause *that was struck by lightning* in (63) elaborates—describes more specifically—the participant in the main clause event denoted by *the tree*. Langacker's more general notion thus captures the similarity between complements and relative clauses more accurately than the predicate–argument notion does.

Certain relative clause types found in the world's languages support the e-site elaboration analysis of relative clauses (see Lehmann 1984, 1986 and Comrie 1989, ch. 7, for surveys of relative clause constructions). In many languages, the relative clause construction is identical to the headless relative clause construction which means 'the one that S'. For example, in Supyire, a Relative Clause with or without a Head Noun is formed by a Demonstrative Pronoun (inflected for Noun Class and Number) plus the Clause followed by the Relativizer *ké/gé* (Carlson 1994: 497, 494):

(64) *Headless relative clause:*
[ŋgé   u   à   pyi   na   ɲ-   càà   gé]
that he   PF   PST   PROG   INTR- seek.IMPF   REL
'the one whom he had been seeking, ...'

(65) *Headed relative clause:*
mobílíye   [ɲjé   yi   mpyi   bobo   kúni   ɲàni   na   ké]
trucks:DEF   **those**   they   were   Bobo   road:DEF   walking:DEF   on   REL
'The trucks which were on the Bobo route ...'

In other words, relative clauses in such languages probably arose diachronically from a construction which really does denote a participant, and not simply a property attributed to a participant (see §2.2.3). In fact, it could be argued that a relative clause in such languages still does denote a participant, and is in apposition to the head noun.

Also, in many languages complement structures and relative clause constructions are very similar if not identical. Internally headed relative clauses, such as the Imbabura Quechua examples in §9.1.2, are generally identical in structure to complements. Also noted in §9.1.2 is that fact that in some languages, complementizers and relativizers are identical or similar.

Finally, there is an intermediate subordinate clause type that may be conventionally construed as either a relative clause-like or complement-like construction, not unlike the conditional and comparative types discussed in §9.2.4. In Japanese, one Relative Clause construction type is identical in structure to main clauses, with null instantiation of the Head Noun in the Relative Clause (Comrie 1998: 68; see also Matsumoto 1997):

(66) [gakusei   ga   katta]   hon
     student   NOM   bought   book)
     'the book which/that the student bought'
     (compare *gakusei ga katta* 'The student bought [it]')

Complements of Verbs on the other hand require a Complementizer such as *koto* 'thing' (ibid.: 71):

(67a) [gakusei   ga   hon   o   katta]   **koto**   o   sir-ana-katta
      student   NOM   book ACC bought   thing   ACC know-NEG-PST
      'I didn't know that/*which the student bought the book.'

But so-called NOMINAL COMPLEMENTS use the Relative Clause construction:

(67b) [gakusei   ga   hon   o   katta]   zizitu
      student   NOM   book ACC bought   fact
      'the fact that/*which the student bought the book.'

The English translations of (66)–(67), on the other hand, suggest the opposite is true for that language. The English Nominal Complement, like the Verbal Complement, prohibits the Relative Pronoun *which*, and unlike the Relative Clause, contains no "gap" (it can stand as a main clause on its own; Comrie 1998: 66–7).

Finally, there are languages such as Khmer, in which Nominal Complements of different Head Nouns use either the Complementizer *thaa* 'say' or the invariant Relativizer *dael* (Comrie and Horie 1995: 72–3):

(68) damnəŋ   [**thaa**   qəwpuk   baan   slap]
     news   COMP   father   PST   die)
     'the news that father had died'

(69) riəŋ   [**dael**   ckae   kham   tidaa]
     story   REL   dog   bite   Tidaa)
     'the story that the dog had bitten Tidaa'

The cross-linguistically intermediate status of nominal complements can be explained in terms of e-site elaboration. The head noun and its complement each elaborates a not very salient e-site of the other's semantic structure. Nouns such as 'news', 'story', and 'fact' are nonrelational (§2.4.2), and hence the content of the news, etc.—the e-site of the head noun that is elaborated by the nominal complement—is out of profile. Conversely, the fact of an event occurring, or its constituting news, etc.—the e-site of the nominal complement that is elaborated by the head noun—is also of low salience. Hence, nominal complements can be conventionally construed as either the head noun elaborating an e-site of the subordinate clause (i.e. a relative clause), or as the subordinate clause elaborating an e-site of the head noun (i.e. a complement).

Relative clauses and complements share many structural properties in many languages, and this is due to the fact that they are both elaborations of (relatively) salient e-sites of the situation denoted by the main clause.

9.3.2. *From figure–ground to relative clause*

Relative clauses are figure–ground constructions, as was suggested in §9.2.2. In discussing Old English *þe* constructions, which have both adverbial and relative interpretations (§9.1.2), Wiegand (1987) argues for a semantic analysis based on an analysis originally developed by Larson (1983). Larson analyzes restrictive modification, such as that found with relative clauses, as 'evaluation in a situation'. The relative clause represents an ancillary situation that 'contains information that will help understand some aspect of what I am talking about in the main clause' (Wiegand 1987: 194). The information may involve a shared individual, in which case we get the relative clause interpretation. But it could involve the sharing of other aspects of the situation, including the time reference; hence the simultaneous temporal adverbial interpretation.

Larson's analysis of restrictive modification makes it resemble the figure–ground relation more closely: the modifier is the ground element, providing essential information 'supporting' the figure. The argument for the backgrounding character of attributive (relative) clauses has been made more generally. Reinhart's Gestalt analysis of foregrounding/backgrounding includes relative clauses as indicators of ground (background) events along with adverbial clauses, in keeping with previous research on the discourse function of relative clauses (see §9.2.2).

Relative clauses, like most if not all serial verb constructions, have a shared-argument requirement with the main clause. This is in fact what distinguishes them from adverbial clauses, particularly in the case of the Australian and Old English types described above. However, neither adverbial sentences nor relative clause sentences require the same tense–mood–aspect for both clauses. In fact, as Reinhart and others have argued, aspectual differences between the events in the main clause and in the adverbial or relative clause are responsible for the figure–ground construal of the complex sentences (see §9.2.2). This fact is strong evidence for relative clauses as figure–ground constructions.

There is evidence that at least some relative clauses are historically derived from adverbial clauses. In §9.1.2 I noted that adjoined relative clauses, which are common in Australian languages, are ambiguous between an adverbial interpretation and a relative clause interpretation. Adjoined relative clauses are not as closely integrated with their main clauses as the embedded relative clause type is: as their name indicates, they are adjoined to, not embedded in, the main clause. Adjoined relative clauses in Australian languages may either precede or follow the main clause (Hale 1976: 78). In fact, it is probably better to describe them as adverbial clauses extended to an attributive (relative) clause function, rather than as relative clauses at all.

In at least one Australian aboriginal language, Kunjen, it appears that Adjoined Relative Clauses can also be embedded, that is, interrupt elements of the main clause (Sommer 1972: 58, 57, 56; Sommer's syntactic analysis):[6]

(70) [alk   anen   iyan   ambul] ogŋg alk   alaw agŋganamban al
     spear COMP   make:RL.PRS 1PL.IN first spear rod   look.for   go:RL.PRS
     'When we make a spear, first we go and look for a rod.'

(71) ididay   ay iŋun akaɲar aden [anen elkeŋan   il   olon   Cairns -am]
     wait:RL.PRS I   him   YBr   my   COMP   return:IRR.FUT   he   hither Cairns -from
     'I am waiting for my younger brother, who is (I attest) coming back here from Cairns.'

(72) iṉ   pigipig [fence aden anen ubmar]   egŋ   aden adndelaɣ
     meat   pig   fence   my   COMP break.down:RL.PST   food   my   completely
     id'ar
     eat:RL.PST
     'The pig that I attest broke down my fence, ate up all my vegetables.'

Example (70) illustrates a clearly adverbial use of the Kunjen construction. Example (71) illustrates a relative clause use that is adjoined, or at least allows for an adjoined analysis, although it is contiguous with the phrase that would be its Head Noun if it were embedded. Example (72), however, is analyzed as an embedded Relative Clause: the Relative Clause is contiguous with its Head and interrupts the elements of the Main Clause. The Papuan and Kunjen examples suggest that the historical development of at least some relative clauses proceeds from an adjoined form, which shares adverbial functions with adverbial clauses, to an embedded one.

Correlative relative clauses might appear to be candidates for complex figure constructions because the clauses are syntactically parallel. However, as noted in §9.1.2, Comrie argues that 'it is preferable to treat them ... as instances of adjoined relative clauses' (Comrie 1989: 146; see §9.1.2). Correlative relative clauses, like adjoined relative clauses, can grammaticalize into embedded relative clauses. They appear to have done so in Avestan (Haider and Zwanziger 1984: 141, 146; see Aristar 1991: 20):

(73) [yō yaom kāraiieiti] hō ašəm kāraiieiti
     'Who tills corn, this one tills truth' (V.3.31)

---

[6] Hale reports another example from Kaititj (Hale 1976: 100), but in fact Kaititj has distinct Adjoined and Embedded Relative Clauses (David Wilkins, pers. comm.).

(74) buuaṯ dama aṣ̌auua yaoždāθrəm [yå̄ həṇti spəṇtahe mainiiə̄uš]
'there happens purification of the righteous beings, which adhere to the holy spirit' (Yt 6.2)
(75) haomō aēibiš [yōi auruuantō hita taxš̌əṇti arənāum] zāuuarə aojā̊sca baxš̌aiti
'Haoma offers to those, who hurry harnessed to their destination (?), power and strength' (Y 9.22)

Example (73) is a Correlative Relative Clause preceding the Main Clause, while in (74) the Correlative Relative Clause follows it, and is contiguous with its putative Head Noun. In (75), the Relative Clause is contiguous with its Head Noun and interrupts the Main Clause, demonstrating that it can be embedded.

There is a process that appears to be the converse: relative clauses becoming adverbial clauses. In many cases, nouns meaning 'place', 'time', etc. plus their relative clause complement grammaticalize into adverbial clauses (Kortmann 1997: 65), as in Irish *nuair* 'when', 'while' from *an uair* 'the hour' (ibid.) The same process is occurring with English *the moment that*:

(76) a. **When** she arrived, it began to rain.
b. **The moment that** she arrived, it began to rain.

This process is not exactly the case of a relative clause becoming an adverbial clause. Instead, a noun denoting the ground circumstances of place, time, etc. (relative to the main clause event figure) grammaticalizes into an adverbial subordinator with its own backgrounded event. The reason that this structure involves a relative clause is because adverbial clauses do elaborate less salient e-sites of the main clause, namely the circumstantial roles of place, time, and manner, and constructions such as (76b) encode the adverbial relation as such. Nevertheless, the conceptual compatibility of the ground function of relative clause and adverbial clause probably facilitates this grammaticalization process.

We now turn to the other complex sentence type that involves e-site elaboration, complements.

9.3.3. From purpose clause to infinitival complement

Complements are somewhat anomalous from the perspective of the Gestalt analysis of other complex sentence types. Complements are not complex figures, at least in the early stages of their grammaticalization: the profiled asserted situation is that of the main clause. But nor are complements figure–ground configurations: the complement does not function as a reference point for the situation expressed in the main clause. It should not be surprising to learn that complement constructions arise from either typically complex figure constructions—serial verbs—or figure–ground constructions—purpose clauses. However, purpose clauses are not a typical example of figure–ground construal, and the final stage of the grammaticalization of complements can be the fusion of the complement to a highly generalized main verb, indicating causation, mood, or aspect.

Haspelmath (1989) argues that the commonest source of infinitival complement structures are purpose clauses (e.g. Old Irish *do*, Persian *be-*, Maori *ki*, Bidjandjadjara *-ku*; Haspelmath 1989: 293–4). Purpose clauses (or final constructions, as they are also called) are also semantically closely related to consecutive chains, the prototypical coordinate structures: 'semantically speaking, final constructions are cognate to C-chains in that both construction types imply a successive ordering between events, and also an intimate relationship between the events in that succession' (Stassen 1985: 72).

Stassen further notes that a typical consecutive chain such as *John stood up and closed the window* pragmatically implicates that John's purpose for performing the first event is to perform the second event (ibid.). Conversely, a final (purpose) construction in the past tense such as *Tony went home for the weekend to see his girlfriend*, without any qualification, implicates that the second event actually did occur. Although there is no construction in English that semantically entails both the actuality and the purposiveness of the second of two consecutive events, the constructions that entail one property implicate the other.

In other languages, such as in the Serial Verb Construction in Mandarin Chinese, both readings are possible, and presumably can coincide (Stassen 1985: 73):

(77) [ta hui 'jiā] [kān qīnqi]
     he return home see parents
     'He returned home and saw his parents/to see his parents.'

Purpose clauses and complements differ from prototypical complex figure constructions in that they do not necessarily obey tense iconicity and only the main clause situation is profiled. In addition the etymological source of purpose clause markers is often a case marker (usually allative or dative), which further implies a figure–ground construal.

However, purpose clauses are semantically unlike other adverbial clauses. Other adverbial clauses have independent specification of tense–aspect–mood, and do not have to share participants with the main clause. But the main clause predetermines the tense–mood of the purpose clause (irrealis future), and the outcome of the purpose clause situation is typically dependent on the agent of the main clause situation, that is, is controlled at least in part by the agent of the main clause situation (Cristofaro 1998: 153). Cristofaro takes these facts as representing a high degree of semantic integration (see §9.4) in purpose clauses which is absent in other adverbial clause types (ibid.).

These facts imply that purpose clauses are not really figure–ground structures. Instead, purpose clauses possess a degree of semantic integration that is typical of the complements they grammaticalize into.

9.3.4. From serial verb to complement

One grammaticalization path that appears to lead from complex figure constructions to complement constructions proceeds through serial verb constructions.

The intermediate structure between syndetic coordination (with a conjunction) and serial verb constructions is represented by types of asyndetic coordination such as the Lango paratactic construction illustrated in §9.1.2.

A clear link between syndetic and asyndetic coordination exists in a language in which the conjunction is optional. Schiller (1990: 38) defines a category of coordinate serial verb constructions that illustrates this type. Syntactically, coordinate serial verb constructions lack a conjunction, but in some languages a conjunction can be optionally inserted, as in Mooré (ibid.: 38):

(78) a ịku sụugā n   wāg nemdā
     he took knife CONJ cut meat
     'He cut the meat with a knife.'

Once the conjunction is lost completely, serial verb constructions are found, with the two verbs syntactically integrated into a single clause to varying degrees.

In many languages, a 'say' verb evolves into a complementizer via a serial verb construction. Lord (1976) illustrates this grammaticalization path for a number of languages; the following examples are from Ewe (ibid.: 179, 182):

(79) me- **be**   me- wɔ   -e
     I-   **say** I-   do   -it
     'I said "I did it"/I said that I did it.'
(80) fia   gbé   **bé**   wómagàvá   o
     chief refuse **say** they.PROH.come NEG
     'The chief forbade that they should come.'

Lord (1993: 151–76) includes a detailed analysis of the evolution of the Twi verb *sɛ:* 'resemble, be like, be fitting, etc.' from a verb to a complementizer, an introducer of clauses of purpose and result, and conditional clauses. The Twi *sɛ:* conditional construction must be tense-iconic (ibid.: 164), like other complex–figure constructions. Lord notes that *sɛ:* is also found with adverbial clauses of reason, but only in combination with the verb *e-fi* 'IMPR-begin from', which introduces a figure–ground conceptualization into the interclausal relation. Lord's examples demonstrate that this latter construction is not tense-iconic, as one would expect (ibid.: 169–72).

Serial verb constructions display a number of constraints which require certain semantic traits to be shared between the two verbal events. Schiller (1990: 33–6) convincingly demonstrates that the criterion of shared subjects is not a necessary condition of serial verb constructions, and restricts himself to a same tense/aspect constraint (ibid.: 47). The existence of shared ARGUMENTS appears to be a necessary though not sufficient condition for serial constructions, however. For instance, Schiller cites a Paamese example (ibid.: 34) in which the subject of the second verb is the action described by the first verb; the second verb denotes a property of the action of the first verb. The same construction is found in Mandarin (Li and Thompson 1981: 604):

(81) [māma   chuān   duǎn   qúnzi]   [bu   hǎo-   -kàn]
     mother wear   short   skirt   not   good-   -look
     'Mother doesn't look good in short skirts.'

In (81), the "shared argument" is the whole first clause.

The Medial Verb constructions in the Papuan languages are also more closely integrated semantically than independently coordinated constructions in other languages are: the two clauses must agree in tense, mood, and illocutionary force (Foley 1986: 194). However, there need not be shared arguments, and in that respect they are more like coordinate structures than serial verb constructions. Nevertheless, it is interesting to note that the Papuan languages that lack medial verbs also lack serial verbs (Foley 1986: 197); as Foley writes, this is 'further evidence that these two grammatical constructions, although distinct, are related' (ibid.).

Finally, serial verb constructions tend to be tense-iconic if the events are in temporal sequence, no matter what the basic word order of verb and subordinate clause is in the language (Croft 1991: 234–6; Durie 1997: 330–9). For example, even though Kalam is an SOV language, the events reported in a Serial Verb sequence are in their iconic order (Pawley 1987: 329):

(82) b   tw   dy   mon   tb   lak-p
     man   axe   having.taken   wood   cut   he.split
     'The man split the wood with an axe.'

In this respect, serial verb constructions retain some traces of the complex–figure structure of coordinate constructions, despite their high degree of syntactic integration.

9.4. The Syntactic Space of Complex Sentences: the Deranking Hierarchy

The domain of complex sentences is a continuum between coordination and subordination largely because of the constructions that cross any of the traditional divisions (see Figure 9.1). In §§9.2–9.3, I have argued that this aspect of the coordination–subordination continuum reflects connections in the conceptual space underlying complex sentence types (Figure 9.2). But the domain of complex sentences also represents a continuum in syntactic space, in at least three dimensions: deranking, embedding, and clause fusion. Only the first dimension has been explored in detail. For this reason, most of this section will concern deranking, with only speculative comments about embedding and clause fusion.

Deranking is defined relative to the normal expression of simple sentences. The properties defining deranking in §9.1.1 are repeated in (83):

(83) a. Elimination of tense, mood, and aspect markings, or use of special forms distinct from those used on simple main clause verbs

b. Elimination of agreement markings, or use of special forms
c. Overt morpheme attached to verb form

The criteria in (83) are criteria of typological markedness: the phenomena in (83a–b) are symptoms of the limited behavioral potential of subordinate forms, and (83c) is the manifestation of the overt structural coding of subordinate forms. These criteria indicate that deranked clauses are typologically marked and balanced clauses are typologically unmarked.

In addition to these properties of the verb form, Croft (1991) also compares the coding of the S/A and P arguments in deranking. S/A and P arguments may be eliminated or coded differently from S/A and P arguments in main clauses, specifically with the possessive or oblique forms characteristic of the phrasal modifiers of nouns.

The dimensions described in (83a–c) and in the last paragraph constitute a multidimensional syntactic space. However, implicational relations hold between some of the properties, which reduces the deranking syntactic space to basically a single dimension, the Deverbalization Hierarchy (Croft 1991: 83):

(84) *Deverbalization Hierarchy*:
tense–mood–aspect   <   S/A possessor/   <   P possessor/
elimination/special form   oblique coding   oblique coding

The Deverbalization Hierarchy states that if a language uses possessor or oblique coding for Ps, then it will use possessor/oblique coding for S/As; and if it uses possessor/oblique coding for S/As, then it will eliminate at least some tense–mood–aspect inflections, or use special forms for them. For example, the English *For-to* Complement in (85) does not inflect for Tense–Mood–Aspect, and uses an Oblique for S/A; and the Russian example in (86) does not inflect, and uses Oblique Case markings for S/A and P (Croft 1991: 84–5):

(85) a. I made it easy **for him** to eat this.
    b. *I made it easy he ate this.
(86) razrušenie   gorod -a   vrag   -om
     destroy:NR   city   -GEN   enemy   -INST
     '(the) destruction of the city by the enemy'

The Deverbalization Hierarchy incorporates in part another manifestation of the accusative participant role hierarchy, following research by Comrie on action word (verb) nominalizations (Comrie 1976b). Comrie defines action nominalizations as verb forms that may take case endings to indicate their role in the main clause, and he observed the ranking S/A < P in the expression of participants. Koptjevskaja-Tamm (1993) uses the same definition of action nominals as Comrie and, in a sample of seventy languages, found evidence for the following implicational hierarchy (Koptjevskaja-Tamm 1993: 257):

(87) word order,
A agreement < S agreement < S case < A case < P agreement < P case

The coding properties on the left are the most NP-like, and those on the right the most main-clause-like.

The hierarchy in (87) can be analyzed into the two hierarchies in (88a–b) (Croft 1995d: 82):

(88) a. S possessor/oblique ?< A < P (3 exceptions in 70-language sample)
    b. word order < agreement < case marking

The hierarchy in (88a) is similar to the accusative participant role hierarchy for typological markedness (§4.2.2). The hierarchy in (88b) is probably related to the Subject Construction Hierarchy (§4.3.2). The Subject Construction Hierarchy does not include word order, but there is some evidence that word order is higher on the Subject Construction Hierarchy than agreement or case marking: for example, experiencers are found in preverbal position in Germanic before triggering nominative agreement and acquiring nominative case marking (see examples in §4.3.3). The presence of all positions on the hierarchy with verb forms that accept case marking for their role in the main clause demonstrates that this latter property does not itself fall in any position on the hierarchy.

Cristofaro (1998) is the broadest study of subordinate clauses so far conducted, examining over 400 subordinate forms for complements, adverbial clauses and relative clauses in eighty languages. Cristofaro tested the Deverbalization Hierarchy on her sample. She found evidence in favor of the initial ranking of tense–mood–aspect elimination (Cristofaro 1998: 226, 233; she did not test the participant role hierarchy):

(89) tense–mood–aspect   <   elimination of agreement
       elimination   (375 confirming, 5 disconfirming)
                         ?<   possessor-oblique encoding of arguments
                               (49 confirming, 10 disconfirming)

Cristofaro also investigated the relative ranking, if any, of tense, mood, and aspect elimination (Cristofaro found that the use of special forms for inflection in deranked clauses is quite rare). There is no strong evidence for a hierarchy of tense, mood, and aspect forms. The only generalizations holding for Cristofaro's sample are that aspect inflections are never the only inflections eliminated in deranked forms, and tense inflections are never the only inflections remaining.

The Deranking Hierarchy, a revised form of the Deverbalization Hierarchy based on the studies surveyed in this section, is presented in (90) (?< indicates at best weakly supported implicational relations):

(90) *The Deranking Hierarchy*
Clause-like (Balanced) ⟵⟶ NP-like(Deranked)

tense ??< mood ?< aspect < $\begin{cases} S\ ?< A < P \\ \text{word order} < \text{agreement} < \text{case marking} \\ \text{case marking on dependent "verb"} \end{cases}$

The Deranking Hierarchy defines the dimension of syntactic space on which the typological universals in this section are based.

Cristofaro investigates the relationship between deranking and the type of semantic relations holding between main clauses and complements, adverbial clauses and relative clauses, building on earlier work by Givón (1980b) and Lehmann (1984, 1986). Cristofaro defines a subordinate clause as a clause that represents a nonassertional proposition (Cristofaro 1998: 38–45; see §9.1.2). Cristofaro investigates each of the three subordinate clause types separately, and then in combination.

Cristofaro identifies a series of implicational hierarchies for the expression of the different types of subordinate events in complex sentences. Two qualifications are necessary before presenting Cristofaro's results. Cristofaro did not test for different degrees of deranking in a single language. Instead, she contrasts any degree of deranking with absence of deranking (i.e. balancing; Stassen 1985: 76). Cristofaro does test each individual criterion of deranking, and finds that each criterion conforms to the hierarchy established by the overall comparison.

Also, Cristofaro's implicational universals are of the existential type (see Cristofaro 1998: 18–20). Universals of the form Y ⊃ X must be quantified if X or Y contain a set of types, for instance the set of complement-taking perception verbs. An existential universal supporting a hierarchical ranking X < Y is to be interpreted as follows: if a language deranks at least one subordinate clause of type Y, then it deranks at least one subordinate clause of type X, that is ∃Y:Derank(Y) ⊃ ∃X:Derank(X). This type of universal is weaker than one in which deranking of any subordinate clauses of type Y implies deranking of all subordinate clauses of type X, that is ∃Y:Derank(Y) ⊃ ∀X:Derank(X).

Cristofaro classifies the semantic relation between a complement clause and its main clause in terms of the semantic class of the main clause verb or predicate. Cristofaro distinguishes the following semantic classes for complements:

(91) a. *Modal*: I **can** play the piano.
 b. *Phasal*: He **began** to dance.
 c. *Manipulative*: She **made** him serve the food.
 d. *Desiderative*: I **want** to go home.
 e. *Perception*: I **saw** her leave the building.
 f. *Knowledge*: I **know** that they finished the job.
 g. *Propositional attitude*: I **believe** that they finished the job.
 h. *Utterance*: She **said** that she would drop by after lunch.

Cristofaro's results for complements largely confirms Givón's Binding Hierarchy (Givón 1980b: 369); Cristofaro included perception verbs and modals, but did not find a relative ranking for manipulative and desiderative complement-taking predicates. Cristofaro's hierarchy is given in (92) (Cristofaro 1998: 109–10; the most deranked type is to the left on the hierarchy):

(92) *Complement Deranking ('Binding') Hierarchy*

modal, phasal < manipulative, desiderative < perception < knowledge, propositional attitude < utterance

Cristofaro classifies the semantic relation between an adverbial clause and its main clause in terms of the semantic relation between the states of affairs denoted by the two clauses. The categories distinguished by Cristofaro are given in (93):

(93) a. *Purpose*: She ran every morning **in order to** keep fit.
b. *Before*: I finished the book **before** going back to Germany.
c. *After*: I bought the groceries **after** picking up my bike from the shop.
d. *When*: **When** the guests came, we served them hors d'œuvres.
e. *Reason*: I left **because** it became unbearable for me there.
f. *Reality condition*: **If** the bread is left out, it will get moldy.

Cristofaro discovered the hierarchy for the semantic relations of adverbial clauses given in (94) (Cristofaro 1998: 151)):

(94) *Adverbial Deranking Hierarchy*
purpose < before < after, when < reason, reality condition

The semantic relations in the Adverbial Deranking Hierarchy are of course the same semantic relations found in coordinate constructions: temporal simultaneity and sequence, cause (reason), conditional (see §9.2.4), and arguably purpose (see §9.4.5). Cristofaro does not investigate the relationship between coordination and deranking). Stassen, however, reports that deranking of consecutive temporal clause chains is found if and only if deranking of simultaneous temporal clause chains is also found (Stassen 1985: 99). This may correspond to the joint ranking of 'after' (consecutive) and 'when' (simultaneous) adverbial clauses on the Adverbial Deranking Hierarchy.

The classification of semantic relations in relative clauses operates on a quite different principle. Cristofaro, like Lehmann before her (Lehmann 1984, 1986), classifies relative clauses in terms of the participant role of the relativized (head) noun phrase in the relative clause:

(95) a. *Subject (S/A)*: the girl$_i$ [that $\emptyset_i$ left early]; the girl$_i$ [that $\emptyset_i$ kissed me]
b. *Object (P/T)*: the book$_i$ [that I bought $\emptyset_i$]; the book$_i$ [that you sent $\emptyset_i$ to me]
c. *Indirect Object (G)*: the girl$_i$ [that he sent the card to $\emptyset_i$]
d. *Oblique*: the pen$_i$ [that I wrote the letter with $\emptyset_i$]

Cristofaro's results also confirms Lehmann's, which conform to the accusative and direct object participant role hierarchies (Cristofaro 1998: 184–5; see also §§4.2.2–4.2.3):

(96) *Relative Clause Deranking Hierarchy*
   subject (S/A) < object (P/T) < indirect object (G) < oblique

Cristofaro compared all three subordinate clause types, and found the following partial implicational hierarchy (Cristofaro 1998: 202):

(97) *Subordinate Clause Deranking Hierarchy*

modal, manipulative,
phasal < purpose < desiderative < perception < before <
              reason,   knowledge,

< { after, when < reality condition < prop. attitude < utterance
    S/A rel. < P/T rel. < G rel. < oblique rel.

In other words, complement and adverbial relations form a single implicational hierarchy, while relative clause relations form a separate hierarchy, which is no more deranked than temporal adverbial relations.

The Deranking Hierarchy defines a one-dimensional syntactic space for the syntax of subordinate clauses. The Subordinate Clause Deranking Hierarchy links the one dimension of the syntactic space with the two-dimensional conceptual space for complex sentences sketched in Figure 9.2. As we did for voice in §8.5.2, we may lay out the syntactic space of deranking (in 90) onto the conceptual space of complex sentence types in Figure 9.2. One can capture the relationship between the one-dimensional syntactic space of deranking and the two-dimensional conceptual space of complex sentences by using a polar coordinate mapping, as in Figure 9.7 on p. 360 (the position of the relative clause roles in the figure is only approximate).

A main clause, as in a simple sentence or a coordinate (complex figure) construction is balanced, and various types of subordinate clauses are deranked relative to it. Figure 9.7 represents deranking as radiating outward from the typologically unmarked main clause type, and each circle represents another step on the Subordinate Clause Deranking Hierarchy.

Cristofaro argues that a number of semantic properties determine the hierarchies in (87)–(89) (Cristofaro 1998: 210, and personal communication; compare Givón 1980b: 335). The first three steps in the hierarchy (up to perception complements) are ranked in terms of degree of semantic integration. Cristofaro defines semantic integration as the degree of interconnectedness of the two situations. The degree of interconnectedness is influenced by the number and role of shared participants in the situations denoted by the two clauses, and by the degree of control over the realization of the subordinate clause situation on the part of a participant in the main clause situation. For modals and phasals, participants are identical. Manipulative, desiderative, and perception complements add a participant; for manipulatives and purpose clauses, the participant has some degree of control over the realization of the subordinate clause situation.

For complex sentence situation types lower in the hierarchy, semantic integra-

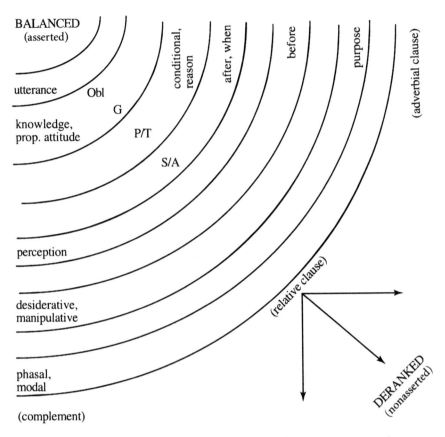

Figure 9.7. Syntactic-conceptual space mapping for complex sentence constructions

tion is absent. The semantic factor that appears to determine their ranking is predetermination of the time reference and/or the modal status of the subordinate clause situation. Temporal adverbials (before, after, when) predetermine the time reference of the subordinate clause situation. In reason, reality conditional, knowledge, and propositional attitude constructions, but not utterance complements, the modal status of the subordinate clause state of affairs is predetermined. Semantic integration is absent in relative clauses also. The deranking of relative clauses is instead sensitive to the centrality of the referent of the head noun in the relative clause event, as defined by the participant role hierarchy in (96).

In conclusion, I will make some speculative remarks about two other syntactic properties associated with subordinate clauses that are not represented in Figure 9.7, embedding and clause fusion. It appears that both embedding and clause fusion conform to the same dimension as deranking. Embedding is definable cross-linguistically in terms of (non)separability of the main clause by the subordinate clause (see §5.3.2). If this is true, then embedding would be iconically motivated by degree of semantic integration.

Clause fusion also occurs with all types of subordinate clauses. It is common for relative clauses to become grammaticalized as simple attributive constructions, particularly with property words (see §2.4.2). Also, relative clauses in cleft constructions and questions lose their biclausal status (Harris and Campbell 1995, chs 7 and 10). Regarding complements, it is also common for manipulatives, modals, and phasals to grammaticalize into auxiliaries and even clitics or verbal affixes (Lehmann 1982b/1995: 27–8; Harris and Campbell 1995: 173–82; Cristofaro 1998). Finally, adverbial clauses may develop into adverbs or adposition. For example the participial form *Regarding* in the previous sentence but one appears to be grammaticalizing into a topic marking preposition; and *notwithstanding* now functions as a postposition. These observations also suggest that clause fusion is iconically motivated by degree of semantic integration.

9.5. Conclusion

The typology of complex sentences is extremely complex. However, the complexity and the continua found in the typology of complex sentences can be organized into a conceptual space defined by a Gestalt distinction between complex figure and figure–ground constructions, and by the property of e-site elaboration. The syntactic continuum of deranking is ordered by the Deranking Hierarchy, which in turn conforms to the universals of typological markedness. The Deranking Hierarchy allows us to reduce the syntactic space to one dimension, which can then be mapped onto the conceptual space in terms of the conceptual dimension of semantic integration. Moreover, it appears that embedding and clause fusion follows the same conceptual dimension, which is not surprising because semantic integration iconically motivates embedding and clause fusion.

The analyses in this chapter have necessarily been drawn with a broad brush. However, the research reported here suggests that we may systematically and universally link the structural diversity of complex sentences to the structured conceptual space that complex sentences encode.

10

Syntactic Theory and the Theory of Language

In this book, I have presented the case for Radical Construction Grammar. I have argued that virtually all aspects of syntactic structure are language-specific, indeed, construction-specific. I believe that the structural diversity of the world's languages calls for nothing less than a Radical Construction Grammar approach. Likewise, I have argued that the only tenable syntactic structure of constructions is found in the meronomic relations of syntactic elements to the construction as a whole. Again, the structural diversity of the world's languages requires us to replace syntactic relations with syntactic roles and symbolic relations linking form and meaning.

By this, I mean the structural diversity of *all* languages. Not just little-known endangered languages from the jungle and the desert, but also English, the language discussed in most syntactic theorizing. All languages have a wide array of constructions whose distribution patterns do not line up, and which have complex mappings of form to meaning. A model of syntax with atomic primitive elements and with various kinds of syntactic relations will not succeed in capturing the empirical facts of grammar without adding dozens of features and multiple levels of syntactic structure, and even so rarely accounts for more than the few languages it was designed to account for. A fresh start is needed.

Dealing with grammatical diversity requires rebuilding syntactic theory almost from scratch. Fortunately, the development of construction grammar in the last decade and a half has pointed the way to a model of syntactic representation amenable to the cross-linguistic facts. At least as important, a substantial and growing body of research in linguistic typology over the past four decades, some of which is reported in these pages, has also contributed to the rebuilding of grammatical theory.

Radical Construction Grammar is disarmingly simple—it is a genuinely minimalist model of syntactic representation. It can be summarized in five points:

1 *Primitive grammatical units in the model.* The only type of primitive grammatical units are CONSTRUCTIONS—pairings of form and meaning which may be atomic or complex, schematic or substantive (§1.3.1, Table 1.4).

   In fact, Radical Construction Grammar is more restrictive than this. Complex constructions, made up of multiple elements, may have either schematic or substantive elements, or a combination of the two. But atomic "constructions" can only be substantive, that is, they can only be specific WORDS. There are no atomic schematic elements—syntactic categories. Syntactic categories are defined within (complex) constructions, that is, as schematic elements playing a role in some construction.

There is no universal finite inventory of syntactic construction types; constructions are language-specific (Chapters 8–9). Constructions can range freely over regions of SYNTACTIC SPACE, the space of possible syntactic types.

2 *Primitive syntactic relations in the model.* The only type of syntactic relations within a construction are the MERONOMIC (part–whole) relations between the construction on the one hand and the ELEMENTS that fill the ROLES of the construction. Since syntactic roles are defined relative to constructions, there is no universal finite inventory of syntactic role types.

The only type of syntactic relations allowed between constructions are the TAXONOMIC (schema-instance) relations between whole constructions and between an element of one construction and an element of another construction. That is, all relations between constructions are CATEGORIZING relations, and therefore conform to the principles of human categorization. (Semantic structures, on the other hand, are much richer and more complex; see §§3.3, 6.4.3.)

3 *The relation between form and meaning.* A construction joins its form and meaning via SYMBOLIC relations (Figure 1.4 in §1.3.2). Symbolic relations hold between the construction's formal structure as a whole and its meaning as a whole. Symbolic relations also hold between the elements of a construction's formal structure and COMPONENTS of its semantic structure. The possible types of mapping patterns are not restricted (Chapters 5–6), although some mapping patterns (e.g. ICONIC mappings) tend to be found more widely than others.

4 *Generalizations within and across languages.* One type of generalization within languages are categorizing relations, referred to above. A second type of generalization is found across constructions and across languages. These are systematic patterns of variation, such as PROTOTYPES and IMPLICATIONAL HIERARCHIES, that characterize cross-constructional and cross-linguistic diversity and constrain the distribution and even the form of constructions used for particular functions (Chapters 2, 4, 8, 9). That is, valid cross-linguistic generalizations are generalizations about how function is ENCODED in linguistic form. Moreover, the variation within and across languages is governed by the same generalizations.

5 *Explanations of linguistic generalizations.* The patterns described above are accounted for by the hypothesis of a largely universal CONCEPTUAL SPACE (Chapters 2–3) which represents structures in the human mind. Distribution patterns are overlapping SEMANTIC MAPS on conceptual space. Language universals are accounted for by constraints on the TOPOGRAPHY of conceptual space which predict what sort of patterns can be found within and across languages, and what sorts of diachronic grammatical changes may occur.

Nothing more is needed for the formal representation of grammatical structures. But everything more is needed to understand and explain the full range of diversity of grammatical constructions in English and all languages. This volume, large as it is, is only the beginning of this exploration, critically examining the fundamental concepts in syntactic theory: parts of speech and other syntactic categories; "grammatical relations" (syntactic roles); syntactic relations and how they are represented; heads, arguments, and adjuncts; grammatical voice; and complex sentence structures. Contemporary linguistics, even typological research, is only at the stage of the early global explorers in mapping out conceptual space and the syntactic space of constructions that encode it.

Both construction grammar and typological theory have emphasized the central role of the relationship between form and function in grammatical knowledge. This relationship is the linguistic sign. A fundamental principle in linguistics for a century is that the linguistic sign is arbitrary (Saussure 1916/1966: 67–8). The validity of this principle is not in doubt. But the arbitrariness of the linguistic sign is superimposed on a structure that is largely universal, that is, the conceptual space that linguistic signs are mapped onto. The conceptual space is the geography of the human mind, which can be read in the facts of the world's languages in a way that the most advanced brain scanning techniques cannot ever offer us. This is one of the great joys of studying languages, which is—or should be—doing linguistics.

The universality of conceptual space does not deny the arbitrariness of the linguistic sign, or the role that language-specific (and construction-specific) categories play in human cognition (§3.4). Again, only the study of the diversity of human languages can allow us to understand the interplay of the universal and the particular in cognition and communication.

And COMMUNICATION is the operative word here, despite the emphasis on mental representation in this book. Radical Construction Grammar, like any other syntactic theory, is just a syntactic theory. A syntactic theory is a theory of the representation of grammatical knowledge in the mind. This has been a central concern of linguistics for the past century. But a theory of syntax is not a theory of language. A theory of syntax without a theory of language is just a notational system, or at best a model of what goes on inside a speaker's head. Radical Construction Grammar is no exception to this fact.

Explaining Language Change: An Evolutionary Approach (Croft 2000a) presents a theory of language; Radical Construction Grammar can be seen as part of that larger enterprise. Language is a fundamentally dynamic phenomenon and a fundamentally interactional phenomenon. Language is the totality of the events of language use, every utterance that has or ever will be spoken to someone, and every shared experience among human beings that each utterance creates. The theory of the evolution of utterances is a theory of language in all of its facets.

A scientific approach to language that captures the totality of language can be developed using a generalized model of evolution (Hull 1988). The generalized model is based on two fundamental insights of evolutionary theory in biology: the POPULATION definition of biological categories and the theory of SELECTION. However, the generalized model is *not* simply a biological theory. The generalized model is a theory of evolving systems, in any empirical domain, whether it is organisms or languages. The generalized model spans all disciplines that study evolving systems.

A biological species is not defined by a set of necessary and sufficient features; it cannot be, because a species evolves, acquiring and losing "essential" features. A species is defined as a POPULATION of individual organisms that are reproductively isolated from other organisms (that is, they do not interbreed with other organisms). This interactional property defines a species as a population. More generally, evolving populations must be defined by some interactional property, not inherent properties that can appear and disappear in the course of evolution.

The interbreeding of members of a biological species allows the population to exist across time and space until the population either splits or goes extinct. It also defines another population, the population of GENOMES—the full complement of genes of any particular individual—of the species. That population in turn defines another population, the GENE pool—the population of genes (gene tokens)—of the species. All of these populations are what Hull calls SPATIOTEMPORALLY BOUNDED INDIVIDUALS: they are real, existing, finite, empirical entities.

In Croft 2000a, I argue that the proper definition of speech community is a population of individual speakers who are COMMUNICATIVELY ISOLATED from other speakers. The communicative interaction of speakers defines another population: the population of UTTERANCES produced by the speakers in a speech community. A LANGUAGE is a population of utterances—not possible utterances, but actual utterances, just as the species is a population of actual organisms. Utterances contain tokens of linguistic structures: constructions, words, morphemes, phonemes. These tokens of linguistic structures are LINGUEMES. The language defines the lingueme pool—the population of linguemes in the utterances of the speech community. The lingueme pool is sampled by sociolinguists: sociolinguists study the structure and evolution of the lingueme pool. All of these populations are also spatiotemporally bounded individuals: real, existing, finite, empirical entities.

How do utterances come into being in conversation? Utterances are a means of sharing experience, a journey through a region of the speaker's mind. The means by which this sharing is achieved are the structures of utterances. Whenever an utterance is produced by a speaker, the linguistic structure of the utterance is REPLICATED from prior utterances that the speaker has experienced, which possessed those structures or variants of those structures. That is, the linguistic structure of this utterance involves the replication and recombination of linguemes—words, morphemes, constructions—used in prior utterances, in order to communicate a new experience in a new utterance.

Linguemes are REPLICATORS, like genes, and 'replicators exist in nested systems of increasingly more inclusive units' (Hull 1988: 449; see Croft 2000a: 33–4). This is the structure of the genome, and I have argued that exactly the same structure is found in utterances. In Radical Construction Grammar, grammatical constructions have only meronomic structure: the construction is the more inclusive unit that contains its elements, which are in turn constructions—units including other units until one reaches the level of words and morphemes (see points 1 and 2 above).

Lingueme replication is thus the process of using language. As such, replication is subject to all the vagaries of communication and social context. A speaker replicates linguemes in the way intended by her; the hearer understands those replications based on the context of the discourse situation, and his experience of prior replications of those structures—an experience which may not be the same as the speaker's, and which may involve misunderstandings and negotiations of meaning. But the production of any utterance involves a speaker replicating existing morphosyntactic structures to encode the current experience, and the hearer using his knowledge to map the morphosyntactic structures onto a conceptual structure.

In other words, the production of utterances—communication—centrally involves the mapping of meaning onto form (and vice versa for the hearer): that is, the symbolic relations in a construction. I have argued that symbolic relations, not syntactic relations, are central to the internal structure of constructions. I have also argued that the universals of language are found in patterns of the mapping of meaning onto linguistic form. Constructions and their elements are mapped onto corresponding semantic structures in conceptual space in systematic ways. This is a central tenet of Radical Construction Grammar (see points 4 and 5 above). It is plausible to hypothesize that language universals are found in the most crucial step in communication, where communication has the greatest potential of breaking down.

And communication is not perfect. The mapping of constructions onto conceptual space, and the region of conceptual space onto which they are mapped, must be renewed in each utterance. In the process of communication, reanalysis of the form–function mapping may occur, leading to grammatical INNOVATION (Croft 2000a, chs 4–6). The replication of linguemes may also alter their structure; in particular linguemes may be recombined in an utterance in a novel way. The real locus of innovation in language change is in symbolic relations: the employment of linguemes in an utterance to convey a meaning. The remapping of symbolic relations between form and function is the primary mechanism for innovation or ALTERED REPLICATION in grammatical structures.

Language change, like any evolutionary change, is a two-step process. The two-step process is described by the generalized theory of selection. The generalized theory of selection was developed by Hull to model any process in which change occurs by replication, and involves the evolution of populations. As noted above,

References

ABNEY, Stephen P. (1987). 'The English noun phrase in its sentential aspect', Ph.D. dissertation, MIT.
AIKHENVALD, Alexandra. (2000). *Classifiers: A Typology of Noun Categorization Devices.* Oxford: Oxford University Press.
AISSEN, Judith. (1980). 'Possessor ascension in Tzotzil', *Papers in Mayan Linguistics*, ed. Laura Martin. Columbia, MO: Lucas Publishers, 89–108.
AISSEN, Judith. (1987). *Tzotzil clause structure.* Dordrecht: Kluwer.
AKMAJIAN, Adrian. (1984). 'Sentence types and the form–function fit', *Natural Language and Linguistic Theory* 2: 1–23.
ALTENBERG, Bengt. (1987). *Prosodic Patterns in Spoken English: Studies in the Correlation between Prosody and Grammar for Text-to-speech Conversion.* Lund Studies English, 76. Lund: Lund University Press.
ANDERSON, Lloyd B. (1974). 'Distinct sources of fuzzy data: ways of integrating relatively discrete and gradient aspects of language, and explaining grammar on the basis of semantic fields', *Towards Tomorrow's Linguistics*, ed. Roger W. Shuy and Charles-James N. Bailey. Washington, D.C.: Georgetown University Press, 50–64.
ANDERSON, Lloyd B. (1982). 'The "perfect" as a universal and as a language-particular category', *Tense–Aspect: Between Semantics and Pragmatics*, ed. Paul Hopper. Amsterdam: John Benjamins, 227–64.
ANDERSON, Lloyd B. (1986). 'Evidentials, paths of change, and mental maps: typologically regular asymmetries', *Evidentiality: The Linguistic Encoding of Epistemology*, ed. Wallace Chafe and Johanna Nichols. Norwood: Ablex, 273–312.
ANDERSON, Lloyd B. (1987). 'Adjectival morphology and semantic space', *Papers from the 23rd Annual Regional Meeting of the Chicago Linguistic Society, Part One: The General Session*, ed. Barbara Need, Eric Schiller, and Ann Bosch. Chicago: Chicago Linguistic Society, 1–17.
ANDERSON, Stephen R. (1971). 'On the role of deep structure in semantic interpretation', *Foundations of Language* 7: 387–96.
ANDERSON, Stephen R. (1976). 'On the notion of subject in ergative languages', *Subject and Topic*, ed. Charles Li. New York: Academic Press, 1–24.
ANDERSON, Stephen R. (1992). *A-morphous Morphology.* Cambridge: Cambridge University Press.
ANDREWS, J. Richard. (1975). *Introduction to Classical Nahuatl.* Austin: University of Texas Press.
ANNAMALAI, E. (1970). 'On moving from coordinate structures in Tamil', *Papers from the Sixth Regional Meeting of the Chicago Linguistic Society*, ed. anon. Chicago: Chicago Linguistic Society, 131–46.
ANWARD, Jan, Edith A. MORAVCSIK, and Leon STASSEN. (1997). 'Parts of speech: a challenge for typology', *Language Typology* 1: 167–83.
ARIEL, Mira. (1990). *Accessing Noun Phrase Antecedents.* New York: Routledge.
ARIEL, Mira. (1998). 'Mapping so-called "pragmatic" phenomena according to a

Differential replication—propagation—is governed by the social factors well-known to sociohistorical linguists (for a summary, see Croft 2000a, chs 6–8). That is, the speaker (the interactor) replicates a lingueme variant (a replicator) in part for social reasons, of which the most general is the act of identifying with a particular community that the variant is associated with. These social factors are the causal mechanisms for the process of selection in the realm of language.

This brief outline of the theory of language described in *Explaining Language Change* is intended to demonstrate to the reader that Radical Construction Grammar—a theory of grammatical knowledge—is just one part of a broader theory of language in which language is construed as and treated as an integrated whole. Grammatical knowledge is acquired through the use of language in utterances. Language—the population of utterances—evolves through continued social interaction. That social interaction determines the macroprocesses of language change: variation, propagation, language contact, language divergence, language shift. At the microlevel, constructions arise and evolve in the course of language use, and the locus of innovation is the symbolic relation between form and function, which is also the locus of universals of grammar. Syntax cannot be separated from its context.

References

ABNEY, Stephen P. (1987). 'The English noun phrase in its sentential aspect', Ph.D. dissertation, MIT.
AIKHENVALD, Alexandra. (2000). *Classifiers: A Typology of Noun Categorization Devices.* Oxford: Oxford University Press.
AISSEN, Judith. (1980). 'Possessor ascension in Tzotzil', *Papers in Mayan Linguistics*, ed. Laura Martin. Columbia, MO: Lucas Publishers, 89–108.
AISSEN, Judith. (1987). *Tzotzil clause structurei.* Dordrecht: Kluwer.
AKMAJIAN, Adrian. (1984). 'Sentence types and the form–function fit', *Natural Language and Linguistic Theory* 2: 1–23.
ALTENBERG, Bengt. (1987). *Prosodic Patterns in Spoken English: Studies in the Correlation between Prosody and Grammar for Text-to-speech Conversion.* Lund Studies English, 76. Lund: Lund University Press.
ANDERSON, Lloyd B. (1974). 'Distinct sources of fuzzy data: ways of integrating relatively discrete and gradient aspects of language, and explaining grammar on the basis of semantic fields', *Towards Tomorrow's Linguistics*, ed. Roger W. Shuy and Charles-James N. Bailey. Washington, D.C.: Georgetown University Press, 50–64.
ANDERSON, Lloyd B. (1982). 'The "perfect" as a universal and as a language-particular category', *Tense–Aspect: Between Semantics and Pragmatics*, ed. Paul Hopper. Amsterdam: John Benjamins, 227–64.
ANDERSON, Lloyd B. (1986). 'Evidentials, paths of change, and mental maps: typologically regular asymmetries', *Evidentiality: The Linguistic Encoding of Epistemology*, ed. Wallace Chafe and Johanna Nichols. Norwood: Ablex, 273–312.
ANDERSON, Lloyd B. (1987). 'Adjectival morphology and semantic space', *Papers from the 23rd Annual Regional Meeting of the Chicago Linguistic Society, Part One: The General Session*, ed. Barbara Need, Eric Schiller, and Ann Bosch. Chicago: Chicago Linguistic Society, 1–17.
ANDERSON, Stephen R. (1971). 'On the role of deep structure in semantic interpretation', *Foundations of Language* 7: 387–96.
ANDERSON, Stephen R. (1976). 'On the notion of subject in ergative languages', *Subject and Topic*, ed. Charles Li. New York: Academic Press, 1–24.
ANDERSON, Stephen R. (1992). *A-morphous Morphology.* Cambridge: Cambridge University Press.
ANDREWS, J. Richard. (1975). *Introduction to Classical Nahuatl.* Austin: University of Texas Press.
ANNAMALAI, E. (1970). 'On moving from coordinate structures in Tamil', *Papers from the Sixth Regional Meeting of the Chicago Linguistic Society*, ed. anon. Chicago: Chicago Linguistic Society, 131–46.
ANWARD, Jan, Edith A. MORAVCSIK, and Leon STASSEN. (1997). 'Parts of speech: a challenge for typology', *Language Typology* 1: 167–83.
ARIEL, Mira. (1990). *Accessing Noun Phrase Antecedents.* New York: Routledge.
ARIEL, Mira. (1998). 'Mapping so-called "pragmatic" phenomena according to a

"linguistic-extralinguistic" distinction: the case of propositions marked "accessible"', *Functionalism and Formalism in Linguistics, vol. II: Case studies*, ed. Michael Darnell, Edith Moravcsik, Frederick Newmeyer, Michael Noonan and Kathleen Wheatley. Amsterdam: John Benjamins, 11–38.

ARIFF, Syed Zainal Jamaluddin. (2002). 'The Evolution of the Grammatical Meaning and Function of the Prefixes *per-*, *ber-* and *memper-* between the Seventeenth and Twentieth Centuries in Malay'. Ph.D. dissertation submitted to the University of Manchester.

ARISTAR, Anthony Rodrigues. (1991). 'On diachronic sources and synchronic patterns: An investigation into the origin of linguistic universals', *Language* 67: 1–33.

ARISTAR, Anthony Rodrigues. (1997). 'Marking and hierarchy types and the grammaticalization of case-markers', *Studies in Language* 21: 313–68.

ARNDT, P. P. (1931). *Grammatik der Sika-Sprache*. Ende, Flores.

ASHTON, E. O., E. M. K. MULIRA, E. G. M. NDAWULA, and A. N. TUCKER. (1954). *A Luganda Grammar*. London: Longmans, Green and Company.

BAILLEUL, C. (1977). *Cours pratique de Bambara t.III*. Bobo-Dioulasso, Upper Volta (Burkina Faso): Imprimerie de la Savane.

BARLOW, Michael. (1988). 'A situated theory of agreement', Ph.D. dissertation, Stanford University. (Published by Garland Press, New York.)

BARSALOU, Lawrence R. (1992). *Cognitive Psychology: An Overview for Cognitive Scientists*. Hillsdale, New Jersey: Lawrence Erlbaum Associates.

BARSS, Andrew and LASNIK, Howard. (1986). 'A note on anaphora and double objects', *Linguistic Inquiry* 17: 347–54.

BAUER, Laurie. (1990). 'Be-heading the Word', *Journal of Linguistics* 26: 1–31.

BERLIN, Brent. (1968). *Tzeltal Numeral Classifiers*. The Hague: Mouton.

BIBER, Douglas, JOHANSSON, Stig, LEECH, Geoffrey, CONRAD, Susan, and FINEGAN, Edward. (1999). *Longman Grammar of Spoken and Written English*. Harlow, Essex: Longman.

BIRD, Charles S. (1968). 'Relative clauses in Bambara', *Journal of West African Languages* 5: 35–47.

BIRNER, Betty J. and Gregory WARD. (1998). *Information Status and Noncanonical Word Order in English*. Amsterdam: John Benjamins.

BLOOMFIELD, Leonard. (1933). *Language*. New York: Holt, Rinehart and Winston.

BLOOMFIELD, Leonard. (1962). *The Menomini Language*. New Haven: Yale University Press.

BOLINGER, Dwight. (1967). 'Adjectives in English: attribution and predication', *Lingua* 18: 1–34.

BOLINGER, Dwight. (1977). *Meaning and Form*. London: Longmans.

BOLINGER, Dwight. (1980a). *Syntactic Diffusion and the Definite Article*. Bloomington: Indiana University Linguistics Club.

BOLINGER, Dwight. (1980b). *Language, the Loaded Weapon*. London: Longmans.

BOWERMAN, Melissa. (1996). 'The origins of children's spatial semantic categories: cognitive versus linguistic determinants', *Rethinking Linguistic Relativity*, ed. John J. Gumperz and Stephen C. Levinson. Cambridge: Cambridge University Press, 145–76.

BRAINE, Martin D. S. (1976). *Children's First Word Combinations*. Monographs of the Society for Research in Child Development 41, no. 1.

BRESNAN, Joan (ed.). (1982). *The Mental Representation of Grammatical Relations*. Cambridge, MA: MIT Press.

BRESNAN, Joan and Samuel A. MCHOMBO. (1987). 'Topic, pronoun and agreement in Chichewa', *Language* 63: 741–82.

BRESNAN, Joan and Jane SIMPSON. (1982). 'Control and obviation in Warlpiri', *Proceedings of the First West Coast Conference on Formal Linguistics*, ed. Daniel P. Flickinger et al., 280–91.
BYBEE, Joan L. (1985). *Morphology: An Inquiry into the Relation between Meaning and Form*. Amsterdam: John Benjamins.
BYBEE, Joan L. (1998). 'The emergent lexicon', in M. Catherine Gruber, Derrick Higgins, Kenneth S. Olson, and Tamra Wysocki (eds.). *Papers from the Panels, 34th Annual Meeting of the Chicago Linguistic Society*. Chicago: Chicago Linguistic Society, 421–35.
BYBEE, Joan L. and Östen DAHL. (1989). 'The creation of tense and aspect systems in the languages of the world', *Studies in Language* 13: 51–103.
BYBEE, Joan L., Revere D. PERKINS, and William PAGLIUCA. (1994). *The Evolution of Grammar: Tense, Aspect and Modality in the Languages of the World*. Chicago: University of Chicago Press.
CARLSON, Robert Joel. (1994). *A Grammar of Supyire* (Mouton Grammar Library, 15.) Berlin: Mouton de Gruyter.
CHAFE, Wallace. (1977). 'Caddo texts', *Caddoan Texts* (IJAL Native American Text Series, 2.1), ed. Douglas R. Parks. Chicago: University of Chicago Press, 27–43.
CHAFE, Wallace. (1979). 'The flow of thought and the flow of language', *Discourse and Syntax* (Syntax and Semantics, Vol. 12), ed. Talmy Givón. New York: Academic Press, 159–82.
CHAFE, Wallace (ed.). (1980). *The Pear Stories*. New York: Ablex.
CHAFE, Wallace. (1988). 'Linking intonation units in spoken English', in Haiman and Thompson (1988), 1–27.
CHAFE, Wallace. (1994). *Discourse, Consciousness and Time: The Flow and Displacement of Conscious Experience in Speaking and Writing*. Chicago: University of Chicago Press.
CHOI, Soonja and Melissa BOWERMAN. (1991). 'Learning to express motion events in English and Korean: The influence of language-specific lexicalization patterns', *Cognition* 41: 83–121.
CHOMSKY, Noam. (1957). *Syntactic Structures*. The Hague: Mouton.
CHOMSKY, Noam. (1965). *Aspects of the Theory of Syntax*. Cambridge, MA: MIT Press.
CHOMSKY, Noam. (1970). 'Remarks on nominalization', *Readings in English Transformational Grammar*, ed. Roderick Jacobs and Peter S. Rosenbaum. Boston: Ginn, 184–221.
CHOMSKY, Noam. (1981). *Lectures on Government and Binding*. Dordrecht: Foris.
CHOMSKY, Noam. (1986). *Barriers*. Cambridge, MA: MIT Press.
CHOMSKY, Noam. (1991). 'Some notes on the economy of derivation and representation', *Principles and Parameters in Comparative Grammar*, ed. Robert Freidin. Cambridge, MA: MIT Press, 417–54.
CHOMSKY, Noam. (1995). *The Minimalist Program*. Cambridge, MA: MIT Press.
CHUNG, Sandra. (1976). *Case Marking and Grammatical Relations in Polynesian*. Austin: University of Texas Press.
CHUNG, Sandra. (1977). 'On the gradual nature of syntactic change', *Mechanisms of Syntactic Change*, ed. Charles Li. Austin: University of Texas Press, 3–55.
CHURCHWARD, C. Maxwell. (1953). *Tongan Grammar*. Nuku'alofa, Tonga: Taulua Press.
ČIKOBAVA, Arnold and Ilia CERCVADZE. (1962). *Xundzuri ena*. Tbilisi: Universit'et'i.
CLARK, Eve V. (1978). 'Existentials, locatives and possessives', *Universals of Human Language, Vol. 4: Syntax*, ed. Joseph H. Greenberg, Charles A. Ferguson, and Edith A. Moravcsik, Stanford: Stanford University Press, 85–126.

CLARK, Eve V. (1993). *The Lexicon in Acquisition*. Cambridge: Cambridge University Press.
CLARK, Eve V. and Herbert H. CLARK. (1979). 'When nouns surface as verbs', *Language* 55: 767–811.
CLARK, Herbert H. (1996). *Using Language*. Cambridge: Cambridge University Press.
COLE, Peter. (1982). *Imbabura Quechua*. Lingua Descriptive Studies 5. Amsterdam: North-Holland.
COLE, Peter. (1984). 'Clause reduction in Ancash Quechua', *Syntax and Semantics 16: The Syntax of Native American languages*, ed. Eung-Do Cook and Donna B. Gerdts. New York: Academic Press, 105–21.
COLE, Peter, Wayne HARBERT, Gabriella HERMON, and S. N. SRIDHAR. (1980). 'The acquisition of subjecthood', *Language* 56: 719–43.
COMRIE, Bernard. (1975). 'The antiergative: Finland's answer to Basque', *Papers from the Eleventh Regional Meeting of the Chicago Linguistic Society*, ed. Robin E. Grossman, L. James San, and Timothy J. Vance. Chicago: Chicago Linguistic Society, 112–21.
COMRIE, Bernard. (1976a). *Aspect*. Cambridge: Cambridge University Press.
COMRIE, Bernard. (1976b). 'The syntax of action nominals: a cross-language study', *Lingua* 40: 177–201.
COMRIE, Bernard. (1977). 'In defense of spontaneous demotion: the impersonal passive', *Grammatical Relations*. (Syntax and Semantics, Vol. 8.), ed. Peter Cole and Jerrold M. Sadock. New York: Academic Press, 47–58.
COMRIE, Bernard. (1978). 'Ergativity', *Syntactic Typology*, ed. Winfrid Lehmann. Texas: University of Texas Press, 329–94.
COMRIE, Bernard. (1980a). 'Inverse verb forms in Siberia: evidence from Chukchee, Koryak and Kamchadal', *Folia Linguistica* 1: 61–74.
COMRIE, Bernard. (1980b). 'Agreement, animacy and voice', *Wege zur Universalien Forschung* (Sprachwissenschaftliche Beiträge zum 60. Geburtstag von Hansjakob Seiler), ed. Gunter Brettschneider and Christian Lehmann. Tübingen: Gunter Narr, 229–34.
COMRIE, Bernard. (1982). 'Grammatical relations in Huichol', *Studies in Transitivity*, ed. Paul Hopper and Sandra Thompson. New York: Academic Press, 95–115.
COMRIE, Bernard. (1986). 'Markedness, grammar, people and the world', *Markedness*, ed. Fred R. Eckman, Edith A. Moravcsik, and Jessica R. Wirth. New York: Plenum Press, 85–196.
COMRIE, Bernard. (1989). *Language Universals and Linguistic Typology* (2nd edn). Chicago: University of Chicago Press.
COMRIE, Bernard. (1998). 'Rethinking the typology of relative clauses', *Language Design* 1: 59–86.
COMRIE, Bernard and Kaoru HORIE. (1995). 'Complement clauses versus relative clauses: some Khmer evidence', *Discourse Grammar and Typology: Papers in Honor of John W. M. Verhaar*, ed. Werner Abraham, T. Givón, and Sandra A. Thompson. Amsterdam: John Benjamins, 65–75.
COOREMAN, Ann. (1987). *Transitivity and Discourse Continuity in Chamorro Narratives*. Berlin: Mouton de Gruyter.
COOREMAN, Ann. (1994). 'A functional typology of antipassives', *Voice: Form and Function*, ed. Barbara Fox and Paul Hopper. Amsterdam: John Benjamins, 49–88.
CORBETT, Greville. (1979). 'The agreement hierarchy', *Journal of Linguistics* 15: 203–24.
CORBETT, Greville. (1991). *Gender*. Cambridge: Cambridge University Press.

CORBETT, Greville and Alfred G. MTENJE. (1987). 'Gender agreement in Chichewa', *Studies in African Linguistics* 18: 1–38.
CORBETT, Greville, Norman FRASER, and Scott MCGLASHAN (eds.). (1993). *Heads in Grammatical Theory*. Cambridge: Cambridge University Press.
COWPER, Elizabeth. (1992). *A Concise Introduction to Syntactic Theory*. Chicago: University of Chicago Press.
CRAIG, Colette. (1986). 'Jacaltec noun classifiers: a study in language and culture', *Noun Classes and Categorization*, ed. Colette Craig. Amsterdam: John Benjamins, 263–93.
CRISTOFARO, Sonia. (1998). 'Subordination strategies: a typological study'. Revised version of Ph.D. dissertation, University of Pavia.
CROFT, William. (1984). 'Semantic and pragmatic correlates to syntactic categories', *Papers from the Parasession on Lexical Semantics, Twentieth Regional Meeting of the Chicago Linguistic Society*, ed. D. Testen, V. Mishra, and J. Drogo, 53–71.
CROFT, William. (1986). 'Categories and relations in syntax: the clause-level organization of information'. Ph.D. dissertation, Stanford University.
CROFT, William. (1988). 'Agreement vs. case marking and direct objects', *Agreement in Natural Language: Approaches, Theories, Descriptions*, ed. Michael Barlow and Charles A. Ferguson. Stanford: Center for the Study of Language and Information, 159–80.
CROFT, William. (1990a). *Typology and Universals*. Cambridge: Cambridge University Press.
CROFT, William. (1990b). 'A conceptual framework for grammatical categories (or, a taxonomy of propositional acts)', *Journal of Semantics* 7: 245–79.
CROFT, William. (1990c). 'Possible verbs and event structure', *Meanings and Prototypes: Studies on Linguistic Categorization*, ed. S. L. Tsohatzidis. London: Routledge, 48–73.
CROFT, William. (1991). *Syntactic Categories and Grammatical Relations: The Cognitive Organization of Information*. Chicago: University of Chicago Press.
CROFT, William. (1993a). 'A noun is a noun is a noun—or is it? Some reflections on the universality of semantics', *Proceedings of the Nineteenth Annual Meeting of the Berkeley Linguistics Society*, ed. Joshua S. Guenter, Barbara A. Kaiser, and Cheryl C. Zoll. Berkeley: Berkeley Linguistics Society, 369–80.
CROFT, William. (1993b). 'Case marking and the semantics of mental verbs', *Semantics and the Lexicon*, ed. James Pustejovsky. Dordrecht: Kluwer Academic, 55–72.
CROFT, William. (1994a). 'Voice: beyond control and affectedness', *Voice: Form and Function*, ed. Paul Hopper and Barbara Fox. Amsterdam: John Benjamins, 89–117.
CROFT, William. (1994b). 'Semantic universals in classifier systems', *Word* 45: 145–71.
CROFT, William. (1995a). 'Autonomy and functionalist linguistics', *Language* 71: 490–532.
CROFT, William. (1995b). 'Modern syntactic typology', *Approaches to Language Typology: Past and Present*, ed. Masayoshi Shibatani and Theodora Bynon. Oxford: Oxford University Press, 85–143.
CROFT, William. (1995c). 'Intonation units and grammatical structure', *Linguistics* 33: 839–82.
CROFT, William. (1995d). 'Review of Maria Koptjevskaja-Tamm, *Nominalizations*'. *Nordic Journal of Linguistics* 18: 75–83.
CROFT, William. (1996a). '"Markedness" and "universals": from the Prague school to typology', *Multiple Perspectives on the Historical Dimensions of Language*, ed. Kurt R. Jankowsky. Münster: Nodus, 15–21.

CROFT, William. (1996b). 'What's a head?' *Phrase Structure and the Lexicon*, ed. Laurie Zaring and Johan Rooryck. Dordrecht: Kluwer, 35–75.

CROFT, William (1997). 'Intonation units and grammatical structure in Wardaman and English'. Paper presented to the Santa Barbara Workshop on Constituency.

CROFT, William. (1998a). 'Linguistic evidence and mental representations', *Cognitive Linguistics* 9: 151–73.

CROFT, William. (1998b). 'Event structure in argument linking', *Projecting from the Lexicon*, ed. Miriam Butt and Wilhelm Geuder. Stanford: Center for the Study of Language and Information, 1–43.

CROFT, William. (1999). 'Some contributions of typology to cognitive linguistics (and vice versa)', *Cognitive Linguistics: Foundations, Scope and Methodology*, ed. Theo Janssen and Gisela Redeker. Berlin: Mouton de Gruyter, 61–93.

CROFT, William. (2000a). *Explaining Language Change: An Evolutionary Approach*. Harlow, Essex: Longman.

CROFT, William. (2000b). 'Parts of speech as typological universals and as language particular categories', *Approaches to the Typology of Word Classes*, ed. Petra Maria Vogel and Bernard Comrie. Berlin: Mouton de Gruyter, 65–102.

CROFT, William. (in press). 'Lexical rules vs. constructions: a false dichotomy', *Motivation in Language: Studies in Honour of Günter Radden*, ed. Hubert Cuyckens, Thomas Berg, René Dirven, and Klaus-Uwe Panther. Amsterdam: John Benjamins.

CROFT, William. (in preparation). *Verbs: Aspect and Argument Linking*. Oxford: Oxford University Press.

CROFT, William, Hava Bat-Zeev SHYLDKROT, and Suzanne KEMMER. (1987). 'Diachronic semantic processes in the middle voice', *Papers from the 7th International Conference on Historical Linguistics*, ed. Anna Giacalone Ramat, Onofrio Carruba, and Giuliano Bernini. Amsterdam: John Benjamins, 179–92.

CRUSE, D. Alan. (1986). *Lexical Semantics*. Cambridge: Cambridge University Press.

CRUSE, D. Alan. (1992). 'Monosemy vs. polysemy', (review article on Ruhl, *On Monosemy*), *Linguistics* 30: 577–99.

CRUSE, D. Alan and William CROFT. (in preparation). *Cognitive Linguistics*. Cambridge: Cambridge University Press.

CRYSTAL, David. (1975). *The English Tone of Voice: Essays on Intonation, Prosody and Paralanguage*. London: Edward Arnold.

CULICOVER, Peter and Ray JACKENDOFF. (1997). 'Semantic subordination despite syntactic coordination', *Linguistic Inquiry* 28: 195–217.

DAHL, Östen. (1979/1987). 'Case grammar and prototypes', *Concepts of Case*, ed. René Dirven and Günter Radden. Tübingen: Gunter Narr, 147–61.

DAYLEY, Jon P. (1985). *Tzutujil Reference Grammar*. (University of California Publications in Linguistics, 107.) Berkeley and Los Angeles: University of California Press.

DELANCEY, Scott. (1981). 'An interpretation of split ergativity and related patterns', *Language* 57: 626–57.

DELANCEY, Scott. (1982). 'Aspect, transitivity and viewpoint', *Tense–Aspect: Between Semantics and Pragmatics*, ed. Paul Hopper. Amsterdam: John Benjamins, 167–84.

DE LEÓN, Lourdes. (1987). 'Noun and numeral classifiers in Mixtec and Tzotzil: a referential view', Ph.D. dissertation, University of Sussex.

DIESSEL, Holger. (1999). *Demonstratives: Form, Function and Grammaticalization*. Amsterdam: John Benjamins.

DIK, Simon C. (1997). *The Theory of Functional Grammar*, ed. Kees Hengeveld (2 vols.). Berlin: Mouton de Gruyter.
DIMMENDAAL, Gerrit Jan. (1983). *The Turkana Language*. Dordrecht: Foris.
DIXON, R. M. W. (1972). *The Dyirbal Language of North Queensland*. Cambridge: Cambridge University Press.
DIXON, R. M. W. (ed.). (1976). *Grammatical Categories in Australian Languages*. Australian Institute of Aboriginal Studies.
DIXON, R. M. W. (1977). 'Where have all the adjectives gone?' *Studies in Language* 1: 19–80.
DIXON, R. M. W. (1979). 'Ergativity', *Language* 55: 59–138.
DIXON, R. M. W. (1980). *The Languages of Australia*. Cambridge: Cambridge University Press.
DIXON, R. M. W. (1994). *Ergativity*. Cambridge: Cambridge University Press.
DOWTY, David. (1991). 'Thematic proto-roles and argument selection', *Language* 67: 547–619.
DRYER, Matthew. (1986). 'Primary objects, secondary objects and antidative', *Language* 62: 808–45.
DRYER, Matthew. (1995). 'On the intransitivity of passive clauses'. Paper presented at the Conference on Functional Approaches to Grammar, Albuquerque, New Mexico.
DRYER, Matthew. (1997a). 'Why statistical universals are better than absolute universals', *CLS 33: Papers from the Panels*, ed. Kora Singer, Randall Eggart, and Gregory Anderson. Chicago: Chicago Linguistic Society, 123–45.
DRYER, Matthew. (1997b). 'Are grammatical relations universal?' *Essays on Language Function and Language Type*, ed. Joan Bybee, John Haiman, and Sandra A. Thompson. Amsterdam: John Benjamins, 115–43.
DUBOIS, John A. (1985). 'Competing motivations', *Iconicity in Syntax*, ed. John Haiman. Amsterdam: John Benjamins, 343–66.
DURIE, Mark. (1985). *A Grammar of Acehnese on the Basis of a Dialect of North Aceh*. Dordrecht: Foris.
DURIE, Mark. (1986). 'The grammaticization of number as a verbal category', *Proceedings of the Twelfth Annual Meeting of the Berkeley Linguistics Society*, ed. Vassiliki Nikiforidou, Mary VanClay, Mary Niepokuj, and Deborah Feder. Berkeley: Berkeley Linguistics Society, 355–70.
DURIE, Mark. (1988). 'The so-called passive of Acehnese', *Language* 64: 104–13.
DURIE, Mark. (1995). 'Towards an understanding of linguistic evolution and the notion "has a function Y"', *Discourse Grammar and Typology: Papers in Honor of John W. M. Verhaar*, ed. Werner Abraham, T. Givón, and Sandra A. Thompson. Amsterdam: John Benjamins, 275–308.
DURIE, Mark. (1997). 'Grammatical structures in verb serialization', *Complex Predicates*, ed. Alex Alsina, Joan Bresnan, and Peter Sells. Stanford: Center for the Study of Language and Information, 289–354.
ELBERT, Samuel H. (1988). *Echoes of a Culture: A Grammar of Rennell and Bellona*. Honolulu: University of Hawaii Press.
ELBERT, Samuel H. and MOMBERG, T. (1965). *From the Two Canoes*. Copenhagen: Danish National Museum.
ELMAN, Jeffrey L. and James L. MCCLELLAND. (1984). 'Speech perception as a cognitive process: the interactive activation model', *Speech and Language, Vol. 10*, ed. Norman Lass. New York: Academic Press, 337–74.

ELMAN, Jeffrey L., Elizabeth A. BATES, Mark H. JOHNSON, Annette KARMILOFF-SMITH, Domenico PARISI, and Kim PLUNKETT. (1996). *Rethinking Innateness: A Connectionist Perspective on Development*. Cambridge, MA: MIT Press.

EMENEAU, Murray B. (1951). *Studies in Vietnamese (Annamese) Grammar*. Berkeley: University of California Press.

ENGLAND, Nora C. (1983). *A Grammar of Mam, a Mayan Language*. Austin: University of Texas Press.

ENGLAND, Nora C. (1988). 'Mam voice', *Passive and Voice*, ed. Masayoshi Shibatani. Amsterdam: John Benjamins, 525–45.

FAUCONNIER, Gilles. (1985). *Mental Spaces*. Cambridge, MA: MIT Press.

FILLMORE, Charles J. (1975). 'An alternative to checklist theories of meaning', *Proceedings of the First Annual Meeting of the Berkeley Linguistics Society*, ed. Cathy Cogen et al., 123–31.

FILLMORE, Charles J. (1977). 'Scenes-and-frames semantics', *Linguistic Structures Processing* (Fundamental Studies in Computer Science, 5), ed. Antonio Zampolli. Amsterdam: North-Holland, 55–81.

FILLMORE, Charles J. (1982). 'Frame semantics', *Linguistics in the Morning Calm*, ed. The Linguistic Society of Korea. Seoul: Hanshin, 111–37.

FILLMORE, Charles J. (1985). 'Frames and the semantics of understanding', *Quaderni di semantica* 6: 222–54.

FILLMORE, Charles J. (1986). 'Pragmatically-controlled zero anaphora', *Proceedings of the Twelfth Annual Meeting of the Berkeley Linguistics Society*, ed. Vassiliki Nikiforidou et al., 95–107.

FILLMORE, Charles J. and Paul KAY. (1993). *Construction Grammar Coursebook, Chapters 1 thru 11 (Reading Materials for Ling. X20)*. University of California, Berkeley.

FILLMORE, Charles J., Paul KAY, and Mary Kay O'CONNOR. (1988). 'Regularity and idiomaticity in grammatical constructions: the case of *let alone*', *Language* 64: 501–38.

FOLEY, William A. (1986). *The Papuan Languages of New Guinea*. Cambridge: Cambridge University Press.

FOLEY, William A. (1991). *The Yimas Language of New Guinea*. Stanford: Stanford University Press.

FOLEY, William A. and Mike OLSON. (1985). 'Clausehood and verb serialization', *Grammar Inside and Outside the Clause*, ed. Johanna Nichols and Anthony Woodbury. Cambridge: Cambridge University Press, 17–60.

FOLEY, William A. and Robert D. VAN VALIN, Jr. (1984). *Functional Syntax and Universal Grammar*. Cambridge: Cambridge University Press.

FORD, Cecilia E. and Sandra A. THOMPSON. (1986). 'Conditionals in discourse: a text-based study from English', in Traugott et al. 1986, 353–72.

FORD, Cecilia E., Barbara A. FOX, and Sandra A. THOMPSON. (1997). 'Increments in conversation and their relevance to constituency'. Paper presented at the Workshop on Constituency, University of California, Santa Barbara.

FORREST, Linda B. (1994). 'The de-transitive clauses in Bella Coola: Passive vs. Inverse', in Givón 1994, 147–68.

FOX, B. J. (1979). *Big Nambas Grammar*. (Pacific Linguistics, B60.) Canberra: Australian National University.

FOX, Barbara A. (1987). 'The Noun Phrase Accessibility Hierarchy revisited', *Language* 63: 856–70.

Fox, Barbara A. and Paul HOPPER (ed.). (1994). *Voice: Form and Function*. (TSL, 27.) Amsterdam: John Benjamins.

Fox, Barbara A. and Robert JASPERSON. (1995). 'A syntactic exploration of repair in English conversation', *Alternative Linguistics: Descriptive and Theoretical Modes*, ed. Philip W. Davis. Amsterdam: John Benjamins, 77–134.

GALLOWAY, Brent D. (1993). *A Grammar of Upriver Halkomelem*. (University of California Publications in Linguistics, 96.) Berkeley: University of California Press.

GATHERCOLE, Virginia C., MUELLER, Eugenia, SOTO, Sebastián, and SOTO, Pilar. (1999). 'The early acquisition of Spanish verbal morphology: across-the-board or piecemeal knowledge?' *International Journal of Bilingualism* 3: 133–82.

GENETTI, Carol. (1986). 'The development of subordinators from postpositions in Bodic languages', *Proceedings of the Twelfth Annual Meeting of the Berkeley Linguistics Society*, ed. Vassiliki Nikiforidou, Mary Van Clay, Mary Niepokuj, and Deborah Feder. Berkeley: Berkeley Linguistics Society, 387–400.

GENETTI, Carol. (1991). 'From postposition to subordinator in Newari', *Approaches to Grammaticalization*, ed. Elizabeth Closs Traugott and Bernd Heine. Amsterdam: John Benjamins, 227–55.

GIBBS, Raymond W. Jr. (1990). 'Psycholinguistic studies on the conceptual basis of idiomaticity', *Cognitive Linguistics* 1: 417–51.

GIVÓN, Talmy. (1976). 'Topic, pronoun and grammatical agreement', *Subject and Topic*, ed. Charles Li. New York: Academic Press, 149–89.

GIVÓN, Talmy. (1979). *On Understanding Grammar*. New York: Academic Press.

GIVÓN, Talmy. (1980a). *Ute Reference Grammar*. Ignacio, CO: Ute Press.

GIVÓN, Talmy. (1980b). 'The binding hierarchy and the typology of complements', *Studies in Language* 4: 333–77.

GIVÓN, Talmy (ed.). (1983). *Topic Continuity in Discourse*. Amsterdam: John Benjamins.

GIVÓN, Talmy. (1984). *Syntax: A Functional-Typological Introduction, Volume I*. Amsterdam: John Benjamins.

GIVÓN, Talmy. (1991). *Syntax: A Functional-Typological Introduction, Volume II*. Amsterdam: John Benjamins.

GIVÓN, Talmy. (1994). *Voice and Inversion*. Amsterdam: John Benjamins.

GIVÓN, Talmy. (1995). *Functionalism and Grammar*. Amsterdam: John Benjamins.

GLINERT, Lewis. (1989). *The Grammar of Modern Hebrew*. Cambridge: Cambridge University Press.

GLOVER, Warren W. (1974). *Sememic and Grammatical Structures in Gurung (Nepal)*. Norman, Oklahoma: Summer Institute of Linguistics.

GOLDBERG, Adele E. (1995). *Constructions: A Construction Grammar Approach to Argument Structure*. Chicago: University of Chicago Press.

GOLDSMITH, John. (1985). 'A principled exception to the Coordinate Structure Constraint', *Papers from the General Session at the Twenty-First Regional Meeting, Chicago Linguistic Society*, ed. William H. Eilfort, Paul D. Kroeber, and Karen L. Peterson. Chicago: Chicago Linguistic Society, 133–43.

GREENBERG, Joseph H. (1959/1990). 'The origin of the Masai passive', *Africa* 29: 171–6. (Reprinted in Greenberg 1990, 412–18.)

GREENBERG, Joseph H. (1966a). *Language Universals, With Special Reference to Feature Hierarchies*. (Janua Linguarum, Series Minor 59.) The Hague: Mouton.

GREENBERG, Joseph H. (1966b). 'Some universals of grammar with particular reference to the order of meaningful elements', *Universals of Grammar*, ed. Joseph H. Greenberg, 2nd edition. Cambridge, MA: MIT Press, 73–113.

GREENBERG, Joseph H. (1977). 'Numeral classifiers and substantival number: problems in the genesis of a linguistic type', *Linguistics at the Crossroads*, 276–300. (Originally published in *Working Papers in Language Universals* 9: 1–40, 1972; reprinted in Greenberg 1990, 166–93.)

GREENBERG, Joseph H. (1978a). 'How does a language acquire gender markers?' *Universals of Human Language, Vol. 3: Word Structure*, ed. Joseph H. Greenberg, Charles A. Ferguson, and Edith A. Moravcsik. Stanford: Stanford University Press, 47–82. (Reprinted in Greenberg 1990, 241–70.)

GREENBERG, Joseph H. (1978b). 'Generalizations about numeral systems', *Universals of Human Language, Vol. 3: Word Structure*, ed. Joseph H. Greenberg, Charles A. Ferguson, and Edith A. Moravcsik. Stanford: Stanford University Press, 249–96.

GREENBERG, Joseph H. (1990). *On Language: Selected Writings of Joseph H. Greenberg*, ed. Keith Denning and Suzanne Kemmer. Stanford: Stanford University Press.

GREGORES, Emma and Jorge A. SUÁREZ. (1967). *A Description of Colloquial Guaraní*. The Hague: Mouton.

GROSS, Maurice. (1979). 'On the failure of generative grammar', *Language* 55: 859–85.

GUNDEL, Jeannette K., Nancy HEDBERG, and Ron ZACHARSKI. (1993). 'Cognitive status and the form of referring expressions in discourse', *Language* 69: 274–307.

HAEGEMAN, Liliane. (1994). *Introduction to Government and Binding Theory* (2nd edn). Oxford: Basil Blackwell.

HAIDER, Hubert and Ronald ZWANZIGER. (1984). 'Relatively attributive: the 'ezāfe'-construction from Old Iranian to Modern Persian', *Historical Syntax*, ed. Jacek Fisiak. Berlin: Mouton, 137–72.

HAIMAN, John. (1978). 'Conditionals are topics', *Language* 54: 564–89.

HAIMAN, John. (1980a). 'The iconicity of grammar: isomorphism and motivation', *Language* 54: 565–89.

HAIMAN, John. (1980b). *Hua: A Papuan Language of the Eastern Highlands of New Guinea*. Amsterdam: John Benjamins.

HAIMAN, John. (1980c). 'Dictionaries and encyclopedias'. *Lingua* 50: 329–57.

HAIMAN, John. (1983a). 'Paratactic *if*-clauses', *Journal of Pragmatics* 7: 263–81.

HAIMAN, John. (1983b). 'On some origins of switch-reference marking', in Haiman and Munro 1983, 105–28.

HAIMAN, John. (1983c). 'Iconic and economic motivation', *Language* 59: 781–819.

HAIMAN, John. (1985). *Natural Syntax*. Cambridge: Cambridge University Press.

HAIMAN, John. (1986). 'Constraints on the form and meaning of the protasis', in Traugott et al. 1986, 215–27.

HAIMAN, John. (1987). 'On some origins of medial verb morphology in Papuan languages', *Studies in Language* 11: 347–64.

HAIMAN, John and Pamela MUNRO (ed.). (1983). *Switch-Reference and Universal Grammar*. Amsterdam: John Benjamins.

HAIMAN, John and Sandra A. THOMPSON. (1984). '"Subordination" in universal grammar', *BLS* 10: 510–23.

HAIMAN, John and Sandra A. THOMPSON (ed.). (1988). *Clause Combining in Grammar and Discourse*. Amsterdam: John Benjamins.
HALE, Kenneth. (1973). 'Person marking in Walbiri', *A Festschrift for Morris Halle*, ed. Stephen R. Anderson and Paul Kiparsky. New York: Holt, Rinehart and Winston, 308–44.
HALE, Kenneth. (1976). 'The adjoined relative clause in Australian languages', *Grammatical Categories in Australian Languages*, ed. R. M. W. Dixon. Canberra: Australian Institute of Aboriginal Studies, 78–105.
HALE, Kenneth. (1982). 'Some essential features of Warlpiri verbal clauses', *Papers in Warlpiri Grammar in Memory of Lothar Jagst*, ed. S. Swartz. Canberra: SIL-AAB Work Papers, 217–315.
HALE, Kenneth. (1983). 'Warlpiri and the grammar of nonconfigurational languages', *Natural Language and Linguistic Theory* 1: 5–47.
HARRIS, Alice C. and Lyle CAMPBELL. (1995). *Historical Syntax in Cross-linguistic Perspective*. Cambridge: Cambridge University Press.
HARRIS, Zellig S. (1946). 'From morpheme to utterance', *Language* 22: 161–83.
HARRIS, Zellig S. (1951). *Methods in Structural Linguistics*. Chicago: University of Chicago Press.
HARRISON, Sheldon P. (1976). *Mokilese Reference Grammar*. Honolulu: University Press of Hawaii.
HASPELMATH, Martin. (1989). 'From purposive to infinitive—a universal path of grammaticalization', *Folia Linguistica Historica* 10: 287–310.
HASPELMATH, Martin. (1990). 'The grammaticization of passive morphology', *Studies in Language* 14: 25–72.
HASPELMATH, Martin. (1992). 'Grammaticization theory and heads in morphology', *Morphology Now*, ed. Mark Aronoff. Albany: State University of New York Press, 69–82 and 194–8.
HASPELMATH, Martin. (1993). 'More on the typology of inchoative/causative verb alternations', *Causatives and Transitivity*, ed. Bernard Comrie and Maria Polinsky. Amsterdam: John Benjamins, 87–120.
HASPELMATH, Martin. (1994). 'Functional categories, X-bar theory, and grammaticalization theory', *Sprachtypologie und Universalienforschung* 47: 3–15.
HASPELMATH, Martin. (1995). 'The converb as a cross-linguistically valid category', *Converbs in Cross-linguistic Perspective: Structure and Meaning of Adverbial Verb Forms—Adverbials, Participles, Gerunds*, ed. Ekkehard König and Martin Haspelmath. Berlin: Mouton de Gruyter, 1–55.
HASPELMATH, Martin. (1997a). *Indefinite Pronouns*. Oxford: Oxford University Press.
HASPELMATH, Martin. (1997b). *From Space to Time: Temporal Adverbials in the World's Languages*. München: Lincom Europa.
HASPELMATH, Martin. (1999). 'Long distance agreement in Godoberi (Daghestanian) complement clauses', *Folia Linguistica* 23: 131–51.
HASPELMATH, Martin. (to appear). 'The geometry of grammatical meaning: semantic maps and cross-linguistic comparison', *The New Psychology of Language, vol. 2*, ed. Michael Tomasello. Mahwah, N. J.: Lawrence Erlbaum Associates.
HEATH, Jeffrey. (1976). 'Substantival hierarchies: addendum to Silverstein', *Grammatical Categories in Australian Languages*, ed. R. M. W. Dixon. Australian Institute of Aboriginal Studies, 172–90.

HEINE, Bernd. (1993). *Auxiliaries: Cognitive Forces and Grammaticalization*. Oxford: Oxford University Press.

HEINE, Bernd and Mechthild REH. (1984). *Grammaticalization and Reanalysis in African Languages*. Hamburg: Helmut Buske Verlag.

HEINE, Bernd, Ulrike CLAUDI, and Friederike HÜNNEMEYER. (1991). *Grammaticalization: A Conceptual Framework*. Chicago: University of Chicago Press.

HENGEVELD, Kees. (1992). *Non-verbal Predication: Theory, Typology, Diachrony*. Berlin: Mouton de Gruyter.

HERSKOVITS, Annette. (1985). 'Semantics and pragmatics of locative expressions', *Cognitive Science* 9: 341–78.

HOBBS, Jerry. (1990 [1985]). 'On the coherence and structure of discourse', *Literature and Cognition*. Stanford: Center for the Study of Language and Information, 83–114. (Originally published as Report No. CSLI-85-37, Center for the Study of Language and Information, Stanford University, Stanford, California.)

HOFFMAN, Carl. (1963). *A Grammar of the Margi Language*. London: Oxford University Press.

HOFFMANN, J. (1903). *Mundari Grammar*. Calcutta: Bengal Secretariat Press.

HOLISKY, Dee Ann. (1987). 'The case of the intransitive subject in Tsova-Tush (Batsbi)', *Lingua* 71: 103–32.

HOLTON, David, Peter MACKRIDGE, and Irene PHILIPPAKI-WARBURTON. (1997). *Greek: A Comprehensive Grammar of the Modern Language*. London: Routledge.

HOOK, Peter Edwin, and Mohabhat Singh Man Singh CHAUHAN. (1988). 'The perfective adverb in Bhitrauti', *Word* 39: 177–86.

HOPPER, Paul. (1979). 'Aspect and foregrounding in discourse', in Givón 1979, 213–41.

HOPPER, Paul. (2000). 'Grammatical constructions and their discourse origins: prototype or family resemblance?' Paper presented at the 28th LAUD Symposium, Landau, Germany.

HOPPER, Paul and Sandra A. THOMPSON. (1980). 'Transitivity in grammar and discourse', *Language* 56: 251–99.

HOPPER, Paul and Elizabeth TRAUGOTT. (1993). *Grammaticalization*. Cambridge: Cambridge University Press.

HORN, Larry. (1979). 'Remarks on Neg-raising', *Pragmatics (Syntax and semantics 9)*, ed. Peter Cole. New York: Academic Press.

HUDSON, Richard A. (1984). *Word Grammar*. Oxford: Basil Blackwell.

HUDSON, Richard A. (1987). 'Zwicky on heads', *Journal of Linguistics* 23: 109–32.

HUDSON, Richard A. (1990). *English Word Grammar*. Oxford: Basil Blackwell.

HULL, David L. (1988). *Science as a Process: An Evolutionary Account of the Social and Conceptual Development of Science*. Chicago: University of Chicago Press.

HUTCHISON, John P. (1981). *The Kanuri Language: A Reference Grammar*. Madison: University of Wisconsin African Studies Program.

JACKENDOFF, Ray. (1977). *X' Syntax: A Study of Phrase Structure*. Cambridge, MA: MIT Press.

JACKENDOFF, Ray. (1990a). *Semantic Structures*. Cambridge, MA: MIT Press.

JACKENDOFF, Ray. (1990b). 'On Larson's treatment of the double object construction', *Linguistic Inquiry* 21: 427–56.

JACKENDOFF, Ray. (1997). 'Twistin' the night away', *Language* 73: 534–59.

JACOBSEN, William H., Jr. (1979). 'Noun and verb in Nootkan', *The Victoria Conference on*

Northwestern Languages. (British Columbia Provincial Museum Heritage Record No. 4.) Victoria, B. C.: British Columbia Provincial Museum, 83–155.

JAMES, Deborah. (1984). 'Raising to subject in Moose Cree: a problem for Subjacency', *Syntax and Semantics 16: The Syntax of Native American languages*, ed. Eung-Do Cook and Donna B. Gerdts. New York: Academic Press, 205–13.

JELINEK, Eloise. (1984). 'Empty categories, case, and configurationality', *Natural Language and Linguistic Theory* 2: 39–76.

JELINEK, Eloise and Richard A. DEMERS. (1983). 'The agent hierarchy and voice in some Coast Salishan languages', *International Journal of American Linguistics* 49: 167–85.

JELINEK, Eloise and Richard A. DEMERS. (1994). 'Predicates and pronominal arguments in Straits Salish', *Language* 70: 697–736.

JESPERSEN, Otto. (1924). *The Philosophy of Grammar*. New York: Norton.

Joos, Martin (ed.). (1957). *Readings in Linguistics I*. Chicago: University of Chicago Press.

JOSEPHS, Lewis S. (1975). *Palauan Reference Grammar*. Honolulu: The University Press of Hawaii.

KAPLAN, Ronald M. and Joan BRESNAN. (1982). 'Lexical Functional Grammar: a formal system for grammatical representation', *The Mental Representation of Grammatical Relations*, ed. Joan Bresnan. Cambridge, MA: MIT Press, 173–281.

KAY, Paul. (1997). Construction grammar feature structures (revised). http://www.icsi.berkeley.edu/~kay/bcg/FSrev.html

KAY, Paul and Charles J. FILLMORE. (1999). 'Grammatical constructions and linguistic generalizations: the *What's X doing Y?* construction', *Language* 75: 1–33.

KAY, Paul and Willett KEMPTON. (1984). 'What is the Sapir-Whorf Hypothesis?' *American Anthropologist* 86: 65–79.

KAZENIN, Konstantin I. (1994). 'Split syntactic ergativity: toward an implicational hierarchy', *Sprachtypololgie und Universalienforschung* 47: 78–98.

KEENAN, Edward L. (1976). 'Towards a universal definition of "subject" ', *Subject and Topic*, ed Charles Li. New York: Academic Press, 303–34.

KEENAN, Edward L. (1985). 'Passive in the world's languages', *Language Typology and Syntactic Description, Vol. 1: Clause Structure*, ed. Timothy Shopen. Cambridge: Cambridge University Press, 243–81.

KEENAN, Edward L. and Bernard COMRIE. (1977/1987). 'Noun phrase accessibility and universal grammar', *Universal Grammar*, ed. Edward L. Keenan. London: Croom Helm, 3–45. (Originally appeared in *Linguistic Inquiry* 8: 63–99.)

KEMMER, Suzanne. (1993). *The Middle Voice*. Amsterdam: John Benjamins.

KEPPING, Ksenia Borisova. (1979). 'Elements of ergativity and nominativity in Tangut', *Ergativity*, ed. Frans Plank. New York: Academic Press, 362–278.

KHRAKOVSKY, V. S. (1973). 'Passive constructions', *Trends in Soviet Linguistics*, ed. Ferenc Kiefer. Dordrecht: Reidel, 59–76.

KIMENYI, Alexandre. (1980). *A Relational Grammar of Kinyarwanda*. (University of California Publications in Linguistics, 91). Berkeley and Los Angeles: University of California Press.

KINKADE, M. Dale. (1983). 'Salish evidence against the universality of "noun" and "verb" ', *Lingua* 60: 25–40.

KLAIMAN, M. H. (1991). *Grammatical Voice*. Cambridge: Cambridge University Press.

KOFFKA, Kurt. (1935). *Principles of Gestalt Psychology*. New York: Harcourt, Brace & World.

KÖHLER, Wolfgang. (1947). *Gestalt Psychology* (rev. edn). New York: Liveright.
KONESKI, Blaze. (1967). *Gramatika na Makedonskiot literaturen jazik*. Skopje: Kultura.
KOPTJEVSKAJA-TAMM, Maria. (1993). *Nominalizations*. London: Routledge.
KOPTJEVSKAJA-TAMM, Maria. (2001). '"A piece of the cake" and "a cup of tea": partitive and pseudo-partitive nominal constructions in the Circum-Baltic languages', *The Circum-Baltic Languages Vol. 2: Grammar and Typology*, ed. Östen Dahl and Maria Koptjevskaja-Tamm, 523–68.
KORTMANN, Bernd. (1997). *Adverbial Subordination: A Typology and History of Adverbial Subordinators Based on European Languages*. Berlin: Mouton de Gruyter.
KROSKRITY, Paul V. (1985). 'A holistic understanding of Arizona Tewa passives', *Language* 61: 306–28.
KUIJPERS, Aert. (1968). 'The categories verb–noun and transitive–intransitive in English and Squamish', *Lingua* 21: 610–26.
KUNO, Susumu. (1973). *The Structure of the Japanese Language*. Cambridge, MA: MIT Press.
KUNO, Susumu. (1987). *Functional Syntax: Anaphora, Discourse and Empathy*. Chicago: University of Chicago Press.
LABOV, William. (1972). 'The transformation of experience in narrative syntax', *Language in the Inner City*. Philadelphia: University of Pennsylvania Press, 354–96.
LAFITTE, Pierre. (1962). *Grammaire Basque*. Bayonne: Editions des "Amis du Musée Basque" et "Ikas".
LAKOFF, George. (1986). 'Frame semantic control of the coordinate structure constraint', *Papers from the Twenty-second Annual Regional Meeting of the Chicago Linguistic Society*, ed. Ann M. Farley et al. Chicago: Chicago Linguistic Society, 152–67.
LAKOFF, George. (1987). *Women, Fire and Dangerous Things: What Categories Reveal about the Mind*. Chicago: University of Chicago Press.
LAMBDIN, Thomas Q. (1971). *Introduction to Biblical Hebrew*. New York: Charles Scribner's Sons.
LAMBRECHT, Knud. (1990). '"What, me worry?"—"Mad Magazine" sentences revisited', *Proceedings of the Sixteenth Annual Meeting of the Berkeley Linguistics Society*, ed. Kira Hall, Jean-Pierre Koenig, Michael Meacham, Sondra Reinman, and Laurel A. Sutton. Berkeley: Berkeley Linguistics Society, 215–28.
LANGACKER, Ronald W. (1976). 'Semantic representations and the linguistic relativity hypothesis', *Foundations of Language* 14: 307–57.
LANGACKER, Ronald W. (1987). *Foundations of Cognitive Grammar, Vol I: Theoretical Prerequisites*. Stanford: Stanford University Press.
LANGACKER, Ronald W. (1988). 'A view of linguistic semantics', *Topics in Cognitive Linguistics*, ed. Brygida Rudzka-Ostyn. Amsterdam: John Benjamins, 49–90.
LANGACKER, Ronald W. (1991a). *Foundations of Cognitive Grammar, Vol II: Descriptive Application*. Stanford: Stanford University Press.
LANGACKER, Ronald W. (1991b). *Concept, Image, and Symbol: The Cognitive Basis of Grammar*. Berlin: Mouton de Gruyter.
LANGACKER, Ronald W. (1995). 'Raising and transparency', *Language* 71: 1–62.
LANGACKER, Ronald W. (1997). 'Constituency, dependency, and conceptual grouping', *Cognitive Linguistics* 8: 1–32.
LARSEN, Thomas W. (1981). 'Functional correlates of ergativity in Aguacatec', *Proceedings of the Seventh Annual Meeting of the Berkeley Linguistics Society*, ed. Danny K. Alford et al. Berkeley: Berkeley Linguistics Society, 136–53.

LARSON, Richard. (1983). 'Restrictive modification: relative clauses and adverbs', Ph.D. dissertation, Department of Linguistics, University of Wisconsin at Madison.
LARSON, Richard. (1988). 'On the double object construction', *Linguistic Inquiry* 19: 335–91.
LARSON, Richard. (1990). 'Double objects revisited: reply to Jackendoff', *Linguistic Inquiry* 21: 589–632.
LAZDIŅA, Terēza Budiņa. (1966). *Latvian*. London: English Universities Press.
LEE, Penny. (1996). *The Whorf Theory Complex: A Critical Reconstruction*. Amsterdam: John Benjamins.
LEHMANN, Christian. (1982a). 'Universal and typological aspects of agreement', *Apprehension: Das sprachliche Erfassen von Gegenständen*, vol. II, ed. Hansjakob Seiler and Franz Josef Stachowiak. Tübingen: Gunter Narr, 201–67.
LEHMANN, Christian. (1982b). *Thoughts on Grammaticalization: A Programmatic Sketch, Vol. I*. (Arbeiten des Kölner Universalien-Projekts, 48.) Köln: Institut für Sprachwissenschaft. (Reprinted by LINCOM Europa, München, 1995.)
LEHMANN, Christian. (1982c). 'Directions for interlinear morphemic translations', *Folia Linguistica* 16: 199–224.
LEHMANN, Christian. (1984). *Der Relativsatz: Typologie seiner Strukturen, Theorie seiner Funktionen, Kompendium seiner Grammatik*. Tübingen: Gunter Narr.
LEHMANN, Christian. (1985). 'Grammaticalization: synchronic variation and diachronic change', *Lingua e Stile* 20: 303–18.
LEHMANN, Christian. (1986). 'On the typology of relative clauses', *Linguistics* 24: 663–80.
LEHMANN, Christian. (1988). 'Towards a typology of clause linkage', in Haiman and Thompson 1988, 181–226.
LEVIN, Beth C. (1993). *English Verb Classes and Alternations*. Chicago: University of Chicago Press.
LEVIN, Beth and Malka RAPPAPORT HOVAV. (1994). 'A preliminary analysis of causative verbs in English', *Lingua* 92: 35–77.
LEWIS, David. (1969). *Convention*. Cambridge, MA: MIT Press.
LEWIS, G. L. (1967). *Turkish Grammar*. Oxford: Oxford University Press.
LI, Charles and Sandra A. THOMPSON. (1981). *Mandarin Chinese: A Functional Reference Grammar*. Berkeley and Los Angeles: University of California Press.
LICHTENBERK, Frantisek. (1983). 'Relational classifiers', *Lingua* 60: 147–76.
LIEVEN, Elena V. M., Julian M. PINE, and Gillian BALDWIN. (1997). 'Lexically-based learning and early grammatical development', *Journal of Child Language* 24: 187–219.
LORD, Carol. (1976). 'Evidence for syntactic reanalysis: from verb to complementizer in Kwa', *Papers from the Parasession on Diachronic Syntax, Chicago Linguistic Society*, ed. Sanford B. Steever, Carol A. Walker, and Salikoko S. Mufwene, 179–191.
LORD, Carol. (1993). *Historical Change in Serial Verb Constructions*. (Typological Studies in Language, 26.) Amsterdam: John Benjamins.
LORIMER, David Lockhart Robinson. (1935). *The Burushaski Language* (3 vols.). Lisse: The Peter de Ridder Press.
LUCY, John A. (1992a). *Language, Diversity and Thought: A Reformulation of the Linguistic Relativity Hypothesis*. Cambridge: Cambridge University Press.
LUCY, John A. (1992b). *Grammatical Categories and Cognition: A Case Study of the Linguistic Relativity Hypothesis*. Cambridge: Cambridge University Press.
LYNCH, John. (1978). *A Grammar of Lenakel*. (Pacific Linguistics, B55.) Canberra: Australian National University.

MASICA, Colin. (1976). *Defining a Lingustic Area: South Asia*. Chicago: University of Chicago Press.
MASICA, Colin. (1991). *The Indo-Aryan Languages*. Cambridge: Cambridge University Press.
MATHIASSEN, Terje. (1996). *A Short Grammar of Lithuanian*. Columbus, OH: Slavica.
MATSUMOTO, Yoshiko. (1997). *Noun Modifying Constructions in Japanese: A Frame-semantic Approach*. Amsterdam: John Benjamins.
MATTHEWS, Peter H. (1981). *Syntax*. Cambridge: Cambridge University Press.
MATTHEWS, Stephen and Virginia YIP. (1994). *Cantonese: A Comprehensive Grammar*. London: Routledge.
MATTHIESSEN, Christian and Sandra A. THOMPSON. (1988). 'The structure of discourse and "subordination"', in Haiman and Thompson 1988, 275–330.
MBOTELA, J. (1934). *Uhuru wa Watumwa*. London: Nelson [1966 reprint].
MCCAWLEY, James D. (1991). *A Linguistic Flea Circus*. Bloomington: Indiana University Linguistics Club.
MCCAWLEY, James D. (1998). *The Syntactic Phenomena of English* (2nd edn). Chicago: University of Chicago Press.
MCCLENDON, Sally. (1978). 'Ergativity, case, and transitivity in Eastern Pomo', *International Journal of American Linguistics* 44: 1–9.
MCGREGOR, William B. (1997). *Semiotic Grammar*. Oxford: Clarendon Press.
MEILLET, Antoine. (1915/1921). 'Le renouvellement des conjonctions', *Linguistique historique et Linguistique générale*. Paris: Klincksieck. (Originally published in *Annuaire de l'École pratique des Hautes Études*, section historique et philologique, 1915.)
MERLAN, Francesca. (1994). *A Grammar of Wardaman*. Berlin: Mouton de Gruyter.
MICHAELIS, Laura A. and Knud LAMBRECHT. (1996). 'Toward a construction-based theory of language functions: the case of nominal extraposition', *Language* 72: 215–47.
MINASSIAN, Martiros. (1980). *Grammaire d'arménien oriental*. Delmar, New York: Caravan Books.
MIRIKITANI, Leatrice T. (1972). *Kapampangan Syntax*. (Oceanic Linguistics Special Publication No. 10.) Honolulu: The University Press of Hawaii.
MITHUN, Marianne. (1984). 'The evolution of noun incorporation', *Language* 60: 847–94.
MITHUN, Marianne. (1988). 'The grammaticization of coordination', in Haiman and Thompson 1988, 331–59.
MITHUN, Marianne. (1991). 'Active/agentive case marking and its motivations', *Language* 67: 510–46.
MITHUN, Marianne. (2000). 'Noun and verb in Iroquoian languages: multicategorisation from multiple criteria', in Petra M. Vogel and Bernard Comrie (eds), *Approaches to the Typology of Word Classes*. Berlin: Mouton de Gruyter, 397–420.
MONDLOCH, James L. (1978). *Basic Quiché Grammar*. (Institute for Mesoamerican Studies, Publication 2.) Albany: Institute for Mesoamerican Studies.
MORAVCSIK, Edith A. (1978). 'On the distribution of ergative and accusative patterns', *Lingua* 45: 233–79.
MULDER, Jean Gail. (1994). *Ergativity in Coast Tsimshian (Sm'algyax)*. (University of California Publications in Linguistics, 124.) Berkeley: University of California Press.
MUNRO, Pamela. (1982). 'On the transitivity of "say" verbs', Paul Hopper and Sandra A. Thompson (ed.), *Studies in Transitivity* (Syntax and Semantics, Vol. 15). New York: Academic Press, 301–18.

MUNRO, Pamela. (1984). 'Floating quantifiers in Pima', *Syntax and Semantics 16: The Syntax of Native American Languages*, ed. Eung-Do Cook and Donna B. Gerdts. New York: Academic Press, 269–87.
MYHILL, John. (1988a). 'Categoriality and clustering', *Studies in Language* 12: 261–97.
MYHILL, John. (1988b). 'Nominal agent incorporation in Indonesian', *Journal of Linguistics* 24: 111–36.
MYHILL, John and Junko HIBIYA. (1988). 'The discourse function of clause-chaining', in Haiman and Thompson 1988, 361–98.
NAKHIMOVSKY, Alexander. (1988). 'Aspect, aspectual class and the temporal structure of narrative', *Computational Linguistics* 14: 29–43.
NANDRIS, Grigore. (1945). *Colloquial Rumanian*. London: Routledge & Kegan Paul.
NAPOLI, Donna Jo. (1981). 'Semantic interpretation vs. lexical governance: clitic climbing in Italian', *Language* 57: 841–87.
NEWMAN, Stanley. (1944). *Yokuts Language of California*. (Viking Fund Publications in Anthropology, 2.) New York: Viking Fund.
NEWMEYER, Frederick J. (1992). 'Iconicity and generative grammar', *Language* 68: 756–96.
NEWMEYER, Frederick J. (1998). *Language Form and Language Function*. Cambridge, MA: MIT Press.
NICHOLS, Johanna. (1984). 'Direct and oblique objects in Chechen-Ingush and Russian', in Plank 1984, 183–209.
NICHOLS, Johanna. (1986). 'Head-marking and dependent-marking grammar', *Language* 62: 56–119.
NIDA, Eugene A. (1949). *Morphology*. Ann Arbor: University of Michigan Press.
NOONAN, Michael. (1985). 'Complementation', in Shopen 1985b, 42–140.
NOONAN, Michael. (1992). *A Grammar of Lango*. Berlin: Mouton.
NUNBERG, Geoffrey. (1979). 'The nonuniqueness of semantic solutions: polysemy', *Linguistics and Philosophy* 3: 143–84.
NUNBERG, Geoffrey, Ivan A. SAG, and Thomas WASOW. (1994). 'Idioms', *Language* 70: 491–538.
O'GRADY, William, Michael DOBROVOLSKY, and Mark ARONOFF. (1997). *Contemporary Linguistics: An Introduction* (3rd edn). New York: St. Martin's Press.
OATES, Lynette Francis. (1964). *A Tentative Description of the Gunwinggu Language (of Western Arnhem Land)*. Oceania Linguistic Monographs No. 10. Sydney: University of Sydney.
OHORI, Toshio. (2001). 'Clause integration as grammaticalization: a case from Japanese *Tokoro-* complements', *Cognitive-functional linguistics in an East Asian context*, ed. Shigeru Sato and Kaoru Horie, 279–301. Tokyo: Kuroshio.
OUHALLA, Jamal. (1991). *Functional Categories and Parametric Variation*. London: Routledge.
PATZ, Elizabeth. (1991). Djabugay. *The Handbook of Australian Languages*, vol. 4, ed. R. M. W. Dixon and Barry J. Blake. Oxford: Oxford University Press, 245–347.
PAWLEY, Andrew. (1987). 'Encoding events in Kalam and English: different Logics for reporting experience', in Russell Tomlin (ed.), *Coherence and Grounding in Discourse*. Amsterdam: John Benjamins, 329–60.
PAWLEY, Andrew. (1993). 'A language which defies description by ordinary means', *The Role*

of Theory in Language Description, ed. William A. Foley. Berlin: Mouton de Gruyter, 87–129.

PAYNE, Doris. (1987). 'Information structuring in Papago narrative discourse', *Language* 63: 783–804.

PAYNE, Doris. (1994). 'The Tupí-Guaraní inverse', *Voice: Form and Function*, ed. Barbara Fox and Paul J. Hopper. Amsterdam: John Benjamins, 313–40.

PAYNE, Doris, Misuyo HAMAYA, and Peter JACOBS. (1994). 'Active, inverse and passive in Maasai', *Voice and Inversion*, ed. Talmy Givón. Amsterdam: John Benjamins, 283–315.

PAYNE, John R. (1980). 'The decline of ergativity in Pamir languages', *Lingua* 51: 147–86.

PAYNE, Thomas E. (1994). 'The pragmatics of voice in a Philippine language: actor-focus and goal-focus in Cebuano narrative', *Voice and Inversion*, ed. Talmy Givón. Amsterdam: John Benjamins, 317–64.

PAYNE, Thomas E. (1999). 'A functional typology of inverse constructions', *Tipologiya i teoriya yazyka ot opisaniya k ob"yasneniyu*, ed. Ekaterina V. Rakhilina and Yakov G. Testelets. Moscow: Yazyki Russkoy Kul'tury, 245–54.

PAYNE, Thomas E. and Thomas LASKOWSKE. (1997). 'Voice in Seko Padang', *Essays on Language Function and Language Type*, ed. Joan Bybee, John Haiman, and Sandra A. Thompson. Amsterdam: John Benjamins, 423–36.

PERLMUTTER, David M. and Paul M. POSTAL. (1983). 'Toward a universal characterization of passivization', *Studies in Relational Grammar 1*, ed. David M. Perlmutter. Chicago: University of Chicago Press, 3–29.

PINE, Julian and Elena V. M. LIEVEN. (1997). 'Slot and frame patterns and the development of the determiner category', *Journal of Child Language* 18: 123–38.

PINE, Julian, Elena V. M. LIEVEN, and Caroline F. ROWLAND. (1998). 'Comparing different models of the development of the English verb category', *Linguistics* 36: 4–40.

POLINSKY, Maria and Bernard COMRIE. (1999). 'Agreement in Tsez', *Folia Linguistica* 23: 109–30.

POLLARD, Carl and Ivan A. SAG. (1987). *Information-based Syntax and Semantics, Vol. 1: Fundamentals*. Stanford: Center for the Study of Language and Information.

POLLARD, Carl and Ivan A. SAG. (1993). *Head-driven Phrase Structure Grammar*. Chicago and Stanford: University of Chicago Press and the Center for the Study of Language and Information.

PRINCE, Ellen F. (1978). 'A comparison of WH-clefts and *it*-clefts in discourse', *Language* 54: 883–906.

PULKINA, I. and E. ZAKHAVA-NEKRASOVA. (n.d.). *Russian*. Moscow: Progress.

QUIRK, Randolph, Anne P. DUCKWORTH, J. SVARTVIK, J. P. L. RUSIECKI, and A. J. T. COLIN. (1964). 'Studies in the correspondence of prosodic to grammatical features in English', *Proceedings of the IX International Congress of Linguists*. The Hague: Mouton, 679–91.

RADFORD, Andrew. (1988). *Transformational Grammar: A First Course*. Cambridge: Cambridge University Press.

REED, Irene, Osahito MIYAOKA, Steven JACOBSON, Paschal AFCAN, and Michael KRAUSS. (1977). *Yup'ik Eskimo Grammar*. Anchorage: University of Alaska, Alaska Native Language Center.

REESINK, Ger. (1987). *Structures and their Functions in Usan*. (SLCS, 13.) Amsterdam: John Benjamins.

REHG, Kenneth L. (1981). *Ponapean Reference Grammar*. Honolulu: University Press of Hawaii.
REINHART, Tanya. (1984). 'Principles of gestalt perception in the temporal organization of narrative texts', *Linguistics* 22: 779–809.
RHODES, Richard. (1977). 'Semantics in a relational grammar', *Papers from the Thirteenth Regional Meeting, Chicago Linguistic Society*, ed. Woodford A. Beach, Samuel E. Fox, and Shulamith Philosoph. Chicago: Chicago Linguistic Society, 503–14.
RICE, Sally A. (1987). 'Towards a cognitive model of transivity', Ph.D. dissertation, University of California, San Diego.
RIJKHOFF, Jan. (1992). *The Noun Phrase: A Typological Study of its Form and Structure*. Amsterdam: IFOTT.
ROBERTS, John R. (1987). *Amele*. London: Croom Helm.
ROBERTS, John R. (1988). 'Amele switch-reference and the theory of grammar', *Linguistic Inquiry* 19: 45–63.
ROBINS, R. H. (1958). *The Yurok Language: Grammar, Texts, Lexicon*. Berkeley and Los Angeles: University of California Press.
ROBINS, R. H. (1980). 'Grammatical hierarchy and the Yurok bipersonal verb', *Wege zur Universalienforschung*, ed. Gunter Brettschneider and Christian Lehmann. Tübinger: Gunter Narr, 360–4.
ROSCH, Eleanor. (1978). 'Principles of categorization', *Cognition and Categorization*, ed. Eleanor Rosch and Barbara Lloyd. Hillsdale, N. J.: Lawrence Erlbaum Associates, 27–48.
ROSEN, Carol. (1984). 'The interface between semantic roles and initial grammatical relations', *Studies in Relational Grammar 2*, ed. David M. Perlmutter and Carol G. Rosen. Chicago: University of Chicago Press, 38–77.
Ross, John R. (1967). 'Constraints on variables in syntax', Ph.D. dissertation, MIT.
ROWLANDS, Evan Colyn. (1969). *Yoruba*. Sevenoaks, Kent: Hodder and Stoughton.
RUBINO, Rejane B. and Julian M. PINE. (1998). 'Subject–verb agreement in Brazilian Portuguese: what low error rates hide', *Journal of Child Language* 25: 35–59.
RUHLEN, Merritt. (1991). *A Guide to the World's Languages, Vol. 1: Classification*. Stanford: Stanford University Press.
SADOCK, Jerrold M. (1991). *Autolexical Syntax*. Chicago: University of Chicago Press.
SALTARELLI, Mario. (1988). *Basque*. London: Croom Helm.
SAPIR, Edward. (1921). *Language*. New York: Harcourt, Brace & World.
SASSE, Hans-Jürgen. (1988). 'Der irokesische Sprachtyp', *Zeitschrift für Sprachwissenschaft* 7: 173–213.
SASSE, Hans-Jürgen. (1991). 'Predication and sentence constitution in universal perspective', *Semantic Universals and Universal Semantics* (Groningen-Amsterdam Studies in Semantics, 12), ed. Dietmar Zaefferer. Berlin: Foris, 75–95.
SAUSSURE, Ferdinand. (1916/1966). *Cours de linguistique générale*, ed. Ch. Bally and A. Sechehaye. (*Course in General Linguistics*, transl. Wade Baskin. New York: McGraw-Hill, 1966.)
SCATTON, Ernest A. (1983). *A Reference Grammar of Modern Bulgarian*. Columbus, Ohio: Slavica.
SCHACHTER, Paul. (1973). 'Focus and relativization', *Language* 49: 19–46.
SCHACHTER, Paul. (1974). 'A non-transformational account of serial verbs', *Studies in African Linguistics*, supplement 5: 253–70.

SCHACHTER, Paul. (1977a). 'Constraints on coordination', *Language* 53: 86–103.
SCHACHTER, Paul. (1977b). 'Reference-related and role-related properties of subjects', *Syntax and Semantics 8: Grammatical Relations*, ed. Peter Cole and Jerrold M. Sadock. New York: Academic Press, 279–306.
SCHACHTER, Paul. (1985). 'Parts-of-speech systems'. *Language Typology and Syntactic Description, Vol. 1: Clause Structure*, ed. Timothy Shopen. Cambridge: Cambridge University Press, 3–61.
SCHEVILL, Isabel M. (1970). *Manual of Basic Spanish Constructions*. Stanford: Stanford University Press.
SCHILLER, Eric. (1990). 'An autolexical account of subordinating serial constructions', Ph.D. dissertation, Department of Linguistics, University of Chicago.
SEARLE, John R. (1969). *Speech Acts: An Essay in the Philosophy of Language*. Cambridge: Cambridge University Press.
SEARLE, John R. (1979). 'Literal meaning', *Expression and Meaning*. Cambridge: Cambridge University Press, 117–36.
SENFT, Gunter. (1986). *Kilivila: The Language of the Trobriand Islanders*. Berlin: Mouton de Gruyter.
SHIBATANI, Masayoshi. (1985). 'Passive and related constructions: a prototype analysis', *Language* 61: 821–48.
SHIBATANI, Masayoshi. (1988). 'Voice in Philippine languages', *Passive and Voice*, ed. Masayoshi Shibatani. Amsterdam: John Benjamins, 85–142.
SHOPEN, Timothy (ed.). (1985a). *Language Typology and Syntactic Description, Vol. 1: Clause Structure*. Cambridge: Cambridge University Press.
SHOPEN, Timothy (ed.). (1985b). *Language Typology and Syntactic Description, Vol. 2: Complex Constructions*. Cambridge: Cambridge University Press.
SHOPEN, Timothy (ed.). (1985c). *Language Typology and Syntactic Description, Vol. 3: Grammatical Categories and the Lexicon*. Cambridge: Cambridge University Press.
SHORE, Susanna. (1988). 'On the so-called Finnish passive', *Word* 39: 151–76.
SIEWIERSKA, Anna. (1984). 'Phrasal discontinuity in Polish', *Australian Journal of Linguistics* 4: 57–71.
SIEWIERSKA, Anna. (1985). *The Passive: A Comparative Linguistic Analysis*. London: Croom Helm.
SIEWIERSKA, Anna. (1997). 'The formal realization of case and agreement marking: a functional perspective', *Reconnecting Language: Morphology and Syntax in Functonal Perspectives*, ed. Anne-Marie Simon-Vandenbergen, Kristin Davidse, and Dirk Noël. Amsterdam: John Benjamins, 181–210.
SILVERSTEIN, Michael. (1976). 'Hierarchy of features and ergativity', *Grammatical Categories in Australian Languages*, ed. R. M. W. Dixon. Australian Institute of Aboriginal Studies, 112–71.
SJOBERG, Andrée F. (1963). *Uzbek Structural Grammar*. (Uralic and Altaic Series, 18.) Bloomington: Indiana University Press.
SOHN, Ho-min. (1975). *Woleaian Reference Grammar*. Honolulu: University Press of Hawaii.
SOMMER, Bruce. (1972). *Kunjen Syntax: A Generative View*. Canberra: Australian Institute of Aboriginal Studies.
SPENCER, Andrew. (1993). 'Review of Rochelle Lieber, *Deconstructing Morphology*', *Language* 69: 580–7.

STASSEN, Leon. (1985). *Comparison and Universal Grammar*. Oxford: Basil Blackwell.
STASSEN, Leon. (1997). *Intransitive Predication*. Oxford: Oxford University Press.
STOCKWELL, Robert P., J. Donald BOWEN, and John W. MARTIN. (1965). *The Grammatical Structures of English and Spanish*. Chicago: University of Chicago Press.
STUMP, Gregory T. (1984). 'Agreement vs. incorporation in Breton', *Natural Language and Linguistic Theory* 2: 289–348.
SVARTVIK, Jan. (1966). *On voice in the English Verb*. The Hague: Mouton.
SWEET, Henry. (1891). *A New English Grammar, Logical and Historical*, Part I. Oxford: Clarendon Press.
TALMY, Leonard. (1972). 'Semantic Structures in English and Atsugewi', Ph.D. dissertation, Department of Linguistics, University of California, Berkeley.
TALMY, Leonard. (1974). 'Semantics and syntax of motion', *Syntax and Semantics 4*, ed. John Kimball. New York: Academic Press, 181–238.
TALMY, Leonard. (1976). 'Semantic causative types', *The Grammar of Causative Constructions*, ed. Masayoshi Shibatani. New York: Academic Press, 43–116.
TALMY, Leonard. (1978). 'Figure and ground in complex sentences', *Universals of Human Language, Vol. 4: Syntax*, ed. Joseph H. Greenberg et al. Stanford: Stanford University Press, 625–52.
TALMY, Leonard. (1988). 'Force dynamics in language and cognition', *Cognitive Science* 12: 49–100.
TALMY, Leonard. (1991). 'Path to realization: a typology of event integration', *Buffalo Working Papers in Linguistics* 91-01: 147–87.
TANNEN, Deborah. (1989). *Talking Voices: Repetition, Dialogue, and Imagery in Conversational Discourse*. Cambridge: Cambridge University Press.
TAYLOR, John R. (1989). 'Possessive genitives in English', *Linguistics* 27: 663–86.
TAYLOR, John R. (1995). *Linguistic Categorization: Prototypes in Linguistic Theory* (2nd edn). Oxford: Oxford University Press.
TCHEKHOFF, Claude. (1981). *Simple Sentences in Tongan*. (Pacific Linguistics, B-81.) Canberra: Australian National University.
THOMPSON, Chad. (1994). 'Passive and inverse constructions', Givón 1994, 47–63.
THOMPSON, Sandra A. (1987). '"Subordination" and narrative event structure', Tomlin 1987, 435–54.
TIKKANEN, Bertil. (1995). 'Burushaski converbs in their South and Central Asian areal context', *Converbs in Cross-linguistic Perspective: Structure and Meaning of Adverbial Verb Forms—Adverbials Particles, Gerunds*, ed. Ekkehard König and Martin Haspelmath. Berlin: Mouton de Gruyter, 487–528.
TOMASELLO, Michael. (1992). *First Verbs: A Case Study of Early Grammatical Development*. Cambridge: Cambridge University Press.
TOMASELLO, Michael. (2000). 'Do young children have adult syntactic competence?' *Cognition* 74: 209–53.
TOMASELLO, Michael, Nameera AKHTAR, Kelly DODSON, and Laura REKAU. (1997). 'Differential productivity in young children's use of nouns and verbs', *Journal of Child Language* 24: 373–87.
TOMLIN, Russell. (1985). 'Foreground–background information and the syntax of subordination', *Text* 5: 85–122.
TOMLIN, Russell (ed.). (1987). *Coherence and Grounding in Discourse*. Amsterdam: John Benjamins.

TRAUGOTT, Elizabeth Closs. (1985). 'Conditional markers', *Iconicity in Syntax*, ed. John Haiman. Amsterdam: John Benjamins, 289–307.

TRAUGOTT, Elizabeth Closs and Bernd HEINE. (1991). *Approaches to grammaticalization* (2 vols.). Amsterdam: John Benjamins.

TRAUGOTT, Elizabeth Closs, Alice ter MEULEN, Judy Snitzer REILLY, and Charles A. FERGUSON. (eds.). (1986). *On Conditionals*. Cambridge: Cambridge University Press.

TSUKIASHI, Ayumi. (1997). 'A usage-based analysis of the Japanese passive construction', M.A. dissertation, University of Manchester.

TUCKER, A. N. and M. A. BRYAN. (1966). *Linguistic Analysis: The Non-Bantu Languages of North-Eastern Africa*. London: Oxford University Press.

TUCKER, A. N. and J. Tompo Ole MPAAYEI. (1955). *A Maasai Grammar with Vocabulary*. London: Longmans, Green & Co.

UEHARA, Satoshi. (1998). *Syntactic Categories in Japanese: A Cognitive and Typological Introduction*. Tokyo: Kurosio Publishers.

VAN der AUWERA, Johan and Vladimir A. PLUNGIAN. (1998). 'Modality's semantic map', *Linguistic Typology* 2: 79–124.

VAN EIJK, Jan P. and Thom HESS. (1986). 'Noun and verb in Salish', *Lingua* 69: 319–31.

VAN VALIN, Robert D. Jr. (1990). 'Semantic parameters of split intransitivity', *Language* 66: 221–59.

VAN VALIN, Robert D. Jr. (1993). 'A synopsis of Role and Reference Grammar', *Advances in Role and Reference Grammar*, ed. Robert D. Van Valin, Jr. Amsterdam: John Benjamins, 1–164.

VAN VALIN, Robert D. Jr. and Randy J. LAPOLLA. (1997). *Syntax: Structure, Meaning and Function*. Cambridge: Cambridge University Press.

VERHAAR, John W. M. (1995). *Towards a Reference Grammar of Tok Pisin: An Experiment in Corpus Linguistics*. (Oceanic Linguistics Special Publication, 26.) Honolulu: University of Hawai'i Press.

WATKINS, Laurel J. (1984). *A Grammar of Kiowa*. Lincoln: University of Nebraska Press.

WEINER, E. Judith and William LABOV. (1983). 'Constraints on the agentless passive', *Journal of Linguistics* 19: 29–58.

WERTHEIMER, Max. (1950). 'Laws of organization in perceptual forms', *A Source Book of Gestalt Psychology*, prepared by Willis D. Ellis. New York: Humanities, 71–88.

WESTERMANN, Diedrich. (1912/1970). *The Shilluk People*. Westport, Conn.: Negro Universities Press. (Reprinted from original edition by the Board of Foreign Missions, United Presbyterian Church N. A.)

WETZER, Harrie. (1992). '"Nouny" and "verby" adjectivals: a typology of predicative adjectival constructions', *Meaning and Grammar: Cross-linguistic Perspectives*, ed. Michel Kefer and Johan van der Auwera 223–62. Berlin: Mouton de Gruyter.

WETZER, Harrie. (1996). *The Typology of Adjectival Predication*. Berlin: Mouton de Gruyter.

WHITNEY, Arthur. (1944). *Colloquial Hungarian*. London: Routledge & Kegan Paul.

WIEGAND, Nancy. (1987). 'Causal connectives in the early history of English: a study in diachronic syntax', Ph.D. dissertation, Department of Linguistics, Stanford University.

WIERZBICKA, Anna. (1980). *Lingua mentalis: The Semantics of Natural Language*. New York: Academic Press.

WIERZBICKA, Anna. (1986). 'What's in a noun? (or: how do nouns differ in meaning from adjectives?)', *Studies in Language* 10: 353–89.

WIERZBICKA, Anna. (1987). 'Boys will be boys', *Language* 63: 95–114.
WIERZBICKA, Anna. (1988). *The Semantics of Grammar*. Amsterdam: John Benjamins.
WILLIAMS, C. J. (1980). *A Grammar of Yuwaalaraay*. Canberra: Australian National University.
WILLIAMS, Edwin. (1981). 'On the notions "lexically related" and "head of a word"', *Linguistic Inquiry* 12: 245–74.
WILLIAMS, Marianne Mithun. (1976). *A Grammar of Tuscarora*. New York: Garland.
WOLFART, H. Christoph and Janet F. CARROLL. (1981). *Meet Cree: A Guide to the Cree Language* (2nd edn). Lincoln: University of Nebraska Press.
WOOLLAMS, Geoff. (1996). *A Grammar of Karo Batak, Sumatra*. (Pacific Linguistics, C-130.) Canberra: Australian National University.
ZEPEDA, Ofelia. (1983). *A Papago Grammar*. Tucson: University of Arizona Press.
ZOLOTOVA, G. A., N. K. ONIPENKO, and M. Ju. SIDOROVA. (1998). *Kommunikativnaja grammatika russkogo jazyka*. Moscow: Russian Academy of Sciences.
ZWICKY, Arnold M. (1985). 'Heads', *Journal of Linguistics* 21: 1–29.
ZWICKY, Arnold M. (1993). 'Heads, bases and functors', *Heads in Grammatical Theory*, ed. Greville G. Corbett, Norman M. Fraser, and Scott McGlashan. Cambridge: Cambridge University Press, 292–315.

Index of Authors

Abney, Stephen P. 257, 263
Afcan, Paschal 140
Aikhenvald, Alexandra 120, 232
Aissen, Judith 209
Akhtar, Nameera 58
Akmajian, Adrian 16
Altenberg, Bengt 191
Anderson, Lloyd B. 93
Anderson, Stephen R. 149–52, 156, 248, 269
Andrews, J. Richard 215
Annamalai, E. 323
Anward, Jan 85
Ariel, Mira 72, 235
Ariff, Syed Zainal Jamaluddin 306
Aristar, Anthony Rodrigues 235
Arndt, P. P. 340
Aronoff, Mark 10
Ashton, E. O. 215, 250

Bailleul, C. 293
Baldwin, Gillian 58
Barlow, Michael 140, 229–31, 247
Barsalou, Lawrence R. 121
Barss, Andrew 43
Bates, Elizabeth A. 98, 367
Bauer, Laurie 268
Berlin, Brent 120
Biber, Douglas 40
Bird, Charles S. 326
Birner, Betty J. 16
Bloomfield, Leonard 36, 41, 255, 292
Bolinger, Dwight 75, 111
Bonch-Osmolovskaya, Anastasia 165
Bowen, J. Donald 293
Bowerman, Melissa 130–1
Braine, Martin D. S. 58
Bresnan, Joan 3, 156, 208, 227, 228
Bryan, M. A. 266
Bybee, Joan L. 56, 169, 237

Campbell, Lyle 260, 361
Carlson, Robert Joel 347
Carroll, Janet F. 286–7
Cercvadze, Ilia 260
Chafe, Wallace 191, 329
Chauhan, Mohabhat Singh Man Singh 210
Choi, Soonja 130–1
Chomsky, Noam 3, 11, 48, 132–3, 208
Chung, Sandra 303–4
Churchward, C. Maxwell 140

Čikobava, Arnold 260
Clark, Eve V. 74, 111, 216, 238
Clark, Herbert H. 72, 74, 238
Claudi, Ulrike 126
Cole, Peter 157–9, 218, 325
Colin, A. J. T. 191
Comrie, Bernard 7, 51, 134, 146, 168, 211, 224, 235, 290, 291, 296, 297, 299, 301, 326, 347, 348, 350, 355
Conrad, Susan 40
Cooreman, Ann 279, 315–16
Corbett, Greville G. 230
Cowper, Elizabeth 178–9
Craig, Colette 60
Cristofaro, Sonia 60, 321, 323, 352, 356–9
Croft, William 7, 9, 13, 28, 51, 56, 57, 59, 60, 63, 66, 71, 72, 73, 74, 75, 78, 86–7, 89, 91, 93, 97, 100, 101, 103, 104, 107, 108, 117, 118, 126, 127, 133, 139, 140, 145, 153, 156, 160, 162, 163, 164, 191–3, 197–9, 220, 235, 265, 285, 312, 317, 321, 332, 354, 355, 356, 364–8
Cruse, D. Alan 14, 28, 62, 72, 103, 117
Crystal, David 191
Culicover, Peter 328
Culy, Christopher 293

Dabrowska, Ewa 109
Dahl, Östen 116–17, 169, 291, 328
Dayley, Jon P. 201
De León, Lourdes 120
DeLancey, Scott 169, 290, 296, 319
Demers, Richard A. 31–2, 227, 288
Deshpande, Madhav 344
Diessel, Holger 261
Dik, Simon C. 3, 263
Dimmendaal, Gerrit Jan 292
Dixon, R. M. W. 86, 99, 134, 138, 152–3, 160, 165, 167, 265, 309
Dobrovolsky, Michael 10
Dodson, Kelly 58
Dowty, David 248
Dryer, Matthew 8, 32–3, 45, 50, 85, 106, 143, 206, 305, 315
DuBois, John A. 118
Duckworth, Anne P. 191
Durie, Mark 166, 236, 303, 354

Elbert, Samuel H. 251, 254
Elman, Jeffrey L. 98, 367
England, Nora C. 246, 271, 279

Fauconnier, Gilles 217
Fillmore, Charles J. 3, 14–17, 20, 28, 57, 59, 74, 276–9
Finegan, Edward 40
Foley, William A. 3, 227, 243, 283, 301–2, 322, 323, 324, 327, 334, 343, 354
Ford, Cecilia E. 193, 339–40
Forrest, Linda B. 294
Fox, B. J. 342
Fox, Barbara A. 193, 194–5, 237

Galloway, Brent D. 293–4
Gathercole, Virginia V. C. 58
Genetti, Carol 329, 345
Gibbs, Raymond W. Jr. 182
Givón, Talmy 9, 62, 159, 160, 196, 198, 235, 292, 321, 342, 357, 359
Glover, Warren W. 192
Goldberg, Adele E. 14, 16, 27, 57, 59, 122, 184, 248
Goldsmith, John 346
Greenberg, Joseph H. 89, 120, 261, 292, 339
Gregores, Emma 163, 298–9
Gross, Maurice 36
Gundel, Jeannette K. 229

Haegeman, Liliane 10, 13, 64, 84, 208, 228
Haider, Hubert 350
Haiman, John 108, 111, 328, 329, 339–40, 341–2
Hale, Kenneth 186, 187, 226, 227, 249, 324, 350
Hamaya, Misuyo 292, 299
Harbert, Wayne 157–9
Harris, Alice C. 260, 361
Harris, Zellig S. 11, 36, 41
Harrison, Sheldon P. 198
Haspelmath, Martin 93, 211, 263, 268, 269, 279, 313, 317, 326, 342, 345, 352
Hawkins, John A. 206
Heath, Jeffrey 300
Hedberg, Nancy 229
Heine, Bernd 113, 126, 260, 261, 267
Hengeveld, Kees 65–71, 73, 74, 84, 86, 87, 227
Hermon, Gabriella 157–9
Herskovits, Annette 60
Hess, Thom 31–2, 78
Hibiya, Junko 343
Himmelmann, Nikolaus 123
Hobbs, Jerry 334
Hoffman, Carl 225
Hoffmann, J. 340
Holisky, Dee Ann 163
Holton, David 120
Hook, Peter Edwin 210, 344
Hopper, Paul 7, 126, 195, 332
Horie, Kaoru 348
Hudson, Richard A. 3, 241
Hull, David L. 365–7
Humboldt, Wilhelm von 109

Hünnemeyer, Friederieke 126
Hutchison, John P. 140, 228

Jackendoff, Ray 16, 42–4, 48, 328
Jacobs, Peter 292, 299
Jacobsen, William H., Jr. 74, 76–8
Jacobson, Steven 140
James, Deborah 214, 217
Jasperson, Robert 194–5, 237
Jelinek, Eloise 31–2, 226, 227, 288
Jespersen, Otto 255
Johnasson, Stig 40
Johnson, Mark H. 98, 367
Joos, Martin 84
Josephs, Lewis S. 252

Kalinina, Elena 210
Kaplan, Ronald M. 208, 228
Karmiloff-Smith, Annette 98, 367
Kay, Paul 3, 14–17, 20, 24, 28, 57, 59, 130, 276–9
Kazenin, Konstantin I. 153, 155, 156, 160
Keenan, Edward L. 51, 148–9, 215, 216
Kemmer, Suzanne 93
Kempton, Willett 130
Kepping, Ksenia Borisova 296
Kimenyi, Alexandre 146
Kinkade, M. Dale 78
Klaiman, M. H. 283, 295
Koffka, Kurt 47, 329, 332, 333, 337
Kühler, Wolfgang 47, 337
Koneski, Blaze 224
Koptjevskaja-Tamm, Maria 261, 263, 321, 355
Kortmann, Bernd 93, 351
Krauss, Michael 140
Kroskrity, Paul V. 295
Kuijpers, Aert 78
Kuno, Susumu 250

Labov, William 237, 329
Lafitte, Pierre 253
Lakoff, George 14, 16, 27, 346
Lambdin, Thomas Q. 74
Lambrecht, Knud 16, 184
Lang, Ewald 123
Langacker, Ronald W. 9, 14, 16, 17, 18, 20, 21, 25, 26, 28, 59, 62, 64, 75, 93, 104, 109–10, 112, 128, 133, 175, 184, 190, 214, 238, 255–7, 258, 259, 262, 265, 274–5, 280, 341, 346–7
LaPolla, Randy J. 3, 62, 263
Larsen, Thomas W. 142, 154
Larson, Richard 42–4, 349
Laskowske, Thomas 300
Lasnik, Howard 43
Lazdina, Tereza Budina 139
Lee, Penny 109
Leech, Geoffrey 40

Lehmann, Christian 126, 228, 263, 265, 266, 270, 321, 326, 329, 347, 357, 358
Levin, Beth C. 59, 60, 247, 317
Lewis, David 72
Lewis, G. L. 75
Li, Charles 114, 223, 323, 326, 353
Lichtenberk, Frantisek 199
Lieven, Elena V. M. 58
Lord, Carol 265, 353
Lorimer, David Lockhart Robinson 323
Lucy, John A. 109, 119–20, 121
Lynch, John 342

Mackridge, Peter 120
Martin, John W. 293
Masica, Colin 344–5
Mathiassen, Terje 286
Matsumoto, Yoshiko 348
Matthews, Peter H. 272–3, 276
Matthews, Stephen 196
Matthiessen, Christian 332, 334, 336
Mbotela, J. 342
McCawley, James D. 13, 186, 188–9, 190, 191
McClelland, James L. 98, 367
McClendon, Sally 165
McGregor, William 20
Mchombo, Samuel A. 227
Meillet, Antoine 329
Merlan, Francesca 29, 187, 192–3, 300
Michaelis, Laura A. 16, 184
Minassian, Martiros 235
Mirikitani, Leatrice T. 308
Mithun, Marianne 68, 78, 125, 127, 163, 192, 267, 280, 316, 338
  see also Williams, Marianne Mithun
Miyaoka, Osahito 140
Momberg, T. 251
Mondloch, James L. 74, 114, 141, 144, 269, 289
Moravcsik, Edith A. 85, 165
Mpaayei, J. Tompo Ole 292
Mtenje, Alfred G. 230
Mueller, Eugenia 58
Mulder, Jean Gail 166
Mulira, E. M. K. 215, 250
Munro, Pamela 209–10, 324–5
Myhill, John 267, 306, 343

Nakhimovsky, Alexander 332
Nandris, Grigore 198, 232
Napoli, Donna Jo 218
Ndawula, E. G. M. 215, 250
Newman, Stanley 145
Newmeyer, Frederick J. xiv, 208
Nichols, Johanna 141, 197–8
Nida, Eugene A. 29
Noonan, Michael 78–80, 324
Nunberg, Geoffrey 73, 176, 179–85, 201–2

O'Connor, Mary Kay 14–17
O'Grady, William 10
Oates, Lynette Francis 239
Ohori, Toshio 73, 324
Olson, Mike 323
Onipenko, N. K. 291
Ouhalla, Jamal 263

Pagliuca, William 169
Parisi, Domenico 98, 367
Patz, Elizabeth 270
Pawley, Andrew 239–40, 354
Payne, Doris 197, 292, 299, 301
Payne, John R. 138, 199
Payne, Thomas E. 300–1, 307–8
Perkins, Revere D. 169
Perlmutter, David M. 283
Philippaki-Warburton, Irene 120
Pine, Julian 58
Plungian, Vladimir A. 93
Plunkett, Kim 98, 367
Polinsky, Maria 211
Pollard, Carl 3, 20, 243
Postal, Paul M. 283
Prince, Ellen F. 16
Pulkina, I. 123, 199

Quirk, Randolph 191

Radford, Andrew 63, 64, 182
Rappaport Hovav, Malka 317
Reed, Irene 140
Reesink, Ger 201
Reh, Mechthild 260, 261, 267
Rehg, Kenneth L. 263, 280
Reinhart, Tanya 332–3, 336, 349
Rekau, Laura 58
Rhodes, Richard 240
Rice, Sally A. 248
Rijkhoff, Jan 119
Roberts, John R. 144, 345
Robins, R. H. 254, 297–8
Rosch, Eleanor 52–3, 73, 118
Rosen, Carol 133
Ross, John R. 346
Rowland, Caroline F. 58
Rowlands, Evan Colyn 144
Rubino, Rejane B. 58
Rusiecki, J. P. L. 191
Ryder, Mary Ellen 40

Sadock, Jerrold M. 199, 224, 259
Sag, Ivan A. 3, 20, 176, 179–85, 201–2, 243
Saltarelli, Mario 253
Sapir, Edward 34, 102
Sasse, Hans-Jürgen 78, 110, 113, 115, 124–5
Saussure, Ferdinand de 364

Scatton, Ernest A. 223, 246
Schachter, Paul 38, 64, 66, 67, 108, 250, 308, 347
Schiller, Eric 353
Searle, John R. 66
Senft, Gunter 222
Shibatani, Masayoshi 145, 286, 305, 307–8, 310, 316, 317
Shore, Susanna 291
Shyldkrot, Hava Bat-Zeev 93
Sidorova, M. Ju. 291
Siewierska, Anna 138, 155, 165, 187, 214, 310
Silverstein, Michael 160, 300
Simpson, Jane 156
Sjoberg, Andrée F. 211
Sohn, Ho-min 140, 198
Sommer, Bruce 350
Soto, Pilar 58
Soto, Sebastián 58
Spencer, Andrew 269
Sridhar, S. N. 157–9
Stassen, Leon 64, 74, 85–6, 93, 96, 97, 266, 321, 323, 340–1, 344, 352, 358
Stockwell, Robert P. 293
Stump, Gregory T. 228
Suárez, Jorge A. 163, 298–9
Svartvik, Jan 286, 305
Sweet, Henry 254

Talmy, Leonard 130, 164, 329–31, 336
Tannen, Deborah 237
Taylor, John R. 53
Tchekhoff, Claude 68
Thompson, Chad 310, 315–16
Thompson, Laurence C. 29
Thompson, Sandra A. 114, 193, 223, 323, 326, 327, 329, 332, 334, 336, 339–40, 353
Tikkanen, Bertil 323
Tomasello, Michael 58
Tomlin, Russell 334–5

Traugott, Elizabeth Closs 7, 126, 339–40
Tsukiashi, Ayumi 219
Tucker, A. N. 266, 292

Uehara, Satoshi 74–5, 81–3, 94, 103

Van Valin, Robert D. Jr. 3, 62, 162, 263, 283, 322, 327
van der Auwera, Johan 93
van Eijk, Jan P. 31–2, 78
Verhaar, John W. M. 215, 249

Ward, Gregory 16
Wasow, Thomas 176, 179–85, 201–2
Watkins, Laurel J. 253
Weiner, E. Judith 237
Wertheimer, Max 47, 330, 333
Westermann, Diedrich 305–6
Wetzer, Harrie 85–6, 96
Whitney, Arthur 139
Wiegand, Nancy 324, 349
Wierzbicka, Anna 16, 60, 75, 97, 189, 256, 336–7
Williams, C. J. 134
Williams, Edwin 268
Williams, Marianne Mithun 68
  see also Mithun, Marianne
Wolfart, H. Christoph 286–7
Woollams, Geoff 304–5

Yip, Virginia 196

Zacharski, Ron 229
Zakhava-Nekrasova, E. 123, 199
Zepeda, Ofelia 252, 253
Zolotova, G. A. 291
Zwanziger, Ronald 350
Zwicky, Arnold M. 10, 241, 242–54, 255–7, 273, 276

Index of Languages

Note: The entries are given in the format 'Language (Family/Genus)', where 'Family' is the highest-level genetic unit given in Ruhlen (1991:380) and 'Genus' is the genetic unit of approximately the same time-depth as a major branch of Indo-European (Dryer 1989). In cases where the entry refers to a group of languages, only the family name is given; if the highest-level genetic unit in Ruhlen is genus level, only the family-cum-genus name is given; if the language is an isolate at the family level according to Ruhlen, it is indicated as an Isolate. Names of language varieties (e.g. Modern Eastern Armenian) are listed under the language name (Armenian, Modern Eastern). The spelling of the sources has been retained for the most part.

Abaza (Caucasian/Northwest) 150, 151
Acehnese (Austric/Sundic) 303, 311, 313, 314
Aguacatec (Amerind/Mayan) 141–2, 154, 156
Akan, *see* Twi
Alamblak (Indo-Pacific/Sepik-Ramu) 324
Amele (Indo-Pacific/Madang) 144
Ancash Quechua (Amerind/Quechuan) 218
Arabic, Modern Standard (Afroasiatic/Semitic) 231, 232
Arawakan (Amerind/Maipuran) 165
Armenian, Modern Eastern (Indo-European/Armenian) 235
Asiatic Eskimo (Eskimo-Aleut) 156
Australian languages 324, 349–50
  see also Bidjandjadjara; Dyabugay; Dyirbal; Galali; Gunwinggu; Kaititj; Kalkatungu; Kunjen; Ngandi; Nunggubuyu; Twiw; Wangkumara; Wardaman; Warlpiri; Warrungu; Yidiny; Yuwaalaraay
Avar (Caucasian/Northeast) 156, 210, 260
Avestan (Indo-European/Iranian) 350–1

Bambara (Niger-Kordofanian/Mande) 293, 311, 313, 326
Barai (Indo-Pacific/Koairian) 323–4
Bare (Amerind/Maipuran) 156
Bartangi (Indo-European/Iranian) 199
Basque (Isolate) 156, 253
Beja (Afroasiatic/Beja) 266
Belauan, *see* Palauan
Bella Coola (Amerind/Bella Coola) 294–5, 311, 313, 314
Bidjandjadjara (Australian/Pama-Nyungan) 352
Big Nambas (Austric/Central-Eastern Malayo-Polynesian) 144, 342, 343
Bodic languages (Sino-Tibetan/Tibetic) 329, 345
Breton (Indo-European/Celtic) 228
Bulgarian (Indo-European/Slavic) 223, 246
Burushaski (Isolate) 323

Cahuilla (Amerind/Takic) 324–5
Cambodian, *see* Khmer

Cantonese (Sino-Tibetan/Chinese) 196
Cashinawa (Amerind/Panoan) 137, 167
Caucasian languages 210
  see also Abaza; Avar; Chechen-Ingush; Tsakhur; Tsez
Cayuga (Amerind/Iroquian) 124–6
Cebuano (Austric/Philippine) 307–8, 311, 313
Chavante (Amerind/Macro-Ge) 155
Chechen-Ingush (Caucasian/Northeast) 141
Chichewa (Niger-Kordofanian/Bantoid) 227, 230–1
Chickasaw (Amerind/Muskogean) 324–5
Chinese, *see* Mandarin Chinese
Chinook (Amerind/Chinookan) 300, 314
Chol (Amerind/Mayan) 168–70
Chukchi (Chukotko-Kamchatkan) 156, 299–300, 301, 311, 313, 314, 318, 319
Coast Tsimshian (Amerind/Tsimshian) 156, 166
Cree (Amerind/Algonkian) 286–7, 288, 290, 295, 311, 313

Djabugay (Australian/Pama-Nyungan) 270–1
Dyirbal (Australian/Pama-Nyungan) 152, 156, 309–10, 311, 313, 314, 318

Eastern Mono (Amerind/Numic) 238
English (Indo-European/Germanic) 11–14, 16–17, 20–2, 24, 25, 27, 29, 30, 35–40, 41, 42–4, 50, 51, 52, 55, 57, 63, 69, 70–3, 74, 75, 78, 80–1, 85, 88–9, 96, 98–9, 104, 111, 113–14, 115, 119–24, 125, 129, 130–1, 132–3, 134–7, 141, 142–3, 148–9, 152–4, 156, 158, 159, 168, 177–86, 188, 189–95, 197, 213–15, 216–17, 223, 236–7, 238, 243, 244, 245, 247–9, 250, 251, 252, 254, 256, 258, 259, 262, 263–4, 269, 271, 272–80, 285–6, 288, 290, 305, 308, 311, 313, 317, 318, 320–2, 323, 324–5, 326, 328–38, 339–40, 343, 344, 347, 351, 352, 355, 357–8, 362, 363
  British English 71, 127–8, 230
  Early Middle English 157, 200
  Early Modern English 339
  Old English 16, 324, 349

Ewe (Niger-Kordofanian/Western South Central Niger-Congo) 261, 265, 353

Fante, *see* Twi
Finnish (Uralic-Yukaghir/Finnic) 116–18, 291, 311, 313, 314
French (Indo-European/Romance) 36, 111, 113, 115, 231, 251, 261

Galali (Australian/Pama-Nyungan) 138
Georgian, Modern (Kartvelian) 158–9
Georgian, Old (Kartvelian) 158
German (Indo-European/Germanic) 157, 248
Gothic (Indo-European/Germanic) 157
Greek, Classical (Indo-European/Greek) xiii
Greek, Modern (Indo-European/Greek) 157
Guaraní (Amerind/Tupí-Guaraní) 298–9, 301, 311, 313, 314, 319
Gunwinggu (Australian/Gunwinyguan) 239
Gurung (Sino-Tibetan/Tibetic) 192

Hebrew, Biblical (Afroasiatic/Semitic) 74
Hebrew, Modern (Afroasiatic/Semitic) 111, 215, 216
Hindi (Indo-European/Indic) 326
Hittite (Indo-European/Anatolian) 155
Hua (Indo-Pacific/East New Guinea Highlands) 324, 339, 341–2
Huichol (Amerind/Corachol) 146
Hungarian (Uralic-Yukaghir/Ugric) 139, 144, 253–64

Iatmul (Indo-Pacific/Sepik-Ramu) 324
Imbabura Quechua (Amerind/Quechuan) 325, 347
Indo-Aryan languages (Indo-European) 210, 344–5
  see also Hindi; Marathi; Sinhalese
Indonesian (Austric/Sundic) 306, 311, 313, 314
Irish, Old (Indo-European/Celtic) 352
Iroquoian languages (Amerind) 65, 78, 126
  see also Cayuga; Mohawk; Tuscarora
Italian (Indo-European/Romance) 218

Jacaltec (Amerind/Mayan) 156, 338
Japanese (Isolate) 50, 75, 81–3, 90, 94–5, 219, 229, 250, 251, 316–17, 324, 343, 348

K'iche' (Amerind/Mayan) 74, 104, 114, 141, 144, 268, 269, 289–90
Kaititj (Australian/Pama-Nyungan) 350
Kalam (Indo-Pacific/East New Guinea Highlands) 239–40, 354
Kalkatungu (Australian/Pama-Nyungan) 156
Kanuri (Nilo-Saharan/Saharan) 140, 228, 232
Kapampangan (Austric/Philippine) 308, 311, 313, 314

Karo Batak (Austric/Sundic) 304–5, 306, 308, 311, 313, 314
Kayteetye, *see* Kaititj
Kewa (Indo-Pacific/East New Guinea Highlands) 165
Khmer (Austric/Khmer) 339, 348
Kilivila (Austric/Central-Eastern Malayo-Polynesian) 222
Kimbundu (Niger-Kordofanian/Bantoid) 292
Kinyarwanda (Niger-Kordofanian/Bantoid) 145
Kiowa (Amerind/Tanoan) 253
Kituba (Niger-Kordofanian/Bantoid) 260
Korean (Isolate) 130–1
Koryak (Chukotko-Kamchatkan) 299
Kunjen (Australian/Pama-Nyungan) 350
Kutenai (Amerind/Kutenai) 50

Lakhota (Amerind/Siouan) 162
Lango (Nilo-Saharan/Nilotic) 78–80, 90, 96, 100–2, 103, 324, 353
Latin (Indo-European/Romance) xiii, 261, 344
Latvian (Indo-European/Baltic) 139
Laz (Kartvelian) 165
Lenakel (Austric/Central-Eastern Malayo-Polynesian) 342
Lillooet (Amerind/Coast Salishan) 31–2
Lithuanian (Indo-European/Baltic) 286, 311, 313
Luganda (Niger-Kordofanian/Bantoid) 215, 216, 250
Lummi (Amerind/Coast Salishan) 288–9, 290, 314
Lushootseed (Amerind/Coast Salishan) 31–2

Maasai (Nilo-Saharan/Nilotic) 291–2, 299, 311, 313, 314
Macedonian (Indo-European/Slavic) 224
Makah (Amerind/Wakashan) 30–1, 33, 74, 76–8, 84, 85, 90, 104
Malay, Classical (Austric/Sundic) 306
Mam (Amerind/Mayan) 156, 246, 271, 279
Mandarin Chinese (Sino-Tibetan/Chinese) 67, 70, 114, 223, 251, 323, 326, 339, 352, 353–4
Maori (Austric/Central-Eastern Malayo-Polynesian) 352
Marathi (Indo-European/Indic) 145, 210
Margi (Afroasiatic/Biu-Mandara) 225
Mayan languages (Amerind) 153
  see also Aguacatec; Chol; Jacaltec; K'iche'; Mam; Tzotzil; Tzutujil; Yucatec
Menomini (Amerind/Algonkian) 292–3, 311, 313
Minangkabau (Austric/Philippine) 120
Mohawk (Amerind/Iroquoian) 338
Mokilese (Austria/Central-Eastern Malayo-Polynesian) 198
Mooré (Niger-Kordofanian/Gur) 353

Index of Languages

Moose Cree (Amerind/Algonkian) 214, 217, 218
Mundari (Austric/Munda) 340

Nahuatl, Classical (Amerind/Aztecan) 215, 216
Ngandi (Australian/Gunwinyguan) 300, 314
Nguna (Austric/Central-Eastern Malayo-Polynesian) 104
Nootkan (Amerind/Wakashan) 65, 76, 78
 see also Makah
Nunggubuyu (Australian/Nunggubuyu) 300, 314

O'odham (Amerind/Pimic) 197, 223, 252, 253–4
Oceanic languages (Austric/Central-Eastern Malayo-Polynesian) 140
 see also Big Nambas; Kilivila; Lenakel; Maori; Mokilese; Nguna; Paamese; Ponapean; Pukapukan; Rennellese; Tongan; Woleaian
Ojibwe (Amerind/Algonkian) 240

Paamese (Austric/Central-Eastern Malayo-Polynesian) 353
Palauan (Austric/Philippine Austronesian) 252
Papago, see O'odham
Papuan languages (Indo-Pacific) 324, 334, 339, 341, 343, 350, 354
 see also Alamblak; Amele; Barai; Hua; Iatmul; Kalam; Kewa; Usan; Wambon; Yimas
Persian (Indo-European/Iranian) 352
Philippine languages (Austric) 51, 65, 306–8
 see also Cebuano; Kapampangan; Minangkabau; Tagalog
Pima (Amerind/Pimic) 209–10, 325
Pitjantjatjara, see Bindjandjadjara
Polish (Indo-European/Slavic) 187
Polynesian languages (Austric/Central-Eastern Malayo-Polynesian) 65, 126
 see also Maori; Pukapukan; Rennellese
Pomo, Eastern (Amerind/Pomo) 165
Ponapean (Austric/Central-Eastern Malayo-Polynesian) 263, 280
Pukapukan (Austric/Central-Eastern Malayo-Polynesian) 303–4, 311, 313, 314, 318

Quechua (Amerind/Quechuan) 66, 67, 69, 70–2, 250, 256
 see also Ancash Quechua; Imbabura Quechua
Quiché, see K'iche'

Rennellese (Austric/Eastern-Central Malayo-Polynesian) 251, 252, 254, 276
Romance languages (Indo-European) 329
 see also French; Italian; Latin; Rumanian; Spanish
Rumanian (Indo-European/Romance) 198, 232, 234

Rushan (Indo-European/Iranian) 138
Rushi (Indo-European/Iranian) 228
Russian (Indo-European/Slavic, Russia) 29, 116–18, 123–4, 165–6, 198, 199–200, 225–6, 244, 248, 250, 251, 291, 311, 313, 355

Salishan languages (Amerind) 65, 78
 see also Bella Coola; Lillooet; Lummi; Lushootseed; Straits Salish; Upriver Halkomelem
Santali (Austroasiatic/Munda) 199
Sarcee (Na-Dene/Athapaskan-Eyak) 338
Seko Padang (Austric/Philippine) 300–1, 311, 313, 314
Serbian-Croatian (Indo-European/Slavic) 224, 230
Shilluk (Nilo-Saharan/Nilotic) 305–6, 311, 313, 314
Sika (Austric/Central-Eastern Malayo-Polynesian) 340
Sinhalese (Indo-European/Indic) 345
Sm'algyax, see Coast Tsimshian
Soddo (Afroasiatic/Semitic) 104, 343
Spanish (Indo-European/Romance) 69, 140, 188, 227, 271, 293, 311, 313, 314
Straits Salish (Amerind/Coast Salishan) 31–2
Sumerian (Isolate) 155
Supyire (Niger-Kordofanian/Gur) 347
Svan (Kartvelian) 165
Swahili (Niger-Kordofanian/Bantoid) 342–3

Tagalog (Austric/Philippine) 308
Tamil (Dravidian/Dravidian Proper) 323, 344, 345
Tangut (Sino-Tibetan/Burmic) 296–7, 311, 313
Tariana (Amerind/Maipuran) 165
Tewa, Arizona (Amerind/Tanoan) 295, 311, 313, 314
Tibetan, Lhasa (Sino-Tibetan/Tibetic) 165
Tiwi (Australian/Tiwi) 338
Tok Pisin (English Creole) 215, 216, 249
Tongan (Austric/Central-Eastern Malayo-Polynesian) 68, 69, 70–2, 74, 124–6, 140, 150, 151, 156
Tsakhur (Caucasian/Northeast) 210
Tsez (Caucasian/Northeast) 211
Tsou (Austric/Tsouic) 165
Turkana (Nilo-Saharan/Nilotic) 292, 314
Turkish (Altaic/Turkic) 75
Tuscarora (Amerind/Iroquoian) 68, 69, 71
Twi (Niger-Kordofanian/Western South Central Niger-Congo) 353
Tzotzil (Amerind/Mayan) 209, 212
Tzutujil (Amerind/Mayan) 201, 269

Upriver Halkomelem (Amerind/Coast Salishan) 293–4, 295, 311, 313, 314

Index of Languages

Usan (Indo-Pacific/Adalbert Range) 201
Ute (Amerind/Numic) 196–7, 198–9
Uzbek (Altaic/Turkic) 211

Vietnamese (Austric/Viet-Muong) 29, 30–1, 33, 339

Wambon (Indo-Pacific/Central & South New Guinea) 70
Wangkumara (Australian/Pama-Nyungan) 138
Wardaman (Australian/Gunwinyguan) 29, 153, 187, 191–3, 200, 300, 314
Warlpiri (Australian/Pama-Nyungan) 156, 186–7, 200–1, 226, 249, 324
Warrungu (Australian/Pama-Nyungan) 156
Welsh (Indo-European/Celtic) 290–1, 311, 313

Woleaian (Austric/Central-Eastern Malayo-Polynesian) 140, 198

Xokleng (Amerind/Macro-Ge) 155

Yidiny (Australian/Pama-Nyungan) 156, 265–6
Yimas (Indo-Pacific/Sepik-Ramu) 243, 301–2, 318, 319
Yokuts (Amerind/Yokuts) 145
Yoruba (Niger-Kordofanian/Yoruba-Northern Akoko) 144–5
Yucatec (Amerind/Mayan) 119–22, 124, 129
Yup'ik (Eskimo-Aleut, Alaska) 140, 142
Yurok (Amerind/Yurok) 297–8, 311, 313, 314, 318, 319
Yuwaalaraay (Australian/Pama-Nyungan) 134–7, 138

Index of Constructions, Categories, and Features

Note: Constructions and features are named as such; the default entry is a category. Grammatical categories and constructions are given in uppercase, since they are language-specific; semantic categories are in lowercase. However, grammatical entries include references to classes of grammatical categories or constructions defined cross-linguistically by functional prototypes (see §1.6.3; Croft 1990:11–18); these are lowercase in the text. Subtypes of constructions are listed under constructions. Categories have separate entries, unless they are associated with specific constructions. Values of inflectional categories are listed under the category. Category/construction labels specific to certain languages or families have the language (family) name given in parentheses. Theories with which certain categories are specifically associated are also given in parentheses following the term.

Absolutive (chaining) construction 323
   Ablative Absolute (Latin) 344
Absolutive-Dative Alternation construction (Warlpiri) 249
action (semantic class) 63, 67, 70, 74–5, 76–7, 79–80, 87–9, 92, 96–100, 103, 104, 107
   see also events
Active, *see* Voice
Adjective xiv, 10, 12, 17, 29, 30, 31, 37–8, 63–71, 75–82, 85, 89, 95, 103, 104, 186–7, 227, 228, 230, 243, 250, 261, 266
   Adjectival inflection (Japanese) 81–3
   Adjectivalization 88
   Attributive Adjective 230
Adjective Phrase 243
Adposition 198, 199, 226, 234, 263–5, 329, 344, 345
   see also Preposition; Postposition
Adpositional Phrase 263–5
   see also Prepositional Phrase
Adverb 30, 40, 65, 76, 77, 78, 193, 210–11, 243
   Additive Adverb 338
   Negative Adverb 213
   Sequential Adverb 338
   Temporal Adverb 122
Adverbial Subordination construction 321–3, 324, 326, 327, 328–35, 338–41, 344–6, 349–52, 356, 358–9, 360
   Adverbial Subordinator 329
   see also Converb construction; Gerund; Conjunctive Participle
Agreement 13, 14, 30, 78, 150, 153, 157–9, 161, 166, 168, 170, 177, 198, 200, 210–11, 220, 226, 227, 230, 269, 292, 296, 298, 300, 303, 308, 342
   3rd Person Subject Number Agreement (Georgian) 158–9

   Actor Agreement 162
   Feminine Singular Agreement 231
   Nonperson Agreement 199, 227
   Number Agreement 102, 155, 230
   Object Agreement 243, 244
   Person Agreement 198, 199, 201
   Special A Agreement 104–5, 311, 313
   Special P Agreement 294–5, 298, 311, 313
   Subject Agreement 79, 102, 103, 134, 148, 200
   Undergoer Agreement 162
   see also agreement (*in Subject Index*); Pronominal affixes
animacy:
   human 159–60
   inanimate 159–60
   natural forces 291
Antipassive, *see* Voice
Anticausative construction 317
   see also Spontaneous construction
Applicative 284
Apposition construction 192, 347
Argument Linking/Argument Structure constructions 25, 57, 59, 60, 132, 168, 197, 247–8
   see also Absolutive-Dative alternation; Locative Alternation; Voice
Article 31, 39, 88, 98, 123, 124, 128, 223–4, 246, 254, 258, 259, 261, 267, 268
   Definite Article 223
   Indefinite Article 121, 128
   see also Definiteness
Aspect 25, 30, 31, 32, 90, 91, 103, 169, 171, 253, 268, 305, 351, 354–7
   Durative 76–7
   Habitual 79–80, 103
   Imperfective 169, 171, 319
   Inchoative 74

Aspect (*cont.*):
  Momentaneous (Makah) 76–7
  Perfective 79, 169, 171, 319
  Progressive 79, 168
  see also Perfect; Present Perfect
Attributive 230
  see also Modifier
Attributive Particle (Lango) 78–80, 100, 102
Auxiliary 10, 25, 26, 76, 77, 78, 125, 168, 215, 217, 218, 220, 223, 224, 236, 242, 248–9, 251, 253, 258, 259, 260–1, 267, 268, 271, 325
  Modal Auxiliary 26

Bare Singular construction (English) 39–40, 121
Bipersonal construction (Yurok) 297–8
Bodily State construction 115

Case (K; generative grammar) 225
Case (marking) 29, 116–17, 135, 142, 144–5, 153, 177, 186, 200, 225, 228, 244, 248, 249, 250, 270–1, 295
  Ablative 344, 345
  Absolutive 126, 153, 167, 209, 212, 260, 309–10
    Absolutive Noun Phrase 210–11
  Accusative 116–17, 143, 148, 157, 167, 225, 244, 309–10
  Comitative 338
  Dative 143, 145, 152, 157–9, 244, 264
  Ergative 153, 167, 201, 260, 309–10
  Genitive 75, 81, 88, 98, 125, 126, 166, 211, 225, 235, 261, 264, 307
    see also Modifier, Genitive; Noun Phrase, Genitive
  Illative Case 116–17
  Inessive Case 116–17
  Instrumental 238, 244
  Locative 116–17, 235, 264
  Nominative 13, 14, 148, 157, 198, 200, 295
  Objective 145, 157, 200, 324
  see also case marking (*in Subject Index*)
Case Phrase (KP; generative grammar) 225
⟨cat⟩ feature (Head-driven Phrase Structure Grammar, Construction Grammar) 48
Causative 284
Causative Verb construction (Eastern Mono) 238
Class, *see* Noun Class
Classifier 234, 263, 267
  Arrangement Classifier 119
  Group Classifier 119
  Measure Classifier 119, 120, 262
  Numeral Classifier 119–22, 124, 199, 232, 262–3
  see also Numeral Classifier construction
  Partitive Classifier 119, 120
  Possessive Classifier 199
  Sortal Classifier 119–20
Clausal Syntactic Roles:

Actor 59, 303
Direct Object 35–6, 41, 46, 52, 143, 214, 218, 264, 273
Indirect Object 143, 209
Nonsubject 308
Object 10, 13, 29, 32, 40, 43, 49, 59, 77, 132–4, 133–7, 142, 156, 178, 188, 196–7, 217, 234, 243–6, 247, 248, 249, 251, 252, 253, 260, 264, 277–8, 285–7, 291–4, 297, 300, 303, 308, 311–13, 315, 330
Oblique 35, 49, 143, 156–7, 264, 265, 285, 288–9, 291, 294, 295, 303–6, 311–13, 355–7, 358–60
Subject 10, 11, 13, 20, 22, 23–4, 25, 26, 29, 30, 31, 32, 35–6, 49, 57, 109, 59, 132–8, 142, 149–52, 155, 156–9, 162–5, 170, 184, 195, 196–7, 198, 200, 211, 213–17, 219, 234, 243, 251, 253, 260, 277, 278, 284–8, 291, 293–7, 299–300, 202–3, 206, 208, 311–13, 315, 330
  Plural Subject 231
  Pronominal Subject 195
Undergoer 59
"Unergative" 316, 317
Clause construction 22, 23, 24, 25, 30, 57, 124, 125, 137, 152, 154, 185, 194–5, 196, 201, 214, 216, 223, 324, 328–9, 338, 347
  Finite Clause 198, 321
  see also Finite Relative Clause construction
  see also Ditransitive construction; Intransitive Clause construction; Main Clause construction; Transitive Clause construction
Clause Chaining constructions:
  ka Tense Chaining (Swahili) 342
  m- Chaining (Soddo) 343
  Stem Form Chaining (Japanese) 343
  -te Chaining (Japanese) 343
  -to Chaining (Japanese) 343
  see also Absolutive (Chaining) construction; Coordination construction
Cleft construction 26, 153, 154
Clitic Climbing construction (Italian) 218
Comparative construction 340–1
Complement Clause 59, 60, 88, 150, 217, 223, 265–6, 277, 321–2, 323–4, 327, 346–9, 351–4, 356, 357–8, 359–60
Complementizer 98, 141, 223, 242, 265–6, 267, 324, 329, 348
Direct Speech Complement 322, 324–5
DNI Complement construction (English) 278
Infinitival Complement construction 29, 88, 150, 178, 214, 326, 352
Nominal Complement construction 348–9
Nonfinite Complement 321
Sentential Complement 256
Sentential Complement 211, 219
Complex Nominal construction 75, 238, 262

Index Constructions, Categories, and Features 403

Conditional construction 339–40, 342
Conjunction Reduction construction 13, 14, 29, 189, 337, 343
Conjunctive Participle/Verb form 323, 342, 344–5
Constituent Negation construction 154
Control suffixes (Upriver Halkomelem) 294
Converb construction 323, 345–6
Coordinate Sentence, see Coordination
Coordination construction 29, 148, 152, 154–60, 170–1, 189, 192, 256, 320–1, 322–4, 326–9, 336–44, 346, 352, 353–4
   Asyndetic Coordination 353
   Coordinating Conjunction 267, 341–2
   Coordinating Suffix 345
   Syndetic Coordination 353
   see also Absolutive chaining construction; clause chaining construction; Conjunction Reduction construction; cosubordination construction; Gapping construction; Paratactic clause construction; Right Node Raising construction; Serial Verb construction; Stripping construction; switch reference construction
Copula 37, 79–80, 81–3, 88, 90, 96, 98, 103, 184, 214, 216, 266, 267
Cosubordination construction 322–3, 327
Countability constructions 60
Counting construction 121, 122, 129

Dative Shift transformation (generative grammar) 43–4
Dative Subordination suffix (Yidiny) 265
Declarative construction 26, 277
Definiteness:
   Definite 197, 228, 254
   Indefinite 197, 201
Degree 91
   Comparative Degree 80
   Simple Degree 80
   Superlative Degree 80
Demonstrative 17, 77, 103, 154, 227, 228, 230, 246, 261, 347
Determination construction 31, 32
   Determiner 123, 185, 242, 246, 250, 252, 254, 257, 259
   see also Article; Demonstrative
Determiner Phrase (DP) 257–8
Diathesis 284
   see also Applicative; Causative; Voice
Directional 114
Distributive construction 171
Distributive construction 166
   Distributive Preposition (Russian) 166
Ditransitive construction 26, 42–4, 75, 143, 145, 247

DNI Prepositional Object construction (English) 278
Double Object construction, see Ditransitive construction
DP, see Determiner Phrase
DS, see Switch Reference construction

each . . . the other construction (English) 43
Emphatic Sentence construction 228
Equative construction 260
Ergative construction 303, 304
events:
   ditransitive event 142–7, 164
   inactive action 117–18
   intransitive event 134, 137, 142, 163–4, 166, 317–18
   motion event 116–19
   transitive event 134, 137, 142, 164, 284–314, 317–18
   see also actions
Evidential Complement Subject Passive construction (Japanese) 219
Extraction constructions 153–4
   see also Cleft; Constituent Negation; Information Question

Focus constructions 51
   Actor Focus (Philippine languages) 51, 307–8
   Focus Antipassive (Mayan languages) 142, 154
   Goal Focus (Philippine languages) 51, 307–8, 311, 313, 314
   Instrumental Focus (Mayan languages) 201

Gapping construction 189, 280, 337
Gender 29, 91, 200, 227, 229–30
   Feminine 200, 231, 260
   Masculine 231
Gender/Animacy/Classifying constructions 60
Gerund 79, 88, 103
go + Destination construction (English) 113
"Grammatical Relations", see Clausal Syntactic Roles

Imperative construction 13, 14, 148, 152–3
Indefinite ("Passive") construction (Finnish) 291, 311, 313
indefinite human referent 291
Indirect Object construction 42, 143
Infinitive 79–80, 150
   Bare Infinitive (English) 248–9
   Infinitival Predicate 214
   to Infinitive (English) 248–9
Information Question 11, 153, 201
INI Object construction 279
   INI Object 279–80

Index of Constructions, Categories, and Features

Interrogative Sentence construction 26
Intransitive Clause construction 20, 23, 25, 53–7, 247
  Intransitive Subject 55–6, 134
  Intransitive Verb 54–6, 162
Izafet construction (Turkish) 75

kick construction (English) 25, 27

Locative Alternation constructions 44, 248

Main Clause 213, 214, 217, 324, 338, 345, 346, 350, 351
  Main Clause Subject 13
  Main Verb 178, 211, 213, 214, 217, 218, 260, 351
  Perfective Main Clause (Cebuano) 307
Medial Verb constructions (Papuan languages) 323, 343, 354
  Nonfinal Verb form 345
Modifier 37, 38, 84, 88, 90, 199, 215, 228, 243
  Genitive Modifier 246, 247
  Phrasal modifier 193
Mood 25, 30, 31, 90, 91, 103, 253, 342, 351, 354–7
  Subjunctive 79–80, 321

±N feature (generative grammar) 48, 64
N to D movement (generative grammar) 123
Neg-raising construction 213
Negative construction 25–6, 166, 171, 213
Nominal Adjective (Japanese) 81–3, 103
Nominalization 88, 98, 326, 327, 329
  Action Nominals 88, 355–6
  Agent Nominalization 269, 270
  Nominalizer 324, 325
Nontopicalized Declarative Transitive Active construction (English) 236
Noun 10, 17, 29, 30, 31, 32, 33, 37–8, 50, 57, 63–71, 75–8, 85, 89, 90, 95, 102, 104, 108, 109, 121, 123, 124, 185, 186–7, 198, 199, 201, 224, 225, 227, 228, 230, 238, 243, 250, 252, 253, 257–8, 263, 265, 266, 269, 271, 292, 306
  Common Noun 167, 232, 289
  Count Noun 37, 39–40, 119–22
  Deadjectival Nouns 88
  Group Nouns (British English) 230
  Mass Noun 37, 39, 119–22
  Relational Noun 264, 271, 329
Noun Class 211, 243, 347
  see also Gender
Noun Incorporation construction 239, 280, 306, 316
  External Noun 239
  Incorporated Noun 239
  Type I Noun Incorporation 280
Noun Phrase 13, 14, 16, 17, 22, 23, 25, 30, 35, 37, 39, 43, 44, 53, 123, 125, 137, 140, 148, 153, 154, 177, 185, 188, 191, 192–3, 194–5, 196,

  197, 200, 217, 222, 223, 226, 228, 235, 242, 243–5, 247, 250, 251, 257–8, 261–3, 324
  Anaphoric Head 38
  Genitive Noun Phrase 38–9, 75, 262
  Head Noun 37, 78, 211, 228, 246, 324, 347, 348, 350, 351
  Independent Noun Phrase 227
  Subject Noun Phrase 211, 215, 226
  see also Modifier
NP, *see* Noun Phrase
NP movement (generative grammar) 42–3
Null Anaphora 251, 276
Number 23, 29, 78, 91, 122, 200, 211, 227, 254, 347
  Dual 301
  Dual Survival form (Serbian-Croatian) 230
  Nonsingular 302
  Plural 37, 78, 100, 128, 230, 254
  Singular 78, 100, 128, 230
  see also Verbal Number
Numeral 39, 121–2, 224, 230, 232, 261–3
  Base 224, 232
Numeral Classifier construction 129
  see also Classifier, Numeral

Object, *see* Clausal Syntactic Roles
objects (semantic class) 63, 67, 69, 74–5, 76–7, 87–90, 92, 96–9, 104, 107, 166
Obviation:
  Obviative (Algonkian languages) 287
  Proximate (Algonkian languages) 287

Paratactic construction 322, 323, 324
participant role clusters:
  A (transitive "agent") 135, 146–7, 150, 152, 153, 159, 164–5, 167, 168–9, 200, 279, 284–319, 320, 338, 355–7, 358–60
  absolutive (S + P) 135–6, 140–2, 147, 150, 160, 161, 165–6, 200
  accusative (P) 59, 136–42, 143, 147, 150, 154–6, 161
  direct object (P + T) 143–7, 265
  ergative (A) 59, 136, 140–2, 147, 150, 154–6, 313, 314
  experiencer 155–9, 164, 356
  G (ditransitive "goal") 143–7, 164–5, 358–60
  indirect object (G) 143–7, 209
  nominative (A + S) 135, 136–42, 147, 160, 200
  P (transitive "patient") 135, 136–42, 143, 146–7, 150, 152, 153, 159, 164–5, 166, 167, 168–9, 200, 220, 284–319, 320, 338, 355–7, 358–60
  primary object (P + G) 143–7
  S (intransitive "subject") 135, 146–7, 152, 166, 168–9, 200, 338, 355–7, 358–60
  Sa ("actor" intransitive) 162–5, 303, 316
  secondary object (T) 143–7
  stimulus 155–9, 164
  Su ("undergoer" intransitive) 162–5

T (ditransitive "theme") 143–7, 164–5
Participle 88, 253, 260, 325, 326, 344–5
 Nonfinite Participle/Verb form 141, 148, 168, 248
 Past Participle (English) 52, 220, 236, 248–9
 Present Participle (English) 248–9
Particle (English) 40
Partitive construction 166, 171
Passive, *see* Voice
Passive rule/transformation (generative grammar) 18, 43
Perfect construction 162, 168, 218
Person 23, 30, 169, 211, 228, 271, 342
 1st Person 209, 211, 226, 229, 284, 287, 289–90, 294–302, 308, 309–10, 318–19
 2nd Person 284, 287, 289–90, 294–302, 308, 309–10, 318–19
 3rd Person 23, 137, 298, 209, 284, 287, 289–90, 294–302, 305, 309–10, 318–19
  3rd Person Singular Habitual (Lango) 78
Politeness:
 Familiar 290
 Formal 289–90
Possession construction 112–13, 115, 125
 Headless Possession construction 280
Possessive 32, 38, 76
Possessor 209, 212, 254, 355–7
Possessor Ascension construction 209, 211, 212
Postposition 235
Potential construction 316
Predication construction 31, 32
 Nonverbal Predication construction 74, 215
 Predicate 20, 57, 63, 88, 213–15, 230
  see also Verb Phrase
 Predicate Adjective construction 88, 112–13, 125, 184, 266
 Predicate Nominal construction 88, 251, 266
Preposition 35, 40, 44, 49, 78, 88, 98, 114, 122, 143, 150, 156, 185, 225, 232, 234, 236, 242, 250, 262, 264, 269, 271, 306, 330
 Locative Preposition 144, 232
 see also Adposition; Distributive Preposition; Postposition
Prepositional Phrase 177, 185, 194–5
Present Perfect 27
Primary Person affixes (Seko Padang) 300–1
Pronominal affixes 125, 126, 239
 see also Agreement
Pronoun 13, 24, 126, 134, 135, 137, 140, 158, 167, 177, 188, 196, 218, 224, 232, 244, 250, 265, 270–81, 289, 300, 305, 347
 Anaphoric Pronoun 230
 Bound Pronoun 227
 Independent Pronoun 228–9, 269
 Personal Pronoun 122
 Possessive Pronoun 230
  Attributive Possessive Pronouns 38–9

Pronominal Possessive/Possessive Pronouns 38–9
Reflexive Pronoun 150, 153, 293, 348
Subject Pronoun 271
see also Demonstrative
Proper Name 124, 232
properties (semantic class) 63, 67, 69, 70, 74–5, 76–81, 87–9, 92, 96–101, 103, 104, 107
propositional act constructions 59–60
 see also Modifier; Noun Phrase; Predication construction
Pseudocleft construction 195
Psych Verbs, *see* Verbs, Mental
Purpose construction 154–6, 159–60, 170, 322, 326, 351–2
Putting constructions 130–1

Quantifier 209–10, 261–3, 264, 267
Quantifier Float construction 209–10, 212
Quantifier Phrase 264

Raising to Object construction 213–14
Reflexive construction 153, 284
 Reflexive morpheme 148, 150
 see also Voice, Reflexive
Relative Clause construction 51, 78–80, 88, 141–2, 154–6, 159–60, 170, 191, 192, 200, 211, 322, 324–6, 327, 342, 346–51, 356, 358–9, 360
 Adjoined Relative Clause 322, 349–50
 Correlative Relative Clause 322, 326, 350–1
 Embedded Relative Clause 350
 Extraposed Relative Clause construction (English) 191
 Finite Relative Clause 141
 Headless Relative Clause 256, 347
 Internally Headed Relative Clause 312, 325, 347
 Relative Clause Subject 211
 Relative Pronoun 88, 98, 100, 102, 199–200, 230
 Relativizer 223, 347, 348
Right Node Raising construction 189, 337

semantic classes, *see* actions; events; objects; properties
 aspectual semantic classes 60
Sequential Verb form 342
Serial Verb construction 264, 323, 326, 352, 352–4
 Coordinate Serial Verb construction 353
size 91
spatial relations 60
Split Ergative constructions 309–10, 311, 313
Spontaneous constructions 316–17
 see also Anticausative constructions
SS, *see* Switch Reference construction
Stripping construction 189

406 Index of Constructions, Categories, and Features

Subject, see Clausal Syntactic Roles
Subject-Auxiliary Inversion construction
    (Germanic languages) 213
Subordinate Clause construction 213, 320, 321,
    329, 342, 356–60
    see also Adverbial Subordination;
        Complement; Relative Clause
Switch Reference construction 341–2
    Different Subject construction 341–2
    Different Subject (DS) forms 341, 342
    Same Subject (SS) forms 341, 342

Tense 12, 17, 25, 30, 31, 79, 90, 91, 103, 253, 354–7
    Future 113
    Past 28, 138, 169, 171
    Present 134, 138, 168, 169, 171
    Present I (Chukchi) 299–300
    Present II (Chukchi) 299
    see also Perfect; Present Perfect
Tense-Agreement construction (English) 55–6
    3rd Person Singular Present Tense (English)
        12, 24, 122
thematic roles, see participant role clusters
There-construction (English) 27, 200
    Central Deictic There-construction (English)
        27
    Perceptual Deictic There-construction
        (English) 27
    Presentational Deictic There-construction 27
Topic 325
Tough-Movement construction 214
Transitive (Active) Clause construction 25, 52,
    53–7, 247–8, 273, 278, 306, 312, 314, 318
    Transitive affix 249
    Transitive Object 57
    Transitive Subject 55–7, 134
    Transitive Verb 49, 54–6, 251, 260
    Transitive Verb inflections 297–302, 318
    Transitive Verb Phrase 252
Transitive Animate conjugation (Algonkian
    languages) 292
Transitive DNI construction (English) 278, 279
    DNI Object 277–8
Transitive Inanimate conjugation (Algonkian
    languages) 292

Unipersonal construction (Yurok) 297–8

V, see transitive event
±V feature (generative grammar) 48, 64
Verb 10, 13, 14, 17, 22, 23, 24, 25, 26, 28, 29, 30, 31,
    33, 44, 50, 53–5, 63–5, 67–82, 85, 89, 102,
    104, 114, 122, 124, 125, 128, 134, 139, 143,
    157, 166, 177, 178, 185, 188, 192, 194, 196–7,
    198, 199, 200, 211, 215, 217, 219, 22, 223,
    236, 242, 243–6, 247–9, 251, 252, 253, 258,
    259, 260–1, 264, 265, 268, 271, 277–8, 298,
    321, 324, 342, 343, 348
Mental Verbs 155–9
Morphological Verb 55–6
Stative Verbs 65
Verb movement (generative grammar) 42
Verb Phrase 22, 23, 25, 44, 177, 183–4, 185, 194–5,
    196, 223, 242, 243–6, 251, 252
    see also Predication construction
Verb Phrase Deletion construction 188, 189, 251
Verbal Number 166, 171
    Plural Verb 166
Verbal Operator 215
Voice affix 268
Voice constructions 60, 283–319, 364
    Active 35–6, 49, 142, 154, 220, 284–6, 288–90,
        292–4, 295, 302, 303, 304–6, 311, 313, 314,
        316–19
        Active Object 220, 285
        Active Subject 52, 215, 285
        Perfect Active (Shilluk) 305
    Antipassive construction 279, 299, 316–17,
        319
        Antipassive Verb form 152
    Direct 286–7, 288, 308, 315, 318
        Direct Subject 300
    Direct Passive (Menomini) 292
    Impersonal Passive 290–1
    Inverse 286–8, 289, 295–6, 298–302, 307, 310,
        311, 313, 314, 316, 318
        Inverse Active (Menomini) 292–3
        Inverse Passive (Menomini) 292–3
    Middle 284, 294, 314
    Passive xiii, 11, 17, 35–6, 41–4, 46, 49, 50, 52,
        72, 178, 215, 219, 220, 236, 278, 284, 285–6,
        287, 288–95, 297–8, 303, 304–6, 311, 313–
        14, 316, 317, 318
        Agentless Passive 237
        Passive Agent Phrase 236
        Passive Auxiliary 49, 215, 216
        Passive Subject 50, 52, 209, 215, 220
        Passive Verb 216
        Predicated Passive 215, 216
    Passive/Inverse (Arizona Tewa) 295–6
    Reflexive Middle 293
    Reflexive Passive 293
    Subjectless Passive (Karo Batak) 305
    see also Bipersonal construction; Evidential
        Complement Subject Passive
        construction; Focus constructions;
        transitive verb paradigms; Unipersonal
        construction
VP, see Verb Phrase
VP/NP 49

Index of Subjects

Note: In the case of multiple references, definitions and major explications are cited in boldface.

accessible referent 235, 276, 277, 278, 279, 280
accusative languages 137
accusativity, *see* ergativity/accusativity
activation network model 28, 98, 367
addressee 284, 315
  see also hearer; speaker
adjunct 46, 188, 194, **272–80**, 364
  see also argument, semantic; argument, syntactic
affix 198, 199, **268–71**, 342, 361
  see also root
agreement 23, 24, 29, 31, 91, 139, 141, 142, 144–6, 148, 150, 151, 153, 154–6, 158–9, 161, 162–5, 166, 170, 186, **198–9**, 200, 216, **226–32**, 234, 239–41, 246–7, 273, 275, 288, 294, 296–302, 312, 356
  anaphoric agreement 229
  anomalous agreement 210–11
  controller **226**, 227, 228
    absence of controller 226–32
  local agreement 229
  NP-internal agreement 228
  portmanteau agreement forms 295, 298, 302
  target **226**, 227, 242, 243
  see also bound pronoun analysis; coded dependency, relational; discourse referent; double indexation; one syntactic argument per semantic referent assumption; special agreement forms
altered replication
  see also innovation 366
arbitrariness 7–8, 9, 72, 118, 364
argument:
  semantic 26, 88, 217, 247, 273, 346
  syntactic 46, 57, 188, 194, 218, 241, 267, **272–80**, 364
argument (methodology), *see* argumentation; criteria; distributional analysis/method
argumentation xiii–xiv, 3, **13**, 179, 185
atomic **16**, 17, **47**, 48, 53, 362–3
atomic primitives 4, 10, 13, 14–15, **45–6**, **47–8**, 49, 57–8, 83, 84, 131, 149, 362
  see also atomic; primitives
Autolexical Syntax 259
  see also Clitic Principle; Incorporation Principle

backgrounding, *see* foregrounding
backwards pronominal anaphora/control 345
balanced/balancing **321**, 322, 325, 326, 341–6, 355, 357, 359, 360
  see also deranked/deranking; Hierarchy, Deranking
base (headedness) 242, **244–5**, 252
basic-level category 118
basic type (of a construction in a language) **285**, 286, 290, 294, 296, 304–6, 312, 315, 318, 321
behavior, *see* distribution pattern
behavioral constructions/properties/criteria **148–9**, 151, 153, 157–60
  see also coding constructions
behavioral potential **66**, 90, 91, 98–102, 103, 105, 114–15, 140–2, **146**, 147, 318, 355
  see also Behavioral Potential Map Hypothesis; structural coding; typological markedness
Behavioral Potential Map Hypothesis **98**, 99, 101
binary branching analysis 221–2
Binding Hierarchy, *see* Hierarchy, Complement Deranking
biology 365
bound pronoun analysis 227
box notation **20**, 23, 182
bracket notation **20**, 22, 53, 185
building block metaphor 238
  see also scaffolding metaphor

C-chain, *see* consecutive chain
case marking 29, 91, 116, 134, 139–40, 144–5, 148, 149, 150, 151, 153, 154–6, 158–9, 160, 162–3, 170, 186, **198–9**, 200, 226, 263–5, 297, 303, 312, 319, 344, 356
  see also coded dependency, relational
case marking systems 137–47
  neutral case marking system 137, 138, 139
casual speech 304
categorial grammar 49, 184
categories, syntactic/grammatical 4, 8, **12–13**, 18, 20–1, 24, 29–62, 108, 114, 175, 363, 364
  category boundary 103
  covert categories 75

categories, syntactic/grammatical (*cont.*):
  global (cross-constructional)
    categories/relations **45**, 55, 58, 61, 105, 106, 147–52, 153, 162, 179, 186, 189, 202, 241, 254
  "lumping" approach to 32, 65–75, 78, 84, 105
  necessary and sufficient conditions for categories 71–2, 117
    see also monosemy
  population definition of 365, 366
  radial categories **104**, 116
    see also prototypes
  "splitting" approach 32, 65, 75–83, 105
  universal (cross-linguistic)
    categories/relations **32**, 33, 34, 61, 92, 106, 108, 146–7, 149–52, 162, 254
  see also atomic primitives; criteria; Grammatical Category Structure Hypothesis; label; multiple class membership; name; prototype; subclasses; taxonomic links, between categories
categorization 4, 27–8, 52, 55–6, 76, 363, 367
causal chain 164
centrality of relative clause head to relative clause event 360
circumstantial dependent 193, 272, 351
classification (minor propositional act) 94
clause collapsing/fusion 216–20, 354, 360, 361
clitic 218, 308, 343, 361
  enclitic 187, 271, 303
  proclitic 188, 218, 300–1
Clitic Principle (Autolexical Syntax) 259
closure (Gestalt psychology) 332–3
clustering 267
coded dependency 6, **176–7**, 178, 179, 184, 187, **197–201**, 202, 232–3
  indexical coded dependency **199**, 202–3, 226–32, 275, 312
    see also agreement
  overtly coded dependency 197–201, 234
    absence of **232–3**
    optionality of 232–3
  relational coded dependency **199**, 202, 312
    nested relational coded dependencies 224–6
    see also case marking
  see also collocational dependency
coding constructions/properties/criteria **148**, 151, 157–9
  see also behavioral constructions
coequal event 160, 161
Cognitive Grammar 6–7, 14, 59, 104, 109, 184, 268, 367
  see also content requirement; parts of speech, conceptual analysis of; semantic structure; sequentially scanned; summary scanning; valence, semantic
cognitive linguistics 7, 109, 116
cognitive map, *see* conceptual space
Coherence Condition (Lexical-Functional Grammar) 208
collective entity 127–8
collocational dependency 5–6, 176, **177–85**, 186, 201, 225–6, 272
  see also coded dependency
collocations 180
common denominator 336–7, 338, 344
  see also good continuation
communication 364, 366
communicative isolation 365
competing motivations 7–8, 118
complementary distribution 287
Completeness Condition (Lexical-Functional Grammar) 208
complex (vs. atomic) **16**, 17, 362
complex figure structure 327, **336–8**, 339–46, 351–4, 361
complexity (of a grammatical unit) 192–3
component (semantic) 6, **21**, 23, 62, 183, 187, 204–5, 274, 276, 278–9, 280, 363
componential model (of a grammar) **14–15**, 16, 17, 19–20, 175, 180, 182, 202, 205
compositionality, semantic **180**, 181–4
compounding 269, 271
conceptual grouping 189
conceptual space 8, 28, 61, 62, 65, 86, 90, **92–8**, 99–102, 105, 108, 118, 123, 128, 130, 137, 146–7, 149, 159–61, 163, 169–70, 283, 284, 287, 288, 289, 294, 295, 298, 301–2, 303, 309–10, 312, 314–15, 316, 317–18, 319, 320, 327–8, 359–60, 361, 363, 364, 366, 367
  connected region in 96
  see also semantic map
conceptual structure **109**, 128, 130
  see also semantic structure
conceptualization, *see* construal
concord, *see* agreement
conjoinability 189
consecutive chain **336**, 352, 358
  see also simultaneous chain
constituency 5, **22**, 46, 47, 134, 176, **185–90**, 196, 202
  see also constituent structure; "discontinuous constituents"; grouping, formal
constituent structure 42–3
construal 75, 104, 109, 112–13, 117, 119–20, 125, 127–9, 130, 133, 213–20, 230–1, 265, 330, 336, 340, 349, 353
construction 4, 5, 8, **11–12**, **16–17**, 18–62, 77, 83, 84–5, 87, 93, 103, 104, 108, 113, 114, 123, 126–7, 128, 130, 137, 146, 148, 149, 154–85, 170–1, 175, 180, 181, 182, 188, 191, 202,

203–40, 243, 257, 260–7, 276–80, 283–4, 310–19, 322, 362–3, 365, 366, 367, 368
derived structural definition of **285–6**, 321
identification/categorization of **51–3**, 236–27, 283
instance of 20, 25, 52
partial specification of 26
senses of 27
structural type of 283–4, 285
structured inventory of 25
universal constructions 6, 50, 283, 288, 310, 319, 363
see also behavioral constructions/properties/criteria; coding constructions/properties/criteria; idiomatic phrase; idiomatically combining expression; idiom
construction grammar **14–29**, 58–9, 122, 148, 175–6, 179, 180, 182, 184, 185, 199, 202, 203–6, 208, 212, 218, 233, 247–50, 362
see also construction; Construction Grammar; Radical Construction Grammar
Construction Grammar 3, 20, 28, 48
content requirement (Cognitive Grammar) 6, 367
contiguity, syntactic 190, 200–1, 202
see also constituency; grouping, formal
continuum:
syntactic 313, 314, 322, 326, 327, 361
see also syntactic space
syntax-lexicon **17**, 58
Contrast, Principle of **111**, 112, 127, 216
convention/conventionality 19, 60, 62, 71–2, 93, 104, 109–12, 127–9, 133, 180, 183, 196, 239, 256, 279, 329, 341
conventional universalist position/hypothesis 110, 115, 127–9, 341
see also radical relativist position
criteria/arguments/tests **13**, 17–18, 34–47, 64, 68, 81, 84, 153, 179, 188–9, 202, 241–54
argument vs. adjunct 272–80
constituency 185–90
coordination vs. subordination 320–7
cross-linguistic validity of 10, 84, 89, 91, 179, 185, 197–9, 253, 254, 272, 275, 312, 321
global categories 11–14, 34–44
grammatical relations (syntactic roles) 134–6, 148–52
headhood 242–54
multiple class membership 38–9
parts of speech 65–83
subclasses 36–8
transformations 178–9, 184–5
universal categories 11–14, 29–32
voice types (active, passive, inverse) 285–8, 290–302

see also behavioral constructions/properties/criteria; coding constructions/properties/criteria
cross-linguistic comparison 91, 108, 136
cross-linguistic methodological opportunism, *see* methodological opportunism
cue-validity **52**, 89, 118

D-structure 178
see also deep structure
deep structure 151, 178
deixis (minor propositional act) 97, 319
dependency (syntactic representation) 5, **22**, 46, 47, 176, **197–201**
see also coded dependency; collocational dependency; constituency
dependent, syntactic 197–201, 241, 244, **272–80**
see also adjunct; argument, syntactic; head
dependent-marking 197–8
see also head-marking
deranked/deranking **321**, 322, 325, 341–6, 354–60
see also balanced/balancing; hierarchy, Deranking
derivation 269, 270, 293
see also zero derivation
determination 94, 97
diachrony 257–68, 269, 327, 329, 338, 341–6, 363
see also grammatical change; grammaticalization; language, dynamic nature of; language change, gradualness of; typological theory, dynamicization of
differential replication 368
see also propagation; selection
"discontinuous constituents" 186–8, 189
discourse xv, 9, 19, 52, 194, 227, 233, 237, 239–40, 258, 259, 335, 338, 366
function 60, 86, 93, 96, 187, 197, 308, 343, 349
referent 229
discovery procedure xiv, 11
distance 193
distribution pattern 5, **12**, 78, 82, 92, 100, 103, 104, 105, 106, 108, 134–5, 144, 147, 149–50, 153, 155, 161, 166, 169, 171, 252, 279, 283, 287, 295, 362, 363
distributional analysis/method 4, **11–14**, 17, **29–47**, 61, 73, 75, 78, 83, 84–104, 113–15, 125, 151
distributional equivalent 242, **245**, 246, 250–2
diversity, structural 7, 33, 61, 283, 288, 310, 312, 319, 320, 362
DNI, *see* null instantiation, definite
double indexation 229
dynamic character of language, *see* language, dynamic character of

e-site, *see* elaboration site
elaboration **274**, 327, 346–9, 351, 361

elaboration site (e-site) **274**, 346, 348, 351
element (syntactic) 6, 12, **21**, 23, 24, 53–62, 93, 126, 175–90, 192, 197, 203–8, 220, 243, 276, 363, 366
elimination of agreement forms 321, 355
elimination of tense-aspect-mood markings 321, 354, 356, 360–1
ellipsis 188–9, 245, 251–2
embedding, syntactic 345, 346, 347, 350–1, 354
empathy 159
empirical science 9, 10
endpoint (in causal chain) 164, 169, 319
   see also initiator (in causal chain)
entrenchment 28
enumeration (minor propositional act) 97
environment 367
ergative languages 137, 149–52, 303
ergativity/accusativity **134–71**
   "deep" ("syntactic") 151–2
   "superficial" ("morphological") 151
   see also accusative languages; ergative languages; split ergativity; split ergativity, split morphological ergativity; split ergativity, split syntactic ergativity
evaluative comment 334–5
event quantification 165–7, 171
event-participant structure 220
evolution 365
exocentric constructions 256–7
extension:
   formal semantics 259
   in grammatical change 117, 126–9, 130
   of an utterance 193–4
extraction 153, 345

features, syntactic 48–9, 63
field linguistics xviii, 7, 52, 59–60
figure (Gestalt psychology) 274, **329–38**, 339, 351
   see also ground
figure-ground structure 327, **329–35**, 338, 339–46, 351–2, 361
flexible language **66–7**, 68, 69, 70
   one-way flexible language **69**
   see also rigid language; parts of speech
FNI, see null instantiation, free null instantiation
focus 187
focus of attention 333
force-dynamic structure (of events) 164
   see also causal chain; endpoint; initiator
foregrounding **160–1**, 170–1, 307, 332–3, 343, 349
formal grouping, see grouping, formal
formal register 304
formal semantics 123, 259, 346
formalist theories xiii, xiv, 9, 11, 33–4, 132–3, 148
   see also categorial grammar; generative grammar; Government and Binding Theory; Head-driven Phrase Structure Grammar; Lexical Functional Grammar; Minimalism
frame, see semantic frame
"free" word order 196–7
frequency 28, 103–4, 105, 118, 142, 146, 285, 304–7, 315, 318
   token frequency 28
   type frequency 28
Full Grammatical Unit Condition 192, 194
function, mathematical 247–8
function-indicating morphosyntax, see structural coding
functional:
   dependency (Gestalt psychology) 333, 346
   explanation 97
   Functional Grammar 3, 65, 263
   see also term
   motivation 108, 208–13
   overkill 236–7
   underkill 237
functionalist theories xiii, xiv, xv, 9, 11, 32–4, 132–3
functor, semantic 242, **243–4**, 273

gene 365, 367
general formula 189, 337
generality, condition of 11
generative grammar 9, 20, 22, 23, 25, 34, 64, 86, 134–5, 186, 225, 247, 255, 257, 263
   see also Government and Binding Theory; Minimalism; transformational theory
genome 365, 366
Gestalt analysis of complex sentence constructions 327, **328–38**
Gestalt psychology 47, 329
   see also closure; common denominator; complex figure structure; figure; figure-ground structure; functional, dependency; good continuation; ground
given information 334
good continuation (Gestalt psychology) 332–3, 337
government (traditional grammar) 241, 242, **244**, 248–50, 273
Government and Binding Theory 3, 208, 228
   see also Projection Principle; Theta Criterion; X-bar Theory
gradability (semantic) **87**, 115
gradualness of language change, see language change, gradualness of
grammar 9, 11, 15, 32, 36, 45, 57–8, 59–60, 81, 95, 103, 203, 230, 367
   see also componential model; knowledge of grammar/language; syntax
Grammatical Category Structure Hypothesis 103, 105, 118–19

grammatical change 313–14, 363
grammatical organization 24–9, 92–3
  see also conceptual space; taxonomic hierarchy; taxonomic network
"grammatical relations" 32, 46
  see also syntactic role, clausal
grammatical unit (GU) 192–3
grammaticalization 7, 61, 126–7, 130, 159, 169, 216, 217–18, 259–68, 270, 307, 341–6, 350–4, 361
  see also diachrony; grammatical change; paradigmaticization
ground (Gestalt psychology) 278, **329–35**, 338, 351
  see also figure
grounding event 160
grouping, formal **190–7**, 200–1, 202
GU, see grammatical unit

head 46, 59, 94, 197–9, 241, **242–71**, 273, 280, 364
  functional head 259, 269
  see also base; functor; primary information-bearing unit; profile, determinant; profile, equivalent
Head-driven Phrase Structure Grammar 3, 20, 48, 179
head-marking 197–8
  see also dependent-marking
hearer 19, 204–5, 233–4, 366
  see also addressee; speaker
hierarchy, implicational 61, 91, 107
  accusative (case marking) hierarchy **139**, 142, 162, 355, 358
  Adverbial Deranking Hierarchy 358
  Agreement Hierarchy **230**, 231
  animacy hierarchy 159
  Complement Deranking Hierarchy 358
  Deranking Hierarchy 356–60, 361
  Deverbalization Hierarchy 355
  direct object hierarchy **143**, 358
  ergative (case marking) hierarchy **141**, 142, 162
  hierarchy:
    of intransitive participant role coding **163**
    of participant role clusters 138–47, 161–9, **165**, 171, 234, 235, 359, 360
    of properties 96
    of propositional acts **97**, 107
  number hierarchy 299
  primary object (case marking) hierarchy 145
  Relative Clause Deranking Hierarchy 359
  SAP hierarchy **284**, 287, 288, 297, 298–9, 301, 308, 315, 320
    SAP hierarchy constraints 288–90, 294, 295, 301, 307, 308
  Subject Construction Hierarchy 149, **155**, 159–61, 166–7, 170, 304, 356
  diachronic reality of 156–9
  Subordinate Clause Deranking Hierarchy 359
homonymy 115

iconicity **108**, 126, 186, **208–20**, 236, 240, 361, 363
  diagrammatic iconicity 208
  tense-iconicity **328**, 329, 336, 337–8, 341, 343, 344–5, 352, 353, 354
  see also noniconicity in grammar
idiom 5–6, **15–16**, 175–85
  extragrammatical idiom 15
  schematic idiom/construction 15–17
  substantive idiom/construction 15, 56, 362–3
idiom chunk **178**, 181
idiomatic phrase **183**, 184
idiomatically combining expression **181**, 182–5
important information 353
Incorporation Principle (Autolexical Syntax) 259
induction 7, 58, 367
inflection 29–31, 55, 58, 66, 76, 79–82, 85, 90, 103, 125, 129, 225, 245, 251, 253, 258, 266, 268, 270
information status, see topicality
information structure 15, 187, 197, 201, 220, 236
inherent, see transitoriness
inheritance 27
INI, see null instantiation, indefinite
initiator (in causal chain) 164, 169, 319
innateness 9
innovation 366, 368
  see also altered replication
instantiation, syntactic 275–80
  see also nonnull instantiation; null instantiation
interactor 367, 368
intonation unit (IU) 187, **191–3**, 202
  see also IU Storage Hypothesis
IU, see intonation unit
IU Storage Hypothesis 193

knowledge of grammar/language 8, 9, 26–7, 46, 92, 95, 105–6, 117, 204–5, 367, 368

label (vs. name) **50–1**, 54, 85
labeled bracketing, see bracket notation
lack of exclusive partitioning of lexical items **39–40**, 83
language 364–8
  dynamic character of 8, 126–9, 364
  interactional character of 8, 364
  see also knowledge of grammar/language
language change, gradualness of 312, 314
  see also diachrony
language use 8, 203–5, 364, 366
language-internal methodological opportunism, see methodological opportunism

language-particular facts 4, 84
latency **273**, 275–6
  see also null instantiation, definite; required
Lexical Functional Grammar 3, 22, 208, 228
  see also Coherence Condition; Completeness Condition; Uniqueness Condition
lexical item 16, 36, 63, 71, 73, 85, 88, 125–6, 277–8
lexicon **15**, 18
linear order 12, 23, 24, 43, 148, 177, **196–7**, 202, 222, 223–4, 328, 329, 356
  see also "free" word order; position
lingueme 365, 366, 367, 368
linguistics 364
  see also field linguistics
linking rules **15**, 19, 205–6, 207–8, 212
localist metaphor 169, 319
"lumping" approach, *see* categories, "lumping" approach to

markedness, *see* Prague School markedness; typological markedness
meaning:
  conventional 19, 366
  figurative 182
  truth-conditional 331, 338
mental map, *see* conceptual space
mental space 217, 259, 338
meronomic links 54, 59
meronomic structure 5, **20**, 24, 53–7, 59, 283, 362, 363, 366
meta-comment 334–5
metaphor 27, 59, 116, 169
methodological opportunism 61, 70, 72, 84, 147, 149, 151, 189, 202, 272
  cross-linguistic **30–2**, 33
  language-internal **41–4**, 186
methodology xiii–xv, 64
  see also argumentation; criteria
Minimalism 3
minor propositional acts, *see* deixis; determination; enumeration; quantification; selection; situating
mismatches among overtly coded dependencies, contiguity, and linear order 199–201
mismatches in distribution between constructions **34–9**, 41, 45, 46
  see also criteria
model-neutrality xv
modification 37, 65, **66**, 67, 69, 74–5, 76–7, 78, 81, 88, 93, 94, 95, 97, 98–102, 104, 119, 141, 241, 243, 261, 272, 322, 345, 346, 355
  restrictive modification 349
modifier, *see* modification
monosemy **113**, 115–19, 133, 216, 231
morphology 15, 17, 59, 252, 268–71
morphosyntactic locus 242, **243**, 252–4
multiple class membership **38–9**, 83

multiple parents 26
  see also taxonomic network

name (vs. label) **50–1**
narrative line 332, 334–5, 343
NNI, *see* nonnull instantiation
node (in network) 25
nonbasic type, *see* basic type (of a construction in a language)
noniconicity in grammar 208–20
  see also iconicity
nonnull instantiation (NNI) 277
nonredundancy, *see* redundancy
nontransformational syntactic theories 179, 185
nonuniversality of constructions, *see* construction, universal constructions
notational variants 48–9, 206
null element 186, 188, 227, 251, 276
  see also null instantiation
null instantiation 276–80
  definite null instantiation (DNI) **276**, 277
  free null instantiation (FNI) **276**, 278–9
  indefinite null instantiation (INI) **276**, 279–80
  see also nonnull instantiation

obligatoriness 242, **244–5**, 250–2, 273, 275–6, 279
one syntactic argument per semantic referent assumption 228–9
optionality 243
oral narrative 104

paradigm, transitive verb 295–302
paradigmatic contrast 270
paradigmaticization 270
parallelism (in grammatical units) 192
parenthetical element 190, 195
part–whole structure, *see* meronomic structure
participant roles 52, 133, **136**, 137, 141, 146–7, 149, 152, 160, 165, 218, 222, 283, 347
  clusters of participant roles **136–7**, 143, 170
  core participant roles 132, 264
particle 198, 199, 307, 325
parts of speech 29, 30, 33, 48, **63–107**, 123–4, 132, 136, 364
  conceptual analysis of 104
  heuristic criteria for **64**, 80, 81
  minor parts-of-speech classes 69–70
  notional analysis of **63**, 64
  universal-typological theory of 78, **86–92**, 123–4
  see also flexible language; propositional act; relationality; rigid language; semantic compatibility; semantic shift; sequentially scanned; summary scanning; word classes
percolation 253

performance 191, 193, 194
periphrastic expression 81, 91
phonological form 15
phonology 61–2
phrase structure, *see* constituent structure
PIBU, *see* primary information-bearing unit
pivot 152
polysemy 27, 59, **73**, **116–19**, 126, 127, 133, 136–7, 143, 234
  see also monosemy; categories, syntactic/grammatical
position 223
  second position phenomena 223–4
  variable position **196–7**, 345
  see also linear order
possible worlds 338
pragmatic principles 72
pragmatics 19, 93, 96, 230
Prague School markedness 89–90
  see also typological markedness
predetermination of time reference/modal status 351, 360
predicate–argument structure 26, 201, 346–7
predication 31, 37, 65, **66**, 68, 74, 76–7, 79, 81, 85, 88, 93, 94, 95, 97, 98–102, 124–5, 130, 214–16, 266, 283
  of identity 96, 97
  of location 96, 97, 116–17
primary information-bearing unit (PIBU) **258**, 259–71
  see also head
primitives 4, 5, **47**, 48, 51–2, 62, 85, 362
  see also atomic primitives
processing, language 203–5, 283
productivity 28
profile (concept denotation) **255**, 256, 259, 260–7, 349, 351–2
  profile determinant 256
  profile equivalent **257**, 258–67, 268, 269, 271
  see also head
Projection Principle (Government and Binding Theory) 208
pronominalization 188
propagation
  see also differential replication; selection 368
proposition 214
  asserted **323**, 338, 351–2
  nonassertive **323**, 357
  presupposed 334
  unchallengeable 334
  see also state of affairs
propositional act (pragmatic function) 59, 60, **66**, 73, 87–102, 104, 105, 321
  see also modification; predication; reference
prototype 53, 61, 73, 87, **89**, 92, 99, 100, **102–4**, 105, 117–19, 123, 129, 161, 234, 257, 317, 318, 363
  passive 317

subject 161, **162–5**
  see also categories, radial
psycholinguistics 28, 103, 130–1, 182
psychology 4, 5, 52–3, 73, 121, 205

quantification 94, 97, 165–7

Radical Construction Grammar **3–7**, 14, 18, 23, 25, 29, **46–62**, 63, 85–107, 110, 129–31, 136, 138, 149, 155, 159, 160, 161, 165–7, 170, 175, 179, 183, 195, 202, 203–6, 212, 219, 226, 233, 241–2, 243, 246, 257, 272, 283, 303, 312, 314, 327, 362–3, 364, 366, 367, 368
  see also Radical Frame Semantics; Radical Templatic Phonology
Radical Frame Semantics 62
radical relativist position **110**, 111, 115, 119–20, 123, 125–6
  see also conventional universalist position
Radical Templatic Phonology 62
reanalysis 366
recycling (in conversation) 194
reduction of a clause 327
redundancy:
  in expression **119–24**, 129, 216, 236–7, 258
    see also syntagmatic parsimony
  in representation xiv, 28
reference 65, **66**, 67, 69, 74, 76–7, 86, 93, 94, 97, 98–102, 108, 123–5, 283, 347
reference tracking 149, 152, 235, 295
referentially disjoint arguments 284
referring expressions, *see* reference
relationality **87**, 104, 262, **273–5**, 348
relations, *see* linking rules; meronomic links; semantic relations; spatial relations; symbolic relations; syntactic relations; taxonomic links
repetition (in conversation) 237
replicate mass 262
replication 365, 366
replicator 368
representation:
  semantic 62
  syntactic xiii, xiv, **3**, 7, 9, 13, 16, 17, 18, 23, 45–6, 55–6, 62, 95, 105–6, 108, 151, 184–5, 204, 221
required (constituent) **245**, 251–2, 276
  see also latency; null instantiation, definite
rigid language **67**, 68, 69, 70
  see also flexible language; parts of speech
Role and Reference Grammar 3, 263
root **268–71**
  see also affix

S-chain, *see* simultaneous chain
S-structure 178
  see also surface structure

Index of Subjects

salience 235, 262, 275, 315, 317, 319, 320, 349, 351
  see also topicality
SAP, see speech act participant
SAP alignment 318–19
scaffolding metaphor 237–40
  see also building block metaphor
schema/schematic **15**, 25–8, 55, 57, 58, 183, 184, 196, 259, 266, 362–3
selection:
  generalized theory of 365, 366–7
  in language change 367
  minor propositional act 94
  see also differential replication; propagation
selectional restrictions **179–80**
self-repairs 237
semantic:
  class 30, 67, 73, 85, 86–102, 124
  compatibility (of word with part of speech category) 70–1
  component, see component (semantic)
  compositionality, see compositionality, semantic
  dependencies, see semantic, relations
  frame 62, 74
  integration 352, **359**, 361
  interpretation 15, 16, 17, 18, 60, 122, 182, 183–4, 207–40, 244, 249
  map 8, 92, **94–104**, 105–7, 108, 118, 130–1, 138–47, 161, 170, 289, 290, 294, 296–302, 309–10, 314, 363
    see also Behavioral Potential Map Hypothesis; conceptual space; Grammatical Category Structure Hypothesis; Semantic, Semantic Map Connectivity Hypothesis; Structural Coding Map Hypothesis
  relations 6, 21, 25, 59, 62, 175–85, 186, 201–6, 283, 328–9, 330, 338, 357–9
  relativity **108–31**
    see also conventional universalist position; radical relativist position; semantic, Semantic Uncertainty Principle
  restrictiveness 345
  shift 249, 250
    in part of speech derivation **67–75**, 76, 104
  space, see conceptual space
  structure 19, 21, 61, 62–84, 108, **109**, 129, 175–85, 203–40, 274, 363, 366
    autonomous semantic structure **275**, 279, 346
    dependent semantic structure **275**, 279, 346
    see also conceptual structure
Semantic Map Connectivity Hypothesis **96**, 100, 105, 118
Semantic Uncertainty Principle 111, **126**, 130, 216
semantics xv, 9, 52, 60, 88, 93, 96, 115, 230, 256
  universal semantics 108–9, 124–6, 129

Semiotic Grammar 20
separability, see contiguity; grouping, formal
sequentially scanned (Cognitive Grammar) 104
shared:
  arguments (in complex sentence constructions) 338, 349, 353
  knowledge 237, 258, 340
  tense–aspect–mood (in complex sentence constructions) 338, 343–4, 354
sign, linguistic 364
  see also symbolic unit
simultaneous chain **336**
  see also consecutive chain
situating (minor propositional act) 94
social interaction 365–8
sociolinguistics 365, 367, 368
spatial relations 330
spatiotemporally bounded individuals 365
speaker 3, 8, 19, 58, 315, 364, 366
  see also addressee; hearer
special agreement forms 321, 355
special forms of tense–aspect–mood markings 321, 354
speech act participant (SAP) **284**, 319
  see also hierarchy, SAP hierarchy; SAP alignment
speech community 367, 368
split ergativity 167–70
  animacy-/person-based 167, 309–10
  aspect-/tense-based 167–70
  split morphological ergativity 153
  split syntactic ergativity 154
  see also ergativity
split intransitivity 162–5
"splitting approach", see categories, "splitting" approach
state of affairs 214, 217, 236, 265, 358
  see also proposition
stativity 74, **87**, 115
structural coding **66**, 68, 75, 88, **90**, 91, 98–102, 103, 139, **146**, 147, 285, 318
  overt structural coding 68, 69, 71, 75, **88**, 90, 98, 100, 101, 139, 144, 167, 309–10, 312, 314, 355
  zero structural coding 75, 76, **89**, 90, 99, 100, 139, 154, 165, 167, 268, 309–10, 312, 318
  see also behavioral potential; Structural Coding Map Hypothesis; typological markedness
Structural Coding Map Hypothesis **98**, 99, 100, 105
structuralism xiii, 3, 11, 29, 34, 36, 84, 85, 86, 255
structure, see conceptual space; conceptual structure; deep structure; force-dynamic structure; information structure; meronomic structure; predicate–argument structure; semantic,

structure; surface structure; syntactic, structure; taxonomic, hierarchy; taxonomic, network
subcategorization 242, **243–4**, 247–8, 273
  lexical subcategorization 243
  subcategorization frame 25, 247–8
subclasses **36–8**, 80–1
summary scanning (Cognitive Grammar) 104
suppletion 81, 91
surface structure
  see also S-structure 151, 178
symbolic:
  relations 6, 21, 23, 25, 59, 61, 146, 175, 176, 202, **204–40**, 280, 283, 362, 363, 366, 368
  unit **18**, 20, 21, 52, 58, 60, 203
syntactic:
  category determinant 242, **245**, 252–4
  element, see element (syntactic)
  relations 5, **22**, 23, **24**, 59, 132, **175–240**, 283, 362, 364, 366
    abstract syntactic relations **22**, 23
    logical argument against 203–5
  role 5, **11**, 12, 13, **24**, 24, 29, 46, 59, 65, 92, 94, 107, 114, **132–71**, 175, **220–33**, 362, 363, 364
    clausal syntactic roles **132–72**
    see also categories, global categories/relations; categories, universal categories/relations
  space 6, 288, **312–13**, 314, 318, 319, 320, 327, 357, 359, 360, 361, 363, 364
  structure 5, 12, 13, 15, 19, 21, 26, 45, 108, 129, 149, **175–240**, 362
    see also construction
syntagmatic parsimony **120–1**, 129
  see also redundancy, in expression
syntax xiii–xv, 3–4, 61, 202, 362–4, 368
  acquisition of 57–8, 367
  self-containedness of 9
  see also D-structure; deep structure; element (syntactic); knowledge of grammar/language; representation; S-structure; surface structure; theory

tail-head linkage 334
taxonomic hierarchy 25–6, 56–7
taxonomic:
  links:
    between categories **55–7**, 59, 363
    between constructions **25–6**, 54–7, 363
  network **25–6**, 52, 58, 367
term (Functional Grammar) 65, 69, 86
  see also reference
tests, see criteria
theory xiii–xv, 3–10, 18, 47, 54, 61, 62, 64, 110, 132–3, 134, 151, 170, 184–5, 238, 283, 288, 312, 362–8

elegance xiv
nonreductionist theory 5, **47**, 48, 53–7, 61–2
reductionist theory 10, **47**, 48, 53–5, 61–2, 122, 151, 202
simplicity xiv
theory-neutrality xv
  see also formalist theories; functionalist theories; nontransformational syntactic theories; transformational theory; typological theory
Theta Criterion (Government and Binding Theory) 208, 228
  see also frequency
topicality 159–61, 187, 287, 307–8, 315–16, 319, 340, 361
  see also salience
traditional grammar 10, 63, 85, 257
  see also agreement; case marking; government; head
transformational theory 42–3, 159, 178
  see also formalist theories; generative grammar; Government and Binding Theory; Minimalism
transitivity 307
transitoriness **87**, 115
turn constructional unit (TCU) 194, 237
typological:
  markedness 61, 88, **89–92**, 98, 103–4, 105, 118, 139–47, 162, 317–19, 355, 359, 361
  theory **7–8**, 93, 96, 107, 170, 283, 362, 364
    dynamicization of 101–2

uniqueness (of role) 243
Uniqueness Condition (Lexical-Functional Grammar) 208, 228
unit, see symbolic, unit
unit of first-position self-repair **194–5**, 202
unitization 119–22
Universal Grammar xiv, 7, **9–11**, 29, 31, 32, 34, 60–1, 86, 105
universals of language xiii–xv, 5, 7, 8, 61, 73, 84, 86, 98, 100, 105, 110, 136, 138, 146–7, 153, 155, 258, 275, 283–4, 294, 310, 314–15, 319, 320, 361, 366, 368
  cross-linguistic universals 5, 7, 34, 63, 138, 310
  implicational universals 61, 86, 90–1, 139–41, 143, 145, 155, 258, 259, 268, 355, 357–9, 363
  probabilistic universals 8
  smorgasbord approach to universals **10**, 136, 152
  unrestricted universals 86
  see also categories, universal categories/relations; construction, universal constructions; hierarchy, implicational; prototype; typological, markedness; typological, theory

unlikely semantic dependencies 209–20
unmarked, *see* typological, markedness; Prague School markedness
usage-based model **28**, 57, 59
utterances 11, 52, 58, 203, 204–5, 233–4, 364–8

vagueness analysis 71–2
  see also monosemy
valence (semantic; Cognitive Grammar) 274–5, 346
variation:
  linguistic 7, 127
    cross-constructional (language-internal) 5, 7, **106–7**, 161, 175, 179
    cross-linguistic 7, 29–33, 72, 90, **106–7**, 146, 161, 169, 170, 179
  see also diversity, structural
  sociolinguistic 107, 367, 368
verbal attraction 267

Word Grammar 3, 22
word:
  classes 30, 60, 96
    see also categories, syntactic
  order, *see* linear order
  rank 242

X-bar theory 63

zero derivation 73
zero structural coding, *see* structural coding, zero structural coding